Perform, Repeat, Record

Perform, Repeat, Record

Live Art in History

Edited by Amelia Jones and Adrian Heathfield

intellect Bristol, UK / Chicago, USA

First published in the UK in 2012 by
Intellect, The Mill, Parnall Road, Fishponds, Bristol, BS16 3JG, UK

First published in the USA in 2012 by
Intellect, The University of Chicago Press, 1427 E. 60th Street,
Chicago, IL 60637, USA

A catalogue record for this book is available from the British Library.

Front and Back Cover: Janez Janša, Life [in Progress], Ljubljana, 2009-2010.
Photography Nada Žgank. Copyright Maska, Ljubljana.
Cover designer: Holly Rose
Copy-editor: Macmillan
Index: Lyn Greenwood
Typesetting: Mac Style, Beverley, E. Yorkshire

ISBN 978-1-84150-489-6

Printed and bound by Latimer Trend, UK.

This book has been developed and published in collaboration with the Live Art Development Agency, London. Financially assisted by Arts Council England. www.thisisliveart.co.uk

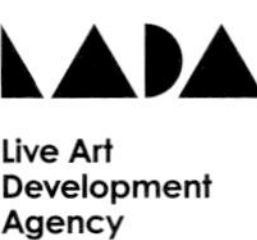

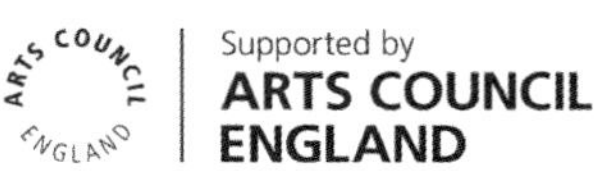

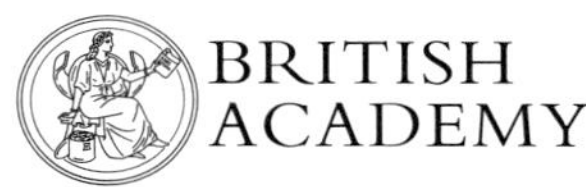

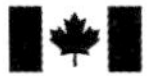

Social Sciences and Humanities Research Council of Canada

Conseil de recherches en sciences humaines du Canada

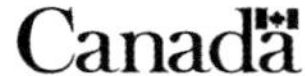

Contents

DIALOGUES

Introductions

The Now and the Has Been: Paradoxes of Live Art in History

Amelia Jones

> [E]very image is in the last analysis plastic, and [...] every artwork is in the end a stature – a stoppage of time, or rather its delay behind itself.
>
> Emmanuel Levinas[1]

> [T]he theatre is the only place in the world where a gesture, once made, can never be made the same way twice.
>
> Antonin Artaud[2]

Our being in the world unfolds in relation to temporality, embodiment, and experience, phenomena at the intersection of live performance and the visual arts. As thinkers and writers coming from differing disciplinary points of view, Levinas and Artaud both articulate the impossibilities thrown in the face of human understanding by the passage of time and the role of representation, and "art," in this conflicted aspect of human experience. This volume takes such insights (which always remain questions, never to be answered fully) and addresses the conundrum of how the live event or ephemeral art work – the act that can "never be made the same way twice," as Artaud puts it – gets written into history. This conundrum is productively exposed in the sites where the intersection between art and the performative is activated: from performance art and theater proper to music and dance to installations and artworks that beg for a durational engagement over time.

The exploration of these complex issues takes place here through a multitude of voices: from the editorial (a scholar initially trained in art history and a scholar trained in theater and performance studies) to a range of disciplinary and interdisciplinary intellectual points of view from dance, performance studies, cultural studies, theater studies, and art history and visual culture studies to creative interventions on the part of artists, theorists, and historians, through a range of methods and modes of writing/enacting/visualizing.

In inviting performance-studies scholar Adrian Heathfield to join me in this project, it was (and remains) my hope that, in particular, the editorial stretch and pull between a perspective growing from a base in art historical training and expanding into performance and a point of view developing out of performance studies (including practice and theory) would benefit this volume by crossing over a (typically art historical) focus on the objects of art analysis – the artwork, object, or *image* (noted by Levinas as a *delay* that stops time) – with an attention to the performative modes of cultural enactment that have come to be central to performance studies.

There is one obvious way in which this crossing of art historical and performance studies perspectives opens up new models for thinking about how visual and embodied cultural expressions come to *mean*. The performative, loosely understood here via theorists from J. L. Austin to Roland Barthes, Jacques Derrida, and Judith Butler as the reiterative enactment across time of meaning (including that of the "self" or subject) through embodied gestures, language, and/or other modes of signification, opens the supposedly static work of art constructed by art history to the temporal, and to the vicissitudes of invested and embodied engagement by visitors to, participants in, or viewers of the work. On the one hand, while performance studies tends to *dematerialize*, to think of all culture as equally performative and open to what literary theorist Roland Barthes called *writerly* interventions, art history at its best can provide rigorous ways of thinking about how specific objects, images, performance works function culturally, and about how to understand the interconnectedness of such material/materials and the vicissitudes of social and political history.[3] On the other hand, while art history, with its connected institutions and discourses (the art exhibition, art gallery and market, curatorial practice, and art criticism), insists on containing the artwork as a discrete and knowable "object," a consideration of the performative "de-contains" the work, reminding us that its meaning and value are contingent. This is no small thing.

The Resurgence of the "Live"

In the past decade, there has been a wholesale resurgence of interest in body art, performance art, or live art – particularly in relation to their histories and limits; as Heathfield has pointed out elsewhere, we are obsessed with "immediacy and interactivity," driven to "bring close all that is now distant to us."[4] Body art, performance art, and live art are all terms wielded in various discourses and in various sites to point to works that activate a body or bodies temporally – either for an audience present at the time ("live art") or for audiences who engage the work through representational modes such as video installation.[5] In each of these modes of creative expression the body has a central role to play (I would say not only central but incontrovertible, if completely baffling and ultimately not fully determinable: this is a body that is always already a thinking subject, with memories, emotions, and moving through time). In spite of attempts by supposedly objective art critics to repress or disavow the body in visual arts discourse, it has never fully disappeared from the visual and performing arts.

Since the late 1990s, however, its role – in activating the viewer, in bringing history to "life," in securing (or refusing) the possibility of knowing one's experience in the present (or past) and projecting future hopes for cultural change – has become newly vibrant, surfaced, put *in your face*. This burgeoning interest (which since 2000 has verged on art world obsession) in the body, in the live act, in the histories and meanings of performance and the performative, is testified to by the timeline I have organized in this volume.

Attempting to explain definitively *why* this "obsession" has occurred would in fact betray the very mode of open inquiry this volume hopes to keep open; it is truly impossible to say with any finality what the relationship is or was between political events or vast economic and social shifts (however these are understood) and cultural effusions (themselves only recognizable through the *stopping of time*, through putting a frame around something and calling it a "tendency"). At the same time, the worst kinds of histories (say, traditional "art histories") are precisely those that pretend that culture (say: art, performance) has nothing to do with other modes of human experience, circuits of economic exchange, and expressions of power.

Therefore, it is surely better to err on the side of at least attempting to posit historical relationships than to ignore altogether the interrelationship of cultural "tendencies" (such as the resurgence of the interest in live art and issues of time and history) and ideological, cultural, social, political, and economic formations (again, however these might be "known"). Scholars of the vicissitudes of the *event*, such as dance theorist Mark Franko, have been assertive in positing specific arguments about such relationships. Franko situates the terrorist attacks of 9/11 as exemplifying a kind of epochal *event* that operates historically as a theoretical rupture point, encouraging artists and intellectuals to seek new ways of relating to past histories.[6] To break out of the limits of Franko's US-oriented context, it is worth noting that the collapse of the Soviet bloc has clearly been a similar "event" for Eastern Europeans rethinking identities in the wake of the end of the Cold War (see the Harutyunyan et al. chapter and timeline in this volume for elaboration on this crucial point). And surely just the passing into a new millennium (those of us on the Christian calendar must not forget the "Y2K" hysteria that accompanied the passage from the twentieth- to the twenty-first centuries) was another point of perceived rupture with beliefs and assumptions associated with modernity and modernism on the part of Euro-Americans.

Perhaps we feel just a little unstable and so questions are being asked. Perhaps after four (coming on five) decades of theorizing/writing into being/experiencing the "postmodern," the end of modernity, the collapse of colonial empires, the rise of the rights movements with their attendant discourses, the burgeoning of "globalization" (presumably in forms differentiated from those previous ones such as medieval trade routes), the blossoming of networks of information exchange and (relatedly) networked ways of thinking and being, the explosion of screen-life, and the expansion of cheap travel, we have begun to understand that we understand very little about ourselves, about other parts of the world, or about the past. In the best-case scenario this situation might be understood as an embrace of insecurity, an acknowledgment that we know nothing (but that it is still worth "re-enacting," making attempts to "know" the mistakes and achievements of the past). In the worst-case scenarios (currently enacted globally) we might see a reactionism: a resurgence of fascist political parties in Europe; a cycle of attempted improvements and violent collapse in various "post"-colonized African countries; a violently repressed soft revolution in 2009 Iran; a wholesale economic collapse throwing in question previously accepted values in late capitalist cultures. And, rather than its abrasive refusal of the structures of late capital, a packaging of the live as commodity, as the perfect spectacle (see Sven Lütticken's chapter in this volume).

At its best, the return to the live via complex modes of re-enactment, re-staging, reiteration, might be seen to be sparked by (and eliciting of) openness and hope, by way of presenting new possibilities of intervention and by activating fresh ways of thinking, making, being in the world. Many of us have invested in just this idea of the politically radical potentialities of the live body in action; as performance theorist André Lepecki has argued, with a utopian yearning: a live art practice such as "conceptual" dance instantiates the "intertwining and conflicting discourses informing and challenging the [previously accepted] notions of 'presence' and 'body,'" and live art works can thus function "as complicated sites where subjectivity challenges subjection, where resistance initiates its moves."[7]

Temporality and Aesthetics

Here, from an art historical point of view, a rumination on the potential of liveness to disrupt the containing function of aesthetics (stemming from eighteenth-century German philosophy, particularly Immanuel Kant's 1790 *Critique of Judgment*) is useful. In this dominant form in Euro-American thought, aesthetics argues for the work of art as fully contained, framed, and thus as "universal" in its effects (while also, Kant admits, obviously only comprehensible through the "subjective" senses).[8] The aesthetic functions to contain: as Kant's compatriot G. F. W. Hegel put it shortly after Kant's formulation, art proceeds "from the absolute Idea," traceable back to a divine origin; and Kant's model of aesthetics, hugely influential in attenuated and oversimplified modernist forms of art criticism in the twentieth-century, asserts that the trained interpreter can in a disinterested fashion "contain" its supposedly universal meaning and value through a correct interpretation.[9] As Derrida notes, in Kant's *Critique of Judgment*, "the concept of art is also constructed with just such a guarantee in view."[10]

The live and/or performance work seems to refuse such containment. But does it do so inherently or inevitably? Certainly not. As counter examples of how the performative can function as containment, the highly aestheticized Nazi marches choreographing bodies according to National Socialist ideals in 1930s Germany come to mind, as do certain kinds of conventional theater relying on the "classics" or even now institutionalized forms of "performance art" as confessional self-expressive narrative, which arguably reconfirm a belief in the body as a transparent conveyor of intended meaning (although the latter two modes are hardly coterminous with fascism!). Lütticken argues persuasively in this volume, too, that certain modes of live public art (such as the works of Tino Sehgal) function precisely to recontain, paralleling the commodification of "performance" in the currently dominant service economy of big business (where "performance reviews" function as the nth-degree functioning of the uncontrollability of human action into the tick-box structures of bureaucratic late capitalism).[11]

Not to put too fine a point on it: with works that function by taking place across time, works that exaggeratedly foreground the *time* it takes to engage with them, the question of meaning and the related question of value – both hinging on temporality and the aesthetic – are up for grabs. Live and/or performance art, the mode of synaesthetic enactment that appears in physical space at particular moments of time, provokes openings to such questions, but also poses some very useful dilemmas for trying to understand how visual and performance cultures *work*. Precisely because it claims both to be "art" and to be "live" (or in some cases to be "performance" or "performative" but not necessarily "live"), live and/or performance art presses together modes of being, meaning, and value that have historically been considered incompatible.[12] Live and/or performance art enact and engage bodies across time and, as such, insistently remind us that, as Henri Bergson pointed out over a century ago, it is through memory (as enacted through our cognitively and emotionally driven bodies) that we connect with the world around us.[13]

At the very least, in terms of temporality and aesthetics, the live/performance art work thus activates the spectatorial (and often auditory and tactile) relation to pose difficult questions. What is the nature of the performance event? Is it more "real" or "authentic" than the various kinds of documentation (textual, photographic, videographic, filmic, re-stagings) through which it is passed down through time? Is the live body more "authentic" than the body represented in photographs, film, or video? (My answer to these queries would be: clearly no.) How does live body art differ from theater, dance, and music productions in its relationship to liveness, the real, documentary and textual (including digital) regimes, and beliefs about presence? How have definitive live art events been narrated in art versus performance theory, and how have these works and their readings altered our perceptions of the history of art, theater, dance, and music?[14] And, perhaps most importantly to a project on "live art in history": How does live art get remembered? How does this remembering manifest itself in documents and in re-enactments of performance events? Who gets to decide how to write the histories of these events? These questions are only, as the richness of this volume suggests, the tip of the proverbial iceberg.

Re-Enactments

The notion of re-enactment is in the air. Many of the contributors to this volume deal, in practice or in theory, with the complex consequences of the redoing of cultural or artistic events. One could argue that all culture, even human experience in general, is necessarily a re-enactment. As Adam Mendelsohn argues, "[u]nderpinning re-enactment art is the implication that the activity of making art itself, participating in cultural production, is …a kind of historical re-enactment – an activity that preserves heritage through ritualized behavior."[15] Or, as Robert Blackson puts it, reflecting on the phenomenon of false memory in relation to artistic re-enactments, "memory, like history, is a creative act."[16] If history and memory are creative acts, as the British historian R. G. Collingwood in fact famously argued fifty years ago, history itself is always re-enactment. For Collingwood, history can only be known through the performative identification of the historian with his subjects: "how does the historian discern the thoughts which he is trying to discover? […] There is only one way in which it can be done: by re-thinking them in his own mind."[17]

If history is performative re-enactment, what about histories of art and of performance and live art themselves? Drawing on theories of performativity by authors from Austin to Derrida to Butler, one could argue that the arts are *all* redoings of one kind or another: either repetitious re-stagings based on a script (as in a classical music concert, a dance event, a conventional theater production, or even performative Fluxus art works from the 1960s), or a process of reworking past styles and themes to move art forward in a fantasy of increasing sophistication and/or aesthetic improvement as in modernist Euro-American models of art. But, with its roots in theater and visual arts production, and with its new popularity under the rubric of live art, performance art has a particularly strong, if also contradictory, relationship to the idea of enunciation as "redo" or as repetitive "iteration."[18] The live event, one could argue, both exemplifies the iterative nature of all bodily enactment (or even of all human experience tout court) and the yearning for authenticity and presence that continues to encourage us to privilege the "live" over the "representational." Yet the live event also, as Philip Auslander's work articulates in the essay in this volume and elsewhere, makes clear the failure of the re-enactment to secure authenticity.[19]

Pil and Gallia Kolletiv have noted that there is a way for this failure of authenticity to function critically: "a historical moment is never new, which means that there is no original to repeat." They continue, drawing on Michel Foucault's notion of history without "landmark," to argue that a "successful re-enactment would therefore [produce a disloyalty to the point of origin which] does not amount to historical relativism, but rather activates history from within the present, allowing us to move away from the sterile attempt to cut through the infinite mediations of the spectacle."[20] I would add to this that re-enactments that do not acknowledge these paradoxes get caught up in the discourse of authenticity and genius, ultimately resting on an impossible (yet still intransigently common) notion of retrievable original meaning and artistic intentionality.

Histories of performance art proper have tended to devolve around a handful of iconic photographs and textual descriptions, or in some cases film or video footage. Until recently, this reliance on these documents and descriptions was rarely put under scrutiny – or exposed for the way in which it paradoxically reduces the celebrated "live" act to singular (and commodifiable) objects of display and exchange. In contrast, what is notable in the context of this volume is that the resurgence of interest in performance or live art since the mid-1990s has often been worked through in relation to some variation on a newly developed re-enactment format – whether this means literal performance works, redone by the same or a different author (such as Marina Abramović's well-known *Seven Easy Pieces* project, performed at the Guggenheim Museum in New York in 2005), or re-stagings of political protests or events (the work of Jeremy Deller, who re-staged the 1984 British miner strike in his 2001 *Battle of Orgreave* as an art event, or of Sharon Hayes, whose recent project has involved having herself photographed with signs from historic protests standing on the sites of the original events). While, at their most compelling, re-enactments presented in visual arts and/or performance contexts interrogate the previously accepted bases for documenting live acts, they are also ironically (as with Deller's *Battle of Orgreave* project) themselves turned into conventional aesthetic displays in their presentation in galleries via forms of documentation, or (also as with Deller's piece) turned into feature films screened in commercial cinemas or on mainstream television.[21] At the same time, the mere fact of performing a historical or artistic event *again* does encourage a critical relationship to liveness – at the very least, a questioning of the status of the event itself both within performance and more general histories.[22] And of course the point made by re-enactments, whether this is the intention of the re-enactor or not, is that the past is impossible to retrieve as it existed in the past (that in fact the event is always already "over").

In thinking about the significance of this burgeoning of re-enactment practices, a crucial question arises: how do the current re-enactments relate to previous arts movements appropriating and reworking images, themes, or materials from previous art and/or from the mass media? While critical re-enactments in an art or performance context are clearly concerned with the "original" act, this concern has more to do with origins in a hermeneutic sense of *what can be known about the event*, and less to do with specific identifications associated with particular structures of authorship and value as was the case in 1980s appropriation art. Sherrie Levine's 1980s remakings of "masterpieces" by modernist photographers and painters, for example, interrogated the structures by which marks on paper or canvas (usually by white men) are given value by the institutions of art. While Abramović's re-stagings might seem at first glance to pivot around similar strategies of "appropriating" works by famous performance artists (in this case both male and female), the *Seven Easy Pieces* project contrasts strongly with this avant-gardist gesture of "critiquing" structures of authorship (certainly Abramović's published comments suggest otherwise, privileging the greatness of the artists, such as Joseph Beuys, whose works she chose to redo). As it was presented and received, and (now) is being historically framed, *Seven Easy Pieces* itself becomes constructed and viewed as a set of "original" acts, pivoting around the name Abramović.[23] Such re-enactments as currently presented and institutionalized in exhibitions, books, and films are thus definitively *not* presented as critiques of modernist structures of authorship and value but come to be about the very way in which live acts come to mean and have value through authorial structures of ratification and commodification. Such works point to the way in which cultural value is ascribed in relation to embodied acts of doing – always already (and to some degree unavoidably) overdetermined by the marketplace.[24]

The visual arts have a fraught relationship to the live – one could argue the impulse to "re-enact" or document the live act results precisely from the pressure of the global art market attached to the visual arts. This pressure of the market, as much as the motivation to secure works in "history" (and after all art history is a part of the market so the writing into history of particular works of art is itself linked to marketing), inspires the range of methods that have been developed to "document" the work and/or its re-enactments and thus to secure the work a place in the marketing of objects and images and, by extension, of particular histories. Music, dance, and theater have an entirely different relationship to temporality, the body, objecthood, and structures of history making. These arts have traditionally acknowledged their reliance on the *script* that passes down through time to be "redone."[25] Re-enactments, like the live in general, might seem to promise an escape from commodification, but the re-enactment often (if not always) ends up congealing into structures of capital – often via its own documentary traces. As Sven Lütticken asks,

> [l]ike other performances, re-enactments generate representations in the form of photos and videos. Is it the fate of the re-enactment to become an image? And are such representations just part of a spectacle that breeds passivity, or can they in some sense be performative, active?[26]

Never inherently eschewing the market (far from it), nonetheless the performative re-enactment reminds us of how such value systems function in historical terms, of how historians write certain things into the present, exclude others, and continually fix and re-fix the meaning of objects as well as events in order to bring them into a continually refreshed "present" (with that "present" inevitably including the circuits of the marketplace, which itself makes and informs "histories" as we know them). Crucially, re-enactments remind us that all present experience is only ever available through subjective perception, itself based on memory; all "events" – those we participated in as well as those that occurred before we were born – can only ever be subjectively enacted (in the first place) and subjectively retrieved later. There is no singular, authentic "original" event we can refer to in order to confirm the true meaning of an event, an act, a performance, or a body – presented in the art realm or otherwise.

Body, Abject, the Uncontainable

More on containment. Aesthetics is one primary parent of art history; the other is "history" itself, but as articulated in a hybrid anthropological form that draws its claims of truth value on its capacity to identify authentic "facts" in relation to the formal qualities of objects displayed in an "art" context (this is art; that is not; this is a masterpiece; that is kitsch). I say "parent" rather than mother/father because this might be a very queer alliance; in fact, there could well be more than two parents involved if performance and live art tell us anything at all. More questions: What happens when the "object" presented to the "(art) historian" (who is always covertly also a "critic," making judgments of value as she chooses which objects to write about, to stake her career on) is a live body? And what happens when the object already presents and in some ways encompasses (while it is also encompassed or enacted by) a confusingly complex subject of making?

In the European and North American context, aesthetics already collided with liveness and performance at least as early as the 1910s, when renegade avant-garde movements such as Futurism and Dada proclaimed the museums "dead" while activating their bodies on stages and in public.[27] These artists, writers, and impresarios intuited that such an activation of the corporeal would be the most effective nail in the coffin of the pretenses associated with high art – pretences that were clung to with particular tenaciousness in the visual arts domain because of its investment in "unique" objects that were bought and sold on the increasingly international art market, all secured through the aesthetic as a mode of containment (becoming institutionalized by the late nineteenth century in the developing new discipline of "art history" and its corollary "art criticism"). The messy, deliberately obnoxious body of the avant-gardist was forced in the face of bourgeois audience members, invited to witness their own humiliation *and thus their own participation* in the making of the work and its meanings and values. This technique reached its apogee in Paris in the early 1960s *Anthropometries* performance series of Yves Klein. In the most famous of these performances, Klein invited upper class art aficionados to witness an event consisting of him in tuxedo smearing the bodies of naked female models with "Yves Klein Blue" (patented as YKB) paint, then pressing and dragging them across canvases on the floor – all to the accompaniment of live classical music.

The body's inevitable grotesqueness, its uncontainability – not to mention the *gendered* and *sexed* nature of this abjection – was both marked and recontained. Klein notably "controlled" the otherwise passive women involved (reiterating the age-old tendency in European art to contain female sexuality through the trope of the female nude).[28] The recontainment is further confirmed by the now iconic photographs and film footage documenting the *Anthropometries*, which seem to prove that the event definitively took place at the claimed time and venue. At the same time these documents freeze the event in perpetuity, reducing it to a few recognizable "moments," slices of time that can be mounted on a wall or shown in a brief clip on a monitor, themselves now commodified as YK "art." Klein, through connoisseurial judgments across the Euro-American art market, has been identified as a master. His act of containment (of the models; of himself) renders him marketable and, ironically, ensures his persistent "presence" in histories of body and performance art – as testified to, in fact, by the numerous re-enactments of his work in more recent practice.[29]

But what of the uncontainably abject bodies of both artists/makers and viewers – often feminine, queer, uncanny, or otherwise grotesque, wounded, or leaking? Is any body totally uncontainable? I have argued elsewhere that for brief moments and in specific contexts particular kinds of performative acts can pierce, wound, and affect the viewer or participant through their violation of the body as container, which can function (if momentarily) as a refusal of the containment of aesthetics. But is not even this act of *writing about* the uncontainable wounded or abject body itself *recontaining* such works, and in turn *marketing* them in ways that substantiate my own authority as a scholar?[30]

I will leave the answer to such questions open at this point, except to remind myself and my readers that *no body, no act, is inherently resistant to recontainment*. And, correlatively, *no body, no act, is inherently and fully containable* whether through state-sponsored torture, prison architecture, or ideological formations such as the aesthetic. After all, if we were to argue or imply that acts or bodies or objects had "inherent" values we would be right back where we started from with eighteenth- and nineteenth-century aesthetics, comfortable with Hegel's model of a history of art "as the [...] unfolding of Spirit whose trace is legible in art objects," a legibility of which is bound and determined by one's position in a class-determined social hierarchy.[31] We would be right back at a situation where the fact that wealthy white men ruled the western world was considered to be inherently "right." A world before Obama.

Reciprocity

A faddish, and quite simplistic, embrace of "relational" aesthetics has emerged over the past few years.[32] This embrace is, to say the least, disingenuous and, to say the most, superficial and unhelpful as a critical formulation. The idea of relational aesthetics ignores a vast and complex history of contemporary art's increasingly assertive opening of artwork to participant (see Allan Kaprow's 1958 article "The Legacy of Jackson Pollock"), and to "situation," "dematerialization," "intermediality," and a general *reciprocity* among maker, work, and interpreter.[33] I insist that reciprocity is more useful than the "relational" in that it automatically pays homage to the rise, after WWII, of theories of interrelatedness in understanding the human subject's complex modes of being in the world in European philosophy, most notably the work of Maurice Merleau-Ponty, culminating in his 1961 essay "The Intertwining, The Chiasm" – where he articulates a model to understand the reciprocal constitution of bodies (themselves fully subjectified) and what he calls the "flesh of the world."[34]

One could argue that it is in fact body/live/performance art, out of all forms of art making, that activates most aggressively the reciprocity that is at least latent in all art making and viewing. So much is my claim in my 1998 book *Body Art/Performing the Subject*, where I activate Merleau-Ponty's notion of the chiasm and attempt also to reanimate historical body art works. Still, by insisting that I was (re)telling their history in relation to a new framework, that of post-structuralist philosophy itself (particularly its not coincidental simultaneous development of theories of reciprocal subject/object relations along with body art), I was of course recontaining these "uncontainable" works. But at the same time I was *changed by them*. The book ended up creating frameworks via Merleau-Ponty that occurred to me *reciprocally* (chiasmatically) through engaging the works, often (because of my generational position as a younger scholar) through their documentary traces (including single- and multiple-channel video and installation formats) rather than "live" versions.

Merleau-Ponty articulated reciprocity via the "chiasm": a crossing over of the visible and invisible (what we think we know by seeing and that which can never be fully grasped in vision). With the notion of chiasm Merleau-Ponty began to explore how humans relate to the world that surrounds us, a question fundamental to aesthetics (which, again, attempts to bridge the gap between the "subjective" senses, necessary for apprehending the object, and the supposedly necessary "objectivity" of the value of things we believe to be art). And yet with the notion of the chiasm Merleau-Ponty ultimately addresses the *impossibility* of bridging the gap between self and world, subject and object, present and past, the impossibility of understanding fully (making a final meaning, making an incontrovertible value) what we think we *see*:

> It is as though our vision were formed in the heart of the visible, or as though there were between it and us an intimacy as close as between the sea and the strand. And yet it is not possible that we blend into it, nor that it passes into us, for then the vision would vanish at the moment of formation, by disappearance of the seer or of the visible [...] vision is question and response [...] The openness through flesh: the two leaves of my body and the leaves of the visible world [...] It is between these intercalated leaves that there is visibility [...] MY BODY model of the things and the things model of my body: the body bound up to the world through all its parts, up against it.[35]

Reciprocally, the live and/or performative artwork opens us temporally to an exchange. No wonder so many women, blacks, queers, and others excluded from conventional institutions of display and historical narrative (as justified and confirmed through the supposedly disembodied "truths" of art criticism, as founded in Kantian aesthetics) have turned to such modes of making from the 1960s to the present. Although plenty of apparently "white men," who would be assumed to be enfranchised but in various ways enacted precarious relationships to dominant structures of subjectivity and artistic meaning, also partook in the invigorating potential of the performative as well: from Allan Kaprow's Jackson Pollock of the late 1950s to Klein and his mentor Georges Mathieu (playing on the performative practice of the Japanese Gutai group) in 1950s and early 1960s Paris.

Beyond this formative moment in 1960s and 1970s Europe and North America, however, a burgeoning group of dancers/artists/filmmakers/actors/poets comprising a range of newly self-enfranchised artistic subjects (including women, blacks, and queers) began *performing* themselves across a range of sites, through an ever expanding range of media and forms from live performance to installations drawing in visitor participation to video art: Yoko Ono, Vito Acconci, Adrian Piper, Gina Pane, Carolee Schneemann, Valie Export, Jack Smith, Yayoi Kusama, Senga Nengudi, Dave Hammons, and many, many others. These artists explosively expanded the parameters of live, body, performance, video and/or installation art to redefine what could be done within the aegis of the aesthetic.

In this way, the intersections of the modes of experience called forth by the terms "live," "body," and "art" put pressure on our deepest assumptions about living, making, and how these become "history." In other words, experiments with the live body over the past century have radically interrogated modes of containment that continue to dominate the most basic understanding of how humans live and create in the world. It is the potential for "uncontaining" that must be reasserted at every moment in engaging with such works – even in producing a "book" that is a "container." I hope that this volume's inevitable containing function (of making sense of a complex range of phenomena linked to live art), then, is also an opening to the messy vicissitudes of desire and remembering that have the potential of productively destabilizing every engagement with visual and performing artworks.

In this way, I invite the reader in. Let us hope the reading/viewing is as reciprocal a process as possible, and that you feel enfranchised to bring yourself in the most bodily and temporally dynamic ways into the process of making new meanings from the performative works and arguments laid out in this volume. In this way, crossing over the present and the historical past in which I am now writing (but which you will, inevitably, receive "later"), your very attention to this project is itself a reciprocal bringing to life of my ideas so clumsily articulated here. I wish you the best of luck in uncontaining this containing.

Notes

1. Emmanuel Levinas, "Reality and Its Shadow" (1948), in Seán Hand (ed.), *The Levinas Reader*, trans. Alphonso Lingis, Oxford: Blackwell, 1989, p. 137.
2. Antonin Artaud, *The Theater and Its Double* (1938), New York: Grove Wiedenfeld, 1958, p. 75.
3. See Roland Barthes, *S/Z* (1970), trans. Richard Miller, New York: Farrar, Straus, Giroux, 1991, pp. 4–5.
4. Adrian Heathfield, "Alive," *Live: Art and Performance*, London: Tate Publishing, 2004, p. 7.
5. I elaborate on the term "body art" in relation to "performance art" in my 1998 book *Body Art/Performing the Subject*, Minneapolis: University of Minnesota Press, pp. 12–14. The term "performance art," more common than "live art" in North America, commonly designates works that are usually live and are more or less theatrically presented either in public spaces or in now institutionalized venues such as Highways Performance Space in Los Angeles or Franklin Furnace in New York City (which exists now only as an archive of performance art). "Live art" is used more frequently in the United Kingdom and has been developed by the hugely influential Live Art Development Agency, which has of course played a role in supporting this publication, and in the work of my co-editor Adrian Heathfield; see the latter's edited *Live: Art and Performance*, also an initiative of the Live Art Development Agency.
6. Mark Franko, "Given Movement: Dance and the Event," in André Lepecki (ed.), *Of the Presence of the Body: Essays on Dance and Performance Theory*, Middletown, Connecticut: Wesleyan University Press, 2004, see pp. 113–15. Important theorists of the "event" as a rupture with the past include Jean-François Lyotard, Gilles Deleuze, and Alain Badiou; see in particular Geoff Bennington, *Lyotard: Writing the Event*, Manchester: Manchester University Press, 1988; and Yve Lomax, "Thinking Stillness," in David Green and Joanna Lowry (eds), *Stillness and Time:*

Photography and the Moving Image, Brighton: Photoforum and Photoworks, 2006, pp. 55–63. I am grateful to Christopher Bamford, who is writing a Ph.D. at University of Manchester on Lyotard's philosophies in relation to art and performance, for raising my awareness of this discourse on the event.

7. André Lepecki, "Introduction," in Lepecki (ed.), *Of the Presence of the Body*, pp. 1–2.
8. Kant's theory is actually extremely complex and foregrounds the inevitable contradiction between the necessary claim for universality of any aesthetic judgment and the fact that such a judgment can only occur through the subject's own apprehension of the artwork through his/her *senses* (an apprehension that is thus inherently subjective): the aesthetic judgment "must involve a claim to validity for all men," but such a "claim to *subjective universality*" can only ever be "an idea," since his judgment is wielded first and foremost through his subjective senses. See *The Critique of Judgment* (1790), James Creed Meredith (tr.,), Whitefish, Montana: Kessinger Publishing, 2007, SS 6, p. 36.
9. Hegel, *Philosophy of Fine Art* (1835), as reprinted in Donald Preziosi (ed.), *The Art of Art History: A Critical Anthology*, Oxford: Oxford University Press, 1998, p. 97.
10. Derrida's critique of Kant here is from "Economimesis," *Diacritics*, Summer 1981, vol. 11, no. 2, pp. 2–25. See also his extended deconstruction of Kantian aesthetics in *Truth in Painting* (1978), trans. Geoff Bennington, Chicago: University of Chicago Press, 1987.
11. On this point see also Jon McKenzie, *Perform or Else: From Discipline to Performance*, London, New York: Routledge, 2001. I am grateful to Gavin Butt for bringing this source to my attention.
12. Certain art practices exacerbate these impossible confluences: as in Hayley Newman's late 1990s *Connotations* series of performative photographs documenting non-existent durational live artworks; or Daniel J. Martinez's 2002 *Happiness is Overrated*, a life-sized robotic "self" that moves in space and over time but is not, strictly speaking, "alive."
13. See Henri Bergson's *Matter and Memory* (1896), trans. Nancy Margaret Paul and W. Scott Palmer, translation from fifth edition of 1908, New York: Zone Books, 2002.
14. For an important historical take on the specific ontology of performance as "repertoire" and the relationship between this ontological basis of live performance and the specific development of performance theory and performance studies, see Diana Taylor, *The Archive and the Repertoire: Performing Cultural Memory in the Americas*, Durham, NC: Duke University Press, 2003.
15. Adam Mendelsohn, "Be Here Now," *Art Monthly*, October 2006, vol. 300, pp. 13–16.
16. Robert Blackson, "Once More … With Feeling: Re-Enactment in Contemporary Culture," *Art Journal*, Spring 2007, vol. 66, n. 1, p. 31.
17. R. G. Collingwood, *The Idea of History*, Oxford: Oxford University Press, 1956, p. 215. See also William Dray, *History as Re-Enactment: R. G. Collingwood's Idea of History*, Oxford: Oxford University Press, 1995.
18. The notion of iteration, taken from linguistic theory, is central to the theorization of the performative on the part of Jacques Derrida and later Judith Butler. See the latter's "Performative Acts and Gender Constitution: An Essay in Phenomenology and Feminist Theory," *Theatre Journal*, December 1988, vol. 40, no. 4, reprinted in Amelia Jones (ed.), *Feminism and Visual Culture Reader*, second edition, London: Routledge: 2010, 482–491.
19. See Auslander's book, *Liveness: Performance in a Mediatized Culture*, 2nd edn., New York: Routledge, 2008. On this point, see also my essay "'Presence' in *absentia*: Experiencing Performance as Documentation," *Art Journal*, Winter 1997, vol. 56, no. 4, pp. 11–18.
20. Pil and Gallia Kollectiv, "RETRO/NECRO: From Beyond the Grave of the Politics of Re-Enactment," in *ART PAPERS*, 2008. Available at: http://www.kollectiv.co.uk/Art%20Papers%20 feature/reenactment/retro-necro.htm, accessed 26 May 2008.

21. Deller's *Battle of Orgreave* was made into a film by Mike Figgis and screened on Britain's Chanel 4 television in 2002. The work has been exhibited in various shifting formats in galleries; the *Battle of Orgreave Archive*, 2004, one version of this documentation, is owned by the Tate Art Gallery in London.
22. On the status of the event in visual arts discourse, see Charles Merewether and Johns Potts (eds), *After the Event: New Perspectives on Art History* in the series "Rethinking Art's Histories" I am co-editing with Marsha Meskimmon (Manchester: Manchester University Press, 2010).
23. This tendency has been exacerbated in Abramović's efforts such as the large-scale performance event titled *Marina Abramović Presents*, which took place in 2009 at the Whitworth Art Gallery, University of Manchester, as part of the Manchester International Festival; she co-organized the event with Festival organizers and the Director of the Whitworth, Maria Balshaw. Here, the work of thirteen internationally known artists (including Alistair MacLennan and Kira O'Reilly) were subsumed under the Marina Abramović author-name. Another example of what might be called the "Abramović effect" (which merges structures of authorship from high modernism with claims of authenticity from performance art discourse) is her 2010 retrospective at the Museum of Modern Art, usually considered the most traditional bastion of high modernist values, titled *The Artist is Present*. The work consisted of a retrospective of her earlier works (including re-enactments of pieces she did in the 1970s with her partner Ulay by younger artists and dancers) and a "live" element with Abramović herself sitting in the central atrium of the museum offering herself for visitations by museum-goers, who would sit across from her in silence as she sat vigil during all of the opening hours of the museum. For more on the tensions between claims made for live art and this kind of institutionalization, see my essay "'The Artist is Present': Artistic Re-Enactments and the Impossibility of Presence," *TDR: The Drama Review* 55: 1 (Spring 2011), 16-45.
24. On *Seven Easy Pieces*, including Abramović's comments about the work, see Abramović, *Seven Easy Pieces*, Milan: Edizioni Charta, 2007, as well as her interview in this volume, and the critical review by Joanna Burton, "Repeat Performance," *Artforum*, January 2006, pp. 55–6.
25. On music, performance art, and liveness, see Auslander's *Liveness* and Jonathan Sterne, *The Audible Past*, Durham: Duke University Press, 2003. And for an interesting take on the script or "scenario" in relation to the archive and the ephemerality of the live event, see Taylor, chapter 2, "Scenarios of Discovery," *The Archive and the Repertoire*, pp. 53–78.
26. Sven Lütticken, "Introduction," in Lütticken (ed.), *Life, Once More: Forms of Re-Enactment in Contemporary Art*, Rotterdam: Witte de With, 2007, p. 5.
27. See Michael Kirby, *Futurist Performance*, New York: E. P. Dutton, 1971; and Mel Gordon, *Dada Performance*, London: PAJ Publications, 1987.
28. See my discussion of Klein's "Anthropometries" in *Body Art*, pp. 86–92. On the aesthetic as containing, and the tendency to represent the female body as a mode of containment, see Lynda Nead's *The Female Nude: Art, Obscenity and Sexuality*, London: Routledge, 1992.
29. Taiwanese performance artist Tehching Hsieh, for example, re-staged Klein's *Leap into the Void*, documented in a famous 1960 photograph by Harry Shunk; see Adrian Heathfield's discussion of this work in his essay "Impress of Time," *Out of Now: The Lifeworks of Tehching Hsieh*, Cambridge, MA: MIT Press, 2009, p. 14; the piece is illustrated with a photograph on p. 323. In his *Leap into the Yard* (2004), Keith Boadwee redid Klein's pseudo-heroic *Leap*, but with himself flying through the air naked and vulnerable; and Rachel Lachowicz re-staged Klein's *Anthropometries* in her 1992 *Red not Blue*, in which she (as the painting artist) reversed the gender of artist and models. On the Lachowicz piece, see my essay "*Not*: Rachel Lachowicz's *Red Not Blue* 1992," *Rachel Lachowicz*,

Santa Monica: Shoshana Wayne Gallery, forthcoming. On Boadwee, who became notorious in the 1990s for his queering of Jackson Pollock painting by squirting paint from his asshole, see my discussion in *Body Art*, pp. 99–102.

30. See my essay, "Performing the Wounded Body: Pain, Affect, and the Radical Relationality of Meaning," *Parallax*, November 2009, vol. 15, no. 4, pp. 45–67, and my attempt to remain "wounded," and to leave the work "uncontained," in my "Holy Body: Erotic Ethics in Ron Athey and Juliana Snapper's *Judas Cradle*," *TDR (The Drama Review: The Journal of Performance Studies)*, Spring 2006, vol. 50, no. 1, pp. 159–69.
31. This is art historian Donald Preziosi paraphrasing Hegel in his "The Other: Art History and/as Museology," in Preziosi (ed.), *The Art of Art History*, p. 451.
32. Curator Nicholas Bourriaud first developed the notion of "relational aesthetics"; see *Relational Aesthetics* (1998), trans. Simon Pleasance, Fronza Woods, with participation of Mathieu Copeland, Paris: Les Presses du réel, 2002.
33. See, respectively, Allan Kaprow "The Legacy of Jackson Pollock," *Art News*, October 1958, vol. 57, no. 6, pp. 24–6, 55–7; Victor Burgin, "Situational Aesthetics," *Studio International*, October, 1969, vol. 178, no. 915, p. 119; Lucy Lippard, *Six Years: The Dematerialization of the Art Object from 1966–1972* (1973), Berkeley: University of California Press, 1997; Dick Higgins, "Statement on Intermedia," in Wolf Vostell (ed.) *Dé-coll/age (décollage)* * 6, Frankfurt: Typos Verlag, and New York: Something Else Press, 1967, available at: http://www.artpool.hu/Fluxus/Higgins/intermedia2.html, accessed 10 May 2011.
34. Maurice Merleau-Ponty, "The Intertwining – the Chiasm," in Claude Lefort (ed.), *Visible and the Invisible* (1964), trans. Alphonso Lingis, Evanston: Northwestern University Press, 1968.
35. Ibid., p. 131.

Then Again

Adrian Heathfield

> There is no archive without a place of consignation, without a technique of repetition, and without a certain exteriority. No archive without outside.
>
> Jacques Derrida[1]

> [B]etween tradition and oblivion [the archive] reveals the rules of a practice that enables statements both to survive and to undergo regular modification. *It is the general system of the formation and transformation of statements.*
>
> Michel Foucault[2]

Let us suspend for the moment questions of the cultural necessity of performance art and live art raised so often in discussions such as these. What is certain with regard to performance's insistent presence in twentieth- and early twenty-first century western art is that its occurrence is invariably accompanied by forceful evidentiary and epistemological drives. From the manifestos of Futurism and Fluxus, through the scores and instructions of Happenings and Conceptual Art and the residual objects of body artists, to the performance scripts of experimental theater and the testimonies and digitized traces of contemporary live artists, where performance arises it is accompanied by its registration in textual and material forms. Whilst these remains are different from the events they register, they reiterate, extend, and transform the "life of performance," securing its relations to the visible and the legible.[3] Aside from the powers of the witnessed performance to bring its objects into question, the traces of performance prompt further questions and proliferate discourses around what exactly was done, seen, and understood.

Performance bears a temporal paradox: it exists both now and then, it leaves and lasts; its tendencies toward disappearance and dematerialization are countered by its capacities to adhere, mark, and trace itself otherwise. Performance art is now variously manifested in global documentary, archival and discursive re-presentations, so much so that we might say that it carries with(in) itself the means of its historicization. Performance imprints itself in the memories of its spectators, in their testimonies, in material objects and spaces, in numerous forms of "text": it is recursively disseminated. The complicities between performance and repetition, the instance and its iteration, performance's becoming-matter and its becoming-text are the subject of this volume's investigations.

In the 1980s when I first encountered performance art of the late 1950s and 1960s, performance's integral relation to the mechanisms of historical record was not entirely evident or culturally accepted. Performance art was an alluring, rarefied and elusive art form; arduous investigation was required to uncover its histories. It felt like a secret. At the same time it also appeared to be a marginal, volatile, and somewhat stigmatized mode for contemporary artists whose inclinations were often anti-textual, anti-materialist, anti-commercial, and passionately presentist. This critical perception proved temporary, perhaps because historical and institutional incorporation is always quietly in motion, or the perception was simply produced by the time lag inherent in all forms of historical narration. The attitudes that characterized the performance scene of the time, however, remain vital to the cultural force of live art, in part because they revivify the texts, materials, economies, and histories they critique. In the interceding time, between the 1980s and the 2010s, there has been a global information explosion and there have been profound shifts in the physical status of the commodity and expansions and transformations in the scenes of performance production and scholarship. Now, whatever historical narrative or genealogy of performance and live art you subscribe to, wherever and whenever you locate its "origins," performance cannot be made, experienced, researched, or understood without some recourse to its complex enmeshment within historical, material, and discursive formations.

Unfolding Time

The anti-capitalist drive that has formed such a significant impetus in the generation of twentieth-century art (though accompanied by relentless, subtle, and sometimes brutal assimilation) has found many particular manifestations in the historical subcultural scenes of performance, a form that has been consistently perceived as an art of time *par excellence*. In the cultural logics of late capitalism, time itself is a highly exploitable commodity. As Jean-François Lyotard noted: "Money is nothing other than time placed in reserve, available."[4] Capitalism seeks to regulate, homogenize, and accelerate time in the interests of productivity. This "capitalized time" was evident to artists in the 1960s and 1970s, for whom the exploration and use of unregulated temporalities (chance operations, contingent forms, and improvisations) was a means to assert "inassimilable" values. Performance offered to return art value to the agency of the artist, locating value within the witnessed passage of the artist's body and actions, rather than in the exchange or reception of the artist's finalized and exteriorized objects. Or it offered self-loss, sacrifice; it was a wasteful or excessive form of expenditure. The physical giving (of one's self) that performance required, seemingly without reserve or recompense, set it aside as a modality marked by an escape from predominant economies. It embodied a certain contrary valuing of the fleeting moment, of the meanings approached, lost and found therein, of the ephemera of communal gathering and exchange.

In artworks of long duration in the 1970s and 1980s, performance art became a vital form of cultural resistance to orders of temporal regulation and acceleration.[5] Taking time itself as a subject and a malleable phenomenon, durational works made the spectator aware of time as an alterable construct. By stalling the cultural economies of instantaneous meaning and reception, by reasserting the living labor of meaning-making, performance enacted what Pamela M. Lee has, in other art historical contexts, called an "ethics of slowness."[6] De-naturalizing and de-habitualizing perceptions of time, durational aesthetics gave access to other temporalities, excluded or marginalized within culture's increasingly rigorous temporal organization. Of course performance art's relation to the object, to materiality and representation was always much more ambivalent than this account admits: it produced objects, it was invested in the materiality of the body, it was both presentation and representation, it found itself represented and consequently circulated.

The time of performance art and live art has often been conceived as that of an event, a term which has its own history in relation to modernity, alongside complex psychoanalytic and philosophical connotations. The psychoanalytic notion of an event, derived from Freudian and Lacanian analyses and inflected most acutely in contemporary trauma theory, proposes that an event is always in excess of the subject that witnesses it, creating a breach in experience and comprehension, a breach that instigates the repetitious return of the event for its witnesses. The past returns repeatedly within the present. An event thus emerges as a kind of rupture in experience, knowledge, and history. Whilst notions of eventhood are often recursive, then, they do suggest a bracketing of time, a designation of "uneventful" times through which the event as heightened experience must necessarily be constituted.

In the early twentieth-century work of Henri Bergson a somewhat different understanding of time emerges. Bergson was similarly concerned with the nature of the inner experience of time, which he distinguished from its social organization in "clock time." He conceived this subjective time as resolutely inaccessible to thought and language, since it is composed of sensations and emotions, qualities not quantities, in a constant, indivisible state of movement and flux. Bergson termed this temporality "duration," since it is always ongoing; it is experienced as a radical form of heterogeneity, no sensation ever being the same as a previous sensation. For Bergson the past lives on inside the present, and is only separated from it by thought. Thoughts, language, representations operate on time by spatializing it (sectioning, containing, and cutting it); thus time is equated with incessant and irreducible movement.[7]

What might these temporal dynamics imply for the practices of historicizing live art through documents, archives, and critical narratives? Whether conceived through the optics of duration or eventhood, the timeliness of performance emerges as a force of abundance and excess that perturbs its rendition in thought, memory, historical record, and narration. Moreover, the rhetorical operations of history have themselves been called into question in part through postmodernity's much discussed and lingering condition of "incredulity toward metanarratives."[8] This pervading disbelief in the underlying organizing logics of history leads an art theorist such as Jan Verwoert to declare:

> On a phenomenological level the experience of history in crisis is also the experience of a crisis of time [...] in the time of crisis two different and essentially contradictory dimensions of temporality coincide: the time of empty duration and the time of absolute urgency.[9]

In Verwoert's analysis contemporary western societies are still gripped by violent historical upheaval, but their cultures now lack the capacity/belief to tell of these changes, and so for those cultures' citizens the experience of time is marked by both an ongoing aimlessness and a quality of perpetual emergency, both of which are profoundly disempowering. Art may be one means through which this impasse can be surpassed, if it is able justly to imagine other "potential historical realities" and thereby "open up a different future."[10] Part of this reinvention of historical sense, I would assert, is the very work of contemporary performance and live art practices, whose capacity to activate and open the past within the present, whose versatility in addressing and transforming the experience of time as it is sensed and made into sense is a vital cultural and historical value.

Much of the onus in relation to the task of revivifying historical sense rests of course with historians, of which art and performance historiographers are but a minor (though growing) breed. How then might performance, with its excessive events and indivisible durations best be historicized? The outlook of this volume would suggest that the crisis in historical narration is not one that could be solved by a return to the old forms of stable objective narrative, instead historiography must enact a questioning encounter with its own narratological structures, with its grip upon its object and with its own fragile tenure. As Eleonora Fabião phrases it in her chapter here on performance historiography, historical narration must honor the multiplicity and singularity of events through "an experiential practice of history writing." As British performance artist Stuart Brisley has noted in relation to the photography of performance: "The issue is not one of the ephemeral versus the permanent. Nothing is forever. It is the question of the relative durations of the impermanent."[11] Brisley's comment is equally applicable to other registrations of performance whether imagistic, textual, or actional and it is an important reminder of the temporality of all historical record, indeed of all matter.

Lure of Presence

The present time/tense has often been seen as inherent within the philosophical (and theatrical) notion of presence, of being present. "Being there," so the story goes, is dependent on being in and of the moment. For much of its life throughout the twentieth-century, the presence of performance art (of the performer) has been both the proposed source of its cultural appeal and value, and the cause of its suspicion, marginalization, and denigration within many critical and institutional contexts.[12] The desire for a condition of unmediated Being and pure presence, of a fleshly existence outside of representation, was famously marked and unravelled by Derrida as the motivating force of one of the twentieth-century avant-garde theater's most influential thinkers Antonin Artaud.[13] Many performance artists of the 1960s up to those of the present day – if not citing Artaud's influence consciously as the renowned Polish experimental theater-maker Jerzy Grotowski did – have attributed powers to performance that hold to notions of self-coincident, unitary, and extra-linguistic Being: the very conditions Derrida cast into a movement of infinite deferral.

In the later decades of the twentieth-century, global cultures and art practices were transformed through rapid technological saturation. Performance became a paradigmatic modality of postmodern aesthetics, where interdisciplinarity, mediation, and self-reflexivity were its prevalent and resilient companion tropes. The 1990s resurgence of Body Art with its emphasis on the opening and materiality of the flesh, its reverberations of "traumatic" and "carnal" affects, was also accompanied in the West by a proliferation of live art and experimental theater practices deploying technologies of mediation and simulation, dense layering of texts, aesthetic techniques of self-interrogation, evident duplicity and haptic spectacle. Contemporary art scenes are now characterized, as this volume reflects, by a complex diversity of live art practices, many of which can no longer be located unequivocally on either side of binarized drives toward exposure or concealment, the embodied or the textual, essence or appearance, reality or illusion, the figural or the literal.

In this context the nature of the experience of "being there" for both the performer and the spectator is, to say the least, critically slippery. As the consequences of post-structuralist thought have reverberated through performance scholarship from the 1970s on, performance theorists have wrestled in Derrida's shadows with the notion of theatrical presence, as a somewhat suspect, but troublingly appealing sub-condition of the questioned philosophical concept.[14] One consequence of these understandings, as the chapters in this volume attest, is that the phenomenological affects of performance are no longer seen as separable from their linguistic and discursive construction. And yet, for all of these determinations, questions of the "life force" of performance persist, and are still brought into relation with critical notions of performance's intrinsic value. As Amelia has noted in a 1997 article, the problem that recurs for theorists of performance looking for "the intrinsic" is the reification of the event above its other eventual recurrences, the tendency to ascribe authenticity to an originary performance, whereby it acquires a truth-value.[15] Here distinctions between forms such as primary and secondary, live and mediated, become redundant in the acknowledgment of the recursive condition of all events of interpretation.

The dilemma for performance critics and spectators alike goes something like this. The witnessed event appears to assert qualities of experience that are singular, irreducible, unrepresentable; and yet there is a cognizance even in "the heat" of the event that the event will be repeated, albeit differently, in thought, memory, historical record. The understanding of a performance proceeds through a temporal paradox, between the "specificity of knowledges [...] in a live performance event" and their subsequent and no less specific revision in other instances of knowing.[16] Experience cannot be detached from thought. The thought of the event is inseparable from its afterthought. So despite the unique affects of a performance, it is impossible to locate the experience of the event, or indeed experience itself, as somehow pure, direct, unmediated, non-contingent, untouched by cultural and ideological conventions. Nonetheless, it was "an experience," it retains "for us" an "otherly" force that secures its return in knowledge, and "our" return to it.

Whether one thinks of performance as founded in "disappearance," "reappearance," or "the viral" – just some of the foundations referenced and proposed in the many chapters assembled here – such definitions are caught in the characteristic dilemma of ontology itself: whether one can define the Being of some thing, without recourse to essence or to a final truth. Performance, it seems, is never far from this lure. But the multiple lives of performance, dissected, represented, re-performed by this volume suggest that one of performance's most consistent and recurring conditions is *transformation*. Perhaps then, one should search less for its ontology and more for its ontogeneses: the many natures of its becomings. A simpler way of saying this is that one can look for and delineate the "life forces" of performance without thinking that they constitute its "only life."

The numerous recurrences of performance in image, text, object, and echo-events presented here suggest that every rendition of a performance, whatever its form, is itself a different event. This difference is more than formal, as forms take place, are received, and understood in the movement of time, a force that is, as Bergson noted, a relentless differentiation of things. This is not to deny similarities and continuities between times and between recursive forms – that, for example, a video recording of a performance event may substantively deliver the meanings and affects of the said event to new spectators – but rather it is to assert that the relation of the two events is marked by some evident and unknowable differences. Each event in each differently functioning form is produced in and by the complex intersubjective and inter-sensorial co-minglings of its participant-spectators/readers. Such contexts are not pre-discursive, and whether or not they involve "solitary reception" (a "single" body watching a pre-recorded body on a screen for example) they are inherently social: involving numerous subjectivities, numerous active beings in and of numerous times, diverging and converging in the times of the event of reading. The bodies assembled here, before each other, actually, virtually, sense and communicate in the flux of simultaneously absent and present corporealities.

Without an Archive

One way of thinking of this volume then, and of reading it, is as a modest archive of a selection of late twentieth- and early twenty-first century performance and live art. Though it is a place, a "container" as Amelia phrases it, from which you may learn about these cultural phenomena, it is distinct from a common cultural archive in a number of ways. *Perform, Repeat, Record* works through its own "technique of repetition": It is wilfully partial, provisional, and turned self-consciously toward its outsides.[17] As Derrida has noted in his work on the archive, one of the unfortunate consequences of the archival impulse is to "place" that which it holds under "house arrest," a consignment that threatens to fix and extract from performance its vitalities, and potentially its cultural, political, and epistemological forces. One answer to such operations within the logic of the archive that this volume (indeed any volume, necessarily) follows is to produce archival forms whose containment is questioned by their evident divergence and fragmentation, by their presentation of paradox, forms that present their inevitable contingency, opening themselves to what they are not.

The dynamics that are inherent to the contingent archive that is *Perform, Repeat, Record* thus remind us of the promissory force of "the performative" and quite specifically of one of its definitive characteristics, as articulated by Derrida in his deconstruction of J. L. Austin's influential work on the subject.[18] While Austin distinguished speech acts or "performatives" from other forms of linguistic expression according to their ability to enact as they say, these articulations or "utterances" as Derrida has it cannot be conceived as pure or outside of a system of citation. The intention (or origin) of speech acts cannot be identified or secured; they are part of an infinitely recurring system of iterations, characterized in each instance by their deferral and difference. The paradox of "the performative" then, like the paradox of performance itself, or indeed the paradox of the "holding place" that is the archive/book, is that it is both double and singular, a "formation" and a "transformation," a conformation and a departure, old and new, echoing and propagating.

This archive is organized into three temporary zones. You will find in the Theories and Histories zone a set of critical investigations that deal with the existing cultural archive of performance and live art, testing out its composition and limits, its organizing logics. Here the volume diversely foregrounds another kind of archive from the ones that have been presented to date, including previously absented works, forms, oeuvres, histories. To take but one important example, we have commissioned accounts and investigations of Eastern European, Asian, and South American performance histories that have been barely acknowledged in other volumes surveying the scenes of recent live art. There is, as one would expect with this kind of restoration, a good deal of corrective work: inclusion requires a revision of the exclusionary terms through which previous narrations operated. Our "technique" is not solely "critical." In the Documents zone of the volume, we have assembled an extensive set of documentary pieces, working directly with artists to explore the possibilities of re-presenting performance works in the limited form of a book. Here the nature of the document is also in question, as the assembled and documented performances are embroiled in a wrangle with the mechanisms of historical record. Which modes and forms of description, depiction, capture and release to deploy and why? How to navigate the narration of a work of performance or a life's work of performances? How to wrestle creatively with the event and the remainder as an artistic source, with the relentless operations of the archive, and the uncanny dynamics of the redo? This work of opening up the archive is further extended in our final zone of Dialogues, where an oft-suppressed dynamic of creative and historical production is foregrounded: dialogic exchange. Here the dialogues enable Amelia and myself, as critical theorists, to engage with artists' narrations of their work, and their perceptions of the mechanisms of their work's historicization. But importantly this zone also allows for the voices of others in exchange, for the acknowledgment of dialogue as a generator of the artwork, and as a performance form in and of itself.

Every archive has its outsides, every book draws boundaries that are exclusive, some known to us as editors, others not. Both Amelia and I could swiftly think of the work of scores of contemporary artists, aesthetic trajectories, and critical voices whose absence here is regrettable. Yet the object of this work is not to represent a comprehensive picture of performance art's history, but to mark performance and live art's potentials as they enter historicization. In this respect the volume is concerned not just with the presentation of under- or un-narrated works, the revision of past narrations, but the opening of critical possibilities, connectivities, and trajectories of thought that will grow and be superseded by new histories of performance and live art. Our hope is, that like the performances it repeats, records, and re-performs, this volume prompts future acts and promises other scenarios.

Notes

1. Jacques Derrida, *Archive Fever: A Freudian Impression*, Chicago, Illinois: University of Chicago Press, 1996, p. 12.
2. Michel Foucault, "The Historical *a priori* and the Archive," *The Archaeology of Knowledge*, New York: Harper & Row 1976 (1971), p. 130.
3. The phrase "life of performance" is derived from Peggy Phelan's axial essay on the ontology of performance in *Unmarked: The Politics of Performance*, Routledge, 1993, with which this introduction quietly dialogues.
4. Jean-François Lyotard, *The Inhuman: Reflections on Time*, trans. Geoffrey Bennington and Rachel Bowlby, Stanford: Stanford University Press, 1991 (1988), p. 66.
5. I explore concepts and aesthetics of duration in much more detail in Adrian Heathfield and Tehching Hsieh, *Out of Now: The Lifeworks of Tehching Hsieh*, Cambridge, MA: MIT Press, 2009.
6. Pamela M. Lee, *Chronophobia: On Time in the Art of the 1960s*, Cambridge, MA: MIT Press, 2004.
7. Henri Bergson, *Time and Free Will: An Essay on the Immediate Data of Consciousness* (1913), London: Elibron Classics, 2005.
8. Jean-François Lyotard, *The Postmodern Condition: A Report on Knowledge* (1979), Manchester: Manchester University Press, 1984.
9. Jan Verwoert, "The Crisis of Time in Times of Crisis," in Anke Bangma, Steve Rushton and Florian Wüst (eds), *Experience, Memory, Re-enactment*, Rotterdam: Piet Zwart Institute and Revolver, 2005, pp. 37–40.
10. Ibid. p. 38.

11. Stuart Brisley, "The Photographer and the Performer," in Alice Maude-Roxby (ed.), *Live Art on Camera: Performance and Photography*, Southampton: John Hansard Gallery, 2007.
12. I am thinking not only of the association of the material presence of the body with notions of corruption and theatricality in influential theories of modernist art such as those of Michael Fried, but also performance art's historical designation as unruly and unwarranted in numerous major art institutional contexts throughout the 1980s and 1990s.
13. Jacques Derrida, "The Theatre of Cruelty and the Closure of Representation," *Writing and Difference*, trans. Alan Bass, Chicago, Illinois: University of Chicago Press, 1978.
14. Philip Auslander, *Presence and Resistance: Postmodernism and Cultural Politics in Contemporary American Performance*, Ann Arbor: University of Michigan Press, 1994.
15. Amelia Jones, "'Presence' in *absentia*: Experiencing Performance as Documentation," *Art Journal*, Winter 1997, vol. 56, no. 4, pp. 11–18.
16. Ibid. p. 12.
17. Jacques Derrida, *Archive Fever: A Freudian Impression*, Chicago, Illinois: University of Chicago Press, 1996, p. 12.
18. Jacques Derrida, "Signature Event Context," *Limited Inc*, Evanston, IL: Northwestern University Press, 1988 (1972).

I

Theories and Histories

Introduction

Amelia Jones

> The modality of the event is a time of loss: as bodies, we are lost to it.
> In asserting a hold on these fleeting, death-bound movements, we cling to the consolations by which the document lays claim to the ephemeral.[1]

In this eloquent, performative statement, performance artist and scholar Dominic Johnson cuts through the dilemmas posed by the live event in terms of its "presence" in history. In spite of these dilemmas, however, a myriad of historical narratives have been drafted to create lineages of official Euro-American performance art history in the past half a century. These histories, by scholars such as, most prominently, New York-based RoseLee Goldberg, have thus constructed a teleology beginning with the performative effusions of Futurists and Dadaists in WWI-era Paris, going relatively quiet over the period of the 1920s–1940s (with the turmoil of WWII and the establishment of abstract painting as the privileged mode of artistic creativity), and reemerging with the development of performance art as a distinct genre in the 1960s.[2] These official histories – *which have themselves constituted the field of performance art proper as a separate discipline (of making and of study)* – have been dominated by a visual arts (art historical) rather than theater studies perspective, although both function as the twin "parent" disciplines of the practices of performance and live art. The "art" perspective in official histories has encouraged the focus on determinable lineages and individual authors, as the art market demands these in order to turn cultural into economic value.

I have argued in my 1998 book *Body Art/Performing the Subject* that this lineage, if we are willing to accept it for the moment, is incomplete without a consideration of the coterminous, but much less marketable, discursive enactment of painting as performance in the career of Jackson Pollock – the performative dimension of which was activated in the 1950 film and photographs of the artist painting by Hans Namuth and from the mid-1950s onwards by the Gutai artists in Japan and by the French painter Georges Mathieu (teacher of Yves Klein). This discursive enactment took place in two key articles as well: Harold Rosenberg's 1952 "The American Action Painters" and Allan Kaprow's 1958 "The Legacy of Jackson Pollock," both of which write Pollock's body into motion as actively painting rather than consigning it to the status of an invisible origin of the work.[3]

Kaprow in particular presciently offered a new way of thinking about painting via Pollock's "diaristic gesture," which he argues established art as a *process* rather than a final product. Most strikingly, Kaprow identified a new situation in which those who approach Pollock's paintings become "participants rather than observers" – marking a very early awareness in visual arts discourse of art as open to interpretive engagement (rather than putatively fixed in its meaning as modernist formalist criticism would have it).[4] Through this new way of seeing and thinking about art as a process of *making* rather than as static *object*, artists and theorists began exploring various modes of foregrounding the body as visible to the making of and encounter with the work of art.

Interestingly, the opening of art to what we might call the performative in these art discourses around 1950 coincided with the development of performance theory in the English-speaking world. It is tempting to say something was in the air (the hoary notion of *Zeitgeist* comes to mind). The important posthumously published book of the British historian R. G. Collingwood, *The Idea of History* first came out in 1946 and was reprinted in 1956. In this series of lectures, Collingwood articulated a theory of history as performative – with the historian necessarily re-telling (and thus creatively re-enacting) events from the past through his or her present point of view: "[H]ow does the historian discern the thoughts which he is trying to discover? [...] There is only one way in which it can be done: by re-thinking them in his own mind."[5] Meanwhile, in the mid-1950s Collingwood's colleague at Oxford, J. L. Austin, was actively theorizing what would become his highly influential theory of linguistic performatives, given first as a series of lectures at Harvard University in the United States in 1955, then published in 1962 in his book *How to Do Things with Words*. And, in the United States, sociologist Erving Goffman was presenting his theory of human behaviour as performative, as published in his 1959 book *The Presentation of the Self in Everyday Life*.[6] Here, Goffman argues that the social self is a *performance* in relation to others, a negotiation involving complex intersubjective cues and behaviors. The self, Goffman asserts,

> does not derive from its possessor, but from the whole scene of his action. [...] A correctly staged and performed scene leads the audience to impute a self to a performed character, but this imputation–this self–is a *product* of a scene that comes off, and is not a *cause* of it. The self, then, as a performed character, is not an organic thing that has a specific location [...] it is a dramatic effect arising diffusely from a scene that is presented.[7]

After WWII, the nascent theory of the "performative" was being articulated (particularly in the Anglophone context) across art making, art theory, philosophy, and modes of theorizing about the writing of history itself. Over the next three decades, Austin's theory of "speech-acts" in particular – partly as elaborated in the work of John Searle – permeated into anthropology, literary criticism, and philosophy.[8] Most influential for discussions of visual and performing arts cultures has been the development of Austin's theory in the work of Jacques Derrida and Judith Butler. In his important 1977 essay "Signature Event Context," Derrida critiques Austin by exposing the assumption of intentionality built into speech-act theory as impossibly invested in the "presence" of the source of utterance. Derrida makes use of written communication to point to the absence of the addressee for the writer, and of the writer for the later reader. Derrida argues that this schism evident in writing exposes the contingency of the performative, and the impossibility of confirming a unified source of meaning: "[T]he performative's referent [...] does not describe something which exists outside and before language. It produces or transforms a situation, it operates."[9]

In her highly influential books *Gender Trouble* (1990) and *Bodies that Matter* (1993), Butler, in turn, adopts Derrida's critical reworking of the Austinian notion of "iteration" to argue that identity (gendered identity in particular) is performative. Butler argues, famously, "the body becomes its gender through a series of acts which are renewed, revised, and consolidated through time."[10] These arguments, which staged the body as a non-essentialized locus of the enactment of linguistic and gestural identifications, were crucial in the highly fruitful intersection of identity theory and performance theory academic discussions of performativity in the 1990s.

The chapters collected in "Theories and Histories" show the expansion of these more philosophically oriented debates into performance theory proper – and it is important to note the crucial role of this trajectory of theory in the institutional formation of Performance Studies as a discipline. The anthropologist Victor Turner, one of the key figures in the extension of a reworked version of Austin's theory of performativity into the ethnographic study of ritual, worked collaboratively with Richard Schechner, a key figure in the founding of the first major Performance Studies department at New York University in 1980. Peggy Phelan, whose 1993 book *Unmarked: The Politics of Performance* has shaped debates in the field for the past seventeen years, taught at NYU in the 1990s and there, with her PhD students, organized the first "Performance Studies international" (PSi) conference in 1995.[11] Phelan's most famous claim in *Unmarked* proposes that performance, *as* live event is, in its very Being, distinct from its subsequent rendition in other forms: "Performance's only life is in the present. [...] To the degree that performance attempts to enter the economy of reproduction it betrays and lessens the promise of its own ontology."[12] This identification of performance as intrinsically resistant to commodification is one that has since preoccupied and troubled many art and performance theoreticians, and it is an assertion that the contributors here variously contend with, as they anatomize the many "lives" of performance in its documentary, archival, and representational forms[13].

"Theories and Histories" is perhaps best read in a non-linear fashion, as the contributors discuss a kaleidoscopic array of problems inherent in the multiple modes of the historicization of performance. The section features a range of chapters addressing theories and histories of performance and performativity, as well as work by art critics and historians exploring the surge of attention toward the live in contemporary art since the turn of the millennium. For example, examining the recent rise of interest in displaying documentation in art contexts, German scholar Boris Groys in a sense extends the logic of Phelan's arguments but gives them a twist, noting that "art documentation," by putting "images and texts that are reproducible" into an art context, "acquires through the installation an aura of the original, the living, the historical" – effectively turning documentation into "historical event." Rebecca Schneider, in contrast, rejects what she argues to be Phelan's reliance on the logic of the archive (in opposition to which the performance distinguishes itself in Phelan's theory as "live"), arguing, rather, that performance might present entirely other kinds of knowing. Christopher Bedford critiques and builds on Phelan's insights in relation to the work of Chris Burden; as a visual arts curator Bedford argues that, rather than having the static ontological status of an "original event" implied by Phelan's model, performances are "viral" – they take their meaning from (and spread virally into) future debates via a range of discourses, including art criticism, journalism, curatorial practices, as well as leftover objects or (as Burden called them) "relics."

Drawing on Gilles Deleuze's notion of repetition as "a skin which unravels," Jane Blocker, trained as an art historian, expands on Schneider's critique in this new chapter on the repetition at the heart of performance to examine how visual artworks can operate performatively. Blocker explores the effects of performative artworks such as Bruce Nauman's and Steve McQueen's video and film installations and, more broadly, argues that an attention to this dimension of performance as a kind of archive itself can serve productively to rethink modes of history-writing. In his 2006 essay "The Performativity of Performance Documentation," Philip Auslander, working in the interfaces among performance, media and music theory and history, looks again at this ontology but through the question of documentation. Like Bedford, he notes the performativity of documentation itself, and critically asserts the impossibility of an event somehow ontologically pre-existing its documentation: we cannot know the event *but* through such fragments and traces or, at least, through the inevitably self-conscious enactment of the event as potentially able to be documented in photography or film. Documentation, Auslander argues, "does not simply generate images/statements that describe an autonomous performance [...] it produces an event as performance."

Performance curator and theorist Sven Lütticken intervenes in these debates to reject wholesale the claims of inherent radicality posed for performance, often via Phelan's arguments or through more naïve, utopian claims for the genre's "resistance to all forms of domination."[14] Applying a rigorous and nuanced Marxist model, Lütticken traces the history of theories of "dematerialization" (a concept first elaborated by Lucy Lippard in her classic 1973 book by this title), examining the dematerialized contemporary performances of artists such as Tino Sehgal (who refuses any documentation of his public events). Lütticken argues that, rather than debunking or overthrowing the circuits of capital, such projects emphasize (and make money from) the workings of the service (or "experience") economy so central to late capitalism – suggesting that, in fact, performance art "has never been a real threat to the spectacle."

Other contributions in this section offer new modes of practice and new theories as well as new histories and new modes of the writing of the histories of live and performance art. Armenian art historian Angela Harutyunyan, with the research input of Vardan Azatyan, Tevž Logar, Vesna Madzoski, Joanna Sokołowska and Eszter Lázár, contributes a two-part timeline addressing from their point of view the complex (and, in the Anglophone context, up to this point unknown) histories of Soviet and post-Soviet era performance in Eastern Europe. Performance and dance theorist and curator André Lepecki reflects on his orchestration of the restaging of Allan Kaprow's *18 Happenings in 6 Parts*, a repeatedly cited "originary" Happening first performed at the Reuben Gallery in New York in 1959. Lepecki dissects the haunted and conflicted nature of working in the creative space of historical re-enactment. Here the redo becomes the site of new understandings of Kaprow's approach to performance, revealing the surprising dependency of the event upon its score, upon non-spontaneous elements and upon restrictions in place that conditioned the parameters of the 1959 performance. The art historian Hannah B Higgins returns to the histories of the Fluxus movement (frequently narrated as a progenitor of contemporary performance) to question the reduction of this complex international network of artists, acts and art propositions to the principles and figure of its supposed *auteur*, George Maciunas. Moving past such narrations, which Higgins sees as being produced by the individualizing imperatives of the art market and conventional art criticism and its related institutions (including the art gallery and art history), she puts forward a reading of Fluxus as a plural activation of intermedial forms and multi-sensate encounters, where the visual can no longer be privileged as the primary mode of communication and understanding.

The reverse of Higgins's critical gesture critiquing the reduction of a past movement to a singular author is found in Brazilian performance artist and performance theorist Eleonora Fabião's chapter which transects the still largely untold and unrecognized histories of South American performance. Fabião recovers for the record the figure of Arthur Bispo do Rosario, a prolific Afro-Brazilian artist who was diagnosed as a schizophrenic and interned in psychiatric institutions for most of his life. Bispo's multi-form, highly crafted artworks recycling trash materials are analyzed by Fabião as a vast archival performance project. Erased from institutional and historical recognition, Bispo's condition of illegibility is seen by Fabião as a key to opening up another mode of historiography that would be constantly attentive to its margins and outsides, a mode that would keep the past moving by reinvesting in and reinventing it in the present. Artist and curator Monica Mayer extends this narration of Latin American performance with a detailed account of the genesis and dynamics of performance art in the Mexican context (as it interfaces with various genres and movements) stretching back into the 1920s. Mayer stresses the complex affinities between documentation and event, the complexities of the relationship of performance to institutions of validation and registration and the ways in which contemporary artists in Mexico have looked to the past and referenced a regional legacy.

After completing extensive interviews and archival research in Austria, Mechthild Widrich looks again at a classic piece of European performance art, VALIE EXPORT's 1969

Genital Panic, to expose the way in which the actuality and provenance of this "performance" (in which EXPORT supposedly wore crotchless pants and stalked men in a porn theater while holding a large gun) is highly questionable; whatever this work consisted of is and was largely signalled by a separate performance for a photograph, tirelessly re-circulated and re-contextualized by EXPORT and others through the contradictory mythical discourses that surround it. Widrich's scholarly project in a sense proves the explanatory value of Bedford's notion of performance as "viral": as existing in and through discourse, rather than as having some originary status as "real."

Meiling Cheng, whose work focuses on Californian as well as Chinese performance art, here looks closely at three Chinese performance projects within the context of contemporary Chinese history to argue that they displace the "*live* into the *once-lived*," through documentation taking on new meanings beyond their immediate (and highly policed) cultural context. Documentation in this context, she argues, produces "a virtual performance event." Collectively Cheng, with the other theorists, historians, and artists whose writings are represented in this section, interrogates and expands upon the intertwined problems posed (or opportunities provided?) by the "live" and the "performative" in relation to economies of image- and object-making, as well as history-writing, in the visual arts context, economies that tend to reduce meaning to simplistic circuits of value. The importance of bringing these voices together lies in stressing the impossibility of resolving how performance and/or live art *works* in relation to the passage of time. Careful theories and histories provide nuanced ways of navigating this question – themselves becoming open-ended *performances*, explorations rather than final or definitive answers.

Notes

1. Dominic Johnson, "Geometries of Trust: Some Thoughts on Manuel Vason and Photographic Conditions of Performance," *Dance Theatre Journal*, 2004, vol. 20, no. 4, pp. 12–19.
2. See for example RoseLee Goldberg, *Performance: Live Art 1909 to the Present*, New York: Harry N. Abrams, 1979.
3. See Amelia Jones, "The Pollockian Peformative," *Body Art/Performing the Subject*, Minneapolis: University of Minnesota Press, 1998, pp. 53–102; Harold Rosenberg, "The American Action Painters," *Art News*, December 1952, vol. 51, no. 8, pp. 22–3, 48–50; and Allan Kaprow, "The Legacy of Jackson Pollock," *Art News*, October 1958, vol. 57, no. 6, pp. 24–6, 55–7, reprinted in Allan Kaprow, *Allan Kaprow: Essays on the Blurring of Art and Life* (1993), Berkeley: University of California Press, 2003, pp. 1–9.
4. Kaprow, "The Legacy of Jackson Pollock," p. 6.
5. Collingwood, *The Idea of History* (1946), Oxford: Oxford University Press, 1956, p. 215. See also William Dray, *History as Re-Enactment: R. G. Collingwood's Idea of History*, Oxford: Oxford University Press, 1995.
6. J. L. Austin, *How to Do Things with Words*, Oxford: Clarendon Press, 1962; Erving Goffman, *The Presentation of Self in Everyday Life*, Garden City, New York: Doubleday, 1959.
7. Goffman, op. cit., pp. 252–3.

8. See Searle's *Speech Acts: An Essay in the Philosophy of Language*, Cambridge: Cambridge University Press, 1969. On the development of speech-act theory within anthropology, where ethnographers have criticized the theory for presenting a universalizing model of linguistic performance in its focus on intentionality, see Kira Hall, "Performativity," *Journal of Linguistic Anthropology*, 2000, vol. 9, no. 1–2, pp. 184–7. Importantly, Victor Turner, key to the founding of Performance Studies, is cited here as developing Austin's theory in works such as his 1984 article "Liminality and Performative Genres," in J. J. MacAloon (ed.), *Rite, Drama, Festival, Spectacle: Rehearsals toward a Theory of Cultural Performance*, Philadelphia: Institute for the Study of Human Issues, 1984, pp. 19–41.
9. Derrida, "Signature Event Context" (1977), *Margins of Philosophy*, trans. Alan Bass, Chicago: University of Chicago Press, 1982, p. 321. The three artists who changed their names to that of the then-prime minister of Slovenia (Janez Janša) produced a performative installation piece playing off of Derrida's essay, entitled *Signature Event Context*, for the performance festival transmediale '08, which took place in Berlin in 2008. On this piece, see http://www.aksioma.org/sec/press.html, Janez's contribution in this volume, and my essay "Naming the Power of the Name: Janez Janša Performs the Political in/for the Art World," *NAME Readymade*, Ljubljana: Moderna galerija and Aksioma Press, 2008, pp. 31–50.
10. Judith Butler, "Performative Acts and Gender Constitution: An Essay in Phenomenology and Feminist Theory," *Theatre Journal*, December 1988, vol. 40, no. 4, p. 523; this essay was reworked and included in her *Gender Trouble: Feminism and the Subversion of Identity*, New York: Routledge, 1990. See also Judith Butler, *Bodies that Matter: On the Discursive Limits of "Sex"*, New York: Routledge, 1993.
11. I discuss the founding of Performance Studies in my essay "Live Art in History: A Paradox?," in Tracy C. Davis (ed.), *The Cambridge Guide to Performance Studies*, Cambridge: Cambridge University Press, 2008, pp. 151–65.
12. Peggy Phelan, *Unmarked: The Politics of Performance*, New York: Routledge, 1993, p. 146.
13. Others have provided ways of rethinking this ontology, including myself (see Jones, "'Presence' *in absentia*: Experiencing Performance as Documentation," *Art Journal*, Winter 1997, vol. 56, no. 4, pp. 11–18); Meiling Cheng, *In Other Los Angeleses: Multicentric Performance Art*, Berkeley: University of California Press, 2002; and Camilla Jalving, "On Truth and Lies in the Work of Hayley Newman," in Rune Gade and Anne Jerslev (eds), *Performative Realism: Interdisciplinary Studies in Art and Media*, Copenhagen: University of Copenhagen/Museum Tusculanum Press, 2005, pp. 145–80.
14. Here, Lütticken is citing art historian Kristine Stiles from her "Performance," in Robert S. Nelson and Richard Shiff (eds), *Critical Terms for Art History*, 2nd edn, Chicago: University of Chicago Press, 2003, p. 85.

Chapter 1

The Performativity of Performance Documentation

Philip Auslander

Consider two familiar images from the history of performance and body art: the documentation of Chris Burden's *Shoot* (1971), the notorious piece for which the artist had a friend shoot him in a gallery, and Yves Klein's famous *Leap into the Void* (1960), which shows the artist jumping out of a second-story window into the street below. It is generally accepted that the first image is a piece of performance documentation, but what is the second? Burden really was shot in the arm during *Shoot*, but Klein did not really jump unprotected out of the window, the ostensible performance documented in his equally iconic image. What difference does it make to our understanding of these images in relation to the concept of performance documentation that one documents a performance that "really" happened while the other does not? I shall return to this question below.

As a point of departure for my analysis here, I propose that performance documentation has been understood to encompass two categories, which I shall call the *documentary* and the *theatrical.* The documentary category represents the traditional way in which the relationship between performance art and its documentation is conceived. It is assumed that the documentation of the performance event provides both a record of it through which it can be reconstructed (though, as Kathy O'Dell points out, the reconstruction is bound to be fragmentary and incomplete[1]) and evidence that it actually occurred. The connection between performance and document is thus thought to be ontological, with the event preceding and authorizing its documentation. Burden's performance documentation, as well most of the documentation of classic performance and body art from the 1960s and 1970s, belongs to this category.

Although it is generally taken for granted, the presumption of an ontological relationship between performance and document in this first model is ideological. The idea of the documentary photograph as a means of accessing the reality of the performance derives

Originally published as Philip Auslander, "The Performativity of Performance Documentation," *Performing Arts Journal* (*PAJ* 84), 2006, vol. 28, no. 3, pp. 1–10.

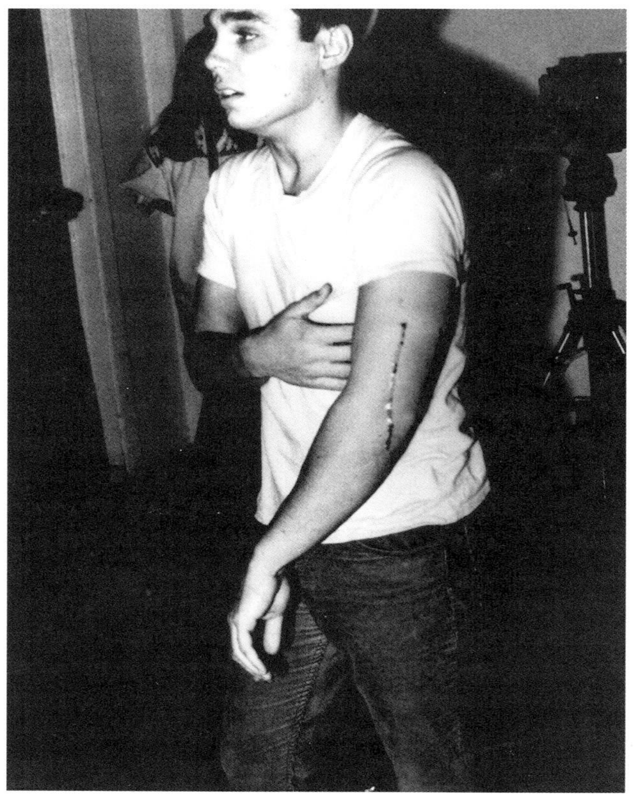

Chris Burden, *Shoot*
F Space, Santa Ana, CA, November 19, 1971
At 7:45 p.m. I was shot in the left arm by a friend.
The bullet was a copper jacket .22 long rifle. My
friend was standing about fifteen feet from me.

from the general ideology of photography, as described by Helen Gilbert, glossing Roland Barthes and Don Slater:

> Through its trivial realism, photography creates the illusion of such exact correspondence between the signifier and the signified that it appears to be the perfect instance of Barthes' "message without a code." The "sense of the photograph as not only representationally accurate but ontologically connected to the real world allows it to be treated as a piece of the real world, then as a substitute for it."[2]

(In relation to Slater's notion that the photograph ultimately substitutes for reality, it is worth considering whether performance recreations based on documentation actually recreate the underlying performances or perform the documentation. *Poor Theatre*, in which the Wooster Group recreates performances by Jerzy Grotowski and William Forsythe, and Marina Abramović's re-enactments of other artists' performances in *Seven Easy Pieces* are recent examples of work that clearly plays with this slippery question.)

Jon Erickson suggests that the use of black and white photography in classic performance documentation enhances photography's reality-effect (for Erickson, color photographs assert themselves more strongly as objects in their own right).

> There is a sense of mere utility in black-and-white, which points to the idea that documentation is really only a supplement to a performance having to do with context, space, action, ideas, of which the photograph is primarily a reminder.[3]

Amelia Jones takes up the idea of the documentary photograph as a supplement to the performance to challenge the ontological priority of the live performance. She offers a sophisticated analysis of "the mutual supplementarity of […] performance or body art and the photographic document. (The body art event needs the photograph to confirm its having happened; the photograph needs the body art event as an ontological 'anchor' of its indexicality.)"[4] While this formulation questions the performance's status as the originary event by suggesting the mutual dependence of performance and document (the performance is originary only insofar as it is documented), it also reaffirms the status of the photograph as an access point to the reality of the performance, a position on which Jones must insist since she argues it to defend her own practice of writing about performances she never saw in the flesh (a situation with which I am in complete sympathy).

In the theatrical category, I would place a host of artworks of the kind sometimes called "performed photography," ranging from Marcel Duchamp's photos of himself as Rose Selavy (1920–1) to Cindy Sherman's photographs of herself in various guises to Matthew Barney's *Cremaster* films. (Other recent examples include the work of Gregory Crewdson and Nikki Lee.) These are cases in which performances were staged solely to be photographed or filmed and had no meaningful prior existence as autonomous events presented to audiences. The space of the document (whether visual or audiovisual) thus becomes the only space in which the performance occurs. Klein's *Leap* belongs to this category. Klein had no audience apart from "close friends and photographers" when he jumped (which he did several times, "attempting to get the desired transcendent expression on his face") and used a protective net that does not appear in the photograph, which is actually a composite of two different shots unified in the darkroom.[5] (It is an open question whether the friends were there to witness a performance or a photo shoot – in either case, they did not see the event depicted in the photograph.) The image we see thus records an event that never took place except in the photograph itself.

From a traditional perspective, the documentary and theatrical categories are mutually exclusive. If one insists upon the ontological relationship by demanding that to qualify as a performance, an event must have an autonomous existence prior to its documentation, then the events underlying the works in the second category are not performances at all and the images are not documents, but something else, another kind of artwork perhaps (the phrase "performed photography," for instance, suggests that such works be understood as a kind of photograph rather than as performances). Erickson gestures toward such a position

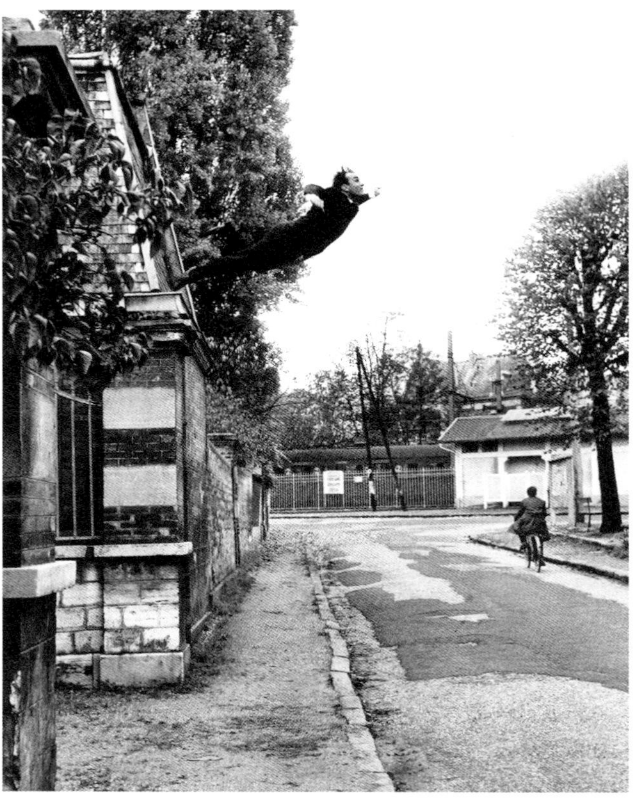

Yves Klein, *Le Saut dans le Vide* (*Leap into the Void*), 1960. Image courtesy Yves Klein Archives. Photo Shunk-Kender. © Estate of Yves Klein / SODRAC (2011). Photo © Roy Lichtenstein Foundation.

(without actually adopting it) in his review of RoseLee Goldberg's book *Performance: Live Art Since 1960* when he poses the question: "[D]oes [the book] defeat its own premise when it includes the 'performed photography' of Cindy Sherman, video, film stills (Matthew Barney's *Cremaster*), and even the drawings and sculptures of Robert Longo?"[6] Since these are all recordings of one sort or another, how can they qualify as "live" art?

From a different perspective, however, the two categories appear to have much in common. Although it is true that the theatrical images in the second category either had no significant audience other than the camera or could have had no such audience (because they never took place in real space), it is equally true that the images in *both* categories were staged for the camera. Although some of the early documentation of performance and body art was not carefully planned or conceived as such, performance artists who were interested in preserving their work quickly became fully conscious of the need to stage it for the camera as much as for an immediately present audience, if not more so. They were well aware of what Jones describes as performance's "dependence on documentation to attain symbolic status within the realm of culture."[7] Burden, for example,

> carefully staged each performance and had it photographed and sometimes also filmed; he selected usually one or two photographs of each event for display in exhibitions and catalogs. [...] In this way, Burden produced himself for posterity through meticulously orchestrated textual and visual representations.[8]

As another example, the European body artist Gina Pane describes the role of photography in her work in the following terms:

> It creates the work the audience will be seeing afterwards. So the photographer is not an external factor, he is positioned inside the action space with me, just a few centimeters away. There were times when he obstructed the [audience's] view![9]

It is clear, then, that such archetypal works of performance and body art as Burden's and Pane's were not autonomous performances whose documentation supplements and provides access to an originary event. Rather, the events were staged to be documented at least as much as to be seen by an audience; as Pane observes, sometimes the process of documentation actually interfered with the initial audience's ability to perceive the performance. In this respect, no documented piece is performed solely as an end in itself: the performance is always at one level raw material for documentation, the final product through which it will be circulated and with which it will inevitably become identified, justifying Slater's claim that the photograph ultimately replaces the reality it documents (or, as O'Dell puts it, "performance art is the virtual equivalent of its representations"[10]). In the end, the only significant difference between the documentary and theatrical modes of performance documentation is ideological: the assumption that in the former mode, the event is staged primarily for an immediately present audience and that the documentation is a secondary, supplementary record of an event that has its own prior integrity. As I have shown here, this belief has little relation to the actual circumstances under which performances are made and documented.

Before drawing conclusions about these issues, I shall place one more piece of evidence into the mix: a performance by Vito Acconci titled *Blinks* (1969) that raises some trenchant questions about the relationship between performance and documentation.[11] Acconci's verbal description of the performance is simple:

> Holding a camera, aimed away from me and ready to shoot, while walking a continuous line down a city street.
>
> Try not to blink.
>
> Each time I blink: snap a photo.

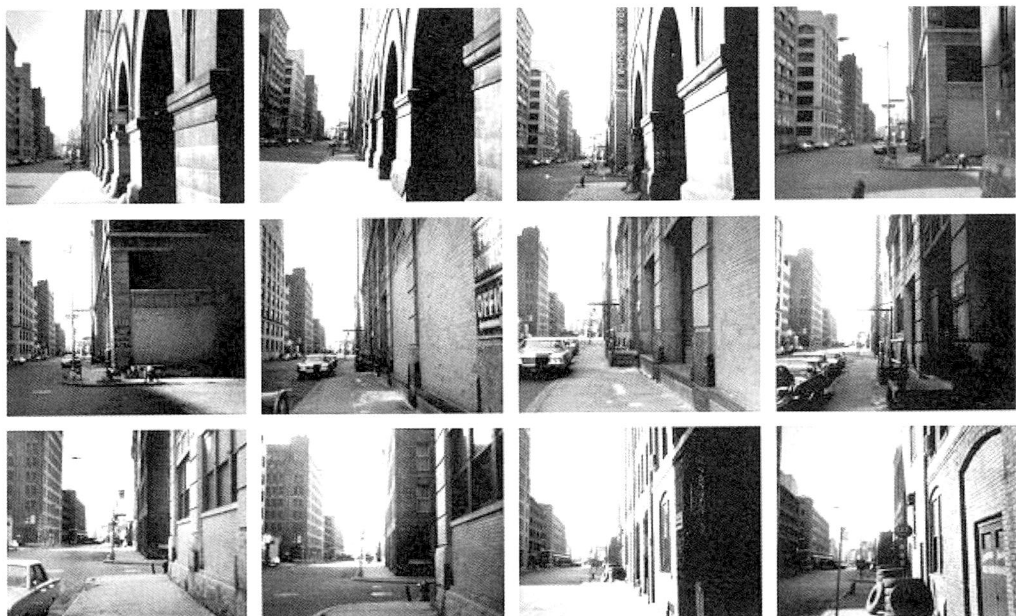

Vito Acconci. *Blinks*, Nov 23, 1969; afternoon. Photo-Piece, Greenwich Street, NYC; Kodak Instamatic 124, b/w film. © Vito Acconci.

The documentation of the piece displays a grid of twelve black and white photographs of a fairly desolate stretch of Greenwich Street in New York City above the verbal instruction. Like many of Acconci's performances of this time, *Blinks* was premised on failure, since it is obviously impossible that Acconci could walk down a street for any length of time without blinking.[12] It also has to do with achieving a high level of self-consciousness in mundane circumstances, as Acconci must become hyper-aware of an autonomic function (and perhaps equally aware of his surroundings) as he walks. Furthermore, as artist Seth Price suggested to me, Acconci was making art out of nothing, an art without content.

This performance confounds the already shaky distinction between the categories of documentary and theatrical images. On the one hand, the photos Acconci produced serve the traditional functions of performance documentation: they provide evidence that he actually performed the piece and allow us to reconstruct his performance. They do not do so in the traditional manner, however, because they do not actually show Acconci performing: they are photographs *by* Acconci, taken while performing, not photographs *of* Acconci performing. They partake of the traditional ontology of performance documentation nevertheless. Since the action of the piece consisted of taking photographs, the existence of the photographs serves as the primary evidence that Acconci executed his own instructions: because the photographs were produced *as* (or perhaps *by*) the performance (rather than *of* the performance), the ontological connection between performance and document seems exceptionally tight in this case.

On the other hand, Acconci's performance was also very like those in the theatrical category inasmuch as it was not available to an audience in any form apart from its documentation. A look at the photographs shows that the street was deserted – there were no bystanders to serve as audience. More important, the only thing bystanders would have seen was a man walking and taking pictures: they would have had no way of understanding they were witnessing a performance. Acconci's photographs thus are more theatrical than documentary, for it is only through his documentation that his performance exists qua performance.

Acconci's *Blinks* points toward a central issue: the performativity of documentation itself. I am using the term performative in J. L. Austin's most basic sense. Speaking of language, Austin calls statements whose utterance constitutes action in itself *performatives* (e.g., saying "I do" in a marriage ceremony). Distinguishing performative utterances from constative utterances, Austin argues that "to utter [a performative sentence] is not to *describe* my doing of what I should be said in so uttering to be doing or to state that I am doing it: it is to do it."[13] If I may analogize the images that document performances with verbal statements, the traditional view sees performance documents as constatives that describe performances and state that they occurred. I am suggesting that performance documents are not analogous to constatives, but to performatives: in other words, *the act of documenting an event as a performance is what constitutes it as such*. Documentation does not simply generate image/statements that describe an autonomous performance and state that it occurred: it produces an event as a performance and, as Frazer Ward suggests, the performer as "artist."[14]

Perhaps this point will be clearer when articulated through a straightforward definition of performance such as Richard Bauman's:

> Briefly stated, I understand performance as a mode of communicative display, in which the performer signals to an audience, in effect, "hey, look at me! I'm on! watch how skillfully and effectively I express myself." That is to say, performance rests on an assumption of responsibility to an audience for a display of communicative virtuosity. [...] In this sense of performance, then, the act of expression itself is framed as display: objectified, lifted out to a degree from its contextual surroundings, and opened up to interpretive and evaluative scrutiny by an audience both in terms of its intrinsic qualities and its associational resonances. [...] The specific semiotic means by which the performer may key the performance frame – that is, send the metacommunicative message "I'm on" – will vary from place to place and historical period to historical period. [...] The collaborative participation of an audience, it is important to emphasize, is an integral component of performance as an interactional accomplishment.[15]

I will not discuss the issues of skill and communicative virtuosity as they apply to performance and body art here, except to say that in an earlier consideration of Acconci's work, I observed, "critical standards for 'body art' are hard to articulate."[16] The virtuosity of this kind of performance, as well as most performance and body art from the 1960s and

1970s, clearly does not reside in the performer's mastery of conventional performance skills: perhaps it resides in the originality and audacity of conception and execution.

Bauman's other points concerning the framing of an event as performance and the concept of responsibility to the audience are directly germane to *Blinks*, however. Since there was no audience for the "live" performance and the event was not framed as performance for whatever accidental audience may have been present (that is, Acconci provided no metacommunication to tell that audience he was performing, not just walking and taking pictures), it is solely through the documentation that Acconci's actions are "framed as display" and "lifted out [...] from [their] contextual surroundings." It was also through the acts of documenting and presenting the documentation that Acconci assumed responsibility to an audience. It is crucial that the audience in question is the one that perceived his actions solely by means of the documentation rather than the incidental audience that may have seen him walking and photographing on Greenwich Street. It is this documentation – and nothing else – that allows an audience to interpret and evaluate his actions as a performance.

I realize that Acconci's performance is a special case but it is not as special as it may seem. All of the works in the theatrical category I posited earlier have the same relationship to performance as *Blinks*: in all cases, the actions undertaken by the artist and depicted in the images become available to an audience as performances solely through their documentation, and it is by virtue of presenting the photographs of their actions that the artists frame the depicted actions as performances and assume responsibility to the audience. As with the Acconci piece, the audience to whom they assume responsibility is the audience for the documentation, not for the live event.

The performances in the documentary category work differently, at least to an extent, because they generally have a dual existence: they are framed as performances by being presented in galleries or by other means and there is an initial audience to which the performer assumes responsibility as well as a second audience that experiences the performance only through its documentation. But this difference is much less substantial than it may appear. Consider the status of the initial audience with respect to documentation. Whereas sociologists and anthropologists who discuss performance stipulate, like Bauman, that the presence of the audience and the interaction of performers and audience is a crucial part of any performance, the tradition of performance art documentation is based on a different set of assumptions. It is very rare that the audience is documented at anything like the same level of detail as the art action. The purpose of most performance art documentation is to make the *artist's work* available to a larger audience, not to capture the performance as an "interactional accomplishment" to which a specific audience and a specific set of performers coming together in specific circumstances make equally significant contributions. For the most part, scholars and critics use eyewitness accounts to ascertain the characteristics of the performance, not the audience's contribution to the event, and discussions of how a particular audience perceived a particular performance at a particular time and place and what that performance meant to that audience are rare.[17] In that sense, performance art documentation participates in the fine art tradition of the reproduction of *works* rather than the ethnographic tradition of capturing *events*.[18]

I submit that the presence of that initial audience has no real importance to the performance as an entity whose continued life is through its documentation because our usual concern as consumers of such documentation is with recreating the artist's work, not the total interaction. As a thought experiment, consider what would happen were we to learn that there actually was no audience for Chris Burden's *Shoot*, that he simply performed the piece in an empty gallery and documented it. I suggest that such a revelation would make no difference at all to our perception of the performance, our understanding of it as an object of interpretation and evaluation, and our assessment of its historical significance. In other words, while the presence of an initial audience may be important to performers, it is merely incidental to the performance as documented. As the statement from Gina Pane I quoted earlier makes abundantly clear, when artists decide to document their performances, they assume responsibility to an audience other than the initial one, a gesture that ultimately obviates the need for an initial audience (who, in Pane's case, could not really participate fully as an audience because of the exigencies of documentation). In the long run, it makes no more difference whether there actually was a physically present audience for *Shoot* or any number of other classic works of performance art than it does whether someone happened to see Acconci on Greenwich Street or wandered into the studio while Cindy Sherman was shooting one of her disguised self-portraits. In that sense, it is not the initial presence of an audience that makes an event a work of performance art: it is its framing as performance through the performative act of documenting it as such.

I return now to the question I posed at the beginning: What difference does the fact that the image of Chris Burden documents something that really happened and the image of Yves Klein does not make to our understanding of these images in relation to the concept of performance documentation? My answer: If we are concerned with the historical constitution of these events as performances, it makes no difference at all. It follows from my assertion that the identity of documented performances as performances is not dependent on the presence of an initial audience, that we cannot dismiss studio fabrications of one sort or another from the category of performance art because they were not performed for a physically present audience. My suggestion that performance art is constituted as such through the performativity of its documentation is equally true for both Burden's piece and Klein's. The fact that one could and did occur before a live audience while the other could not and did not is not a significant difference in this context. This also seems to be the case in more pragmatic terms: this difference between the images has had no consequence in terms of their iconicity and standing in the history of art and performance.

If we are concerned not just with the determination of what makes an event a performance, but also with the notion of authenticity in performance, then the distinction between the two images may seem more significant. I alluded earlier to a position that would treat the Klein photograph as something other than a performance because it documents an event that never actually occurred as we see it in the image. This position seems to me ultimately untenable, however. If I may be permitted an analogy with another cultural form, to argue that Klein's leap was not a performance because it took place only within photographic space would be equivalent to arguing that the Beatles did not perform the music on their *Sgt Pepper's Lonely Hearts Club Band* album because that performance exists only in the space of the recording: the group never actually performed the music as we hear it.[19] I would consider any such claim absurd: of course the Beatles performed that music – how else are we to understand it if not as a performance by the Beatles? And of course Yves Klein performed his jump.

Those who are particularly concerned with recorded music have discussed the whole question of the relationship between performance and its documentation extensively. The two basic categories of that discussion are similar to the ones I have posited here: *documentary* and *phonography*, where documentary recordings are assumed to be straightforward capturings of real sonic events and phonography consists in the "sonic manipulation" of music to produce recordings of performances that never really happened that way. Lee B. Brown, an American philosopher who has addressed these issues, suggests that phonography produces "works of phonoart," a new category of "musical entities" to be considered in their own terms as artworks distinct from traditional musical performances.[20]

This is a version of an argument I have already rejected, of course, since Brown solves the problem of the relationship between performances and documentation by insisting that phonography, the aural equivalent of the performed photography I have been discussing, is not a form of performance but constitutes a new kind of musical event altogether. For me, by contrast, phonoart is a species of musical performance, albeit a species that exists only in the space of recording. But Brown acknowledges an important point: the phenomenological boundaries between documentary and phonography are blurry; it is not always clear "whether a given product is to be understood as a piece of phonoart or a transparent document of a performance." He cites as an example "the albums of 'duets' that Frank Sinatra recorded a few years before his death. They *sound* documentary" even though Sinatra never actually sang with his partners and "the impression of two singers in dialogue with one another is sheer illusion."[21]

One could say exactly the same thing about the Klein photograph: it *looks* documentary even though the impression that Klein leaped unprotected from the window is sheer illusion. At the phenomenal level, there is not necessarily any intrinsic way of determining whether a particular performance image is documentary or theatrical. And even if one does know, precisely what difference does that knowledge make? Are we deprived of the pleasure of hearing Sinatra sing with his duet partners because he did not actually do that? Similarly, is our appreciation of Klein's image of himself leaping into the void sullied by the fact that he erased the safety net from the photograph? Can we not appreciate Sherman's particular ways of embodying an enormous range of characters and images because we never have direct access to her performing body? If we are to insist on a criterion of authenticity when contemplating performance documentation, we must ask ourselves whether we believe authenticity to reside in the circumstances of the underlying performance, which may or may not be evident from the documentation.

Brown implies another possibility worth considering: the crucial relationship is not the one between the document and the performance but the one between the document and its audience. Perhaps the authenticity of the performance document resides in its relationship to its beholder rather than to an ostensibly originary event: perhaps its authority is phenomenological rather than ontological. Just as one can have the pleasure of hearing Sinatra sing duets with singers with whom he had no real interaction, so one can have the pleasure of seeing Klein leap into the void or that of contemplating the implications of Burden's allowing himself to be shot. These pleasures are available from the documentation and therefore do not depend on whether an audience witnessed the original event. The more radical possibility is that they may not even depend on whether the event actually happened. It may well be that our sense of the presence, power, and authenticity of these pieces derives not from treating the document as an indexical access point to a past event but from perceiving the document itself *as a performance* that directly reflects an artist's aesthetic project or sensibility and for which we are the present audience.

Notes

1. Kathy O'Dell, "Displacing the Haptic: Performance Art, the Photographic Document, and the 1970s," *Performance Research*, 1997, vol. 2, no. 1, pp. 73–4.
2. Helen Gilbert, "Bodies in Focus: Photography and Performativity in Post-Colonial Theatre," *Textual Studies in Canada*, 1998, vol. 10–11, p. 18.
3. Jon Erickson, "Goldberg Variations: Performing Distinctions," *PAJ: A Journal of Performance and Art*, 1999, vol. 21, no. 3, p. 98.
4. Amelia Jones, "'Presence' in *absentia*: Experiencing Performance as Documentation," *Art Journal*, 1997, vol. 56, no. 4, p. 16.
5. Amelia Jones, "Dis/playing the Phallus: Male Artists Perform Their Masculinities," *Art History*, 1994, vol. 17, no. 4, p. 554. Jones points out that Klein actually exposed the theatricality of his image by publishing two different versions of it, one with a bicyclist on the street and one without, thus tacitly revealing its constructed nature.
6. Erickson, op. cit., p. 99.
7. Jones, "'Presence' in *absentia*", p. 13.
8. Jones, "Dis/playing the Phallus", p. 568.
9. Quoted in O'Dell, op. cit., pp. 76–7.
10. O'Dell, op. cit., p. 77.
11. Some might take exception to my categorizing Acconci's work as performance. While it is true that his work from this period is often classified under the rubric of conceptual art (and could also be considered process art) I make no apology for claiming it for performance. I am hardly the only one to do so: O'Dell, for instance, includes Acconci in the category of performance art without comment. Frazer Ward (see note 14) argues that the two categories should be seen as intertwined and engaged in an ongoing dialogue rather than as distinct.

12. For a brief discussion of the centrality of predictable failure to Acconci's work, see Philip Auslander, "Vito Acconci and the Politics of the Body in Postmodern Performance," in *From Acting to Performance*, London, New York: Routledge, 1997, pp. 89–97.
13. J. L. Austin, "Lecture I in *How to Do Things with Words*," in Philip Auslander (ed.), *Performance: Critical Concepts in Literary and Cultural Studies*, vol. I, London: Routledge, 2003, p. 93.
14. Frazer Ward, "Some Relations between Conceptual and Performance Art," *Art Journal*, 1997, vol. 56, no. 4, p. 40.
15. Richard Bauman, *A World of Others' Words: Cross-Cultural Perspectives on Intertexuality*, Malden: Blackwell, 2004, p. 9.
16. Auslander, op.cit., p. 96.
17. This observation is intended only to mark disciplinary differences, not to suggest that the ethnographic bent of performance studies provides a superior perspective on performance than the fine art tradition embedded in art history.
18. To speak of *recreating* a performance suggests the reconstruction of an object. By contrast, the term *revival* used in English to describe theatrical productions of existing plays suggests the reawakening of an organic entity rather than the rebuilding of a lost object.
19. For a brief discussion of the idea that recordings constitute the primary experience of music in a mediatized society and that such recordings must be understood as performances in themselves, see Philip Auslander, "Performance Analysis and Popular Music: A Manifesto," *Contemporary Theatre Review* 2004, vol. 14, no. 1, p. 5. I am suggesting that the cultural situation of performance art is similar to that of popular music: Its audience experiences it primarily through documentation, rather than live performance, and the documents effectively become the performances.
20. Lee B. Brown, "Phonography," in David Goldblatt and Lee B. Brown (eds), *Aesthetics: A Reader in Philosophy of the Arts*, 2nd edn, Upper Saddle River: Pearson-Prentice Hall, 2005, pp. 214, 216.
21. Ibid., p. 216.

Chapter 2

Dead Mannequin Walking: Fluxus and the Politics of Reception

Hannah B Higgins

When proponents of avant-garde art think about Fluxus, we often think of its nihilistic aspect, or its fluxing of boundaries between artistic disciplines, between audience and artist, between museum and broader world, between novice and expert, and between artist and activist. This view of Fluxus is substantiated by George Maciunas's 1963 "Purge Manifesto", which, in its visual form, is the most repeated image that appears on a Google® search for "Fluxus." The presence of a manifesto, like its language, is familiar to art writers; here, the stated goal is to "promote a revolutionary flood," resonating with the well-established antics of the historic avant-garde, which likewise sought to "purge the world of bourgeois sickness." Bourgeois sickness: that cultural pestilence of decadence and illegitimate wealth that treats art as one bauble among many. Off with its head! What could be better? Imagine an art world purged of its self-important professionalism and vacuous commercialism and connected to our everyday life. This was the guiding principle of Maciunas, the erstwhile Fluxus co-founder and impresario, and I am deeply sympathetic with it.

Nam June Paik's notorious performance event *One for Violin (Solo)* consists of a simple action. As annotated on a photograph by Maciunas, the performer slowly raises a violin over his head, "in concentrated manner & then" smashes it "BANG!" on a tabletop in front of him. The decisive action is pure catharsis and always garners loud applause and raucous laughter. The spray of splinters makes the purge real, the sharp splinters lacerating the conventions of orchestral violin performance. No conductor. No virtuosic performance. All that remains of the violin in the performer's hands is its broken neck. As the piece concludes we are left with the live artist and a table and stage scattered with debris. During the action each member of the audience anticipates this result. Nevertheless, it is impossible to know the exact moment it will happen, so the crashing and splintering is always something of a

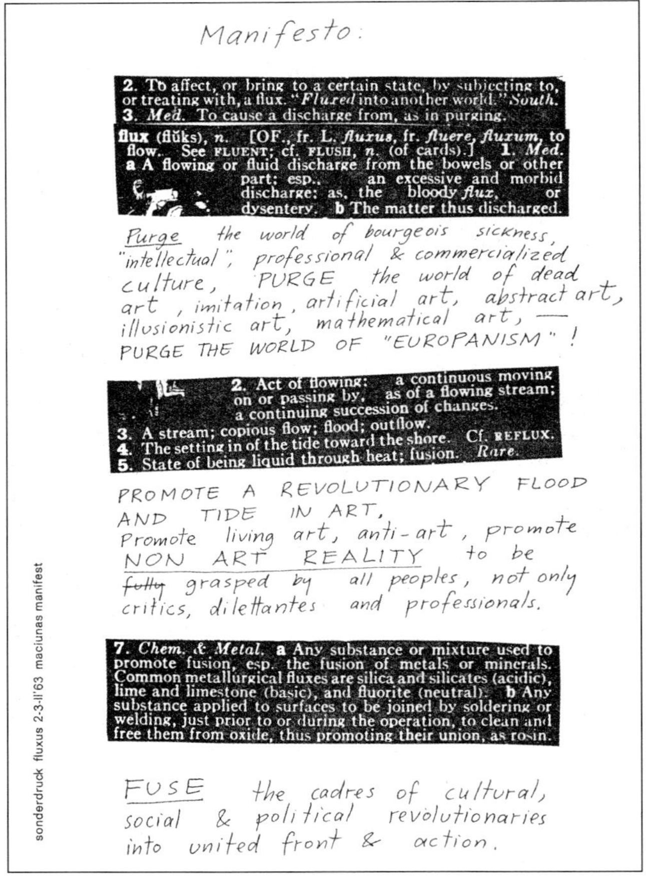

Manifesto:

2. To affect, or bring to a certain state, by subjecting to, or treating with, a flux. "*Fluxed* into another world." *South.*
3. *Med.* To cause a discharge from, as in purging.

flux (flŭks), *n.* [OF., fr. L. *fluxus*, fr. *fluere, fluxum*, to flow. See FLUENT; cf. FLUSH, *n.* (of cards).] **1.** *Med.* **a** A flowing or fluid discharge from the bowels or other part; esp., an excessive and morbid discharge: as, the bloody *flux*, or dysentery. **b** The matter thus discharged.

Purge the world of bourgeois sickness, "intellectual", professional & commercialized culture, PURGE the world of dead art, imitation, artificial art, abstract art, illusionistic art, mathematical art, — PURGE THE WORLD OF "EUROPANISM"!

2. Act of flowing: a continuous moving on or passing by, as of a flowing stream; a continuing succession of changes.
3. A stream; copious flow; flood; outflow.
4. The setting in of the tide toward the shore. Cf. REFLUX.
5. State of being liquid through heat; fusion. *Rare.*

PROMOTE A REVOLUTIONARY FLOOD AND TIDE IN ART, Promote living art, anti-art, promote NON ART REALITY to be ~~fully~~ grasped by all peoples, not only critics, dilettantes and professionals.

7. *Chem. & Metal.* **a** Any substance or mixture used to promote fusion, esp. the fusion of metals or minerals. Common metallurgical fluxes are silica and silicates (acidic), lime and limestone (basic), and fluorite (neutral). **b** Any substance applied to surfaces to be joined by soldering or welding, just prior to or during the operation, to clean and free them from oxide, thus promoting their union, as rosin.

FUSE the cadres of cultural, social & political revolutionaries into united front & action.

sonderdruck fluxus 2-3-II'63 maciunas manifest

George Maciunas, Fluxus Manifesto, 1963. The Museum of Modern Art, New York, The Gilbert and Lila Silverman Fluxus Collection Gift, 2008. Digital Image © The Museum of Modern Art, Licensed by SCALA / Art Resource, NY.

shock: we escape the humdrum life collectively, if briefly. In that moment of shared surprise and reaction, the audience joins the "revolutionary tide." Bang!: in one instant Paik's *Solo* converts Maciunas's call for the destruction of the professional and commercialized culture of classical music into something tangible.

Typical of a good political manifesto, the Purge platform's strength is an uncompromising clarity of purpose that dictates unequivocally both what is wrong with the world it attacks and how to read the work that responds to said world. One worldview engenders one experience and one correct interpretation of it. With the Purge Manifesto as a guiding light, Fluxus events and objects become the most singularly virulent, anti-art forms associated with the neo-avant-gardes of the 1960s. In addition to the Purge Manifesto, Maciunas circulated dozens of newsletters and historic diagrams; visual mappings of Fluxus historicize, contextualize, and generally reinforce the value of the purge.[1]

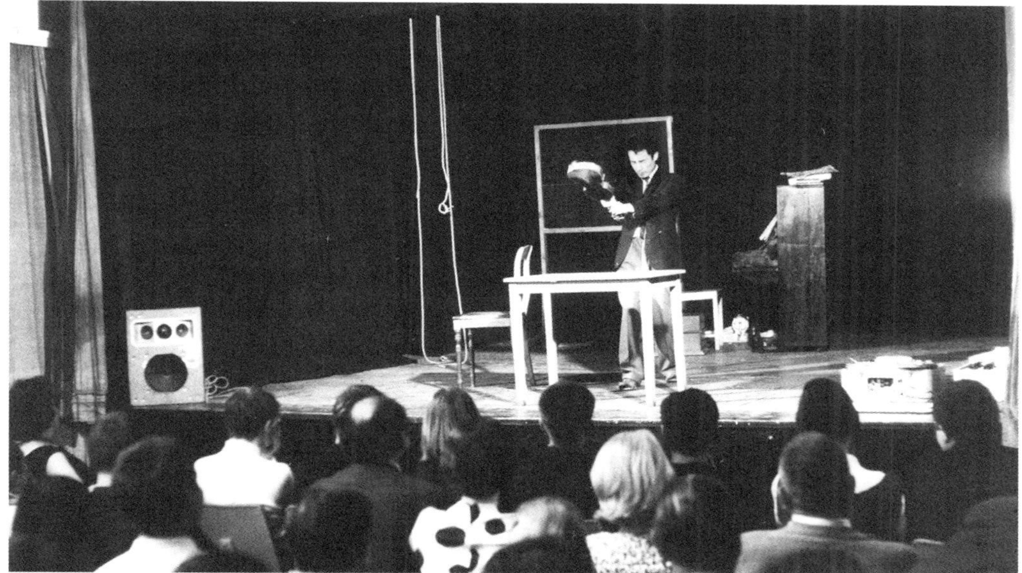

Nam June Paik performs, *One For Violin (Solo)*, 1962. Performed by the artist at Neo-Dada in der Musik, Kammerspiele Düsseldorf, Germany, June 16, 1962. Gelatin silver print, by George Maciunas. The Museum of Modern Art, New York. Digital Image © The Museum of Modern Art, Licensed by SCALA/Art Resource, NY.

When paired with the relative obscurity of Fluxus, the close relationship between Maciunas's manifestos and diagrams and his tireless promotion of the group suggests a homologous framework consistent with a professional art world that defines art history as a sequence of clearly defined movements with singularly discernible styles and intentions. And it did so, with some nostalgia for the halcyon days of the 1960s with which Fluxus was associated. Distortions and omissions have occurred in the reporting of Fluxus events when something fell outside of this narrow framework. For example, a memorial concert at the Kitchen in New York celebrated Maciunas's life with a range of performances that included historic and new works by Fluxus artists and friends. A typical critic wrote in terms that equated the death of Maciunas with the passing of the group, "It was a style that drew miniscule audiences and no critics when it was alive. And it is a matter of some nostalgia today."[2] Most of the artists were still alive at the time and working together. Fluxus no doubt seemed moribund because the artist most associated with its publicity wing had moved on. The critic continues:

> I would like to discuss the recent work by Alison Knowles that was also included in the program [at the Kitchen]. And I would like to go into detail about her particularly memorable performance [...] But it seems preferable to focus on 60s pieces [...] it is a matter of some nostalgia today.[3]

Why it would be preferable to omit works by artists other than Maciunas or outside of the timeframe inscribed by the dates of his activity as a Fluxus artist is never explained, though the shift in focus contained in that little phrase "but it seems preferable" suggests a more comfortable armchair through which to assess the dashed dreams of a radical past.

With this as the back story, it comes as no surprise that in 1983, Fluxus friend and curator Jon Hendricks offered a definition of the group that reflects both his enduring friendship with Maciunas and the common view that Maciunas = Fluxus: "At its inception, Fluxus was intended by George Maciunas to be a publication." He goes on to provide "several quotations taken from George Maciunas's letters to various Fluxus artists which clearly demonstrate the underlying political purpose of Fluxus," without including other positions.[4] Hendricks has been a lifelong friend to many Fluxus artists, as well as the curator of the Gilbert and Lila Silverman Collection, the source collection for virtually every museum exhibition of note of the last thirty years and the permanent Fluxus room at the Museum of Modern Art, which opened in 2009. Clearly, there is documentary support for the perspective, which establishes a nearly seamless homology between the neo-avant-garde view of Fluxus and the exhibiting practices that demonstrate Fluxus principles for the mainstream art audience.

Sympathetic though I may be with these politics, however, things are not that simple. How could they be where scores of artists in a loose network are concerned? Schisms early in the history of Fluxus suggest that Fluxus has never been as straightforward as the preceding account suggests. These breaks found material expression in publication and presentation ventures by artists other than Maciunas: Wolf Vostell's *Dé-collage* Magazine, Charlotte Moorman's Annual New York Festival of the Avant-Garde, Felipe Ehrenberg's Fluxshoe, and my father, Dick Higgins's, Something Else Press. We also see these schisms in the increasing number of voids that appear in Maciunas's coverage of Fluxus: throughout the 1960s, most of the artists were terminated from Maciunas's famous Fluxus timelines. Being unwilling to sign the manifestos or to join in his protests could result in a simple line being drawn through the name on a timeline at a give year: a specious amputation since the artists continued to work together. Recently, German art historian Thomas Kellein has addressed the problem obliquely in his book *George Maciunas: The Dream of Fluxus*, which articulates a view of Fluxus as Maciunas's projection, a working in the name of Fluxus, which, if only potentially, allows for other Fluxus practices since the artists are also free to work in its name.[5]

The socially fractious nature of Fluxus is expressed in the afterlife of the Purge Manifesto, which was unsigned and argued against by most of the artists. In question was whether or not Fluxus is serious culture, whether it should have a relationship to the profession of art (which is particularly bizarre, since the 1962 concerts began in a museum in Wiesbaden Germany), and whether it is intellectual in the learned sense.[6] Fissures appear repeatedly along these lines: when the manifesto was published in 1963, when a protest was organized against German composer Karlheinz Stockhausen's *Originale* in 1964, and when artists wrote in response to a series of position statements sprinkled throughout the *Fluxus Newsletters* of 1962–4.[7] Among many such responses was Fluxus poet Jackson MacLow's angry 1962 letter to Maciunas:

> I am not opposed to serious culture – quite the contrary. I am all for it & I hope & consider that my own work is a genuine contribution to it [...] No blunderbuss attack against culture (serious or otherwise) as a whole [...] will do anything to remedy what's wrong with the present situation.[8]

Not surprisingly, other manifestos followed that were in the apt words of historian Clive Phillpot, "significantly different in tone."[9] The later manifestos nevertheless sought "to establish artists' nonprofessional, nonparasitic, nonelite status in society."[10]

Clearly, the version of Fluxus presupposed in my opening comments and the manifestos appeals because many in a generation of cultural critics, art historians, and artists (including myself) are sympathetic with its rage. But this sympathy does little to recommend its declarative truth. Indeed, much is to be gained from analysis of a more particularizing sort. From the beginning, many Fluxus artists rejected their developing status as purveyors of neo-avant-garde antics, no matter how justified the anger or invigorating the action might feel in the short term or for a few of them. Divesting the Fluxus audience of that view has proven no easy task, however, since Maciunas was particularly gifted at awakening the audience of Fluxus to the oppressive norms of art institutions and acculturated manners through humor, gags, and political demonstrations. He knew we should be outraged at how the professional art world operates, how money dictates visibility in the arts, how even the most apparently liberal state institutions promote and silence through funding, and how the professional world of galleries, museums, criticism, and the publishing industry are anathema to radical forms of innovation. In giving voice to that anger, the narrow view of Fluxus is an important one even as it creates distortions in the variably structured, lived experiences of individual group members.

Fluxus artist George Brecht described Fluxus in precisely these terms. "Something about Fluxus" was written in 1964.

> Whether you think that concert halls, theaters, and art galleries are the natural places to present music, performances, and objects, or find these places mummifying, preferring streets, homes, and railway stations, or do not find it useful to distinguish between these two aspects of the world theater, there is someone associated with Fluxus who agrees with you.[11]

The agreements Brecht refers to do not boil down to an uncritical pluralism. Far from it. Ideological and practical differences in Fluxus make necessary a mechanism for writing history that is argumentative to the core. In such a history these many attitudes would coexist or, since most of these artists have since passed, would be shown to have coexisted uncomfortably. We have here, in small scale, a noisy battlefield that contains a range of combatants: more or less authoritarian, more or less destructive, more or less institutional, more or less anarchic, more or less socialist. Clearly, it is a mistake to take Maciunas's manifestos and dictates as a descriptive umbrella for Fluxus in any sort of unified sense.

Rather, they should be seen as one node, even an admittedly steady point of reference, in a complex and contested network.

Over the years there have been a very few gallerists and critics sympathetic to the task of challenging the overdetermined view of Fluxus.[12] In 1989, for example, Bruce Altschuler wrote a critical review of the magnum opus of the Silverman Collection, the *Fluxus Codex*, in *Arts* magazine. In response to the book's introductory statement that "Fluxus' resident genius was George Maciunas [...] Fluxus begins with the foundation of the Fluxus press in 1961–2, abruptly terminating in May of 1978 when Maciunas dies,"[13] Altschuler counters "Restricting Fluxus to Maciunas related material [...] creates an arbitrary division within the work of many artists. More importantly, to follow Maciunas in taking a narrow view of Fluxus is to limit our understanding of its significance."[14] Written twenty-plus years ago, Altschuler's criticism assessed the vital and collaborative work that continued to be made by Fluxus artists and which remains utterly obscure. The difficulty many Fluxus artists face showing work made since 1978 testifies to the practical consequences of the determinist misreading on the careers of these artists, few of whom have gallery representation.

But there is more to it. Maciunas becomes isolated in the commanding role of definer and leader, resulting a streamlining of both Fluxus and Maciunas that amounts to a decorporealization of the group and its works. The title of this chapter, "Dead Mannequin Walking," refers to the phrase "dead man walking" toward the death chamber in American prisons.[15] Where Maciunas is overdetermined, he becomes isolated from the rich and complex network of artists and arguments that make his work more interesting than its manifestos and multiples are as merely anti-aesthetic objects. More specifically, if we take him for a latter day André Breton, we lose the sense of dialectical and material confrontations in the constitution of Fluxus. I am reminded of the second stanza of a famous 1905 poem called "Dead Man Walking," by Thomas Hardy:

> I am but a shape that stands here,
> A pulseless mould,
> A pale past picture.[16]

As described in detail by Peter Starr in his astute account of the apparent failure of the 1960s and the impact of this "failure" on postmodern philosophy, two patterns emerged in the 1970s which are useful for understanding the reception of Fluxus and the negative function of the mannequin version of Maciunas. Describing the two theoretical commonplaces that deny the efficacy of political (and I would add artistic) action in the 1960s, Starr writes:

> [A]ccording to the first of these, a "logic of recuperation," to oppose the Master (in specifiable ways) is merely to consolidate the Master's power. According to the second, a "logic of substitution," any figure that sets itself up as an alternative to the Master risks becoming a Master in its turn.[17]

As regards Fluxus, we are faced with a familiar and marketable model of artistic practice oriented toward the genius that apparently marries Maciunas's social critique to the extraordinary wealth of his patron Gilbert B. Silverman (a recuperation), while at the same time Maciunas becomes a tyrant in his own small universe (a substitution) in a manner that compromises the socially reflexive basis of both Fluxus and the flesh-and-blood Maciunas.[18] The audience is left with a familiar critique consisting of one voice where there should be many, one practice where the depth of meaning resides across a shared if contested terrain, and the collapse of discourse associated with a group of people as linked to the death of one, admittedly important, member. Nostalgia is a predictable response: it speaks to an impossibly simplified world that is yearned for because things were apparently simpler then.

This apparent failure obscures the profound effect of the broader Fluxus group on the art world, including the collectors who have loved and learned from it. As described by curator and scholar Julia Robinson, "Fluxus is in the DNA of the art world today."[19] Fluxus has become foundational, not only because it evokes an activist past for which we may collectively (and nostalgically) yearn, but also because it evokes a complex, anti-authoritarian sense of community practice, multidisciplinary experimentation, and an art within the everyday. Primarily through teaching and its informal engagement with networks of artists, one important influence of Fluxus lies in its early articulation of what has recently been theorized as relational aesthetics, artistic practices that have complex and contested social relationships as a feature of their communicative standard.[20] These aesthetics exist both in terms of an influence on other artists, but equally importantly as regards the evolution of ideas among Fluxus artists engaged in nearly fifty years of dialogue – in the variety of encounters made possible by a comparative reading of the works and writings of MacLow and Maciunas, among many other possible examples.

The resulting reduction of the decade (and by extension Fluxus) to a few broad, failed intentions results in the familiar accounts of the absolute failure of 1960s political and artistic movements that are often politically simplistic or nostalgic. By this account, Fluxus should never find safe haven in the Museum of Modern Art – it should be forever outside, as a quick survey of lamentations about the arrival of the Silverman Collection in the blogosphere amply demonstrate. The idea is absurd since the first Fluxus titled concerts were in museums in Europe, and being both for and against the professional art system, or for and against specific parts of it, has characterized Fluxus since its beginnings. Consistent with this logic of failed revolt, Fluxus appears in criticism, perversely, as a success and failure, or rather as a success because of its apparent failure alongside the other failed idealistic movements of the 1960s.

The view linking Fluxus exclusively to Maciunas not only collapses the ties to work done since Maciunas's death, it also obscures the networks of practicing artists already associated with the group before Maciunas got involved in 1961–2. A quick look at the early history of Fluxus suggests with some clarity what is, by definition, left out of the conventional account.[21] Instead of beginning with the foundation of the Fluxus press in 1961–2, Fluxus emerged from many contexts in the late 1950s: the Darmstadt circle of concrete poets and Karlheinz

Stockhausen's composition courses in Darmstadt, Germany (Paik, LaMonte Young); the Cologne atelier of his wife, the painter Mary Bauermeister (Paik, Ben Patterson, Wolf Vostell); visual poetry circles in France and Germany (Emmett Williams, Ben Vautier); and artists working in No theater, Group Ongaku and Gutai in Japan (Chieko (Mieko) Shiomi, Yasunao Tone, Takehisha Kosugi).[22] In addition, among these many Fluxus components was a course offered by John Cage in music composition at the New School for Social Research in New York in 1958, which was attended by the young chemist and inventor, George Brecht, as well as by Al Hansen, Dick Higgins, and Robert Watts. The impact of Cage's classes was profound, and indirectly the work of many others in the 1960s, such as Yoko Ono, LaMonte Young, and Alison Knowles.

The rest of this chapter offers an analysis of the wider kind of experiences made possible by events if we bracket, for the moment, the negative aesthetics of Fluxus. In Cage's course, for example, Brecht invented the performance Event, a short, instructional score that alters everyday perceptions. [23] A close reading of one of these is particularly useful in demonstrating that Fluxus is characterized by disputes that mattered enough that they could generate meaningful, competing positions that take the form of art. Nam June Paik's *One for Violin (Solo)* and George Brecht's *Solo for Violin, Viola, Cello or Contrabass* (1962) compare in terms of a network of multisensory feedback mechanisms that link both the destructive and constructive impulses of touch, sight, and sound. In looking at these two works a view of Fluxus practice emerges whose implications exceed the rancor of manifestos and wholesale acts of rage.

George Brecht's *Solo for Violin, Viola, Cello or Contrabass* (1962) reads simply "polishing." Any stringed instrument will do. This work suggests active engagement with the object: to sit and quietly polish the musical instrument. *Solo* relies on sensory feedback mechanisms that produce a simultaneously sonic and tactile experience for the audience and performer. For the audience the work is entered at the inquisitive visual–auditory level: "What is that sound? Is it the oil and cloth squeaking over the surface of the strings? His knuckle just hit the body of the violin. How loud! I hear a hum-m-m." For the performer, this curiosity functions differently than for the audience: "What sound will this oiled cloth make here or there?" Or, "What does polishing the back tell me about how the violin amplifies sound?"

Instead of merely overturning culture, or pretending to, as the flood of Maciunas's manifesto dictates, comparing Brecht and Paik's events suggests something more interesting and subtle in Fluxus than one would expect to find if we measure encounters with Fluxus exclusively through its failed revolutionary tide. Paik's work changes considerably by this account. According to the score and unlike its adaptation in the mainstream, the violin is lifted as slowly as possible, about five minutes, creating an attenuated sense of time that precedes the destructive action. This slowly ascending violin carves out an experiential space filled with pregnant silence – the intensified listening associated with waiting for the moment of the object's demise. As the violin is raised, the ear cues in with anticipation – a jingle of keys, a cough, a squeaky chair, and a shuffle of soft soled shoes become remarkably loud in this hypersensitive state. The ears are in this hypersensitive state as the thing is

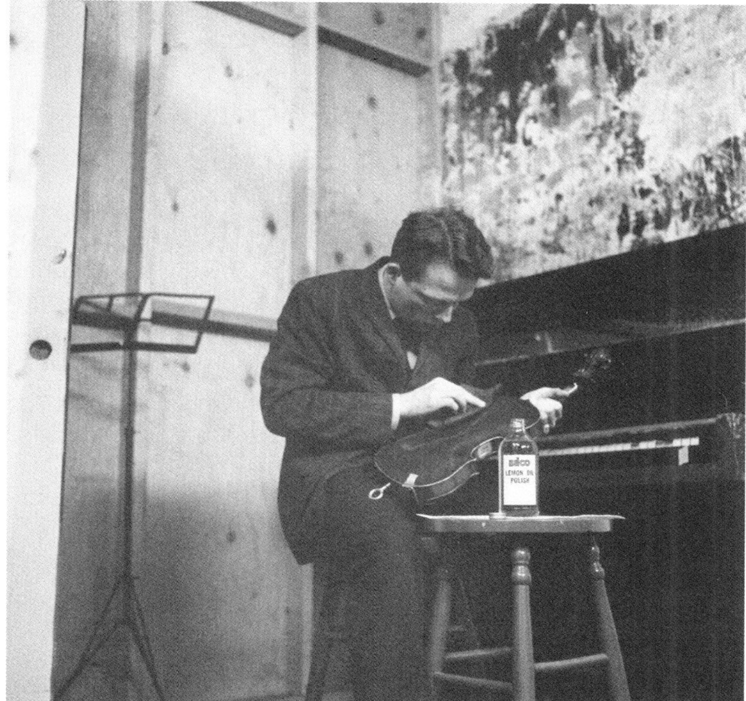

George Brecht, *Solo for Violin, Viola, Cello, or Contrabass*, July 1962 Performed by the artist at Fully Guaranteed 12 Fluxus Concerts, Canal Street, New York, April 25, 1964. Gelatin silver print, by George Maciunas. The Museum of Modern Art, New York. Digital Image © The Museum of Modern Art, Licensed by SCALA/Art Resource, NY.

smashed: Hearkening and the bracing awakening are inextricably bound up throughout the duration of the work in a Fluxus concert.

In *Being and Time* Martin Heidegger theorized a close association between music and the experience of perceptual awakening in terms that resonate with a shared reading of Brecht's and Paik's violin Events. He writes, "Hearkening too has the kind of Being of the hearing which understands. What we first hear is never noises or complexes of sounds, but the creaking wagon, the motorcycle. We hear the column on the march, the woodpecker tapping, the fire crackling."[24] This attentive form of listening evokes curiosity a sound one might never have otherwise heard, noticed, or recognized. Heidegger writes, "Curiosity [...] does not seek the leisure of tarrying observantly, but rather seeks restlessness and the excitement of continual novelty and changing encounters."[25]

Hearkening, however, is not exclusively auditory. Inquisitive listening involves attention to the sources of the sounds as well. Brecht's *Solo* inscribes the experience with an expression of the unique ability of touch to explore and alter materials, creating a feedback system that links touch to the auditory and the visual.[26] The inclusion of touch is significant because touch is a perceptual system that is largely ignored in western culture, where it is normally associated with its utilitarian and puerile dimensions. According to sense scientist J. J. Gibson,

"We are not accustomed to thinking of the hand as a sense organ since [...] we grasp, push, pull lift, carry, insert, or assemble for *practical* purposes."[27] Polishing, close touching, and examination of the object, perfecting its sheen, and feeling its curves relies on the sensory capacity of the hand at the same time as the action establishes a strong connection between the hand and an object in the world.

According to Gibson, as one human sense affects the function of another, it forms an "overlapping field," put into play by the observer in a kind of "feedback,"[28] or active inquiry. Each sense has specific types of information at its disposal such that what is learned or can be learned by one sense (for example, listening) is both biologically and culturally different from what is learned by seeing, smelling, touching, or tasting.[29] For example, the basic orienting system involves mechanoreceptors acting to equilibrate the body by obtaining information about gravity. By looking, the visual system creates information about distance and action that contributes to the function of these receptors. In summary, it is the combined effect of the interacting sense organs and the culture of their hosts that produces the complex of meanings we call perception.

Other Events by Brecht exploit interrelationships of two or more cognitive–sensory systems as a mechanism through which the experience is made possible. For example, *Dresser* is a pun – drawers (also slang for pants) are below what we normally think of as the selves we dress, the torso we see in the mirror above. The simple pun translates into words what could be described as a visual pun: I am the "dresser" both as a person getting dressed and object. I keep my private things below, in a set of drawers – pants. The score illustrates that the piece of furniture both reflects and recreates the parallel organization of parts. The logic of the work inheres in the interferences between the verbal and visual puns, which draws on the suggested visual image of a person dressing.

Five Places, on the other hand, takes its logic from museum and gallery displays, by using the term "exhibit," which appears on five small cards that have the effect of directing the visitor to the proper point of attention at virtually any (art or non-art) location. The seemingly simple action of moving an exhibit label to a non-museum place brings with it the instruction for a certain type of competent viewing. We could call it aesthetic or focused viewing and see it as a logical counter to Marcel Duchamp's readymades, which transformed everyday objects into artworks by relocating them to the museum. Brecht has performed a simple reversal: the museum, or at least the exhibiting practice, is extended back into the world, which begs the question, have the museum walls been merely purged as Maciunas would have it? Not quite. The card could be put in a museum. The piece functions by calling forth an idea of the museum, both by affirming and subverting it.

Brecht's simple instruction presses even further with a few minutes of attention: as with many Events, exhibit is both a noun and a verb. Could it be a request that the performer should somehow exhibit him-or-herself at five different places? Or is it that an entire place in all its myriad complexity, as opposed to a single readymade object, is the point of focus? Taken alongside other Fluxus works that engage smells and touch, the exhibit can extend across the many features of human sensory apparatuses. Brecht, after all, was a chemist; in the field of chemistry the term "exhibit" carries with it the principle of scientific proof. Even insofar as the work is a one word piece, it partakes of a complex network of simultaneously overlapping linguistic, sensory, and institutional frameworks.[30]

Taken together, these Events ebb and flow across the range of human sensory–cognitive formats, dragging habits of language, physical life, and institutional norms along with them and causing us to see each element anew. Sometimes the habit is isolated, made strange, as when we "expect" an exhibit to be in a museum or a violin to be carefully played. At other times, the habit is exploited for its ability to recede into the background sufficiently that primary sensation emerges, as when the scents and sounds of polishing a violin become the artwork. The simplicity of the Event – a word or a few words isolated from the world for a moment's perceptive engagement – always ties the myriad of formats back to a precise location, the Event itself, much like the perceptual tether noted above that holds together, if only for a moment, structures of apparently dissimilar cognitive systems.

The global context of Fluxus and the Event suggests acculturated readings of the primary information present in all locations where the physiological dimension of the Event is shared. Walter Ong has provided useful terminology for this multinational, cross modal experience, wherein social contexts impact the sensorium, meaning the ratio of senses of human beings. In "The Shifting Sensorium" he describes culturally unique relationships between the perceptual systems in each society:

> These relationships must not be taken merely abstractly but in connection with variations in cultures. In this connection, it is useful to think of cultures in terms of the organization of the sensorium. By the sensorium we mean the entire sensory apparatus as an operational complex. The differences in cultures which we have just suggested can be thought of as differences in the sensorium, the organization of which is in part determined by culture at the same time as it makes culture.[31]

Viewing Fluxus in general and the Event in particular as an art of the global sensorium makes particular sense for artists who engaged with the internationalism of the group as a key element of their practice.

Japanese Fluxus artist Mieko Shiomi, for example, wrote nine "spatial poems" which consisted of instructions sent to friends, whose replies were then flagged with pins on a map of the globe. *Spatial Poem No. 1* (1965), for example, consisted of an instruction mailed to friends around the world to "write a word (or words) on the enclosed card and place it somewhere. Please tell me the word and place, which will be edited on the world map." She received sixty-nine responses for her map. *Spatial Poem No. 2* (1965), by contrast, details the different direction people were facing at their locations around the world at one moment: 10:00 pm Greenwich time on 15 October 1965. Whether as a travel log, performance work, conceptual art piece, or mapping exercise, the *Spatial Poems* chart a moment and action relationally in shared space or time. Significantly, the words and actions would mean different things at the different locations where they originated, a difference emphasized by their placement on a map that would diagram this effect within a globally conceived sensorium. Who faced Mecca? Who New York? What does North mean for someone in the South, and vice versa? Did someone face anyone else over the space of continents? How would time zones affect this possibility?

This gives an expanded sense of context to new theories of human intelligence which address both the systematic and adaptive or creative aspects of the human mind. Recent theories of human intelligence include the conventional forms of intelligence associated with the academic disciplines (the linguistic and logical–mathematical intelligences required by writers and mathematicians for example), as well as so-called embodied and emotional intelligence types (the musical, spatial, bodily-kinesthetic, interpersonal and intrapersonal intelligences required by musicians, athletes, artists, dancers, and therapists).[32] This theory of multiple intelligences, MI as it is known, offers a variety of ways to rethink the dualism in western thought, with two modes of intelligence historically located in the separate mind and body, as well as various artists' translations of conceptual material through MI. What's more, MI implies that all forms of aesthetic experience associated with the arts are based in intelligence itself.

For the foremost scholar in this area of cognitive science, Howard Gardner, qualifying as *intelligence* requires that a cognitive/sensory activity be potentially systematic or codifiable, and that the system also be adaptive and transformable. This latter aspect, the manipulability of the intelligence system, is therefore directly relevant to the matter of human creativity, which might be described as the engine behind the manipulability of an intelligence system or group of systems. Indeed, cultural history can be described as expressing evolution across the full range of human intelligences, dance corresponding to kinesthetic, literature to verbal, image making to spatial, music to musical, intelligences, etc. Even if these categories would be justifiably criticized for overdetermining the separation of senses and therefore dividing the art forms that exploit them, as used by educators, MI are useful as a mechanism that expands the capacities of intelligences to address each other, as when music is used to teach mathematical principles, dance to teach geometry to non-math students, the visual arts to expand the reading capacity of dyslexic students, and so on.

More specifically, the close link between Fluxus and experimental composition associated with Cage suggests that the musical score functions in Fluxus, or at least among those artists involved with Cage's work, as a vehicle for MI since it performs an act of translation that links reading to performance experience for the performer at the same time as its interactive aspect establishes a wide range of possible ontological exchanges between the performer and the audience. We have seen the Event as an example of the process of systemization for intelligent, experiential encounters. In each of the works detailed thus far, multisensory feedback systems organize information and enable the interplay of systematic intelligences. It should be clear by now that each medium far exceeds the limitations of a specific sense as habitually laid out by art historians.

Musicality, and more specifically, the musical score as it is used by a classical performer to precisely perform a repeatable skill, is distinct from this habit. In contrast, the Fluxus score functions as a mechanism for cross modal experiential encounters, encounters that multisensate, as opposed to primarily visual. As such, Fluxus works confuse the emphasis on the visual foundational of the professional art system discussed at the beginning of this chapter. By this framing, if art is not primarily visual, it is anti-visual, meaning anti-art. Far from limited to the visual arts, this categorizing behavior is typical of the modern era, with its particularly rigid hierarchy of the senses.[33] A quick perusal of modern culture's maps, ledgers, and screens suggests that an objectifying visuality has dominated the foundations of expertise in the modern era in Europe and its related cultures. Heidegger scholar David Michael Levin has famously criticized the objectifying gaze of western culture, while offering an alternative that promotes better understanding: "Informed by an interactive and receptive normativity, listening generates a very different episteme and ontology [than the visual norm], a very different metaphysics," one based on "communicative rationality."[34] The point is not that vision is inherently evil, but that it has been used to drive the wedge in the subject/object divide.

In an historic essay published in 1965 in the *Something Else Newsletter*, Dick Higgins – another member of the Cage class, Fluxus artist, founder of the Something Else Press and, as noted, my father – revived a term used by Samuel Taylor Coleridge in 1812: *intermedia*.[35] His "Intermedia" statement is also a manifesto in the sense that it articulates a position critical of many aspects of the art world of that time. The similarity to most manifestos breaks down, however, at the level of the term's adaptability and social resilience. Higgins used the term intermedia to describe artwork that made use of structural continuities between the arts in a manner that suggests precisely the kinds of communicative rationality and interactivity theorized by Heidegger and Levin: poetry that was both read and seen as form (visual poetry), poetry that was both read and heard as sound (sound poetry), theater with musical and painterly elements (happenings), and all manner of other arts in between. Higgins wrote, "I would like to suggest that the use of intermedia is more or less universal throughout the fine arts, since continuity rather than categorization is the hallmark of our new mentality."[36] Thirty years later, these intermedia relationships were given graphic form as the schematic "Intermedia Diagram" of 1995.

In its implied resistance to specialized skill sets, the intermedia concept partakes of the anti-establishment orientation of much elite and popular culture of the 1960s. It is a diagram of flux or change:

> The concept of the separation of media arose in the Renaissance. The idea that a painting could be made of paint on canvas or that a sculpture should not be painted seems characteristic of the kind of social thought, categorizing and dividing society [...] which we call the feudal conception of the Great Chain of Being [...]The scene is not just characteristic of the painting world as an institution, however. It is absolutely natural to (and inevitable in) the concept of the pure medium.[37]

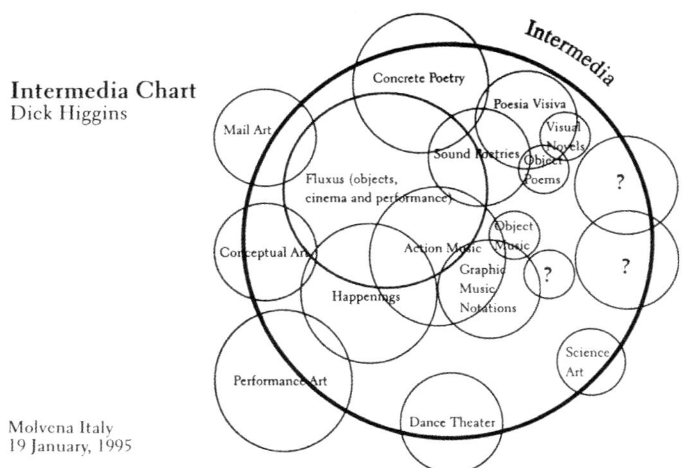

Dick Higgins, *Intermedia Diagram*, postcard, 1995. Courtesy of the Estate of Dick Higgins.

In other words, for Higgins intermedia work is an historic necessity, functioning as a foil for the specialization of the arts, as well as a foil for the overdetermination of painting as *the* art of the mid-century United States – characterized in the field of the visual arts by a near hegemonic dominance of abstract painting.

Higgins is suggesting that the hierarchy of specialized arts is the product of specific historical circumstances that categorized and defined human experience for the modern era and that such divisions are not so much natural as cultural. The historiography of art, literature, and music bear this out as they mirror the processes of disciplinary specialization and industrial mechanization. Perhaps for this reason, fine arts disciplines and sensation-hierarchies run roughly parallel to each other, from the emphasis on the visual in relation to painting and the narrative basis for the literary arts, through music being characterized purely as sound, to the "baser" art forms of movement (dance), taste (the culinary arts), and scent (perfumery). The implication of intermedia as mixing, in other words, suggests a fundamental shift in the sensorium as described by Walter Ong.

Higgins's diagram shows the interaction of Sound Poetries, which emphasize the sound component of language and poetic association, and Concrete Poetry, which is based on a homology of visual form and verbal content such that poetry is structured visually in a coming together of the communicative motive of graphic design and verbal content. Unlike the hard edges of the fractured plane of the Purge Manifesto, the hovering bubbles of the *Intermedia Diagram* (whose sizes seem indeterminate) imaginarily expand, contract, pass over and through each other in a visualization of the fluidity inherent to the intermedia arts, according to Higgins. Question marks demonstrate that other intermedia are still emerging.

Intermedia work, it could be said, occurs between media categories and perceptual categories as well. In summary, a cross modal aesthetics of all senses is needed to understand the power of intermedia work in general, and the Event in particular, as based in the interactions among hearing, touch, smell, taste, and sight. This consideration of intermedial (and therefore intersensory) art therefore requires a simultaneously physiological and cultural framework for each sense as a cross modal perceptual system.

In summary, whether through the overlapping of touch, taste, smell, sound, or speech, Fluxus intermedia works have, at some level, the principle of directness, non-mediation, and unprocessed experience at their core. This does not, however, mean that they stand outside of the cultures of the artists that produced the Events. Far from it. They activate subtle differences in the global sensorium. As Brecht's "Exhibit" cards and Chieko Shiomi's *Spatial Poems* illustrate, the Event adapts itself to many contexts even as its structure privileges perceptual systems over overtly semiotic ones. This recognition goes some way toward explaining the difficulty people have in describing (or translating into words) a Fluxus Event work.

By exploiting the fact that human animals sense in common, and that communities are established where certain sensory experiences are shared, intermedia aesthetics suggest applications far beyond Fluxus specifically, and beyond the specialized context of Fluxus in the art world generally. Great art expands the human sense of community and the sensory mechanisms human beings use to express themselves, connect to each other, and address the complex problems of the day. By expanding the global sensorium manifestly, albeit within the specialized domain of art, Fluxus Events are masterpieces in just this way. Through them the body asserts itself against the machining of the mind, of language, and the mass manufactured sensory spectacle. The current ways that Fluxus is generally understood, while suggesting positive values like cultural critique, resistance, and transformation, miss this important point.

It is in terms of the absence of hearkening, conceived broadly enough to include Gibson's sensory feedback systems and Gardner's MI, that we should regret the historic tendency displayed by the majority of critics, curators, and collectors to treat Maciunas, his manifesto, and the most overtly destructive works as defining the core logic of Fluxus. The version of Fluxus we find on the Internet and in the curatorial mainstream is a fiction, a group of artists circling a parody of the real Maciunas that struts about in the place of Fluxus and the art world making grand gestures and totalizing statements. He is a man without organs, weirdly fleshless or a dead mannequin walking.

Notes

1. For details, see "Charting Fluxus: Picturing History" in my book *Fluxus Experience*, Berkeley, CA: University of California Press, 2002, pp. 69–100.
2. Tom Johnson, "Paper Airplanes and Shattered Violins," *Village Voice*, 9 April 1979, vol. 9, pp. 71–2.
3. *Ibid.*, 32.
4. Jon Hendricks, "Aspects of Fluxus from the Gilbert and Lila Silverman Collection," *Art Libraries Journal*, Autumn 1983, vol. 8, no. 3,, pp. 8–13. Emphasis mine.
5. Thomas Kellein, *George Maciunas: The Dream of Fluxus, An Artist's Biography*, London: Thames and Hudson, 2007.
6. Maciunas later responded to these critics with subsequent manifestos of less narrow bent. These are described admirably by Clive Phillpot, in "Fluxus: Magazines, Manifestos, Multum in Parvo," in Clive Phillpot and Jon Hendricks, *Fluxus: Selections from the Gilbert and Lila Silverman Collection*, New York: The Museum of Modern Art, 1988, p. 13. See http://www.georgemaciunas.com/fluxus-to-george/fluxus_phillipot.html.
7. For details, see *Fluxus Experience*, pp. 69–100.
8. Jackson MacLow in a letter to George Maciunas, 25 April 1962. Located in Archiv Sohm, Staatsgalerie Stuttgart.
9. Clive Phillpot, "Fluxus: Magazines," p. 14.
10. George Maciunas, *Fluxmanifesto*, 1965 (version 1), Gilbert and Lila Silverman Fluxus Collection, Museum of Modern Art, New York.
11. George Brecht, "Something about Fluxus," *Fluxus Newspaper*, no. 4, June 1964.
12. See for instance, Robert C. Morgan, "Fluxus, Museum of Modern Art," *Flash Art International*, May-June 1989, no. 146, p. 14.
13. Robert Pincus-Witten, "Introduction," *Fluxus Codex*, Jon Hendricks, ed., New York: Abrams, 1988, p. 15.
14. Bruce Altschuler, "Fluxus Redux," *Arts*, September 1989, vol. 14., pp. 66–70.
15. See Helen Prejean, *Dead Man Walking*, New York, Random House, 1993, and *Dead Man Walking* (film), Senn Penn and Susan Sarandon, 1995.
16. "The Dead Man Walking," *Time's Laughingstocks and Other Verses*, Thomas Hardy, "The Dead Man Walking," *Time's Laughingstocks and Other Verses*, London: Macmillan and Co., 1909.
17. Peter Starr, *Logics of Failed Revolt: French Theory After May '68*, Stanford, CA: Stanford University Press, 1995, p. 15.
18. Perhaps the ultimate expression of recuperation is the movement today in Lithuania to make a postage stamp in Maciunas's honor and to base a Guggenheim in the capital, Vilnius, with a wing dedicated to the artist.
19. Julia Robinson, conversation with the author, 16 April 2010.
20. Nicolas Bourriaud, *Relational Aesthetics*, Dijon, France: Les Presses du réel, 1998.
21. This is fleshed out in my article "Transflux," in *Not the Other Avant-Garde: The Transnational Foundations of Avant-Garde Performance*, James Harding, ed., Ann Arbor, MI: University of Michigan Press, 2006.
22. Hannah Higgins, "Fluxus Fortuna," in *The Fluxus Reader*, Ken Friedman, ed., West Sussex, UK: Academy Editions, pp. 31–62.
23. For more on Brecht, see Julia Robinson, "From Abstraction to Model: In the Event of George Brecht & The Conceptual Turn in the Art of the 1960s," doctoral dissertation, Princeton University, 2008.

24. Martin Heidegger, *Being and Time* (Sein und Zeit), trans. John Macquarrie and Edward Robinson, New York: HarperCollins, 1962, p. 207.
25. *Ibid.*, p. 216.
26. James Jerome Gibson, *The Senses Considered as Perceptual Systems*, Boston: Houghton Mifflin Company, 1966 [1983], p. 99.
27. Ibid., p. 123. My emphasis.
28. Ibid., p. 31.
29. Ibid., p. 41.
30. For detailed analysis of this phenomenon in 1960s art more generally, see Liz Kotz, *Words to be Looked at: Language in 1960s Art*, Cambridge, MA: MIT Press, 2007.
31. Walter Ong, "The Shifting Sensorium," David Howes (ed.), *The Varieties of Sensory Experience*, Toronto, CA: University of Toronto Press, 1991, p. 28.
32. Howard Gardner, *Frames of Mind: The Theory of Multiple Intelligences*, New York: Basic Books, 1993 [1983].
33. Martin Jay has argued convincingly that this "scopic regime of modernity" (his term) is largely a fiction and that actually vision is more complex culturally and perceptually than most postmodern philosophers would have it. It remains as a cultural commonplace, however, regardless of its being challenged. For a quick summary of Jay's extensive work on this problem, see "Scopic Regimes of Modernity," in Hal Foster (ed.), *Vision and Visuality*, Seattle, WA: Bay Press, 1995, pp. 3–28. For the perspective that vision has been the predominant model for truth and cognition since the Renaissance, see Paul Virilio, *The Vision Machine*, Bloomington, IN: Indiana University Press, 1988.
34. David Michael Levin, *Modernity and the Hegemony of Vision*, Berkeley, CA: University of California Press, 1993, p. 212.
35. Dick Higgins, "Intermedia," *Something Else Newsletter* (1965), reprinted in *Horizons: The Poetics and Theory of the Intermedia*, Carbondale and Edwardsville, IL: Southern Illinois University Press, 1983. The term "intermedium" is adapted from Samuel Taylor Coleridge, "Lecture No. 3, On Edmund Spencer," reprinted in Coleridge's *Miscellaneous Criticism*, T. M. Raysor, ed., London: Constable, 1936, p. 35.
36. Ibid., p. 22.
37. Ibid., p. 18.

Chapter 3

The Viral Ontology of Performance

Christopher Bedford

"Performance's only life," Peggy Phelan contends in her now classic argument in the 1993 book *Unmarked*, "is in the present." She continues:

> Performance cannot be saved, recorded, documented, or otherwise participate in the circulation of representations *of* representations: once it does so, it becomes something other than performance. To the degree that performance attempts to enter the economy of reproduction it betrays and lessens the promise of its own ontology. Performance's being [...] becomes itself through disappearance.[1]

Phelan's contention is as eloquent as it is seductive, predicated as it is on her insistence that performance is inherently "nonreproductive," and thus irreconcilable with the "machinery of reproductive representation necessary to the circulation of capital."[2] More importantly perhaps, Phelan distinguishes performance art in its purest ontological form from all other media on the basis that it (the performance) is by nature traceless.[3] To transcribe the events of that moment into a textual or imagistic format, she implies, is to subject the radical logic of a single moment to the rationalizing frameworks of language and static images, forms which are answerable to normative social codes and are thus antithetical to the free, speculative stage of performance.

In what follows I would like to use Chris Burden's most iconic performance work, *Shoot* (1971), to elaborate upon this very persuasive, landmark thesis, but also to contest the value of insisting that the traceless, nonreproductivity of performance art is the only mark of the medium's conceptual and social radicality. In fact, I argue, *there is no* performance outside its discourse. As a curator invested in finding fresh means to present and animate performance art in a gallery setting, I argue here that art history, art criticism, art practice, and even popular journalism all participate in the extension and reproduction of performance art in the public sphere and are, therefore, in the absence of a conventional "object," as potent and performative as the originary work. In Burden's case these critical texts often incorporate photographs of performances produced or sanctioned by the artist, but I want to demonstrate that it is the *integration* of these images into descriptive and analytical texts that most effectively extends the reach of the performance, not the visual evidence or the text alone. While Burden's photographs are unquestionably indices of his performances, it is the specific interplay of text and image that animates the imagination and activates the performance as an event unfolding in the present.

Whether or not Burden's performances resist or contest the cycles of production and consumption that characterize the art market, and whether, as a result, his work defies the language and values of that system – as Phelan argues – is not a question I will take up here. Nor will the issue of how Burden himself conceives of the duration of his performances be a salient question in the context of this chapter. Rather, following Amelia Jones' suggestion that "there is no possibility of an unmediated relationship to any kind of cultural product, including body art,"[4] through a selective historiographic survey of the reception of Burden's *Shoot*, I want to draw attention to a new concept of the ontology of performance art, one in which a given performance – in this case Burden's now-infamous work – splinters, mutates, and multiplies over time in the hands of various critical constituencies in a variety of media, to yield a body of critical work that extends the primary act of the performance into the indefinite future through reproduction. This approach in turn forces us to relinquish our attachment to the performance as primary act and instead submit to the notion that the object of performance art is in fact a long, variegated trace history that begins with the performance, but whose manifestations may extend, theoretically, to infinity. This extended trace history I will refer to as the *viral ontology* of performance art.

Shoot has one of the richest and most contested historiographic records of any performance to date and will thus serve as a vivid illustration of this principle: the re-performance of *Shoot*, as we shall see, is and was indiscriminate, viral, and utterly unbound by any ontological category. It is not my claim that the analyses, descriptions, and reprisals of *Shoot* that I cite here preserve the authenticity of the performance or safeguard the artist's intention; far from it. Rather, my interest lies in the conviction that through the reproductive function of discourse, these works become *performances through time* that reflect the shifting imperatives of art history and more broadly (and importantly), the ideologies of the social worlds in which they intervene and of which they ultimately become a part.

One of the earliest extended considerations of Burden's performance work appeared in 1973, not in a specialized art publication but in the *New York Times*. Peter Plagens, the author of the histrionically titled story, "He Got Shot – For His Art," begins with a quote from Maurice Merleau-Ponty's *The Phenomenology of Perception*, and thus implicitly declares his intention to understand Burden's work according to the theoretical terms popularized in the United States by the Minimalists during the 1960s.[5] Having ostensibly claimed Burden's theoretical pedigree by implying a link between the artist and Merleau-Ponty – a link he

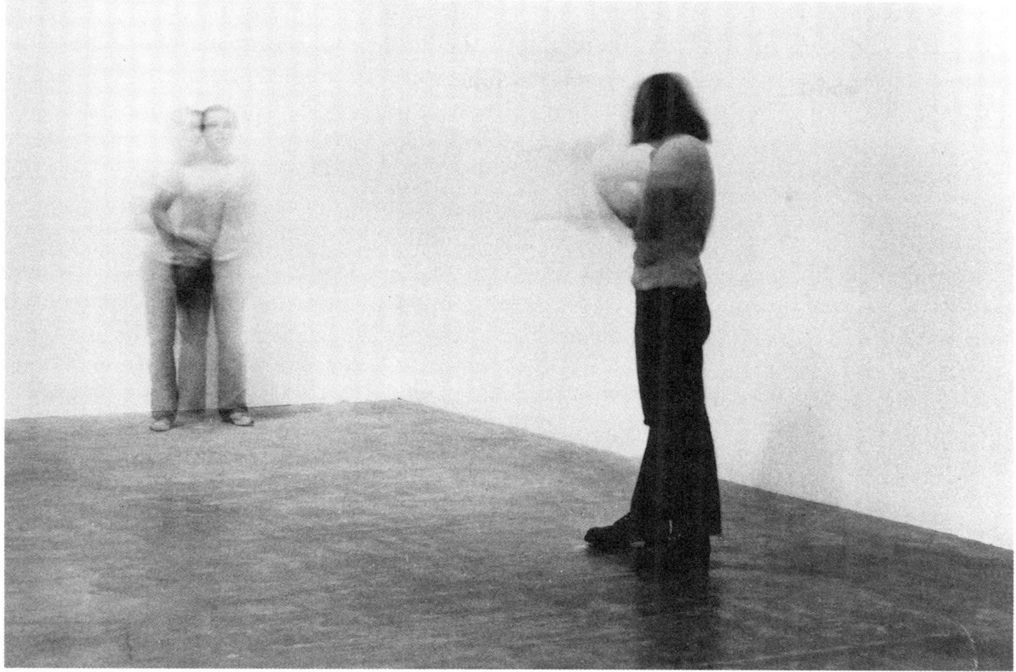

Chris Burden, *Shoot*. F Space, Santa Ana, CA, November 19, 1971. At 7:45 p.m. I was shot in the left arm by a friend. The bullet was a copper jacket .22 long rifle. My friend was standing about fifteen feet from me. © Chris Burden. Courtesy Gagosian Gallery.

does not address or explore in the remainder of the lengthy article – Plagens then proceeds to cast Burden as a pioneering trailblazer with the requisite dash of outsider panache:

> Under hazy, gray skies women looking like retired strippers somnambulate in muumuus while a distant bongo concert continues unabated, and a few artists take a break from their white studios and watch the spacey parade from walkway benches. Chris Burden lives down there in a former hotdog stand (fully converted, heavily padlocked). Burden is a Conceptual-performance artist who does *things* (an appropriately ambiguous term) often involving pain/danger to himself; although he's the product of a European childhood and high school hard by Harvard, his work, looks and mien have the same slightly sinister insouciance as the neighborhood.[6]

Plagens follows this passage of flowery prose with a self-consciously philistine account of Burden's rise to prominence on the back of his performance, *Shoot*. Plagens notes: "Burden is a minor legend because of *Shoot* (1971), a 'piece' (one of the great justifying art-world words) in which a marksman-friend shot Burden in the upper left arm with a .22 long-jacket before an audience of 12 intimates."[7]

Plagens' clear objective is to relate the circumstances of *Shoot* in barebones, sardonic terms, and in doing so illustrate the difficulty inherent in assessing this elusive turn in art production: a performance one has not and cannot witness poses a unique set of rhetorical challenges for the writer, especially when that writer must find a way to evoke the drama of an artist who willingly submitted to being shot in the arm in front of a live audience of his peers. Notably absent from Plagens' discussion, therefore, is any consideration of the aesthetic attributes of the performance – a description of the artist, the marksman, the audience, the gallery space, the wound, the sound of the gunfire, even something as presumably dramatic as gushing blood – because, we must assume, he did not feel qualified to discuss an event he did not himself see. Plagens opts instead to treat the performance not as an art event, but as a historical occurrence, using dry reportage and anecdotal evidence to evoke the dangerous, guerilla spirit of the work. Following this pattern, Plagens then proceeds to catalogue a selection of Burden's performance works, issuing brief descriptions of each, and drawing attention to the real world social implications of, for example, Burden's decision to wrap himself in tarpaulin and lie inert under the wheels of a parked car in a performance entitled, *Dead Man* (1972).

Plagens' account of Burden's work departs from the bulk of the literature in one important respect. Unlike most of the essays and reviews considered here, Plagens ends his article on a note of aggressive skepticism, first drawing attention to the disruptive potential of Burden's practice, then charging that the artist's work "bothers" him "because his freedom – 'to think up things and to do them' – may be entirely illusory; he may be [...] a product of art-world art history – backed further into some untenable corner because all the other novelty territory has been claimed." "If," Plagens continues, "you want to be a heavy artist nowadays, you have to do something unpleasant to your body, because everything *else* has been done."[8] Ultimately, "He Got Shot – For His Art" reflects two curious, inconsistent desires. On the one hand, Plagens is eager to associate Burden with legitimizing thinkers like Merleau-Ponty and Jean-Paul Sartre (whose work he also cites but does not expound upon) in order to establish Burden's seriousness as an artist, an attribute Plagens does not contest. On the other hand, Plagens' critical arsenal, contingent as it is on the language deployed by art criticism to describe and understand objects, stalls when faced with the relative immateriality of Burden's work. Resultantly, he treats Burden's performances not as an art critic might address an art object, but as an historian might treat an historical event. Thus, while his article gestures toward the sociopolitical agency of Burden's performances, he does not connect the visual aspect of the artist's practice with the way meaning is made by his performances. Plagens' ultimate skepticism toward Burden's practice then results more from the limitations of his critical skill-set than from the shortcomings of Burden's performances as visual events, since they are not addressed as such.

However, while Plagens may not have grasped, acknowledged, or attempted to describe the distinguishing visual features of Burden's practice, the conjunction of his empiricist approach to Burden's performances and his stinging criticism of their masochistic extremity, along with the image chosen to accompany his article, activates Burden's presence as a performer far more vividly than Plagens' words alone. Representing Burden, below the caption declaring that "He Got Shot – For His Art" is a sinister image of the artist's face floating against a field of black, veiled by a sinister white woolen ski mask, his eyes dead and expressionless, his mouth down-turned and solemn.[9] An arresting image in and of itself, this fabricated mugshot not only demonstrates Burden's facility with traditional image-making, but also operates as a haunting talisman for his performances: here, we are presented with the guerilla artist Chris Burden, reproducing himself as a performer, aided and abetted by a critic who, like the reader, participates in the reproduction and circulation of the myths that are Burden's performances. The grainy portrait printed on rumpled newsprint reads more as a "Wanted" sign than as a self-portrait, and, in conjunction with Plagens' rhetoric, elaborates upon the elusive threat that so often characterizes Burden's performances. This use of text and image to activate a virtual performance space in which Burden's work might be re-imagined is a strategy that is repeated throughout the literature on the artist and, as we shall see, is informed by a text/image format Burden himself employed in the early part of his career.

Until the dawn of the so-called new art history and particularly the rise of psychoanalytic approaches in the discipline, articles and exhibition catalogues devoted to Burden's work relied heavily on the artist's own words to animate the photographs taken during his performances.[10] The layouts chosen for such articles and exhibition catalogues foreground the narrative generated by the conjunction of image and text, implicitly deferring to Burden as the principle authority on his work. Functioning as would a storyboard, these essays and articles present grainy, blurry, occasionally overexposed images replete with terse descriptions written by Burden, which, in clipped, basic-Hemingway prose, absolutely devoid of adjectives, provide only the most basic information, just enough in fact to permit a skeletal narrative to emerge. An *Arts Magazine* article published in 1975 is a signal example of this strategy. "Chris Burden: Through The Night Softly," an unorthodox article co-authored by Jan Butterfield and Burden, is arranged into three columns, with the narrow outer columns written by Butterfield and providing biographical details, and the much broader middle column devoted to Burden's own descriptions of his performances.[11] Black and white photographs are positioned throughout the article adjacent to Burden's characteristically scant prose descriptions.

This model reprises a text/image layout designed by Burden to disseminate his own work in a self-published artist book issued in 1974, simply titled, *Chris Burden, 71–73*, and recalls gallery presentations wherein the "relics" from performances were presented next to documentary photographs and Burden's texts.[12] With no critical interlocution whatsoever, this book, frequently understood as a simple documentary resource, reproduces photographs of performances from this period, juxtaposed directly with the attendant text, composed exclusively by Burden. Far more than simply an expedient layout, the clear, uninterrupted juxtapositions of image and text in this publication propose a specific relation between the two elements through which the viewer is enticed to generate an imaginary narrative in the space implied between the textual description and the image. The plates that document *Shoot* serve as a perfect example of this interactive ploy.[13]

Burden provides the title of the performance represented – *Shoot* – and the place and time of its execution: F-Space, Santa Ana, California, 19 November 1971. Directly below this simple information are three brusque sentences: "At 7:45 p.m. I was shot in the left arm by a friend. The bullet was a copper jacket 22 long rifle. My friend was standing about fifteen feet from me."[14] Without the nominal interpretive help provided by the text, the photograph reproduced on the page directly opposite would be unintelligible. With it, however, suggestive narrative details emerge from an image that is otherwise unyielding, austere, and almost Minimalist in its rhetoric. A diminutive figure we can identify as Chris Burden appears as a hazy mirage against a white gallery wall. Facing him is a tall, slender person of indeterminate gender aiming a rifle, though this latter detail is not immediately evident from the image alone. The rest of the image is largely without narrative incident; a towering white gallery wall dominates the right of the frame, and to the left is an expanse of dark flooring. Even with so little detail, however, the space is unmistakably a gallery.

Up to a certain point, this simple integration of short text with a rough, black and white photograph is a startling example of the putting forth of "sheer authorial intention."[15] The concept of the performance was Burden's; he played the central role in its realization, and he subjected himself to the very real threat of death to realize his concept. He then wrote the descriptive text, selected the photographic image for publication, laid out those elements on the page and published the book under his own auspices – the level of control borders on tyrannical.[16] Purged of all extraneous narrative details and betraying no obvious agenda beyond the clear, expeditious, and above all brief communication of basic information, one can see why such photographs have been understood as simple documentation. Indeed Burden himself has questioned the use-value of his photographs, noting that

> between the photograph and the performance, I will go for the performance [...] The photograph is nothing but a symbol, everybody knows that, and that's why I like still photographs. Everybody knows that they are lies [...] they are just a hint of the real thing, just a tidbit, a tip of the iceberg.[17]

It is however the enticement of this chosen "tidbit" coupled with the strategic omission of most narrative details that activates the page as a performative space. And, in spite of his attempts to control the presentation of the work through image and text, it is paradoxically through this conjunction of elements that Burden cedes control of his image to the viewer. Like journalistic photographs which are understood as metonyms for a broader, invisible narrative beyond the frame, or images of sculpture that imply three dimensions but record only two, or like photographs of paintings that capture the basic pictorial composition but lose the intricacy of surface detail, the interface of word and image that comprises Burden's discursive performance of *Shoot* remains incomplete and seduces viewers' minds into an act of spurious reproduction: they must conjure an event they never witnessed, based on the selective evidence presented by Burden. Accordingly, viewers might summon the various narrative details absent from the official record of *Shoot*: the tension before the

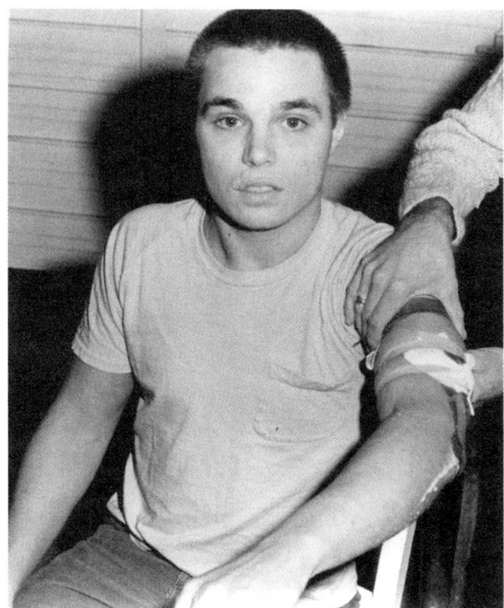

Chris Burden, *Shoot*. F Space, Santa Ana, CA, November 19, 1971. At 7:45 p.m. I was shot in the left arm by a friend. The bullet was a copper jacket .22 long rifle. My friend was standing about fifteen feet from me. © Chris Burden. Courtesy Gagosian Gallery.

performance, the sound of rifle fire in an enclosed space, the subsequent panic of the audience, Burden's response, even the reaction of the marksman. It is, then, the absence of detailed information in Burden's textual re-performance that is the ultimate enticement to the viewer's imagination.

What I am calling the reproduction of *Shoot* is not confined to articles, interviews, artist books, and exhibition catalogues. Indeed, reproduction has assumed a number of forms, including quite literal transcriptions of Burden's now ubiquitous photo-documentation. Israeli painter Rueven Zahavi, for example, executed a rich, brushy acrylic on canvas painting of Chris Burden immediately after performing *Shoot*, based on an image published in Lucy Lippard's widely read text, *Six Years: The Dematerialization of the Art Object from 1966 to 1972; a cross reference book of information on some esthetic boundaries* (1973).[18] In the painting, as in the photograph, Burden walks from right to left, his wounded arm dangling inertly at his side, a small rivulet of blood running almost elegantly down his arm, an expression of unaffected petrified shock on his face.[19]

Working at a considerable remove not only from the originary event but the specifically American context in which it emerged, Zahavi first encountered American performance art as an art student in Jerusalem during the 1970s, and then only through still, documentary images made available in Lippard's book. Returning to those images in 1999, Zahavi's painting, *Chris Burden Shoot 1971*, as the title indicates, frames Burden's performance as an event made available through documentation. The transcription of Burden's photographic likeness captured in the immediate aftermath of *Shoot* into an acrylic on canvas painting made twenty-eight years after the performance does not shed any particular light on Burden's experience of that moment, nor does it register as an important piece of documentary evidence. It does, however, extend the ontology of the performance temporally and geographically, and claims, however implicitly, that the only access to *Shoot* is through images and statements that exist at a greater and greater remove from the event they ostensibly record.

Los Angles-based artist Tom LaDuke's tongue-in-cheek, mixed-media sculpture *Self-Inflicted Burden* (2004) is a jocular rejoinder to the elusive character of performance art. The sculpture is a three-foot tall self-portrait rendered with disarming verism in various plastic resins. The artist is shown shirtless in casual sweatpants and slippers, his skin translucent and waxy and dotted with pores and blemishes. His left arm raised and his bald head cocked inquisitively, he inspects a thin rivulet of blood emerging from an angry wound just below his bicep. Dangling casually in his right hand is a Daisy pellet pistol.[20] The sculpture is accompanied by a low-cost, camp "how to" manual entitled "Instructions for Assembling Self-Inflicted Burden." Two pages in length, the document provides the buyer with step by step instructions on how to assemble his or her kit, and details the materials needed to "assure yourself a perfect model every time!" Significantly, the document also features a photograph of LaDuke himself in precisely the pose captured by the sculpture, in effect the artist's document of his own transient, originary event, which, of course, derives its logic from Burden's performance and its various multimedia reprisals.

LaDuke makes no attempt to capture his action on film or by any other real time means. Consequently, in the context of *Self-Inflicted Burden* the moment LaDuke actually shot himself with a pellet gun remains imaginary and necessarily fugitive, mimicking the myth-making ontology of Burden's *Shoot*. Instead, what he offers is a carefully curated conjunction of text and image through which the action is constituted as absent, while the sculpture and instructional guide operate as talisman animating the event in the mind of the viewer. Though irreverent, playful, and self-consciously deconstructive, LaDuke's project emphasizes and reproduces the iconicity of Burden's performance, and its status as an immaterial template – the ghost of an action – available for continual appropriation and re-performance.

The critical reproduction of *Shoot* assumed a literal and indeed performative dimension in 2005 when Joseph Deutch, a University of California, Los Angeles (UCLA) studio art graduate student in visiting instructor Ron Athey's class introduced what appeared to be a loaded weapon into a performance class. "The student," *Artforum* correspondent Jeffrey Kastner writes,

> wearing a coat and tie, produced either a gun or a convincing replica of one, put what looked like a bullet into the weapon, spun the cylinder, and held it to his head, Russian-roulette style. He pulled the trigger, but the gun did not fire. The student left the room; while he was out of view, a shot was heard, at which point he returned, now apparently unarmed.[21]

According to Deutch, speaking through his lawyer, Howard R. Price, he in fact dashed into an adjoining room and did not fire a gun, but rather set off a firecracker inside a large can, thereby simulating the deafening noise of gunfire.[22]

Seen in the light of Phelan's argument that the potency of performance art lies in its essential ethereality – its tracelessness – Deutch's decision to leave the room and simulate the sound of gunfire, while offering the audience no visible evidence of his actions, might very well be understood as a clever riff on the notion that the essential ontology of performance is realized through disappearance. In the case of Deutch's untitled work, the crescendo of the performance was actualized as an invisible act, one that evaded the visual record altogether, only to be re-imagined and re-performed first by the audience and then – unexpectedly or not – in the spectacular, virtual realm of popular journalistic discourse.

To an even greater extent than Burden's 1971 performance, Deutch's enigmatic work ignited a storm of media controversy fueled largely, and perhaps unwittingly, by the objections of Chris Burden, then a professor in the art department at UCLA, to Deutch's work. Burden's dismissal of the performance, which he made quite deliberately public, was followed avidly by the New York and Los Angles presses, and the emerging details of the story – including shifting renditions of the performance – were recorded and parsed in exquisite detail. Speaking through his dealer, Gagosian Gallery in Beverly Hills, Burden charged that in the context of the then current (just post-9/11) political climate, Deutch's work represented a sort of "domestic terrorism," and the university's refusal to properly sanction the student, Burden claimed, was deeply irresponsible.[23] In a letter to the *Los Angeles Times*, Burden explained that Deutch's work violated the spirit and decorum of a university atmosphere and created for his fellow students a "hostile and violent work environment." Since UCLA was unwilling to take immediate action, Burden wrote, he felt honor bound to tender his resignation and asserted that he did not want to be "associated with an institution that condones such behavior."[24] Preempting the charge of hypocrisy, Burden also added that what distinguished *Shoot* from Deutch's work is the simple fact that his audience was forewarned about what they would witness and were therefore afforded a choice. With his decision to retire in protest, Burden ensured that Deutch's work would be understood through the prism of the originary act, namely, *Shoot*.

Speaking explicitly about the much-discussed connection between his work and that of the embattled UCLA graduate student in a phone interview with the *New York Times*, Burden claimed that he was "sure the student was referencing the work I did. He was also trying to co-opt and demean it and parody."[25] Though it is not clear whether Deutch anticipated the press attention his work would generate, and though he claims that his project was not a conscious reprisal of *Shoot*, the collision in the press of these two performances – separated by more than thirty years – represents not only a provocative testimonial to the persistent interest in Burden's radical early practice, but also a vivid illustration of the very different political climate in which we live today, one in which the use of a gun in a performance – once the basis for a speculative phenomenological discussion in the popular press – is now cause for immediate alarm and harsh sanctions.

What this account of Burden's *Shoot* proposes is a wholesale dissolution of disciplinary and medium-based boundaries, and a concomitant embrace of the interrelated notions of mutation, transformation, and inauthenticity in the study and presentation of performance art. The photographs, descriptions, analyses, anecdotes, and performances that constitute *Shoot*'s performance over time claim a new ontology of performance art that extends far beyond the evanescent primary act: a viral ontology. As such the study of performance calls not only for the reconstruction of discrete historical moments, but for a systematic historiographic approach that charts the life and afterlife of a given work.

Performances like Burden's continue to assert themselves in the present, to extend their own ontology through discourse and reproduction, reestablishing their pertinence and agency over and over again. Performance is a myth-making medium and as such essentially viral in nature. It extends indefinitely through history, its auratic charge often gaining traction and potency, just as the originary act recedes and recedes. It is the absence of the event, the absence of an object, which makes the work available for rewriting, and it is this quality that permits the work to travel through time and space, absorbing and assimilating the conditions of history. The moment of performance, then, is simply the beginning point, the source of the myth, one of its functions being the foundation of a viral chain, the ontology of which is predicated on perpetual revision, by historians and practitioners.

Phelan's critical interest in the ethereality of performance art, articulated so influentially in *Unmarked*, is motivated by a desire to claim an experimental space in which, for a fleeting moment, a community of people can together experience and accept – if only transiently – a reality incompatible with the conditions of the broader social world. While rhetorically convincing, influential, and of enduring value, Phelan's ontology of performance, like all other paradigms, presupposes its own negation, or at least expansion. The afterlife of Chris Burden's *Shoot* – 1971 to the present – reveals the need for a revision of this paradigm, and for a new theoretical model that can account for the demonstrable fact that a performance which lasted for a few seconds thirty-five years ago, through various permutations and mutations, lives on today.

Notes

1. Peggy Phelan, *Unmarked: The Politics of Performance*, London and New York: Routledge, 1993, p. 146.
2. Ibid., p. 148.
3. Ibid., p. 149.
4. Amelia Jones, "'Presence' *in absentia*: Experiencing Performance as Documentation," *Art Journal*, Winter 1997, vol. 56, no. 4, p. 11.
5. Maurice Merleau-Ponty, *The Phenomenology of Perception*, London: Routledge & K. Paul, 1962.
6. Peter Plagens, "He Got Shot – For His Art," *New York Times*, 2 September 1973, p. 87.
7. Ibid.
8. Ibid.
9. This image is photograph taken from his performance *You'll Never See My Face in Kansas City*, performed in the Morgan Gallery, 6 November 1971. See *Chris Burden, 71–73*, Los Angeles: Chris Burden, 1974, pp. 20–1.
10. Amelia Jones, "Dis/playing the Phallus: Male Artists Perform Their Masculinities," *Art History*, December 2004, vol. 17, no. 4, pp. 546–84, and Frazier Ward, "Gray Zone: Watching Shoot," *October*, Winter 2001, vol. 95, pp. 114–30, remain the two most developed revisionist accounts of Burden's practice.
11. Jan Butterfield, "Chris Burden: *Through the Night Softly*," *Arts Magazine*, March 1975, vol. 49, pp. 68–72.

12. See *Chris Burden, 71–73.*
13. This formula hues closely to that used in a comprehensive catalogue of Burden's work in all media produced recently by Gagosian Gallery and Fred Hoffman in close collaboration with the artist; see *Chris Burden*, Newcastle upon Tyne: Locus + Publishing, 2007.
14. See *Chris Burden, 71–73*, p. 24. There are in fact twelve additional documentary images included in *Chris Burden, 71–73*, immediately following the double page spread that introduces *Shoot*. Among these images, not reproduced in any obvious narrative order, are some extremely gruesome details of Burden's arm as it is treated and bandaged by a member of the audience after the performance. On page 30, there is also photograph of Burden setting up what appears to be a camera in preparation for the performance.
15. This phrase is borrowed from Michael Fried's analysis of Thomas Demand's photographs of his sculptural models in "Without a Trace," *Artforum*, March 2005, vol. 43, no. 7, p. 200.
16. By his own admittance, Burden is scrupulous in his selection of the photographic imagery to document his performance work: "When I did a performance," he notes, "and there was a series of photographs, I'd take them home and study them for a l-o-o-o-ng time. And usually I'd select one image to represent the whole thing." See Jan Tumlir, "First Break: Chris Burden," *Artforum*, December 2001, vol. 40, no. 4, p. 23.
17. Chris Burden quoted in Marc Selwyn, "Chris Burden: I think museums function in the way churches function for religion – it's the place where you go to do it," *Flash Art*, January/February 1989, no. 144, pp. 90–1.
18. Smadar Sheffi, "Jaffa: Reuven Zahavi at Mary Faouzi," *Art in America*, April 2000, vol. 88, no. 4, p. 127.
19. The best reproduction of the original image can be found in *Chris Burden, 71–73*, p. 27.
20. On LaDuke's work, see Christopher Knight, "A Lush Landscape of Vast Alienation," *Los Angeles Times*, Friday 8 October 2004, E20; Suvan Geer, "Tom LaDuke at Angles Gallery," *Artweek*, November 2004, vol. 35, no. 9, pp. 18-19; November 2004, vol. 35, no. 9; Constance Mallison, "Tom LaDuke at Angles," *Art in America*, April 2005, p. 159.
21. Jeffrey Kastner, "Gun Shy," *Artforum*, 20 January 2005; available online at: http://www.artforum.com/diary/id=8299; accessed 23 June 2011.
22. Mike Boehm, "The 'shot' Heard 'round UCLA; Student Joseph Deutch says he was testing perceptions when he played Russian roulette as performance art," *Los Angeles Times*, 9 July 2005, E1.
23. Ibid.
24. Ibid.
25. Jenny Hontz, "Gunplay, as Art, Sets Off a Debate," *New York Times*, 5 February 2005, B7.

Chapter 4

Can Photographs Make It So? Repeated Outbreaks of VALIE EXPORT'S Genital Panic since 1969

Mechtild Widrich

"Presence," in its dual significance of immediacy and being in the right place at the right time, has long been considered the key term for artists and historians conceptualizing performance art. In recent years, however, the intense interest in the status of the documentation of performances – mostly photographs and films – has challenged the dominance of this term. While some dismiss these documents as commodification of an originally irreproducible encounter between the performer's and the audience's bodily presence, others have concluded that the document is an equal ally or even a privileged link between performer and the public. Simultaneously, artists have begun to destabilize the one-time experience of performance art by re-enacting their own or their colleagues' works. Mike Kelley and Paul McCarthy's desublimatory look at the 1970s in their *Fresh Acconci Portfolio* from 1996 (in which they hire aspiring Hollywood actors to redo key Acconci works), Dan Graham's reflection on his own 1975 videotaped performance *Performer/Audience/Mirror* under the title *Video/Architecture/Performance* in 1995, and Yoko Ono's redoing of her most famous performance, the mid-1960s *Cut Piece*, in a small theater in Paris in 2003 as a protest against the war in Iraq are some of the most prominent examples of this recent trend.

In my case study, an "action" by Austrian artist VALIE EXPORT from 1969 that was re-performed by Marina Abramović in 2005, I will neither advocate "presentness," nor attempt to efface all differences between mediated and unmediated modes of interaction. Rather, I will show how ephemeral art practices create more than just one performative moment. We need to differentiate discrete levels of mediation, without simply favoring one of them a priori. Considerations of medium specificity do not play a prominent role in my discussion – though photographic practice is important – because labels such as "photo-performance," or "performance for the camera" do more to obscure the complexity of the performative action that unfolds than to reveal the actual dynamics of the interaction between the piece, its context, and its audience(s).

Therefore, I will draw upon another set of "specificities," namely reception, history, and memory. These terms are neither interchangeable nor strict analogues, although they fuse at times to play their part in the field of representation. Because of its centrality to the historical reception of live art, the document will surface in all of these settings – and with it the question of whether it is self-contained or discursive in its effects and to what extent it can reach its own audience. In my reading of re-performance, the body in public will become legible as a monument to past eventness, participating in the performative unfolding of the so-called original rather than offering a belated repetition.

First, let me address the construction of presence where it is most emphatically asserted: in a catalogue text on Marina Abramović, performance scholar RoseLee Goldberg finds "presence" to be the artist's "overriding obsession."[1] Indeed, Abramović has been famous since the 1970s for exhausting, often dangerous performances, some of which have depended on direct audience participation – for example *Rhythm 0*, 1974, in which the spectators were asked to use tools, among them knives, a gun with one bullet, and scissors, on the "objectified" body of the artist, until the performance ended in disarray.

In the fall of 2005, Abramović staged and re-performed six performances of the 1960s and 1970s, five of which were initially not her own, together with a newly created performance, under the title *Seven Easy Pieces*. Among the chosen pieces were Joseph Beuys' 1965 *How to Explain Pictures to a Dead Hare*, Bruce Nauman's 1974 *Body Pressure*, and EXPORT's *Genital Panic*. One could read these re-enactments along the lines sketched out by Goldberg, arguing that Abramović replaced the body of the original performer with her own, painstakingly redoing the action decades after the fact, in order to overcome (for herself and the audience) the most obvious limitation of performance art, namely the unavailability of the "original" experience for all those not present at the earlier event. But things are not so simple. An investigation of the different relocations and re-emergences of *Genital Panic*, from its first occurrence in 1969 to Abramović's re-enactment in the Rotunda of the Guggenheim Museum in 2005, will allow me to interrogate the concept that the live act provides unmediated access to performance through the artist's body.

Performative Panic Attacks

It is said that, in 1969, VALIE EXPORT went into a cinema in Munich, wearing jeans with a triangular cutout in the pubic area. Once inside the auditorium, she walked slowly through the rows, with her "crotch and [the audience's] nose on the same level."[2] The intention of this "action," as EXPORT herself described it, was to confront the voyeuristic male moviegoer with a "real" female body, instead of the mediated one that could be consumed clandestinely – thus anticipating and inverting Laura Mulvey's famous 1975 feminist manifesto "Visual

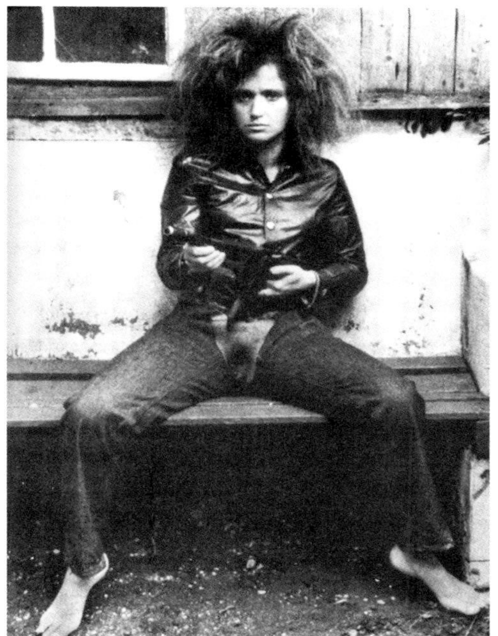
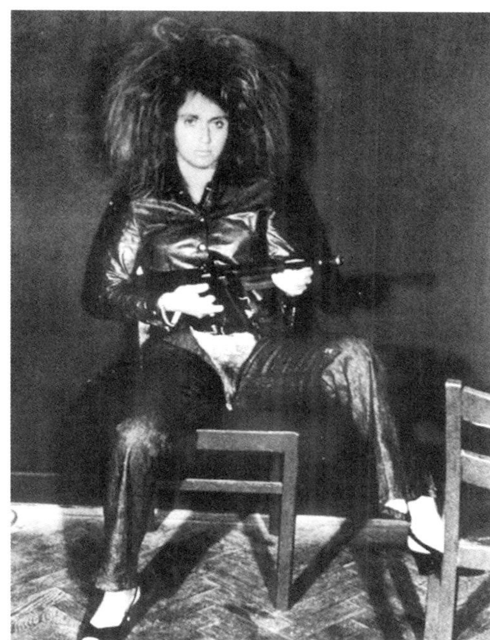

VALIE EXPORT, *Action Pants: Genital Panic*, 1969. Photo: Peter Hassmann. Courtesy Charim Galerie, Vienna.

Pleasure and Narrative Cinema" by several years. "People in the back of the cinema got up and fled the situation, because they were afraid I would come up to them as well," EXPORT recalled in a recent interview, thus confirming that the titular "panic" had in fact taken place, and stressing that the presence of the real woman was pivotal.[3]

Let us examine the images associated with this "action" of VALIE EXPORT's more closely. Two of them became the stand-ins for *Genital Panic* in surveys of postwar art throughout Europe and the United States. Taken in 1969, one photograph shows EXPORT, with teased hair, seated on a bench outside what looks like a house in rural Austria, with bare feet, her crotch in the center of the composition, pointing a machine gun in the general direction of the camera. In the second photograph we see EXPORT inside the same building, sitting with one leg propped aggressively on the wooden crossbeam of a second chair, thus emphasizing her pubic area, the gun's barrel directed at the ceiling. A third photograph, with EXPORT standing in front of the bench, has also been published in recent years.[4]

None of the photographs is a document taken during the actual performance. None tries to re-stage the ostensible setting of the performance. On the contrary, all three focus on the carefully posed artist, exchanging the cinema in the metropolis for a suburban milieu – in fact the studio of the photographer, Peter Hassmann, located on the northern outskirts of Vienna. The compositions resemble movie posters, while the grainy texture links them to the mid-twentieth-century tradition of documentary photography. They seem to be a distillation of the *idea* of the action rather than film stills, and, given the iconic nature of the images, it is no surprise that Hassmann became locally famous at the time for political advertisements commissioned by the Austrian Socialist Party (SPÖ).[5]

The photographs are detached from the supposed location of the original performance, begging the question of how we know what took place during the action. Thus this particular case reflects larger issues attendant on any study of live art: how does one link textual or verbal descriptions of the event, which often circulate in conflicting versions, with the few documentary images or films that remain? What, in short, does the *picture* have to do with the *narrative explanation* of the event? Accounts of *Genital Panic* from the time of its execution do not exist, which is surprising, given the fact that EXPORT received extensive, often outraged press coverage for other actions such as *Touch Cinema* in 1968. EXPORT's own extant accounts tend to appear a few years later. Take the following interview from 1979, in which EXPORT describes the situation in a way that closely follows the photographs in some respects (supplying a gun) while elaborating on other aspects of the 1969 performance (the movie theater):

> Genital Panic was performed in a Munich theater that showed pornographic films. I was dressed in a sweater and pants with the crotch completely cut away. I carried a machine gun. Between films I told the audience that they had come to this particular theater to see sexual films. Now, actual genitalia was available, and they could do anything they wanted to it.[6]

Twenty years later, however, EXPORT renounced this combative stance, stating: "I never went in a cinema in which pornographic movies are shown, and NEVER with a gun in my hand," a position she confirmed in an interview in February 2007, contradicting her own 1979 description of the event and instilling confusion about the origin of the description of the theater as "pornographic." Almost parenthetically, EXPORT remarked that if she had actually gone into the theater with a gun, "[t]he security would have shot me."[7] The weapon in the photograph - confirmed by Hassmann to have been an actual firearm - seems unlikely indeed to have been wielded in public, given the politically tense German climate of the time, with the terrorist Red Army Faction about to launch their first attacks, and particularly in conservative Bavaria.[8]

What are we to make of these multiple revisions, besides the commonplace that art historians should not trust the oral accounts of artists or interviewers, or, more accurately, should not trust published narratives claiming to be artists' oral accounts? Most conspicuous is the correlation of EXPORT's 1979 interview to the photo-pieces featuring the machine gun, a prop that appeared also in Abramović's re-performance in 2005. If EXPORT could not have used the gun in public, then is Abramović's gun an *Ergänzung* (addition, or replenishment) to the 1969 performance, as EXPORT characterized it when asked about Abramović's re-

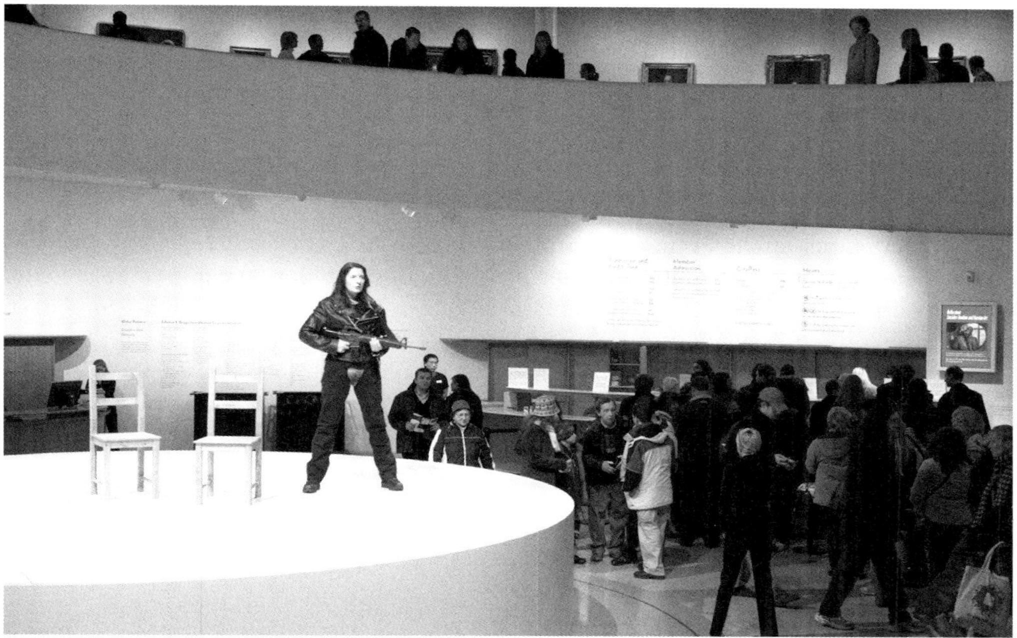

Marina Abramović performing VALIE EXPORT, *Action Pants; Genital Panic*, Solomon R. Guggenheim Museum, New York, 2005, photograph by Kathryn Carr.

enactment?[9] Abramović's use of the weapon clearly derives from the photographs, and her stance is an exact merging of EXPORT's in the images.

I will return to the significance of the machine gun in a moment. First, however, I want to propose that EXPORT's 1979 account of her own piece is not simply a true or false statement; rather we have to consider it an accomplice in the performative production of meaning. The pornographic cinema, the weapon, her role as the feminist warrior – is a performance in its own right, detached from the bodily presence of performer and audience in the "here and now" (ten years later, *there and then*) of the Munich theater.[10]

The interview becomes performative by re-instantiating the earlier performance. British philosopher J. L. Austin describes performative speech in the following manner: "by saying or in saying something, we are doing something" (e.g. the wedding vow, "I hereby take you to be my husband").[11] In this sense, although legally her statements might have been dubious or false (being unverifiable by witnesses and contradicted by her own later accounts), EXPORT is not *narrating* the performance either truthfully or untruthfully, nor are we dealing with a "fake" work of art. On the contrary, EXPORT's statements in the 1979 interview must be considered what Austin calls a "happy performative," namely an utterance being taken for the action of that which is being uttered, an utterance with concrete consequences in contrast to a descriptive statement.

One of the requirements that Austin wishes to find in every "happy performative" is "appropriate circumstances" or a "situation" that makes possible the concrete consequences of the performative. In this case, the situation encompasses the public nature of the magazine in which the interview was printed and the willingness of members of the art world to historicize the event in the reassuring form of the pictures, and also, through these pictures, to forget that they were not present at the "original" event.

These "circumstances," however, are not arbitrarily plucked out of an infinite "context," as Jacques Derrida argues in his post-structuralist reading of Austin.[12] Rather than the concrete conditions serving as a crutch for stabilizing an infinite and shifting range of performed meanings, we should, with Austin, conceive the utterance and its conditions interacting without hierarchy in the "total speech act."[13] The total speech act in the case of EXPORT's *Genital Panic* ranges from the embodied act in 1969, through the 1979 interview (contextualized in its specific site and through its particular disseminations), up to Abramović's re-enactment and beyond. In this sense, the 1979 interview in its mediated condition, as it was received at the time or as we read it today (for example, through my citation of it here), draws its authority from but also itself *enacts* the belief in the bodily presence of the artist, which is thus retrospectively projected back into the event. The interview, along with other re-articulations of the work, thus creates a new form of audience to which that body is (imaginatively) "present," a *reading audience*. The readers of 1979 could thus connect the event to the photograph, affirming or even producing a new historical version of the performance ten years after it was done: an audacious and aggressive act in public.

Happiness is a Warm Gun

The question of motivation remains, however, haunting our relationship to *Genital Panic*. Why would EXPORT insist on the shock value of the real in a 1969 *Genital Panic* "action," and also produce an image of it, only to question the visual "facts" she thus established in her later reminiscences about the piece? Why does the gun enter the picture at all, and why does EXPORT then dispute its "presence" in the original performance in her later statements? EXPORT, I want to claim, needed to alter the set-up of the action for the photographs in order to achieve a functioning performative action in itself. The photographs in fact circulate under a slightly different title, namely *Aktionshose: Genitalpanik* (*Action Pants: Genital Panic*), instead of the mere *Genitalpanik* of the performance, as if EXPORT were presenting to us the *prop* or the remnants of the action. The most conspicuous addition, the machine gun, is crucial to the performativity of the photographic piece: it must be seen as a necessary substitute for the most prominent "loss" in the photographic version of the work, namely the absent bodies of her presumably male audience in an encounter outside the art world.

In short, the machine gun brings the potential aggression of the encounter with the audience in public space symbolically into the picture, appropriating the signs of sexual

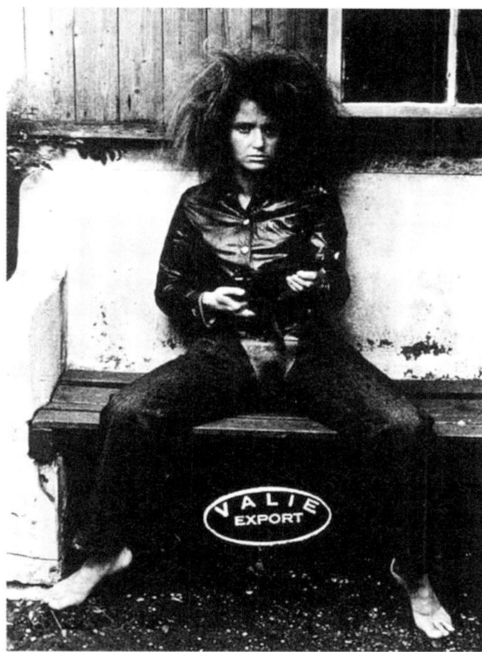

VALIE EXPORT, *Action Pants: Genital Panic*, 1969. Silkscreen poster by Kari Bauer. Courtesy of Charim Galerie, Vienna and of VALIE EXPORT.

VALIE EXPORT, *Action Pants: Genital Panic*, Installation in public space in Berlin, 1994/95. Photo: Torsten Monschein. Courtesy of Charim Galerie, Vienna and of VALIE EXPORT.

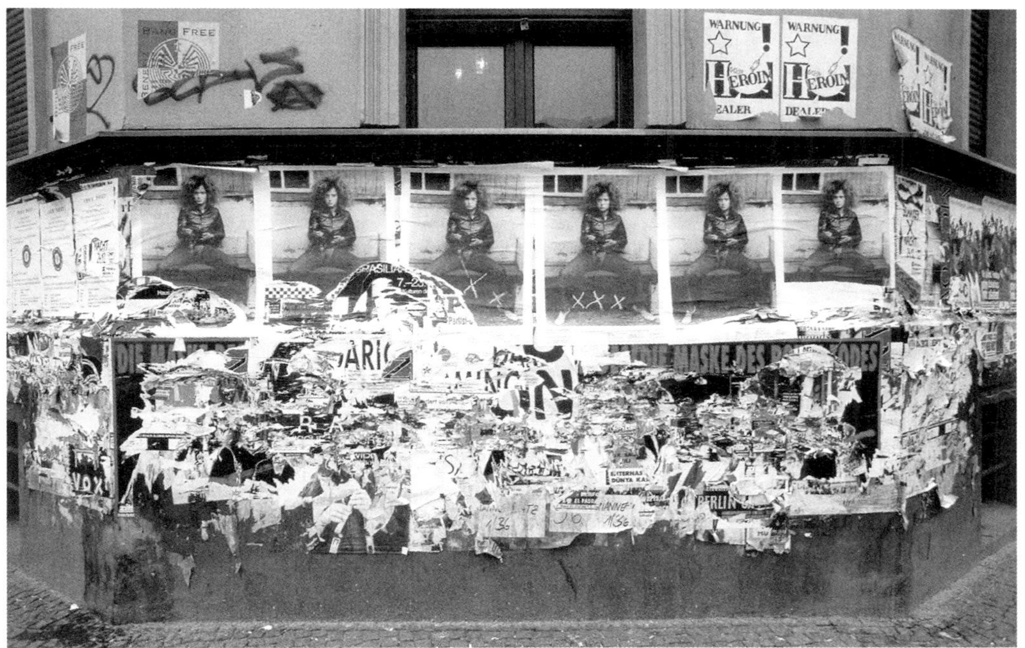

aggression (generally coded as male) for the female protagonist; in the photographs EXPORT returns the putative male gaze directed toward her genitals with a feminist appropriation of an obvious phallic symbol. For the reading audience this prop was and is the necessary cue, providing the tension within the picture that performs and thereby instantiates the tension of the movie-theater action. EXPORT had to transfer the gender conflict into the photograph through visual cues in order for the confrontation to remain legible.

At the same time, however, the machine gun redirects the gaze away from the genitals, transforming the genital panic into a possibly terrorist one, replenishing the effect of the original performance by introducing what Austin might call fresh circumstances, through the performative function of the photographs. The complexity of the (narrated) encounter is recreated in the photographs, which indeed means that the images stand as solid performative pieces on their own. The performative utterance can, as Austin points out, be conveyed in written form or through a gesture, and also, I would argue, be transposed from a gesture into a photograph, as long as the narrative conventions and the situational cues enable one to make sense of the action. In fact, photography must be seen as a privileged medium of performance, due to its dual capacity of acting as quasi-legal document of the past (applicable even when the photographs are staged) and at the same time as a persistent re-enactment.

Indeed, the balance of autonomy and reference in the photograph has underwritten the long and varied history of *Genital Panic*. EXPORT's idea after producing the photographs was to disseminate the bench image as a poster in public space in Vienna.

Silkscreen posters of this image, reversed, as if to bring in another perspective, and stamped with EXPORT's name logo, were printed by Kari Bauer the same year. As EXPORT claimed in a recent interview, however, after having the posters made she was not able to get the necessary permission from the city to disseminate the posters publicly, nor did she have the means and the workforce to put them up; she thus ended up "giving them to friends."[14]

EXPORT had a similar poster displayed in the streets of Berlin as a contribution to the 1994 exhibition *Gewalt/Geschäfte* (*Violence/Business)* of the Neue Gesellschaft für Bildende Kunst. Both of the original photographs were sold as photo editions in galleries, shown in exhibitions, and of course disseminated in volumes such as this one.

I have been arguing that these images cannot be seen as documentary proof of the performance. But are they still dependent on it, their meaning inherently linked to the original "action," or are they self-sufficient art projects? EXPORT did experiment with photographic stagings around the time of *Genital Panic* that resemble the ones Cindy Sherman would produce years later, notably the *Identitätstransfer (Identity Transfer)* of 1968, in which she presents herself in a stereotypical male posture for the camera. From the beginning of her career, photography was never simply a medium for documenting her actions, but one that self-reflexively opened up complex performative interactions – anticipating the current tendency of staging performances expressly for the camera.[15]

EXPORT's persistent use of photography might at first glance suggest that she privileges the photograph over the actual performance. Some performance scholars have in fact recently argued for the general priority of documentation for performance art and its after-life. Is in fact the image the performance "as such?" A provocative conclusion not far from this has been drawn by Philip Auslander in a discussion of work by Yves Klein and Chris Burden: "*The act of documenting an event as a performance is what constitutes it as such.*"[16] Auslander ascribes the performative content of a live act exclusively to its documentation.

Taking Auslander literally, in our case the contradictions between versions of the event would be irrelevant, since the photograph would constitute the performance itself: it would be of little interest that EXPORT's photo pieces are not of the public performance, nor that the gun is present in the pictures and then reported in the Munich action in her 1979 interview but disclaimed in recent publications and statements of the artist. It would also be of little interest whether the artist ever went into a cinema with her "Action Pants." True, the photographs have all the ingredients of a performative gesture, as we have seen, and they seem perfectly to illustrate EXPORT's oral utterance (or verbal performance) of the piece in the first interview. And yet, Auslander's argument rules out the complexity inherent in the tension between acts and performative documents. He cannot account for what I am interested in, namely the oscillations between different instances of the performative, oscillations that in turn reveal the different audiences and the different meanings produced in each instance.

A subtler argument might insist that the radicality of performance art lies precisely in its ability to bridge bodily presence and its image. Amelia Jones writes:

> Precisely by using their bodies as primary material, body or performance artists highlight the "representational status" of such work rather than confirming its ontological priority. The representational aspects of this work – this "play within the arena of the symbolic," and, I would add, its dependence on documentation to attain symbolic status within the realm of culture – expose the impossibility of attaining full knowledge of the self through bodily proximity.[17]

Jones justly points out that the documentation of performance art plays its role in "enacting the artist as public figure," and acknowledges that it is the moment of the performance where cultural representation, and thus history, begins.[18] One could add that history continues to be built through palimpsests of discourse and image that continue inexorably from this moment – including critical reviews, interviews and artist's statements, art historical texts, exhibitions and catalogue essays, and a range of performative enunciations and visual images from the artist's documents of the supposed original event to later reproductions of these images and re-enactments. How can we then bind this reception history to the performative force of the images?

I have made the case that photographs refer not so much to the staged version of the performance, the mechanical reproduction of which we are allowed to see, but to an "imaginary" performance, one that is performatively defined through its descriptions, disseminations, and other permutations in the public sphere. The reading and viewing public uses the image to point (imaginatively) back to the action; the photograph becomes a metaphorical version of an indexical sign: a sign causally connected to its referent, not necessarily resembling it.[19] The photograph provides the imaginary performance with an image. If we accept this broader concept of the index as a sign pointing to an action, as a sign that indicates an event has occurred, we can allow into the interpretation of photographs of performative acts such as EXPORT's a broader context of historical references inside and outside the image. This context is not a supplement, but the medium within which performative action unfolds – which is also how Austin understood the "circumstances" of his "total speech act."

A Monument to Performance Art

When Marina Abramović re-performed *Genital Panic*, she based her seven-hour-long performance consciously on the photographic documents she knew. The body she "brought back" was yet another imaginative constitution of presence for a viewing public, informed by mediated historical fragments rather than ensuring at last an "authentic" return to bodily presence. Abramović herself wrestled with the problem of historical amnesia, as we can gather from a statement about her motivation for the *Seven Easy Pieces*:

> I'm one of these artists of the 70s and I'm just fed up with the copying of not just my work – of all the artists of the 70s in different ways in MTV, in theater, in dance, in fashion, in young artists, I'm also fed up with young critics who actually evaluate the young artists' work and tell us they are original, without referring to the past works at all. They deny history.[20]

Abramović's attention to history is a model to artists and scholars, and yet, her suggestion that somehow there is an authentic version of the performance that is waiting to be excavated for history (and that this version can be retrieved through the work's re-enactment by an artist such as herself) contradicts the fact that the circumstances have changed since the original performance. In addition, Abramović's claim that amnesia has fully removed the famous pieces from history is not convincing, since the works she re-enacted in 2005 have had pronounced historical visibility (otherwise, her versions would hardly be recognizable as "redos"). I would argue, rather, that history itself has transformed and recontextualized them.

Abramović's 2005 project is extremely complex in terms of how it shifts our historical understanding of re-enacted works such as EXPORT's *Genital Panic*. First of all, there is the issue of reconstruction of the "original" event itself. The organizers of *Seven Easy Pieces* at the Guggenheim Museum ran into various difficulties while trying to unearth the original course of events. The confusion reached a climax when EXPORT stated in a 2005 e-mail to curator Nancy Spector that she "did it [*Genital Panic*] two times, one time in a Art Cinema in München and second for the poster," but only then with the weapon.[21] Abramović herself

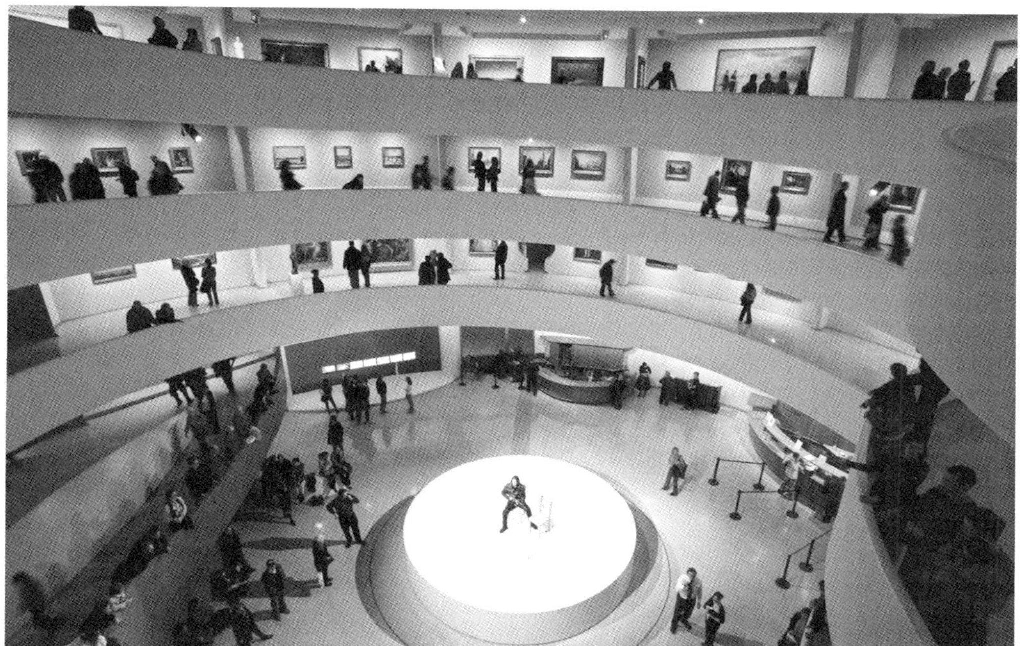

Marina Abramović performing VALIE EXPORT, *Action Pants; Genital Panic*, Solomon R. Guggenheim Museum, New York, 2005, photograph by Kathryn Carr.

recently recalled the difficulty of accessing the performance through the oral descriptions of the artist:

> I was the most critical and most careful about this piece because in reality she stated that she originally performed the piece in this theater at the erotic film festival in Vienna, but at the same time she made the poster as well. *Genital Panic* is a great contradiction because she also made the photograph in her studio and there are lots of different images of that poster.[22]

Having rather unclear information, Abramović decided in her re-enactment to carry the gun, thus indicating that the images had become central to the historical imagining of *Genital Panic*. The solution at the Guggenheim was to title the evening *Action Pants: Genital Panic*, after the photographic work, but to describe the Munich action as a historical reference point both on the website and in the catalogue.[23]

These complex and often competing histories of *Genital Panic* make it clear that audience members approaching performance must mobilize a version of history that we might call mnemohistory – a history that is not necessarily based on facts (whatever these may be), but rather on the myths or traditions associated with the "original" performance but also with its subsequent narrations and documentations. Abramović understood very well that she performed *her Genital Panic* for a new public. The already-historical sources were therefore made transparent by Abramović's choice to explicitly "quote" EXPORT's images. Consequently, the performance consisted of Abramović posing statically as if doing a *tableau vivant* – using the props of the chairs, the gun, and the cutout pants, alternating her posture in accordance with EXPORT's several photo pieces.

Occasionally – every hour or so – Abramović slowly rose from her seat, walked to the edge of the platform, paused, and walked back to the chair to sit down again.

Abramović's re-enactment of history, in a distillation of reception and memory (prompted and informed by photographs and EXPORT's reminiscences), proposed a new canonical status for the performance pieces she staged. The weapon – according to the files at the Guggenheim a replica of an American M16 rifle – played a particular role for Abramović. It externalized the potentially violent gender conflict the photographs had staged – an important strategy of visualization since the Guggenheim public was also not the fabled male audience of the supposed porn theater. On the other hand, because it appeared only in the photographic versions of the piece (according to EXPORT's later claims at least), the gun became an inverted index making us aware of the reception history of the performance. Abramović as the female protagonist becomes the re-enactor as well as the transmitter of history and the guarantor of recollection – a recollection that changes our conception of the "original" once again.[24]

In the European culture of commemoration, female bodies have always played an important part, most manifestly in the iconography of the monument as abstract personifications of virtues or countries. Could we say that Abramović is monumentalizing EXPORT's performance, and performance art in general? After all, she decided to re-stage the performances in the Guggenheim Museum – an institution known for canonizing works of art. Aside from the change of venue and audience, the obvious particularity of the re-performance – apart from the props fairly closely matching the photograph – was Abramović's bodily presence, a presence that was tempered by the use of a tall white cylindrical platform, which served as her base. Instead of the intimate encounter between the audience's faces and EXPORT's crotch – which, EXPORT had argued, was supposed to have ensured the shock value with the original piece – Abramović was now visible from all sides but untouchable. The audience walked around as in any museum setting, and Abramović's operational zone was additionally demarcated as "forbidden" by the use of black tape on the floor.

At one point during the performance a young man with a ponytail tried to climb onstage and was immediately removed by the museum's security personnel. This attempted interaction, prevented by the guards, did not stir Abramović. She sat in her chair, impassive as a statue – or photograph. She had to, because the intruder did not understand the recreated piece, which was not, as in EXPORT's case, about a "real encounter," about acting out gender relations. Rather, Abramović made herself into what we might call a performative monument

– what in German is termed a *Denkmal*, a mark for thinking or remembering. A monument does not ensure "authentic" remembering, since it addresses an audience with disparate experiences of the past. What a monument allows is *commemoration*: a conventional act establishing a new, public version of the past event. The very length of Abramović's version of *Genital Panic* served to bring together a temporally disjointed public at the Guggenheim around an idealized feminist performance from the 1960s.

With *Action Pants: Genital Panic*, as with each of the other re-enactments in *Seven Easy Pieces*, Abramović consolidated the consequences of different performative actions, mediating through her body both the document and the imagined historical gesture of the action. Abramović infused the performance with her own memory, which has evolved almost solely through mediation – Abramović was not present at any of the performances which form the "score" for her *Seven Easy Pieces*, excepting her own earlier piece, *Lips of Thomas* (called *Thomas Lips* in 1975).[25] In this adaptation, the artist split complex actions into smaller units that were repeated several times, as if fragmented pieces of memory had been reactivated. This suggests that even her own memory was combined with the reception of the piece, including the images that have circulated in the decades since.

In Abramović's re-enactment, documents and memories merged into a performative monument that refers to the past by re-instantiating it in the present. Abramović acted for a historically informed public, not because its members might have been present at the event in the Munich cinema, but rather because they heard or read about it (or *will* hear or read about it in the Guggenheim publications). History and memory, or to be more exact, cultural memory based on mediated experience, were embodied equally in the performer and the audience.

One question remains. Did EXPORT's *Genital Panic* ever actually take place as a performance? Certainly, it continues to do so. But the act of the artist in a movie theater in Munich might not have taken place. An indication that *Genital Panic* remained in the planning stage is the entry on the piece in the anthology of Actionist works co-edited by EXPORT in 1970, which printed the bench photograph for the first time with a text that uses the conditional "should happen."[26] This indicates the work's preliminary status; but *should* (in German *sollte*) can also be taken as an imperative. This ambiguity is at the center of the piece. The "should happen" may become an Austinian "it is so," and indeed it has in the brief history of this performance. It is for this reason that the "original" continues to work in our heads, and is inseparable from the later performative utterances that we again and again connect to a presupposed live act.

Notes

1. RoseLee Goldberg, "Here and Now," in *Marina Abramović: Objects, Performance and Video Sound*, exh. cat., Oxford: Museum of Modern Art Oxford, 1995, p. 11.
2. Peter Weibel and VALIE EXPORT, *Bildkompendium Wiener Aktionismus und Film*, Frankfurt am Main: Kohlkunstverlag, 1970, p. 290. Translation by the author.
3. VALIE EXPORT, interview by author, audio file, New York, 19 February 2007. Translation by the author.
4. The lesser known photograph of EXPORT standing is published in Roswitha Mueller, *VALIE EXPORT: Fragments of the Imagination*, Bloomington and Indianapolis: Indiana University Press, 1994, p. 18, and in Hedwig Saxenhuber (ed.), *VALIE EXPORT*, exh. cat., National Centre for Contemporary Art and Ekaterina Foundation, Moskow, Vienna , Bolzano: Folio, 2007, p. 32.
5. The outdoor photographs were taken in the secluded courtyard of a house in the 22nd district of Vienna. Hassmann used a Pentax 35mm camera, which explains the grain when blown up to poster size. Peter Hassmann, interview by author, audio file, Vienna, 13 August 2007.
6. "VALIE EXPORT interviewed by Ruth Askey in Vienna 9/18/79," *High Performance Magazine*, Spring 1981, p. 15.
7. The first quote is EXPORT cited by Kristine Stiles, "Corpora Vilia: VALIE EXPORT's Body," *Ob/De+Con(Struction)*, ,exh. cat., Philadelphia: Moore College of Art and Design, 1999, note 7; the 2007 quote is from my interview with EXPORT noted above. EXPORT described the theater as an art cinema; this is consistent with the Guggenheim catalogue.
8. While Hassmann did not remember the details, Hermann Hendrich, photographer of EXPORT's *Body Configuration* series as well as producer of some of her films, recalled that the gun was acquired from Udo Proksch, businessman and weapon collector, who was later convicted of murder in the course of one of the greatest insurance frauds in Austria's history, the shipwreck of the *Lucona* in 1977. Hermann Hendrich, interview by author, audio file, Vienna, 29 January 2008. Translation by the author.
9. VALIE EXPORT, interview by author (see note 3).
10. The phrase "here and now" could serve as a talismanic summation of the concerns of early performance studies; it is also the title of Goldberg's text on Abramović, who herself uses the phrase (see note 1).
11. J. L. Austin, *How to Do Things with Words*, Cambridge, MA: Harvard University Press, 1962, p. 12.
12. Jacques Derrida, "Signature, Event, Context," in *Margins of Philosophy*, trans. Alan Bass, Chicago: University of Chicago Press, 1982, p. 322, esp. note 11.
13. Cf. Austin, op. cit., p. 52.
14. VALIE EXPORT, interview by author (see note 3).
15. This trend is finely exemplified in Jens Hoffmann and Joan Jonas (eds), *Art Works Perform*, New York: Thames and Hudson, 2005.
16. Philip Auslander, "The Performativity of Performance Documentation," *PAJ: A Journal of Performance and Art*, September 2006, vol. 84, 5, pp. 1–10, and reprinted in this volume.
17. Amelia Jones, "'Presence' *in absentia*: Experiencing Performance as Documentation," *Art Journal*, Winter 1997, vol. 56, no. 4, p. 13; with the phrase "play within the arena of the symbolic," Jones cites Kathy O'Dell, "Toward a Theory of Performance Art: An Investigation of its Sites," PhD dissertation, City University of New York, 1992, pp. 43–4.
18. Amelia Jones, *Body Art/Performing the Subject*, Minneapolis, London: University of Minnesota Press, 1998, p. 6.

19. On the index, see Charles Sanders Peirce, *Collected Papers of Charles Sanders Peirce*, vol. 2, Cambridge: Harvard University Press, 1960, pp. 147–9 and 304.
20. Marina Abramović, Q & A Session at the conference *Feminist Future* at the Museum of Modern Art, New York, 26 January 2007, audio file available online at: http://www.wps1.org/include/shows/moma.html, accessed 1 April 2007.
21. Email from VALIE EXPORT to Nancy Spector on 3 January 2005, The Solomon R. Guggenheim Museum Archive, New York.
22. Marina Abramović in dialogue with Amelia Jones, "The Live Artist as Archaeologist," New York, 5 August 2007; in this volume.
23. *Marina Abramović: Seven Easy Pieces*, Milano: Edizione Charta, 2007, p. 118; and available online at: http://www.guggenheim.org/exhibitions/abramovic, accessed 23 July 2008.
24. Abramović gives us a hint to the task she had in mind through her title. *Easy Pieces* is a common title for musical compositions: Ferdinando Carulli (eighteenth century), Niccolo Paganini (nineteenth century), and Ernst Krenek (twentieth-century) wrote musical works called *Seven Easy Pieces*. They are often used to instruct children or beginners, which means that Abramović is alluding ironically to herself as a beginner, but also as the instructor of the audience. Abramović herself cited Richard P. Feynman, *Six Not So Easy Pieces: Relativity, Symmetry and Space-Time*, 2004, based on the physicist's lectures at Caltech in the 1960s, as a text pivotal to her production. From a selection of artist reading lists originally in *Frieze*, reprinted in Lioba Reddeker (ed.), *ACA Art Critics Award Lesebuch*, Vienna: basis wien, 2007.
25. The change of title to *Lips of Thomas* is another interesting episode in reception history. See my dissertation, *Performative monuments: public art, commemoration, and history in postwar Europe*, PhD dissertation, Massachusetts Institute of Technology (MIT), 2009.
26. "Anstelle einer vorführung sollte ich mich mit entblösster fut (an der Hose ausgeschnitten) durch die zuschauerreihen drängen, ergo fut und nase in gleicher höhe, indirekter sexueller kontakt mit dem publikum. VALIE EXPORT." [Instead of a screening I was supposed to push through the rows of the audience with exposed crotch (cut out from the pants), ergo crotch and nose on the same level; indirect sexual encounter with the audience. VALIE EXPORT] Text printed in Weibel and EXPORT, op. cit., p. 290. Translation by the author. The ostensible date of the performance remains unclear. The Guggenheim Museum and some other recent sources date the original action 22 April 1969. EXPORT performed her *Touch Cinema* in Munich on 15 April 1969, not for the first time, a performance that is well documented, for example, in the article "Exhibitionisten an die Front," *Der Spiegel*, 21 April 1969, p. 194. She performed in Zurich on 18 and 25 April 1969 (cf. Archive of the Generali Foundation, Vienna), making an appearance in Munich on 22 April possible but unlikely. The Guggenheim catalogue gives the theater *Augusta Lichtspiele* as location (*Marina Abramović: Seven Easy Pieces*, p. 118). The live performance of *Genital Panic* in a cinema has not been questioned in the literature: Roswitha Mueller describes the performance briefly in the context of "sexual liberation," without mentioning the gun (Mueller, op. cit., p. 18). A recent Austrian publication revives the myth of the porn cinema: Carola Dertnig and Stefanie Seibold (eds), *Let's Twist Again: Performance in Wien von 1960 bis heute*, Gumpoldskirchen: DEA, 2006.

Chapter 5

Macular Degeneration: Some Peculiar Aspects of Performance Art Documentation[1]

Mónica Mayer

I will focus on Mexican performance art because it is what I know best, but will sprinkle this account with contextual information from the rest of Latin America.

I have always thought it is paradoxical that half the time I produce ephemeral art, and the rest of the time I document it in as many ways as possible. For me, as for most performance artists I know, keeping a record of our work and that of our colleagues has always been important because apart from registering our process, we realize it is raw material for history and theory. To reach that stage, it must first penetrate institutions where it can be classified and safeguarded. This has not always been easy.

In the following pages, I will discuss some of the problems faced in relation to documentation and I will let you in on a strange phenomenon: performance art is such a lethal virus that it has even infected the ways in which we register it.

We Did Not Lose Our Memory; We Never Had One

Non-objectual arts,[2] understood as "new ways of thinking reality from the point of view of art,"[3] have been around since the early twentieth-century. Their journey has been marked by how they have been documented or made invisible. I imagine this process as a chain of knowledge with links that have become shapelessly elastic to try to avoid breaking, although sometimes breakage has been inevitable. One of the reasons is money. Documenting is expensive. You need the tools and the resources to update the document every time corporations change formats, and you need enough money to pay someone to do it. This can be an obstacle for institutions and individuals.

Home Alone

The problem of documentation is also conceptual and ideological. Performance art is rich and complex, but the ways we have registered it and theorized it are not. This is not surprising. As Juan Acha said, the basic weakness of Latin American art theory is that "we believe that phenomena and things are products to be taken or discarded, and not long and rugged processes embarked upon."[4] The work has always been there, but we have still not built a solid critical apparatus to study it, and when viewed from the framework of European or US theory, it inevitably seems derivative. I do not mean to imply that we have to think in isolation. Art is joyfully promiscuous, open to influences from all over the world and from every field. It is capable of highlighting our differences and turning them into similarities. Nevertheless, in order for this to happen, we must first know ourselves. Artists have traditionally tried to patch the weaknesses of the art system.[5] We have taken over its distribution by opening artist-run galleries and its consumption by forming collections that end up in museums.[6] In performance, we have gone even further. We have been the first to document it and write about it.

From Oblivion to Fame

The Estridentistas were a group of poets, painters, and musicians, among whom were Manuel Maples Arce and Germán Cueto; between 1922 and 1927 they experimented with technology and performance. After a first powerful impact, the Estridentistas were forgotten, probably because the concepts needed to understand them did not exist. The theoretical framework has shifted since, allowing us to see their contributions under a new light.

In the 1970s Luis Mario Schneider[7] recovered the Estridentistas for literature, generating so much interest that they are now cult figures. In 1994, when artist Maris Bustamante outlined the history of performance art, she considered them the starting point.[8] It was logical for her to begin with the Estridentistas because of their parallelism to Futurism, for the strong connection that has existed between visual poetry and performance art,[9] and because after interviewing Germán Lizt Arzuvide, the last of the Estridentistas, she found important conceptual similarities with them, such as wanting to "take the image to unexpected territories."[10]

Today, the Estridentistas are inspiring new works, such as Jesse Lerner's 2004 experimental video based on the Luis Quintanilla's 1924 poem/performance ... *IU IIIUUU IU...* In this piece, Juan José Gurrola delivers the poem that simulates the tuning of an old radio, whose fragmented sounds take us to different countries and situations – from a slaughterhouse in Chicago to Gandhi in the middle of a crowd – in a world that technology was beginning to connect. According to Rubén Gallo, Lerner's work is "a collage of archive images that illustrate the scenes described by the poet."[11] By recreating Quintanilla's work, Lerner reactivated and documented it. He patched a broken link through art.

Day of the Dead

To feed the myth that Mexicans have a unique way of seeing death, I now share with you the story of a performance archive in the shape of a grave. Bustamante considers Conchita Jurado (1865–1931) as an example of the "performance impulse"[12] of the early twentieth-century. After the Revolution, between 1926 and 1929, Jurado created a fictitious character called Don Carlos Balmori to perform her famous *balmoreadas*, which were extravagant tricks played upon members of the bourgeoisie, politicians, and the *nouveau riche*. Dressed as a man, Jurado, who was in her sixties, showed up as a Spanish millionaire willing to share his money if his victims agreed to act immorally or be humiliated. Jurado and her accomplices, including many past victims, created performatic situations. The *balmoreadas*[13] have a peculiar archive: Conchita Jurado/Don Carlos Balmori is buried at the Panteón de Dolores, an old cemetery in Mexico City. The grave – which is more like a monument – is covered by mosaics that are decorated by drawings and texts illustrating their performances.

A Woman's View

Who has created a character more successfully than Frida Kahlo? Are Kahlo's paintings documentation of her great performances? Could we understand Orlan without Kahlo?[14] Why are there so many films, choreographies, plays, and operas on her life? Why does everybody want to enact her? Did she create a template personality people want to perform? Everything is possible with Kahlo, even a strange story like that of Colombian photographer Leo Matiz who visited Mexico in the 1940s and started a series on Kahlo but had to leave unexpectedly; he returned in the 1990s, long after she had died, to conclude the series using a model.[15]

From the Muralist Movement to Performance Art?

David Alfaro Siqueiros, one of the foremost Mexican muralists of the twentieth-century founded the famous Siqueiros Experimental Workshop (SEW) in New York in the 1930s. One of his students was Jackson Pollock.

According to Irene Herner,[16] at the SEW they experimented with new types of quick-drying industrial paint and an array of tools that changed their approach to the canvas. Siqueiros developed what he called "controlled accidents" which he applied during the first stage of his works where "the whole body had to be in action because it was like starting a piece as if it were a ritual, unpredictable, liberating dance." In an interview with Jeffrey Potter, Reuben Kadish, who was a member of the SEW, mentions how this influenced Pollock: "Eventually, this would make him think of the whole canvas as an arena on which to create."[17]

If we consider Pollock's action painting as one of the stepping-stones to performance art, his relationship to Siqueiros is particularly interesting.

Siqueiros was also working on what he called "a functional Revolutionary art." He considered easel painting dead and used any surface necessary to transmit his message, including "wood, metal, sand and paper, or on concrete walls and even surfaces completely foreign to art, such as a float or a silk screen."[18] One such piece was the Hearst-Hitler political float with which they paraded in a demonstration at Coney Island. This work is a precedent of works like Suzanne Lacy and Leslie Labowitz's *Take Back the Night* float in San Francisco 1978.

Siqueiros' painting process was also very performative. He often posed and took photographs for his "living sketches." As Herner says, "[h]is theatrical personality led him to explore (invent) realistic compositions based on fantasy, which he staged himself before a camera prior to painting them."[19] In August 2002, the Sala de Arte Público Siqueiros presented *Matrices fotogénicas*, an exhibition including this material. The show was interesting from the point of view of Siqueiros' relationship to performance art, but, more importantly, it revealed how art history is being revised from a performance-informed perspective.

On Tours and Detours

The 1950s and 1960s should have marked the full acceptance of performance art. By then, the muralists' experimental attitude was complemented by the playful spirit of the Surrealists who arrived in Mexico in the 1940s, among them Remedios Varo, Leonora Carrington, and Kati Horna. In 1940, André Breton, Wolfgang Paalen, and César Moro organized the *Exposición Internacional de Surrealismo* [International Exhibition of Surrealism] at the Galería de Arte Mexicano. Isabel Marín performed *La esfinge de la noche* [*Night's effigy*], generally accepted as the first Mexican protohappening.

In the 1950s, we had Poesía en Voz Alta [Poetry Out Loud], a project of multidisciplinary experimental events that included poets, playwrights, and visual artists such as Octavio Paz and Leonora Carrington. It ended in 1963, and was forgotten until 1981 when Roni Unger wrote *Poesía en Voz Alta in the Theater of Mexico*, which was not translated into Spanish until 2007.[20] This is what I call the grand tour phenomenon: we often embrace our art history only after it has been accepted abroad.[21] This milieu was enhanced by the presence of German born artist Mathías Goeritz and Chilean playwright Alejandro Jodorowsky, with whom Manuel Felguérez and José Luis Cuevas, members of La Ruptura, collaborated.[22]

Felguérez participated actively in Jodorowsky's "ephemeral panic acts,"[23] multidisciplinary stage productions based on spontaneity and chance. Some of them are legendary, like the one at the sports club Deportivo Bahía, where a helicopter was supposed to transport Jodorowsky in a grand entrance, but crashed into the swimming pool during rehearsals, three hours before the performance began. They simply left the aircraft there as part of the set. Although Felguérez usually collaborated as a stage designer, he also performed:

> I had a model wearing several layers of white clothes and had to undress her by cutting pieces of material off and nailing pieces of fabric (white, red, black) on a board to make a kind of abstract painting, while the play was taking place on stage.[24]

In 1961, Cuevas was part of *Los Hartos*,[25] the famous "exhibition" organized by Goeritz. This foundational conceptual piece against Dada and the *avant-garde* questioned what the definition of art was and who made it. The "hartists" participated as representatives of their trade. Kati Horna was an "hobject maker" and Beningno Alvarado a "hworker." They even included "Hinnocence" the hen. The letter H before each word marked their membership in the *Los Hartos* movement. According to Francisco Reyes Palma, this event was a provocation that resulted in an involuntary happening. The audience threw drinks at the wall and surrealist artist Alice Rahon "destroyed one of the works (an egg), regardless of the fact its author, Innocence, was present."[26] *Los ecos de Mathias Goeritz*, an exhibition at the Antiguo Colegio de San Ildefonso in 1997, brought together some of the objects of that mythical work, partly recreating its atmosphere. It was an early exercise in documenting an ephemeral event museographically.

Throughout his career, Cuevas has done many performances and conceptual pieces such as his famous ephemeral mural in 1967, which he "dictated" to a house painter. He has also photographed himself every day for years and published his personal journal in major newspapers for decades alongside his column *Cuevario*. Like Kahlo, he has made his character his best creation.[27]

Both these artists should have been strong links in the history of performance art, but Felguérez ended up rejecting performance, even as audience:

> I have never seen anything else again, maybe it's the nostalgia of thinking that the past is always better. They were spectacular and so violent, so full of spirit and determination that I feel what is done today is too prepared, quite preconceived.[28]

Cuevas has never considered himself as a performance artist, but he is clear about his role as a predecessor:

> [A] lot of things being done today in contemporary art in Mexico probably wouldn't have happened without my presence. Even expressions that seem distant from my work, such as installations and other products apparently derived from conceptual art – and I say apparently because I was doing those kinds of things long ago, such as the ephemeral mural, tattooing women, the *Signs of Life* exhibition where, for example, I exhibited my semen, the electrocardiogram taken during sex [...] all this relates to what is being done today.[29]

Why did Felguérez, Cuevas, and other members of their generation pull back? Was it loyalty to the object? Market pressures? Politics? There is a possible answer in the catalogue *La era de la discrepancia* (*The Age of Discrepancy*) and the exhibition itself implies another one. In her essay, Pilar García de Germeños[30] tells the story of the Salón Independiente (SI) that started in 1968 as a reaction against the official cultural program of the Olympic Games and its *Exposición Solar.*[31] Thirty-five artists, among them Felguérez, Cuevas, Marta Palau, and Gunther Gerzso, refused to participate in this exhibition, among other reasons, because they were against the organizers' traditional definition of art. Their refusal was also a silent way to support a growing student movement that ended in the Tlatelolco massacre on 2 October 1968.

The SI lasted three years, each more radical than the one before. They used unusual materials such as newspaper to make art and abandoned the gallery space to interact with the people. According to García, the SI ended because of disagreements among the artists. Maybe this artistic detour was caused by personal problems. Once the collaborative impulse evaporated, each artist went back to his or her studio.

The existence of this exhibition and its catalogue imply another answer. In over thirty years as an artist, I had heard many rumors of the SI but had never before been able to see the work in an exhibition or a book. No information was available. The SI was up against institutions that were becoming overtly and covertly more repressive. Being ignored was an effective form of censorship.

Crossroads

Institutional silence is never innocent. The Tlatelolco massacre and the authoritarianism that followed marked our culture. A positive aspect of the massacre was that opposition to the repressive regime eventually led to what is still our young and fragile democracy. According to Elizabeth Romero a negative aspect is that it deformed our history, including that of performance art, and this will only begin to change when the oppressors account for their actions legally and society begins to heal.[32] As institutions became more entrenched, the older artists backed off and younger ones became more radical politically and artistically. The *Generación de los Grupos* (*Generation of the Groups*) emerged in the 1970s. They were more politicized and less playful. They worked in collectives. For them, form and content were political. Some, such as Germinal, who did banners for demonstrations, militated in political organizations. For others, such as Mira, Suma, and Proceso Pentágono, activism was reflected in the political content of their work. The first artists to devote themselves exclusively to performance belong to this generation. For Rubén Valencia, Melquiades Herrera, Alfredo Núñez, and Maris Bustamante of the No-Grupo, or for individuals like Marcos Kurtycz, performance art was not an experiment any more.

I had never quite understood how this change had occurred until I read Miguel López and Emilio Tarazona:

> The history of contemporary Peruvian art has still not overcome a sort of split which only recently seems to be noted between the avant-garde scene originated in the mid sixties

> and another one that emerged to a great degree disassociated from the first one at the end of the seventies.[33]

They mention that Chile had experienced a comparable, although more violent process. As each of our local histories is written, we will probably find a similar pattern in other Latin American countries with repressive governments during this period. Latin American performance art dealt frontally with this repression. It has even based its identity on politics. As Aracy Amaral said at the Primer Coloquio Latinoamericano de Arte No objectual in Medellín (First Latin American Non-Objectual Art Congress) in Columbia in 1981:

> It seems possible to affirm that the actions that distinguish non-objectual art in Latin America from those in Europe and the US since the sixties are works that along with creativity, have a political connotation in a wide sense (both directly and through metaphors).[34]

Although I agree with Amaral, I think performance art everywhere is always political. Extreme circumstances, such as those in Latin America, made artists respond to repression overtly and, as a political act, critics focused on this aspect of the work. The problem is that, unless we underline their artistic contribution, we risk being stereotyped, we grant too much authority to political power and we neglect the fact that diversity is one of Latin America's strongest characteristics.

Scary Scars

Among the most internationally successful recent Latin American performances are those of women artists who turn their bodies into archives of violence, marked by the crimes of political power and the most ferocious misogyny. In 2003, Lorena Wolffer presented *Mientras Dormíamos* (*While We Slept*) at the Museo universitario del Chopo in Mexico City. She drew on her body the wounds inflicted upon some of the hundreds of women who have been murdered in Ciudad Juárez since the 1990s. In 2005 Guatemalan artist Regina José Galindo carved the word PERRA (Bitch) on her right leg with a knife. In her country, women's corpses have turned up tortured and inscribed with knife marks. I found both works very moving and intriguing: how do we keep the balance between making violence visible and making a permanent backup copy of it in our bodies? When are these types of works politically effective and when do they become a spectacle or a stereotype?

Tragedy versus Triviality

In 1984, I participated in the *Obras Nuevas en la Sala Permanente. Arte Contemporáneo Mexicano* (*New works at the Permanent Hall. Contemporary Mexican Art*), an exhibition at the Museo de Arte Moderno, at the time directed by artist Helen Escobedo, one of the first installation artists in Mexico, who was a member of the SI and a strong promoter of the Generation of the Groups. Like all participants, I was asked to donate my work to the museum, badly in need of updating its collection. The exhibition included the work of artists from the 1960s and 1970s, even some of the collectives and performance artists. When the show closed, they returned our works with no explanation and not long after, Escobedo stepped down as director. The museum's collection is still incomplete and, with it, so is the history of our recent art. Years later I asked Helen what had caused this twenty-year delay in the documentation and legitimating processes of art.[35] Apparently, Paloma de la Madrid, the President's wife, had visited the exhibition and was upset by some of the foul language used by the Tepito Arte Acá group in their work.[36] I leave the rest to your imagination.

On Archives and Collections

The attitude of institutions toward performance documentation has been, to put it mildly, erratic. In 1993, the Instituto Nacional de Bellas Artes (INBA, National Institute of Fine Arts) opened Ex-Teresa: Arte Actual, a museum dedicated exclusively to non-objectual art, that has organized important international performance and sound art festivals. Ex-Teresa has an important archive that has always been surrounded by rumors that past directors have ransacked it when they left, even though they are committed artists and curators who understand the importance of documentation and, within institutional limitations, have built it up.[37]

Concerned about this situation, I paid them an independent surprise inspection visit.[38] I was pleased to see the archive had finally been placed in a room that could be locked and documents were not being lent out anymore. I also found out the INBA did not have a legal definition for these materials.[39] They are not part of a collection or even protected as government property: chairs and trash bins are inventoried and regularly audited, but books, catalogues, magazines, photographs, videos, DVDs and CDs, sound tapes, and artists' files are only safeguarded by a list and the goodwill of employees.

Institutions are slowly changing. The Museo Universitario de Ciencias y Artes (MUCA; The University Museum of Sciences and Arts) Roma, Mexico City – a university museum for young, experimental art – was renovated in 2006. The new facilities include a documentation center run by contemporary art conservation specialists who know how to preserve material works and document ephemeral ones. MUCA Roma is part of the UNAM Universidad Nacional Autónoma de México [National Autonomous University of Mexico], the institution that has led the discussion on how to exhibit and present non-objectual works. One of the parallel events to the above-mentioned *La era de la discrepancia* exhibition, was the international symposium *Recargando lo contemporáneo. Estrategias curatoriales de rescate del arte reciente* [*Reloading the contemporary. Curatorial strategies to rescue recent art*], which took place in September 2007 and included international curators who have presented exhibitions that recover work from the 1960s and 1970s. They all faced similar challenges, such as difficulties in finding information and the need to create guidelines to recreate works from the past that do not exist anymore.

Among the projects discussed were *La persistencia de lo efímero* (*The Persistence of the Ephemeral*) curated by Miguel López and Emilio Tarazona for the Centro Cultural España in Lima, Perú, *Orígenes del arte conceptual en Colombia (1968–1978)* (*The Origins of Conceptual Art in Colombia (1968–1978)*) curated by Álvaro Barrios for the Museo de Antioquia in Medellín, Colombia and *Lygia Clark de l'oeuvre a l'événement. Nous sommes le moule. A vous de donner le souffle* (*Lygia Clark from Work to Event. We are the mold. To you breath is given*) curated by Suely Rolnik for the Musée des Beaux-arts in Nantes, France.

Infected!

Performance art has infected curatorial practice, and Suely Rolnik is one of its victims. Faced with the challenge of presenting the work of Brazilian artist Lygia Clark, whose objects and performances involved the spectator in a sensitive and sensorial experience, Rolnik came up with a solution that enabled her to avoid turning objects into fetishes and documentation into a death certificate. In tune with her experience as a psychoanalyst, the exhibition Rolnik curated included sixty-four interviews with different people close to Clark, her work, and her context. This allowed her to suggest what Clark's work had meant. To reactivate the work, Rolnik inverted the object/context relation accepted in traditional exhibitions where the former is regarded as fundamental and the latter as anecdotal. Performance art is anchored in life, even though its ephemeral character constantly makes us face death. In this game, context is everything. Rolnik understood that if we want to capture the complexity of works of art that involve the promotion of social or personal artistic relationships rather than the creation of aesthetic objects, whatever memory of them we create through written or visual documents, recollections, and even legends must reflect this.

Love Letters

Whereas institutions and historians have not been good accomplices of performance art, the media has been a faithful lover. They have been platform and document. According to Ruben Gallo, "the first radio transmission began with Manuel Maples Arce reading his 'T.S.H,' an Estridentista poem on the wireless telegraph."[40] Television has also been a platform for performance art. In 1987, the feminist art group Polvo de Gallina Negra made several performances on television, such as *Madre por un Día* (*Mother for a Day*).[41] In 1988, Melquiades Herrera had a performance section in a program called *La Caravana* (*The Caravan*).[42]

Newspapers have played a basic role in documenting performance art. As Lorena Wolffer wrote:

> Although over the past few years many books have been published on the theory, practice and the role of performance art in contemporary society (mainly in the United States and Europe), the lack of documentation – and therefore of memory – that still exists around this genre in Mexico is, to say the least, dramatic. The documentation of performance art has happened in journalism, not in art criticism or analysis.[43]

Let me illustrate this: while fewer than ten books have been printed on Mexican performance art as I write this text in 2007, between 1991 and 2005, newspapers in Mexico City alone have published approximately 1500 articles on performance art[44] and three performance artists have had weekly columns in different papers.[45] Television has also played an important role in documenting performance art. In the 1990s Galería Plástica focused on the work of young artists and many did performance art.[46] In 2004, Lorena Wolffer created La Caja Negra, a program she conducted and wrote with Norma Lazo on issues such as the body and madness as articulated through different arts. Performance was a constant reference. In 2006, they both produced *Las 7 nuevas artes* for TV UNAM and one of the programs was on performance art.

Hope

There is hope for performance art documentation in Mexico because in recent years more scholars are specializing in this field of study, for example, Antonio Prieto, Elia Espinosa, and Josefina Alcázar, who has broken all records by publishing three books and editing a documentary series in CDs.[47] They have fought an uphill battle. In addition, as of 2000, art schools have sprouted at universities all over the country. Some, like the Escuela Superior de Artes de Yucatán, founded by artist Monica Castillo, base the first year of their curricula on performance art. Non-objectual arts are finally penetrating institutions.

Shared Stories

The 1950s and 1960s saw the rise of multidisciplinary artwork, which was left out of the HISTORY OF ART. Fortunately, the idea of a history of art with capital letters that includes everything has vanished and specialized art histories have proliferated. To trace the history of performance art today, one has to visit parallel fields. For example, one would have to read the texts of musician and sound artist Manuel Rocha. In *Arte Sonoro en México* (*Sound Art in Mexico*), he writes about the work of Ulises Carrión and Felipe Ehrenberg, both important to performance art.[48]

Photographers

Several photographers have specialized in performance art since the early 1990s, among them Monica Naranjo and Antonio Juárez. Their work has become a hybrid product that is both documentation and art. Naranjo presented the first exhibition of performance art photographs in 2003, *Fotografías de performance* at the Galería José María Velasco, and Juárez has exhibited his performance documentation in Mexico and abroad since 2004, most recently in 2011 with *F.isuras* at the Casa de la Primera Imprenta Gallery in Mexico City.[49]

Documentation as Art

Documenting performance is so important that some performances deal with the problems of documentation and others *are* documentation. In 1989, Victor Lerma and I founded *Pinto mi Raya*, an applied conceptual art project whose purpose is to lubricate the art system. The core of our project is an archive. In 1997 we made a piece called *El Balcón del CENIDIAP* (*The CENIDIAP Balcony*. CENIDIAP stands for the National Art Center for Research, Documentation and Information). Concerned about the lack of documentation and research on performance art, we visited this official institution to find out what they were doing. We discovered that the National Art Library did not have a single document on performance art and none of the CENIDIAP's scholars specialized in this field. The situation was so desperate we decided to invite a witch to make a "*limpia*," a *cleansing*, a ritual to cure an evil spell. In a crossed ritual, she cast her spell while we read a text explaining the importance of documenting performance art and demanding a more professional approach from the institution.

We have also trained as storytellers to make performances where we tell stories about performance. In an oral culture such as ours, it seems an adequate way of documenting. Oral narrative is also analogous to performance art in that storytellers do not act and the work is a collaborative creation between the narrator and the audience. The 2006 *Performance a Domicilio* (*Home Delivered Performance*) was a project by several artists, including Debora Carnevali, Omar Góngora, Edgar Canul, and Omar Euan. They felt photographs and video documentation were unable to transmit the experience of a performance, so they opened a site with a menu of pieces that members of the public could request at their convenience. These included their covers of the works of artists such as Marina Abramović and Esther Ferrer. For them, re-enactment was a way of sharing history.

Now for the Good News

Then came technology and everything changed. Not long ago, it was difficult to find information on Latin American performance art. Luckily, the Internet distributes and archives information. Today resources on the Internet are multiplying so fast that the amount of information available may soon be overwhelming. Take, for example, Performancelogía (http://performancelogia.blogspot.com/), a blog created by Venezuelan artists Amira Tremont, Aidana Rico, and Ignacio Pérez in 2006 with the purpose of compiling performance documentation, mostly from Latin America. In 2007, Performanceología asked its collaborators, among them Soledad Sánchez Goldar (Argentina), Paula Darriba (Brasil), Carlos Zerpa (Venezuela), and Yto Aranda[50] (Chile) to write about the importance of documentation.[51]

This discussion has addressed three issues. The first was the need to analyze, document, and define performance art from a Latin American perspective. There is a general interest in developing or strengthening the necessary tools and institutions to achieve this. Some artists, like Clemente Padín (Uruguay), insist on the importance of marking our differences: "We have to let it be known that 'we were and we are here,' and that our role will not be meaningless, but dynamic, and inevitably bonded to the interests of our communities." The second is the importance of documentation in terms of education. Everyone agrees this aspect of performance art documentation is imperative. For Alexander Del Re (Chile), it is even more so: using documentation to teach performance means "creating a 'new performance' that will only exist in this new space/time, suspended in the minds of the students listening to me." Apparently, performance has also infected art education. The third is the eternal debate on whether the document is part of the work or whether performance art resists documentation. Of all these ideas, what Gustavo León (Venezuela) wrote struck me as particularly true to my experience: "I confess I am a documentator, and an addict to registering." I would only add that there is a growing epidemic of this disease.

Notes

1. Macular degeneration is a medical condition that leads to the loss of central vision.
2. Non-objectual-art is a term that refers to ephemeral and non-traditional arts used by Peruvian critic and theorist Juan Acha. This term is often used in Latin America to refer to installation and performance art.
3. Maris Bustamante, "Arbol genealógico de las formas pías," *Revista Generación N° 20 year X, El Performance Art*, Mexico DF, 1998.
4. "Problemas artísticos de América Latina" by Juan Acha. Text with which the Peruvian art critic and theorist participated in the XVII Coloquio Internacional de Historia del Arte in Zacatecas in 1993. Available at: www.unam.mx/latinart/latin4.htm (accessed September 2007). Translated by the author.
5. My book *Escandalario: Los artistas y la distribución del arte* (AVJediciones, México, 2006) refers to the participation of artists in the distribution of art.
6. Many museums in Mexico were founded by artists who donated their collections to the country. Examples of them are the Museo José Luis Cuevas in Mexico City and Museo de Arte Abstracto Manuel Felguérez in Zacatecas.
7. Schneider, who was a poet, writer, and researcher, wrote several books on the Estridentistas, among them *El Estridentismo: México 1921–1927*, Universidad Nacional Autónoma de México, 1985.

8. Bustamante has written several articles on this subject, such as "Non-Objective Arts in Mexico 1963–83," published in Coco Fusco, *Corpus Delecti: Performance Art of the Americas*, London: Routledge, 2000, pp. 204–217.
9. For more than two decades César Espinosa and Araceli Zúñiga have organized the Bienal de Poesía Visual (Visual Poetry Bienal), which was mostly performance art.
10. Bustamante, op. cit.
11. Rubén Gallo and Ignacio Padilla, *Heterodoxos mexicanos*, Mexico: FCE, 2006.
12. Ibid.
13. Balmori's tricks were so well known that the word *balmoreada* now stands for a practical joke.
14. I wrote about Frida as a performance artist and a precedent to Orlan's work in my article "¿Cuándo se convirtió Frida en FRIDA?" (When did Frida become FRIDA) published in *El Universal* on 18 October 2003, p. 5. If you need a certified First World opinion, Germaine Greer also wrote on this phenomenon in her text "Patron Saint of Lipstick and Lavender Feminism," published in *TATEetc, Visiting and Revisiting Art, etcetera*, Summer 2005, issue 4. Available at: http://www.tate.org.uk/tateetc/issue4/kahlo.htm (accessed 23 June 2011): "This is her achievement – the lifelong performance of Frida Kahlo." and "It is no small praise to say that Kahlo was the first ever true performance artist"; and "Orlan is probably not a great fan of Frida Kahlo, yet, in many ways her art practice is an elaboration on the Mexican's precedent."
15. The Museo Casa Estudio Diego Rivera y Frida Kahlo in Mexico City presented the exhibition *El encanto enigmático de Leo Matiz* showing these photographs in 2003.
16. Irene Herner, "Siqueiros, del paraíso a la utopia," *Arte e Imagen*, México: Consejo Nacional para la Cultura y las Artes, 2004.
17. Ibid. According to Herner, this 2 December 1983 interview is at the Pollock/Kasner House and Study Center archive at the University of New York.
18. Ibid.
19. Ibid.
20. Roni Unger, *Poesía en Voz Alta in the Theater of Mexico*, EU: Missouri Press, 1981; Roni Unger, *Poesía en Voz Alta* (translated by Silvia Peláez) published by the Dirección General de Publicaciones y Fomento Editorial and the Centro Nacional de Investigación, Documentación e Información Teatral Rodolfo Usigli, INBA, 2007.
21. I will be writing more about the *Discrepancias* exhibition later, but it is worth noting here that in the catalogue Olivier Debroise and Cuauhtémoc Medina argue that one of the motivations behind this exhibition was that, as Gabriel Orozco became famous, his "international career was tied to specific historical distortions, a result not only of a lack of information on modern art and avant-garde movements in 'peripheral' nations, but also a reflection of the desire of certain critics to control artistic discourse from the center." They mention that "the new artistic circuits were producing a new mythology about local practices too often based on superficial and careless 'instant histories' that had to be challenged." While I agree with them, it is sad that they only decided it was important to rescue the recent art history of Mexico after a few artists broke the underdog barrier and critics abroad noticed them. This is another version of the grand tour phenomenon. Both citations: Olivier Debroise and Cuauhtémoc Medina, "Genealogy of an Exhibition," in Olivier Debroise (ed.), *The Age of Discrepancies*, UNAM, 2007, p. 26.
22. The Ruptura [Rupture] generation broke away from the Muralist Movement. Cuevas and Felguérez are part of it, as are Arnaldo Coen, Vicente Rojo, and Lilia Carrillo.
23. Alejandro Jodorowsky, "Teatro pánico," México: Ed. Era, DF, 1965.

24. Dulce María de Alvarado Chaparro, *Performance en México. Historia y Desarrollo.* Visual Arts BA thesis, UNAM. This document can be found in the publications section at http://www.17.org.mx/index.php?cont=6, accessed 2 May 2011.
25. Hartos is a play on words between "harto" (fed up) and "arte" (art).
26. Francisco Reyes Palma, "La exposición de Los hartos." In the catalogue *Los Ecos De Mathías: Catálogo De La Exposición.* Compiled by Ferruccio Asta, Catalogue of the exhibition at the Antiguo Colegio de San Ildefonso, Mexico. Instituto Nacional de Bellas Artes-Universidad Nacional Autónoma de México-Consejo Nacional para la Cultura y las Artes- Instituto Goethe-Patronato de la Industria Alemana para la Cultura, 1997, p. 172. Translated by the author.
27. José Luis Cuevas, "El mural efímero," *Letras Libres*, February 1999. Available at: http://www.letraslibres.com/index.php?art=5671 (accessed September 2007).
28. Dulce María de Alvarado Chaparro, op cit.
29. Claudia Díaz Rivera, "Las tendencias del arte actual mexicano quizá no existirían sin mi influencia: Cuevas," *GACETA*, a magazine of the Universidad Veracruzana. Nueva época no. 64–5. Xalapa, Veracruz, Mexico, May 2003. Available at: http://72.14.253.104/search?q=cache:fBplFs8M8NUJ:www.uv.mx/gaceta/Gaceta64/64/ventana/ventana02.htm+cuevario,+semen&hl=es&ct=clnk&cd=2&gl=mx (accessed September 2007).
30. LA ERA DE LA DISCREPANCIA, catalogue of the exhibition of the same name that was shown at the Museo Universitario de Ciencias y Artes at the Universidad Nacional Autónoma de México in 2007. Pilar García de Germeños's essay in this catalogue is "Salón Independiente: una relectura." Pilar García de Germenos, "The *Salón Independiente*: A New Reading," in Olivier Debroise (ed.), *The Age of Discrepancies*, UNAM, 2007, pp. 49–57.
31. Solar Exhibition. The Exposición Solar took place at the Palacio de Bellas Artes (Palace of Fine Arts). It was a thematic art competition.
32. I had heard Romero, who is an artist and a writer, express this idea in lectures, and she confirmed it in a telephone interview on 12 December 2006.
33. Paper by Miguel Lopez and Emilio Tarazona presented on 9 September 2007 at the International Symposium *Recargando lo contemporáneo* [*Reloading the Contemporary*] at the UNAM. It was one of the parallel activities to the exhibition *La era de la discrepancia.* Translated by the author.
34. As quoted by Clemente Padín in his essay "La Performance Desde La Perspectiva Latinoamericana" in the virtual magazine *Escáner Cultural*, no. 77. Clemente *Padín*, *Desde la perspectiva latinoamericana*, Escáner Cultural: http://www.escaner.cl/escaner77/acorreo.html (accessed 16 March 2007). Amaral's words at this Congress are quoted by almost everyone who writes about Latin American performance art. They have become like a mantra. You can also find them in: Víctor Muñoz, "Notes on Action Art in Latin America" in Richard Martel (ed.), *Art action 1958–1998*, Québec: Éditions Intervention, 2001, p. 212.
35. I was preparing my paper "The Seventies are Dead: Long Live the Seventies" for Los no objetualismos en México 1963–1983, a panel on the history of non-objectual art in Mexico for ARCO in 2005.
36. Tepito Arte Aca is a group headed by artist Daniel Manrique which still exists and works in Tepito, one of the oldest poor districts in the city, known for its community life and its black market.
37. The directors until 2007 were Eloy Tarcisio (artist), Lorena Wolffer (artist), Guillermo Santamarina (curator), and Juan Carlos Jaurena (artist).
38. After that visit I wrote "La memoria del arte contemporáneo" for El Universal newspaper, 17 September 2006, cultural section, p. 5.

39. These other museums have shown performances and installations since the 1970s, but for the first two decades they kept no records and even in the 1990s they did not have a clear documentation policy.
40. Rubén Gallo, Ignacio Padilla, op. cit.
41. Maris Bustamante and I founded Polvo de Gallina Negra in 1983 and many of our pieces were media oriented. In this particular piece we named anchorman Guillermo Ochoa "Mother for a Day" during the Nuestro Mundo program which was seen all over Latin America on Channel 2.
42. Melquiades Herrera (1994–2003) was a member of the No-Grupo with Maris Bustmante, Alfredo Núñez, and Rubén Valencia. *La Caravana* was transmitted on Channel 13.
43. Lorena Wolffer, "Construyendo Mitos: El Performance En México," Nexos On-line. *Revista Nexos*, no. 327, Marzo de 2005, http://betanexos.webcom.com.mx/spip.php?article264 (accessed 14 September 2006).
44. Information obtained from the Pinto mi Raya archive on contemporary Mexican art that Victor Lerma and I began in 1991, specifically the compilation *Performance en el archivo de Pinto mi Raya 1991–2005*, which includes performance reviews published in the most important newspapers in Mexico.
45. Pancho López in *Crónica*, Lorena Wolffer in *Séptimo Día* magazine and mine in *El Universal*.
46. Galería Plástica was a TV series produced by Jorge Prior from Producciones Volcán for Channel 22.
47. Elia Espinosa works for the Instituto de Investigaciones Estéticas and Josefina Alcázar is a sociologist, researcher at the Centro de Investigación Teatral Rodolfo Usiglil del Instituto Nacional de Bellas Artes. *Performance y arte-acción an América Latina* [Performance and Action Art in Latin America], Ediciones Sin-Nombre, México, 2005 is co-edited by Alcázar and Fernando Fuentes and her documentary series *Serie Documental de Performance: Mujeres en Acción* [Documentary Series on Performance: Women in Action] is a collection of 15 CDs on three generations of women performance artists in Mexico.
48. Rocha was co-founder and curator of the Internacional Sound Art Festival held at Ex-Teresa: Arte Actual between 1999 and 2002. His *Sound Art in Mexico* was published by *Curare* magazine in 2005, available at Rocha's web page at: http://www.artesonoro.net/soundartwritings.html (accessed September 2007).
49. *f.isura. Fotografías de Antonio Juárez*, Editorial Fogra, FONCA, ExTeresa 2007.
50. Yto Aranda directs Escáner Cultural (http://www.escaner.cl/), which has ample information on contemporary Latin American art, including performance art.
51. Citations of Alexander Del Re, Gustavo Leon are included in the blog: http://performancelogia.blogspot.com/2007/04/colaboradores.html (accessed 22 August 2007). Translated by the author.

Chapter 6

History and Precariousness: In Search of a Performative Historiography

Eleonora Fabião

It is about words. It is about *língua*.

In Portuguese *língua* means both language and tongue; its double meaning relates word and flesh, writing and muscle, speech and taste. *Língua*: an elucidative semantic coincidence. It is about *língua*, about searching, saying, listening, reading, inventing, copying, copyrighting, writing the necessary words to formulate a momentary answer for the recurrent question: what are the relations between language and body? Or, in the context of this volume: what are, or can be, the reciprocities between history and performance? And, specifically in this essay: how does performance art challenge, charge, and change contemporary historiography?

To associate historiography and performance art, to emphasize the performativity of history and the historicity of performance, is a delicate operation given history's tradition as a form of conservation (despite its living condition) and performance art's tradition as a form of expenditure (despite its immense documentary production). Performance art, the artistic practice that forces representation toward unpredictable extremes, the paradoxical practice that dismantles strict separations between art and non-art, inspires rethinking modes of "historiographing". The performance artist – the one who uses his or her embodied self as matter and way, the one who has a particular talent both to expose and to create context through emphatic actions, the corporeal poet of politics – inspires specific modes of acting historiography.

A preliminary goal here is to explore ways out of the well-known dichotomy between *scientific history* and *literary history*. To refuse the notions that history is either a scientific work of research, examination, objective exposition, and explanation of sources, or that "historical narratives are verbal fictions, the contents of which are as much invented as found and the forms of which have more in common with their counterparts in literature than they have with those in the sciences" (as argued by Hayden White and others).[1] Rejecting the rigidity of both perspectives, David Carr proposes a phenomenological approach to history. In his 1986 book Time, Narrative and History, Carr suggests that *historical experience* lies behind and precedes both the narrator's creative act and the scientist's objectivity. He evokes Wilhelm Dilthey's argument: "[W]e are historical beings first, before we are observers [*Betrachter*] of history, and only because we are the former do we become the latter."[2] "The historical world is there," said Dilthey, "and the individual not only observes it from the outside but is intertwined with it [*in sie verwebt*]."[3] The phenomenological move intertwines subject and world (historian and archive), such that subjectivity and objectivity become inseparable in the phenomenological realm of historical experience. It is precisely the phenomenological sense of history as experience, as active involvement and awareness (all necessarily corporeal), that animates the approximation between historiography and performance art proposed here. The ultimate importance of experience[4] as a privileged way of accessing and generating knowledge differentiates a performative approach of history from a literary and a scientific one.

A historical parallel elucidates the sense of experience's relevance for both performance art and performatively oriented historiographies: the gradual decline of storytelling coincides with the gradual growth of extremely corporeal performance practices and the further consolidation of these practices as an art genre. Walter Benjamin famously asked after WWI: "Was it not noticeable at the end of the war that men returned from the battlefield grown silent – not richer but poorer in communicable experience?"[5] Benjamin associated the end of the ability to narrate, the end of "the art of storytelling," with a growing incapacity to exchange experiences. Benjamin emphasized that "one reason for this phenomenon is obvious: experience has fallen in value. And it looks as if it is continuing to fall into bottomlessness."[6] Thus storytelling's decay is associated not only with a diminishment in the capacity to communicate experience but with a drastic decrease in the capacity to experience; a decline of the experience of experiencing. The two world wars and their related catastrophes not only debunked western illusions of cultural development, historical progress, and advancing civilization, but also diluted the experience of creating and sharing narration. Nevertheless, this same post-war scenario is precisely the landscape for performance art's growth, the environment for the development of a radical eulogy of psychophysical experience and political experimentation. As articulated by Paul Schimmel:

> The era following World War II saw a veritable explosion of activity which brought process and performance directly to bear as the subject of works themselves. The line between action, performance and a work of art became increasingly indistinguishable and irrelevant.[7]

He adds:

> The possibility of global annihilation made human beings more aware than ever before to the fragility of creation, subject as it was to forces of destruction of unprecedented magnitude. In this regard, it also made them more cognizant of the primacy of the act.[8]

The experience of massive death, atomic explosions, the Holocaust, thus became major references for a certain approach to "body," "scene," "art," and "experience" investigated by performers thereafter.

Accordingly, any writing on performance art, or any writing inspired by actions proposed and enacted by performance artists, calls for a consideration of storytelling's political and poetic force. In contrast to the novelist who isolates her or himself to write, the storyteller "takes what he tells from experience – his own or that reported by others. And he in turn makes it the experience of those who are listening to his tale."[9] Closer to the figure of the storyteller than the novelist, the performative historian forces the limits of solipsism, of bookish phantasmagoria, of traditional narratography and pushes words and tongue toward an experiential practice of history writing. To recover the sense of experience – the experience of narrating, the narration of experiences and the experience of narratives—is a key theoretical concern in the search of a performative historiography.

It is also important to consider the ways performance artists conceptualize narrative. Due to a general disinvestment in fiction, performance art usually does not articulate narratives, plots, characters, but rather, it implements a *program*.[10] This program needs not be previously rehearsed and will not be improvised but experienced. Performance artists tend not to perform improvisations, they create programs and program themselves to act them out. While experiencing the program, frequently, organism and context are de-programmed. Performance artworks are often dramaturgically open and relational enough to leave space for as many reactions, interferences, co-creations, interpretations, and narrative-derived productions as the number of their spectators. The more performance art slows down fiction and narrative, the more it leaves room for the witness to engage in an experience of creating significance rather than deciphering and understanding something previously conceived. Frequently performers don't want to communicate a specific content to be decoded but to promote an experience through which contents will be elaborated.

Performance art's openness suggests that there will never be just one fact to be experienced and narrated by many. Historiographies, similarly, are not just multiple narrative versions of a single monological object. Rather, there will always already be, within the very "singularity" of the event, a multiplicity of simultaneous fact*s* already taking place*s*. In a performative sense, this is historicity itself. Again, it is not a matter of one historical fact that may be read by multiple voices in a sort of semantic polyphony, but rather, multiplicity is constitutive of the event. This is why the historical fact always unfolds and multiplies in as many relational ramifications, in as many co-creators, and in as many contextual destinies as there might potentially be (just as the body unfolds and multiplies in as many relational ramifications, in as many co-presences, and in as many contextual destinies as there might potentially be).

Therefore it is legitimate to consider, as many already have, that there is no "History" but multiple historiographies, as many historiographies as historiographers and readers.

Benjamin described the historiographic desire to objectively present "the past as it had actually occurred,"[11] as "the strongest narcotic of the [nineteenth] century."[12] In fact, "the past" did not exactly, or not only, "actually occur"; the disturbing simple fact is that "the past" also continues passing. "The past" is not a monolithic block waiting to be moved by the omnipresent, omniscient, and omnipotent historian demiurgic recording machine; "the present," as well, is not a static and neutral receptacle ready to didactically accommodate the historical lesson. Gilles Deleuze clarifies: "A scar is the sign not of a past wound but of the 'present fact of having been wounded.'"[13] History making is vertiginous because it is the creation of a force field, a system of extremely mobile forces that through their interactions are permanently becoming via one another. Henri Bergson, while relating memory and matter, argued that past and present are not necessarily successive but simultaneously produced: "[E]ach past is contemporaneous with the present that it was, so that all of the past coexists with the new present in relation to which it is now past."[14] Michel de Certeau provides the elucidatory epistemological response by identifying another narcotic in western historiography: "Modern Western History essentially begins with the differentiation between the present and the past."[15]

In a corporeal sense, the so-called past is neither gone nor actual, it is neither exactly accumulative nor does it simply vanish – the body intertwines imagination, memory, sensorial perception, and actuality in very sophisticated ways. The body itself moves according to these intertwinements while permanently producing new mnemonic, sensorial, actual, and imaginative connections that generate movement. In a corporeal sense, the past is a becoming.

Informed by the body's psychophysical intertwinements and performance art's dramaturgical deconstruction of representation, the search for a performative historiography is not a discussion on fictive vs. non-fictive aspects of historiography but rather, an experience of the perception of history and the phenomenology of narrative, which takes the body as paradigm. To put it another way: the purpose is to investigate and expose the inseparability of memory, imagination, sensorial perception, and actuality of which the embodied self is the model, rather than to invest in differentiating "fiction" and "reality" or in stimulating the conflict between the aim of preservation (scientific history) and the impossibility of reconstitution (literary history). Here, I associate history and performance art due to my interest in highlighting their acute investment in experience and precariousness. I am particularly interested in the experience of historiographers, their experience with time, space, objects, corporeality, writing, and *língua*. I am interested in the generative force of historiographic performance. I want to approximate the figures of the performance artist and the historian, their common interest in experiencing facts, in embodying sources, in making their bodies available for the enactment of all sorts of performances. Just as with the performer's body, the historian's body will evoke, be traversed by, and cross several other bodies – existing and nonexistent, phantasmatic, and palpable, present, future, and past, actual, imaginary, sensorial, and mnemonic, theoretical and factual, individual and collective.

In search of a performative historiography, my interest lies in the paradoxical possibility of creating not a history of the past but a history of the present. In his unfinished *Arcades Project* Benjamin suggests: "Say something about the method of composition itself: how everything one is thinking at a specific moment in time must at all costs be incorporated into the project then at hand."[16] Inspired by corporeally and politically charged performance art works, performative historiography posits history as existing only as a political statement in a social context – in a permanently renewing dialogue with the different contextual and personal perspectives with which it will be confronted. The writing of history is a performative act under specific historical, political, identitary, and aesthetic conditions of production. The reading of history is a performative act under specific historical, political, identitary, and aesthetic conditions of reception. Historiographic performances are eminently critical, sensorial, affective, mnemonic, imaginative, and relational; they envision the recreation of the polis rather than its reconstitution or preservation. In his famous "Nietzsche, Genealogy, History" Michel Foucault proposes: "Knowledge is not made for understanding; it is made for cutting."[17]

The project of performance art is related to making fluid and dynamic not only art itself, but highly stratified and inflexible states-of-things. Performance art disorders a culture based on the principles of solids: reproduction, mimetic representation, durability, monumentality, guarantees, diplomas, certitude. It works against reproduction in its broadest subjective sense: it deconstructs automatic modes of behavior, works against habit, suspends fixed meanings. Taken together, performance art as a methodological-theoretical paradigm and the body as model propose a poetics and politics of precariousness. Performance art is engaged with the instantaneous, the irreproducible, and the acutely transient, as the historical fact itself. Meaningfully, it is a practice that, due to its emphatic experiential tonus, can be identified with a historical fact per se. Performance art provokes a short-circuit of strict differentiations between fact and representation, that is, it turns representation into a fact itself and shows the fact's representational latency. In search of a performative historiography, a question keeps resonating: what is the politics of representation in the making of history?

In this context, the archive must be approached phenomenologically and theorized according to Maurice Merleau-Ponty's concept of the flesh. In his unfinished 1961 text *The Visible and the Invisible*, Merleau-Ponty writes: "We have to reject the age-old assumptions that put the body in the world and the seer in the body, or, conversely, the world and the body in the seer as in a box. Where are we to put the limit between the body and the world, since the world is flesh?"[18] The intimacy of flesh applied to flesh, of a shared elementality, is the condition of possibility for subjects and objects to intertwine in endless rearrangements. Merleau-Ponty continues: "[M]any painters have said, I feel myself looked at by the things, my activity is equally passivity […] the seer and the visible reciprocate one another and we no longer know which sees and which is seen."[19] Phenomenologically speaking, the work of the painter and of the performative historiographer have some analogous characteristics. A historian feels equally "looked at" by the archive; a historian equally works with both "passivity" and "activity"; a historian hears the archive's voices; a historian feels impregnated by the archive. Historians perform by finding successive different distances from the object of study, to the extreme of fusing with it, of becoming it, of becoming not-it. Or still, if relationality is a major concern as proposed here, if perception is understood as a mode of relation, the historian is inescapably part of the archive and researching is part of the fact being researched. The historian is not a mere collector of data but a producer of affects and effects and, reciprocally, the archive is not a mere collection of data but a producer of affects and effects. In this phenomenological intertwinement, archives are formed by "objectacts," that is, objects energized as transitive verbs. In a performative sense, the archive is not only, or not exactly, a documentary source but a source of historical experience and experimentation.

It was Brazilian artist Hélio Oiticica who proposed the concept of what he called the "objectact." Oiticica theorized that "the object is the discovery of the world every instant. [...] a bridge to access the instant, *objectact*."[20] Even if Oiticica was specifically referring to the sensorial and relational objects created by artist Lygia Clark, his theoretical sensibility is precise in clarifying my point: the object-archive while activated by a historian aware of her or his contextual presence is a "quasi-corporeal" open circuit of acts, of object-acts. The expression "quasi-corporeal" also springs from Brazilian art. Lygia Clark used to refer to some of her objects as "quasi-corporeal." Poet and art critic Ferreira Gullar wrote in "Manifesto Neoconcreto" (an important Brazilian art movement of the late 1950s in which Clark and Oiticica participated as main figures): "We do not conceive a work of art as a 'machine' or as an 'object,' but as a 'quasi-body' [...] which can only be understood phenomenologically."[21] The same argument holds for object-archives and their performative experiential and experimental relationality, corporeality, and precariousness.

Because of the ways he challenges history, performs archivization, and resists critical and disciplinary definition, I would like to introduce a man and his work. His name is Arthur Bispo do Rosario – *Arthur* (with the English spelling, as the king), *Bispo* (Bishop, as the cleric or the chess piece), *do Rosario* (of the Rosary, as the string of beads to count the prayers) – Arthur Bishop of the Rosary, so to speak. Date of birth unknown – maybe 14 May 1909, according to the Brazilian Navy's official register; maybe around 5 July 1909, according to his baptism certificate issued by Igreja Matriz de Nossa Senhora da Saúde (Church of Our Lady of Health) in Japaratuba his hometown; maybe 16 March 1911 as indicated in the admission sheets of "Light" (the electric power company in Rio de Janeiro that employed him from 1933 to 1937); or maybe simply sometime during the years 1911and 1912 according to two different patient's files at Colônia Juliano Moreira, the psychiatric hospital where, between comings and goings, Bispo lived from 1939 till his death, in 1989.[22] Who knows?

According to these different archives, it is also impossible to define with certainty Bispo's filial origin. In different documents, one finds different names. And, surprisingly (or not), in the psychiatric hospital's papers neither of his parents' names are recorded. His archival history appears, from its start, ruptured and dissociated, disturbingly precarious. Does this

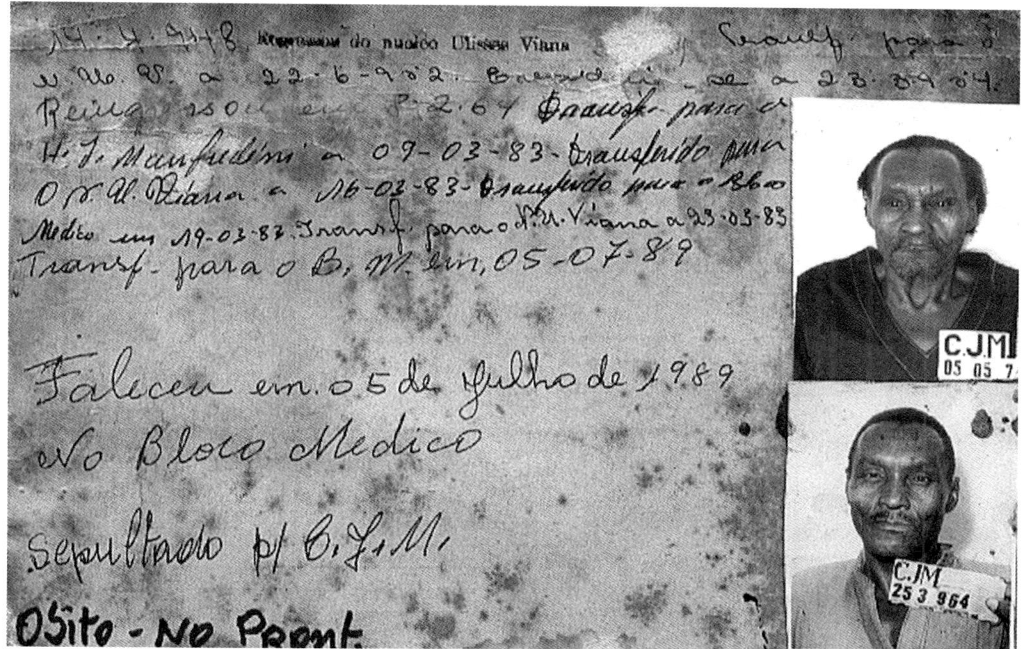

Colônia Juliano Moreira's File: Transfers and death register of Arthur Bispo do Rosario on 5 July 1989. Courtesy of Museu Bispo do Rosario Arte Contemporânea, Prefeitura da Cidade do Rio de Janeiro.

archival disruption happen only because Bispo, a model of mental and moral tortuousness according to the parameters of normative subjectivity, is the subject in question? Or is it that any history is necessarily incomplete and archives something other than comprehensive deposits of proofs? Or, is it maybe that Bispo's history is a paradigmatic case to focus on the not so functional and transparent relations between historiography and factuality, history and language, archives and accuracy, institutions and their subjects? Calling Arthur Bispo do Rosario.

Against this noise in the archive, against this official mismanagement of memory and identity, against precariousness, Bispo repeatedly affirmed, as if to clarify and dismiss any factual doubts about his origin: "One day I simply appeared." Arthur Bispo do Rosario (date of birth unknown – 1989) was an Afro-Brazilian man diagnosed as paranoid schizophrenic before he reached his thirties. He was first interned in a psychiatric hospital in 1938 after working as a shipmate in the Brazilian Navy, fighting as a professional boxer, working as a security guard, and then as housekeeper. After 1938, Bispo spent most of his life interned at Colônia Juliano Moreira Asylum in Rio de Janeiro, where he produced around nine hundred pieces including embroideries, clothes, banners, and sculptures using the hospital's trash and everyday objects as raw material. Despite his extraordinary needlework Bispo never worked with sewing machines; if necessary he would unravel patients' uniforms and bed sheets to obtain threads to manufacture his pieces. He also asked or blackmailed other patients to collect objects and bring them to him: mugs, magazines, spoons, necklaces, hats, rubber boots, balls, bottles. These objects were usually paid for with cigarettes (acquired in the asylum's black market). He also did favors to the hospital staff in order to get materials, protection, and permission to keep his works (also known as *Xerife*, the Sheriff, Bispo was encouraged by the asylum's staff to use his boxer's expertise to help them to keep order). Other materials he obtained from visitors, from other patients' family members or friends. According to the hospital's archive no one from Bispo's family ever came to visit during his approximately fifty years of psychiatric confinement. Calling Arthur Bispo do Rosario.

Bispo's declared objective as a maker was not to create artworks – he did not consider himself an artist – but "to represent everything that exists."[23] I repeat: *to represent everything that exists*. Following commands from the voices he heard, especially Virgin Mary's voice, Bispo's lifelong project was to build an archive of the human world to be presented to God on the Day of the Final Judgment. As commented by art critic and historian Waldir Barreto, everyday objects would be removed from their utilitarian flow and transmuted by an aesthetic act of faith: "[T]he object suffers deep interference being visually and spiritually enriched until partially or totally missing its original, mundane and prosaic attributes."[24]

Inspired by the combined performative power of representing and creating, Bispo do Rosario doggedly fulfilled a religious mission that was also an archival, anthropological, aesthetic, and magical task: archival – he collected, catalogued, and preserved; anthropological – his archival making represents the world, the culture, and the group of which he was a member; aesthetic – he aesthetically acted upon and (re)created the group, the culture, and the world in which he partook while making his anthropological-aesthetic archive;

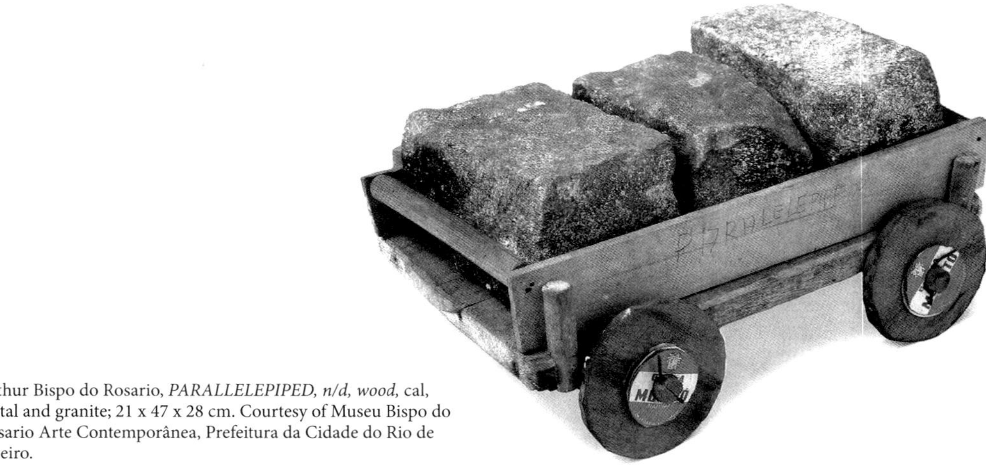

Arthur Bispo do Rosario, *PARALLELEPIPED, n/d, wood,* cal, metal and granite; 21 x 47 x 28 cm. Courtesy of Museu Bispo do Rosario Arte Contemporânea, Prefeitura da Cidade do Rio de Janeiro.

magical – he not only recycled but actually transubstantiated the asylum's garbage and his own body through his religious–anthropological–aesthetic performance. His concern was not to invent but rather, to copy, order, catalog, describe, list, and classify every-thing-of-the-world. But while copying, ordering, cataloguing, describing, listing, and classifying things, he constructed and invented a unique world with its own measures, morals, and logics. Bispo's voluminous archive is also a private world, a thicker skin, a protective shell, a regulated environment, the materialization of his paranoiac and grandiloquent exercise of power, control, and endless productivity.

Bispo's world making indicates an ethical posture on how to recycle colonialism's residues and capitalism's excesses. His condition is evidently related to a larger cultural problem, a social pathology typical of the cultural logic of colonialism and of capitalism. Not by coincidence, the majority of Colonia Juliano Moreira's patients are African descendents from low-income social segments. By coincidence (or not), Juliano Moreira Asylum's many sections are built upon a large old plantation. A visitor can still find the ruins (some of them well preserved) of the *casa grande* (the lord's big house), the aqueduct, the *Igreja Nossa Senhora dos Remédios* (Church of Our Lady of Medicines) and the *senzala* (the plantation slave quarters). The architecture, the memories, the corpses, the voices, the politics, the corporeality, the violence: they still haunt the place. As demonstrated by postcolonial theorists such as Franz Fanon, Ann Cheng, Homi Bhabha, and others, the colonial project is not only a project of exploitation but of schizophrenization; of fractioning people's identity and imposing new models of identification and desire that can put them in constant combat against their own image, or, in extreme cases, make impossible the experience of identification, signification, and (self)integration. Bispo's work is, at the same time, a creative resistance to the system he is part of – perhaps an attempt to express his experience, memory, and corporeality – and a paranoiac mimicry of this system – since he identifies with and reproduces the hierarchic, bureaucratic, authoritarian, and monumental models of the Navy, the state, and the hospital.

Bispo's production disturbs critical and historiographic projects while challenging the possibility of being classified according to conventional theoretical models. Just as with a performance artist, his actions are those of a *cultural complicator*. On one hand, Bispo's work cannot be analyzed according to art history's parameters and methodologies because it fundamentally resists classification as art: it does not participate in the historical discourse that defines art making; it is not intentionally dialoguing with this tradition. On the other hand, the work's extraordinary artistry has to be considered not only because of its unique aesthetic power and meaningfulness, but also due to the simple and unavoidable fact that it has been largely perceived, presented, appraised, and consumed as contemporary art. As Ricardo Aquino reminds us:

> Bispo's work represented Brazil at the Venice Biennale in 1995 and occupied a prominent position in the *Mostra do Redescobrimento Brasil +500* (Rediscovery Brazil +500) exhibition staged in several venues. It has also been shown at Foundation Cartier in

> Paris; Fundación Proa in Buenos Aires; the Guggenheim in New York; Mexico City and Stockholm, to mention only venues outside Brazil.[25]

However, it can be considered a violation to move Bispo's inventories away from their mystic purpose. But, it would be outrageous to keep them confined and forgotten, or worse, to let them rot, abandoned in the storage room of a sanatorium. The singular power of Bispo's work itself poses the question: is there any appropriate place for this work in the inflexible structure of contemporary western culture which divides secular from religious, sane from insane, art from life? What matters here is to refuse falling into a classificatory trap. Inspired by performance art's political verve, what matters is to engage in a critical revision of canons, rules, and ethics regulating western art and health discourses and procedures. The fact is that the madman's obsessive lucidity mobilizes both unconscious productions and conscious acts of the one who faces it. It is impossible to stay indifferent before "the archive of the human world." Personally, after experiencing this work, I started conducting body-oriented practices with chronic patients as a volunteer at Juliano Moreira Asylum, frequenting Museu Bispo do Rosario (Museum Bispo do Rosario) located at Colônia Juliano Moreira, writing about the archive, and literally writing in Bispo's former cell.

Allen S. Weiss, while discussing "Art Brut" and the theoretical ways of addressing its specificities, poses the question: "How would we have to modify our aesthetic theories and our histories of art to accommodate such works?"[26] Like Weiss, I continually ask myself about consequent and productive ways to articulate Bispo's "appearing" into historiography. A possible answer is to make a *historical assemblage* exposing the impossibility of generating any sort of complete history of Bispo's life and work. This approach reflects the belief that the gaps between references call for the reader's voice, that room should be left for the reader to occupy. Completeness is not only factually unachievable – as already indicated by the conflicts found in the official archive – but epistemologically undesirable – as already indicated in my approximation of historiography to performance art's modes of relationality.

As performance art and the phenomenological body both keep recalling, there is no stable ground, no static archive, no frozen meaning. Therefore the present historiographic operation is based on the idea of keeping Arthur Bispo do Rosario "appearing." There is no such thing as a full and homogeneous subject interacting with a full and homogeneous

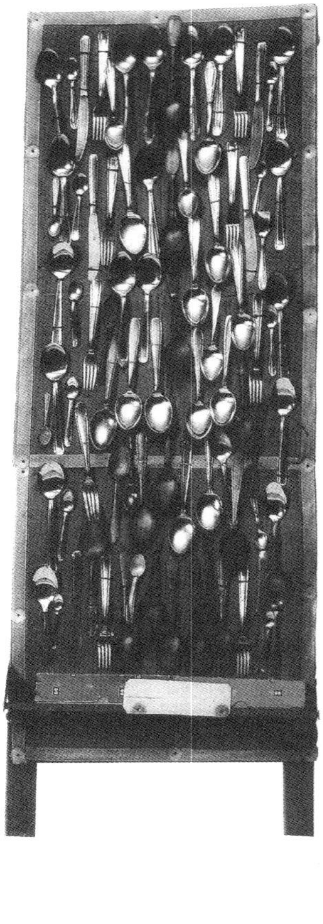

Arthur Bispo do Rosario, *Silverware*, n/d, wood, metal, paper, cloth and plastic; 197 x 70 x 9 cm. Courtesy of Museu Bispo do Rosario Arte Contemporânea, Prefeitura da Cidade do Rio de Janeiro.

archive and reflecting a full and homogeneous reality. It is precarious. Thus, the historian's goal becomes not one of summarizing fifty years of feverish work, but to continue Bispo's task of representing the world, to historiographically represent worlds, and to reflect on what representation means – specifically, on what historical representation in a performative sense signifies. Performances and bodies cannot be historically reproduced but only historiographically presented in and as language, recreated in and as language, constructed in and as language. Linguistic representation's experiential force opposes historical reproduction's reconstitutive drive. The more the historiographer experiences the object while critically (and objectively) showing the representational experience of it, the more performative will be the results. It is about words; it is about *língua*, about the relations between language and tongue, word and flesh, writing and muscle, narrative and taste. Forcing the body of language, forming language as body, performance art, once again, makes meaning move.

The existence of the archive radically presupposes the inexistent in it, and what is visible in the archive clearly points to its phantasmatics. Objectacts. The experience of the archive exposes the "constitutive paradox" of physical beings conceptualized by Merleau-Ponty: the condition of simultaneous presence and absence, visibility and invisibility. What is particularly meaningful to stress in this search of a performative historiography grounded in phenomenology, is the vibratory condition of objects and subjects, or better, of objectacts and subjectacts in their paradoxical energetics, and their vibrating intertwinements. Bispo clarifies: "[M]y corporeal action is the brightness that I put in the pieces."[27]

To perform the archive is also to be confronted with the epistemological force and the energetics of the fragment. The archive's performative mode, its objectivity and its temporality, are those of the fragment. To recall Hélio Oiticica's words, the fragmentary archiveact is "the discovery of the world every instant. [...] a bridge to access the instant." Different from a detail, a fragment does not evoke a supposed whole of which it was originally a part, but rather, it generates in and by itself successive provisory wholes. The fragment ontologically threatens not only the notion of completeness but also, and meaningfully, the sense of temporal linearity related to it. Fragments challenge totalitarian orders; they resist unification and linearity by affirming themselves as open force fields that attract and repel other fragments composing mobile systems of relational meaning. There is no possible unity to be achieved out of fragments; a fragment will never become a totality; the final puzzle is necessarily incomplete. A fragment is not melancholically searching for a lost completeness but vividly reinforcing its precariousness, that is, its relativity and relationality. A fragment retains the full energy of the explosion that formed it: it is a blast, a pandemonium, a dismemberment, a flight, and a rearrangement. A fragment performs neither in favor of an economy of efficacy, efficiency, and effectiveness, nor in favor of its own definition, but only in terms of movement. In its associative performance, the fragment activates multiple circuits of references in unpredictable ways. In short, fragmentary order is always provisory, under construction, in transition, associative, mobile, and open: it is precarious. It disturbs because it explodes everything that "touches" it. It disturbs because of its endless associative energy.

Bispo's archive of the human world to be presented to God on the Day of Final Judgment is an enormous fragment of fragments. However, his motivation was completeness (recalling Benjamin's proposition for his own historiographic voraciousness in the *Arcades Project*, cited earlier in this text: "[H]ow everything one is thinking at a specific moment in time must at all costs be incorporated into the project then at hand"). Bispo's parameter was the absolute, but his psychophysical experience was that of blasting. Bispo sometimes used to voluntarily ask the guards to incarcerate him in his cell:

BISPO: Imprison me because I am transforming myself.
ALTAMIRO: Into what?
BISPO: Into a King. Imprison me because I will start a war.[28]

The voluntary prisoner needed a walled confinement to not lose his parameters, the parameters of his embodied self. On these occasions, the hospital staff would leave him quiet, isolated, working on the objects, working on reconstituting and loosening limits. His cell (2 x 3 m) had walls with small, high, rectangular grid-covered windows (sized around 150 x 50 cm, more or less the same size of the "Silverware" piece (see page 130) and many other similar assemblages of objects he made) through which Bispo could only see the sky. Bispo could stay in this situation for months, usually not accepting food, rarely accepting fruit, sometimes just drinking few glasses of sugared water.

"I NEED THESE WORDS. WRITTEN." is a banner embroidered with the figure of a man. As far as I know, this is Bispo's only work where a human body is figuratively represented and emphasized. The embroidery was made on a thick hospital sheet from the Ulisses Viana Section (the initials "UV" are printed on the other side of the sheet among many other embroideries), the section of the hospital reserved for the most aggressive patients, where Bispo used to live. It is supported at the top by a thin wood plank so that it could be carried as a religious procession banner. The masculine figure is in the middle-bottom of the surface. The body floats at the top of a sort of staircase which has a phrase written under it: "I NEED THESE WORDS. WRITTEN." His arms are slightly opened and the hand palms turned out. Three dots define nipples and belly button. A horizontal line in the middle of the torso, as a diaphragmatic line, divides upper and lower bodies. This filament also "dresses" the figure; it gives the sensation that this man is wearing pants, especially because the genitals are not indicated. The masculine name "CLOVES" is embroidered underneath the heart. But "CLOVES"? "CLOVES" who? The floating man is surrounded by a sky of written words and encircled by a line. This contour outlines his force field: his energetic, verbal, and auditory surrounding mass; his aura/aural/aureole/auricle. On the top of his simple oval head the words "DORSAL SPINE" vertically zigzag as if escaping and/or piercing. Curvilinear shaped on the left side and almost straightly aligned on the right side, groups of words seem to be irradiating from and/or attracted by the magnetic field. Those complete or incomplete words, accurately or inaccurately written, refer to body parts, organs, fluids, body actions. The floating man, besides a small drawing on the left upper corner representing the Sugar

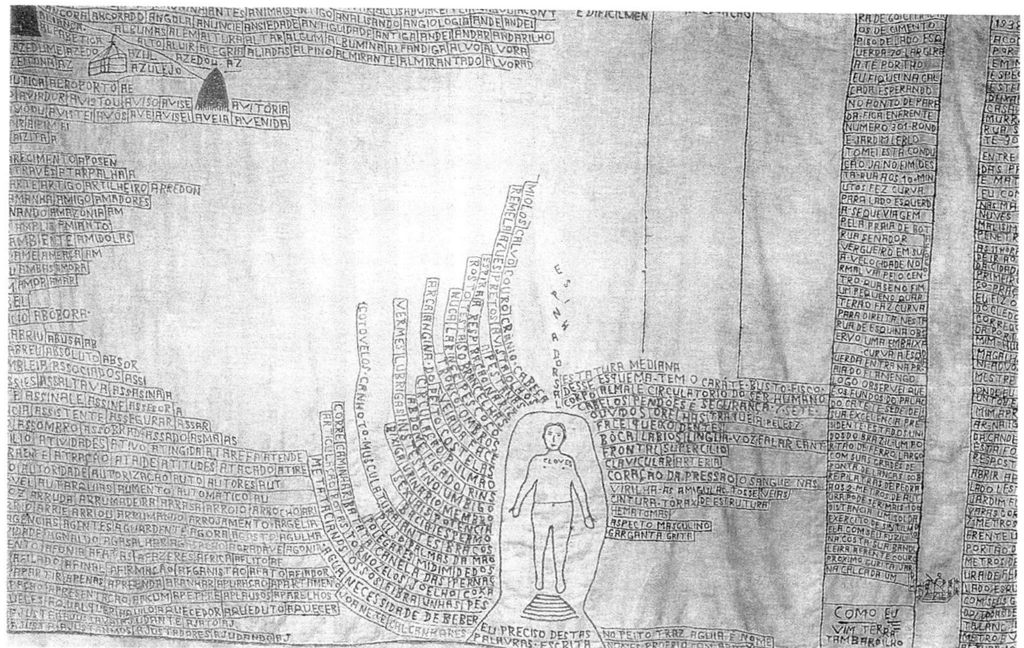

Arthur Bispo do Rosario, I NEED THESE WORDS. WRITTEN, n/d, wood, cloth, metal, thread and plastic; 120 x 189 cm. Courtesy of Museu Bispo do Rosario Arte Contemporânea, Prefeitura da Cidade do Rio de Janeiro.

Loaf mountain in Rio de Janeiro and a very, very small drawing of a guardian at the right bottom of the surface are the only embroidered drawings on this side of the panel. All the rest are words and lines; on the extreme left a list of around 300 words beginning with letter "A," and on the right side two columns with complete or semi-complete sentences, composing a narrative of fragmented episodes lived by him. In this embroidery, letters also become forms; the alphabet, tiny geometrical matter; phrases, lines to be bent according to the writer-sculptor-embroiderer's necessities. Sentences flexible enough to be curved, grammatically raw enough to be torqued. Being called by Arthur Bispo do Rosario.

Words are everywhere, like vermin, always there, outside of the auratic shield but in the heart of this linguistic body and at its base; the body of a boxer schizo sailorman – a nomad in fact (a traveler) and in mind (a traveler), an archetypal storyteller. A man that does not forget and cannot remember. A man whose words unite to form an order to leave nothing outside itself. A man in a world of history and language, steeped in processes of linguistic representation and voices, of writing with needles and listening commands, of historiophonics, as if nothing could escape from him. Bispo represents every-thing-that-exists-in-the-world following a mixed impulse of retention and liberation characterized by a compulsive process of organization. A body of language – light enough to float. An empty body – its insides became language. The transmuted thick hospital sheet suggests that body and language are made by the same substance, that language is also fleshy and constitutive of bodies, that bodies are also immaterial and vibratory and constitute language, that words can be representational entities capable of materializing the signified as much as bodies can be made of language. A fleshy body that is also voices, listenings, storytelling, history, and written words. He *needed* to materialize language into embroidered-piercing-writing, he *needed* to see and to touch the voiced world. He needed these words. Written. And I listen to Merleau-Ponty's voice: "The word and speech must somehow cease to be a way of designating things or thoughts, and become the presence of that thought in the phenomenal world, and, moreover, not its clothing but its token or its body."[29]

The sense of precariousness so determinant in Bispo's work, as well as in the performative historical approach that is being claimed here, is very much related to the city where "the archive of the human world" was produced, the city where I was born and grew up. Lygia Clark, a contemporary of Bispo do Rosario, who also created the major part of her work in Rio de Janeiro but possibly never heard about Bispo's apparition, convokes: "We propose the precarious as a new concept of existence against any form of static crystallization in duration."[30] Works and words such as those of Lygia Clark and Bispo do Rosario offer the possibility to conceptualize precariousness as potency rather than mere debility, to identify precariousness' temporal vibration, political vigor, aesthetic potency, and philosophical energy. They also offer the possibility to dislocate performance studies discourses, predominantly dominated by European and North American cultural values, academic environments, and political contexts, offering new references to reframe and recreate the debate.[31]

My interest in the theoretical verve embedded in the notion of precariousness derives from the ways it differs from, as well as adds to, the notion of "ephemerality" (the term frequently applied to conceptualize the temporal aspect of performance). If the ephemeral is transient, momentary, brief (the opposite of what is permanent), the precarious is unstable, risky, dangerous (the opposite of what is secure, stable, and safe). If the ephemeral is diaphanous, the precarious is shaky. If "ephemerality" denotes disappearance and absence (thus, predicating that at a certain moment, something was fully given to view), "precariousness" denotes the incompleteness of every apparition as its corporeal, moving, constitutive condition. If the ephemeral can open spaces of melancholy, the precarious' materiality and emergency violently innervates. If the ephemeral rehearses death, precariousness lives life. If the ephemeral refers to the non-lasting, the precarious discovers that "what is under construction is already a ruin."[32] If the ephemeral leaves traces, the precarious is by itself a remainder and leaves what it is. The precarious does not exactly announce or resemble its disappearance, it performs the latency of past and future as presence. It simply appears.

Notes

1. Quoted by Georg G. Iggers in *Historiography in the Twentieth Century*, Middletown, Connecticut: Wesleyan University Press, 1997, p. 119, from Hayden White, "Historical Texts as Literary Artifact," in *Tropics of Discourse*, Baltimore: John Hopkins University Press, 1978, p. 82.
2. David Carr, *Time, Narrative, and History*, Indianapolis: Indiana University Press, 1986, p. 4.
3. Ibid.
4. Victor Turner articulates an elucidative etymology for the word "experience":

   > Scholars like Julius Pokorny trace "experience" right back to hypothetical Indo-European base or root **per-*, "to attempt, venture, risk" whence the Greek *peira*, "experience," the source of our word "empirical." It is also the verbal root from which derives the Germanic **feraz*, giving rise to Old English *faer*, "danger, sudden calamity," whence Modern English "fear." [...] But more directly "experience" derives via Middle English and Old French, from the Latin *experientia*, denoting "trial, proof, experiment," itself generated from *experiens*, the present participle of *experiri*, "to try, test," from *ex-*, "out"+ base *per* as in *peritus*, "experienced," "having learned by trying." The suffixed extended form of **per-* is **peri-tlo*, whence the Latin *periclum*, *periculum*, "trial, danger, peril." Once more we see experience linked with risk, straining towards "drama," crisis, rather than bland cognitive learning! [...] If we put these various senses together we have a "laminated" semantic system focused on "experience," which portrays it as a journey, a test (of self, of suppositions about others), a ritual passage, an exposure to peril or risk, a source of fear.

   According to this etymological approach, experience is a mode of relationality obviously not related to a distancing cognitive process but to personal and psychophysical engagement. *From Ritual to Theater*, New York: PAJ Publications, 1982, pp. 17–18.
5. Walter Benjamin, *Illuminations*, New York: Schocken Books, 1968, p. 84.
6. Ibid., pp. 83–4.
7. Paul Schimmel (ed.), *Out of Actions: Between Performance and the Object 1949–1979*, Los Angeles: Thames and Hudson, The Museum of Contemporary Art, 1998, p. 11.
8. Ibid., p. 17.
9. Benjamin, op. cit., p. 87.
10. The inspiration for this word choice comes from Gilles Deleuze and Félix Guattari, "How to Create for Yourself a Body Without Organs?" in *A Thousand Plateaus*, Minneapolis: University of Minnesota Press, 1987, p. 151, where they propose that the "program" is the motor of experimentation.
11. Leopold von Ranke cited by Iggers, op. cit., p. 2.
12. Walter Benjamin, *The Arcades Project*, Cambridge and London: Harvard University Press, 1999, p. 463.
13. Gilles Deleuze commenting on Stoicism in *Difference and Repetition*, New York: Columbia University Press, 1994, p. 77.
14. See Gilles Deleuze's comment on the Bergsonian idea that "each present present is only the entire past in its most contracted state." Ibid., p. 82.
15. Michel De Certeau, *The Writing of History*, New York: Columbia University Press, 1988, p. 2.
16. Benjamin, *Arcades Project*, p. 456.
17. Michel Foucault, "Nietzsche, Genealogy, History," in Paul Rabinow (ed.), *The Foucault Reader*, New York: Pantheon, 1984, p. 88.

18. Maurice Merleau-Ponty, *The Visible and the Invisible*, Evanston: Northwestern University Press, 1964, p. 138.
19. Ibid., p. 139.
20. *Hélio Oiticica*, GAM – Galeria de Arte Moderna, Rio de Janeiro, 1968, pp. 26–7.
21. "Manifesto Neo Concreto," facsimile Jornal do Brasil 22 March 1959. It is important to note that Lygia Clark and Hélio Oiticica are integral to any discussion of performance art/body art in Brazil and Latin America. See, for example, Guy Brett's "Life Strategies" in *Out of Actions: Between Performance and the Object 1949–1979*, Los Angeles: Thames and Hudson, The Museum of Contemporary Art, 1998, pp. 197–225.
22. For a thorough biography of Bispo do Rosario, see Luciana Hidalgo, *Arthur Bispo do Rosario: o Senhor do Labirinto*, Rio de Janeiro: Ed. Rocco, 1996.
23. Arthur Bispo do Rosario quoted by Waldir Barreto, *Arthur Bispo do Rosario*, Goiás: Museu de Arte Contemporânea de Goiás, 1999, p. 9.
24. Waldir Barreto, "A Contemporaneidade de um Extemporâneo," in *Ibid.*, p. 7.
25. Ricardo Aquino, "Arthur Bispo do Rosario: artista," in *Ordenação e Vertigem*, São Paulo: Centro Cultural Banco do Brasil, 2003, p. 76.
26. Allen S. Weiss, "Nostalgia for the Absolute: Obsession and Art Brut," in *Parallel Visions*, Los Angeles County Museum of Art: Princeton University Press, 1992, p. 281.
27. Excerpt from an interview with Hugo Denizart, in Hugo Denizart, Video: "O Prisioneiro da Passagem," Museu Bispo do Rosario Arte Contemporânea Archive, 1980.
28. Quote from Luciana Hidalgo's *Arthur Bispo do Rosario: o Senhor do Labirinto*, p. 25. Translation by the author. (I got similar information from interviews I did at Colônia Juliano Moreira with nurses, doctors, security guards, and patients, 2003.)
29. Maurice Merleau-Ponty, *Phenomenology of Perception*, London and New York: Routledge, 1962, p. 163.
30. See Lygia Clark's "Nós recusamos ..." (We refuse ...) in *Lygia Clark*, exh. cat., Barcelona: Fundació Antoni Tàpies, 1998, p. 211.
31. For more information on Clark and Bispo as well as on the relations between performative historiography, performance art, and body studies, see my PhD dissertation "Precarious, precarious, precarious: the works of Lygia Clark and Arthur Bipo do Rosario in Rio de Janeiro," New York University, 2006.
32. Verse from Caetano Veloso's song *Fora da Ordem* (Out of Order).

Chapter 7

Performance Remains

Rebecca Schneider

> The peculiar burden and problem of the theater is that there is *no original artwork at all.* Unless one maintains that the text is the art work (which repudiates the entire history of the theater), there seems no way of avoiding this difficult fact. Every other art has its original and its copies. Only music approximates the theatrical dilemma, but notation insures that each musical performance will at least come close to the composer's intention.
>
> Richard Schechner (1965)[1]

> Dance exists at a perpetual vanishing point. […] It is an event that disappears in the very act of materializing.
>
> Marcia Siegel (1968)[2]

> In theater, as in love, the subject is disappearance.
>
> Herbert Blau (1982)[3]

> Performance originals disappear as fast as they are made. No notation, no reconstruction, no film or videotape recording can keep them. […] One of the chief jobs challenging performance scholars is the making of a vocabulary and methodology that deal with performance in its immediacy and evanescence.
>
> Richard Schechner (1985)[4]

A revised version of Rebecca Schneider, "Performance Remains," *Performing Research,* 2001, vol. 6, no. 2, pp. 100–08. For the latest "re-do" of this essay, see Rebecca Schneider, *Performing Remains: Art and War in Times of Theatrical Reenactment,* New York: Routledge, 2011, pp. 87–110. This essay is altered somewhat from the original publication, modifications that bear the marks of the essay's promiscuous afterlife, including references to texts that post-date 2001.

> Performance cannot be saved, recorded, documented, or otherwise participate in the circulation of representations of representations: once it does so it becomes something other than performance. […] Performance […] becomes itself through disappearance.
>
> Peggy Phelan (1993)[5]

> We need a history that does not save in any sense of the word; we need a history that performs.
>
> Jane Blocker (1999)[6]

This chapter is about performance and the archive, or the positioning of performance in archival culture. It takes up the long-standing invitations of many in performance studies to consider performance "always at the vanishing point."[7] Taking up these invitations, I've set myself the following question: if we consider performance as "of" disappearance, if we think of the ephemeral as that which "vanishes," and if we think of performance as the antithesis of "saving,"[8] do we limit ourselves to an understanding of performance predetermined by a cultural habituation to the patrilineal, west-identified (arguably white-cultural) logic of the Archive?

Troubling Disappearance

The archive has long been habitual to western culture. We understand ourselves relative to the remains we accumulate, the tracks we house, mark, and cite, the material traces we acknowledge. Jacques Le Goff stated the western truism quite simply, noting that history, requiring remains, has been composed of documents because "the document is what remains." Even as the domain of the document has expanded to include "the spoken word, the image, and gesture," the fundamental relationship of remain to documentability remains intact.[9] But the "we" of this mode of history as remains is not necessarily universal. Rather, "archive culture" is appropriate to those who align historical knowledge with European traditions, or, even more precisely, those who chart a (mythic) descent from Greek Antiquity.[10] As Derrida reminds in *Archive Fever*, the word archive stems from the Greek and is linked at the root to the prerogatives of the archon, the head of state. Tucked inside the word itself is the house of he who was "considered to possess the right to make or to represent the law," and to uphold, as Michel Foucault has written, the "system of its enunciability."[11]In the theater the issue of remains as material document, and the issue of performance as documentable, becomes complicated – necessarily imbricated, chiasmically, with the live body. The theater, to the degree that it is composed in live performance, seems to resist remains. And yet, if live theater in the west is approached as that which refuses to remain, as performance studies scholars have quite fulsomely insisted, it is precisely in live art and live theater that scores of late twentieth- and early twenty-first century artists explore history – the recomposition of remains in and as the live.[12] If we consider performance as of disappearance, of an ephemerality read as vanishment and loss, are we limiting ourselves to an understanding of performance predetermined by our cultural habituation to the logic of the archive?

According to the logic of the archive, what is given to the archive is that which is recognized as constituting a remain, that which can have been documented or has become document. To the degree that performance is not its own document (as Schechner, Blau, and Phelan have argued), it is, constitutively, that which does not remain. As the logic goes, performance is so radically "in time" (with time considered linear) that it cannot reside in its material traces and therefore "disappears."

The definition of performance as that which disappears, which is continually lost in time, is a definition well suited to the concerns of art history and the curatorial pressure to understand performance in the museal context where performance appeared to challenge object status and seemed to refuse the archive its privileged "savable" original. Arguably even more than in the theater, it is in the context of the museum, gallery, and art market that performance appears to primarily offer disappearance. Particularly in the context of visual art, performance suggests a challenge to the "ocular hegemony" that, to quote Kobena Mercer, "assumes that the visual world can be rendered knowable before the omnipotent gaze of the eye and the 'I' of the Western cogito."[13] Thus there is a political promise in this equation of performance with disappearance: if performance can be understood as disappearing, perhaps performance can rupture the ocular hegemony Mercer cites. And yet, in privileging an understanding of performance as a refusal to remain, do we ignore other ways of knowing, other modes of remembering, that might be situated precisely in the ways in which performance remains, but remains differently? The ways, that is, that performance resists a cultural habituation to the ocular – a thrall that would delimit performance as that which cannot remain to be seen.

The predominant performance-studies-meets-art-history attitude toward performance as disappearance might overlook different ways of accessing history offered by performance. Too often, the equation of performance with disappearance reiterates performance as necessarily a matter of loss, even annihilation. Curator Paul Schimmel made this perspective clear in his essay "Leap into the Void," writing that the orientation toward "the act," which he historicizes as a post-World War II preoccupation, is an orientation toward destruction. "Although there are instances of lighthearted irreverence, joy, and laughter in this work, there is always an underlying darkness, informed by the recognition of humanity's seemingly relentless drive toward self-annihilation."[14] In his analysis, performance becomes itself a void. It may be a medium of creation, but a creation subservient to a disappearance understood as loss, "destruction," and "darkness."

If we adopt the equation that performance does not save, does not remain, and apply it to performance generally, to what degree can performance interrogate archival thinking? Is it not the case that it is precisely the logic of the archive that approaches performance as of disappearance? Asked another way, does an equation of performance with impermanence, destruction, and loss follow rather than disrupt a cultural habituation to the imperialism inherent in archival logic? A simple example may serve us well: on a panel at a Columbia University conference in 1997 on documentation, archivists Mary Edsall and Catherine Johnson bemoaned the problems of preserving performance, declaring that the practices of "body-to-body transmission," such as dance and gesture, mean that "you lose a lot of history."[15] Such statements assume that memory cannot be housed in a body and remain, and thus that oral storytelling, live recitation, repeated gesture, and ritual enactment are not practices of telling or writing history. Such practices disappear. By this logic, being housed always in the live, "body-to-body transmission" disappears, is lost, and thus is no transmission at all. Obviously, the language of disappearance here is hugely culturally myopic. Here, performance is given to be as antithetical to memory as it is to the archive.

Should we not think of the ways in which the archive depends upon performance, indeed ways in which the archive performs the equation of performance with disappearance, even as it performs the service of "saving"? It is in accord with archival logic that performance is given to disappear, and mimesis (always in a tangled and complicated relationship to the performative) is, in line with a long history of antitheatricality, debased if not downright feared as destructive of the pristine ideality of all things marked "original."[16]

Performing the Archive

> It is thus in [...] *domiciliation*, in [...] house arrest, that archives take place.
>
> Jacques Derrida[17]

If the twentieth-century was famous for, among other things, criticizing the concept of historical facticity, such criticism has not resulted in the end of our particular investments in the logic of the archive. Rather, we have broadened our range of documents to include that which we might have overlooked and included the stockpiling of recorded speech, image, gesture in the establishment of "oral archives" and the collection of "ethnotexts." The important recuperation of "lost histories" has gone on in the name of feminism, minoritarianism, and its compatriots. In light of this, what does it serve to remind ourselves that this privileging of site-able remains in the archive is linked, as is the root of the word archive, to the prerogatives of the archon, the head of state? In what way does the housing of memory in strictly material, quantifiable, domicilable remains lead both backward and forward to the principle of the archon, the patriarch? The Greek root of the word archive refers to the archon's house and, by extension, the architecture of a social memory linked to the law. The demand for a visible remain, at first a mnemonic mode of mapping for monument, would eventually become the architecture of a particular social power over memory.[18] Even if the earliest Greek archive housed mnemonics for performance rather than material originals themselves, archive logic in modernity came to value the document over event. That is, if ancient archives housed back-ups in case of the failure of localized knowledge, colonial archives participated in the failure of localized knowledge – that failure had become a given. The document, as an arm of empire, could arrest and disable local knowledges while simultaneously scripting memory as necessarily failed, as Ann Laura Stoller has amply illustrated. The archive became a mode of governance against memory.[19] The question becomes: does the logic of the archive, as that logic came to be central to modernity, in fact demand that performance disappear in favor of discrete remains – material presented as preserved, as non-theatrical, as "authentic," as "itself," as somehow non-mimetic?

In the archive, flesh is given to be that which slips away. According to archive logic, flesh can house no memory of bone. In the archive, only bone speaks memory of flesh. Flesh is blind spot.[20] Dissimulating and disappearing. Of course, this is a cultural equation, arguably foreign to those who claim orature, storytelling, visitation, improvisation, or embodied ritual practice as history. It is arguably foreign to practices in popular culture, such as the practices of US Civil War reenactors who consider performance as precisely a way of keeping memory alive, of making sure it does not disappear. In such practices – coded (like the body) primitive, popular, folk, naive – performance does remain, does leave "residue."[21] Indeed the place of residue is arguably flesh in a network of body-to-body transmission of affect and enactment – evidence, across generations, of impact.

In scholarly treatments, the question of the performance remains one of history, or more specifically history that remains in performance practice (versus written or object remains) generally falls under the rubric of memory versus history, and as such it is often labeled "mythic." Oral history also often falls under the rubric of ritual. In turn, "ritual" generally (or historically) has fallen under the rubric of "ethnic" – a term which generally means race- or class-marked people but which Le Goff cites as "primitive" or "peoples without writing."[22] Clearly, concatenations of primitivism and attendant racisms attach, in turn, to attempts to acknowledge performance as an appropriate means of remaining, of remembering. Is this perhaps because performance threatens the terms of captive or discrete remains dictated by the archive? Is this in part why the logic of the archive – that utopic "operational field of projected total knowledge" – scripts performance as disappearing?[23] Because oral history and its performance practices are always decidedly repeated, oral historical practices are always reconstructive, always incomplete, never in thrall to the singular or self-same origin that buttresses archontic lineage. In performance as memory, the pristine self-sameness of an "original," an artifact so valued by the archive, is rendered impossible – or, if you will, mythic.

Performance practice has been routinely disavowed as historical practice.[24] Though historiographers such as Pierre Nora claim that this attitude has shifted in favor of a "new" history that incorporates collective memory and performative practices, nevertheless that "new" history is manifested in the constitution of "radically new kinds of archives, of which the most characteristic are oral archives."[25] The oral is not here approached as already an archive, a performance-based archive. Rather, oral histories are constituted anew, recorded and "saved" through technology in the name of identicality and materiality. Though this "new" archiving is supposedly against loss, doesn't it institute more profoundly than anything the loss of a different approach to saving that is not invested in identicality? Doesn't it further undo an understanding of performance as remaining? Do not such practices buttress the phallocentric insistence of the ocularcentric assumption that if it is not visible, or given to documentation or sonic recording, or otherwise "houseable" within an archive, it is lost, disappeared?

It is interesting to take the example of battle reenactment into account and look at the particular case of Robert Lee Hodge – an avid Civil War enthusiast who participates in reenactments. As Marvin Carlson described him in an essay on theater and historical reenactment, Hodge has attained significant notoriety among reenactment communities for his "ability to fall to the ground and contort his body to simulate convincingly a bloated corpse."[26] The question is obvious: under what imaginable framework could we cite Hodge's actions as a viable mode of historical knowledge, or of remaining? Is Hodge's bloat not deeply problematic mimetic representation, and wildly bogus and indiscreet at that? Does Hodge, lying prone and fake-bloating in the sun, attempt to offer index of – as well as reference to – both the material photograph and the photographed material of Civil War corpses? Is the live bloater only offering a mimetic and perhaps even ludicrous copy of something only vaguely imagined as a bloated corpse? Yet, within the growing "living history" and reenactment movement, Hodge's bloating body is, for many enthusiasts, evidence of something that can touch the more distant historical record, if not evidence of something authentic itself.[27] In the often-ridiculed "popular" arena of reenactment, Hodge's bloat is a kind of affective remain – itself, in its performative repetition, a queer kind of evidence. If the living corpse is a remain of history, it is certainly revisited across a body that cannot pass as the corpse it recalls. If it cannot pass, what kind of claim to authenticity can such a faulty corpse demand?

I am reminded of Charles Ludlam's queer Theatre of the Ridiculous in which the replaying of classics or the "camp" reenactment of the folk art of "vulgar" commercial entertainment (such as B-movies) offers a different though perhaps related kind of "living history." Ludlam's parodic evenings offered a fractured re-entry of remainders – a history of identifications, of role-playing and its discontents. In Ludlam's theater, as Stefan Brecht described it in 1968,

> Removal of cadavers, necessitated by the high onstage death-rate, is done with exaggerated clumsiness, the corpse does not cooperate – but mostly the dead just sit up after a while, walk off, reparticipate in the action.[28]

When we approach performance not as that which disappears (as the archive expects), but as both the act of remaining and a means of re-appearance and "reparticipation" (though not a metaphysic of presence) we are almost immediately forced to admit that remains do not have to be isolated to the document, to the object, to bone versus flesh. Here the body – Hodge's bloated one – becomes a kind of archive and host to a collective memory that we might situate with Freud as symptomatic, with Cathy Caruth with Freud as the compulsory repetitions of a collective trauma, with Foucault with Nietzsche as "counter-memory," or with Fred Moten with Baraka, Minh-ha, and Derrida as transmutation.[29] The bodily, read through genealogies of impact and ricochet, is arguably always interactive. This body, given to performance, is here engaged with disappearance chiasmically – not only disappearing but resiliently eruptive, remaining through performance like so many ghosts at the door marked "disappeared." In this sense performance becomes itself through messy and eruptive re-appearance. It challenges, via the performative trace, any neat antimony between appearance and disappearance, or presence and absence through the basic repetitions that mark performance as indiscreet, non-original, relentlessly citational, and remaining.

Indeed, approached in this way, performance challenges loss. Still, we must be careful to avoid the habit of approaching performance remains as a metaphysic of presence that fetishizes a singular "present" moment. As theories of trauma and repetition might instruct us, it is not presence that appears in the syncopated time of citational performance but precisely (again) the missed encounter – the reverberations of the overlooked, the missed, the repressed, the seemingly forgotten. Performance does not disappear when approached from this perspective, though its remains are the immaterial of live, embodied acts. Rather, performance plays the "sedimented acts" and spectral meanings that haunt material in constant collective interaction, in constellation, in transmutation.

Death and Living Remains

Let us not too rapidly dispose of the issue of disappearance. If Schechner, Blau, Phelan, and others are correct and performance is given to become itself through disappearance – to resist document and record, to deny remains – we find ourselves in a bit of an awkward bind regarding the argument so far. In fact, Blau's work on this bind, particularly his *Take Up the Bodies: Theatre at the Vanishing Point,* has been particularly trenchant:

> Whatever the style, hieratic or realistic, texted or untexted – box it, mask it, deconstruct it as you will – the theater disappears under any circumstances; but with all the ubiquity of the adhesive dead, from Antigone's brother to Strindberg's Mummy to the burgeoning corpse of Ionesco's *Amedée,* it's there when we look again.[30]

Upon any second look, disappearance is not antithetical to remains. And indeed, it is one of the primary insights of poststructuralism that disappearance is that which marks all documents, all records, and all material remains. Indeed, remains become themselves through disappearance as well.

We might think of it this way: death appears to result in the paradoxical production of both disappearance and remains. Disappearance, that citational practice, that after-the-factness, clings to remains – absent flesh does ghost bones. We have already noted that the habit of the West is to privilege bones as index of a flesh that was once, being "once" (as in both time and singularity) only after the fact. Flesh itself, in our ongoing cultural habituation to sight-able remains, supposedly cannot remain to signify "once" (upon a time). Even twice won't fit the constancy of cell replacing cell that is our everyday. Flesh, that slippery feminine subcutaneousness, is the tyrannical and oily, invisible-inked signature of the living. Flesh of my flesh of my flesh repeats, even as flesh is that which the archive presumes does not remain.

As Derrida notes, the archive is built on the domiciliation of this flesh with its feminine capacity to reproduce. The archive is built on "house arrest" – the solidification of value in ontology as retroactively secured in document, object, record. This retroaction is nevertheless a valorization of regular, necessary loss on (performative) display – with the document, the object, and the record being situated as survivor of time. Thus we have become increasingly comfortable in saying that the archivable object also becomes itself through disappearance – as it becomes the trace of that which remains when performance (the artist's action) disappears. This is trace-logic emphasizing loss – a loss that the archive can regulate, maintain, institutionalize – while forgetting that it is a loss that the archive produces. In the archive, bones are given not only to speak the disappearance of flesh, but to script that flesh as disappearing by disavowing recurrence or by marking the body always already "scandal."

An instituted loss that spells the failure of the bodily to remain is rife with a "patriarchal principle." No one, Derrida notes, has shown more ably than Freud how the archival drive, which he labels as a "paternal and patriarchic principle," is both patriarchal and parricidic. The archival drive

> posited itself to repeat itself and returned to reposit itself only in parricide. It amounts to repressed or suppressed parricide, in the name of the father as dead father. The archontic is at best the takeover of the archive by the brothers. The equality and liberty of brothers. A certain, still vivacious idea of democracy.[31]

Ann Pellegrini has stated this Freudian schema succinctly: "[S]on fathers parent(s); pre-is heir to post-; and 'proper' gender identification and 'appropriate' object choices are secured backward" – a "retroaction of objects lost and subjects founded."[32]

Elsewhere I have discussed this parricidal impulse as productive of death in order to insure remains.[33] I have suggested that the increasing domain of remains in the West, the increased technologies of archiving, may be why the late twentieth-century has been both so enamored of performance and so replete with deaths: death of author, death of science, death of history, death of literature, death of character, death of the avant-garde, death of modernism, and even, in American playwright Suzan-Lori Parks' brilliant and ironic rendition, *Death of the Last Black Man in the Whole Entire World*.[34] Within a culture that privileges object remains as indices of and survivors of death, to produce such a panoply of deaths may be the only way to insure remains in the wake of modernity's crises of authority, identity, and object. Killing the author, or sacrificing his station, may be, ironically, the means of ensuring that he remains.

For the moment let me simply suggest that when we read this "securing backward" Pellegrini discusses, this "retroaction" of objects, we are reading the archive as act – as an architecture housing rituals of "domiciliation" or "house arrest" – continually, as ritual, performed. The archive itself becomes a social performance space, a theater of retroaction. The archive performs the institution of disappearance, with object remains as indices of disappearance and with performance as given to disappear. If, in Derrida's formation, it is in domiciliation, in "house arrest" that "archives take place" we are invited to think of this "taking place" as continual, of house arrest as performative – a performative, like a promise, that casts the retroaction of objects solidly into a future in which the patriarchic principle Derrida cites will have (retroactively) remained.

To read "history," then, as a set of sedimented acts that are not the historical acts themselves but the act of securing any incident backward – the repeated act of securing memory – is to rethink the site of history in ritual repetition. This is not to say that we have reached the "end of history," neither is it to say that past events didn't happen, nor that to access the past is impossible. It is rather to resituate the site of any knowing of history as body-to-body transmission. Whether that ritual repetition is the attendance to documents in the library (the physical acts of acquisition, the physical acts of reading, writing, educating), or the oral tales of family lineage (think of the African American descendents of Thomas Jefferson who didn't need the DNA test to tell them what they remembered through oral transmission), or the myriad traumatic reenactments engaged in both consciously and unconsciously, we refigure "history" onto bodies, the affective transmissions of showing and telling.[35] Architectures of access (the physical aspect of books, bookcases, glass display cases, or even the request desk at an archive) place us in particular experiential relations to knowledge. Those architectures also impact the knowledge imparted. Think of it this way: the same detail of information can sound, feel, look, smell, or taste radically different when accessed in radically different venues or via disparate media (or when not told in some venues but told in others). In line with this configuration performance is the mode of any architecture or environment of access (one performs a mode of access in the archive; one performs a mode of access at a theater; one performs a mode of access on the dance floor; one performs a mode of access on a battlefield). In this sense, too, performance does not disappear. In the archive, the performance of access is a ritual act that, by occlusion and inclusion, scripts the depreciation of (and registers as disappeared) other modes of access.

Remaining on the Stage

Artists such as Parks and Piper attempt to unpack a way in which performance (or action, or act) remains – but remains differently. Such works are interested in the ways in which history is not limited to the imperial domain of the document, or in which history is not "lost" through body-to-body transmission. Is this less an investigation of disappearance than an interest in the politics of dislocation and relocation? That idea that flesh memory might remain challenges conventional notions of the archive. By this reading, the scandal of performance relative to the archive is not that it disappears (this is what the archive expects, this is the archive's requirement), but that it remains in ways that resist archontic "house arrest" and "domiciliation."

To the degree that it remains, but remains differently or in difference, the past performed and made explicit as (live) performance can function as the kind of bodily transmission conventional archivists dread, a counter-memory – almost in the sense of an echo (as Parks's character Lucy in *The America Play* might call it). If echoes, or in the performance troupe Spiderwoman's words "rever-ber-berations," resound off of lived experience produced in performance, then we are challenged to think beyond the ways in which performance seems, according to our habituation to the archive, to disappear.[36] We are also and simultaneously encouraged to articulate the ways in which performance, less bound to the ocular, "sounds" (or begins again and again, as Stein would have it), differently, via itself as repetition – like a copy or perhaps more like a ritual – like an echo in the ears of a confidence keeper, an audience member, a witness.

Arguably, this sense of performance is imbricated in Phelan's phrasing – that performance "becomes itself through" disappearance. This phrasing is arguably different from an ontological claim of being (despite Phelan's stated drive to ontology), even different from an ontology of being under erasure. This phrasing rather invites us to think of performance as a medium in which disappearance negotiates, perhaps becomes, materiality. That is, disappearance is passed through. As is materiality.

Works in which the political manipulations of "disappearance" demand a material criticism – works such as Diana Taylor's *Disappearing Acts* or José Esteban Muñoz's "Ephemera as Evidence" – thus create a productive tension within performance studies orientations to (and sometime celebrations of) ephemerality.[37] It is in the midst of this tension (or this "pickle" as Parks might put it) that the notion of performance as disappearance crosses chiasmically with ritual – ritual, in which, through performance, we are asked, again, to (re) found ourselves – to find ourselves in repetition.

Pickling
[performance] is trying to find an equation
for time *saved* / saving time
but theater / experience / performing /
being / living etc. is all about
spending time. No equation or …?[38]

Notes

1. Richard Schechner, "Theatre Criticism," *The Tulane Drama Review*, 1965, vol. 9, no. 3, pp. 22, 24, emphasis in original.
2. Marcia B. Siegel, *At the Vanishing Point. A Critic Looks at Dance*, New York: Saturday Review Press, 1968, p. 1.
3. Herbert Blau, *Take Up The Bodies: Theater at the Vanishing Point*, Urbana, IL: University of Illinois Press, 1982, p. 94.
4. Richard Schechner, *Between Theatre and Anthropology*, Chicago: University of Chicago Press, 1985, p. 50.
5. Peggy Phelan, *Unmarked: The Politics of Performance*, New York: Routledge, 1993, p. 146.
6. Jane Blocker, *Where is Ana Mendieta: Identity, Performativity, and Exile*, Durham: Duke University Press, 1999, p. 134.
7. Herbert Blau, op. cit., p.28. The approach to performance as "an ephemeral event" has been a cornerstone to Performance Studies and has been evident as basic to performance theory since the 1960s, as evident in the epigraphs to this essay. Barbara Kirschenblatt-Gimblett, another longstanding member of and influential thinker in the field, employed the term "ephemeral" in 1998 claiming that: "The ephemeral encompasses all forms of behavior – everyday activities, story telling, ritual, dance, speech, performance of all kinds." Barbara Kirshenblatt-Gimblett, *Destination Culture: Tourism, Museums, and Heritage,* Berkeley: University of California Press, 1998, p. 30. In an excellent 1996 essay, "Ephemera as Evidence: Introductory Notes to Queer Acts," Jose Esteban Muñoz turned the table on ephemerality to suggest that ephemera do not disappear, but are distinctly material. Muñoz relies on Raymond William's "structures of feeling" to argue that the ephemeral -"traces, glimmers, residues, and specks of things" – is a "mode" of "proofing" employed by necessity (and sometimes preference) by minoritarian culture and criticism makers. José Esteban Muñoz, "Ephemera as Evidence: Introductory Notes to Queer Acts," *Women and Performance: A Journal of Feminist Theory,* 1996, vol. 8, no. 2, pp. 5–16, this quote p. 10. See also Diana Taylor, *The Archive and the Repertoire*, Durham: Duke University Press, 2003.
8. Building explicitly on Phelan's work, Jane Blocker has employed the equation of performance with disappearance to suggest that performance is the antithesis of "saving" (op. cit., p. 134). See also Blocker's important complication of this position in her subsequent book, *What the Body Cost: Desire, History and Performance*, Minneapolis: University of Minnesota Press, 2004, in which she engages (pp. 105-7) with this essay as it appeared in *Performance Research*, op cit.
9. Jacques Le Goff, *History and Memory*, New York: Columbia University, 1991, p. xvii.
10. See Richard Thomas, *The Imperial Archive: Knowledge and the Fantasy of Empire*, New York: Verso, 1993. The articulation of Greek antiquity as fore-fathering history itself is mythic. The "disremembering" of other lineages ultimately served Eurocentric, geopolitical, racializing agendas. See Martin Bernal, *Black Athena*, New Brunswick, NJ: Rutgers University Press, 1989.
11. Jacques Derrida, *Archive Fever: A Freudian Impression*, Chicago, IL: University of Chicago Press, 1995, p. 2. In the late 1960s, reaching English readers in the early 1970s, Michel Foucault had expanded the notion of "the archive" beyond a material, architectural housing of documents and objects to include, more broadly, structures of enunciability. Foucault articulated "the archive" as essentially discursive – invested of an investment in preservation – determining not only the "system of enunciability" (what can be said) but also the duration of any enunciation (what is given to remain becomes what can have been said). An excerpt from Foucault's *The Archaeology of Knowledge* bears repeating: "The archive is first the law of what can be said, the system that

governs the appearance of statements as unique events. But the archive is also that which determines that all these things said do not accumulate endlessly in an amorphous mass, nor are they inscribed in an unbroken linearity, nor do they disappear at the mercy of chance external accidents; but they are grouped together in distinct figures [. . .] The archive is not that which, despite its immediate escape, safeguards the event of the statement, and preserves, for future memories, its status as an escapee; it is that which, at the very root of the statement-event, and in that which embodies it, defines at the outset the *system of its enunciability.* Nor is the archive that which collects the dust of statements that have become inert once more, and which may make possible the miracle of their resurrection; it is that which defines the mode of occurrence of the statement-thing; it is *the system of its functioning*." In *The Archaeology of Knowledge,* translated by Alan Sheridan, London: Tavistock, 1972, p. 129, emphasis in original.

12. See, for example, Keith Piper's installation *Relocating the Remains* in Keith Piper, *Relocating the Remains*, London: Institute of International Visual Artists, 1997. The work of Suzan-Lori Parks is also exemplary: Suzan-Lori Parks, *The America Play: And Other Works*, New York: Theater Communications Group, 1995. See Harry Elam and Alice Rayner, "Unfinished Business: Reconfiguring History in Suzan-Lori Parks's *The Death of the Last Black Man in the Whole Entire World*," *Theatre Journal,* 1994, vol. 46 no. 4, p. 447–61.
13. Kobena Mercer, "Unburying the Disremembered," in *New Histories*, Boston: Institute of Contemporary Art, 1996, p. 165.
14. Paul Schimmel, "Leap Into the Void: Performance and the Object," in *Out of Actions: Between Performance and the Object*, curated and edited by Paul Schimmel, Los Angeles: Museum of Contemporary Art, 1998, pp. 17-120, this quote p. 17.
15. Comments made at the panel "Documentation in the Absence of Text," during the conference "Performance and Text: Thinking and Doing," sponsored by the Department of Theatre Arts, Columbia University, New York, May 2–4, 1997.
16. See Jonas Barish, *The Antitheatrical Prejudice*, Berkeley: University of California Press, 1981; Samuel Weber, *Theatricality as Medium,* New York: Fordham University Press, 2004. That a distrust of mimesis should develop simultaneously with the development of archives in ancient Greece deserves greater analysis, especially given the fact that the first Greek archives did not house originals but seconds. The first archives were used to store legal documents that were not originals but official copies of text inscribed on stone monuments placed around the city. The documents were copies of stone markers that were themselves "mnemonic aids" – not, that is, the "thing" preserved. See Rosalind Thomas, *Literacy and Orality in Ancient Greece*, Cambridge: Cambridge University Press, 1992, pp. 86-7. Thus the first archived documents backed up a performance-oriented memory that was intended to be encountered live in the form of monuments, art, and architecture. On the classical art of memory as performance-oriented, see Francis Yates, *The Art of Memory,* Chicago, IL: University of Chicago Press, 1966, pp. 1–49.
17. Jacques Derrida, *op. cit.*, p. 2.
18. Jacques Derrida unpacks the meaning of the word archive thus: "The meaning of 'archive,' its only meaning, comes to it from the Greek *arkheion*: initially a house, a domicile, an address, the residence of the superior magistrates, the *archons*, those who commanded. The citizens who thus held and signified political power were considered to possess the right to make or to represent the law. On account of their publicly recognized authority, it is at their home, in that *place* which is their house (private house, family house, or employees' house), that official documents are filed." Ibid., p. 2. But ancient archival practice is more complicated than Derrida lets on. In ancient Greece the word archive was not used to refer to the housing of original documents (cf. James P. Sickinger, *Public Records and Archives in Classical Athens*, Chapel Hill: University of North

Carolina Press, 1999, p. 6). I have alluded to this briefly in the endnote above, but to complicate matters, the first official (though not the only) storeroom for documents in Ancient Greece was called the Metroon – the sanctuary of the Mother of the Gods. The Metroon was established in part to bring some order to official documents which had been scattered in the keeping of the magistrates.

19. See Ann Laura Stoller, "Colonial Archives and the Arts of Governance," *Archival Science*, 2002, vol. 2, nos. 1&2, pp. 87–109; and her *Along the Archival Grain: Epistemic Anxieties and Colonial Common Sense*, Princeton, NJ: Princeton University Press, 2009. See also Richard Thomas, *Imperial Archive*, op. cit.
20. Psychoanalysis certainly posits flesh as archive, but an inchoate and unknowing archive. Is it a given in all circumstances that body memory is "unknowing" and "blind"? See Rebecca Schneider, "Judith Butler in My Hands," in *Bodily Citations: Religion and Judith Butler*, edited by Ellen Armour and Susan St. Ville, New York: Columbia University Press, 2006, pp. 225–251.
21. In his influential book *Orality and Literacy: The Technologizing of the Word*, Walter Ong makes the claim that because they are performance based, oral traditions do not leave "residue," make no "deposit," do not remain. Arguably, this claim is debunked by his own insistence that many habits from oral culture persist (Walter Ong, *Orality and Literacy: The Technologizing of the Word*, New York: Routledge, 1998, p. 11). On the issue of body memory in general see Paul Connerton, *How Societies Remember*, Cambridge: Cambridge University Press, 1989. Connerton surprisingly situates bodily memory as extremely fixed and unchanging. This aspect is critiqued by Neil Jarman in *Material Conflicts: Parades and Visual Displays in Northern Ireland*, Oxford: Berg Publishers, 1997, p. 11.
22. Le Goff's work provides an example of the troubled leap from oral history to ritual to ethnicity and from ethnicity to "peoples without writing." Le Goff, op. cit., p. 55.
23. Richard Thomas, op. cit., p. 11.
24. Cultural historians now accept popular and aesthetic representation generally as social modes of historicization, often under Maurice Halbwachs's rubric "collective memory" (cf. Halbwachs, *On Collective Memory*, Chicago, IL: University of Chicago Press). Still, the process of approaching aesthetic production as valid historiography involves careful (and debated) delineation between "memory," "myth," "ritual," and "tradition" on the one hand and the implicitly more legitimate (or supposedly non-mythic) "history" on the other (cf. Michael Kammen, *Mystic Chords of Memory: The Transformation of Tradition in American Culture*, New York: Vintage Books, 1993, pp. 25–32).
25. Le Goff, op. cit., pp. 95–6.
26. Marvin Carlson, "Performing the Past: Living History and Cultural Memory" *Paragrana* 2000, vol. 9, no. 2, 237–48; see also Tony Horwitz, *Confederates in the Attic: Dispatches from the Unfinished Civil War*, New York: Vintage, 1999, pp. 7-8.
27. See Vanessa Agnew on the myriad problems that arise for historians who attempt to credit live reenactment as any kind of access to history or any kind of complement to the historical record. Agnew accuses reenactment of "theatre." She rather reductively associates theater with one of its historical modes—romantic sentimentalism—rather than, say, associating theater with Brechtian alienated historicization. Agnew's primary critique of living history and reenactment is that the focus on reenactors' experiences sentimentalizes and subjectivizes history. Vanessa Agnew, "Introduction: What is Reenactment?" *Criticism* 2004, vol. 46, no. 3, p. 335. But the case of the corpse is problematic. For, at least as described by Horwitz, op. cit., pp. 7–8, Hodge is not naive enough to think that he fully experiences what it means to be a corpse, even if it is true that his (mock) fallen body may (mock) alarm other (mock) soldiers who come upon it on the (mock) battlefield.

28. Stephan Brecht, "Family of the f.p.: Notes on the Theatre of the Ridiculous," *The Drama Review*, 1968, vol. 13, no. 1, pp. 117–141, this quote p. 120.
29. See Fred Moten and Charles Henry Rowell, "'Words Don't Go There': An Interview with Fred Moten," *Callaloo,* 2004, vol. 27, no. 4, pp. 954–966.
30. Herbert Blau, op. cit., p. 137.
31. Derrida, op. cit., p. 95.
32. Ann Pellegrini, *Performance Anxieties: Staging Psychoanalysis, Staging Race*, New York: Routledge 1997, p. 69.
33. See Rebecca Schneider, "Hello Dolly Well Hello Dolly: The Double and Its Theater," in *Psychoanalysis and Performance*, Patrick Campbell and Adrian Kear (eds.), London: Routledge, 2001.
34. Parks, op. cit.
35. See Tavia Nyong'o, *The Amalgamation Waltz: Race, Performance, and the Ruses of Memory,* Minneapolis: University of Minnesota Press, 2009, pp. 152–3, for engagement with oral history and "official" history in the example of Jefferson's descendents and the "hidden in plain sight" theory of quilting patterns. Nyong'o, reminding us fulsomely throughout his book of the race politics always sedimented in debates about history and memory, writes that "at issue was less a choice between the archive and memory and more a context over black representative space in memory [...] less a competition between 'elite' and 'folk' knowledge and more of a competition between academic and mass culture over the pedagogic stakes of remembrance" (p. 153). Nyong'o's comments of the generative aspects of "myth," "error," and "mistake," and the palimpsest of racial politics that inform the stakes in mistake, are extremely useful as well.
36. See my chapter "Seeing the Big Show," in Schneider, *The Explicit Body in Performance,* New York: Routledge, 1997, pp. 152–175.
37. See Taylor, *Disappearing Acts: Spectacles of Gender and Nationalism in Argentina's "Dirty War,"* Durham, NC: Duke University Press, 1997, and Muñoz, "Ephemera as Evidence," op. cit.
38. Parks, op. cit., p. 13.

Chapter 8

Not as Before, But Simply: Again

André Lepecki

Part One: Scripting

> First Kaprow explained what he wanted and gave each performer copies of the script material.
>
> Michael Kirby[1]

> Room 2, Set 1, Person 1, Movement 28, 2": extend foot ~~again~~ as before and at same time raise right hand to chin and support elbow with left hand; all lines rigid.
>
> Allan Kaprow[2]

In her essay on Allan Kaprow's relation to photography, Judith Rodenbeck notes how, "the problematic of the writerly script had been introduced [by Kaprow] in *18 Happenings in 6 Parts*."[3] In order to write this account of how I approached the 2006 and 2007 authorized redoings of Allan Kaprow's *18 Happenings in 6 Parts* (first commissioned by Haus der Künst, Munich and later presented during PERFORMA 07, NYC), I would like to start by focusing on this "script problematic." Not only because this problematic was at the center of my dramaturgical approach to the redoing, but because I feel "the problematic of the writerly script" at large brings about some important theoretical consequences for current debates on re-enacting performance – particularly on the issues articulated in the epigraphs above: the author as the writer of a meticulous will; and the performer as reader and recipient of an extremely detailed, deeply performative, and intentionally imperative writerly script.

It has been noted by Rodenbeck, but also by Jeff Kelley and others, that Kaprow's deep investment in writerly scripts aligned his work from the late 1950s till the mid 1960s with a whole tradition of American poetry – most notably (for Rodenbeck) with the objectivist poetry of Williams Carlos Williams[4] and (for Kelley) with the "whitmanesque cadence of the writing and its thumping Beat undertones."[5] Moreover, the clear links between poetry, scripting, sculpting, and performing in Kaprow's work already announce soon to follow developments in conceptual art's relationship to language – developments already present in the sculpturally resonant poetic scores of the early 1960s by Kaprow's friend George Brecht, and further explored in the 1970s by other artists, such as Vito Acconci, interested in experimenting with fusing the performativity of the written script with the sculptural poetics of live performance.

What I find striking in the way Kaprow approached this "problematic of the writerly script" during the creation of *18 Happenings in 6 Parts* in the summer and early winter of 1959 is how he found a mode of scripting that aligned his work less with what would soon be conceptual art's investment in language, than with what can only be called a *choreographic* concern with rigorously transmitting intentionality and form. Simply put, choreography can be said to be a writerly device that facilitates the transmission of rigorous, formal, clear, and imperative instructions to performers willing to execute faithfully an author's will. Indeed, as emphasized by Michael Kirby in his seminal description of *18 Happenings in 6 Parts*,[6] as commented even more emphatically by Jeff Kelley in his account of the piece,[7] and as remarked by Kaprow himself,[8] one of Kaprow's main concerns while creating *18 Happenings in 6 Parts* was to secure the faithful execution of a formal composition in time and space carried out by moving bodies. All testify that Kaprow's decision to write scores (along with the intriguing appearance of the figure of "the dancer" in some of his unperformed scores of 1959) coincided with his disappointment with earlier attempts to get participants in his events to take his proposed actions seriously. Describing Kaprow's frustration with a failed event the summer before he started working on *18 Happenings in 6 Parts* – the proto-happening *Pastorale* (1958) created at George Segal's farm – Kelley writes:

> Some [participants] were against the idea of the restrained, deliberate actions envisioned by Kaprow, committed as they were to spontaneity and emotional expressiveness in painting. Besides, it was a hot day and they had all drunk plenty of beer; *veering irreverently from the script was inevitable*. One artist called Kaprow a "fascist" for attempting to direct his participants.[9]

Kaprow himself commented on the *Pastorale* fiasco: "And other people were making out in the chicken coops and not really dedicated. [...] It never stopped being a party. It was never clearly what *I had intended*."[10] Kaprow's solution to have people perform what he had intended was (1) to adopt a mode of transmission where a clear score would lead to a clear expression of his intent; and (2) to work with performers willing to rigorously follow and execute the author's will.

Ironically (but rather tellingly), while trying to create simultaneously a compositional device and an authorial/authoritative mode of transmission for a groundbreaking, avant-garde piece, Kaprow unknowingly arrived at the same solution used by seventeenth-century French dance masters. In other words, when the "problematic of the writerly script" aligns with the need for "telling the performers what he *wanted*" (Kirby), the result is strikingly similar to

> the procedure detailed by a text from the Hardouin-Médor archive in Caen: the city's dancing masters are shut up in a room with paper, writing desk, "mathematics case, etc.," as if for a written examination; they compose [on paper] choreographies for balls or ballets [...]; only afterwards comes the practical test, or "execution."[11]

And this reclusion into a private space in order to create movement on paper is exactly what Kaprow did in the summer of 1959, as he meticulously wrote down movements in the form of (very personal) dance notations based on stick-figures accompanied by time counts and often by verbal descriptions of the actions: "Room 3, Set 3, Person one: at buzzer walks down corridor after other four persons have preceded you. Pause at entrance for count of 3, walk behind partition, turn at far side of room and stand facing audience. Count to 65 and recite." Kaprow's methodology of setting down on paper a choreographically precise distribution of actions, steps, sounds, and words, *even before there were any performers involved in the process, even before there were any rehearsals*, made it possible for him to conceive and then dispatch these parts to (near and far) future activations – while ensuring that these parts could keep their rigorous formal integrity.[12] Contrary to contemporary perceptions, the first Happening[13] was not an occasion for one to freely express oneself – rather, it was a carefully calibrated spatial and temporal frame to experiment with the transmission of intentionality from a formal script into a formal event, and thus to occasion Kaprow's sculptural approach to action in live performance, as well as his performative approach to sculpture as a multisensorial, synesthetic, and deeply social event.

Thus, during the summer of 1959, one year after the infelicitous *Pastorale*, Kaprow "got on a bus each weekday morning and went to work at the gallery"[14] – a rented loft on the third floor of 61, 4th Avenue, NYC, the first location of the soon to be famous Reuben Gallery. Kaprow spent that summer engaged in two peculiar activities for a painter and a sculptor: creating a complex and groundbreaking electronic music composition on tape[15] and generating a huge amount of all kinds of writerly stuff. On the creation of the electronic music tapes, Robert Watts would reminisce, years later in a conversation with Kaprow:

> It was really crazy. The summer before, 1958, Allan was welding some pieces and covering them with cement and tar. The transition from one summer to the next was fantastic. You had a welding set [...] and the next summer you were doing tapes.[16]

He had moved from tar to tape in one year; from drying cement to moving bodies; from paint to sound – but also, as we saw, from participants making out and drinking beer while "veering irreverently from the script" in 1958 to performers sticking rigorously to a script in 1959. Uniting it all was Kaprow's desire for conveying form to live performance – a kind of social sculpture but not quite; a kind of theater of images but not quite; a kind of dance piece, but not quite; a kind of Fluxus opera but not quite; a kind of ritual but not quite; a kind of painting but not quite; a kind of comedy but not quite.

Kaprow's copious work on paper produced throughout that summer and early fall of 1959, and consulted for the redoings of 2006 and 2007, amounts to hundreds of different formatted manuscript sheets. Reading them, it becomes clear that Kaprow used paper as his privileged rehearsal platform, room, or studio. One could even say that a significant part of those eighteen happenings take place only on paper; they belong exclusively to paper: words, and drawings and sketches performing away on dozens upon dozens of pages. On paper, *18 Happenings in 6 Parts* is a dynamic, truly rhizomatic collection of virtual ideas, beautiful poems, impossible actions, architectural dreams, sharp short manifestos on art, music, and theater, hilariously self-aggrandizing narratives, hilariously self-deprecating narratives, brilliantly compact theoretical texts, insightful quasi-ethnographic snapshots of quotidian expressions, acute diagnostics on urban life, and heartbreaking confessions of the artist before the huge challenges posed by the project. They have little to do with the inertia of a dead register. They are in themselves fully dynamic, fully kinetic in their very concrete virtuality.

These papers include: idiosyncratic choreographic notations, many different floor plans, doodles, quickly scribbled budgets, letters for possible financial support, crossed over performance ideas, stream of consciousness poems, silly poems, visual poems, small manifestos, third person descriptions of a yet-to-open and yet-to-be-titled performance, sketches for human-size puppets, grid analysis of the human face in which Kaprow detailed several types of muscle contractions and extensions involved in different kinds of laughter (for instance how "ah!" is distinct from "ha!"), jotted down loose phrases caught from the street, technical inquiries to sound engineers at Columbia University, ideas for a "theater piece," philosophical meditations on time and art, transcriptions of poems by Apollinaire, Mallarmé, Ezra Pound (among other poets), design ideas for small cards and odd costumes that were not used in the event. All this paper stuff being produced by, through, and because of writing and drawing was aimed at the piece opening in October 1959 (even though only a fraction of them were scores that could be performed, or texts that ended up in the piece), which would inaugurate the Reuben Gallery and mark a crucial turn in Kaprow's career, in the history of twentieth-century performance, and in the irreversible performative turn in the visual arts since then. As mentioned, not all scores, notes, and ideas were actualized, or were supposed to be performed – but all of them, together, create a deep resonance, a mood that sets up the atmosphere, pace, and ground for *18 Happenings in 6 Parts*.

A final point regarding the redoing of a piece from its archived papers: even though the production of paper stuff (and the electronic tapes) preceded, propelled, shaped, and guided the yet-to-exist performance, even though all this scribbling, notating, scoring, drawing, transcribing, doodling, and choreographing both enveloped and grounded, formed and then activated the live actualization of *18 Happenings in 6 Parts*, the fact remains that paper is always somehow perceived as a secondary, distant para-phenomenon of a much more *real* "original" – the live event, the "happening," which enjoys a kind of supremacy (or truth value) in relation to writing, scripting, drawing, scribbling. But, as I suggested earlier, those hundreds of pages, those hours of working with pen and pencil in hand, of inventing and planning on paper, were nothing other than a necessary and unavoidable *rehearsal* – and here I agree fully with Kelley, when he notes that in "Kaprow's fluid but matter-of-fact hand, [...] *image-phrases* weigh upon the page with a prosaic (today we might say low-tech) physicality."[17] It is this physicality on paper, this synaesthesia that impresses Kaprow's readers, even today. It also leads to the odd reciprocity between page and performance in Kaprow's scripts, as noted by Kelley: image-phrases create surprising effects. It is as if we find in Kaprow's use of paper already the discovery of a powerful "multimedia," as Kelley implies: "In performance, *as on the page itself*, the sounds made by the instruments and the associations with life that they inevitably produce spill over the strict parameters of the score."[18]

It is striking how this passage describing Kaprow's mode of operating on paper echoes Jacques Derrida's writings in the late 1990s on paper as multimedia: "[P]aper is the support not only for marks but for a complex 'operation' – spatial and temporal; visible, tangible, and often sonorous," which means, for Derrida, that paper's "economy has always been more than that of a medium [...] but also, paradoxically [...] that of multimedia."[19] We can now say that in *18 Happenings in 6 Parts*, the "problematic of the writerly script" derives from its multimedial economy, from its choreographic performativity, and from its authorial/authoritative function, all of which Kaprow's hand and poetics activate (curiously at a time when he, Robert Watts, and George Brecht were actively proposing the term multimedia, as in a 1958 proposal for the Carnegie Foundation[20]). This paper economy (or paper-machine) is precisely what allows future possibilities for reactivating Kaprow's scores not as dead remainders, or crumbling, melancholic "descriptions" of a live event to which they only have a faint relation, but as fully active forces already and forever secreting the possibility of their own redoing, not as before, but simply: again.

Part Two: Activation/Actualization/Again

> The movements scored on paper have much the same feel. They are represented by stick figures very similar to those in the paintings. Kaprow's hand jumps forward not as a mark maker, but as a gatherer, paster, arranger, and composer. In retrospect, his painted stick figures seem like diagrams waiting for the matter-of-fact avant-garde choreography they foreshadow.
>
> Jeff Kelley[21]

Kelley's observation, which I first read months after the last performance of the redoing of *18 Happenings in 6 Parts* for PERFORMA 07 was long over, begs the question: how does one activate waiting diagrams on paper? In practical terms, in strict performative terms, the decision for activation demanded finding a way for Kaprow's papers to escape the law that condemns them to remain fixed as passive representatives of a supposedly irretrievable original performance and bearer of exclusive rights to action and motion. Here, I am simultaneously agreeing with and reversing Judith F. Rodenbeck's observation when she writes (in relation to Kaprow) that "any examination of ephemeral works is necessarily conditioned by the artifacts remaining – photographs, scripts, anecdotes; such apparently secondary texts bear uneasy witness to crucial aspects of the works they describe."[22] If I agree that it is *crucial* to note that these remaining texts are only *apparently* secondary, I emphatically disagree that in the case of *18 Happenings in 6 Parts* (as with much of Kaprow's later happenings and activities of the 1960s), these paper "artifacts," these scripts and texts and notes "bear witness" only, just as I would say that they do not really describe a work. It is only after the actualization of the scores that we can say that Kaprow's notes *describe* the piece; rather, their anteriority is ontologically prescriptive. In the case of *18 Happenings in 6 Parts*, papers are *primary agents* of a work that they do not witness, nor describe, but that they *produce, ground, prescribe, pre-arrange, create* and *launch*, on and from and because of paper.

In other words, between the original performance and the original texts the question is one of determining what is being quoted by what? Is the script quoting (describing) a performance? Or is the live performance quoting (actualizing) the script? Solving this problem of quotation (which, along with the problem of translation is a general problem for any re-enactment or redoing) allows for a reconsideration of what it means to reactivate scores almost fifty years after their first actualization. Jacques Derrida (whose dislike of happenings was notoriously voiced in his essay on Artaud[23]) once wrote that quotation marks have a law: "to stand guard" over the word. He also noted that whenever we remove these diacritical guards a surprising result ensues: the unleashing of spirit.[24] So, if one gets rid of these guards, of the law of quotation marks, by removing the question of what quotes what (the script, the performance) can one find in the scripts a less guarded force?[25] For all of those who (willingly or unwillingly) participate in this odd operation (maybe the right name for it is a *séance*), the only mode is to let spirit enter. What spirit? The spirit of the letter. This leads us to a crucial question for re-enactments in general (or for redoings in particular): the (legal and aesthetic) question of an author's will in regard to the spirit of his or her letter. For, once this spirit of the letter enters, it soon starts to play its tricks, dance its autonomy, and enact its originality or singularity. I would claim that this dance and unguarded play does not follow the logic governing a re-enactment – but one governing a redoing. There is a fundamental difference between re-enacting (understood as performing as before) and doing again (understood as unleashing the stored energy of a diagram-in-waiting into an act, *not as before*, but *once again*).

The only problem is that it is not that easy to stand face to face with a spirit. In the end, as Derrida warns us, "a kind of delegation" still has to take place.[26] Such delegation was performed by Kaprow in 1959, the moment he finally handed the scripts to his performers "two weeks before the first performance,"[27] "in the final week,"[28] or "several months,"[29] and again in 2006, when Kaprow finally delegated someone to direct (again) *18 Happenings in 6 Parts* based on his 1959 scores, for the *Kaprow Exhibition* at Haus der Künst, Munich. I really want to make clear at this point – because this guided in a very practical way the whole directorial and dramaturgical and curatorial approach to the redoing, to the scores, to the paper stuff – the mechanism of such a delegation. It works as follows: from the moment paper crosses hands, from the author's hands to the performers'; from the author's hands to the assigned director's; from the archive's grips to all future directors', it is paper itself that is delegated with authorial authority. The act of transmission confers power not to the recipient of the authorial scripts (he or she will not be a proxy for the author), but *confers authority to the scripts themselves.* It is now the writerly script that takes over the reigns of the performance – with total intentional sovereignty. This is the ultimate problematic of the writerly script: paper takes command – like a living will. This insight was a major directive in my approach to the redoing – the scripts, the papers, the spirit of Kaprow's letter were in command.

Part Three: Into the Future

At the end of a densely (and perhaps nervously) scribbled page-and-a-half summary of all the actions, sounds, texts, light and slide cues, short pauses, and long intervals that would constitute *18 Happenings in 6 Parts* – a summary written by Kaprow right before public performances were about to start at the Reuben Gallery on 4 October 1959, which includes last minute cast modifications, new timings for some of the acts, brief descriptions of each act's soundtrack, and clarifications of some of the actions carried out by performers and technicians – Kaprow wrote, as a kind of signature, or hopeful outburst on the eve of an opening night: "Each of these parts may be re-arranged indefinitely." Thus, at least in early October 1959, as he was about to make history, Kaprow registered his desire for future actualizations of *18 Happenings in 6 Parts* – indefinitely opened ones, for sure, but still composed by meticulously pre-arranged "parts" (or "acts" or "sets"; Kaprow used these terms interchangeably throughout his notes).

Kaprow's concluding sentence, prefacing the public opening of his ambitious piece, reverberates today not only as a directorial note, a choreographic indication, or a permission to redo: it lasts, echoes, and insists as an explicit wish for futurity, a testamentary will written down before the advent of the events it simultaneously produced. The sentence endures as a kind of signature that (con)firms the author's desire for a much longer future for his piece than we now know it had. A question to ponder is why *18 Happenings in 6 Parts*, after its six evening public run (4–10 October 1959) at the Reuben Gallery was not performed again –

despite Kaprow's jotted desire. A clue to this question may be found in the fact that in the most comprehensive anthology of Kaprow's writings, his classic *Essays on the Blurring of Art and Life*, not once is *18 Happenings in 6 Parts* mentioned in any form, shape, or context – including Jeff Kelley's "Introduction" and Kaprow's "Preface to the Extended Edition" (of 2003). This amazing disavowal of *18 Happenings in 6 Parts* can be read as symptomatic, and it bears directly to the correlate question: why should this piece be "revived," "re-enacted," "reconstructed," "performed again," "reactivated," "redone," or "actualized" from its dormant papery state, in 2006 in Munich, and in 2007 in New York? Why would Kaprow authorize the return of a repressed (perhaps even censored) work? And, reciprocally, why would I want to pick up the invitation, once it arrived?

Part Four: The First Redoing

In November 2005, when Stephanie Rosenthal first invited me to co-curate with her, and be the director of, a redoing of *18 Happenings in 6 Parts* for the *Kaprow Exhibition* she was preparing at Haus der Künst, Munich, opening in the Fall of 2006, I hesitated. At the time, I had not yet seen Kaprow's detailed choreographic scores, the drawings, texts, poems, sketches, manifestos, private outbursts, discarded drafts for floor plans, fundraising letters, and cryptic technical exchanges with sound engineers. I had not yet seen Kaprow's very detailed and very peculiar fingering instructions for flute and violin (to be used in part four, room one), nor had I read his outrageously funny ideas for costumes (fortunately, he never used them in performance), nor his descriptions of some of the slides to be projected in room three during five of the six acts or parts or sets. I had not known then that the twenty-four minutes and fifteen seconds of rigorously timed and choreographed actions comprising the six parts of the eighteen happenings were also rigorously framed by a total of thirty-six minutes of intervals and pauses – the two fifteen minute intervals and the three two minute pauses between the parts last longer than the acts or parts (which are also quite sparse in action at times, with totally empty rooms for whole acts). Nor did I know then of Kaprow's desire to have the quirky "Helena Polka" blasting away from a long-play record in part five, room one – at exactly the moment when two guest painters simultaneously paint lines and circles on each side of an unprimed canvas dividing room one from room two, transforming painting (the glorious apex of the fine arts!) into a circus activity. I had not yet read Kaprow's amazingly beautiful text on time, delivered by him in room three, part two. And, of course, I had not yet read his directive to dispatch *18 Happenings in 6 Parts* to unknown, re-arrangeable futures.

All I knew then of *18 Happenings in 6 Parts* was pretty much what is generally (and vaguely) known about it in the field:[30] It was a groundbreaking work responsible for bringing that felicitous word – happening – into the vocabulary of twentieth-century performance practice and theory; that John Cage apparently had disliked it quite a bit, particularly the controlling aspects of it (and that Kaprow had been quite disappointed by Cage's disappointment);[31] that Michael Kirby had published a very meticulous description of the piece (which immediately became, up to today, *the* discursive proxy for the original event, and which I believe was mostly written based on the scripts and personal conversation with participants or Kaprow[32]); that *18 Happenings in 6 Parts* had inaugurated the Reuben Gallery in New York, a venue where soon some budding names of postmodern dance, like Simone Forti and Yvonne Rainer, would perform (albeit in a different location, the gallery moved to 44, East 3rd Street in 1960);[33] that Robert Rauschenberg and Jasper Johns had performed in "the Polka" passage of the piece as guest painters; that Samuel Delaney had stumbled upon an ad for it while walking down Fourth Avenue on an October evening and had most probably been the only black teenager to sit as an audience member among the exclusive Manhattan art crowd. But most of all, I vividly recalled an influential essay by Kaprow, "Happenings in the New York Scene," first published in 1961, two years after he had created *18 Happenings in 6 Parts*, where he clearly defined happenings not only as "events that, put simply, happen," but most importantly (with regard to the question of its redoing) where he had also defined their temporality: "they exist for a single performance, or only a few, and are gone forever as new ones take their place."[34]

Because of such a clear-cut definition, where Kaprow claims ephemerality and uniqueness as the constitutive elements of a happening, my first impulse was to refuse Rosenthal's invitation. Ironically, Rosenthal was also having some doubts about the project. Indeed, how could anyone return to a piece that was so iconic, but that had also been so radically set aside by its own author? Kaprow had even made the point to create, in 1988, a happening under exactly the same title that purposefully not only had nothing in common with the 1959 happening, but was predicated precisely on emphasizing its radical difference to the 1959 piece, by basing it on transient and non-rehearsed actions without a captive audience. Purposefully striking a definitive blow against the overdetermined, rehearsed, and "stiff" original, the 1988 *18 Happenings in 6 Parts* had one simple but very significant setting and a very simple yet very open program. It should take place on the streets, not inside a room or rooms; it should follow chance, not carefully choreographed actions; its timing should be determined by a natural unfolding of the actions, not by a chronometer or a clock (as had been the case in 1959). As for its main conceptual impetus and correlate action, it could not be more different: a first participant fills his or her pockets with dry leaves, walks on the streets of New York until he or she meets another participant; at this point, he or she removes the crumbling dry leaves from his or her pockets and passes them to participant number two; bits inevitably fall during this exchange; participant number two stuffs his or her pockets with the remainder of the leaves and walks looking for participant number three; they meet and the action is repeated; number three looks for number four, etc. The performance continues until no leaf crumble is left to be exchanged. In a preparatory meeting for this *18 Happenings in 6 Parts*, Kaprow stated to his collaborators that a return to the 1959 scores would be for him both "dull" and "totally uninteresting to engage again today."[35]

In light of all this, my hesitation in accepting Rosenthal's invitation increased. Why redo a piece when the *perception* we have of it today is of an extraordinarily innovative idea that somehow did not turn out as well as it should have in its first incarnations, as opposed to later happenings Kaprow would create throughout the 1960s, such as *A Spring Happening* (1961), *Self-Service* (1966), or *Fluids* (1967)? Indeed, art critics in 1959 either ignored it completely (Kaprow's papers at the Getty related to the piece include an unfinished letter to Hilton Kramer where Kaprow demands the art critic explain his absence during the runs of *18 Happenings in 6 Parts* in 1959);[36] or dismissed it. Fairfield Porter, reviewing the piece for *The Nation*, concluded his two-column text with these devastating sentences: "Avant-garde art has the merit of surprise. Kaprow's avant-garde 'event' constantly disappoints one's expectation of surprise. Like so many science fiction movies about the future, his subject matter is the undigested immediate past."[37]

However, in a meeting with Rosenthal in 2005, Kaprow had given his consent for someone other than him to direct a redoing of *18 Happenings in 6 Parts* based on his 1959 scores, in the context of the Munich exhibition. Kaprow had also made it clear to Rosenthal that he did not want to have any direct involvement in the preparations for such a redoing. It was Kaprow's personal consent that became, for me, the crucial event – the singular gesture that all of a sudden echoed and answered the call placed by him almost half a century earlier on a scrap of paper that hurriedly compressed the entirety of *18 Happenings in 6 Parts*: "Each of these parts may be re-arranged indefinitely."

Part Five: Today is a Bad Day

From: Rosenthal@…
Subject: 18/6
Date: April 6, 2006 1:29:11 PM EDT
To: atl1@nyu.edu
Cc: Grundler@ …, lorz@ …,
info@ …

dear andré,

i got the very sad message this morning, that allan died. he just sleeped away, so that's the only consolation.
so today is a bad day.
[…]
let's try to talk next week. all the best, stephanie[38]

Part Six: Continue to Act

> For the written to be written, it must continue to "act" and to be legible even if what is called the author of the writing no longer answers for what he has written, for what he seems to have signed, whether he is provisionally absent, or if he is dead, or if in general he does not support, with his absolute current and present intention or attention, the plenitude of his meaning, of that very thing which seems to be written "in his name."
>
> Jacques Derrida[39]

We had been working since early January on developing a concept for the redoing. Reams of paper. Assembling an artistic team: I invited Noémie Solomon to decode the choreographic scores, actualize them into movement, perform, and be assistant to the director; Shawn Greenlee to work on the sound design and on Kaprow's notations on sound. Rosenthal suggested Christin Vahl for the design of the environment and the construction of objects. (This same team worked together again in the redoing at PERFORMA 07). Backs and forths about the project and its details with Rosenthal, the Kaprow Estate, and the artistic team (but never, at least as far as I am concerned, directly with Kaprow, whom, regrettably, I did not meet). The decision had been made to build a space equal in dimension, materials, and scale to the one Kaprow had built in 1959 inside the Reuben Gallery loft. And then, way into this preparatory process, Kaprow passed away. All of a sudden, our work had completely and irrevocably changed. We were no longer working solely with a temporally distanced performance. Now, the piece had become a dead man's legacy. Now, I was working with the papers left by a man I would never meet. All of a sudden, Kaprow's papers, his marks, his writings, had acquired an incredible force. The death of the author, not as a conceptual or theoretical issue, but as a profoundly affective and pragmatically legal event, clarified and indicated a general dramaturgical path for how to approach the redoing. The death of Kaprow all of a sudden instilled even more energy in the papers pertaining to the piece he had now *left*. His departure approximated those papers further to the hauntological force contained in their deeply choreographic nature. Hence, I could establish my relationship to Kaprow's spirit as one to the spirit of his letter. A spirit filled by particularly strong illocutionary and perlocutionary forces – guiding, leading, and commanding (or perhaps just taking by his hand) those willing to give form to the movements and actions Kaprow had set on paper and that had waited for half a century to be set into motion again. This capacity to animate through the force of a mark is exactly the project and promise of choreography in general in its most strict, onto-historical sense.

Part Seven

What is widely described in the scholarship as "the script" or simply "the score" of *18 Happenings in 6 Parts* (see for instance, the surprisingly misleading use of the definite article in Jeff Kelley's presentation of "the score" of *18 Happenings in 6 Parts*, as reduced to one single page[40]) is rather a massive textual and visual work set on paper. As I mentioned before, it is almost autonomous in its prolific poetic ramifications, internal logic, and performative potentialities. But a few dozen pages are clearly aimed at preserving and transmitting a rigorous performance structure and choreographic score. Yet, even those notes were always, and constitutively, slightly *anexact*: not really inexact, but besides or beyond the problem of exactitude. Indeed, Kaprow's movement and sound scores, despite their meticulousness, were also fraught with small inaccuracies and micro-paradoxes. In their rigorous delivery Kaprow had certainly (purposefully?) created some room to play – a playfulness allowed by the indeterminacy of language, as in the detailed "technical instructions" he handed to the two technicians running sound and lights and slides in the hidden "control room" right behind the large assemblage on the back wall in room three.[41] With the heading "TECHNICIANS: INSTRUCTIONS" and the footer "FINIS," the following commands guide the cadence of slide projections throughout the performance:

Act 1: 16 Slides (rapidly)
Act 3: 13 Slides (rapidly)
Act 4: 11 Slides (fast)
Act 5: 9 Slides (quickly)

To redo *18 Happenings in 6 Parts* would be continually to solve problems similar to the one of finding out what exactly could be the difference between doing something "rapidly," "quickly," and "fast." Thus, I kept as main dramaturgical guideline the following formula: that the scores and choreographic details so carefully annotated by Kaprow, were to be approached (precisely) as being "*rigorous yet anexact*" instructions. I took it as no mere coincidence that this apparently paradoxical formula is also the one used by Gilles Deleuze to describe the dynamics of organic life. Kaprow was already using the anexact nature of semantics and of writing to fuse, or melt, or better still, alloy, art (or representation) and life (or spirit).

Part Eight

Are the ~~gentleman~~ players ready? …
They shall ready themselves …
We shall begin …
The time is near …
Now is the time.[42]

First practical question to solve: space or rather, *place*, where to place the redoing? Kelley notes that Kaprow had accepted the invitation by Anita Reuben to create something for the inauguration of her new gallery "not so much because he wanted to work in a gallery space, but because he felt the Reuben Gallery, a raw loft space, had not yet been 'contaminated' by art."[43] This was clearly not the case in Munich, where the redoing would take place inside a Museum's gallery. This placing had to be carefully and explicitly addressed. Quite early in the process, Rosenthal and I agreed that we wanted to build as accurately as possible the precarious architecture Kaprow had created within the Reuben Gallery loft. How then to deterritorialize our room from the institutional frame of the museum? The aim was to create an object that would invade the gallery while at the same time not reveal itself fully, nor give itself to be contemplated at a distance as a work of art. Moreover, I wanted to place this huge box at an angle, so it wouldn't align with the structure of the building – thus reinforcing its out-of-place quality. The redoing could only take place inside a Museum's gallery as long as it remained slightly misplaced. Vahl responded to this idea by conceiving a large structure made out of cheap construction materials with porous outside walls, like a skin. Plain wood on the outside, white on the inside, roofless. The misalignment of this box with the rest of the building generated a slight sensation of vertigo.

In New York during PERFORMA 07 and PSi (the Performance Studies international Conference), the setting for the box was completely different. As in 1959, the piece would take place in a space not originally intended to host art (an industrial warehouse), still to be adapted to function as a gallery, and not yet open to the public: the large (and at the time unfinished), new space of Deitch/Barney in Long Island City. This warehouse is riddled with evenly spaced columns. To install our box, we opted for a design solution where the structural columns in the space would pierce through the floor of our set, as if pinning it down, emphasizing its exteriority to the hosting space, once again. In New York, I was able to learn much more about Kaprow's relationship to form. The odd mix of high professionalism and high volunteerism that typifies the New York art scene contributed to the creation of a set that conveyed a strict formalism and yet revealed to me for the first time how form and objecthood for Kaprow were the outcome of a serendipitous yet utterly necessary meeting between precarious materials and hard labor, performed in non-ideal conditions. As days progressed (we had a total of 14 performances in 10 days) the panels and partitions slowly but surely started to tilt, going slightly off their orthogonal lines. Halfway through the run, one of the room's panels started to visibly lean. One evening, Vaughan Rachel, who was married to Kaprow at the time he was creating the piece in 1959, honored us with her presence. At the end of that performance, as I accompanied her on her way out, she looked at that particularly pronounced leaning panel and said: "It looks just like it was in 1959. Of course, back then, Allen would just kick the panels so they would look like this." I learned how Kaprow was interested in building, in shaping, in being a formalist through and through, but also in purposefully annoying the monumental aura of the "well-built": what Kelley called Kaprow's "flat-footed" sense of form.[44]

I could also finally pinpoint the cause of the underlying tension between the precarious (yet formal) architecture and (everyday) objects on one hand, and the minimalist, cold, and stiffly choreographed steps and gestures on the other. The tension was this: objects and space and materials appeared to have more life than the human bodies subjecting themselves to the laws of the choreography dictated by Kaprow. The bodies moving in *18 Happenings in 6 Parts* had been described by Michael Kirby as "clear, simple and unspontaneous. Their faces never expressed feeling or emotion. They walked slowly, carefully and always in straight lines and parallel to the walls: all turns, as if marching, would be at right angles." They moved "stiffly," in a "calculated, "expressionless" way, "with the disinterested blankness of someone who is hypnotized."[45] It was from the display of this potential for inhumanity in choreography (despite its great capacity to form and to resist time) that Kaprow fled, immediately after, in his subsequent happenings and events. And, interestingly, it was this element that generated the most amount of resistance from the part of some of the audience in New York. As opposed to the 1958 rambunctious participants of *Pastorale*, or Cage's feeling he was being policed by Kaprow (or by the scores) in 1959, the audience in 2007 seemed fine about being moved around by the dictates of the cards. The main objection was about the disjuncture between what was being performed and the semantic field generated by the word "happening" in American culture since the 1960s (an association with hipness and spontaneity which lead Kaprow to write in 1967, that he was trying "to get rid of the word," without success). The objection was voiced like this: surely Kaprow could not have wanted these stiff, unexpressive, blank, bodies! Wasn't this a *happening*, after all?

Part Nine

Dressed in ordinary street clothes
(a Negro girl wore a black leotard)[46]

I was less struck by the "ordinary street clothes" than by the parenthetical and anachronistic mode of referring to one of the performers as "Negro girl." In 1959, that "Negro girl" was Shirley Prendergast. This is one of the rare social-historical markers that binds Kirby's text to the time it was written. "Negro girl" took me directly to the very specific historical period of the late 1950s in the US. And given the way Kaprow controlled with absolute precision every single detail of the production, the stark differentiation between the way that "Negro girl" was dressed in her skin-tight black leotard and the other white performers in their "street clothes" could not be ignored. A "Negro girl" in black leotard performing, slow, abstract dance movements less than a foot away from an overwhelmingly (if not exclusively, with the exception of Samuel Delaney!) white audience could not be taken as a small detail in the work of a sculptor and a painter so invested in critiquing the history of western art in its relation to figuration (a critique in which *18 Happenings in 6 Parts* partakes fully, particularly in the slides shown in room 3, part 2, which fuse Kaprow's paintings and drawings of figures and nudes with paintings by Great Masters and children's drawings). The "Negro girl's" presence, actions, demeanor in Kaprow's piece could not be seen as a neutral statement in 1959, when the Civil Rights movement was well under way, and when the lack of *visibility* of black women in the downtown avant-garde circles in New York was the rule (interestingly reinforcing this invisibility, Delaney does not mention this other African American in the room with him). It seemed to me that I had to cast the redoing by taking into consideration the ways Kaprow was approaching the politics of racial visibility and invisibility.[47] In the redoing, the black woman could not be replaced by just anyone. So, even though, much later, after a round table at MoMA on Kaprow's art, I was told by one of Kaprow's collaborators in the 1960s that I had gotten this "whole race thing all wrong" (a statement with which I politely insist on disagreeing) another element crept in, coming from the scores, corroborating my decision not to brush aside race as an important element in the redoing: a mechanical toy, used in part four. Kirby describes how a man

> entered the second room, put the mechanical toy on the table and set it in motion. About one foot high, it was the brightly colored figure of a Negro dancing on a drum; the legs jiggled and swung frantically when the toy was started.[48]

Throughout his notes, Kaprow tellingly calls this toy the "Black Sambo" – a crucial character both in the history of that foundational form of US popular entertainment, blackface minstrelsy, and in the history of US racism. Again, the inclusion of this Black Sambo dancing mechanically to the cacophony of an avant-garde orchestra playing in the next room in an environment lit by red, white, and blue light bulbs seemed to me not at all an innocent gesture in 1959. For the redoing, a decision had to be made about what kind of mechanical toy to use. For a while I considered buying an antique (there are plenty tin toy Sambos available on e-bay). But this would be an odd statement, as if the visual economy of racism, and particularly the commodification of blackness as a mechanized subjectivity always ready to provide pure kinetic entertainment, was a thing of the past. It was when I was walking on the streets of Rio de Janeiro, that I stumbled upon the solution on the evening before taking my plane to Munich to start rehearsals. Staring at me, the colorful, one foot tall "Rap Brother" smiled from behind a window in a toy store in Ipanema; yellow jacket, brown face, thick red lips, maniacal grin, wide eyes, gloved hands. Just press his wrist and he hip-hops endlessly, singing and dancing upon command. It flew to Munich with me and performed the redoing with us every night. In New York, its performance drew gasps from the audience. A mechanical toy's music and dance, rippling through the historical surface of US racism. Then and now.

Part Ten

> [T]he sound is made of pure essences
> rather than "music" in the conventional sense.
>
> Allan Kaprow[49]

Kaprow describes his music as based on the principle of treating sounds not as notes but as self-contained "events," thus allowing him to create music that was void of any "compositional" concerns. I had asked Shawn Greenlee, working at the time at Brown University on his doctorate on the relation between electronic music and image, to be responsible for the sound design of the redoing. Then, we got lucky. Peter Kirby contacted us. He had found in a box left in a basement the five reel-to-reel tapes used by Kaprow in 1959. Our task of decoding Kaprow's intentions became easier – even though the discovery of the tapes also made clear that all sounds had to be constantly arranged and rearranged in real time throughout the performance. The tapes were to be played like an instrument – which resulted in a more dynamic sound environment. Throughout the redoing, Greenlee played with Kaprow's "pure essences" every night.

Last Part: Kaprow's Spirit

> *But this is, as I explained in my last letter, only part of my work. I am very busy now working in N.Y. City in a large space in preparation for a performance in the fall. I am building a series of semitransparent compartments in which several scored "happenings" will take place simultaneously. These will be partially visible and completely audible to the audience in each compartment. Therefore I am now deeply involved in preparing words to be recited, choreography, films, electric light "events," collages – in other words – the "works" all at once. I have been trying to raise money for all of this with absolutely no success and so I am unfortunately reduced to a nervous madness that gives me bad dreams and makes life miserable for my wife and child. But I must do things and thus no matter what happens or doesn't happen, I will continue. Eventually things will improve.*[50]

Notes

1. Michael Kirby, "18 Happenings in 6 Parts," in Kirby (ed.), *Happenings: An Illustrated Anthology*, New York: E. P. Dutton, 1965, pp. 53–65.
2. Excerpt from script section of *18 Happenings in 6 Parts*. Getty Research Institute Research Library. Special Collections. Allan Kaprow papers, 1940–1997.
3. Rodenbeck, in Benjamin H. D. Buchloh and Judith F. Rodenbeck, *Experiments in the Everyday: Alan Kaprow and Robert Watts – Events, Objects, Documents*, New York: Columbia University and the Miriam and Ira D. Wallack Art Gallery, 1999, p. 60.
4. Ibid.
5. Jeff Kelley, in Kelly (ed.), *Childsplay: The Art of Allan Kaprow*, Berkeley and Los Angeles: University of California Press, 2004, p. 22.
6. Kirby, op. cit., pp. 67–83.
7. Kelley, op. cit., pp. 29–41.
8. In Buchloh and Rodenbeck, op. cit., pp. 70–1.
9. Kelley, op. cit., p. 27. Emphasis mine.
10. Kaprow in Buchloh and Rodenbeck, op. cit., p. 70. Emphasis mine.
11. Laurenti, Jean-Noel, "Feuillet's Thinking," in Laurence Louppe (ed.), *Traces of Dance*, Paris: Editions Dis Voir, 1994, p. 86.

12. For Kaprow as a "formalist," see most of Jeff Kelley's writings on the artist.
13. Even though there are early works by Kaprow where happening elements emerge, it seems clear that *18 Happenings in 6 Parts* bring those elements to a new coherence.
14. Kelley, op. cit., p. 29.
15. "Allan Kaprow: actually there were five different tapes. Each of the tapes was made up of independent groups of sounds that I had to generate electronically. There was a division into three parts, as I recall. It was made up of little bits of tape spliced together. I remember sorting those little pieces, all very laboriously recorded with generators, filters, etc, according to categories and putting them into boxes – boxes all over the place. Robert Watts: hundreds of boxes. I never saw so many boxes". In Buchloh and Rodenbeck, op. cit., p. 73.
16. Buchloh, ibid.
17. Kelley, op. cit., p. 17. Emphasis added.
18. Ibid.
19. Derrida, *Paper Machine*, trans. Rachel Bowlby, Stanford, CA: Stanford University Press, 2005, p. 42.
20. Buchloh, op. cit., p. 71.
21. Kelley, op. cit., p. 24.
22. Rodenbeck, op. cit., p. 55.
23. "[T]he 'happening' can only makes us smile: it is to the theater of cruelty what the carnival of nice might be to the mysteries of Eleusis. This is particularly so due to the fact that the happening substitutes political agitation for the total revolution prescribed by Artaud." Derrida, *Writing and Difference*, trans. Alan Bass, Chicago, IL: University of Chicago Press, 1978, p. 245.
24. Jacques Derrida, *Of Spirit: Heidegger and the Question*, trans. Goeffrey Bennington and Rachel Bowlby, Chicago, IL: University of Chicago Press 1989, p. 31.
25. Ibid.
26. Ibid.
27. Kirby, op. cit., p. 75.
28. Kelley, op. cit., p. 29.
29. Rodenbeck, op. cit., p. 55. Since I have strong reasons to believe the Kirby's "description" in *Happenings* was written from consultation of the scores and with the help of either Kaprow or Lucas Samaras, I tend to think two weeks was the original time frame of rehearsing the performers. This is also corroborated by my own experience of directing the piece. One week is too short, while several months make no sense and there is no support for this claim.
30. It is outrageous how little is actually known of the piece since it has become the proxy for Kaprow's entire oeuvre (see for instance, the centrality of it in Kaprow's obituaries in major European and North American newspapers). Even more outrageously, the misinformation those reports give on the piece create all sorts of historical short-circuits to the point of total disinformation. *The Guardian*'s obituary proclaimed that John Cage had actually performed in *18 Happenings*.
31. In a 1965 interview with Michael Kirby and Richard Schechner, Cage stated his discontent bluntly:

> So when I go to a Happening that seems to me to have intention in it I go away saying that I'm not interested. I also did not like to be told, in the 18 Happenings in 6 Parts, to move from one room to another. Though I don't actively engage in politics I do as an artists have some awareness of art's political content, and it doesn't include policemen.

Mariellen R. Sandford (ed.), *Happenings and Other Acts*, London: Routledge, 1995, pp. 68–9.

32. I have many reasons to believe that Kirby may not have attended the 1959 performances he describes. I don't want to make a big deal out of this possibility, but alongside some personal communications about Kirby only starting to attend happenings from 1962 onwards (and that Lucas Samaras was the one passing along the scripts to Kirby) and the fact that in the lists of reservations for the 1959 performances (also part of Kaprow's papers), Kirby's name does not appear, I have always felt that the absolute exactitude of Kirby's description indicated that his narrative had to be directly lifted from the scores. Kirby gives details only someone with access to the scores could account for: exact timings of all actions to the second, exact transcription of poems read amidst a cacophony of sounds, including exact rendition of punctuation marks. Moreover, he describes precisely all actions in all three rooms – which implies that he would have had to attend not only all 6 evenings of the 1959 run *but also* that he would have had to either cheat in the card instructions or have had an astronomical luck in getting to all rooms in all parts to see all actions. All these factors together make his presence there questionable and his writing from the scores certain. This is why Kirby's description was considered in the re-doing as a kind of auxiliary score – but, as always, in case of conflict of information or detail, Kaprow's papers would always have the last word. Again, the possible fact that Kirby may not have written his account from first hand witnessing does not trouble me at all – nor should diminish the value and the work of an extraordinary scholar and writer (Portuguese poet Fernando Pessoa wrote a notoriously insightful critical review of a painting by Almada Negreiros without ever setting foot on the gallery where it was being first exhibited). At the same time, I feel that the sheer force in Kirby's description conveys the sheer performativity and amazing detailing we find in Kaprow's scores, those incredible *image-phrases*, in the expression of Jeff Kelley.
33. Simone Forti presented at Reuben her piece *See Saw*, performed by Robert Morris and Yvonne Rainer, December 1960.
34. Kaprow, in Jeff Kelley (ed.), *Allan Kaprow: Essays on the Blurring of Art and Life*, Berkeley and Los Angeles: University of California Press, 2003 (1993), p. 16.
35. Quotes taken from a sound file, courteously provided by Peter Kirby, of a preparatory meeting for the 1988 version of *18 Happenings in 6 Parts* in New York. In that file we can hear Kaprow briefly discussing the 1959 piece. When considering the possibility of doing it again, he tells how it would be "dull" for him to return to the issues he was dealing with in the late 1950s. Those were, mainly, according to Kaprow: how to "transpose" the audience into actively participating in the event; and how to create a "summing up of the avant-garde up to that time" through "a visual assemblage of events that were of an active and yet obviously of a formal sort."
36. Manuscript sheet located in the Getty Research Institute Research Library. Ibid.
37. Fairfield Porter, "Art," *The Nation*, 1959, vol. 189, no. 13, p. 260.
38. From the author's files.
39. Jacques Derrida, "Signature Event Context," in *Margins of Philosophy*, trans. Alan Bass, Chicago, IL: University of Chicago Press, 1982, p. 316.
40. Kelley, op. cit., pp. 30–1.
41. Kirby describes this assemblage camouflaging the control room in 1959:

    [A] large, bold, ragged collage of roughly torn canvas: the lower portion primarily contained crudely lettered words of various sizes [...]; the upper, a band of diagonal stripes and a slated construction that jutted over the chairs. Unseen behind this collage wall was the control room from which the performers would enter and to which they would exit.

Kirby, op. cit., p. 70. Kaprow placed another assemblage, recycling his *Rearrangeable Panels* of 1957, in room one. For the redoings we opted to roughly paint the plastic back wall of room three in black, and to lean one single tall plank of wood with glued apples and pears on it in room one; a structural wooden bar next to it was used to hang the cut canvases with stripes and circles paintings produced in each performance – by the end of a few days, we had a nice volume of fabric hanging on this bar.

42. Spoken text from *18 Happenings in 6 Parts*, as heard coming from an LP originally recorded with Kaprow's voice, Room 2 Set 3 (in the re-doing, an LP with Shawn Greenlee's voice).
43. Kelley, op. cit., p. 29.
44. Ibid., p. 23.
45. Kirby, op. cit., p. 76.
46. Ibid.
47. In the unpublished letter to Fairfield Porter mentioned above, Kaprow accuses the reviewer of being incapable of fully seeing what had surrounded him during the performance. Kaprow phrases this accusation of a kind of selected blindness by comparing Porter with "[T]he British who goes to Hong Kong for the first time and sees his house-boy everywhere he goes, on every street corner, tens of thousands of examples of this poor wretch – concluding that the Chinese are all alike."
48. Michael Kirby, "18 Happenings in 6 Parts," in Kirby (ed.), *Happenings: an illustrated anthology*, New York: E.P. Dutton, p. 77.
49. Handwritten sheet by Kaprow titled: "To the Theater People." Subtitled: INNOVATOR. Getty Research Institute Research Library. Ibid.
50. Excerpt from a manuscript letter to a "Mr. König," asking advice on sound electronic. Kaprow papers *18 Happenings in 6 Parts*.

Chapter 9

The Prosthetic Present Tense: Documenting Chinese Time-Based Art

Meiling Cheng[1]

I. Perceptual Hyperlinks

A stiffened rice paper with a thick inky rectangle in the middle. We see an object resulting from Qiu Zhijie's protracted five-year xingwei piece, *Repeatedly Duplicating a Thousand Times "Lantingxu"* (1990–5).

A photograph; a written journal; a fellow artist as the authenticator. Aside from the artist's oral history, the two documents, plus one entrusted witness, constitute the only extant evidence of Yang Zhichao's *Within the Fourth Ring Road* (26–30 July 1999).

A few selected candid shots and itemized financial accounts posted on a Blogsite; a little grocery shop located in Tongxian, Beijing. These are the ongoing compositional elements of Wang Chuyu and Wang Hong's collaborative project, *"Wang Mian Rice Oil Shop" Document Files* (2006 on).

In the "Documents" section of this volume I have described in more detail these three time-based pieces, which feature a variety of media, experiential interfaces, and performance durations. Qiu's piece is a hybrid between calligraphy and performance. His action score consists of recurrent inscriptions of the same text on the same sheet of paper over an extended period. The primary interface exists in the inscriber's deliberate hand moving through a progressively indecipherable writing surface, which becomes, as it were, a darkened mirror. "A thousand times," chosen "arbitrarily" by the artist,[2] function as the temporal outer frame – one necessarily prolonged due to its copious requirement – for the artwork's flexible duration.

Yang's project is a loose assemblage of endurance body art via psychosomatic self-studies, ethnographic fieldwork, interactive urban ritual, and sociological investigation, deploying a performance mode theorized by Augusto Boal as "invisible theatre."[3] Having

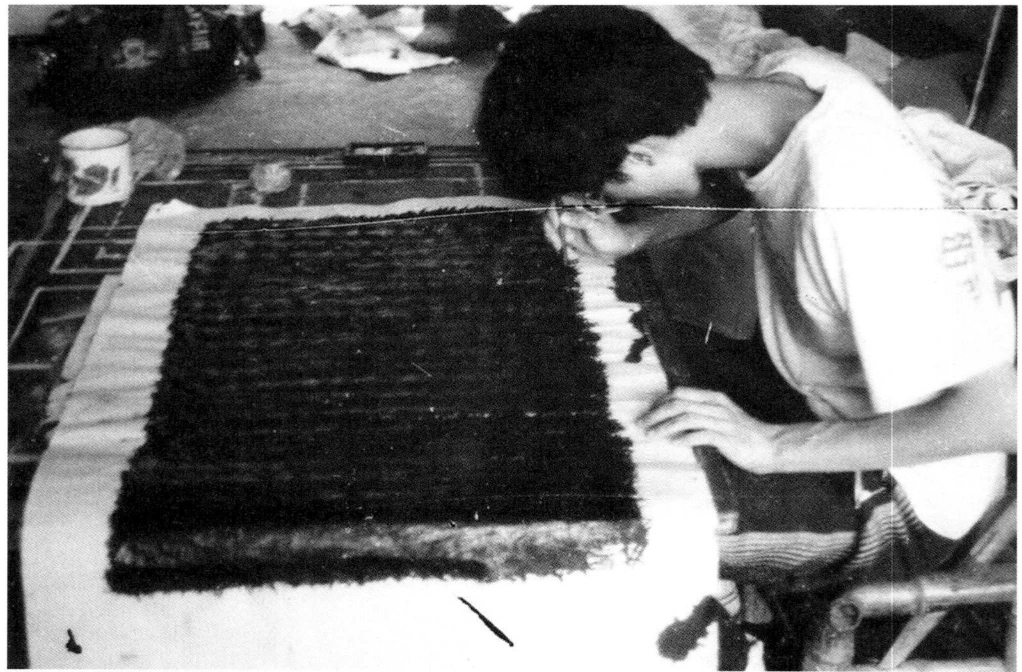

Qiu Zhijie performing *Repeatedly Duplicating A Thousand Times "Lantingxu,"* undated Courtesy of Qiu Zhijie.

chosen "begging" as his project's main action and his sole source of survival during its enactment, Yang binds himself to a compulsory scenario of initiating contact with another person, soliciting the person's help, bearing the humiliation of being rejected, or expressing gratitude. Interactivity mobilizes the artist through his immersion in an unevenly developed postsocialist metropolis. Yet, interactivity also triggers the artist's process of dis-identification, shifting his role from someone who consciously engages in a productive act to an indolent, parasitical, or downtrodden nobody. Befitting his liminal mask as one who withholds the right to self-determination, Yang also rescinds his control over the project's duration. His artwork ended after four days when the law intervened.[4]

"Wang Mian Rice Oil Shop" Document Files has at least a doubled body, which points self-reflexively to the divergent professional credentials and experiential differences between its collaborators: Wang Chuyu, an established independent artist uninvolved in the rice oil shop's daily operation; and Wang Hong, an aspiring artist whose main livelihood depends on the shop's smooth operation. We may consider the project, for Wang Chuyu's part, a classical example of what Gregory Battcock calls "Conceptual or Idea Art," which produces not a commodifiable object, but "some kind of documentation referring to the concept."[5] For Wang Hong, in contrast, a clear-cut distinction between his art, work, and life is elusive; instead, the project approximates what Allan Kaprow has noted as "making nonart into

art": "[W]ork in unrecognizable, i.e., nonart, modes but present the work in recognizable art contexts."[6] Wang Chuyu has enabled Wang Hong's nonart business – running a grocery store – to be reconceptualized as art by presenting its financial documents monthly on an established Chinese art website: *Meishu tongmeng/arts.tom.com*.[7] The project's double status also affects its possible duration. While the project's process-oriented emphasis renders its durational aspect less significant artistically, the artwork's actual duration is contingent upon the quotidian sustainability of "Wang Mian Rice Oil Shop." The shop's potential nonart longevity would ironically keep the artwork incomplete, making its culminating, postmortem art exhibition impossible.

All three Chinese projects I annotate here rely on documentation for display and dissemination. Qiu had pre-set a given number for his calligraphic action, but he allowed an ad-hoc structure for its execution. He had performed the inscription once a day, several times a day, or would at times lapse for days without touching the brush pen; he did the work indoors or out.[8] Because of its extended duration and its semi-improvisational event structure, Qiu's calligraphic xingwei cannot be witnessed live in its entirety by anyone other than the writer himself. Yang's "begging" xingwei depends on the artist's willing suspension of his professional identity so as to experience, as he put it, "a means of survival based on an individual's freely chosen act to lose any human dignity whatsoever."[9] Yang's unwitting co-performers were precisely those who could not recognize his begging as art. Indeed Yang's interactive art could succeed only when those from whom he sought alms failed to discern the artist's disguise. His xingwei is then an openly engaged clandestine action. Even Ai Weiwei, Yang's long-term artistic mentor and the only designated "witness" to *Within the Fourth Ring Road*, served solely as an authoritative guarantor of the project's veracity without having seen Yang's action live. Whereas Qiu's and Yang's artworks depend on documentation to reach virtual, posterior viewers, documentation, and its attendant public display, constitutes the project itself for *"Wang Mian Rice Oil Shop" Document Files*. In this light, the shop and its documented artistic existence become mutually reinforcing. The shop's "real-world" operation permits the documentation to continue; the continuous documentation redistributes the shop's financial protocols as idea art on the Web's citational engines and virtual galleries.

Using documentation to reach a wider, off-site audience is not a novel strategy in time-based art. Documentation, in various formats, has almost always existed alongside enacted artworks as a way for the artist to recollect, record, and disseminate the work. More recently, however, contemporary art worlds have shown a resurgence of interest in documentation, treating it not only as a communicative vehicle for art but also as a unique body of art. This very volume's thematic tenors attest to such a phenomenon. *Perform, Repeat, Record*: three disparate acts find their equal footings in the volume's title; their syntax challenges our acculturated habit to prioritize the original (to *perform*) over the subsequent (to *repeat*) and the supplementary (to *record*). Still, not to utterly surrender the vigor of the live (the once alive) to its documented afterlife, the co-editors Heathfield and Jones arrange these three acts in a tacit chronology. To *perform* comes first; to *repeat* – either through re-enacting the original performance score, or by re-imagining what has been enacted – comes next, perhaps simultaneously or just a moment ahead of the third task: to *record* the performance, thereby initiating the possibilities for the given piece to enter art history.

This tacit chronology nevertheless does not work for the three Chinese artworks that I recall. These pieces' original creative acts are so intertwined with their documentary records that we can hardly distinguish when the artists' performances end and their documentations begin. Qiu's performance is literally a repetition, which simultaneously keeps a record. *Repeatedly Duplicating a Thousand Times "Lantingxu"* cites from a traditional calligraphic technique called *linmo* (tracing/copying/duplicating). This two-word phrase indicates a sequence of close encounters. "*Lin*" evokes proximity at two junctures: where the calligrapher's fingers grasp the brush pen and where the calligrapher's master model – say, Wang Xizhi's breathtaking *xinshu* in "Lantingxu" – is placed near one's hand for reverential imitation. Appropriately, "imitation" happens to be an apt translation for *mo*. Insofar as imitation is repetition, Qiu's piece involves no original act: his creativity lies in his recreativity. Further complication: his recreativity involves a self-defacing mechanism. The more he recreates, the less legible his product becomes, yielding meanwhile a by-product that eventually erases even references to what has been recreated. Qiu's excessive record keeping services his performance by transmuting its traces.

In *Within the Fourth Ring Road*, documentation is both integral and supplementary to the artist's performance. Yang made numerous journal entries on each begging day, describing his encounters, observations, and philosophical meditations. From his futile fight to chase off mosquitoes to his bone-eating loneliness and depression, from his anger at receiving coarse insults to his fear of being physically hurt, Yang's journal narrates, if in a piecemeal and haphazard fashion, the rough goings and small consolations lived by his body. His words recall what we, his remote reader-spectators, did not and cannot see and hear in the flesh. His words stand, therefore, as accessible surrogates for the missing origin. Although the artist's body is absent, his words are here, within our reach. Through their associative flights, his words further extend the body of his performance, leading us into a temporary republic of diachronically conjoined reveries: a conceptual double take not easily achievable at the first sight, were we ever immersed in the live that Yang initiated.

In *"Wang Mian Rice Oil Shop" Document Files*, the artwork is the process and sum total of its documentation. Documentation here exceeds its usual function of record keeping for verification by positively enabling the performance. When infused with an artistic intention, Wang Hong's daily act of documenting some petty cash exchanges is suddenly endowed with a different purpose, if not higher, at least less pragmatic and spirit-constraining. Staying clear of the shop's day-to-day management, Wang Chuyu's performance consists of alchemizing the shop's commercial records into non-commercial art. Although his invented documentary structure does not automatically enhance Wang Hong's pleasure as a shopkeeper, it does abet a conceptual rhythm for him to transmute drudgery into art, tedious repetition of labor into monthly verifications of a merchant's alternative vocation. Wang Hong's record keeping, cognitively reframed, enacts his desired identity as an artist.

As long as the two artists keep replicating this documentary structure, additional project installments will appear. In their collaboration, to perform equals to repeat and to record; the three acts happen in synchronicity.

II. Navigating Live Sites

My three case studies have arguably displaced the *live* into the *once-lived*. If we may consider the "live" in live art a collective sensory ecology surrounding the present-tense interchange between an artist's doing and some viewers' witnessing, then such collectivity becomes drastically dissipated in the *once-lived*, which occupies a private universe, a hermetic time-space shared by an artist and his/her consciously framed art actions. As art, however, the *once-lived* aspires not to become the *already-dead*. Documentation is the *deus ex machina* that intervenes to transform the *once-lived* into the *again-alive*. How does documentation accomplish this mythic feat? The *once-lived* is alive again because its solitude is broken. Documentation's magic lies in its explosive power; it shatters the reclusive planet inhabited by the *once-lived* into a radiating galaxy of asteroids. Each asteroid carries some memories of the *once-lived*; each in turn extends, renews, or replaces the vitality of the *once-lived*; each has the potential to grow into a different planet. Thus, the *once-lived* lives again and lives on, not as itself per se, but as itself altered: dismembered, redone, augmented, partially replicated, diminished, burned into ashes, or consumed as legends.

To me, what is most generative in my just improvised live art mythology is documentation's function as a transmitter, a boundary-blasting messenger that transfers some past information to other ears. Yet, to identify documentation as a Hermes-like agent is to distinguish its ontology from that of performance: just as a messenger is not synonymous with its message, so documentation (as a representational system for a certain once-lived condition) is not identical to what it represents: a given performance (as a once-alive nexus of information). This kind of ontological distinction between performance and documentation is nonetheless untenable for those time-based artworks that have collapsed the temporal sequences between their embodied actions and discursive re-enactments. In *Repeatedly Duplicating a Thousand Times "Lantingxu,"* for instance, Qiu's very first embodied action – as he sat quite still to breathe all energies into a moving brush pen – was already a discursive re-enactment of a writerly action performed by (a very drunk) Wang Xizhi centuries ago. *Within the Fourth Ring Road* provides another prototype, in which Yang's action and documentation are interwoven as his performance's complementary parts. *"Wang Mian Rice Oil Shop" Document Files* pushes this prototype further to the discursive extreme, practically construing Wang Hong's lived experiences as a shopkeeper to be a pretext for his art documentation.

The three Chinese artworks therefore participate in contemporary performance field's manifest interest in documentation. This emergent trend in live art research has implicitly "upgraded" documentation from its traditional status as that which permits a critic/writer/

distant viewer to access retrospectively a vanished artwork into a legitimate, if not fully independent, object of inquiry. Such an upgrade endows – discursively if not literally – a given performance's documentary traces with the aura of the originary live event. Documentation, in this context, produces not only a static archive, nor just a re-enactable score, but also a virtual performance event: it is (virtually) live.

The proposition of a discursive near-equivalence between a performance artwork and its documentary traces forces us to reassess a presumed stable distinction between a live art event and its subsequent multi-sourced (visual, audiovisual, literary, painterly, schematic, or multimedia) performance documents. We now reckon that the relationships between an originary performance (the *live* as well as the *once-lived*) and its documentation exist not in a dichotomy but in a spectrum of possibilities. At one end of this spectrum lies my Chinese examples, in which the embodied art actions and their documentary traces function as coinciding, interdependent, even mutually constituting, counterparts. At the other end appear those instances – most from performance art's earliest practices – wherein the artists desire to stage some ephemeral actions for an onsite audience without leaving behind any (significant) documentation. In between are the majority of cases where certain live events do happen first and their documentations next, or simultaneously, as in a video recording. It is this middle majority that seems to resist most vehemently documentation's usurpation of performance.

The middle majority's impulse for conservation has its rational grounding. Two direct consequences result from loosening the rigid distinction between a time-based art event and its documentation: (1) It permits the (relatively) permanent to impinge upon the (supposedly) ephemeral; (2) It challenges the priority of the live. Combining these two tendencies brings forth an obvious threat to live art, thrusting it back to the fold of commodification: live art documentation is now available for sale, for exhibition, and for canonization. The "live," which thrives formlessly in between some sentient beings who self-select to share a stretch of site-specific temporality together, becomes materialized, solidified, an art object – (yet another) detachable from its communal raison d'être. Is there no escape from the protean grabs of capitalism?

The invisible hand of capitalism, with its current guise as transnational globalization, may be the most omnipotent climate that contributes to the condition of production for all artworks – time-based or not – in our late postmodernist era. Yet, even the bad weather cannot stop those who seek fresh air from going outdoors! Live art practitioners may choose to take the cash-signified forces of commodification as a threat, a temptation, a numbing white noise, an opponent, an oppressor, a patron saint, a goad, or an open challenge. Thus, one can still try thinking outside the box by asking: in addition to its pragmatic and profitable implications, how does the blurring of boundaries between performance and its documentation modify our conceptual mores in live art research?

Most immediately, this blurring compels us to re-evaluate a prized methodology in performance critique, one based on an intensive onsite engagement with a live artwork. While advantageous, this methodology becomes problematic when it is assumed to be the most authoritative, even the minimal, credential for a critic/historian to analyze a performance piece. The logic behind this assumption, I deduce, implies an epistemic collapse between experience and knowledge, corporeal presence and purposeful introspection. Unfortunately, seeing/hearing something live does not guarantee knowing it fully. As Amelia Jones cautions in "'Presence' in *absentia*," not only is there no "unmediated relationship" between a perceiver and "any kind of cultural product," but that it also requires distance for the perceiver to make sense of a live experience through retrospective deliberation. Jones makes a strong case for experiencing performance as documentation by pointing out the analogous exchange process between a viewer watching an artist performing and a viewer/reader examining the performance documents. "While the live situation may enable the phenomenological relations of flesh-to-flesh engagement, the documentary exchange (viewer-/reader–document) is equally intersubjective."[10] Thus, Jones argues, the specific knowledge a spectator gains from participating in a live event, though valuable, should not take precedence over the equally specific knowledge that a critic/historian develops "in relation to the documentary traces of such an event."[11]

Philip Auslander extends Jones's argument from an opposite end, championing the "performativity of performance documentation" to authenticate a posterior spectator's encounter of "the document itself *as a performance*."[12] Auslander's theoretical proposition evokes the preeminence of documentation characteristic of my Chinese case studies. His position shifts the status of a performance document from its normative role as the trace that verifies and preserves a live event to that of a performance in its own right. Auslander further reverses the temporal sequence of a live event and its recording to state that "*the act of documenting an event as a performance is what constitutes it as such*."[13] This analysis effectively repositions the performance document from being an indexical link to the originary event to being a performative entity in dialogue with its present beholder.

Common to Jones's and Auslander's arguments is their defense of the perceptual immediacy, analytical rigor, ethical feasibility, and epistemic validity of a performance critique offered by a viewer/reader who may not have seen the live event itself, but who has studied the performance artwork through its various documentary remnants. Both arguments support my conceptual basis in assessing the Chinese time-based artworks. Before I plead my case again, however, let me first address a zone of contention and power struggle.

The move to highlight the "intersubjective as well as interobjective"[14] exchange between a critic/reader and the performance documents has the potential effect of divesting the artist, who created the performance live, of her/his conceptual monopoly over the given artwork. For the artwork itself, as reflected in its documentary fragments and reconstructed by the critic/writer, is the real object of inquiry, whereas the artist becomes only a source, as the one who had produced – with varying degrees of conscious control – the artwork of interest. In a critique of Jones's "'Presence' in *absentia*," for instance, Catherine Elwes protests precisely what she regards as a reduction of the artist's creative agency by a critic who has chosen, without having seen the live event, to interpret the piece based on its documents. Elwes takes exception especially to Jones's reservation about getting to know an artist personally to ascertain his/

her perceived intentions about the work. "What we were left with," as Elwes objects, "was the primacy of the written word over the visual, the postrational over the immediate non-verbal response and the critic over the person and creative output of the artist."[15]

As a performance critic myself whose primary medium is words, I accept Elwes's charge that to privilege the performance documentation over its vanished referent tends to displace the artist-performer from the center stage to the wing. Moreover, at the spot vacated by the artist/creator now sits the critic/writer, whose action alternates between thumbing through an assortment of performance documents and gazing into thin air. In this scenario revolving around a writerly reader's response, there is an intervention – an intrusion, even – of critical subjectivity into a live artwork's creative domain, effectively "demoting" artistic subjectivity – at least the part embodied by the artist/performer's intentionality and mnemonic agency – to be a mere trace among many the critic/writer consults in evaluating the performance. While a critic/scholar might be justified and indeed compelled to do so when composing a historiographic account about a century-old performance, the situation becomes highly contentious with respect to a contemporary piece when the original author is still alive and open to queries.

Although I cherish learning from an as-yet-accessible creator, I also believe that performance art's conceptual basis fosters the emergence of critical subjectivity as a composite, contingent, and provisional textual embodiment of spectatorial commitment, recreative agency, and interpretive critique. As I have elaborated elsewhere, performance art thrives on a radical incompleteness: it anticipates a spectatorial other's active perceptual, cognitive, and hermeneutic investments to extend its mnemonic affectability.[16] My thesis departs from performance art's intermedia borrowing from theater to constitute its consistent structural ecology: the time-space-action-performer-audience matrix of theatricality. Unlike theater art's communal root, however, performance art's conceptual heritage allows it to elastically remodel each theatrical element, especially what counts as "an audience." Whereas theater cannot sustain itself without a live audience, performance art manages to reconceptualize the dialogic relationship between the performer and the audience as a *promise* rather than an essence. This redefinition grants performance art to seek the polyphonic dynamics of the (theatrical) here-and-now even in the (conceptual) thereafter. My analysis elucidates why performance art, after some initial resistance to documentation, has quickly evolved strategies for posthumous revival by incorporating a technological arsenal for self-memorialization, as if to preempt its own mortality.

From performance art's open invitation for spectatorial others to witness, experience, and share the work's present-tense unfolding comes infinite possibilities for onsite viewers to multiply what the work signifies, or how the live action touches those present. From performance art's desire to document itself for wider and future cultural dissemination comes the prospect of multiplying its audience base to include all those subsequent others provoked by the artwork, however distanced in time and space they are from the originary action, which might have been witnessed only by a camera's lens, the audience of a technological eye. By willingly distributing conceptual ownership among its actual and/

or virtual viewers, performance art has (inadvertently) nourished the rise of performative writing as a discursive mode that enacts – by writing into being – critical subjectivity. Although an artist might feel threatened by a critic's professed adoption of a subject position in critiquing the artwork, I hold that the expression of critical subjectivity remains bound to the analyzed artwork and, as such, communicates nothing but the response to an affective force. Besides, to foreground critical subjectivity merely discloses an ineluctable but rarely exposed process within any analytical project. Critical subjectivity complements, contests, challenges, and supplements artistic subjectivity to jointly locate the performance artwork in its larger sociocultural contexts. The critic and the artist therefore partner in their purpose to articulate and propagate the artwork's significance in discursive memories. This shared purpose, I offer, validates performance research's recent focus on documentation as both a retrospective site, permitting one to access and appraise the originary live artwork, and a generative site, empowering a subsequent critic/writer to discern, imagine, and amplify the cultural resonances of the given piece.

I have earlier compared documentation to a *deus ex machina*, swooping down from its multimedia crane to salvage the hermetic body of the *once-lived* and then to catapult it explosively into space, tearing the *once-lived* apart into myriad star seeds, waiting to sprout again. The critic as an experiential, probing, empathetic, and epistemic subject provides one of those potentially sustainable eco-pods, wherein the *once-lived* – despite being now only smithereens – may come alive again, albeit in an alternatively incarnated form, in the cultural ether. Can we clearly differentiate who owes whom in this exchange? The eco-pod is inert until it is triggered into animation by a wandering star seed and the fragile star seed is lonely until it finds an echo chamber to evolve.

III. Clicking on the Prostheses

In my allegory for the information transfer process that makes possible live art's posthumous circulation in the culture-at-large, I chanced upon the imagery of outer space, conjuring up a boundless vista without national borders, geo-historical diversities, economic, demographic, political, and other regional differences. This picture exists only in the abstraction of a heuristic model. The model illustrates performance documentation's service in facilitating the dissemination of time-based art, but it fails to address, say, why artists in diverse countries may have both similar and different reasons to document their artworks. Ironically, this boundless space with much freedom for movement, play, spontaneity, and self-determination may chime in quite harmoniously with the projection by multinational corporate forces of a globalized world market filled with infinite opportunities.

I realize that my hermeneutic horizon has been subliminally affected – both cultivated and contaminated – by my particularized residency within the United States, which is harried but still complacent at its current historical moment as a relatively affluent, expansionist, self-defensive, post-industrialized nation. Despite conscious vigilance, my role as a critical subject remains complicit with my life's specific propensity, making my encounter with every Chinese artistic subject an intercultural negotiation and my studies of his/her performance a sub-field of Sinology. Complicating this factor is my personal immigration background as a Taiwanese American who had spent her formative years on an island that continues to have an ambivalent and tense political relationship with mainland China. There is more than one way for the Chinese artists to mark me, even before or just when we begin to speak; my accent, here and there, speaks louder than my syntax, English or Chinese. Even presuming that no neutral critical subject exists, my diasporic acculturation still raises the stakes of my transcontinental investigations.

This self-reflexive scrutiny prepares for my coinage of "prosthetic performance," which addresses the complex afterlife of a time-based artwork through a process largely activated by performance documentation. A prosthetic device is above all an entity that stands in substitution for the irretrievable origin; it extends the origin's functionality by metaphorically giving it a second life – one that may survive indefinitely in the hereafter of an expired body of action. A constant reminder of the vanished origin, a prosthesis yearns for the absent body even as it recuperates the body's raison d'être and re-engages with its existential potentials. In a minor usage related to body modification subculture, a prosthetic unit (say, a breast implant) may be added to an existing body to alter the body's images, thereby augmenting, calling attention to, or otherwise transforming its functions.[17] Departing from the prosthetic's instrumentality as a medical or cosmetic technology, I use prosthetic performance to account for the various ways in which a live performance extends its vitality beyond its originary sited and time-based span.

Prosthetic performances belong to the order of documentation. They signify the relatively more accessible and distributable information sources for a live action that has transpired elsewhere. As repossessed mnemonic vehicles appearing in a sporadic chronology and encompassing multiple modality, prosthetic performances empower virtual spectators to imaginarily encounter a past time-based artwork. An eyewitness account, an oral recall, a journalistic review, and a scholarly critique about a given live event are prosthetic performances; so are documentary photographs, written statements, diagrams, or performance scores prepared by the artists. Since a prosthetic performance deals explicitly with the privilege of access, it exists less for itself than to supplement and enrich its source performance. A prosthetic performance's very emergence attends to a vanished antecedent. While not a replica, a prosthetic performance seeks to imitate its origin by emulating its intended cultural efficacy. In prosthetic performance, live art finds an evolutionary answer to its existential dilemma: it lives as it dies and vice versa. A prosthetic performance offers a conciliatory solution to preserving an art/life form that fulfills itself by its own expenditure.

If what an artist makes is a perishable body of performance, then what a critic makes, having sifted through the performance's documentary substitutes to piece together, reconfigure, and extend the source body, is a prosthetic performance. Claiming a critic's analytical as well as inventive response as a *prosthetic performance* rather than an *authentic representation*, I hope to articulate what I regard as the bond between an artist and a critic in producing a live art critique and the ineluctable emanation of critical subjectivity into the historiographic process. Both propositions confront the consequence of mortality and a mortal's attempt not to bypass death but to transfigure its finality. The ethical bond between two voluntary subjects brings up the issue of acquired, in lieu of biological, inheritance: through affinity, an other gifts the self with an act, if not of love, at least of concentrated energy. This observation applies to both the artist/maker as the self, endowed with the creative agency to gift the world with an ephemeral artwork, which then depends on others to make public, and to the critic/writer as the self, inspired by the live presence and/or documentary traces of an other's artwork to operate the recreative license, producing in turn a work that resurrects, however partially, its source of stimulation and gratitude. To expose a critical subject's recreative intervention, moreover, is to acknowledge the entropic tendency within human memories: what we call history is, at its most sincere, an approximation of what has happened. Historical verity is produced rather than retrieved by the historian's scrupulous research, both in the field and on the desk. The prosthesis of this once-lived "verity" is imagination.

My theory of prosthetic performance falters when I turn to my selected Chinese time-based artworks, in which no clear distinctions exist between enactment and documentation. What these artists make as the original pieces already include prosthetic performances. Qiu's calligraphy was at first a prosthetic performance of Wang Xizhi's masterpiece; subsequently he inscribed nine-hundred-and-ninety-nine replicating palimpsests on it. *Repeatedly Duplicating a Thousand Times "Lantingxu"* was therefore nothing but a durational prosthetic performance. *Within the Fourth Ring Road* comprises a table of regulations, the artist's documentary photograph, the social encounters on which he depended for survival, and his diary entries. Is Yang's table of regulations *not* the original performance, for which his actual begging serves as its prosthetic extension? Or, are his diary entries, produced alongside his begging, *not* the originary performances, which end up turning their live referents – the begging that cannot be perceived as art – into prosthetic performances? *"Wang Mian Rice Oil Shop" Document Files* concerns the continuous accumulation of art documents through the nonart action of running a grocery shop. This piece's original action is split into two, both revolving around the documenting act: Wang Hong produces the original documents – his shop's actual financial records – and Wang Chuyu documents Wang Hong's documentation by framing it as art and distributing the artwork on the Internet. The two artists create prosthetic performances for which their respective daily lives are the origins.

My Chinese case studies cause a cognitive crisis in my theorization of prosthetic performance. At most they evoke analogously the "cosmetic" application of prosthetics: to add something extra to an existing body part, not exactly to replace it but to modify, ornament, and enhance it. Wang's "Lantingxu" is the existing "body part" to the prosthetic performances contributed by Qiu. The various parts of Yang's *Within the Fourth Ring Road* serve as one another's compliments or prostheses. The collaborating artists in *"Wang Mian Rice Oil Shop" Document Files* intentionally produce prosthetic performances, whose original live/life source is artistically irrelevant. These artists have chosen to highlight documentation in their time-based art for reasons that seem, nonetheless, weightier in the Chinese context than my cosmetic analogy can suggest.

The use of documentation in these artists' performance works reflect a post-Tiananmen tactic in response to the heightened political tension and official proscription regarding avant-garde art, which China's communist government considered a culprit in inciting the students' pro-democratic mass rally. As Wu Hung notes, the Sichuan art critic Wang Lin invented "the format of the *Document Exhibition* (*Wenxian zhan*) in 1991" to circumvent the official prohibition against experimental art right after the June Fourth incident.[18] These shows, consisting of reproductions of experimental artworks and art writings, toured nationally to provide a communication channel for non-commercial artists. In the late 1990s, when government censorship became less systematic and the technology of dissemination witnessed a qualitative shift, these document exhibitions were effectively replaced by "virtual exhibitions," which served similar purposes via a new cybernetic channel.[19]

Citing Wang's *Document Exhibition* as a precedent, Wu Hung elucidates what he observes as Chinese artists' quest for unconventional ways of exhibiting experimental art in the 1990s. I would extend Wu's inquiry to suggest that documentation likely enjoyed the discursive camouflage of being perceived by China's censors as scholarly, historical, and politically inert. Thus, documentation becomes the very mechanism art practitioners use to initiate cultural circulations of certain artworks deemed too seditious for public display. These radical artworks, presented as themselves to the public, might provoke collective reactions, which the government would not tolerate. In contrast, to display these artworks' documents, as mere prosthetic reminders of what was allegedly "real," is an educational and cultural activity, which the government would encourage, even with funding support.

China's given political circumstance in the first post-Tiananmen decade probably persuaded many time-based artists to seize documentation simultaneously as a means of preserving their ephemeral artworks and the sole vehicle for transferring their art to the public domain. Yet, this general circumstance cannot fully explain my case studies. Qiu began his calligraphic performance in 1990, which preceded *Document Exhibition*. Yang's begging piece happened almost a decade later, when commercialization replaced censorship as the major threat to Chinese experimental art. Wang's documentation project appeared even later; besides, the project speaks to the socially conscious, mass-enlightening ethics of Mao Zedong's cultural heritage, as articulated in his *Yan'an Talks on Literature and Art*.[20] My chosen artworks are weak targets for censorship, but strong candidates for the Ministry of Culture's medals of honor!

Aside from institutional censorship, then, what might be other region-specific reasons for Chinese artists to feature documentation? Reading the selected artworks within China's current sociocultural moment, I submit that documentation serves various epistemic, redressive, pragmatic, and pedagogical functions. Due to rapid modernization and the aggressive mobilization of capital, transience and opportunism have become the order of China's daily urban life, especially since Deng Xiaoping's 1992 reaffirmation of his policy to promote a socialist market economy without tampering with the hegemonic communist ideology.[21] Both modernization and capitalist mobilization aim for building a prosperous future for China; time-based art counters this officially condoned mass rally for the future by intensifying the existential awareness and relish of the present moment. Documenting time-based art amounts to producing certain culturally pertinent but financially unprofitable objects, thereby promulgating the ethical efficacy of non-monetary alternatives for living/being. This subtly dissident proposal goes against the grains of mainstream economic trends and challenges the prevalent attitude toward conspicuous consumption as a sociocultural status symbol.

Returning to prosthetic performance, I will offer one more thought regarding my critical ventures into China's time-based art. The artworks examined here merely sample a prominent motif – documentation – in the respective oeuvres of Qiu Zhijie, Yang Zhichao, and Wang Chuyu. The three artists are heirs to China's literati tradition, which recognizes an intellectual as a poet, a historian, and a philosopher all in one: a "total writer" of sorts. All three artists, for instance, write extensively about contemporary experimental art, including publishing insightful comments on their own works. Their writerly interventions, I suggest, create a split – or, rather, a multiplication effect – in their artistic identities, which have incorporated critical subjectivities in their make-ups. These artists are capable of critiquing and historicizing their own art; their self-documentations rival my critical interpretations of their artworks. Whose prosthetic performance would speak the last word?

Prosthetic performance may then also mark the process of negotiation, even competition, between the artist, who has authored the source performance, and the critic, who wills to author a subsequent critique, in their dialectic struggles and/or alliances to historicize the performance piece. A critic may choose, of course, not to develop any substantial (interpersonal) contact with the artist. I am not making an ethical argument for the need to interview an artist, but rather to describe, should such a contact happen in the critic's research, the intersubjective exchanges that may retrospectively transform the live event, simply by re-accessing it. Prosthetic performance emerges out of such loaded exchanges to alter, augment, and extend the originary live artwork, which is its source, referent, and its object of inspiration and quest.

IV. Interface, Then and Now

I opened the chapter with three moments of experiential distillation; like hyperlinks, they transport me into an altered state of mnemonic immersion. These capstone-like entries lure me into what Alison Lansberg calls, "prosthetic memories,"[22] those that one appropriates not through strictly lived experience, but from one's empathic involvement with the information culture. Focusing on the cinematic experience, Lansberg's analysis nevertheless identifies a cognitive phenomenon resembling my sensory recall of a live performance. By summoning up the event again, I remember a gesture, a tonal inflection, or an accusatory glance that I might or might not have seen then and there. The reverse also holds true: by searching through a performance's documentary traces, I remember how it happened then and there, even though I had not lived through its happening. "But thinking makes it so," as Hamlet once said through Shakespeare (or the other way around). Slanting the thinking otherwise: for one who recognizes memory's property as prosthetic, history is always in the making. This epiphany turns prosthetic memory into a drive for prosthetic performance; both gravitate toward the agency of *now*.

Prosthetic performance invites us to reconsider what we have termed "live" in both *enacting* and *recording* time-based artworks. Suddenly we wonder again what's "live" in live art? Is it "barely live" and "barely art," as Alan Read once wittily put it?[23] Does it indicate the contingent dynamics among various perceptual qualities, identified by Adrian Heathfield as "immediate, immersive, interactive," each addressing the artist's manipulation and contemplation of temporality, spatiality, and corporeality?[24] Does "live" signify the present-tense co-presence of three-dimensional beings, the conscious or coincidental synchronicity between a perceiver-enactor and other entities, sentient or otherwise? Does "live" describe the process of executing a durational task or the condition of presenting/displaying the task?

Re-accessing the live alongside the prosthetic troubles what we habitually presume to be the relations between live performance and documentation, such as their sequentiality and their contrasting original and prosthetic standings. I argue that sensing and behaving "live" is an experiential dimension that happens *both* in creating and in recording time-based art. For an artistic subject, being "live" may be a condition first associated with the duration of making / presenting a performance, and then it emerges as a discontinuous, accumulative, repetitive, and perhaps protracted process in documenting a performance. For a critical subject who missed attending the live event, the sequence of experiencing "live" is somewhat reversed: moving from encountering the prosthetic to producing the meta-original, a referential text simultaneously original and prosthetic.

The live sequences I trace above become further complicated in my Chinese samples. These artworks are either compiled of numerous prosthetic performances, or cannot be witnessed wholly by intentional viewers. As interested spectatorial others, we can only access the source performances via their prosthetic doubles. Thus, if we loosely equate the watching of a live performance to a documenting process for our mnemonic repertoires, then we may approach Qiu's, Yang's, and Wangs' documentary performances as a redoubled process of documentation, a *live* duration in which our experiences with the originary and the prosthetic overlap and through which we may design (*live*) our prosthetic additions to the original prosthetic bodies.

Is there a contradiction in using documentation to create time-based art? On the surface, I believe, a contradiction does exist. If we take ephemerality as the cost of a time-based artwork, then documenting the artwork itself, or rather, performing the artwork via documentation, may be seen as creating a saving account to offset the expense of forgetfulness. Just as live art spends, so documentation salvages and saves. But, underneath the surface, ephemerality, or the sense of ceaselessly losing touch with the evaporating moment-to-moment, is precisely what drives the impulse for documentation. Extravagance inspires and depends on conservation to last. As a prosthetic double to live art, documentation reviews, repeats, records, relearns, and re-imagines a partially memorialized past to generate a present-tense re-encounter with pieces from the past and to facilitate future generations' reliving of these semi-processed pasts in their present moments. What we call "live," then, points to a perceiver's present-tense intertwinement with the fleeting sense of being alive. Documentation offers a storehouse (or, to a more enterprising documenter, a bank) of catalysts, signs, images, mirrors, candles, discursive fragments, and other mnemonic prompters for us to simultaneously engender and live in a prosthetic present tense.

Notes

1. Throughout the text, I have adopted the pinyin system for Chinese titles, followed by the titles' English translations in parentheses. For Chinese names, I follow the local convention of listing the surname first, unless the artists or scholars prefer otherwise. Unless otherwise stated, all translations from Chinese into English are mine, including the artworks' titles and cited passages. Although I follow the artworks' original Chinese titles in my pinyin versions, my translated titles at times differ from those publicized by the artists or by earlier critics.
2. See the artist's personal website Qiu Zhijie.com. Available at: http://www.qiuzhijie.com/homepage.htm, accessed 2010.
3. Augusto Boal, "Invisible Theatre," translated from the French by Susana Epstein, *TDR*, 1990, vol. 34, no. 3 (T127), pp. 24–34 (24). Reprinted in Rebecca Schneider and Gabrielle Cody (eds), *Re:Direction: A Theoretical and Practical Guide*, London: Routledge, 2002, pp. 112–21 (112).
4. See Zhichao Yang, "Dangan 15: Yang Zhichao xingwei yishu dangan," in Wenguang Wu (ed.), *Document/Xianchang*, Guangxi, China: Guangxi shifan daxuei chubanshe, 2005, pp. 6–147 (29) for his journal entry dated 30 July 1999.
5. Gregory Battcock (ed.), *Idea Art: A Critical Anthology*, New York: E. P. Dutton, 1973 [1970], p. 1.
6. Allan Kaprow, "Nontheatrical Performance," in Jeff Kelley (ed.), *Allan Kaprow, Essays on the Blurring of Art and Life*, Berkeley: University of California Press, 1993 [1976], pp. 163–80, at pp. 174–75.
7. Chuyu Wang, interview with the author, 7 July 2006, in Beijing. Wang posted the project's monthly records on the Web regularly during 2006. Afterwards, they have continued to keep physical records, but did not publicize them routinely online.
8. Zhijie Qiu, interview with the author, 5 July 2005, in Beijing.
9. Zhichao Yang, "Dangan 15: Yang Zhichao xingwei yishu dangan," in Wenguang Wu (ed.) *Document/Xianchang*, Guangxi, China: Guangxi shifan daxuei chubanshe 2005, pp. 6–147, at p. 29.
10. Amelia Jones, "'Presence' *in absentia*: Experiencing Performance as Documentation," *Art Journal*, Winter 1997, vol. 56, no. 4, pp. 11–18, at p. 12.
11. Ibid.
12. Phillip Auslander, "The Performativity of Performance Documentation," *PAJ*, 2006, vol. 84, pp. 1–10, at p. 9.
13. Ibid., p. 5.
14. Jones, op. cit., p. 12.
15. Catherine Elwes, "On Performance and Performativity: Women Artists and Their Critics," *Third Text*, 2004, vol. 18, no. 2, pp. 193–7, at p. 194.

16. Meiling Cheng, *In Other Los Angeleses: Multicentric Performance Art*, Berkeley and London: University of California Press, 2002.
17. See Parmod K. Nayar, *Virtual Worlds: Culture and Politics in the Age of Cybertechnology*, London: Sage Publications, 2004.
18. Hung Wu, "A Brief Reflection on the Study of Contemporary Chinese Experimental Art," in Hung Wu (ed.), *Transience: Chinese Experimental Art at the End of the Twentieth Century*, Chicago: The David and Alfred Smart Museum of Art and the University of Chicago Press, 2004 [1999], pp. 176–9, at p. 178.
19. Wu, "Exhibiting Experimental Art in China," in Hung Wu (ed.), *Exhibiting Experimental Art in China*, Chicago: The David and Alfred Smart Museum of Art and the University of Chicago Press, 2000, pp. 9–46, at p. 41.
20. See Xianting Li, "Major Trends in the Development of Contemporary Chinese Art," trans. Valerie C. Doran, in Valerie C. Doran (ed.), *China's New Art, Post-89*, X–XXII, Hong Kong: Hanart TZ Gallery, 1993, pp. xii–xiii.
21. See Kang Liu, "Is There an Alternative to (Capitalist) Globalization? The Debate about Modernity in China," in Frederic Jameson and Masao Miyoshi (eds), *The Cultures of Globalization*, Durham: the Duke University Press 2003 [1998], pp. 164–88; Minglu Gao, "Toward a Transnational Modernity," in Minglu Gao (ed.), *Inside Out: New Chinese Art*, New York: San Francisco Museum of Modern Art and Asia Society Galleries and Berkeley: University of California Press, 1998, pp. 15–40; Xudong Zhang (ed.), *Whither China? Intellectual Politics in Contemporary China*, Durham and London: Duke University Press, 2001.
22. Alison Lansberg, "Prosthetic Memory: *Total Recall* and *Blade Runner*," in Mike Featherstone and Roger Burrows (eds), *Cyberspace, Cyberbodies, Cyberpunk: Cultures of Technological Embodiment*, London: Sage Publications, 1995, pp. 175–90, at p. 175.
23. Alan Read, "Say Performance," in Adrian Heathfield (ed.), *Live: Art and Performance*, London: Tate, 2004, pp. 242–7, at p. 243.
24. Adrian Heathfield, "Alive," in Adrian Heathfield (ed.), *Live: Art and Performance*, London: Tate, 2004, pp. 6–13, at p. 8.

Chapter 10

Progressive Striptease

Sven Lütticken

Performance Ideology: Past and Present

Ever since the late 1950s, when happenings and events first appeared on the art scene, performance art has carried progressive and in some cases revolutionary connotations. Especially from the 1970s onwards, when the term performance became widely used in the art world and a specific discourse developed around it, this ideologization turned into a reflex. "Performance clogs the smooth machinery of reproductive representation necessary to the circulation of capital," Peggy Phelan wrote in 1993, although she might no longer endorse this statement today.[1] Yet Kristine Stiles has recently demonstrated that this discourse is still anything but dead: "Through its emphasis on action, performance recovers the social force of art. It remains one of the last and most effective modes of resistance to all forms of domination, from globalization to totalitarianism," and in this sense continues the work done in the heroic era, from the 1950s to the 1970s, when performance was "the most forceful opposition to capitalism in the visual arts."[2] Only performance can save the world: this is more or less what this discourse amounts to.

It is high time to reconsider this rhetoric and to formulate an alternative to the ideologization of performance as an intrinsically progressive phenomenon. From the 1950s to the 1970s, performance could still be presented as being radically opposed to spectacle, its primitivist quasi-rituals apparently immune to colonization by the media and of the market; as a "progressive" force, performance art in fact opposed progress as defined by capitalism – a future of growth, new products, new markets. By now, the accumulation of economical, social, and environmental havoc suggests that capitalism's future itself is the revival of an archaic past, far removed from the shiny promises made by the postwar spectacle; it is as if the spectacle now stages a grim version of the romantic archaisms of

Originally published as Sven Lütticken, "Progressive Striptease: Performance Ideology Past and Present," in *Secret Publicity: Essays on Contemporary Art*, Rotterdam: NAi Publishers, 2006, pp. 161–80.

much historical performance art. In this situation, performance ideologists such as Tino Sehgal redefine performance's progressive role in capitalist terms: far from being a leftist critique of capitalism, performance now is to save capitalism by deflecting its destructive archaic turn into a more benign primitivist utopia.

Dematerialization

Among other reasons, performance is regarded as progressive because it trades in the object for ephemeral action. It is hence thought to represent a break with the status of art as a commodity. In Lucy Lippard's classic anthology, *Six Years: The Dematerialization of the Art Object from 1966 to 1972*, the author discusses performance along with other "dematerialized" art forms of the period. She lists the principal media as video, performance, photography, narrative, text, and actions, and the first work of art she cites is a book by George Brecht, which combines several of these categories.[3] "Brecht has been making 'events' that anticipate a stricter 'conceptual art' since around 1960," Lippard writes, giving several examples of Brecht's event-texts, including *Time-Table Event, spring, 1961*: "To occur in a railway station. A timetable is obtained. A tabled indication is interpreted in minutes and seconds (7:16 equaling, for example, 7 minutes and 16 seconds). This determines the duration of the event."[4] Works such as this are ambivalent: they are textual works that could in principle give rise to performances, but they could just as well remain entirely textual. Lippard therefore lumps this art form in with Conceptual art, which uses language, photography, film, and video. These media provide her with her archetypal "dematerialized art objects" and true performance plays at most a minor part. But although Lippard believes these art forms imply a critique of the art product as a unique, prestige-laden commodity, they still yield objects which function as commodities – if of a more "democratic" complexion than expensive paintings. It would appear that performance art goes farther, genuinely abandoning the object; after all, performances are not supposed to yield even nugatory objects, but to consist purely of action. As Kristine Stiles puts it:

> Performance [...] developed into a leftist alternative to the production of art objects and was presented in non-traditional spaces as a means to subvert both the market and the regular institutions of art. It confounded the reduction of art to undifferentiated merchandise by displacing objects with artists, subjects whose performances resisted commodification (even as the residue of those acts could still be objectified and sold).[5]

This final qualification rather undermines her argument, and in practice virtually every form of art performance has yielded objects of some kind, whether relics of the action itself or recordings on physical media such as photos or videos.

But what if there were a radicalized performance art which really left no material trace and which survived only in the audience's memory? Would this really amount to a rift with the commodity character of art? Has such a "pure" performance art totally dispensed with commodification? Not if the performance *itself* is sold as a commodity. After all, according to Marxist political economy, a commodity does not have to be a material object: a commodity is anything that is exchanged for money, anything that is sold.[6] From this perspective the ever-rising importance of immaterial commodities such as services in the western economy is an interesting development within advanced capitalism, as an effort to create new areas for the production of surplus value, but it does not really amount to a fundamental break. Services are still commodities, even if they are allegedly more advanced in character than ordinary goods. Of course, liberal economic theory does not claim that services constitute a rift with capitalism either, but it is more inclined to place emphasis on the qualitative difference between goods and services: services are hyped up as a more advanced, progressive economic phenomenon, the very vanguard of capitalism. Tino Sehgal, an artist who is perhaps the leading ideologist of performance of recent years, seems to have concluded from this that performance art is far from being an attack on capitalism: after all, performance seems to bear a similar relation to the modern art object as services do to goods.

Sehgal's works consist mainly of small surprises in art shows, actions which are generally carried out by staff of the institutions concerned: a museum attendant who suddenly starts jumping up and down, for instance, someone rolling over the ground in slow motion, or a girl who unexpectedly sinks to the ground behind the visitor's back and breaks into song. Each of these acts concludes with a pronouncement of the title of the work and the name of the artist. Sehgal's prima facie aim in these highly immaterial works is to dispense with the nature of art as an object, but his stated intentions are ecological rather than anti-capitalist. Unlike earlier performance ideologists, Sehgal does not criticize the object because of art's commodified status but because of the depletion of natural resources and environmental degradation. Industry is now having negative effect on humanity rather than a positive one, and art ought not add to that burden: "The fact that current production is possibly also decreasing the quality of life is in civilizational terms an absolute historical novelty, since the function of production was, of course, to ensure survival and enhance the quality of life."[7] It is on these grounds that Sehgal describes the production of art objects as "reactionary."[8] The implicit suggestion is of course that performance is progressive, but he does not conclude that performance escapes the market's clutches. "My agenda is not necessarily a leftist one," Sehgal explains, and unlike Lippard or Phelan, he accepts that dematerialized art is as much a part of the capitalist economy as any other kind.[9]

While this insight is to his credit, it forms the prelude to a new "progressive" ideologization of performance, which combines the old leftist slogans on dematerialization with a more recent discourse developed by economists who hype advanced capitalism. A typical instance of this tendency is *The Experience Economy* by Joseph Pine and James Gilmore, a book which was briefly hyped up in the art world a few years ago.[10] This book, tellingly subtitled "Every Work is Theatre & Every Business a Stage," sketches a progressive economical spiritualization, leading from "commodities" via "goods" and "services" to "experiences." In

Marxian discourse, the term "commodity" refers to *all* material or immaterial products sold under capitalism, but Pine and Gilmore, and contemporary liberal economics in general, use it exclusively to refer to bulk goods – their, "lowest," most primitive category. The more immaterial the product, the higher its value and status, but higher goods generally depend on the lower ones: even if a fancy coffee shop turns the buying and drinking of a cappuccino into an "experience," the transaction still involves raw materials, goods and services. However, the surplus value is increasingly located in the uppermost category: most of the ten dollars you fork out for drinking a fancy coffee is for the "experience."

Sehgal follows a similar logic of capitalist dematerialization, but he aims to strip advanced commodities of the hybrid, "inconsistent" traits they present in the "experience economy." He also aims to short-circuit the first two steps – the consumption of raw materials and their processing into goods – so as to supply a purely performative service that results in an "experience." To elucidate his outlook on performance, Sehgal points to the example of striptease.[11] Striptease is ephemeral but distinct from other forms of dance:

> [W]hat is specific about striptease is that it is generally done to be bought and sold. It is inherently commercial. It is a product like any other product, with one categorical difference: it is produced by a person transforming his or her actions.[12]

In contrast to other service jobs which use objects (such as computers) or consist of the processing of objects, Sehgal argues that the striptease is almost wholly immaterial: the shedding of material ballast has become its very content. Despite the sexist connotations of striptease, something Sehgal clearly has problems with, it forms a perfect model for the future, and for progressive performance art. The dematerialization of art has completed its capitalist turn. Sehgal's artistic project is not only an attempt to rescue nature and our natural environment, but also an attempt to rescue capitalism from its own destructive tendencies. Only if it relinquishes producing things can capitalism have a future; the performance can prepare and instigate this relinquishment, and that is where its inherent radicalism and progressiveness lie. But the fact that his neo-liberal ecotopia has barely anything to do with actual economic developments, in which industrial production continues to play a significant (if unsexy) part, turns it into a hypocritical fable – an ideological magic mirror held up to the existing order.

Ban on Reproduction

"Classic" performance art was pitched not only against the art object or the material character of art, but also against all forms of reproduction and representation. Performance was typically associated with a discourse that contrasted performance to the alienating, fetishist nature of the mass media and the spectacle. Against these spectacular representations, performance posited, in Peggy Phelan's words, an activating and confrontational "representation without reproduction," while Erika Fischer-Lichte argues that performance attempted to transgress the limits of representation itself in order to seek a liminal experience that was simultaneously presentation and a representation.[13] When Marina Abramović allows her audience to mistreat her, even providing weapons with which she could be killed, representation and presence have indeed become inextricably entwined. This rejection of reproduction too was motivated by anti-capitalism. Performance was trying to detach itself from capitalist spectacle, and the photography or filming of performances was regarded as an inadmissible attempt to reclaim performance and reintegrate it into the capitalist spectacle.

This view has persisted for many years; even in the 1990s, Peggy Phelan still defended performance's by-now-traditional inimicality to reproduction, claiming that performance should serve as a "model for another representational economy":

> Performance's only life is in the present. Performance cannot be saved, recorded, documented, or otherwise participate in the circulation of representations of representations: once it does so, it becomes something other than performance. To the degree that performance attempts to enter the economy of reproduction it betrays and lessens the promise of its own ontology.[14]

In other words, when a performance is reproduced it is no longer a true performance. The persistence of this discourse seems all the more remarkable when we consider that, historically, the ban on reproduction has proved futile – even in the 1960s, when happenings went "pop" and transformed into media events, to the disgust of Allan Kaprow and the delight of Andy Warhol, who himself eagerly took part in the process. It is in any case now clear that the "classic" performance art of Joseph Beuys, Marina Abramović, or Chris Burden owes its enduring impact largely to the black-and-white photos, films, and videos that were made. These images have acquired the status of originals, to such an extent that recent re-enactments of historical happenings, events, and performances continually find themselves in competition with these old images; the re-enactment runs the risk of coming across as the live reproduction of an old photo or video.[15] The best re-enactments are not afraid to take this risk, and in general the more interesting recent performance art tends to undermine the conventional opposition between the live event and the (supposedly inferior) reproduction. Whereas classic performance art generally tried to abandon representation for presentation of a non-reproducible live experience, more recent performances draw lessons from the fact that the classic performances proved unable to avoid media representation. Live performances, photos, and videos are now acknowledged as different manifestations of the same work, which oscillates between presentation and representation in a more complex way than the old performance ideology was willing to contemplate (and the live version is not the form in which that work survives).

The conclusion from this can only be that performance art has never been a real threat to the spectacle; its integration into spectacle as media performance comes as no surprise. Yet if performance artists were to radicalize the anti-production tradition, if they were to really roll up their sleeves and take the fight against reproduction seriously – couldn't this result in a form of performance that was incompatible with capitalism? This line of reasoning rests on the assumption that "the media" are virtually identical with advanced capitalism. Yet following Guy Debord, one can argue that the spectacular character of the capitalist economy is not primarily located in media like film, photography, and video, but in commodity fetishism: commodities seem to maintain whimsical "social" relations due to their exchange value. In the process the commodities become images, hieroglyphic representations of the relations in human society.[16] This primary spectacle of commodities-become-images is thus the prevailing social condition, which is reflected in "the media" in the form of a secondary spectacle of images-become-commodities, which reinforces the primary spectacle. To get rid of the society of spectacle, it is hence not enough to get rid of "the media"; the whole of society must be revolutionized.

Taking the anti-media rhetoric of performance discourse more seriously than was usual in the 1960s and 1970s, Sehgal fights reproduction of his works in photographs or videos with an almost Taliban-like fanaticism, actively trying to prevent pictures of his works being taken and published. However, since Sehgal is not an anti-capitalist, his prohibition of photographic and video reproduction cannot be interpreted as anti-capitalist either. Like Debord, he must have come to the conclusion that a ban on reproduction is not necessarily a threat to the spectacle; indeed, his work is based on the insight that a radical ban on prohibition could have a peerlessly spectacular effect. The aura of such elusive celebrities as J.D. Salinger, Stanley Kubrick, and Howard Hughes has already demonstrated that a one-sided denial of mechanical reproduction fosters mythologization and thus functions as a paradoxical form of publicity. Sehgal applies the same principle to his artistic activities. The works profit from their unavailability; it is precisely because the performance happens only in a specific time and place, and is not visible on demand, that it has an aura comparable to that of Walter Benjamin's cult image – the devotional object which may be viewed only by priests except when paraded publicly on specific feast days.[17] Sehgal's rejection of reproduction and the difficult "findability" of his work in exhibitions turns the work of art back into (the semblance of a) cult image, or rather of a cult act. His ban on reproduction seems to enjoy a strange parallel with the increasingly severe restrictions on the use of images and text imposed by draconic copyright laws; both of them deny freedom to the spectator or user. Sehgal's primitivist model for a benign future capitalism serves as an ideological smokescreen for the spectacle's rather less cute archaisms.

Sehgal is not the only artist to generate an aura through invisibility. Rirkrit Tiravanija's 2004–5 retrospective, shown at Rotterdam's Museum Boijmans Van Beuningen and other venues, consisted entirely of reconstructions of empty spaces where the artist had once installed his work. The actual installations were not shown; they were merely described in texts that recalled the original presentations. It is to Tiravanija's credit that he foregrounded this mystique of absence through the show's didactic approach, thus stimulating the questioning of his own aura-production. In Sehgal's case, the main impression left is one of a deliberately mystifying aesthetic impoverishment. His radical ban on reproduction creates a spectacle of absence. The prohibition on photography stimulates instead the reproduction of the work in the form of rumor. The refusal of mediatization thus becomes mediagenic; the publicity machine of the museums, biennales, and other artistic manifestations ensures that word of Sehgal's ephemeral and largely invisible performances spreads like wildfire. Sehgal's triumph lies in staging the rejection of contemporary media culture in the most mediagenic way imaginable.

At the same time, the fact that Sehgal's work is made public through texts and rumors impedes critical scrutiny and reflection. Its limited visibility makes it harder for the spectator to get involved with it, to charge it with personal meanings and sentiments, and if need be to misread it. Exhibition visitors may have been free to discuss "the market economy" with Sehgal's performers or "interpreters" in the work *This is Exchange* (2004), but the actual course of those conversations is scarcely relevant: all that matters is that such conversations took place within the framework of Sehgal's work, regardless of their content; it is the representation of those conversations in the form of rumor that counts. Sehgal's performances are invisible, intangible commodities that live at a safe, enigmatic remove in their own world, as elusive as electronic capital.

The Performative Imperative

In recent years it has become more and more obvious that the spectacle has taken a "performative turn." Typical of the neo-liberal performance culture is the TV program in which a mediagenic entrepreneur like Donald Trump selects a new appointee from candidates who must perform themselves in a way that will win them a highly paid job. The spectacle of the Situationists, which involved a distinction between a dreamlike theater of commodities and the passive consumer, has been succeeded by a participatory, performative spectacle. Thus we have entered a phase that the Situationists themselves failed to foresee. In spite of the fact that commodities need not be objects, immaterial commodities such as services were somewhat neglected by Marxist theory, including that of the Situationist International, and the transformation of anonymous services into personalized performances is a development that was not seen or foreseen by the Situationists, and perhaps analyzed best by Italian operaists such as Paolo Virno and Antonio Negri with their work on post-Fordism and immaterial labor – even though, quite apart from the problematic aspects of these writings, in their reception their terminology becomes decontextualized and compatible with a neo-liberal hyping of "immaterial" capitalism.[18]

The primary immaterial commodity in Marxist theory was labor power: a statistical average of the amount of labor needed to produce a certain industrial commodity, which is responsible for the exchange value of goods (contrary to the fetishist illusion that they obtain value through mutual relations). In principle, this theory of labor power can also be applied to many services that do not depend on a unique performer. Services too are commodities in which labor has been invested, and in most cases the worker will be paid a wage that represents an abstraction – the amount of labor normally needed to do the job. Today, however, it seems increasingly difficult to base the value of goods on this statistical average – plus the surplus value, which the employer pockets. In the contemporary economy, value has spun completely out of control. A trendy cup of coffee may cost a small fortune because it represents an "experience," a top manager can take home an absurdly inflated bonus because he is a unique performer: he sells a *habitus* with capabilities and personal qualities that are supposedly unique. The value of such performers and their performances can no longer be measured in abstract labor power. If object-commodities become images in classical spectacle, in the performative spectacle the service too turns into an image. Of course, this does not mean that the other, anonymous service jobs no longer exist, but increasingly the performative colonizes labor: even in jobs where wages *are* standardized (and low), the worker is expected to put his or her unique charms and qualities into the job if he or she wants to keep it. As anonymous services become performances, even abstract labor power has to be enacted in a personalized way by individual performers.[19] This turns not only performance into a commodity, but ultimately the performer as well.

The Situationists' conception of the spectacle, which was still based on the model of the western theater with its audience watching a play on a stage, is not sufficient for the performative spectacle. An advert for a film camera reproduced in the *Internationale Situationniste* (SI) portrays a woman who wishes to film "the most beautiful moments of her life." As an industrial product, which produces images, the camera is a symptomatic commodity from a Situationist point of view. The caption, which is mostly about the colonization of time by the spectacle, has the headline "*domination du spectacle sur la vie*," but isn't the point of this ad the transformation of life itself *into* spectacle, rather the domination of life *by* the spectacle?[20] While Debord claimed that life was colonized by the spectacle, he pictured this above all as the infiltration of commodities – and of commodity fetishism – into all aspects of life. While the SI was not blind to the status of film stars or models as commodities, they were seen as more or less equal to cars and vacuum cleaners: commodity-images whose fetishist allure impoverished life, yet in the end distinct from the lives they dominate. And in fact, in the classical spectacle, stars – especially Hollywood stars – were distant and different, seemingly inhabiting a different world. But by the 1960s the inflation of stardom was well under way, as epitomized by Warhol's famous "fifteen minutes of fame" quote. The model in the film camera ad represents this new celebrity culture, just as the camera (although still a film camera, not yet video) announces the increasing availability of means of reproduction.

In the performative spectacle everybody is a potential performer, from movie stars to next-door neighbors. Reality TV, webcams, and similar phenomena are the ultimate consequence of this development. The polarity between performance and media cherished by performance ideologues has been replaced by a capricious dialectic: every profession, every job, every private life – in other words, every performance – can claim an entitlement to reproduction, and at the same time every conceivable media model may be lived out and performed. Performance art, integrated into the spectacle, has become part of this wider performative culture. Salvador Dalí, that consummate media performer, was no less prophetic of this development than Pollock, who – in spite of his qualms – was transformed by Hans Namuth into a media icon, which significantly contributed to the rise of happenings and events. Both Dalí and Pollock symbolize the metamorphosis of the role of the artist into permanent public self-performance. The difference between artist and oeuvre has collapsed: the artists themselves are their main commodity on the performative market. Stiles' statement should actually be inverted: performance has aggravated the reduction of art to undifferentiated merchandise by displacing objects by artists, by subjects whose performances have themselves become commodified. In his striptease utopia, Sehgal distracts attention from the true conditions of the present performative imperative: the culture of Donald Trump and Matthew Barney, of Germaine Greer appearing in *Big Brother* and of the former punk Situationist John Lydon in a jungle show, of countless business people and employees – and of Tino Sehgal. The striptease model has already long been realized, if perhaps in a less utopian way than anticipated; for what is striptease if not an extreme manifestation of the merciless economic drive to perform?

In this culture of mandatory performance, the discourse on performance has entered a new round. On the one hand it has become an academic specialism, meticulously administered by scholarly technocrats; on the other hand the increased focus on this field has entailed a continual inflation of the concept of performance. During the 1990s, performance theorists like Peggy Phelan used elements from the works of J. L. Austin and Judith Butler to develop a broad notion of the performative or performativity.[21] In the days when art was just beginning its own performative turn, with Pollock and the reception of Pollock by Harold Rosenberg, Allan Kaprow and others (and several years before George Brecht's ambiguous "event scores"), Austin called attention to the performative component of certain forms of speech, such as baptizing a ship or declaring a couple man and wife. Although his discourse and practice depend on the classic isolation of "pure performance" as a physical act, Sehgal is a virtuoso language-performer: his ban on reproduction and his notarized sales contracts may well be his most important (linguistic) performances.

By now the terms "performative" and "performativity" have been overstretched like semantic chewing gum: anything can be performative, even art objects and static images. Sehgal's partner, the critic Dorothea von Hantelmann, presents the artist as the apotheosis of the wider definition of "the performative." She argues that *every* work of art should be seen as performative, and hence as political, in that it forces the spectator into an active relationship.[22] Sehgal's piece in which the visitor is invited to make a statement about the market economy is one of Hantelmann's examples of this political, activating character of the performative.[23] But if any statement and any discussion or non-discussion will do, all that seems to matter is the suggestion that everything is performative, and that this insight and its enactment constitute a radical theoretical advance. In this way the performative too becomes progressive – even if it is merely the progressiveness of a new, improved product on the theory market. Hantelmann broadens the performative to include *objects*, since they too can encourage the viewer to take on an active, performative relationship with the object; the glaring contradiction with Sehgal's pursuit of dematerialization carries little weight in the domain of "theory-as-publicity." What it boils down to is rhetoric – and rhetoric can indeed be very performative, particularly in the art world.

The loose way in which contemporary critics and theorists use the notion of the performative owes much of its charm to the magical, animistic suggestion it imparts. In a culture of the performative imperative, the notion of performativity (or at least its sound-bite version) suggests a world that is infinitely malleable. If everything is performative, everything is open to influence and transformation. Performative language becomes the thinking person's magic; if contemporary society often seems to correspond to the grim picture Theodor W. Adorno painted of a modernity as irrational and constraining as the most primitive stages of civilization, the performative alleviates this by returning to the overestimation of the mind's powers which authors such as Edward Burnett Tylor, James George Frazer, and Sigmund Freud considered to be typical for the earliest stages of civilization: magic as an oneiric attempt at controlling a hostile environment.[24] The transformation of the performative into magic is signaled by the refusal to investigate the *conditions* under which an action or speech act may be truly performative; it is nicer to dream of being a heroic performer like Joseph Beuys than to acknowledge that one is an actor in someone else's spectacle. The first step toward preventing the further degeneration of performativity discourse into sham progressiveness is to acknowledge the conditions of the performative spectacle, which also means acknowledging that Tino Sehgal is not that radically different from Matthew Barney, or Donald Trump.

Freedom and Determination

A successful example of an artistic intervention in the performative spectacle is Andrea Fraser's re-enactment of a drunken speech by Martin Kippenberger. Fraser's source for *Art Must Hang* (2001) was a recording of this speech, in German, which Fraser learned phonetically by heart. Fraser's performance is thus a re-enactment of a reproduction of a performance; the work is clearly integral to a performance culture that no longer makes any fundamental distinction between medial representation and live performance. Itself based on a reproduction, her own performance again results in a reproduction: Fraser presents her re-enactment as a life-sized DVD projection (in combination with one or several paintings). It is clear even to someone unfamiliar with the original that Fraser has stuck rigorously to her model. With immaculate self-control, she duplicates Kippenberger's supreme lack of control, and it is this ostensibly slavish imitation that makes her re-enactment into something beyond a mere reproduction of her exemplar, the "original" recording of Kippenberger. By performing Kippenberger, Fraser also performs the performative imperative to which the artist, a manic self-performer, submitted himself.

Speaking about this work, Fraser has stated that the artist's task is,

> to perform the inseparability of freedom and determination: to perform that contradiction without distancing it in facile irony or collapsing it in cynicism, and without forgetting that you can't escape it through an act of will or reflection or a gesture of transgression.[25]

In her case, performance is neither the suggestion of a realm of pure presence without media representation, nor an exercise in fake ecology: she tries to extract a potential of freedom from impure conditions, a freedom that is inseparable from those very conditions. There is perhaps one work, the text piece *This Sentence Already Performed* (2003), in which Sehgal shows signs of a comparable reflexivity. The words THIS SENTENCE ALREADY PEFORMED are scattered over a number of pages, as in Stéphane Mallarmé's *Coup de dés*; this phrase suggests that Sehgal wants to embrace the discourse of universal performativity, but the text appears to consist principally of an inventory of the materials and energy consumed in producing the considerable number of copies of the printed work. The prophet of dematerialization here acknowledges the far from environment-friendly economy and the industrial performance culture in which he participates.[26] Such moments are all too rare in Sehgal's oeuvre.

While the anti-capitalist performance discourse of old would make us blind to the omnipresence of performance culture in the contemporary capitalist economy, contemporary expostulations such as those of Sehgal or Hantelmann develop into a phantasmagoric vision of that culture. Sehgal refuses to perform "the inseparability of freedom and determination" by camouflaging determination – the performative imperative in today's economy – as freedom. Thus the performative spectacle gives birth to an ecological utopia in which all fundamental problems have been magically solved. But performance is not a solution or a promise; it is an obstinate and problematical fact. Only if we avoid presenting today's culture of performance as a prelude to utopia and instead acknowledge its normative character is there a chance of art performance instigating little "truth-events" that highlight tiny fissures in the performative spectacle, and so raise the possibility of a more fundamental break with it.[27]

Notes

1. Peggy Phelan, *Unmarked: The Politics of Performance*, London, New York: Routledge, 1993, p. 148.
2. Kristine Stiles, "Performance," in Robert S. Nelson and Richard Shiff (eds), *Critical Terms for Art History*, 2nd edn, Chicago, London: University of Chicago Press, 2003, p. 85.
3. Lucy Lippard, *Six Years: The Dematerialization of the Art Object from 1966 to 1972 (etc.)*, Berkeley, Los Angeles, London: University of California Press, 1997 [1973], p. xi (1997 preface, "Escape Attempts").
4. Ibid., p. 11.
5. Stiles, op. cit., p. 85.
6. Karl Marx, *Das Kapital: Kritik der politischen Ökonomie*, Stuttgart: Alfred Kröner, 1957 [1867], pp. 127–37 (1957 ed. Benedikt Kautsky).

7. Tino Sehgal, "Jeff Koons, *Hippo*, 1999," in *Artists' Favourites Act II: 30 July–5 September 2004*, brochure, London: ICA: 2004, p. 15.
8. Ibid.
9. Ibid.
10. B. Joseph Pine II and James H. Gilmore, *The Experience Economy: Every Work is Theatre & Every Business a Stage*, Boston: Harvard Business School Press, 1999.
11. Tino Sehgal, untitled text in Mark Kremer, Maria Hlavajova, and Annie Fletcher (eds), *Now What? Artists Write!*, Frankfurt am Main, Utrecht: Revolver/bak, 2004, p. 170.
12. Ibid.
13. Phelan, op. cit., p. 3; Erika Fischer-Lichte, *Ästhetik des Performativen*, Frankfurt am Main: Suhrkamp, 2004, pp. 255–60. See also Stiles, op. cit., p. 90.
14. Phelan, op. cit, pp. 3, 146. It is an indisputable merit of Phelan's more recent writings, in particular her analyses of the presidency of Ronald Reagan, that she has replaced her essentialist anti-production rhetoric by a keen analysis of contemporary media performance. See Phelan, "Performance and Death: Ronald Reagan," Cultural Values, 1999, vol. 3, no. 1, pp. 100–122.
15. See also Sven Lütticken, "An Arena in Which to Reenact," in *Life, Once More: Forms of Reenactment in Contemporary Art*, exh. cat., Rotterdam: Witte de With, 2005, pp. 17–60.
16. Guy Debord, *La Société du Spectacle*, Paris: Gallimard, 1992 [1967], p. 15.
17. Walter Benjamin, "Das Kunstwerk im Zeitalter seiner technischen Reproduzierbarkeit" (1935–1937), in *Gesammelte Schriften*, vol. I.2.: *Abhandlungen*, Frankfurt am Main: Suhrkamp, 1991, pp. 483–4.
18. Paying homage to Debord, Paolo Virno has attempted to take the notion of the spectacle beyond its Debordian horizon, making it suitable for the post-Fordist regime; see Paolo Virno, *A Grammar of the Multitude*, trans. Isabella Bertoletti, James Cascaito, and Andrea Casson, Los Angeles, New York: Semiotext(e), 2004, pp. 59–61.
19. This performative capitalism has absorbed "radical" 1960s notions on the importance of play and creativity. See Luc Boltanski and Eve Chiapello, *Le Nouvel esprit du capitalisme*, Paris: Gallimard, 1999.
20. *Internationale Situationniste*, October 1967, no. 11, p. 57.
21. J. L. Austin, *How to Do Things with Words*, Oxford, New York: Oxford University Press, 1980 [1955/62]. For the reception received by Austin, see Judith Butler, *Excitable Speech: A Politics of the Performative*, London, New York: Routledge, 1997; Peggy Phelan, op. cit., pp. 146–66; Erika Fischer-Lichte, op. cit., pp. 31–42.
22. Dorothea von Hantelmann, "Showing Art Performing Politics: Zum Verhältnis von Kunst, Performativität und Politik," in *I Promise It's Political*, exh. cat., Köln: Theater der Welt, Museum Ludwig, 2002, pp. 12–30.
23. Dorothea von Hantelmann, "Ik beloof je, het is performatief," in *Metropolis M*, August–September 2004, vol. 25, no. 4, p. 80.
24. See for instance Freud on "primitive" people's animistic belief in the "Allmacht der Gedanken" as the basis for magic in "Das Unheimliche" (1919), *Der Moses des Michelangelo, Schriften über Kunst und Künstler*, Frankfurt am Main: Fischer, 1993, pp. 159–60.
25. Andrea Fraser, "Performance Anxiety," *Artforum*, February 2003, vol. 41, no. 6, p. 103.
26. Tino Sehgal, "this sentence already performed" (2003), in Jens Hoffmann and Joan Jonas (eds) *Perform*, London: Thames & Hudson, 2004, pp. 23–31.
27. For the concept of a "truth-event," see Slavoj Žižek, *The Ticklish Subject: The Absent Centre of Political Ontology*, London, New York: Verso, 1999, pp. 141–5.

Chapter 11

Repetition: A Skin which Unravels

Jane Blocker

I

There's a joke that goes like this: Pete and Repeat were sitting on a fence. Pete fell off so who was left? Repeat. Pete and Repeat were sitting on a fence. Pete fell off so who was left? Repeat.

Actor Walter Stevens tells this joke again and again, faster and faster, in Bruce Nauman's 1987 video installation *Clown Torture*. Dressed in a garish clown costume, with ruffled cuffs and multicolored stripes, and made up in white grease paint, a red nose, and exaggerated red lips, Stevens moves quickly from laughter to agitation and panic. He is trapped by the logic of his own joke, by the logic of repetition, from which he cannot find escape. He sweats. He frowns. He claps his hands on his cheeks. He talks faster, as though the outcome of the joke might be different if he could just beat it to the punch.

Nauman's installation, in which four different videotaped sequences of clowns stuck in various repetitive scenarios are projected on walls or shown on television monitors, seems to be the physical realization of a collective childhood revenge fantasy.[1] In that fantasy, repetition operates as a form of torture. Moreover, in this particular scenario, the character called Repeat, and the logic of repetition that he simultaneously names and childishly demands, is the figure of derision, a man with a funny name who continually and ridiculously remains. Pete, by contrast, is the familiar origin who is always dropping away, always experiencing the trauma of the fall. In these terms, then, we might think of Pete as performance, always in the process of disappearing, that is, in Peggy Phelan's terms, as performance in the process of becoming itself.[2] And, to the degree that repetition is a conservative gesture, a mechanism of remembering and retaining, we might think of Repeat as performance's definitive opposite: history, the archive, that which remains. They are original and copy, the thing and its representation, actor and archive, the continuous overflowing present and the incomplete past. Pete and Repeat.

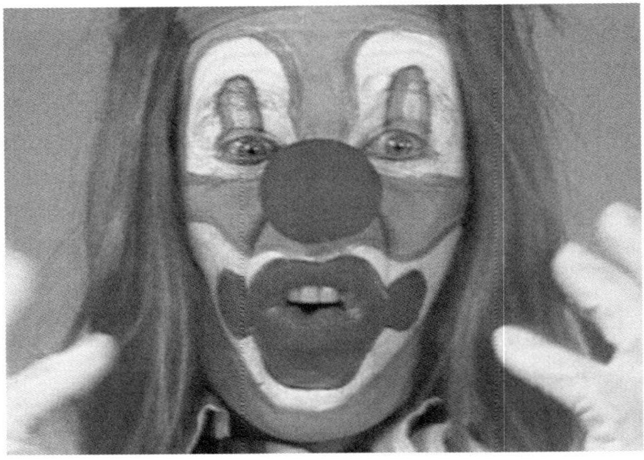

Bruce Nauman, *Clown Torture*, 1987, Tape II, Reel C, "Pete and Repeat," four channel video installation. Courtesy of the Art Institute of Chicago. © 2008, Bruce Nauman, Artists Rights Society (ARS), New York.

To describe Nauman's video in these terms, to use words like "torture" and "loss," is to indulge in archive fever, the symptoms of which Jacques Derrida describes as follows: "It is to have a compulsive, repetitive, and nostalgic desire for the archive, an irrepressible desire to return to the origin, a homesickness, a nostalgia for the return to the most archaic place of absolute commencement."[3] The pathology of archive fever lies in a fundamental contradiction: in one's desire to recapture the lost moment as origin, one develops a "nostalgic desire for the archive" (for the photograph, the film, the document, or record), which is ironically the opposite of that moment, but which offers its promise nonetheless. One might say that performance studies is plagued by this fever, by the desire to return to the moment when the action begins, a search for that moment's remains, and a perpetuation of that desire on account of the vacuities of the archive.

Rebecca Schneider thinks critically about the feverish tendency to mystify performance as a pure, singular origin always already lost, because that tendency implies that the body in performance is inherently excluded from the archive, its logic of origins, the historical knowledge it secures, and the legitimacy it confers. The mystification of performance in turn produces a privileging of its remains and of the archive as the repository of relics. She asks:

> If we consider performance as "of" disappearance, if we think of ephemerality as "vanishing," and if we think of performance as the antithesis of "saving," do we limit ourselves to an understanding of performance predetermined by a cultural habituation to the patrilineal, West-identified (arguably white-cultural) logic of the Archive?[4]

From Schneider's point of view, Pete is no origin – neither solo nor pure; rather he might be described as "the original [that] is always subject to, and the subject of, repetition."[5]

In Schneider's advocacy of history in the form of what she calls (following Mary Edsall and Catherine Johnson) body-to-body transmission, she echoes (or should I say repeats)

Gilles Deleuze, who insists that "difference inhabits repetition."[6] Deleuze's anti-Hegelian project demands that he trouble binary logics that place self and other, origin and copy, identity and difference, Pete and Repeat always in opposition and hierarchical relation. He explains:

> In every way, material or bare repetition, so-called repetition of the same, is like a skin which unravels, the external husk of a kernel of difference and more complicated internal repetitions. Difference lies between two repetitions.[7]

This means that, while repetition is normally understood to denote the recurrence of two or more of the same things at different moments, even those things which appear to be the same – Pete and Pete, for example – are, in Deleuzian terms, different. Their similarity to each other and to themselves is only superficial, like a skin or husk. Thus we can think of Pete's falling as like any action, which, in Schneider's words, "is already a palimpsest of other actions, a motion set in motion by precedent motion or anticipating future motion or lateral motion." For her, a beginning, "by virtue of its 'again-ness,' is never for the first time and never for the only time – beginning again and again in an entirely haunted domain of repetition: image, text, and gesture."[8]

Though it is not tragic, one could argue that the joke Walter Stevens tells is haunted, that in telling it he repeats and re-embodies a former violence that the medium of videotape, and its seemingly endless capacity for repetition, simultaneously preserves, re-enacts, and hollows out. This white man made up in white face tells a joke that, as I understand it, was once a staple of black face minstrelsy. In its earlier incarnation, the joke would be told by two men in the form of a riddle. One man says, "Pete and Repeat were sitting on a fence. Pete fell off, so who was left?" The second man guesses the answer and says "Repeat," thereby unwittingly commanding the first man to begin the joke again and consigning himself to hearing it. When he gets the joke which has been played on him, the repetition stops. But in Nauman's video the telling of that joke is a kind of self-torture, a compulsive repetition from which there seems to be no escape. Stevens thus surrogates in shades of white a legion of earlier black and blackened performers, touches an earlier history in which he becomes entrapped, and at the same time his constant repeating of the joke, his relentless putting into play of the past from which it comes, inures us to its complex historical origins. No one, so far as I know, has ever drawn a connection between Stevens' performance in white face and the tradition of black face minstrelsy.

This fact begs a historiographic question of Schneider's approach: if one body in performance transmits an earlier performance by another body, but does so unintentionally or unknowingly, can it still be said to function as an archive of that earlier action, particularly when the contemporary performance jams the transmission with an endlessly repeating video signal? Schneider puts this question more plainly when she asks: "What kind of historical 'lineage machine' can *fully* adopt this as scholarly practice?" Would it matter if Stevens and Nauman were unaware of the heritage of this joke, that for them the joke's origins lie somewhere else? "Since such a history could not offer a lineage that allows for singularity or discrete or unitary origins," Schneider answers, "'lineage' seems like a profoundly inadequate word. Perhaps an illegitimate history, a history of illegitimacy – that which we leave out, put back – is more (im)precisely the point."[9]

Following Schneider's insights, I am interested in trying to see this performance as an illegitimate history, one in which things (such as the racial heritage of the joke or the racial connotations of the performer in white face) are left out and put back, but I am also concerned about the ways in which the repetition of the video both creates surplus – the proliferation of the joke, the action, the audience – at the same time as it evacuates and empties. (How do we get to skin?) In short, I want to think about the skin that unravels in repetition and about how the body-to-body transmission gets jammed.

II

In 1997 British artist Steve McQueen produced a silent, black-and-white film installation[10] called *Deadpan* in which he stands stock still, unflinching even while the gable-end wall of a house falls down around him and he narrowly escapes being crushed. Mimicking a trick that Buster Keaton performed in the 1920s, he is carefully positioned at precisely the spot where the window opening in the wall will come to rest on the ground. The stunt is shown again and again from a variety of angles, and the entire film runs on a continuous loop, so that a cloud of dust is silently blown into the air over and over every time the wall hits the ground. Wearing a white T-shirt, denim pants, a dark belt, and boots without shoelaces,

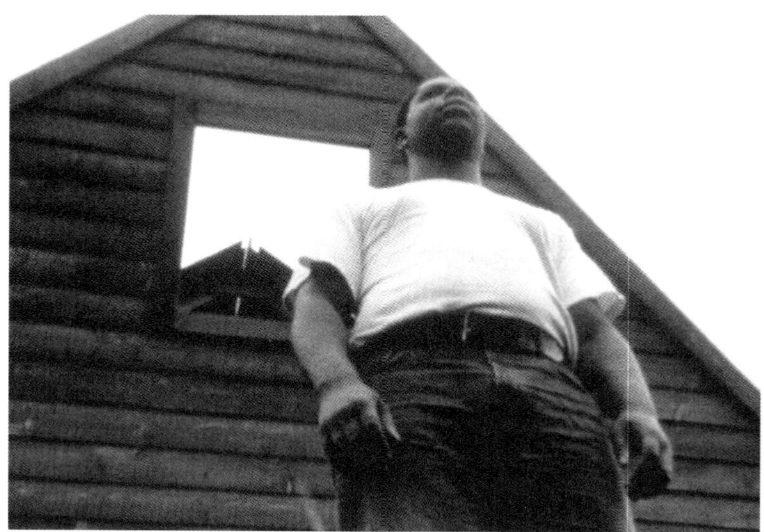

Steve McQueen, *Deadpan*, 1997, 16mm, black & white film, video transfer. Silent, 4:30. Image courtesy of the artist and Marian Goodman Gallery, New York.

McQueen expresses no emotion. As a result of *Deadpan*'s emptied aspects – McQueen's stoic face, which hides a terrible danger, the silent fall, which smothers the sound of tearing wood, the crash of enormous weight – the slapstick scene has been described as stripped of comic effect: "The repetition turns an hilarious lucky escape and spectacular stunt into an ordeal and endurance, implying a sense of entrapment and punishment."[11] Because the scene is filmically deconstructed (shot and re-shot in different ways), and because the film runs continuously, this work, according to critic Michael Archer, "produces a strange sense of suffocation."[12] Like the story of Pete and Repeat, *Deadpan* is the repetitive re-enactment of a fall. It conserves and holds in suspension the lost act, the finality of the wall come down, by replaying it again and again. So here again is repeated the problem of the fall, the problem of performance and bodies for the archive.

"In privileging an understanding of performance as a refusal to remain," Schneider asks, "do we ignore other ways of knowing, other modes of remembering, that might be situated precisely in the ways in which performance remains, but remains differently?"[13] Contemplating performance's ultimate refusal to disappear, she advocates thinking of performance as itself an archive, of the body not as that which eludes archivization but as itself a means of memory and history. It is not difficult to see *Deadpan* in these terms since it quite deliberately archives the famous scene in the Buster Keaton film *Steamboat Bill Jr.* in which Keaton innocently escapes being crushed by the wall of a house in exactly the same manner as McQueen. It is easy to read the deadpan expression that McQueen wears as a surrogation, a transmission of Keaton's face, to see McQueen's body as haunted by Keaton's. *Deadpan* is thus the scene of both internal and external repetitions, a film that pays homage to another film, a performance piece that repeats another, earlier performance. It is the record and re-enactment of a body-to-body transmission. To concede to performance the status of archive, however, only leads to a confrontation with the fact that as an archive it only preserves and remembers to the degree that it alters and forgets.

Therefore, in order to understand this film as an archive, to see it as a history of an earlier performance (or rather an earlier set of performances), it is necessary to think more carefully about the archive. "Let us not begin at the beginning, or even at the archive," Derrida writes,

> but rather at the word "archive" – and with the archive of so familiar a word. *Arkhē*, we recall, names at once the *commencement* and the *commandment*. This name apparently coordinates two principles in one: the principle according to nature or history *there* where things *commence* – physical, historical, or ontological principle – but also the principle according to the law, *there* where men and gods *command, there* where authority, social order are exercised, *in this place* from which *order* is given – nomological principle.[14]

The archive is empowered to create origins, the place from which things commence, the site where history begins. It also names, gives order to, and interprets its "own" contents. "The meaning of 'archive,'" he continues, "its only meaning, comes to it from the Greek *arkheion*: initially a house, a domicile, an address, the residence of the superior magistrates, the *archons*, those who commanded."[15] Derrida asserts that the archive develops from two sources – the home (it is the site of origins) and the law (it is the site of the jussive, that which commands). It shelters artifacts and documents in a place where they can be gathered together, unified, identified, and classified.[16]

In addition to its connections to the house, it is important to note in this context that the architecture of the archive also includes the body. Like the *arkheion*, he argues, the body can be marked with an organizing logic, it can bear the inscription of the law, as, for example, in circumcision, which classifies and draws a line between Jew and Gentile even as it violently imposes its law and remembers the past.[17] Even though it is affiliated with the law (even God's law), with magistrates and hermeneutics, there is one other principle of the archive that we must bear in mind: "The archive always works," Derrida insists, "and *a priori*, against itself."[18] That is, the archive stands as a monument to forgetting.

It is its amnesiac function more than its order, commandment, or law that Carolyn Steedman experiences in the archive. For her, the archive is Kafkaesque: she experiences no origins, only the feeling of being caught in the middle of something vaguely oppressive; she confronts the law, certainly, but finds it incompetent, disorganized, incomplete, and irrational; she finds no ontological or nomological clarity. The archive, she says,

> never has been the repository of official documents alone. And nothing starts in the Archive, nothing, ever at all, though things certainly end up there. You find nothing in the Archive but stories caught half way through: the middle of things; discontinuities.[19]

What is more, as she explains later on,

> in actual Archives, though the bundles may be mountainous, there isn't in fact, very much there [...] And *nothing happens to this stuff, in the Archive*. It is indexed, and catalogued, and some of it is not indexed and catalogued, and some of it is lost.[20]

Steve McQueen's *Deadpan* is, I argue, precisely this kind of archive. While on one hand the film indexes and catalogues the original performance, it also loses hold of that performance's details. In the original film, Keaton plays Willie, the son of a steamboat captain, who was raised on the East Coast and has recently graduated from Harvard. Willie arrives in the fictional Midwestern town of River Junction just in time to help rescue his father's steamboat business, threatened by a wealthy competitor with a brand new steamer. Willie, a hapless nerd dressed in a college sweater and bow tie, is a huge disappointment to his father, and becomes even more so when he falls in love with the daughter of his father's competitor. The famous scene occurs when a cyclone tears through town and blows Willie through the streets while buildings collapse and debris flies through the air. He stops in front of a house, as though trying to decide what to do, while the wind pulls terrifically against him. Suddenly the facade of the two-story house behind him is blown loose and falls down threatening to crush him, but the open second-floor window passes, with only a three inch margin of error, around him. At first he seems completely unaware of what has taken place, but then, after stepping over the collapsed wall, he does a double-take and runs away in terror from other falling buildings and flying debris.

I should mention that even this scene, which forms the origin of McQueen's film, is neither original nor singular. After the wall collapses in *Steamboat Bill Jr.*, the collapse is repeated at least two other times in the tornado sequence, when Keaton emerges through doorways of descending walls. Moreover, all of this repeats an earlier film from 1921 called *One Week*. In that shot, Keaton plays a newlywed who tries to assemble a prefabricated house, which of course results in all manner of calamities, including a brief shot of an unfinished wall falling down on Keaton, who emerges unscathed out of its roughed-in window opening.

Unlike *Steamboat Bill Jr.*, which shows the house falling only once, only from the front, and not in close-up, McQueen's version employs a catalogue of filmic techniques. Michael Newman describes it this way:

> The first shot is from inside the building, beginning when the fall of the wall lets in light; the last shot is of the wall falling onto the camera, and ends in darkness. The shots in between analyse the gag from all points of view: feet from the front (shoelaces missing); centered on the window, which reveals the interior of the building when it falls; the window to the left, with the camera following the movement of the falling wall ending with McQueen's legs; the artist's body in an "American shot" cut above the legs; a side view of the upper torso as the wall passes; a downward shot from the upper window rapidly repeated; a frontal shot of the window cut by the frame; oscillating still-shots of the face; and the face with the wall falling across it.[21]

The sheer proliferation of all these shots and their endless repetition makes the film resemble the "mountainous bundles" that Steedman characterizes as occupying the space of the archive. Indeed, as in the archive, though Keaton's story has ended up there, it is a story caught half way through. "While in the source of the gag," Newman writes, as though emphasizing this point,

> Buster Keaton is in movement, running through the windstorm, McQueen is motionless. Whereas the actions in *Steamboat Bill Jr.* are causally motivated, the repetition of the gag in *Deadpan* eliminates causality. This leaves the gag open for re-inscription: by withholding a plot, it invites interpretation by the viewer.[22]

One of the consequences of this repeating and nonrepeating is that Keaton's film is, to quote Steedman again, "indexed, and catalogued, and some of it is not indexed and catalogued, and some of it is lost." This is evident in the surprising number of descriptions of *Deadpan*'s citational source which remember it incorrectly. Barry Schwabsky, writing in *Art/Text*, describes *Deadpan* as "a set of variations on a famous scene by Buster Keaton, in which the imperturbable silent-film comedian walks *out of a house* falling down around him without noticing that anything has happened."[23] Tim Adams writes in *The Guardian* that "*Deadpan* is a return to Buster Keaton's famous stunt which involves the gable end of a *barn* crashing down over him; the window of the *barn* wall falls around Keaton, and he walks away unscathed."[24] And Robert Storr erroneously claims, in the ICA catalogue on McQueen, that *Deadpan* is a reference to Keaton's earlier *One Week* rather than *Steamboat Bill Jr.*[25]

While from a historical point of view the inaccuracies about Keaton's film that seem to arise from the archive of McQueen's film are troubling, they are not at all unusual. Indeed Steedman argues that history almost always goes awry when we think of it as an accumulation of *stuff*, which we delude ourselves into thinking will help us get the details right. Rather, she suggests that history be thought of more as a process, a process of repetition, if you like.[26] "This is not to say that *nothing* is found [in the archive]," she explains, "but that thing is always something else, a creation of the search itself and the time the search took [...] the object sought is bound to be 'not the lost [one], but a substitute.'"[27] It seems that the repetition and consequent proliferation of elements from Keaton's gag leads ironically to its being emptied out; its original context, details, and significance are lost even in the face of the image's seeming plentitude. And just as it is drained, it is simultaneously filled with something else.

What people seem often to be looking for in this film is something about blackness, a critical commentary about the experience of the black man, perhaps, or the history of racial inequality. Many of the viewers who examine it ponder what it can mean that a black man is performing Keaton. They compare the violence of Keaton's tornado (and all those falling walls) with the violence of a wall falling over and over again, seemingly without cause, around a man whose black face registers no emotion, remains, like Keaton's, deadpan. *This* violence, they reason, is not funny. Holland Carter, in a review for *The New York Times*, claims that "unlike Keaton's film, Mr. McQueen's keeps the idea of disaster rather than comedy to the fore." Moreover, the disaster is something he reads, not in the artist's performance, but in his skin: "Seen in an American context, the house suggests a sharecropper's cabin; its destruction evokes Abraham Lincoln's Civil War caveat, 'a house divided against itself cannot stand,' referring to a nation riven by the question of slavery." Just in case we have missed the connection here, he notes in parentheses, "(Mr. McQueen is black.)"[28] Mark Durden provides another example when he writes that "As his impassive face fills the gallery wall screen, these shots call to mind the frontal and stark portraits of black subjects within colonial anthropometric photography, measured and framed."[29] And describing a show of McQueen's films in 2005, Roberta Smith declares: "One way or another they all return to the theme of race."[30]

It strikes me as odd that, in the case of Nauman's video, the potential emergence of a history of race and racism is forgotten, ignored, or has simply been evacuated by virtue of a repetition so complete as to obliterate origins, and in the case of McQueen's film, the history of race and racism is thought to be so self-evident as to overflow the flickering image. As a result, critics tend to be skeptical when McQueen claims that his film is simply about film itself, about film history and Keaton's role as a major innovator of the medium, and about film aesthetics, what the artist describes as "a building passing through a person; a horizontal passing through a vertical."[31] When asked directly by Tim Adams if he views himself as a black artist, McQueen replies, "I would say no." "But," he continues, referring to his 1993 film *Bear*, "if you watch my film, you see two black men wrestling. If I watch it, I see two men wrestling. If I spit on the floor here, it is black spit. I can't escape from that."[32]

So what is to be found in the archive of McQueen's film? I will tell you. It is the archive. By this I mean that the film both acts *as* an archive of a performance and is *about* the archive's "white-cultural logic" and its relation to performance. It remembers Keaton, yes, but it also remembers a particular form of violence. Perhaps it is the violence of slavery, the sharecropper's cabin, or the ethnographic portrait but, when McQueen describes not being able to "escape" from the connotations of race, that particular word suggests that his film might be as much about the violence of interpretation as anything else. Derrida remarks, "What is at issue here is the violence of the archive itself, *as archive, as archival violence*."[33] Remember that the word "archive" comes "from the Greek *arkheion*: initially a house, a domicile, an address, the residence of the superior magistrates, the *archons*, those who commanded."[34] So when this house falls apart, that is, when the archive falls apart, the gag is that the performer escapes its violence, is saved by a well-placed window. In Steedman's words

> The Archive then is something that, through the cultural activity of History, can become memory's potential space, one of the few realms of the modern imagination where a hard-won and carefully constructed place, can return to boundless, limitless space, and we might be released from the house arrest that Derrida suggested was its condition.[35]

Deadpan is a performance that is an archive, a performance that multiplies and repeats McQueen's and Keaton's actions. In this sense, like the house which is the film's central motif, the archive, the *arkheion*, is repeatedly, obsessively blown open. And yet it remains.

Notes

1. The other video sequences, all shown in continuous loops, are as follows: *Clown Taking a Shit* shows a clown sitting on a toilet in a public bathroom as though captured by a surveillance camera; *Clown with Goldfish* shows a clown balancing a fish bowl on a pole against the ceiling until he is unable to hold it up any longer and it falls; *Clown with Water Bucket* shows a clown walking through a door over and over again as the bucket balanced on the door repeatedly falls and drenches him; *No. No. No. No.* shows a clown shouting "No" in a range of vocal inflections.
2. Peggy Phelan, *Unmarked: The Politics of Performance*, New York: Routledge, 1993, p. 146.
3. Derrida, *Archive Fever: A Freudian Impression*, trans. Eric Prenowitz, Chicago: University of Chicago Press, 1996, p. 91.
4. Rebecca Schneider, "Archives: Performance Remains," *Performance Research*, 2001, vol. 6, no. 2, p. 100. [See the revised version of this essay published in this volume.]

5. Rebecca Schneider, "Solo Solo Solo," in Gavin Butt (ed.), *After Criticism: New Responses to Art and Performance*, London: Blackwell, 2005, p. 40.
6. Gilles Deleuze, *Difference and Repetition*, trans. Paul Patton, New York: Columbia University Press, 1994 (1968), p. 76.
7. Ibid.
8. Schneider, "Solo, Solo, Solo," p. 41.
9. Ibid., p. 37.
10. The film is meant to be projected floor to ceiling, wall to wall in the empty cube of a gallery.
11. Mark Durden, "Viewing Positions: Steve McQueen," *Parachute*, April–June 2000, pp. 18–25.
12. Michael Archer, "Steve McQueen," *Art Monthly*, 20 February 1998, no. 213, p. 20.
13. Schneider, "Archives," p. 101.
14. Derrida, op. cit., p. 1.
15. Ibid., p. 2.
16. Ibid., p. 3.
17. Ibid., p. 10.
18. Ibid., p. 12.
19. Carolyn Steedman, *Dust: The Archive and Cultural History*, New Brunswick, NJ: Rutgers University Press, 2001, p. 45.
20. Ibid., p. 68.
21. Michael Newman, "McQueen's Materialism," in Gerrie van Noord (ed.), *Steve McQueen*, London: ICA, 1999, p. 26.
22. Ibid.
23. Barry Schwabsky, "*Steve McQueen*: Institute of Contemporary Arts, London," *Art/Text*, August–October 1999, no. 66, p. 77. (Emphasis added.)
24. Tim Adams, "Steve McQueen," *The Guardian*, 10 October 1999. (Emphasis added.) Available online at: http://www.guardian.co.uk/turner1999/Story/0,,201738,00.html (accessed 24 February 2006).
25. Robert Storr, "Going Places," in Gerrie van Noord (ed.), *Steve McQueen*, London: ICA, 1999, p. 14.
26. Steedman, op. cit., p. 67.
27. Ibid., p. 77.
28. Holland Carter, "Art in Review," *The New York Times*, 23 January 1998, sec. E, 35.
29. Durden, op. cit.
30. Roberta Smith, "Art in Review: Steve McQueen," *The New York Times*, 28 January 2005, sec. E, 41.
31. Steve McQueen, quoted in Tim Adams, op. cit.
32. Ibid.
33. Derrida, op. cit., p. 7.
34. Ibid., p. 2.
35. Steedman., op. cit., p. 83.

Chapter 12

Art in the Age of Biopolitics: From Artwork to Art Documentation

Boris Groys

In recent decades, it has become increasingly evident that the art world has shifted its interest away from the artwork and toward art documentation. This shift is particularly symptomatic of a broader transformation that art is undergoing today, and for that reason it deserves a detailed analysis. The artwork is traditionally understood as something that embodies art in itself, that makes it immediately present and visible. When we go to an exhibition, we usually assume that what we will see there – whether it is paintings, sculptures, drawings, photographs, videos, readymades, or installations – *is* art. Artworks can, of course, refer in one way or another to something other than themselves – say, to objects in reality or specific political subjects – but they cannot refer to art, because they *are* art. This traditional assumption about a visit to an exhibition or museum is proving more and more misleading. Increasingly, in art spaces today we are confronted not just with artworks but with art documentation. The latter can also take the form of paintings, drawings, photographs, videos, texts, and installations – that is to say, all the same forms and media in which art is usually presented – but in the case of art documentation these media do not present art but merely document it. Art documentation is by definition *not* art; it merely *refers* to art, and in precisely this way it makes it clear that art in this case is no longer present and immediately visible but rather absent and hidden.

Art documentation documents art and refers to art at least in two different ways. It may refer to performances, temporary installations, or happenings, which are documented in the same ways as theatrical performances. In such cases, one might say that these are art events that were present and visible at a particular time, and that the documentation that is exhibited later is merely intended as a way of recollecting them. Whether such a recollecting is really possible is, of course, an open question. Since the advent of deconstruction, if not before, we have been aware that the claim that past events can be recalled in this way must, at the very

Originally published as Boris Groys, "Art in the Age of Biopolitics: From Artwork to Art Documentation," trans. Steven Lindberg, *Documenta 11* Catalogue, Ostfildern-Ruit: Hatje Cantz, 2002, pp. 108–14.

least, be considered problematic. Meanwhile, however, more and more art documentation is produced and exhibited that does not claim to make a past art event present. Examples include complex and varied artistic interventions in daily life, lengthy and complicated processes of discussion and analysis, the creation of unusual living circumstances, artistic exploration into the reception of art in various cultures and milieus, politically motivated artistic actions, and so on. None of these artistic activities can be presented except by means of art documentation, since from the very beginning these activities do not serve to produce an artwork in which art as such could manifest itself. Consequently, such art does not appear in object form – is not a product or result of a "creative" activity. Rather, art is itself this activity, is the practice of art as such. Correspondingly, art documentation is neither the making present of a past art event nor the promise of a coming artwork but the only possible form of reference to an artistic activity that cannot be represented any other way.

To misunderstand and trivialize art documentation as a "simple" artwork would be to overlook its originality, its identifying feature, which is precisely that it documents art rather than presenting it. For those who devote themselves to the production of art documentation rather than of artworks, art is identical to life, because life is essentially a pure activity that does not lead to any end result. The presentation of any such end result – in the form of an artwork, say – would imply an understanding of life as merely a functional process whose own duration is negated and extinguished by the creation of the end product – which is equivalent to death. It is no coincidence that museums are traditionally compared to cemeteries: by presenting art as the end result of a life, they obliterate this life once and for all. Art documentation, by contrast, marks the attempt to use artistic media within art spaces to refer to life itself, that is, to a pure activity, to pure practice, to an artistic life, as it were, without wishing to present it directly. Art becomes a life form, whereas the artwork becomes non-art, a mere documentation of this life form. One could also say that art becomes biopolitical, because it begins to use artistic means to produce and document life as a pure activity. Indeed, art documentation as an art form could only develop under the conditions of today's biopolitical age, in which life itself has become the object of technical and artistic intervention. In this way, one is again confronted with the question of the relationship between art and life – and indeed in a completely new context, defined by the aspiration of today's art to become life itself, not merely to depict life or to offer it art products.

Traditionally, art was divided into pure, contemplative, "fine" art and applied art – that is, design. The former was concerned not with reality but with images of reality. Applied art formed the things of reality themselves. In this respect, art resembles science, which also can be divided into a theoretical and an applied version. The difference between fine art and theoretical science, however, is that science has wanted to make the images of reality that it creates as transparent as possible, in order to judge reality itself on the basis of these images, whereas art, taking another path, has taken as its theme its own materiality, lack of clarity, the obscurity and, therefore, autonomy of images and the resulting inability of these images adequately to reproduce reality. Artistic images – from the "fantastic," the "unrealistic," by way of the Surrealistic and on up to the abstract – are intended to thematize the gap between art and reality. And even media that are usually thought of as reproducing reality faithfully – such as photography and film – are also used in the context of art in a way that seeks to undermine any faith in reproduction's ability to be faithful to reality. "Pure" art thus established itself on the level of the signifier. That to which the signifier refers – reality, meaning, the signified – has, by contrast, traditionally been interpreted as belonging to life and thus removed from the sphere in which art is valid. Nor can it be said of applied art, however, that it concerns itself with life. Even if our environment is largely shaped by applied arts such as architecture, urban planning, product design, advertising, and fashion, it is still left to life to find the best way to deal with all these design products. Life itself as pure activity, as pure duration, is thus fundamentally inaccessible to the traditional arts, which remain oriented toward products or results in one form or another.

In our age of biopolitics, however, the situation is changing, for the principal concern of this kind of politics is the lifespan itself. Biopolitics is often confused with scientific and technical strategies of genetic manipulation that, at least potentially, aim at re-forming the individual living body. In these strategies, however, it is still a matter of design – albeit of a living organism. The real achievement of biopolitical technologies lies more in the shaping of the lifespan itself – in the shaping of life as a pure activity that occurs in time. From begetting and lifelong medical care, by way of the regulation of the relationship between work time and free time, up to death as supervised, or even brought about by, medical care, the lifetime of a person today is constantly shaped and improved artificially. Many authors, from Michel Foucault and Giorgio Agamben to Antonio Negri and Michael Hardt, have written along these lines about biopolitics as the true realm in which political will and technology's power to shape things are manifested today. That is to say, if life is not longer understood as a natural event, as fate, as Fortuna, but rather as time artificially produced and fashioned, then life is automatically politicized, since the technical and artistic decisions with respect to the shaping of the lifespan are always political decisions as well. The art that is made under these new conditions of biopolitics – under the conditions of an artificially fashioned lifespan – cannot help but take this artificiality as its explicit theme. Now, however, time, duration, and thus life too cannot be shown directly but only documented. The dominant medium of modern biopolitics is thus bureaucratic and technological documentation, which includes planning, decrees, fact-finding reports, statistical inquiries, and project plans. It is no coincidence that art also uses the same medium of documentation when it wants to refer to itself as life.

Indeed, one feature of modern technology is that we are no longer able by visual means alone to make a firm distinction between the natural or organic and the artificial or technologically produced. This is demonstrated by genetically modified food, but also by the numerous discussions – particularly intense these days – about the criteria for deciding when life begins and when it ends. To put it another way, how does one distinguish between a technologically facilitated beginning of life, such as artificial insemination, for example, and a "natural" continuation of that life, or distinguish that natural continuation, in turn, from an equally technology-dependent means of extending life beyond a "natural" death? The longer these discussions go on, the less the participants are able to agree on how precisely the line between life and death can be drawn. Almost all recent sci-fi films make a major theme of this inability to distinguish between the natural and the artificial: the surface of a living being can conceal a machine; conversely, the surface of a machine can conceal a living being – an alien, for example.[1] The difference between a genuinely living creature and its artificial substitute is merely a product of the imagination here, of a supposition or suspicion that can be neither confirmed nor refuted by observation. But if the living thing can be reproduced and replaced at will, then it loses its unique, unrepeatable inscription in time – its unique, unrepeatable lifespan, which is ultimately what makes the living thing a living thing. And that is precisely the point at which the documentation becomes indispensable, producing the life of the living thing as such: the documentation inscribes the existence of an object in history, gives a lifespan to this existence, and gives the object life as such – independently of whether this object was "originally" living or artificial.

The difference between the living and the artificial is, then, exclusively a narrative difference. It cannot be seen but only told, only documented: an object can be given a prehistory, a genesis, an origin by means of narrative. The technical documentation is, incidentally, never constructed as history but always as a system of instructions for producing particular objects under given circumstances. The artistic documentation, whether real or fictive, is, by contrast, primarily narrative, and thus it evokes the unrepeatability of living time. The artificial can thus be made living, made natural, by means of art documentation, by narrating the history of its origin, its "making." Art documentation is thus the art of making living things out of artificial ones, a living activity out of technical practice: it is a bio art that is simultaneously biopolitics. This basic function of art documentation was strikingly demonstrated by Ridley Scott's *Blade Runner.* In the film, the artificially produced humans, called "replicants," are given photographic documentation at the time they are produced, which is supposed to certify their "natural origin" – faked photographs of their family, residences, and so on. Although this documentation is fictive, it gives the replicants life – subjectivity – which makes them indistinguishable from the "natural" human beings on the "inside" as well as the outside. Because the replicants are inscribed in life, in history, by means of this documentation, they can continue this life in an uninterrupted and thoroughly individual way. Consequently, the hero's search for a "real," objectively determinable distinction between the natural and the artificial ultimately proves to be futile, because, as we have seen, this distinction can only be established through an artistically documented narrative.

The fact that life is something that can be documented but not immediately experienced is not a new discovery. One could even claim that this is the definition of life: life can be documented but not shown. In his book *Homo Sacer*, Giorgio Agamben points out that the "bare life" has yet to achieve any political and cultural representation.[2] Agamben himself proposes that we view the concentration camp as the cultural representation of the bare life, because its inmates are robbed of all forms of political representation – the only thing that can be said of them is that they are alive. They can therefore only be killed, not sentenced by a court or sacrificed through a religious ritual. Agamben believes that this kind of life outside all laws yet anchored in law is paradigmatic of life itself. Even if there is much to be said for such a definition of life, it must be remembered that life in a concentration camp is generally thought to be beyond our powers of observation or imagination. Life in a concentration camp can be reported – it can be documented – but it cannot be presented for view.[3] Art documentation thus describes the realm of biopolitics by showing how the living can be replaced by the artificial, and how the artificial can be made living by means of a narrative. A few examples will illustrate the different strategies of documentation.

In the late 1970s and early 1980s, the Moscow group Kollektivnye Deystviya [Collective Action Group] organized a series of performances conceived mostly by the artist Andrey Monastyrsky, which took place outside Moscow with only the members of the group and a few invited guests present. These performances were made accessible to a wider audience only through documentation, in the form of photographs and texts.[4] The texts did not so much describe the performances themselves as the experiences, thoughts, and emotions of those who took part in them – and as a result, they had a strongly narrative, literary character. These highly minimalist performances took place on a white, snow-covered field – a white surface that recalled the white background of Kazimir Malevich's Suprematist paintings, which has become the trademark of Russian avant-garde. At the same time, however, the significance of this white background, which Malevich had introduced as the symbol of the radical "non-objectivity" of his art, as a symbol of a radical break with all nature and all narrative, was completely transformed. Equating the Suprematist "artificial" white background with the "natural" Russian snow transposed the "non-objective" art of Malevich back into life – specifically, by using a narrative text that attributed another genealogy to (or rather, imposed that genealogy upon) the white of Suprematism. Malevich's paintings thus lose the character of autonomous artworks and are in turn reinterpreted as the documentation of a lived experience – in the snows of Russia.

This reinterpretation of the Russian avant-garde is even more direct in the work of another Moscow artist from this period, Francisco Infante, who in his performance *Posvyashchenie* [*Dedication*] spread one of Malevich's Suprematist compositions on the snow – once again replacing the white background with snow. A fictive "living" genealogy is attributed to Malevich's painting, as a result of which the painting is led out of art history and into life – as with the replicants in *Blade Runner*. This transformation of the artwork into documentation of a life event opens up a space where all sorts of other genealogies could equally be discovered or invented, several of them quite plausible historically: for example, the white background of the Suprematist paintings can also be interpreted as the white piece of paper that serves as the background for every kind of bureaucratic, technological, or artistic documentation. In this sense, it could also be said that the documentation also has snow as its background – and thus the play of narrative inscriptions can be extended further and further.

Such a drama of narrative inscriptions is also staged in Sophie Calle's installations *Les Aveugles* [*The Blind*] and *Blind Color*. In *Les Aveugles* of 1986 the artist documents a survey of blind people that the artist conducted, in which people who were born blind were asked to describe their conception of beauty. Several responses referred to figurative artworks, about which these blind people had heard, that they depicted the real, visible world in an especially impressive manner. In her installation, the artist confronts the descriptions of these artworks given by the blind with reproductions of the paintings described. For *Blind Color* of 1991 Sophie Calle asked blind people to describe what they see, then wrote their answers on panels, which she juxtaposed with texts on monochrome painting written by artists such as Kazimir Malevich, Yves Klein, Gerhard Richter, Piero Manzoni, and Ad Reinhardt. In these art documentations, which are presented as the results of a sociological research, the artist manages to attribute unfamiliar genealogy to examples of the traditional, figurative, mimetic art as well as to modern paintings that were conceived and traditionally understood as artificial, abstract, and autonomous. For the blind the mimetic, figurative paintings become totally fictional, artificially constructed, one can say even, autonomous. On the contrary, the modernist monochrome paintings become the true depictions of the blind's vision. Here it becomes obvious to what extent our understanding of a particular artwork is dependent on a narrative that relates this artwork to its context.

Finally, we should mention here Carsten Höller's performance *The Baudouin/Boudewijn Experiment: A Large-Scale, Non-Fatalistic Experiment in Deviation*, which took place in the Atomium in Brussels in 2001. A group of people were enclosed in the interior of one of the spheres that make up the Atomium, where they spent an entire day cut off from the outside world. Höller frequently engages in transforming the "abstract," minimalist spaces of radically modernist architecture into spaces for living experience – another way of transforming art into life by means of documentation. In this case, he chose for his performance a space that embodies a utopian dream and does not immediately suggest a domestic environment. Primarily, however, the work alludes to commercial television shows such as *Big Brother*, with its portrayal of people forced to spend a long time together in an enclosed space. But here the difference between a commercial television documentation and art documentation becomes particularly clear. Precisely because television time and again shows images of the enclosed people, the viewer begins to suspect manipulation, constantly asking what might be happening in the space hidden behind these images in which "real" life takes place. By contrast, Höller's performance is not shown but merely documented – specifically, by means of the participants' narratives, which describe precisely that which could not be seen. Here, then, life is understood as something narrated and documented but unable to be shown or presented. This lends the documentation a plausibility of representing life that a direct visual presentation cannot possess.

Topology of the Aura

Some of the examples above are particularly relevant to the analysis of art documentation because they show how famous artworks that are well known from the history of art can be used in a new way – not as art but as documentation. At the same time they also reveal the procedures by which art documentation is produced, along with the difference between the artwork and art documentation. But one important question remains unanswered: if life is only documented by narrative and cannot be shown, then how can such a documentation be shown in an art space without perverting its nature? Art documentation is usually shown in the context of an installation. The installation, however, is an art form in which not only the images, texts, or other elements of which it is composed but also the space itself plays a decisive role. This space is not abstract or neutral but is itself an artwork and at the same time a life space. The placing of documentation in an installation as the act of inscription in a particular space is thus not a neutral act of showing but an act that achieves at the level of space what narrative achieves at the level of time: the inscription in life. The way in which this mechanism functions can best be described by using Walter Benjamin's concept of aura, which he introduced precisely with the intention of distinguishing between the living space of the artwork and its technical substitute, which has no site or context.

Benjamin's essay "The Work of Art in the Age of Mechanical Reproduction" became famous primarily thanks to its use of the concept of aura. Since then, the concept of aura has had a long career in philosophy, especially in the celebrated phrase "loss of aura," which characterizes the fate of the original in the Modern age. This emphasis on the loss of aura is, on the one hand, legitimate, and clearly conforms to the overall intention of Benjamin's text. On the other hand, it begs the question of how the aura is originated at all before it can or must be lost. This, of course, does not mean aura in the general sense, as a religious or theosophical concept, but in the specific sense used by Benjamin. A close reading of Benjamin's text makes clear that the aura only originates by virtue of the modern technology of reproduction – that is to say, it emerges in the same moment as it gets lost. And it emerges for the same reason for which it gets lost.

In his essay, Benjamin begins with the possibility of perfect reproduction, in which it is no longer possible to distinguish materially, visually, empirically between the original and the copy. Again and again in his text, Benjamin insists on this perfection. He speaks of technical reproduction as a "most perfect reproduction" which may not touch the material qualities of the actual work of art.[5] Now, it is certainly open to doubt whether the techniques of reproduction that existed at the time, or even today, ever really achieved such a degree of perfection that it was impossible materially, empirically to distinguish between the original and the copy. For Benjamin, however, the ideal possibility of such perfect reproducibility, or a perfect cloning, is more important that the technical possibilities that actually existed in his day. The question that he raises is: does the extinction of the material distinction between original and copy mean the extinction of this distinction itself?

Benjamin answers this question in the negative. The disappearance of any material distinction between the original and the copy – or, at least, its potential disappearance – does not eliminate another, invisible but no less real distinction between them: the original has an aura that the copy does not. Thus the notion of aura becomes necessary as a criterion for distinguishing between original and copy only because the technology of reproduction has rendered all material criteria useless. And this means that the concept of aura, and aura itself, belongs exclusively to modernity. Aura is, for Benjamin, the relationship of the artwork to the site in which it is found – the relationship to its external context. The soul of the artwork is not in its body; rather, the body of the artwork is found in its aura, in its soul. This other topology of the relationship between the soul and the body traditionally has a place in gnosis, in theosophy, and similar schools of thought, which it would not be appropriate to pursue here. The important realization is that for Benjamin the distinction between original and copy is exclusively a topological one – and as such it is entirely independent of the material nature of the work. The original has a particular site – and through this particular site the original is inscribed into history as this unique object. The copy, by contrast, is virtual, siteless, ahistorical: from the beginning it appears as potential multiplicity. To reproduce something is to remove it from its site, to deterritorialize it – reproduction transposes the artwork into the network of topologically undetermined circulation. Benjamin's formulations are well known: "Even the most perfect reproduction of a work of art is lacking in one element: its here and now; its unique existence at the place where it happens to be."[6] He continues:

> These "here" and "now" of the original constitute the concept of its authenticity, and lay basis for the notion of a tradition that has up to the present day passed this object along as something having a self and an identity.[7]

The copy lacks authenticity, therefore, not because it differs from the original but because it has no location and consequently is not inscribed in history.

Thus, for Benjamin, technical reproduction as such is by no means the reason for a loss of aura. The loss of aura is introduced only with a new aesthetic taste – the taste of the modern consumer who prefers the copy or reproduction to the original. Today's consumer of art prefers the art to be brought – delivered. Such a consumer does not want to go off, travel to another place, be placed in another context, in order to experience the original as original. Rather, he or she wants the original to come to him or her – as in fact it does, but as a copy. When the distinction between original and copy is a topological one, then the topologically defined movement of the viewer alone makes this distinction. If we make our way to the artwork, then it is an original. If we force the artwork to come to us, then it is a copy. For that reason, the distinction between original and copy has, in Benjamin's work, a dimension of violence. In fact, Benjamin speaks not just of the loss of aura but of its destruction.[8] And the violence of this destruction of aura is not lessened by the fact that the aura is invisible. On the contrary, a material injury to the original is much less violent, in Benjamin's view, because it still inscribes itself in the history of the original by leaving behind certain traces on its body. The deterritorialization of the original, its removal from its site by means of bringing it closer represents, by contrast, an invisible and thus all the more devastating employment of violence, because it leaves behind no material traces.

Benjamin's new interpretation of the distinction between original and copy thus opens up the possibility not only of making a copy out of an original, but also of making an original out of a copy. Indeed, when the distinction between original and copy is merely a topological, contextual one, then it not only becomes possible to remove an original from its site and deterritorialize it, but also to reterritorialize the copy. Benjamin himself calls attention to this possibility when he writes about the figure of profane illumination and refers to the forms of life that can lead to such a profane illumination: "The reader, the thinker, the loiterer, the *flâneur*, are types of illuminati just as much as the opium eater, the dreamer, the ecstatic."[9] One is struck by the fact that these figures of profane illumination are also figures of motion – especially the *flâneur*. The *flâneur* does not demand of things that they come to him; he goes to things. In this sense, the *flâneur* does not destroy the aura of things; he respects them. Or rather, only through him do the aura emerge again. The figure of profane illumination is the reversal of the "loss of aura" that comes from siting the copy in a topology of undetermined circulation though the modern mass media. Now, however, it is clear that the installation can also be counted among the figures of profane illumination, because it transforms the viewer into a *flâneur*.

Art documentation, which by definition consists of images and texts that are reproducible, acquires through the installation an aura of the original, the living, the historical. In the installation the documentation gains a site – the here and now of a historical event. Because the distinction between original and copy is entirely a topological and situational one, all of the documents placed in the installation become originals. If reproduction makes copies out of originals, installation makes originals out of copies. That means: the fate of modern and contemporary art can by no means be reduced to the "loss of aura." Rather, the (post)modernity enacts a complex play of removing from sites and placing in (new) sites, of deterritorialization and reterritorialization, of removing aura and restoring aura. What distinguishes the modern age from earlier periods in this is simply the fact that the originality of a modern work is not determined by its material nature but by its aura, by its context, by its historical site. Consequently, as Benjamin emphasizes, originality does not represent an eternal value. In the modern age, originality has not simply been lost – it has become variable. Otherwise, the eternal value of originality would simply have been replaced by the eternal (non)value of unoriginality – as indeed happens in some art theories. All the same, eternal copies can no more exist than eternal originals. To be an original and possess an aura means the same thing as to be alive. But life is not something that the living being has "in itself." Rather, it is the inscription of a certain being into a life context – into a lifespan and into a living space.

This also reveals the deeper reason why art documentation now serves as a field of biopolitics – and reveals the deeper dimension of modern biopolitics in general. On the one hand, the modern age is constantly substituting the artificial, the technically produced, and the simulated for the real, or (what amounts to the same thing) the reproducible for the unique. It is no coincidence that cloning has become today's emblem of biopolitics, for it is precisely in cloning – no matter whether it ever becomes reality or remains a fantasy forever – that we perceive life as being removed from its site, which is perceived to be the real threat of contemporary technology. In reaction to this threat, the conservative, defensive strategies are offered which try to prevent this removal of life from its site by means of regulations and bans, even though the futility of such efforts is obvious even to those struggling for them. What is overlooked in this is that the modern age clearly has, on the other hand, strategies for making something living and original from something artificial and reproduced. The practices of art documentation and of installation in particular reveal another path for biopolitics: rather than fighting off modernity, they develop strategies of resisting and inscription based on situation and context, which make it possible to transform the artificial into something living and the repetitive into something unique.

Notes

1. On this, see Boris Groys, *Unter Verdacht: Eine Phänomenologie der Medien*, Munich: Carl Hanser Verlag, 2000, pp. 54ff.
2. Giorgio Agamben, *Homo Sacer: Sovereign Power and Bare Life*, trans. Daniel Heller-Roazen, Stanford, California: Stanford University Press, 1998, pp. 166ff.; originally published as *Homo sacer: Il potere sovrano e la nuda vita*, Turin: Giulio Einaudi Editore, 1995.
3. See also Jean-François Lyotard, *The Differend: Phrases in Dispute*, trans. Georges van den Abbeele, Manchester, UK: Manchester University Press; Minneapolis, Minnesota: Minnesota University Press, c. 1988; originally published as *Le Différend*, Paris: Editions de Minuit, 1983.
4. See *Kollektivnye Deystviya: Pojezdki za gorod, 1977–1998*, Moscow: Ad Marginem, 1998. See also Hubert Klocker, "Gesture and the Object. Liberation as Aktion: A European Component of Performative Art," in *Out of Actions: Between Performance and the Object, 1949–1979*, exh. cat., Los Angeles: The Museum of Contemporary Art; Vienna: Österreichisches Museum für Angewandte Kunst; Barcelona: Museu d'Art Contemporani de Barcelona; and Tokyo: Museum of Contemporary Art, 1998–9, pp. 166–7.
5. Walter Benjamin, "The Work of Art in the Age of Mechanical Reproduction," *Illuminations*, trans. Harry Zohn, London: Fontana, 1992, pp. 214–15. [Translator's note: This English edition is a translation of the second version of Benjamin's essay.]
6. Ibid., p. 214.
7. Walter Benjamin, "Das Kunstwerk im Zeitalter seiner technischen Reproduzierbarkeit," *Gesammelte Schriften*, vol. 1, pt 2, Frankfurt amd Main: Suhrkamp Verlag, 1974, p. 437. [Translator's note: This is my translation, from the first version of Benjamin's essay, originally published in an altered French translation in *Zeitschrift für Sozialforschung*, vol. 5, Paris, 1936.]
8. Walter Benjamin, "The Work of Art,", p. 217.
9. Walter Benjamin, *Reflections: Essays, Aphorisms, Autobiographical Writings*, ed. Peter Demetz, trans. Edmund Jephcott, New York: Schocken Books, 1986, p. 190; first published as "Der Sürrealismus. Die letzte Momentaufnahme der europäischen Intelligenz," *Die Literarische Welt*, 1929, vol. 5, pp. 5–7.

Chapter 13

The Interstices of History

Angela Harutyunyan with Vardan Azatyan, Tevž Logar, Vesna Madžoski and Joanna Sokołowska, Eszter Lázár

Several years ago my friend and colleague Julian Vigo sent me four photographs from Montreal that she had printed from film that had been left behind in a 1950s camera manufactured in the USSR. After opening the envelope, I was enchanted by the photographs' mysterious quality: they resisted interpretation through their reluctance to give a clue, a hint, a recognizable code for historical reconstruction (Figure 1). The photographer's name, the objects he or she was depicting, the precise time and place in which these photographs were taken could not be known. Looking at these photographs it felt as if I were given a chance to look out from a window back into the past, but that the window was covered with an impenetrable curtain.

Formally and aesthetically the *Other* of Socialist Realism, the photographs do not heroically claim that there is a purer "reality" beneath representation. Their otherness is not alien but rather hovers within the realm of the mundane; they are unintentional messages that seem to emanate from the everyday life of the past, even if we find ourselves temporarily unable to locate what and where this past "was," begging the question of how we "contextualize" them in their conditions of production and reception if we have lost access to these variables.

This attempt at producing a timeline of performance practices in Eastern Europe since WWII is necessarily incomplete. Just as the unidentifiable photographs refuse to tell us a simple narrative of their conditions of production and reception in the former Soviet bloc, so this schematic historical timeline of body art and performance practices from former socialist countries of the Soviet Union and Eastern Europe – filled with ruptures, repressions, tales of arrest, and immigration but also of occasional acceptance and tolerance – does not form a linear chronological narrative that conveniently presents the "other story" to official

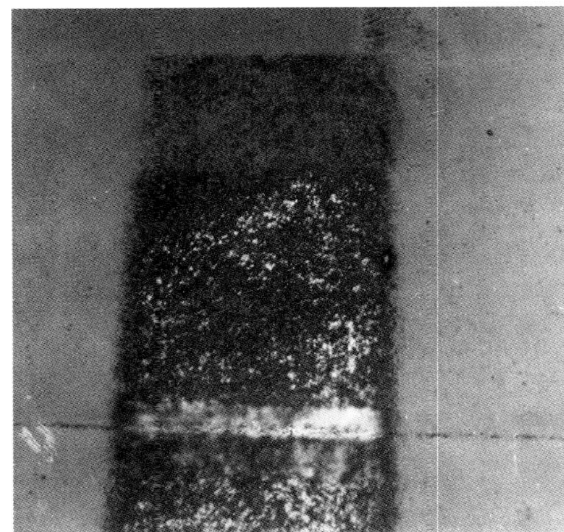
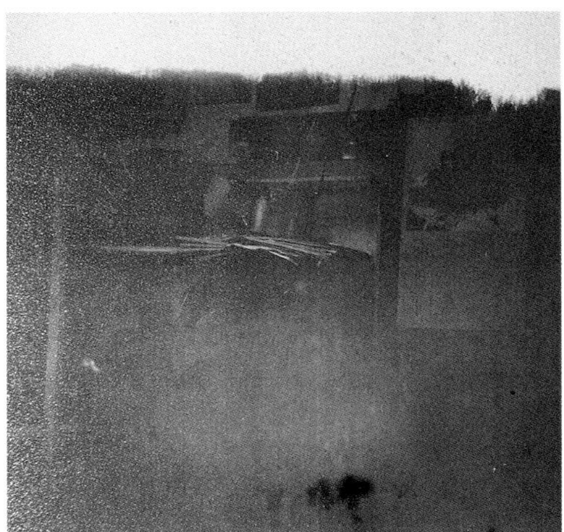
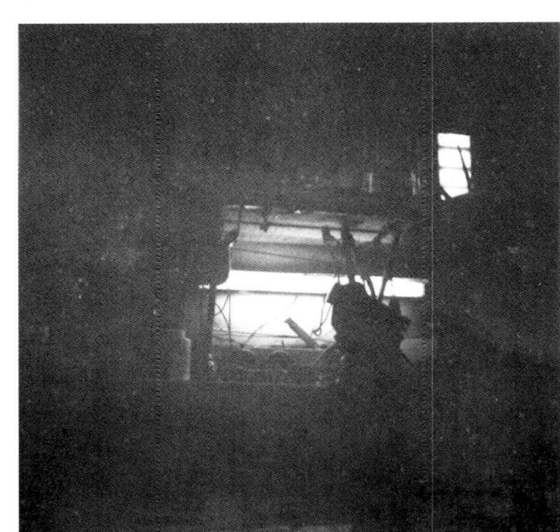

Untitled photographs. Anonymous photographer. Date Unknown. Courtesy of Julian Vigo.

histories of Euro-American art and performance in the post-WWII period. I have, with the consultation of curators and art historians Joanna Sokołowska from Poland, Tevž Logar from Slovenia, Eszter Lázár from Hungary, Vesna Madžoski from Serbia, Vardan Azatyan from Armenia, chosen to embrace the inevitable failure of such histories to be comprehensive – there are many practices, contexts, and countries that are not included here. At times, it was simply beyond the capacities of the authors of this project to excavate the past, to trigger memories of witnesses, or to find pieces of documentation; even in cases in which documents such as photographs, texts, and witnesses' narratives exist, these are often opaque and (like the photographs developed from the negatives found in the Soviet-era camera) function more as sites of erasure than of remembrance. This impossibility of reconstruction as well as the existence of parallel and at times antagonistic histories of the Soviet avant-gardes and the official narrative entails that the way history has been experienced, understood, and narrated has an entirely different meaning in the socialist and post-Soviet contexts than it sustains in Western European and North American cultures.

In elaborating this timeline, we propose it as an example of a historically grounded and context-sensitive curatorial practice, necessarily contingent and incomplete in its conclusions. The artistic practices covered in the timeline include some of the works produced after 1945 (the earliest dating back to 1949) in Armenia, Georgia, Croatia, Hungary, Romania, Russia, Poland, Serbia, and Slovenia. They are presented in parallel to the official timeline of USSR–US relations during the Cold War as illegitimate offspring of these political metanarratives; in a sense they claim different histories without rendering the former histories as false. The chronological sketch of these practices does not simply deconstruct the Cold War's well-sketched linear history of rivalry, power, and the fight between "good" and "evil" (with which nation is on which side depending on which side is writing the history), but rather subtly challenge these "political" narratives, often laid out as if they have nothing to do with "culture." In so doing we are claiming that behind and beyond the meta-discourses there were other stories evolving within the everyday. It is not accidental that many artists in the former Soviet bloc and former Yugoslavia saw possibilities of resisting the communist regime and its manifestations in art and cultural policy through adopting strategies of subverting everyday life and intervening in structures of state power. Nevertheless, as with the photographs, while subverting the very context of their production, these works function as a constituent part of that context by being embedded within it.

The bi-polar world order ended with the collapse of state socialism and artistic practices evolving after 1991 are presented without a meta-discursive "backbone," that is, without the political timeline. This is not to say that after the Wall the era of metanarratives was over or that art was no longer political and politics anesthetized but, rather, that references and associations across cultures from the former socialist bloc are more diffuse and dispersed – from the rise of globalization, capitalism, westernization, "EU-ification," fundamentalism, and traditionalism to the return to a folkloristic pre-modernism. While there are deep contextual differences between the practices of diverse socialist and former socialist contexts, there are also deep-rooted similarities in that what most of the examples share is a response to similar political and ideological meta-discourses. Within this, several thematic lines emerge: Artistic Action and/as Political Action; Interventions into the Everyday; The Body and/as Identity; and Performing History.

Artistic Action and/as Political Action

USSR: in the USSR politically conscious performance practices radically challenged or directly attacked both the political apparatus of the dominant ideology and its aesthetic manifestation in Socialist Realism. However, in many Soviet contexts such attacks took place during the years of Gorbachev's *Perestroika* and *glasnost* (1985–91), where it was already *licensed* by the political power to speak out and voice the need for change ("glasnost" in Russian means to voice). In this regard, such practices, with all their subversive rhetoric, could be called a *retroactive attack* on ideology. Russian artist Yevgeni Yufit's films and performances of the 1980s and 1990s as well as the practices of the Armenian 3rd Floor movement of the late 1980s and 1990s are similar in their retrogressive attacks upon the already dying body of state ideology during the years of *Perestroika*.

Saint-Petersburg-based Yufit's performances and films are dubbed as "necro-realism." Echoing the feeling of the *Perestroika* years that the old system of the Soviet Union was dying, Yufit performed different macabre rituals and filmed them. These included suicide, burial, and ritualized acts of collective punishment which often emerged as excesses of desire for knowledge, or more specifically, of the epistemological quest for a rational scientific language. Some of these episodes were later included in his various experimental films. Sources for his performances, underlined by a sadistic black humor, were as various as psychiatric textbooks, criminology, and archaic rituals.[1]

POLAND: Joanna Sokołowska: around the same time, in the late 1980s Wrocław-based underground anarchic collective Orange Alternative was adopting tactics of carnivalesque mimicry of official celebration and events through major public happenings. One of the most spectacular actions of Orange Alternative took place on 6 November 1987, in the crowded center of Wrocław. Teasing out the state culture of promoting seemingly endless celebrations of different official occasions, they staged "the Eve of the October Revolution" to commemorate the seventieth anniversary of this event. Wearing Russian cavalry caps and racing wooden horses, the participants of the happening performed the battle of Budyonny's army. When the "battle" between "whites" and "reds" began, those who had no red clothes went to buy sandwiches with ketchup in order to have crimson props. When the police realized the meaning of the queue to the sandwich stand, they decided to close it. In the end the confused and embarrassed police arrested approximately 150 "Red" activists.

ARMENIA: Vardan Azatyan and Angela Harutyunyan: paralleling the strategies of Orange Alternative, Armenian artist Grigor Khachatryan adopts the tools of official ideology to subvert this very ideology through over-identifying with its iconographical manifestations. From 1974 to 2007 he performed the *Grigor Khachatryan Award* series in different locations in Armenia. From 1990, on 7 November, the day of the Bolshevik Revolution and the artist's birthday, the award-giving ceremonies became a tradition, mimicking the pathos of similar events of the communist era. The receiver of the award had to lift and hold Grigor Khachatryan in his/her arms to be photographed (Figure 2). The latest ceremony took place in the summer of 2007. The award was granted to Nadja Tsulukidze, member of Khinkali Juice performance artists' duo, in Tbilisi, in Lake Sevan, Armenia.

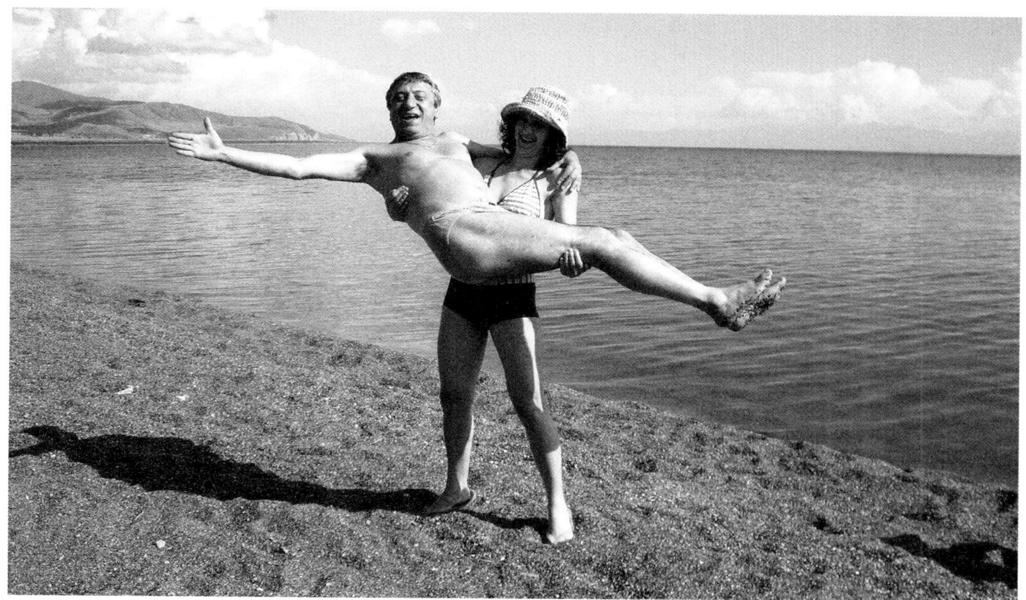

Grigor Khachatryan, *Grigor Khachatryan Award Ceremony: Nadia Tsulukidze*, Lake Sevan, 2007. Courtesy of Joanna Sokolowska's Archive.

Marking the incipient collapse of the Soviet bloc, Armenian artists' movement the 3rd Floor performed "Hail to the Union of Artists from the Netherworld: the Official Art has Died" in 1988. In the happening, they walked silently through an official art exhibition as resurrected ghosts, marking the death of Socialist Realism. The message was quite clear: the dead are the proper audience for an official exhibition of an already dying system.

YUGOSLAVIA: Artists in the former Yugoslavia, under Tito's moderate authoritarianism with relatively open borders, reacted differently to dominant cultural and political conditions. Many of them critically reflected upon a specific regime of oblivion, and particularly, the forgetting of the Nazi past.

Vesna Madžoski: some performance and body art practices in Serbia and Slovenia aimed at destabilizing socially coordinated techniques of managing the body through the narratives of memory and erasure. In Serbia, Dragoljub Raša Todosijević performed his *Was ist kunst Marinela Koželj?* in 1977. In this performance, the artist consistently repeats one question: "Was ist kunst (What is art)?" to a mute and motionless female model seated in front of him. The model becomes his object of investigation and abuse, whereas his voice becomes a parody of police interrogation, until it fails him. According to the artist, this question was only possible in German, evoking a supreme example of totalitarian legacy again and again.

Tevž Logar: in the fall of 1984 the Borghesia group appeared in Cankarjev dom in Ljubljana with the performance *Lustmörder*. In her article on Slovenian art scene, Slavenka – Iliž labeled the performance fascistic:

> [O]ne of the female protagonists placed bloody pieces of liver on the nude chest of a man lying on a elevated part of the stage (an altar). The man was wearing only a leather helmet, leather briefs and chains. Another man, also half naked, with a made-up face, crushed the liver in his hands and smeared it over the supine man. [...] The themes of the video projected on the screens in the background were sadomasochism, violence, fascism, war, army, parade, socialist realism. [...] The expression of violence, of deviant forms of sexuality, transvestism, perversity, indicate in the view of the group, the process of a metaphysical discovery of the concealed essence of repression.[2]

Projected on the back of the set was a poster of Dušan Mandič with the inscription: "1968 is over. 1983 is over. The future lies between your legs."

ARMENIA, post-1991: Vardan Azatyan and Angela Harutyunyan: in 1995, the same year the Armenian people voted for their first constitution, the artists' group ACT (1994–6) obtained an official permit from the City Council of Yerevan to hold a procession of artists in Yerevan. The artists marched carrying placards with slogans in Armenian and English calling for an "Art Demonstration" and an "Art Referendum" and stating that "Creativity will Save Humanity." Parodying the participatory tools of political action from representative democracies and addressing the new concept of citizenship and the ways in which it affected the artists' status in society, ACT members, along the lines of official economic policy, were calling for free market relations in the general economy as well as in the art world.

SLOVENIA/ RUSSIA: Slovenian artists' group IRWIN were typical of a move in the former Eastern bloc to address remnants of the socialist past lingering in the post-socialist period in order to illuminate these shared past experiences for international art audiences.

Tevž Logar: In 1992 IRWIN installed a large black square made of canvas on Moscow's Red Square. The action *Black Square on Red Square*, intended as a living installation, was a part of the NSK (Neue Slowenische Kunst) Moscow Embassy project, which took place in a private apartment at Leninsky Prospekt 12 (the NSK was a multi-disciplinary group that incorporated different departments, including music, art, and graphic design). Besides the documents and artifacts of NSK groups – Laibach, IRWIN, Noordung, New Collectivism Studio, and the Department of Pure and Applied Philosophy – the central event of the project was a one-week program of lectures and public discussions. The encounter of individuals with similar aesthetic and ethical interests and social experiences revealed that the topic arousing the most enthusiastic and intense debate was the art and culture of the 1980s and the specific role it played in the transformation of Eastern Europe.

Angela Harutyunyan: while IRWIN's practices strove to construct an inter-artistic dialogue in relation to former socialist contexts, the Moscow art scene largely oriented itself toward what used to be perceived as the West, with its art market and value system. This is especially true in relation to Alexander Brener and Oleg Kulik's performances. After acting as a dog for five years in performances in Manifesta I (Rotterdam, 1996) and the Interpol exhibition in Stockholm (1996) among other events, Oleg Kulik arrived at Kennedy Airport in New York City in 1997 only to enter a cage to become a "dog" for the entirety of his two-week stay in the US. The cage was placed on view in Deitch Gallery, where visitors were invited to don protective suits to enter the cage and interact with Kulik as a "dog." Kulik's "dog years" reflected upon the condition of the Russian artist as the *Other* of both the western art market and its institutions.

Interventions into the Everyday

Interventions into the everyday in the socialist period in Eastern Europe, at times ephemeral and barely tangible, were a common strategy to react against the elimination of the concept of privacy within the officially controlled and regulated public sphere.

POLAND: Joanna Sokołowska: between 1972 and 1974 the Polish artistic duo KwieKulik created a series of actions with their baby son Maksymilian Dobromierz in their flat, later the site of the Studio for Action, Documentation and Distribution. The resulting piece, *Activities*

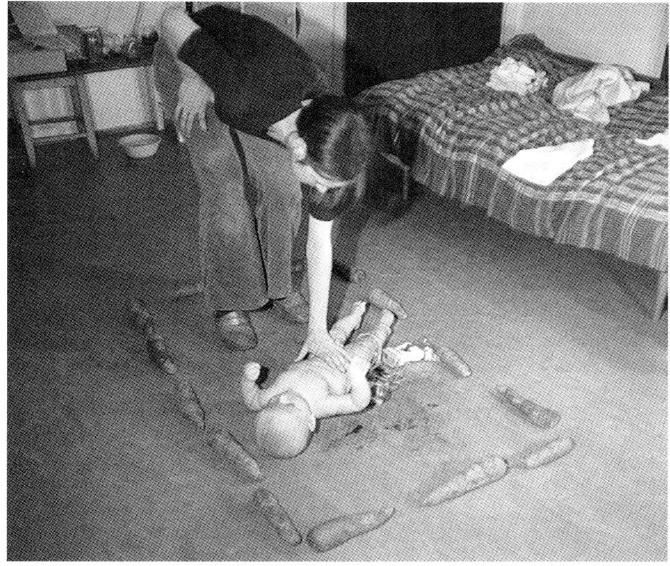

KiewKulik, *Activities with Dobromierz*, 1972–1974, Warsaw. Courtesy of the artists.

with Dobromierz, documented the baby's everyday life in relation to different pre-existing and newly conceived spatial configurations, producing a variety of so called aesthetic time-results (Figure 3). For instance, the artists put their son in the toilet, surrounded him with vegetables, knives, and forks, or blocks of ice from the river. All of these actions were recorded on slides and negatives constituting an archive of over nine hundred images.

CROATIA/former YUGOSLAVIA: Tevž Logar: Croatian artist Tomislav Gotovac similarly produced semi-private, semi-ephemeral performances, integrating processes in real time into the work of art. His actions in the 1980s, such as *Sweeping the Streets*, differed from their everyday counterparts in their demonstrative character, being performed by the artist himself. A performance, however, includes not only the artist's ideas, but also the social context, including structures and beliefs linked to contemporary political ideologies – in this case, beliefs linked to the illusory erasure of individual agency under the guise of collectivism.

The Body and/as Identity

Related to the concept of privacy or the lack of it within the official ideology of the communist regime is the idea of the private body, which functions as the repressed other of state ideology. It is not insignificant that, with the fall of the communist regime in the early 1990s, there was a proliferation of body art practices in many of the countries of the former Eastern bloc. These practices often articulated the body as a site for the construction of desiring gendered subjectivities and often triggered reactions linked to a lingering dominant patriarchal anxiety over the signs of explicit sexuality.

USSR/RUSSIA: Angela Harutyunyan: I Love You, Life! was a St. Petersburg-based women artists' collective, the first of its kind in Russia that operated from 1990–2. Comprised of Marina Alexeeva, Marina Koldobskaya, Marina Teplova, and Eugenia Kamenskaya, the group appropriated Soviet signs and symbols in the organization of parties and public installations (the group's name, "Ya Lyublyu Tebya Jizn,'" in Russian was the name of a song popular in Stalin's times). The 1991 installation *Nonna and Pasha* at the Yubileyni Athlete Center in St. Petersburg of 1991 presented a naked female mannequin, recalling the female statues in Soviet gardens. However, this one had plastic nipples and pubic hair, its sexuality more or less naturalistically represented. After the artists refused to comply with the demand on the part of Center officials to dress up the installation in panties, the mannequin was anonymously vandalized.[3]

SERBIA: Vesna Madžoski: *Personal Space* of 1996 was a performance enacted at the Biennale of Young Artists in Vršac, during which Serbian artist Tanja Ostojić stood still, bold, and naked, covered with white marble powder. This mute and androgynous body is uncanny, seemingly dead while still alive, a still-female body turned simultaneously into the signs of beauty and humility. *Personal Space* reveals the human condition of nakedness and the search for a pure, innocent body at the moment when thousands were violated, decapitated, and shattered just a few hundred kilometers away. Ostojić radically questions the agency of the artist in times of horror and chaos – can the artist merely stand silently in front of the crime scene and be numb and ashamed?

These two examples play with the idea of the gendered body as a cultural sign. In I Love You Life's performative installation, the naked body of the doll is animated through the very act of vandalism in which the attack on the sign is also an attack against the referent. In *Personal Space* the living body of the artist is turned into an inanimate doll: a sign without a referent.

Sites of Memory and Oblivion

This project of constructing a timeline of body art and performance practices in the Eastern European context poses larger questions: what are the modes of recalling the past as history? What traces and kinds of evidence do we look to in this recalling? What do we remember from the past? How do we (not) remember? What can be considered as a historical document or evidence?

CROATIA/Former YUGOSLAVIA: Tevž Logar: a photograph dating back to 1949 shows Croatian artist Seissel, Božidar Tušek, and others, all standing on the beach at Brela, Croatia with stones on their heads while holding another one in their hands. The photograph, reified and fixed as the first ever happening in post-war European art, however, raises many questions: whether this was a happening at all; whether Siessel was the author; how and why and to whom we attribute authorship; what is the role of the interpreter/historian in the work of reconstruction of an event when the documentation resists such reconstructions?

USSR/RUSSIA: historical evidence does not merely consist of material traces but also of bodily re-enactments, thus bringing in the performative aspects of memory. Dmitry Prigov, one of the leading figures on the Moscow conceptual art scene in the 1970s and 1980s, was known for his performances in which he screamed poetry and cited passages from literary and colloquial discourses. His self-published and self-disseminated *Samizdat* poems circulated widely on the Moscow underground scene in the late Soviet years. However, the focus here is not Prigov's artistic personae, but the way in which he is remembered or relived through re-enactments. Prigov died on 16 July 2007. The Voina group, fulfilling Russian funerary traditions, commemorated the fortieth day after Prigov's death by setting up a table filled with pickled salads and candy in the brown line of the Moscow subway. About fifty people attended the performance. As one of the organizers, Oleg Vorotnikov stated: "The Circle Line of the Moscow metro is depicted using the color brown – the color of earth, and the color of feces, waste products. That which is left of you [...] What's left of Dmitry Alexandrovich is his poetry and his body, which is located with us in Moscow, not far from the center."[4]

HUNGARY: performative re-enactment has also been the strategy of Hungarian artists' collective Little Warsaw, which deals with contemporary approaches to the production and representation of historical performance pieces through re-contextualizing the reception of artworks.

Eszter Lázár: in a 2005 work, the group Tableau Vivant enacted a performance in which the artists reconstructed and reinterpreted Tamás Szentjóby's 1972 *Expulsion-Exercise*. In the original work Szentjóby (also called St. Auby) sentenced himself to sit with a bucket over his head; he invited the audience to ask him questions of their own or to choose them from a list provided. St. Auby would try to provide direct and honest answers. Some of the questions included: "Can a person who is not completely free form a collective with other people?" and "Is it the true task of culture to make us aware that our destiny is one with history?" However, the re-enactment was not simply a repetition but an entirely new work of art. "The repetition of this legendary exercise would pose the questions: how do we perceive the same performance after a long time? Would the performance be the same within a different framework of time, way of perception, and changed notion of performance art itself?"[5]

ROMANIA: in the performances of the 1990s in Eastern Europe, not only did artists re-enact earlier artistic actions; they also re-enacted political events belonging to recent history, critically articulating them as sites of artistic interventions. In September 2007, seventeen years after the miners' march to the center of Bucharest in Romania to oppose and halt the revolutionary transformations in society and politics during the decline of the Soviet system, artist Dan Perjovschi performed his *Historia/Histeria-2* piece at the same location where the march took place – in Bucharest's central University Square. The performance took place seven days a week, two hours a day. The artist simply stood still for the first ten minutes, and was subsequently replaced by actors.. The actors became a temporary living monument who retroactively internalized the historical event; the body became a literal carrier of collective memory and history.

ARMENIA: Vardan Azatyan and Angela Harutyunyan: at times history proves to be too traumatic to remember or to return to, as Armenian artist David Kareyan's work of the late 1990s and early 2000s seems to suggest. Kareyan's *No Return* is a multimedia audio-visual installation realized in collaboration with Eva Khachatryan in 2003. The central video projection depicts the artist's figure in a woman's nightgown and dominates both the audience and a live performance of seven females drumming on wooden bases taking place below. On the second screen the video presents different juxtaposed images of political turmoil as well as texts such as "Terror," "Suicide," "You are in a Logic Trap." The aesthetics of pain, ritualistic sacrifice, and bodily suffering became typical for Kareyan's works of the late 1990s and early 2000s. In his videos and performances of the period the figure of the heroically suffering artist emerges through various ritualistic acts such as continuously rubbing blood on his own body (*Dead Democracy*, 1999), tumbling in mud (*The World Without You*, 1999) and axing a cow's head (*Call of Ancestors*, 2001). Here the political dystopia of post-socialist Armenia was traumatically internalized and then expressed through violence.

Instead of a Conclusion or P.S.

The first draft of this project was finished in November 2007, before the 2008 war between Russia and Georgia. The official political timeline, which stops after the collapse of the Soviet Union implies a ray of optimism, suggesting that the Cold War era's polarized world order is over. However, the short war between Georgia and Russia in August 2008 inspired the media and politicians around the world to declare the return of Cold War politics. While the media rhetoric certainly re-staged Cold War propaganda, the events were surely a result of a deep-rooted cycle linked to a variety of colonialism specific to the Eastern European context. On the one hand Russia seemed to be striving to revive its colonial politics masked under the rhetoric of the humanistic but also all-punishing big brother; on the other hand, the Georgian President claimed to be acting autonomously as the head of a sovereign country, but constantly referred to NATO and his American neo-conservative allies within George Bush's regime in order to justify his response to Russian aggression.

GEORGIA: at times artistic practices do not provide a follow-up reflection upon politics but precede it. Nadja Tsulukidze: two weeks before Bush's visit to Georgia in 2006, the houses on the main streets of Tbilisi were painted pink, yellow, blue, and green. A big show, with folk dance and songs, was arranged for the President. He seemed to be satisfied, he smiled and winked to the Georgians, and this moment was immortalized on the billboard exhibited on a big avenue, named George Bush Avenue. In contemporary Georgia the convenient marriage of nationalism and westernization is prevalent in most spheres of life. We – an artists' duo Khinkali Juice – decided to confront this nationalist rhetoric and its paraphernalia by making an artistic/economic intervention. Begging for money in the streets, we were singing the most popular Georgian song, the national anthem, on Europe Square and George Bush Avenue. In ten minutes we managed to earn two Georgian laris, the equivalent of one US dollar, and this was much more than we ever could have gotten from the Ministry of Culture for a contemporary art project.

Notes

1. Viktor Tikhomorov and Yevgeni Yufit, *Tikhomorov and Yufit: An Energetic Pair*; Artists' Catalogue; forward by Olesya Turkina, St. Petersburg: Great Print, 2006. Branislav Dimitrijević, "A Brief Narrative of Art Events in Serbia after 1948" in IRWIN (eds), *East Art Map: Contemporary Art and Eastern Europe*, London and Cambridge, MA: Afterall Books and MIT Press, 2006, p. 271.
2. Zemira Alajbegović, "Ljubezen je hladnejša od smrti. Dokumenti", *Likovne Besede*, Ljubljana, January 1992.
3. Marina Koldobskaya, "Some Provincial Stories," in *East Art Map*, p. 277.
4. The event is documented on the blog "The Accidental Russophile." Available at: http://accidentalrussophile.blogspot.com/2007/09/wake-of-dmitri-prigov.html, accessed 26 February 2009.
5. Artists' statement. Available at: http://labor.c3.hu/wp-content/uploads/Labor_Time_of_an_artwork.pdf. Accessed 2 May 2011 (editor's note).

An Unofficial Timeline of Socialist and Post-Socialist Performance[1]

Angela Harutyunyan with Vardan Azatyan, Tevž Logar, Vesna Madžoski and Joanna Sokołowska, Eszter Lázár

1945: Victory in WWII. The United States and Soviet Union end WWII as allies. **1947: Cold War Begins.** The struggle between the United States and the Soviet Union for domination in certain sectors and parts of the world is dubbed the Cold War. It will last until 1991. **9 May 1948**: The Communist Party takes control in Czechoslovakia. **28 June 1948**: Schism between the Soviet Union and Yugoslavia. **4 April 1949**: NATO (North Atlantic Treaty Organization) was established in Washington. **24 May 1949:** The Federal Republic of Germany (West Germany) was established. **1949**: Josip Seissel (Yugoslavia), *Untitled*, aka Jo Klek, happening, Brela, Croatia. **5 March 1953:** Joseph Stalin dies. **14 May 1955:** The Warsaw Pact is founded by the Soviet Union, Albania, Bulgaria, Czechoslovakia, Hungary, the German Democratic Republic, Poland, and Romania. **14 February–25 February 1956**: The twentieth Congress of the Communist Party of the Soviet Union is held. Nikita Khrushchev denounces the Soviet dictator Joseph Stalin in the Secret Speech. **23 October 1956**: The Hungarian Revolution is suppressed by the Soviet military. **1956:** Miklós Erdély (Hungary), *Unguarded Money*, action, Budapest. The action *Unguarded Money* is realized during the Hungarian Revolution. Erdély places six boxes in the streets of Budapest to collect money for the families of political martyrs. **1957:** The Soviets launch Sputnik, the first manmade object to orbit the Earth. **15 September–27 September 1959**: During the tour of the United States Nikita Khrushchev calls for the peaceful coexistence of communist nations with capitalist nations. **3 June 3–4 June 1961**: John F. Kennedy and Nikita Khrushchev meet in Vienna. **13 August 1961:** The Berlin Wall is built by the Soviets, dividing the city into two sectors. **20 June 1963**: The "Red Telephone" linking Washington and Moscow is established. **14 October 1964**: Nikita Khrushchev is removed and is succeeded by Leonid Brezhnev as the Party First Secretary. **20 August–21 August 1968**: The Prague Spring is suppressed when the Soviet Union and its Warsaw Pact allies invade Czechoslovakia. **1968**: Group OHO

(Yugoslavia), *Mount Triglav*, performance, Ljubljana, Slovenia. Three members of the group are draped by a cloth to reveal their long-haired heads on three different levels, mimicking the three peaks of Mount Triglav in Slovenia. **1969:** The Red Peristil (Yugoslavia), *Untitled*, urban intervention, Split, Croatia. During the night of 11 January 1968 what will later be called The Red Peristil group paints the main square of Diocletian's Palace in Split red. Because of the assumed political intentions of the act, the artists are hunted by the police. **1969**: Theater Pupilija Ferkeverk (Yugoslavia), *Pupilija, papa Pupilio pa pupilčki,* performance, Ljubljana, Slovenia. Rather than being a direct expression of a political protest against a specific ideology, *Pupilija* first and foremost resisted all forms of authority in society, politics and aesthetics. **22 May–30 May 1972:** Richard. M. Nixon becomes the first President of the United States to visit Moscow. **1972–4**: KwieKulik (Zofia Kulik, Przemysław Kwiek) (Poland), *Activities with Dobromierz/Działania z Dobromierzem*,Warsaw. **1972–7**: Slobodan Tišma and Čedomir Drča (Yugoslavia), *The End*, Serbia, a series of time-based performances during which the artists drank American Coca-Cola and Russian Kvass every day with their friends in front of a local store. **1972:** Tamás Szentjóby (or St. Auby) (Hungary), *Expulsion-Exercise*, performance, Balatonboglár Chapel, Lake Balaton. **22 June 1973**: Leonid Brezhnev visits the United States. **1974–ongoing:** Grigor Khachatryan (Armenia), *Grigor Khachatryan Award*, performance, photo, poster, different locations in Armenia. **1974**: Marina Abramović (Yugoslavia), *Rhythm 5*, performance, Belgrade, Serbia, in which Abramović sets fire to a five-pointed star wooden construction, cuts her hair and nails and throws them into the fire, finally entering the flaming star herself. **17 July 1975:** The Apollo-Soyuz Test Project. In the first joined spaceflight of the United States and the Soviet Union Apollo 18 and Soyuz 19 spacecrafts docked. **1977**: Dragoljub Raša Todosijević (Yugoslavia), *Was ist kunst Marinela Koželj?* performance, Serbia. In the performance, the artist consistently repeats one question: "Was ist kunst?" (What is art?) in German, to a mute and motionless female model seated in front of him. **1979**: Stefan Bertalan (Romania), *I Live with a Sun Flower for 130 days*, multimedia action. For 130 days before the action in the gallery, Bertalan carefully observes and documents the patterns and processes of growth of the sunflower. During the action he reads his notes poetically and passionately. **1979**: Sanja Iveković (Yugoslavia), *Triangle*, performance, Zagreb, Croatia. During President Tito's visit to Zagreb, the artist positions herself in her balcony, in view of the police, drinks whiskey, reads a book, and pretends to masturbate. **1979:** Tibor Hajas (Hungary), *Touch*, radio performance, Budapest. In this work Hajas insistently addresses the radio listeners in second person singular. Some of the messages included: "listen carefully," "lean back and relax," "close your eyes." **1980:** The United States and sixty other countries boycott the Summer Olympics (held in Moscow) to protest the Soviet invasion of Afghanistan. **6 September 1980:** The Polish independent trade union federation "Solidarity" was established. **1980**: Ewa Partum (Poland), *Self-Identification/Samoidentyfikacja*, Mała Gallery, Warsaw. Surrounded by the audience, the naked artist reads a manifesto about women's existence within the alienating patriarchal structures of society. Then she leaves the gallery, walking out in the direction of the Wedding Palace located next to it. **20 January 1981:** Ronald Reagan is inaugurated as President of the United States. He refers to the Soviet Union as the "Evil

Empire." **1981**: Tomislav Gotovac (Yugoslavia), *Sweeping the Street*, action, Croatia, Zagreb. **1982**: *Happening*, various artists, curated by Vardan Tovmasyan, Yerevan, Armenia. Due to the lack of available documentation, it is impossible to reconstruct this exhibition at this point.[2] **16 June 1983:** Yuri Andropov is elected the General Secretary of the Communist Party. **1983**: Laibach (Yugoslavia), *Interview*, Slovenia. A documentary by TV Slovenia in 1983 is made to discredit Laibach as a fascistic enterprise. However, the documentary unintentionally becomes a well-staged visual presentation by Laibach in which the editing, lighting, and camera moves transform the group's appearance into a powerful noir-ish performance. **13 February 1984:** Konstantin Chernenko succeeds Yuri Andropov as the General Secretary of the Communist Party. **1984**: The Soviet Union and a handful of countries boycott the Summer Olympics in Los Angeles. **1984**: Borghesia (Yugoslavia), *Lustmörder*, performance, Ljubljana, Slovenia. **11 March 1985:** Mikhail Gorbachev is elected General Secretary of the Communist Party. In June he declares *Perestroika*, which aims at reforming the centrally planned economy. **19 November–20 November 1985**: The Geneva Summit occurs between Ronald Reagan and Mikhail Gorbachev; this is the first American–Soviet meeting since 1979 when Jimmy Carter and Leonid Brezhnev met in Vienna. **1986:** A nuclear power plant in the Soviet Union (Chernobyl, Ukraine) explodes, spreading contamination over a huge area. **1987**: Pomarańczowa Alternatywa/Orange Alternative (Poland), *Eve of the October Revolution* – 6 November, Wrocław. **February 1988:** The Karabakh Movement, which later grows into movement for independence, starts in Armenia. **8 November 1988:** George H. W. Bush is elected the President of the United States. **1988**: The 3rd Floor, *Hail to the Union of Painters from the Netherworld*, happening, Yerevan, Armenia. **4 June 1989**: The Solidarity Party wins the Polish elections. **23 October 1989:** On the thirty-third anniversary of the Hungarian Revolution of 1956 the Hungarian Republic is officially declared. **9 November 1989:** The fall of the Berlin Wall. **25 December 1989:** Execution of the General Secretary of the Romanian Communist Party Nicolae Ceausescu. **29 May 1990:** Boris Yeltsin is elected as chairman of the Presidium of the Supreme Soviet of the Russian SFSR (Soviet Federative Socialist Republic). **3 October 1990:** The unification of East and West Germany. **31 March 1991:** The Warsaw Pact is dissolved. **25 June 1991:** Slovenia declares its independence from Yugoslavia. **19 August 1991:** Soviet coup attempt, in response to a new union treaty to be signed on 20 August. **25 December 1991:** Dissolution of the Soviet Union. **1 February 1992:** George H. W. Bush of the United States and Boris Yeltsin declare a formal end to the Cold War. **1991**: I Love you, Life! (Russia) *Nonna and Pasha*, Installation, Yubileyni Art Center, St. Petersburg. **1992**: IRWIN (Slovenia), *Black Square on Red Square*, urban intervention, Moscow, Russia. **1995**: Karine Matsakyan (Armenia), *The Triumph of Consumerism*, action, Yerevan, in which the artist walks into a butcher's shop in the center of Yerevan, pulls out a toy-gun and starts shooting at hanging meat. **1995:** ACT (Armenia), *Art Demonstration*, action, urban intervention, Yerevan. **1996**: *Personal Space*, by Tanja Ostojić (Serbia), performance, Belgrade, Serbia. **1997**: Oleg Kulik (Russia), *I Bite America and America Bites Me*, Deitch Projects, SoHo, New York. **4 January 1997**: Alexander Brener (Russia), action, Stedelijk Museum, Amsterdam. The artist walks into the museum and sprays a green dollar sign on

Malevich's *Suprematisme* painting (1920–7); he is arrested and brought to trial. **15 December 1999**: Dragan Živadinov's Cosmokinetic Cabinet Noordung Theatre (Slovenia), *Biomechanics Noordung*, 1999, performance, near Moscow, Russia. *Biomechanics Noordung* is performed in a Russian cosmonaut training aircraft just outside Moscow, at an altitude of 6660 meters and at zero gravity, researching the revolutionary changes which take place in the human body in a situation of weightlessness. **1999**: Artur Żmijewski (Poland), *The Game of Tag/Berek*, Warsaw. Żmijewski filmed a group of nude women and men playing a game of tag in two rooms: a basement of a private house and a former Nazi gas chamber. The existence of the latter is revealed only in the captions at the end of the film. **2003:** David Kareyan (Armenia), *No Return*, multimedia performance, Venice and Yerevan. **2004**: Johnny Racković (Serbia), *In the Presence of Art*, performance, Belgrade, a series of performance-actions by Racković performed during art openings in which he reacts to exhibited works of art by kneeling or falling on the ground in awe and admiration. He chokes and "dies" in front of one of them in the end. **2005**: Paweł Althamer (Poland), *Film*, multimedia action, Warsaw. Althamer first presents a trailer of a new movie starring Polish actors in a local cinema, which functions as an invitation to participate in a new project staged later in "real" life in front of a shopping mall. Actors appear alongside a number of extras who perform as ordinary passers-by; their roles re-enact the "action" announced by the trailer. **2005:** Little Warsaw (Hungary), *Tableau Vivant*, Little Warsaw's Studio, Budapest. **2006**: Khinkali Juice (Georgia), *Georgian National Anthem*, action, urban intervention, Tbilisi. **2006:** Peter Halász (Hungary), *Virtual Funeral*, 2006, Kunsthalle, Budapest. While fighting cancer, Halász directs his last performance, which is his own virtual funeral ceremony. In the crowded farewell party, after talking about his illness in an objective manner, he places himself in an open coffin; climbing in and out of his coffin, he gives a spontaneous farewell speech, spiced with humor and wit. **September 2007**: Dan Perjovschi (Romania), *Historia/Histeria-2*, performance, Bucharest. Seventeen years after the miners' march to the center of Bucharest, artist Dan Perjovschi performs his *Historia/Histeria-2* in University Square. The performance takes place seven days a week, two hours a day, during which two actors representing a miner and a student stand still next to each other.

Notes

1. The political Timeline of Cold War events is compiled from the following sources: http://www.cold-war-timeline.com/cold-war-timeline/from-february-7-1984-to-february-1-1992/. Accessed 2 May 2011 (editor's note). After the collapse of the Soviet Union, the political timeline stops while the timeline of performative practices in former communist bloc countries continues.
2. A witness's account testifies: "There was a wonderful poet […] named Belamuki, but the focus was on two actors, who, in a very strange way, resembled Salvador Dali and Picasso." Arman Grigoryan, "Informed but Scared," in Hedwig Saxenhuber and George Schöllhammer (eds), *Adieu Parajanov*, Vienna: Springerin and Authors, 2003, p. 11.

II

Documents

Introduction

Adrian Heathfield

The multiple approaches to the question of how one might document historical and contemporary works of performance and live art deployed in this zone of *Perform, Repeat, Record* reveal the performance archive as a temporary, contingent, dynamic, and transformative site. Gathered together here are documents of performance and live artworks from the late 1960s to the present and from locations as diverse as Eastern Europe, South America, Australia, and the Middle East, alongside works from the Western European and North American axis often privileged in performance art histories. However, this zone does not work as an historically or culturally representative reflection of performance, but rather as a sampling of some key coordinates, some orientation points, in an as-yet-uninstituted archive of global late twentieth- and early twenty-first century performance and live art.

Historically and culturally diverse, numerous forms of documentation are assembled here within the limited confines of the printed page, each with their own dilemmas, tactics, and perspectives on the question of how one might describe, depict, capture, and restore the event of a performance work for historical record. Consequently the reader is invited to move between quite different experiences of documentary and discursive address, between forms of writing such as the manifesto, the performance lecture, the autobiographical account, performative writing, the performance score and script, art theory, and art historical narration. These documents also ask the reader to navigate and think through the numerous indexical relations conjured between photography, text, and event, and their operations upon each other. In each document the goal is not the finalization or truth of an event, its full and transparent recovery, but the provision of a version for future revision. Where text and images contributed by artists required historical, aesthetic, and cultural contextualization, this is provided through short introductions written by Amelia Jones.

In composing this selection of documents in collaboration with our contributors, we have sought to gather materials whose location, form, or content opens intriguing questions for the historicization of performance. In Tim Etchells' account of twenty years of artistic work with Forced Entertainment, historical narration moves through elaborate temporal twists and loops engineered via the academic convention of footnoting, but deployed in an evocative and digressive manner to crisscross between instants, documents, events, and memories, moving insistently in and out of the aesthetic and the biographical. Choosing the more familiar chronological organization of time common to an autobiographical account, Guillermo Gómez-Peña's narration of his work deploys the art historical timeline as a lifeline, connecting and celebrating diverse agents in his artistic journey, and accumulating a dense critique along the way of the logical contortions and practical paradoxes of the global art and performance scenes in their dealings with cultural difference. Lebanese theater and performance artist Rabih Mroué uses the form of the performance lecture to disclose his "personal archive" of images and experiences from conflict-torn streets; here the archive and its re-presentation in the performance lecture emerge as fraught negotiations with the dynamics of the remembering and the forgetting of lives irreversibly marked by violence and loss. For these contributors the archive and the documentary evidence upon which it is instituted are sites where the past is remade in the present, and consequently where the action of memory may be contested.

Other contributions are concerned with the nature of the redo and the kind of correspondence that can be enacted in an artistic gesture that brings a past performance into the present in new times and forms. The original text of Faith Wilding's 1972 performance *Waiting* is counterpointed with its 2007 redo, where the work becomes a site for the articulation of transformations of the cultural status of the feminine subject. In Ming-Yuen S. Ma's reformation of Yoko Ono's 1964 *Cut Piece*, a work that similarly deals with questions of passivity and blankness, the original performance and its iterations become the prompt for multiple contemporary reinterpretations of a piece extensively discussed in histories of art and performance (and redone by Ono herself at the Ranelagh Gallery, Paris, 2003). Hayley Newman, whose work has dealt with the fabrication inherent within the photographic and textual documentation of performance, returns to the rich source of Fluxus (the movement in which Ono participated in the 1960s) in a work that takes original Fluxus scores as an inventory of objects that are miniaturized in sculptural form to create an installation.

If Newman's installation makes plain that performance history is necessarily subject to reduction but is also a site for playful reinvention, Janez Janša's redoing of an influential late 1960s piece of Slovenian avant-garde performance delineates the critical and political coordinates that such reinventions necessarily traverse. The redo becomes a test site for collective memory, the shifting borders between the personal and the public, and the public negotiation of the ethics of violent acts in altered times. Similarly Lucas Ihlein's participation in the Teaching and Learning Cinema's 2007 recreation of Anthony McCall's *Long Film for Ambient Light* (1975) aims to enlighten our understanding of a key historical artwork through its re-practicing, examining the nature of audience experience as a crucial but elusive vector in the critical and aesthetic dynamics of the redo. Each of these works in quite different ways makes evident the dependence of performance on documentation for both its inception and historical survival, but also the significance of these documents as sources for further invention and transformation by artists.

The problematics of the action of documentation are critically addressed in numerous contributions. In works such as *Don't Leave Me This Way* by Franko B, where the event takes place at the limits of hearing and sight, photography and narration are charged with the task of representing a "wounding" experience (for the spectator) that is barely visible and recountable. Jonathan Burrows and Matteo Fargion document two of their complex choreographic duets. The challenge here is to find a form of representation that could give access to an elaborate gestural work set to an inaudible musical score, or to a form of textual enunciation that follows rhythmic musical principles. In Meiling Cheng's accounts of three processual and durational Chinese performances, hybrid documents are required to mark the irretrievable durations of the works; a record of these pieces is formed through their preparatory textual parameters, photographs as indices of the sustained events and open narrations of the engagement with the performances *as documentation*.

The manifestation and proliferation of highly diverse forms of documents and artifacts circulating around an enacted event has been a crucial part of the artistic practice of Lynn Hershman Leeson since the 1970s. The elusive qualities of the event and its charged relation to its remnants are highly evident in her contribution here, as Hershman Leeson's practice is engaged in layers of duplicity and mediation, through the use of surrogate personas and an avatar as a guide in a virtual archive of the artist's work. This interest in duplication and simulation is strikingly manifest in Daniel Joseph Martinez's documentation here of *Call Me Ishmael*, a "performance" enacted by an uncanny robotic rendition of the artist, calling into question the very nature of the "live" or "original" event. For the artist Orlan, the document is a kind of extruded or residual material, produced through the embodied intensity of performance, full of narrative potential and consequently available for re-use and alteration by others. Similarly, for Nao Bustamante, who narrates the evolution of her performance *Given Over to Want* (and related works) in these pages, the remaining artifacts emerging from a performance have an "afterlife" and they are actively put to use in a practice of recycling and transformation in order to generate new works. The history of such acts of reinvention is traced by Blair French, curator and director of Artspace, Sydney, who organized a series of interrelated performances drawing on remainders in his exhibition *Aftermath* in 2007. His contribution catalogues and explores this experiment in an alternative art institution through which the document is performed as a source and aesthetic element to generate new installation works.

If the proliferation of documentation and the multiplication of its forms is a response to the problematics of performance retrieval and representation, the question of how to document performance works that strike a marginal, critical, or interventionist approach to their sites of realization is even more acute. Several works assembled here bring the socio-political dimension of such actions into sharp focus. Here a recurring concern is the relationship between systems of documentation – aesthetic, critical, and juridical – and the bodies and actions of subjects excluded from or unsanctioned by art institutions.

Cai Yuan and Jian Jun Xi's illicit performance actions within the spaces of major art institutions, which playfully reuse the artworks of others and contravene the numerous codes and laws of art definition and exhibition, are necessarily consigned to post-event explanations and journalistic photographic records.

The boundaries crossed in Tanja Ostojić's work are those of nation states. Her numerous testings of the relations between the legal structures that secure national identity and the actualities of bodies whose movement and freedom is constrained by such systems, engage the spectator in the social consequences of being with or without papers, with or without documentary evidence securing the legal right to belong. Ostojić's artistic gestures point not only to the paradoxes of such systems of verification but to the value of lives that are led outside of social, legal, or aesthetic recognition. This dynamic was equally present in Barbara Smith's important but rarely discussed and documented work *Intimations of Immortality* (1974) in which she developed collaborative relations with three homeless women, leading to an action of substitution, in which Smith took the role of living outside on the street while the women performed Smith's role within the art gallery. Such acts of surrogacy and insertions of bodies designated improper to an art space are the recurring subject of Santiago Sierra's works. His piece *Polyurethane Sprayed on the Backs of 10 Workers* (2004) is recorded here. As in Sierra's numerous other works, which play with the dependency of systems of cultural and commercial production on an exploited or undocumented labor force, the objective is the creation of an artwork as a documentary remainder and thus reminder of injustices perpetrated on unrecognized subjects. The assembled documents are then, in many forms and senses, registers of what remains outside of historical and institutional orders of recognition, legibility, and visibility.

Chapter 14

A Text on 20 Years with 66 Footnotes

Tim Etchells

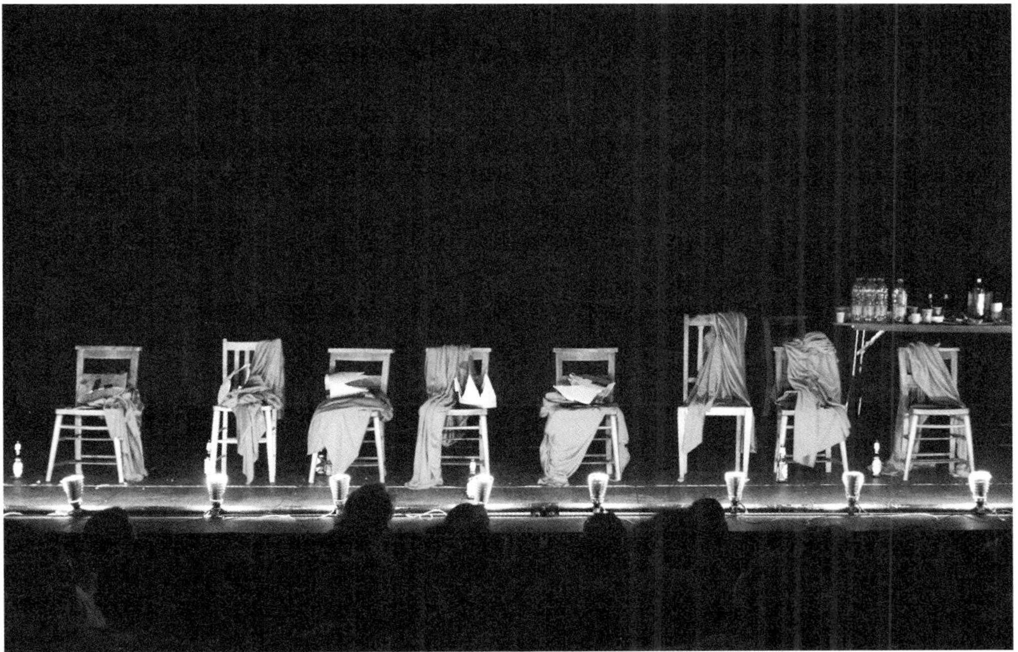

Forced Entertainment, *And on the Thousandth Night*…2007 (2000). Photograph by Hugo Glendinning. © Hugo Glendinning.

Originally published as Tim Etchells, "A Text on 20 years with 66 footnotes," in *Not Even A Game Anymore: The Theatre of Forced Entertainment*, eds. Florian Malzacher and Judith Helmer, Berlin: Alexander Verlag, 2004.

It starts somewhere[1] and rapidly unfolds in many directions.[2]

During very early rehearsals for *Bloody Mess*, Jerry Killick comes to the front of the stage[3] and "explains" to the audience[4] why the atmosphere is completely wrong. As far as the text goes, in fact, Jerry is improvising a version of what he has just heard John Rowley improvising in a previous run-through. And John – when he was onstage about fifteen minutes earlier – was simply improvising around what I'd explained to him of what I could vaguely remember of Cathy's original improvisation of a text for this part of the performance, which she had done about a month beforehand, back in our rehearsal studio.[5] This kind of swapping around of material from one performer to another sometimes takes place at the start of rehearsal processes – either for logistical reasons (such as Cathy is busy in London working on a film script today, or someone is sick, or …) or for "artistic" reasons (such as we think that it would be interesting to change the gender of the performer doing a particular thing, or that it would be "useful" to switch who's doing something because of how it will connect – or disconnect – to some other activity they have at some other point in the piece).[6]

---

1. As it must do.
2. I have told this story, spoken of this history so many, many times that it is hard to approach it afresh. When I do write or speak about it now it can seem to me that I am not telling what happened as much as telling what I have told before – the way a photograph of an event can come to stand in place of a memory of it, or the way that a photograph itself can become a memory. There is a photograph by Hugo Glendinning that shows us on the beach in Gdansk in Poland – we were touring there in 1989 with the theater performance *200% & Bloody Thirsty*. I have no real memory of the day we visited the beach, but sometimes call to mind the picture, believing it to be a memory.
3. We are in the grand gold proscenium and red-velvet auditorium of Sheffield's Lyceum Theatre, squeezing this rehearsal in between what we should actually be doing which is rehearsing the monologues project *The Voices*. It is (the) afternoon, sometime in 2003.
4. In fact, the audience is only me, Tobias Lange (a German performer with whom we've worked on many occasions), Helen Gould (one of the performers in *The Voices*) and Sara Stenström, a Swedish dramaturgy student who is following rehearsals.
5. We have this initial improvisation (and all subsequent ones) on video tape for reference, but at this point in the rehearsals, I am too lazy to find it or we are too short of time in the Lyceum to spend time watching it. In any case, for the moment at least, the fact that John and Jerry will come up with something in the same broad area as Cathy's original version but different in emphasis and detail is probably a useful thing. When the text "returns" to Cathy a month or so hence, she may borrow from the material that John and Jerry have created. "The John version" and "the Jerry version" of this scene (and of the persona at the centre of it) will be useful models in discussions through the process, points of comparison and conjecture against which the unfolding work will be measured and changed.
6. Despite all this, and not to be deliberately confusing, once we're out of the very early stages of making a piece – once some material is attached to a performer in rehearsal – it generally tends to stay with them. Initial decisions about who does what can be arbitrary or pragmatic, but once

It jumps[7] and cuts backwards in time.[8]

Years before, Richard is stood at the long metal table we use for *Speak Bitterness* and he is dealing the texts out along its length. Setting up for the performance, he is isolating special parts of the text that need to be in particular places on the table for particular people at particular times and placing them accordingly, and simply scattering the rest of the papers on the table here and there, covering it completely. The texts are lists of confessions. The piece, we say, is an attempt to confess to everything – a vast catalogue of wrong-doings that includes murder, fraud, genocide, eating the last biscuit in the tin, not washing up properly, hiding the TV remote control, and buggery.[9]

It slides around, becomes non-specific.

We are in a van,[10] in a theater, in a dressing room, in a bar late at night, in a taxi to an airport. We are walking in a strange city looking for somewhere to eat, we are repeatedly drawing diagrams of the structure of a show on paper napkins[11] in the corner of a bar, with furrowed brows and shaking heads, or in a restaurant, rearranging elements, passing paper down the table to get a comment or a raised eyebrow from someone else, we are drinking with ten or more people crammed into a single hotel room.[12]

---

concretized in action, these decisions tend to stick. The particular way that a person does a certain thing, the particular energy they bring to an action or a text becomes a compositional given – an important part of its place in the piece.

7. As it tends, very often, to do.
8. I think of Robin in one section of *Showtime*, being harassed by Cathy crawling on her hands and knees dressed in a dog costume, barking at him. The way I remember him, Robin is naked, except for a stocking mask like those that picture-book bank robbers wear. He holds a red balloon with which he tries to hide his genitals. Inevitably the "dog" is very interested in the balloon. Robin speaks: "I've been thinking a lot about time. It only goes in one direction. It just goes forwards. So you can't go back. It's also supposed to go at the same speed all the time, but that is not true is it, because sometimes it goes more slowly than other times … I mean the thing about time is that …. Time is an important subject. It's one of the fundamentals, isn't it? It's an important subject. It's not meant to be trivialized, it's not meant to be the subject of a cheap joke … Time is a big subject. Time – like space, war, love – is a big topic, with important consequences for everybody."
9. If *Speak Bitterness* is a catalogue of (all?) possible confessions, then *Quizoola!* is a catalogue of all possible questions, *And on the Thousandth Night …* a catalogue of all possible stories, *12am: Awake & Looking Down* a catalogue of all possible characters and costumes, etc. It's not so much the content of any particular confession, story, question, etc. that's of interest, but the way that the nature of the catalogue itself – its boundaries, its built-in agendas, its formal extremities, its *concerns* – is revealed.
10. Soundtrack: Tom Waits' *Raindogs* or Al Green.
11. Or on beer mats or in a notebook.
12. Generic memories – so many variations of the same scene layered one on top of the other that they are by now almost impossible to distinguish. A density blur.

It settles again, at some other point.

Now Terry and Cathy are on the chalk-scrawled set of *Club of No Regrets* in Berlin, placing texts and props on the stage in the right places prior to the performance. I'm watching them from the auditorium.[13] As I watch, I am thinking that their activity on stage looks as if they were doing the piece in schematic form – visiting its places, its positions, each in turn, only in reverse.[14] On the stage, Terry and Cathy are putting the bucket of water at the back, so that later, in the performance, it can be moved to the front by the shoddy wooden house that sits on the stage. When she leaves the stage, job completed, Terry passes Robin on the stairs. Later, for years and years, she will tell the story that Robin looked completely crazy on the stairs[15] and that his eyes were in a very strange state and that he was muttering to himself and that she thought "Oh God. What's he going to be like in the performance …"

It speeds up.

We are in a rehearsal room. We are loading a van. We are checking into a shitty English bed and breakfast. The stench of fifty years worth of cooked full breakfasts has been fried into the brown paint walls. The building shrieks and groans when the taps run, the floorboards creak in incomprehensible ways – unbearable burden of the lives that passed through here; the lights dim whenever anyone takes a shower.

Robin crawls, stripped to the waist, his head in the fun-fur mask of the pantomime horse[16] and he swigs from the whisky bottle through the eyehole of the horse – more like brutal IV drug use than drinking. As Robin pushes the bottle in through the eye, the horse head is bent grotesquely out of shape – driven crazy by drinking,[17] wracked in bewildered cartoon agonies.

13. I don't know what year this is. I spent a lot of time watching people on stage doing things that are not strictly speaking performance – setting up for things, building sets, fooling around, hanging lights.
14. Several times we tried to include walk-throughs of performances as part of performances themselves, but never succeeded. Something fascinating about the energy of these rehearsal activities – the high-speed, casual energy "marking" of positions and lines, the précis, the annotated summary disrupted by the occasional detail of a moment or interaction that someone needs to practice "for real."
15. Whenever it was, this week in Berlin involved quite a lot of parties.
16. This is a pantomime horse costume we borrowed from a local theater when we did a kids' project for them. A spectacularly crappy and comical horse with a goofy expression and teeth too big for its mouth.
17. Normally it would be water in the whisky bottle, not actual whisky, although in shows where there is beer drunk onstage (and there are quite a few of these), people tend to drink beer for real, even in rehearsals. It's an interesting thing that people sometimes manoeuvre a little, "speculate" while improvising so that their role might involve having a beer or two, or smoking the odd cigarette, or having a nice sit-down from time to time.

Terry changes costume.[18]
Cathy addresses the audience.[19]
John shakes his head in disbelief.[20]
Jerry laughs, his face all smashed up from a bicycle accident.[21]
Terry yells in Italian.[22]
Richard puts on a blindfold and stands as if waiting to be shot.[23]
Robin parts the curtains slightly and peers through them at the arriving audience.[24]
It slides in time.[25]
Claire dances in her bra and knickers, midriff wrapped in skimpy, improvised fake feather tutu, a knife in her hands. There is slowed down music from the record player[26] and to go with it, Claire dances kind of suicidal and ultra slow motion.[27] She does not know that this dance will be in the final performance, but already, perhaps, suspects. She knows that "something" is happening, that somewhere in the confluence of what she and the others on stage are doing (improvising) there is a "scene," or that this is some particular nuanced

---

18. *Emanuelle Enchanted.*
19. *Disco Relax.*
20. *First Night* rehearsals.
21. Performance of *And on the Thousandth Night …*, Munster 2003.
22. Performance of *Club of No Regrets* in Italian for Volterra (?) Festival, 1993 (?). Everyone learned most of their texts in Italian, parrot-fashion. The performance took place outdoors, in the grounds of an old monastery. For years afterwards, people would talk about the way the smoke from the performance (talcum powder hurled into the air) rose and drifted up toward the trees, blown on the wind in the moonlight during the show. I was not there but sometimes I find that I talk about it as if I had been.
23. *Hidden J.*
24. A generic memory and one which, in any case, I wouldn't have witnessed. Robin likes to see the audience before they see him – checking them out – weighing the possibilities of how the gig will go. Other performers prefer not to see the public till they get on the stage.
25. As it tends to do.
26. We used the same battered record player in a whole string of shows from *Showtime* to *Disco Relax*. In the first of these it played a number of old 45rpm records that Richard had found at his parents' house. We liked the record player because it meant that the means of producing music and the operation of it were visible on and controlled from the stage. Prior to this, music slammed or drifted in as if controlled by some unseen hand ("from God" we used to say, joking) and we became suspicious of this … preferring that all of the signification (except the lights) remain in control of the performers onstage. Using the record player (and with it "found" songs or music on vinyl) meant that the music was (literally) an object held up for use and scrutiny much like a found text, or a second-hand costume. It meant an end, more or less, to our theater work with composer John Avery who'd done soundtracks for almost all of the performances prior to the arrival of the record player.
27. This is *Pleasure* rehearsals.

articulation of what we have been doing for a month or more.[28] Claire dances and Cathy writes obscenities on the blackboard: Cunt. Get Your Rocks Off. Blow Job.[29] The music is *The Last Mile Home* but because it's slowed down so much, you can hardly hear the words.[30]

As she dances, Claire does not know that years later she will sit on the seating bank in the rehearsal room – close to where I am watching her from now – and she will watch (in the future) as Wendy Houstoun does this dance. Claire will be teaching it to her because Claire will be pregnant and Wendy will be replacing her in some part of the *Pleasure* touring. And Claire does not know that she will be saying to Wendy, "No. Heavier, Make it clumsier. It needs to be worse …" and that Richard will be sat at the front of the stage the whole time[31] loading the gun[32] with his blindfold on and Claire does not know that she will watch Wendy and that as she does so, her hands will be clasped over her belly inside of which will be Ruby May – of whom, at this point in the story of Claire first improvising the dance, there will not even be the tiniest idea.[33]

---

28. It is a big joke in rehearsals and afterwards that the stupidest, most painful or random improvisational move can end up being your fate for a whole show and for a whole year of touring. As in "If I'd have known I was going to end up doing *that* for a year, I wouldn't have done it in the first place."
29. This is a list of dirty words and phrases I have downloaded from the Internet.
30. When performance artist Michael Atavar comes to see a rehearsal one day, he remembers how he and his sister used to play all their parents' records slowed down and scare each other with the messages from the Devil they could hear in there.
31. There is a whole strand of the work where someone (often Richard) "comes to the front" or "takes centre" to frame or MC the pieces. Occupying this place appears something of a structural necessity but is rarely weighted with the kind of actual authority that a narrator/MC might be expected to project. We took to calling the role/position "frame" and then, as it decayed further, etiolated or "weak frame." The storyteller is weak, prone to distraction (like me, here), disorganized, crazed, uncertain. We understood this MC position as a structural tactic – about one (or more) people coming forwards so that others might have the space to live/exist/work in the back. The front provides covering fire (deals with the audience, acknowledges them, speaks to them directly) so that the rest can get on with what they need to do.
32. In rehearsal, any action with the gun has a real tension about it since many of the performers like to fire the bloody thing. The bangs from the gun (which fires real blanks) are horribly, horribly loud in the studio, ripping through the atmosphere of the work and prompting people to nervously keep their fingers near their ears whenever it is in play. Often in these days, I think about William Burroughs in *The Place of the Dead Roads* where he talks about gunshots blowing a hole in the fabric of space and time. I remember in *Marina & Lee* we used audio from movies (gunfights, brawls, kung-fu fights) to interrupt the action on stage – throwing the performers into chaotic and clumsy fight sequences, jumpcutting the piece to a new place.
33. Years later than this even, Ruby May and a bunch of other kids in the general Forced Entertainment entourage – Miles, Seth, Megan, Jacob, Leon, Izzy – play in the rehearsal studio, using a wardrobe which has been crudely fitted with a "secret" door in the back to perform imitation magic tricks. The wardrobe has been used in *First Night* rehearsals during a phase where we think the show will have

It continues to jump.

We are in a hotel room. The technician Andy Clarke is drinking whisky from a toothpaste mug whilst various people add to the uncharacteristic make-up and pink-wig outfit that he is sporting. It is 5 in the morning. I am filming.[34] We are in Columbus, Ohio. Outside there is snow.

We are driving on a road between Berlin and Warsaw in a three-and-half ton truck, overtaking in swirling dense fog on narrow roads. Whoever is in the passenger seat has to spot for oncoming headlamps appearing out of the gloom.[35] It's a nerve-wracking business. You feel close to your death every time we pull out to overtake.
We are in Sheffield, rehearsing in a church hall.[36]

We are in Sheffield, rehearsing in an abandoned school with smashed windows and industrial gas heaters.[37]

We are in a Sheffield, rehearsing in an old factory above which is a boxing gym. When the guys upstairs are training, their skipping sends showers of plaster falling from the decaying ceiling. The dust and plaster settling like a strange rain over everything. When you look from the set of *(Let the Water Run its Course) to the Sea that Made the Promise* to this ice-cold, smashed-up old factory that we call home for five years, you can hardly tell one from the other.

We are making *Some Confusions in the Law about Love*. We seem to change it every time we do a performance. One of those shows that never ever gets finished. Years later, we find texts

---

various solo magic acts or tricks in it. At one point prior to this – for research purposes – Richard, my son Miles and I go to a Magicians' Convention at some seafront hotel in Blackpool on the north-east coast of England. At the convention, we purchase the plans for a number of stage illusions – photocopied plans, which are sold in sealed envelopes. The fronts of the envelopes bear a description of the illusion, but to find out how it is constructed, you have to buy the plans. One night at the same Convention, we watch a very simple close-up magic trick performed by some German guy and we all think it's great. The trick involves a shoe magically appearing in the hands of the conjuror. Six or seven months after the Magicians' Convention, Richard will try to recreate the German guy's shoe trick – we are now in Vienna, drunk, in a bar, following a performance of *Instructions for Forgetting* – a recreation that will end with a predictable melee of destruction and broken glass.

34. The tape is lost.
35. This story gets told in *The Travels* (2002).
36. Soundtrack: The Fall, *Hex-Enduction Hour*.
37. When the guys come to deliver gas canisters, they are wary of Mark Randle and Robin because they are wearing cowboy hats and dresses, and wary of Claire because she has a fake-penis and a beard drawn on her face (costumes for *Marina & Lee*).

and video tapes relating to the show and can't figure out what versions they represent. Was this Nottingham? Was this the ICA version? Who knows.[38]

We are in Munich. Terry drops a glass bottle during *Bloody Mess* rehearsals[39] and the glass shatters everywhere – shards and fragments[40] all over the floor. The rest of the run-through is peppered with attempts to clean the mess up which becomes part of the action.[41]
We are in Beirut. The city is covered in posters for an election – huge portraits, hand painted, almost all of which show these fine-looking Arab guys with extravagant well-groomed moustaches. We are here to do the durational performance *And on the Thousandth Night* ... – six hours of improvised stories – from fairy tales to personal stories and movie plots, each story interrupting its predecessor and none of them allowed to finish. Beirut seems a perfect location for this performance. That night when we do it, there are many stories in response to the posters we have seen on the streets, all the stories fanciful, playful, absurd: a story about a city in which several men are in love with one woman, the various suitors covering the streets with their portraits in an attempt to seduce her; another story about a city in which the king organizes a moustache competition, and so on. People are delighted – seeing the reality of the city outside pass straight into the distorting mirror of the work.[42]

---

38. Sometime in 1999, we lodge all of our rehearsal video tapes at the National Sound Archive of the British Library in London. This includes videos of almost every rehearsal hour of everything we made since *Emanuelle Enchanted*, plus some occasional tapes of earlier stuff. Boxes and boxes of it – most of it uncatalogued in anything but the most rudimentary way – tapes labelled by date or in some cases simply by number or letter. What's for sure is that some of the tapes used to document rehearsals also have other more personal stuff on them. It's weird to think that somewhere in the depths of the British Library there is a Hi-8 tape marked "Dirty Work 9" that also has some footage of Seth and Deb running around in the garden or some footage of a view from a window in a house from years ago.
39. She has been using the water in the bottle to make it look like she has been crying.
40. I am thinking about fragments but in an absolutely different sense. Disconnected from its "original" place, lacking context, lacking "beginning" or "end," lacking place in an argument, lacking "reason" – the fragment is both statement and question.

    We cannot know (and can therefore only guess) what the fragment is, what purpose it has, what intention is behind its production or presentation. In this sense and for our purposes (here and elsewhere), the fragment remains an ideal compositional unit.
41. There is an audience at this rehearsal comprising some people from the Big Art Group (who are performing in the same festival, but who won't be able to see an actual performance) and a couple of Russian guys who we think are also part of the festival, but we aren't sure.
42. And the work, later, will pass right back into the world. After we've been back from Beirut for a couple of months, I bump into Walid Raad, an artist who's from the city. He says that six weeks after we'd done *And on the Thousandth Night* ... performance in Beirut, Vico – who's the technician of the festival there – had been arrested. I asked why and Walid said "something political," then

We are in New York.[43] Richard is in a hotel room putting the finishing touches to a home-made bomb. The bomb is made of broom handles covered in red tape, an alarm clock, and a bit of old circuit board. The whole lot held together on a makeshift harness that goes around the body. It's a kind of perfect "cartoon ticking bomb"-style bomb. We shoot a load of pictures of people holding the bomb in the hotel[44] and then go out to Central Park and shoot some more.[45] There is snow everywhere. Super-beautiful. Various people pose amongst the snowbound trees with the bomb. The suggestion of an explosion from the toy bomb seems so perfect and delicate next to the tree branches, which look like they will shed their snow at the slightest knock. People are walking their dogs and snowballing in the park. They see us – a group of people standing around and a bomb being passed around – and they just smile and go about their business.[46] Lewis Nicholson is with us and we talk about the beautiful publicity objects he used to make for us – wonderful, oblique, and amazing things that were somehow completely at odds with their supposed function as advertising.[47] Later in the early morning, when we have done the gig and have been drinking a lot in the East Village, we step out of the Ukrainian National Home or the Telephone Bar[48] and Cathy and Claire walk across 1st Ave (?) having looked right and not left or something and they come very close (i.e. as close as I have ever seen) to being killed by an oncoming car which squeals and slides to a halt just in front of their drunken lurch, the driver looking with a mixture of anger, disbelief, and distress like he will be tortured by remembering this near-terrible moment for the rest of his life and they (Cathy and Claire), in fact, will forget all of it.[49]

---

laughed – "oh, not political, nothing important, just drunk and disorderly." He said that Vico had spent three days in jail, in a small cell shared with eight other prisoners. He said that there, in the central jail of Beirut, Vico had taught these guys to play the improvised game that makes up the show. They'd passed the days and nights in the cell together that way, telling stories, interweaving tales, none of them ever allowed to finish, moving from true stories and personal stories to fairy tales and movie plots.

43. This is years before.
44. Hotel 17.
45. Hugo is doing the photographs as he has since 1986. When it comes to mid-rehearsal shoots with Hugo, we liked to say that getting the pictures back was a way to see for the first time what you were really doing.
46. This is 1998.
47. A book of burnt matches for *Club of No Regrets*, a note inserted behind the matches bearing supposed directions to the Club itself. A set of price lists for brutal and banal objects and acts for *Hidden J*. A limited edition of handmade maps of an imaginary country for *Emanuelle Enchanted*.
48. Or somewhere else.
49. These near-deaths are a constant part of the story. Once, after we had done the final performances of *Some Confusions in the Law about Love*, at the Leadmill in Sheffield, I watched the lighting designer Nigel Edwards sitting on a scaffolding pole high up in the lighting rig and calmly (without realizing it) undoing the only clamps which were attaching the pole itself to the rig. It was pure cartoon – the guy sawing at the plank on which he himself is standing. I asked Nigel to stop.

I remember that E. M. Forster had the advice *only connect*. But in this history (mine) (like any other) (i.e. yours) anything can be connected to anything else. Or else: everything already contains everything else. Every story is a Chinese box, or a doorway that leads to every other one.[50] *Only connect. Only connect.* Strange – we spent so much of our time in the process not connecting material, but rather trying to keep it separate. Trying to let stuff just sit there as itself, "as objects," as we liked to say. *The thing is the thing is the thing.* Having admitted that anything might be relevant – anything might be connectable, anything might have a productive bearing on what you are currently doing – we wanted tracks of material, blocks of time that sometimes collided or appeared to meet, but which always, in fact, stayed resolutely separate.[51] We wanted something that would not ever reduce down into a single narrative, a single statement. "Oh," we would say, as an insult in rehearsals if the structure ever felt too clear, or too collapsed, "Oh, it's become a play now."[52]

We did not, it seems, want "a play," which, for us, became a byword for the homogenized, the pre-packaged, the performance which somehow wanted to deny presence and performance and liveness and insist instead on writing, closure, absence, and fixity. We wanted the unstable. The trembling. The thrill of live decisions. The collision of different materials, different narratives.[53] A theater that placed you in a world rather than describing one to you. Or which placed you in a situation rather than describing one to you. A theater in which

---

50. Maybe this is in fact what we tried to deal with in the durational performance *And on the Thousandth Night* ... where the performers improvise many stories from midnight to 6am, stealing characters, structures from each other, from the general cultural stockpile, and none of the stories allowed to end – a kind of mad fornication of stories, connections, jumpcuts, reversals.
51. I think about something that Ron Vawter told me once when I did an interview with him in Belgium. Sitting in a café, Ron said: "What we tend to do in the Wooster Group, and in my own work, is to appropriate from several different sources at the same time. That way we can juggle all these separate things until the weights are familiar and then a new kind of theater text is created between these different places."
52. Notebook fragment (dream).

    She has hypermedia and hypertextual links embedded in her body – when you kiss her hands or her elbows or her eyelids, she opens up to streams of data, opening like a doorway to a hidden kingdom. X could never work out if this hypertextual woman was meant as metaphor or not, and never having met her couldn't be sure ... I mean wasn't sex itself always a kind of hypertext ... the body blossoming in memory and enactment of other loves, other beds, previous embraces ... the texts of the past inscribing themselves into the present to create possibilities, impossibilities, structures, doorways ...

53. There was a lot of talk at some point about non-narrative theater. We said we had nothing against narrative at all – in fact, we just wanted lots of it. The best example of this might be the durational performance *12am Awake & Looking Down*, where the circulation and re-circulation of the cardboard signs bearing the names of characters functions as a kind of narrative kaleidoscope. Watching this performance with Miles (in Paris sometime) I realized how very much the work relies on the watcher having certain kinds of cultural knowledge. Most of it was lost on Miles (he

your agency as a watcher was an acknowledged and known part of the performance from the outset. A theater that felt more like event. A theater that made demands. A theater that was ugly, awkward. A theater that liked its ambiguities, its undecidednesses, its disconnections. A theater that was very, very funny, ridiculous, absurd. A theater where the comedy did not ever quite confirm itself as comedy.[54] A theater that did not hide the fact that here, in front of you, were a bunch of people doing something. A theater that critiqued its own language even as it was using it. A theater that divided audiences. A theater that could also bring audiences "together" even as it critiqued that word. A theater constantly looking to breach its own edges, to duck into performance, into installation, into event, into blankness. A vulnerability. A frailty. A provisionality. Home-made. Human-scale. A slipperiness. An air of anti-art. A workman-like attitude. A rawness. A bleakness. A melancholy. An hilarity. An anger. A lack of compromise. A theater that insisted on its own time, brought you into collision with its own temporality. A theater that had no beginning and no end.

And finally it[55] ends, as it must.[56]

The sound of taped gunshots blows a hole in the fabric of space and time.
Robin closes the curtain and leaves off staring at the audience.
Terry changes costume again.[57]

Cathy screams and yells in gibberish language inside the house center stage in *Hidden J*, the curtains drawn across the window so she cannot be seen. The other performers listen, and wait, wait until she is done.

Claire watches her own face on video, expression blank.[58]

Huw Chadbourn smears dirt across his face.[59]
Hugo checks the screen on his camcorder as various people from Forced Entertainment and from Richard Maxwell's company sing together "Goodnight Eileen."[60]

Will Waghorn watches a photographic print emerge from the fluid in a developing tray, timing the procedure by taking his own pulse.[61]

---

was maybe eight or nine at the time) because he didn't know the sources (actual or generic) from which the characters/figures were drawn.

54. This is something of a paraphrase of what the UK performance artist Gary Stevens once said to me.
55. This text, or the rhizome of memories it constructs and contains.
56. In fact nothing actually ends.
57. *Bloody Mess*, 2003.
58. *Some Confusions in the Law about Love*.
59. *The Day that Serenity Returned to the Ground*, 1986.
60. In a bar, very late night, Theatre Mousonturm, Frankfurt, Friday 28 November 2003.
61. *Red Room*, Showroom Gallery, 1988.

Vlatka Horvat learns the tech for *Instructions for Forgetting.*[62]

Robin's spectacles are smashed and smashed again.[63]

Susie Williams throws a chair in Sheffield, 1984[64] and it crashes to the ground in Brussels, May 2004.[65]

Richard (in Vienna in 2000) takes the shoe from his foot, intending a recreation of the magic trick we saw back at the Magicians' Convention back in Blackpool – the trick with the shoe that miraculously appears in your hand. The bar in Vienna is noisy. There is hardly space for this. The trick with the trick is to stand on one leg, secretly slip the shoe off the raised foot into your left hand, and then to bring the shoe slamming round suddenly and into the palm of your raised right hand, right in front of the hapless spectator. Richard moves. And the trick begins, except in this case, at four in the morning and a lot of caipirinhas under the bridge, the shoe comes slamming round and misses the hand. It becomes a size 8 torpedo – a shoe flying across the bar. It crashes into a table that is all mountained up with drinks and the glass goes bursting everywhere.

"Oh. You know," the barmaid says. "It happens all of the time."[66]

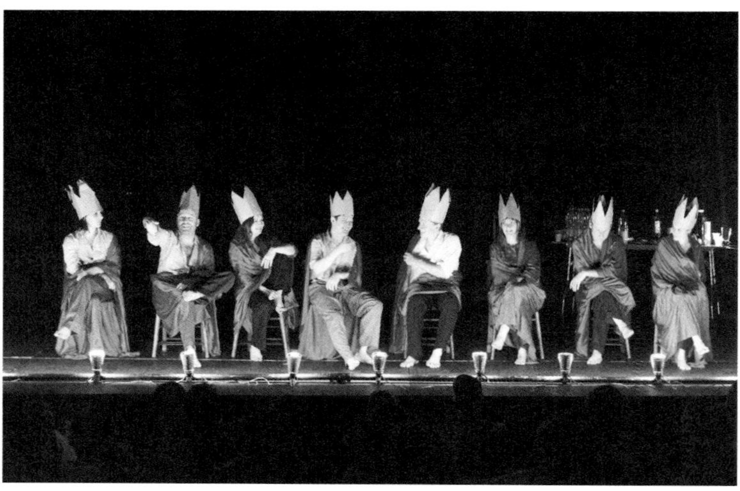

Forced Entertainment is a group of six artists – Tim Etchells, Robin Arthur, Terry O'Connor, Richard Lowdon, Claire Marshall, and Cathy Naden – based in Sheffield, UK. They stage theater performances as well as projects in other media and contexts. Their work varies from projects that are brash and theatrical to works that are minimal and text-based. Since 1984 they have performed in the UK, mainland Europe and around the world, and have become one of Europe's leading theater groups.

Forced Entertainment, *And on the Thousandth Night...*2007 (2000). Photograph by Hugo Glendinning.

62. Ghent, Belgium, 2003.
63. *The Set-up,* 1985.
64. *Jessica in the Room of Lights* rehearsal.
65. I am imagining this, since I am writing in January 2004.
66. And keeps on happening. The glass shards flying out from there in every direction, backwards and forwards in time. Connections spin and multiply. The screen shimmers, cuts to black and then kicks into life again.

Chapter 15

Faith Wilding, Waiting and Wait-With

Faith Wilding has been a major force in the feminist art movement since her role in supporting the founding of the Feminist Art Program in California, one of the most important sites for the development of a politicized approach to the making and theorizing of feminist art.[1] Her 1972 performance piece *Waiting* is an acknowledged classic of early body art; it was originally performed as a centerpiece of the influential installation project *Womanhouse* – a derelict house in central Los Angeles taken over and renovated by the members of the Feminist Art Program such that each room was turned into a feminist installation.[2] As part of the global resurgence of interest in the history of feminist art, Wilding was invited to redo *Waiting* for *Wack! Art and the Feminist Revolution*, an exhibition of 1970s feminist art staged in 2007 at the Museum of Contemporary Art, Los Angeles (and traveling to the Museum of Modern Art's alternative venue P.S.1 Contemporary Art Center, New York City). On receiving the invitation for *Wack!* Wilding's choice was *not* simply to re-enact the *Waiting* piece "accurately," recreating the original costume, poses, and monologue, but to redo the performance from her point of view in 2007.[3]

The script of this re-enactment, titled *Wait-With*, indicates a shift in Wilding's work and in feminist art in general away from the highly specific and politicized concerns of the early 1970s Anglo-American feminist art movement (concerns that often had to do either with exposing and criticizing patriarchal forms of oppression enacted in the visual field – via the fetishizing "male gaze" – or with identifying "women's experience" and finding ways to rearticulate it in positive or more critical forms, as with *Waiting*). The new piece indicates Wilding's development of a sophisticated relationship to different modes of technological mediation, and her sensitive attention to different generational and geographical concerns across global networks of feminist activity in the visual arts.

Rather than exclaiming a litany of events to which, as a woman, she is submitted and subordinated ("waiting" for things to happen or people to do things to her), in *Wait-With* Wilding engages with the voices of Samuel Beckett and her interlocutors in feminism Irina

Aristarkhova and Gregg Bordowitz. The 2007 work is far more affirmative than the rather melancholic 1972 version. As Wilding has noted, *Wait-With* moves away from the negative analysis of waiting as a woman's lot in life (a kind of enforced passivity) toward a more positive reading of the potential of waiting as "non-violent action, as a possibility of identification with activists who have staged waiting demonstrations as political actions; and I'm trying to investigate ideas about positive uses of passivity, of refusal to act or produce."[4] This shift indicates a personal and creative transformation but also points to the fact that it took the bravery of feminists and anti-racist and queer campaigners and artists in the 1970s to lay the groundwork for a more affirmative "re-enactment" of the potential agency of women and other minoritarian subjects in Euro-American culture.

In *Wait-With*, Wilding enacts an agency that goes beyond the relatively simple identification of "women's experience" to perform "a woman artist's body" as "becoming-woman." This "becoming" both refers back to feminist philosopher Simone de Beauvoir's famous argument in *The Second Sex* (1949) that "one is not born a woman, one becomes one" and points as well to Gilles Deleuze and Félix Guattari's notion (in their 1980 book *A Thousand Plateaus*) of "becoming" a gendered or sexed subject as a process of identification with radical potentiality, a kind of subjectivity in process that never remains fixed. Across a range of voices and technologies (for example, the Los Angeles version of the live event has been filmed and is available as a DVD) Wilding enacts herself within a web of discourses and images (including those relating to the original *Waiting*) as becoming-woman. *Wait-With* thus also makes an important intervention into questions of how live art functions in history – elaborating how the performer's body *means* over time.

Amelia Jones

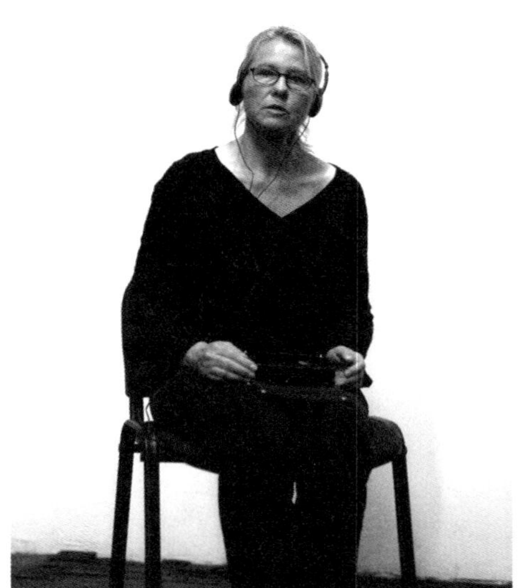

Faith Wilding, *Wait-With*, Centre d'art contemporain, Geneva, 2007. Photograph by Isabelle Meister. © Isabelle Meister.

Notes

1. Spearheaded initially in 1970 by Judy Chicago at California State University Fresno, where Wilding was a graduate student in fine arts, the program was moved to California Institute for the Arts, Valencia, in 1971 where it was co-run by Miriam Schapiro but still guided by the efforts of Wilding and fellow students such as Suzanne Lacy.
2. The best history of the Feminist Art Program was in fact written by Wilding herself; see her "The Feminist Art Programs at Fresno and CalArts, 1970–75," in Norma Broude and Mary Gerard (eds), *The Power of Feminist Art*, New York: Thames & Hudson, 1996.
3. Interestingly, the *Wack!* invitation paralleled Wilding's earlier invitation, for the exhibition *Division of Labor: Women's Work in Contemporary Art*, 1995 at the Bronx Museum of Art in New York, to remake her 1972 *Womb Room*, a room-sized crocheted "womb" and one of the installations at the original *Womanhouse*. In contrast to her response to the *Wack*! opportunity, for the Bronx show Wilding chose to redo the *Womb Room* more or less faithfully.
4. In dialogue with the author, 15 July 2008.

Waiting

A Poem by Faith Wilding

Waiting ...   waiting ...   waiting ...
Waiting for someone to come in
Waiting for someone to hold me
Waiting for someone to feed me
Waiting for someone to change my diaper   Waiting ...

Waiting to scrawl, to walk, waiting to talk
Waiting to be cuddled
Waiting for someone to take me outside
Waiting for someone to play with me
Waiting for someone to take me outside
Waiting for someone to read to me, dress me, tie my shoes
Waiting for Mommy to brush my hair
Waiting for her to curl my hair
Waiting to wear my frilly dress
Waiting to be a pretty girl
Waiting to grow up   Waiting ...

Waiting for my breasts to develop
Waiting to wear a bra
Waiting to menstruate

Waiting to read forbidden books
Waiting to stop being clumsy
Waiting to have a good figure
Waiting for my first date
Waiting to have a boyfriend
Waiting to go to a party, to be asked to dance, to dance close
Waiting to be beautiful
Waiting for the secret
Waiting for life to begin   Waiting …

Waiting to be somebody
Waiting to wear makeup
Waiting for my pimples to go away
Waiting to wear lipstick, to wear high heels and stockings
Waiting to get dressed up, to shave my legs
Waiting to be pretty   Waiting …

Waiting for him to notice me, to call me
Waiting for him to ask me out
Waiting for him to pay attention to me
Waiting for him to fall in love with me
Waiting for him to kiss me, touch me, touch my breasts
Waiting for him to pass my house
Waiting for him to tell me I'm beautiful
Waiting for him to ask me to go steady
Waiting to neck, to make out, waiting to go all the way
Waiting to smoke, to drink, to stay out late
Waiting to be a woman   Waiting …
Waiting for my great love
Waiting for the perfect man
Waiting for Mr. Right   Waiting …

Waiting to get married
Waiting for my wedding day
Waiting for my wedding night
Waiting for sex
Waiting for him to make the first move
Waiting for him to excite me
Waiting for him to give me pleasure
Waiting for him to give me an orgasm   Waiting …
Waiting for him to come home, to fill my time   Waiting …

Waiting for my baby to come
Waiting for my belly to swell
Waiting for my breasts to fill with milk
Waiting to feel my baby move
Waiting for my legs to stop swelling
Waiting for the first contractions
Waiting for the contractions to end
Waiting for the head to emerge
Waiting for the first scream, the afterbirth
Waiting to hold my baby
Waiting for my baby to suck my milk
Waiting for my baby to stop crying
Waiting for my baby to sleep through the night
Waiting for my breasts to dry up
Waiting to get my figure back, for the stretch marks to go away
Waiting for some time to myself
Waiting to be beautiful again
Waiting for my child to go to school
Waiting for life to begin again   Waiting …

Waiting for my children to come home from school
Waiting for them to grow up, to leave home
Waiting to be myself
Waiting for excitement
Waiting for him to tell me something interesting, to ask me how I feel
Waiting for him to stop being crabby, reach for my hand, kiss me good morning
Waiting for fulfillment
Waiting for the children to marry
Waiting for something to happen   Waiting …
Waiting to lose weight
Waiting for the first gray hair
Waiting for menopause
Waiting to grow wise
Waiting …
Waiting for my body to break down, to get ugly
Waiting for my flesh to sag
Waiting for my breasts to shrivel up
Waiting for a visit from my children, for letters
Waiting for my friends to die
Waiting for my husband to die   Waiting …
Waiting to get sick

Waiting for things to get better
Waiting for winter to end
Waiting for the mirror to tell me that I'm old
Waiting for a good bowel movement
Waiting for the pain to go away
Waiting for the struggle to end
Waiting for release
Waiting for morning
Waiting for the end of the day
Waiting for sleep Waiting …

Waiting was performed at Womanhouse in Los Angeles sponsored by the Feminist Art Program, California Institute of the Arts.

Chapter 16

Lynn Hershman and/as Roberta Breitmore

In the mid 1970s the San Francisco-based artist Lynn Hershman (who adopted the additional surname Leeson in the 1980s) took on an alternative persona, *Roberta Breitmore*, across a range of performative activities and domains. These included performances of Hershman and various surrogates as Breitmore, installations in urban spaces (the 1973 *Dante Hotel* installation, in which a hotel room where Breitmore supposedly stayed on her first night in San Francisco was opened as an installation to the public), and numerous legal, literary, medical, epistolary, robotic/cyborg modes of enactment such as her existence as Hershman's avatar who welcomes the visitor to the artist's online archive lodged on the Web's Second Life domain. Such duplicities and duplications present a profound challenge for art history.

What does *Roberta Breitmore* mean historically? How can this wide-ranging performative function or persona be retrieved and retained for the historical record without destroying "her" ambiguity and poignant significance as a complex multi-levelled enactment of contemporary subjectivity? How does Roberta Breitmore relate to Lynn Hershman Leeson? How can we access this project in its range of enactments to gain a sense of its impact and significance in "real" time and space, the spaces of the institution (such as the art gallery), and the virtual spaces of the World Wide Web?

These questions were addressed thoughtfully in the exhibition *Autonomous Agents: The Art and Films of Lynn Hershman Leeson*, 15 September–12 December 2007, at the Whitworth Art Gallery, University of Manchester (an expanded version of a show initiated at the Henry Art Gallery in Seattle, United States). Installed by curator Mary Griffiths in collaboration with the artist, the exhibition explored a range of different ways of making Roberta "present" for the gallery visitor.

At the same time, the constraints of the gallery are all too evident in viewing here, in book form, the second-degree "documentation" of the show itself. The art gallery or museum is, of course, an institution that contains and maps all aspects of the project into an array of

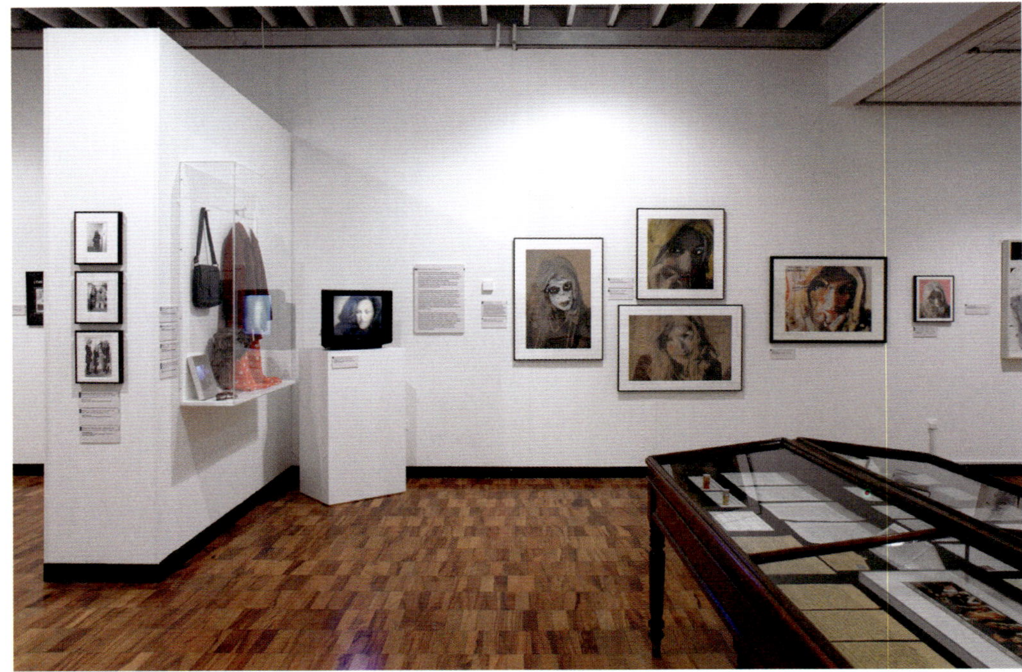

Whitworth Art Gallery, University of Manchester, 2007. View of the gallery showing part of the large Victorian vitrine filled with "Roberta's" personal objects, a wall-mounted vitrine with her clothing, "construction charts" of Hershman as Breitmore, and a looped VHS copy of the 16 mm film by Eleanor Coppola entitled *Constructing Roberta* (1975).

objects to be viewed in a particular order. The book is, in turn, a container for a sequential presentation of text and images. Still, here are some indicators to point to the complexity of this fascinating and crucial performance practice, which cuts across media, time, and space to address and interrogate how the artistic subject is inextricably linked to her practice and how both are sustained historically, through various forms of documentation and critical inquiry.

This view of the gallery shows part of the large Victorian vitrine filled with "Roberta's" personal objects, a wall-mounted vitrine with her clothing, "construction charts" of Hershman as Breitmore, and a looped VHS copy of the 16 mm film by Eleanor Coppola titled *Constructing Roberta* (1975). The wall text in this gallery of the Whitworth notes that Hershman's Roberta Breitmore enacts a "troubling of art history [...] What are the most relevant tools art historians might bring to bear on this proliferation of documents that continues even after the performance has stopped?"

Amelia Jones

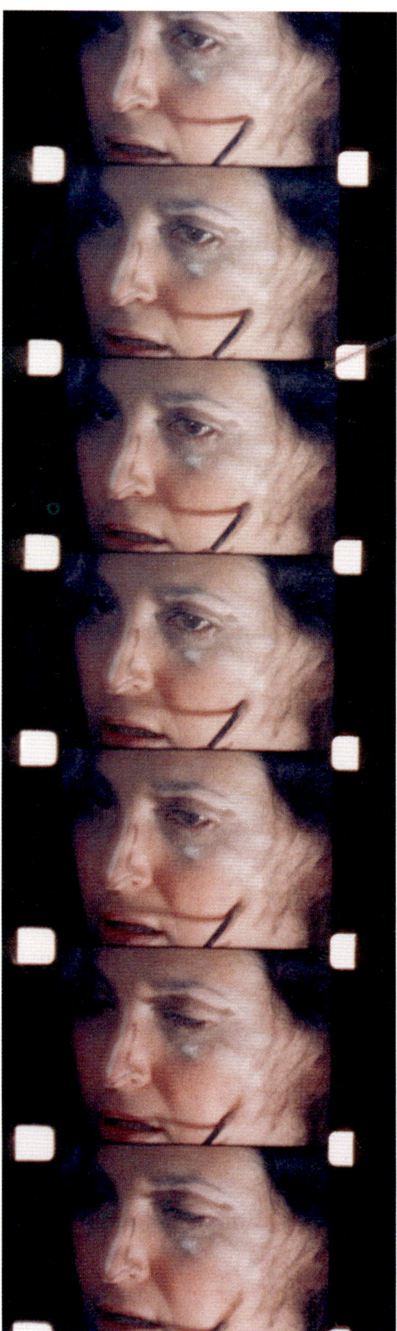

Lynn Hershman, *Roberta: External Transformations*, 1974. Film strip, 16mm, of timed makeup construction.

Closer view of the *External Transformations* and *Articles of Identity* portions of the Breitmore installation: Roberta Breitmore's clothing and wig; and video monitor showing *Constructing Roberta*, as installed in the Whitworth Art Gallery exhibition *Autonomous Agents*, 2007.

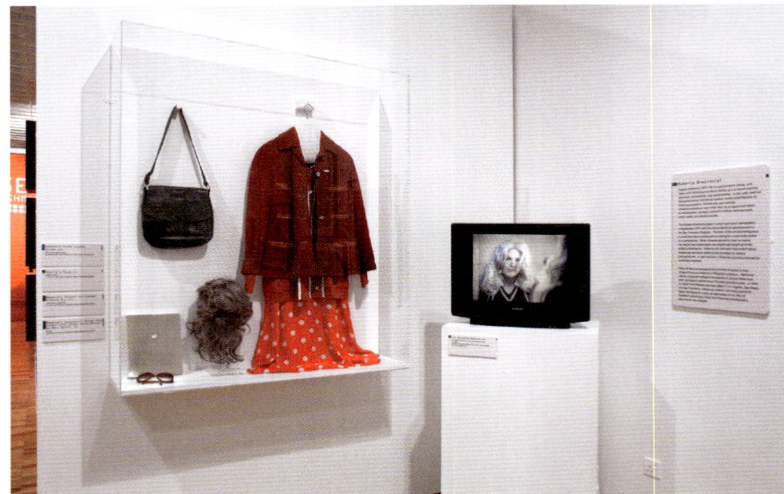

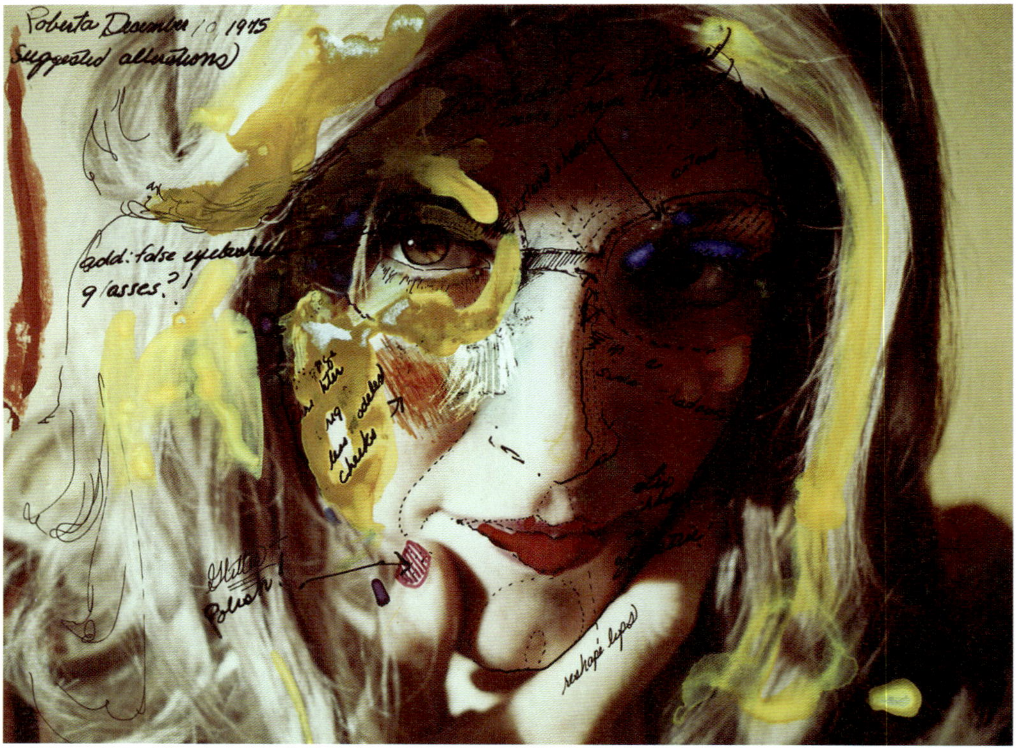

External Transformations, part of the Roberta Breitmore archive; *Roberta's Physical Stcnce #2*, 1976; chromogenic print, acrylic and pen; one edition 3/3, 30 x 40 inches.

STATE OF CALIFORNIA
DEPARTMENT OF MOTOR VEHICLES

INTERIM DRIVERS LICENSE (TEMPORARY)
DIVISION OF DRIVERS LICENSES

VALID FOR 60 DAYS FROM
DATE

Roberta Breitmore
3007 Jackson
San Francisco, CA 94115

SEX	HAIR	EYES	HEIGHT	WEIGHT	PRE LIC EXP
F	Brn	Brn	5-9	155	None

DATE OF BIRTH 3-19-45 SOC. SEC. NO.

CLASSES
ADDITIONAL PRIVILEGES ONLY AS CHECKED BELOW
☐ NONE.
4 ☐ MAY DRIVE 2-WHEEL MOTORCYCLE.
2 ☐ MAY DRIVE ANY SINGLE VEHICLE OR BUS EXCEPT 2 WHEEL MOTORCYCLE.
1 ☐ MAY DRIVE ANY VEHICLE OR BUS EXCEPT 2 WHEEL MOTORCYCLE. MAY TOW ANY VEHICLE OR COMBINATION OF VEHICLES.

OTHER ADDRESS
CLASS 3 3 AXLE HOUSE CAR AND ALL 2 AXLE VEHS. EXCEPT BUS OR 2 WHEEL MOTORCYCLE. MAY TOW VEH. UNDER 6000 LBS. GROSS.

SEE OVER FOR ANY OTHER CONDITIONS ☐ MUST WEAR CORRECTIVE LENSES ☐

X

1-20-76 SnF 1r

FEE $3.25

EXAMINER BADGE NO.

APP. No. DF 219767

TRACER USED { DL22 Date Office

In the *Articles of Identity* part of the Roberta Breitmore archive, as exhibited in the large Victorian vitrine: (above) *Driver's License*, 1976 (original document); and (below) *Diary*, 1976 (original book with handwritten text).

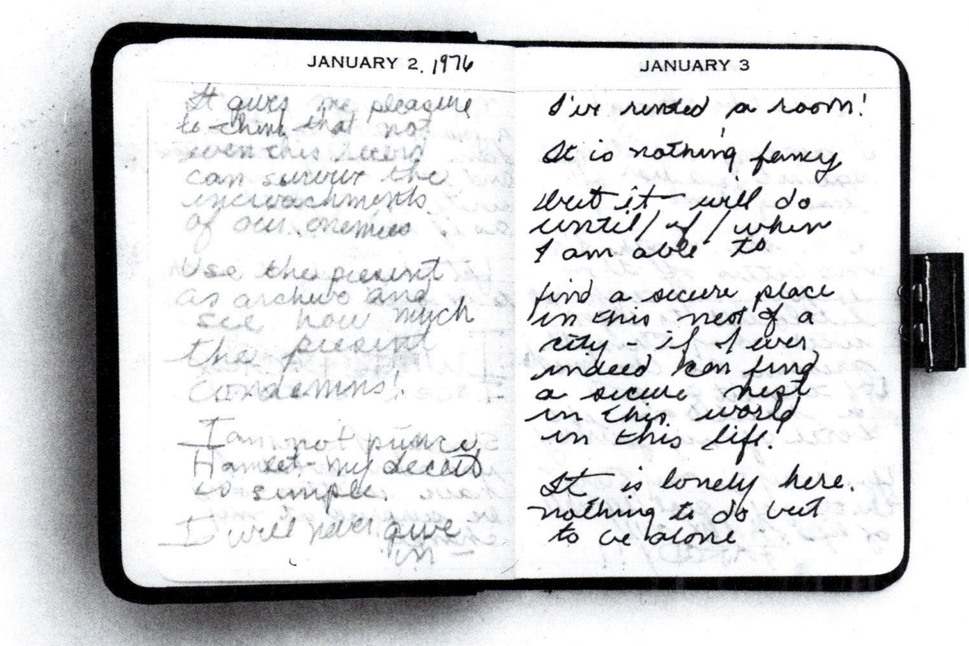
JANUARY 2, 1976

It gives me pleasure to think that not even this diary can survive the encroachments of our enemies.

Use the present as archive and see how much the present condemns!

I am not prince Hamlet - my deceit is simple.

I will never give in

JANUARY 3

I've rented a room!

It is nothing fancy but it will do until/if/when I am able to find a secure place in this nest of a city - if I ever indeed can find a secure nest in this world in this life!

It is lonely here. nothing to do but to be alone

EXCERPTS FROM THE CASE HISTORY
OF MS. R.S.B.

AGE: 30
SEX: female
RACE: white
RELIGION: Jewish
MARITAL STATUS: divorced
OCCUPATIONAL STATUS: unemployed
GENERAL SITUATION:
The patient has been depressed and nervous. Showed signs of inability to concentrate and some impairment of memory.....
APPEARANCE:
Deeply affected posture that quite often puts her into slumped position. Heavy makeup conceals her features. During observation she appeared both passive and eager to please. Prefers to lie down (dramatizing her helplessness). A line is beginning to form between her eyes. Modest signs of dysplasia. Her knees are stiff and feet contracted. Decreasing flexibility of legs. Can curl toes under in prehensile manner. Under the superficial softness one could palpatate tension in deep muscles of the skull. Tensions choke off the flow of blood and energy, thus skin appears tender and dry. Voice is nearly always inaudible. No spontaneity of gesture.....
MEDICAL HISTORY:
Usual childhood diseases. Tonsillectomy at age 11. Remembers having ingrown toenails. Suffers from many accidents. Generally clumsy.....
SEXUAL HISTORY:
Patient admits to incestuous relationship with brother. Began pattern of masturbation. Finds intercourse painful. Achieves no orgasm. No pregnancies. Fearful of pregnancies.....

VITAE

BORN: August 19, 1945
BRIEF SYNOPSIS 1969-75:
Attended Kent State University and majored in English, minors in Art and Drama.
1969: Quits school, marries Arnold Marx. Lives in suburb adjacent to Cleveland. Lonely, depressed. Cannot adjust.
1974: Marriage ends in divorce.
June 1975: Roberta moves to San Francisco. Stays the first two nights at the Dante Hotel. Comes with one suitcase, a flight bag, and $1800.00.
February 1976: Roberta visits San Diego, in hopes of finding happiness/security. She places ad in the San Diego Tribune and meets date at Belmont Amusement Park. Date arrives with five others and asks Roberta to join a prostitution ring.
July-January 1975-76: Roberta begins to establish her identity. She opens a checking account, recieves a driver's license, applies for credit. Rents a room for $54.00 a week including 2 meals daily. Seeks a room mate to help share costs and cut loneliness. Advertises in various papers for room mate. Interviews for room mate. Ventures unsuccessful.
March-July 1976: Roberta has gained 4 lbs. Her depression is continuing. Requires abnormal amounts of sleep. San Diego trauma creates an end to her seeking a room mate. Money running out. Takes odd jobs. Begins visiting nightly encounter session.

From the *Articles of Identity* part of the Roberta Breitmore archive, as mounted on the wall near the vitrine, *Roberta's [Psychiatric Case] History*, 1978; paper and ink; one edition, 8½ x 11 inches.

Mr. America Series, part of "Roberta Breitmore" display at *Autonomous Agents* – this part of the exhibition included a range of documentary materials from the performative action by Hershman/Breitmore following her placement of a classified advertisement to solicit a companion in the newspaper (mostly men replied). The display included the (original) newspaper advertisement, surveillance images of Breitmore meeting men who had answered the advertisement (taken by various photographers enlisted by Hershman), an audiotape documenting one of the meetings, and correspondence between Breitmore and the men answering her advertisement.

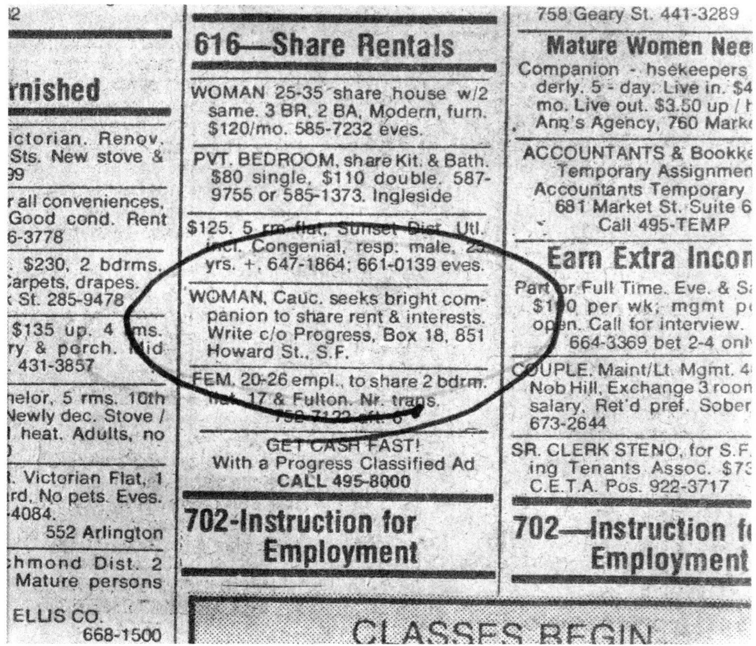

rnished

ictorian. Renov. Sts. New stove & 99

r all conveniences, Good cond. Rent 6-3778

. $230, 2 bdrms. arpets, drapes. St. 285-9478

$135 up. 4 rms. ry & porch. Mid 431-3857

helor, 5 rms. 10th Newly dec. Stove / heat. Adults, no

. Victorian Flat, 1 rd. No pets. Eves. 4084. 552 Arlington

hmond Dist. 2 Mature persons

ELLIS CO. 668-1500

616—Share Rentals

WOMAN 25-35 share house w/2 same. 3 BR, 2 BA, Modern, furn. $120/mo. 585-7232 eves.

PVT. BEDROOM, share Kit. & Bath. $80 single, $110 double. 587-9755 or 585-1373. Ingleside

$125. 5 rm flat, Sunset Dist. Utl. incl. Congenial, resp. male, 25 yrs. +, 647-1864; 661-0139 eves.

WOMAN, Cauc. seeks bright companion to share rent & interests. Write c/o Progress, Box 18, 851 Howard St., S.F.

FEM. 20-26 empl., to share 2 bdrm. flat. 17 & Fulton. Nr. traps.

GET CASH FAST! With a Progress Classified Ad CALL 495-8000

702-Instruction for Employment

758 Geary St. 441-3289

Mature Women Nee

Companion - hsekeepers derly. 5 - day. Live in. $4 mo. Live out. $3.50 up / Ann's Agency, 760 Mark

ACCOUNTANTS & Bookke Temporary Assignmen Accountants Temporary 681 Market St. Suite 6 Call 495-TEMP

Earn Extra Incon

Part or Full Time. Eve. & S $100 per wk; mgmt p open. Call for interview. 664-3369 bet 2-4 onl

COUPLE. Maint/Lt. Mgmt. 4 Nob Hill, Exchange 3 roon salary. Ret'd pref. Sober 673-2644

SR. CLERK STENO, for S.F. ing Tenants Assoc. $7 C.E.T.A. Pos. 922-3717

702—Instruction f Employment

CLASSES BEGIN

Mr. America Series: Clipping of a classified ad placed by "Roberta Breitmore" in the *San Diego Union & Evening Tribune*, 1975; original newspaper clip displayed on the wall in *Autonomous Agents*.

10 Dec 1975

Dear Roberta,

The 18th is fine with me!

If you're not doing anything the following night, would you care to go to Jack Welpott's (the photographer) opening at the S.F. Museum of Art? It's from 5:30 – 7:30 PM. We'll be there, plus drinks, and the arty crowd flowing about.

Sorry you couldn't make it on Tuesday. But two days isn't long to wait,

Best,

Irwin

PS - I like your stationary; sharp colour and design.

Mr. America Series: Letter from "Irwin," one of the respondents to the classified advertisement, to Roberta Breitmore, 10 December 1975.

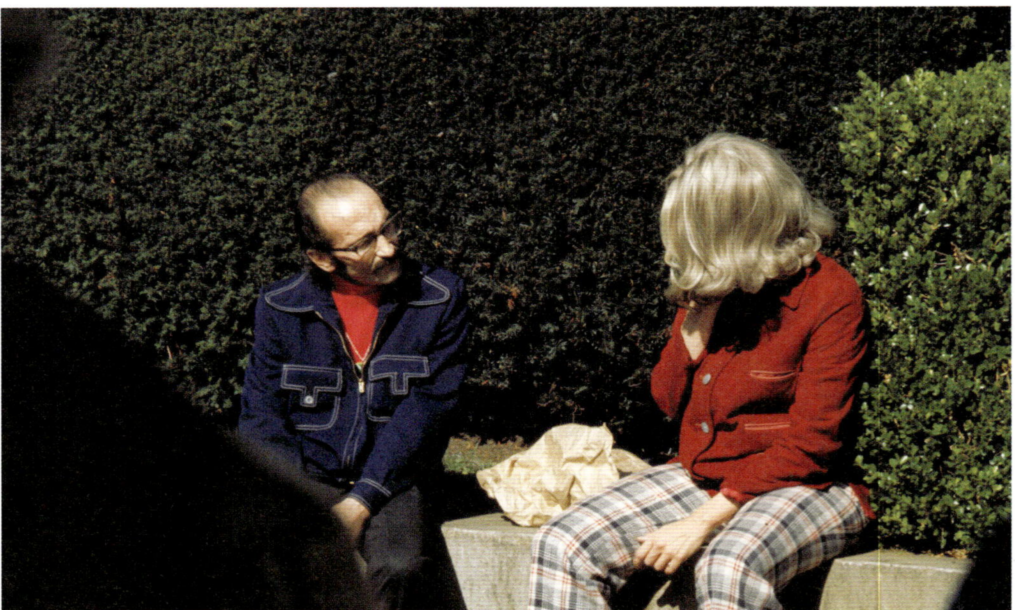

Mr. America Series: Surveillance Shot of Roberta and Blaine, another one of the respondents to the classified advertisement, in Union Square, San Francisco, 1975; Hershman hired photographers to spy on her and the men she was meeting and to photograph them from afar.

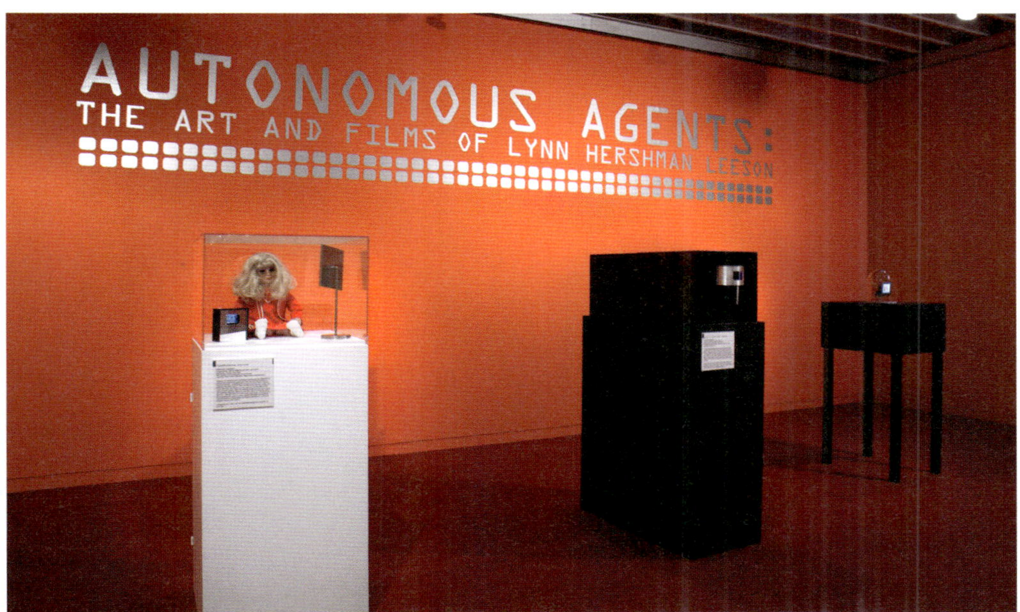

Roberta Breitmore "beyond" the art gallery: View of *Autonomous Agents* exhibition showing *CybeRoberta*, 1995–8. The doll's eyes include a webcam which "watch" visitors to the show and send this footage to Lynn Hershman Leeson's website (see http://lynnhershman.com/doll2/).

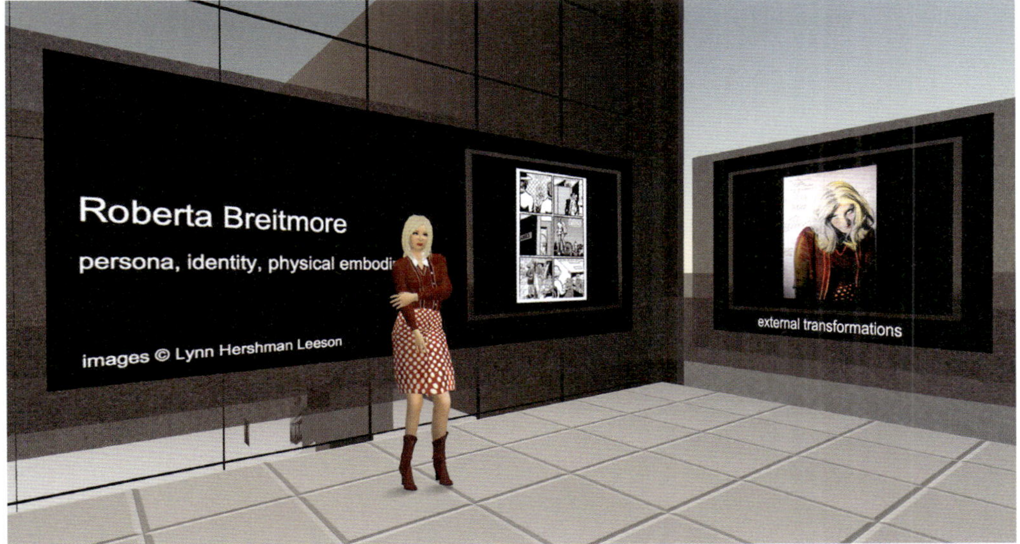

Roberta Breitmore "beyond" the art gallery: Roberta Breitmore welcomes the visitor (the avatar) to Lynn Hershman Leeson's on-line archive in Second Life.

Chapter 17

We Are Formatted Memories

Orlan

We can notice three moments of performance in relation to live art: the moment of the making in front of an audience, a large or a small one, or even without any audience (like the moment of painting); the moment of the display of the remains of the work on a wall; and the achievement that can be a photo, a video or a picture ...

I consider that what is called performance documents, or the traces or remains of performance, are most of the time comparable to Jackson Pollocks' drippings.

Most artworks are the result of a body action (energy, motion, pleasure, anguish ...) that stays as a fossil in the painting, the picture, the sculpture, the photo, the video ...

The "anthropometries" of Yves Klein (from the early 1960s) are not considered as marks of performances, like documents. They have the full status of artworks; nevertheless they are the product of a public performance. Yves Klein could have chosen to realize the same works with his models in the secret space of the studio.

In this case the process of creation wouldn't have been visible.

All my performances or my *Orlan-Corps* actions have been built for a plastic result that is re-composed later within a mise-en-scène to be shown to another kind of audience.

The exhibition *Out of Actions* organized by Paul Schimmel at the Museum of Contemporary Art in Los Angeles (1998) questioned the tendency to make a value distinction between the "live" work and the document. He displayed in this exhibition marks of performances and/or works taken from performances, asking us to estimate them at their own value like any other works.

These objects or documents are full artworks and moreover they carry the stories of their elaborations in and by the intensity of the performance.

Concerning "re-enactment": this new attitude of artists in relation to the art of other artists (or in relation to their own art) is a Fluxus-type approach. Everyone could replay in his own way earlier live artworks, the products of other artists, in a manner of repetition like the interpretation of a musical work that is open to being played by amateurs as well as professional musicians.

A young Parisian artist Pascal Lièvre often replays my 1976–8 work *The Kiss of the Artist* [*Le baiser de l'artiste*], performing it apart from the sculpture-photo through which I practiced the piece originally.

He realized this performance, referring to the text "In front of a society of mothers and merchants" to link it back to my work and to my name. Many artists have made it without citing my name but the Lièvre re-enactment is an homage to my work and to my name; it exemplifies an approach of appropriation like that of Sturtevant or Sherrie Levine.

Before Lièvre, a woman artist re-enacted *The Kiss of the Artist* at a preview but without informing the audience of her "source," an approach I find less interesting and less courageous.

However that's what we do most of the time because we are only formatted memories, trapped by the déjà-vu, the déjà-dit.

I have already myself done several remakes of my earlier performances, for example, I reworked many times my 1979 piece *One-ORLAN-Body-of-Book*.

Artists no longer have the status of authors because of others, because of history, because the time we are living in speaks inside us; we are at best chroniclers of our time and moreover it's the viewer that makes the artwork.

To reactivate one's own work or to replay the work of other artists is sometimes cynical, sometimes unconscious of art history. Re-enactments can feed this magma of the end of illusions and ideologies, the death of utopic ideals and of the era of suspicion.

Has what I call the "know-how of doing one's artist job" replaced the traditional know-how of artistic practice? I don't regret such a shift. But I do regret Fluxus artist Robert Filliou's principle of equivalence "well done, badly done, not done … and the continuous party."

Orlan for Performance!

Orlan, *Omnipresence*, 21 November 1993, Sandra Gering Gallery, New York; seventh surgery-performance.

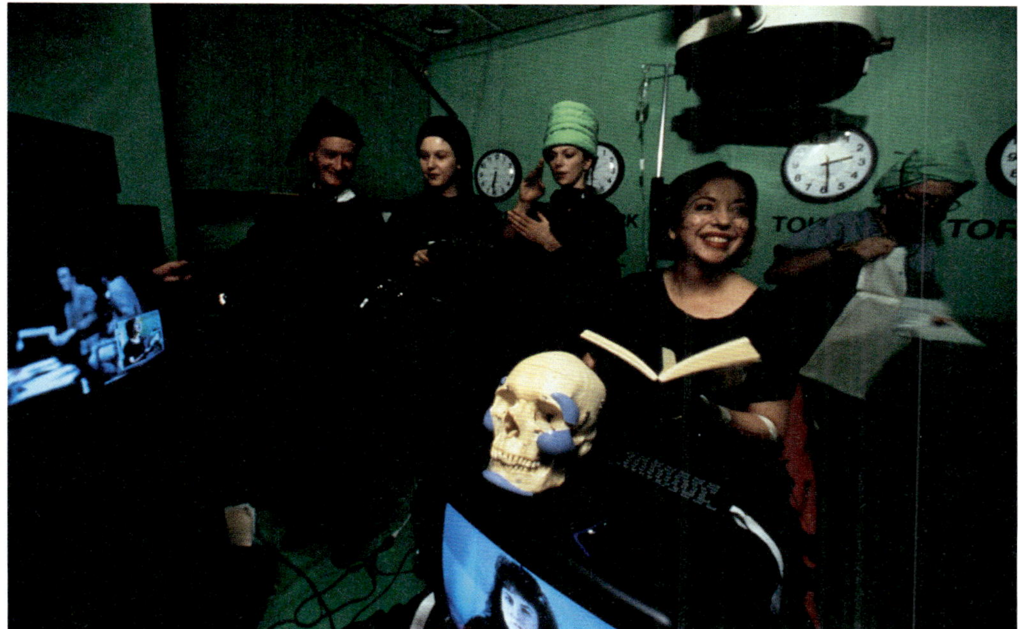

Orlan, *Omnipresence* [*Omniprésence*] performance, photographic document of Orlan in the operating theater reading from a text by Eugénie Lemoine Luccioni, with simultaneous translation into English and sign language; showing monitors streaming live video imagery via satellite. Cibachrome photograph in an edition of seven, by Vladimir Sichov for Sipa-Press.

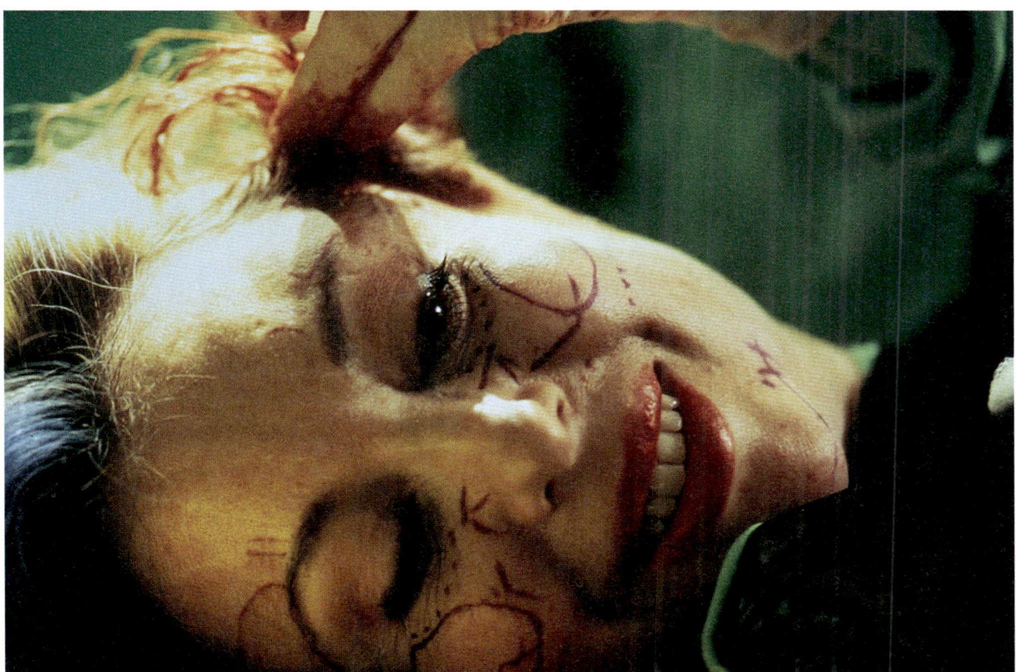

Orlan, *Omnipresence* performance, photographic document showing Orlan smiling while her face is being cut by the surgeon. Cibachrome photograph in an edition of seven, by Vladimir Sichov for Sipa-Press.

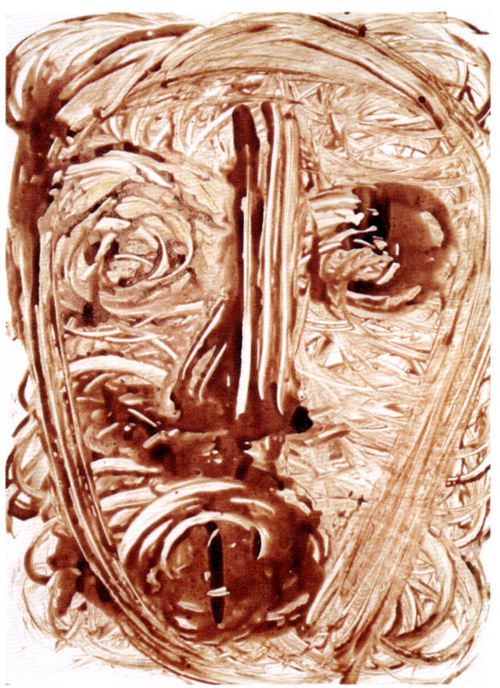

Orlan, *Drawing Done in Blood*, 8 December 1993; blood on paper, enlarged onto oilcloth through the Scanachrome process, edition of nine. Painting made from blood let during the *Omnipresence* surgery.

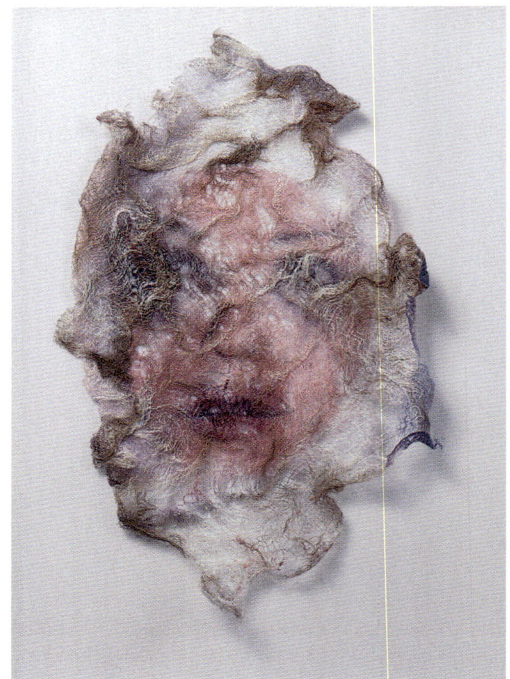

Orlan, *Saint Suaire no. 21*, 1993; photographic transfer onto blood-soaked surgical gauze. The *Saint Suaires* photographs are more frequently exhibited than the original gauze "portraits."

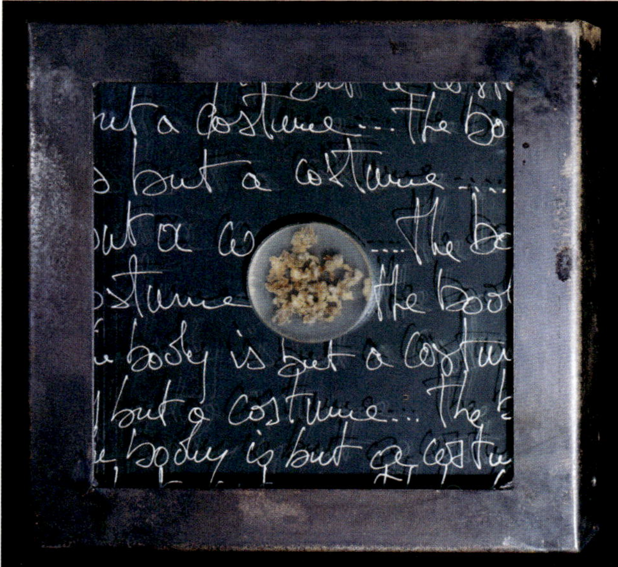

Orlan, *Little Reliquaries [Les petits reliquaries]*, 1993; from the seventh surgical performance, *Omnipresence*; Orlan's flesh preserved in resin, soldered metal, and bullet-proof glass with etched text.

Chapter 18

Franko B and Kamal Ackarie, Don't Leave Me This Way

Franko B is internationally known as a performance artist who works with a range of media to enact, engage, and otherwise document the traces of the human body in its painful and joyful states of being. His best known performance is his *I Miss You!*, which he presented at the Tate Modern's *Live Culture* event in 2003 and at various other venues – here, Franko B, his body painted white, walked slowly and elegiacally up and down a canvas catwalk laid along the floor of the massive void of the gallery's Turbine Hall, the veins in his arms opened by cannulas which allowed the blood to drip and dribble continuously as he moved. Watching the live event, one smelled the blood and heard the sound of the artist's feet sticking to the canvas – a sucking sound that affirmed his "thereness" but that pointed to his imminent absence as the blood drained from his white body.[1] Franko B enacts his body as simultaneously "live" and "representational" – a dual status amplified by his careful use of photographs and digital video footage to document the event, and by his strategy of reusing the blood spattered canvas, making it into objects marred by the signs of his own wounding.

Don't Leave Me This Way, a collaborative work with Australian-British curator and lighting designer Kamal Ackarie, involves Franko B sitting on a raised plinth or altar with his large naked body being revealed through lighting effects either to a small audience or in a one-to-one encounter. Ackarie designs the light to flood the venue periodically; at first Franko B's body emerges to view as a sculptural object (yet the body of a subject, the artist, before us) and then the light continues to increase to a level of such intense brightness that the viewer or viewers are all but blinded by it. As the press release for the piece notes,

> The notion of blinding the audience plays on the ambivalent allure Franko's body holds, in that the glare of floodlights will repeatedly illuminate his form beyond vision, while also returning the gaze in a way, by illuminating the other as spectator [...] Moreover, the aggressive lighting will (safely!) play on the idea of burning his image onto the mind's eye, his outline momentarily existing in each viewing body, in the event's corporeal afterglow.[2]

The press release goes on to note that "Franko B's performances have always left metaphorical marks on the psyches of vulnerable spectators, moving empathetic viewers with the visceral charge of the prone [or wounded] body." In this way, *Don't Leave Me This Way* extends aspects of the investigation played out in *I Miss You!*, drawing the spectator(s) in through extreme bodily "presence" (marked either by wounding or by lighting effects) and dramatically encouraging her, through empathy, to question her own relationship to pain and the bodies of those enacted as radically other (Franko B is tattooed, and often exacerbates his whiteness by covering his body with white paint). At the same time *Don't Leave Me This Way* pushes the earlier work's bid for the authenticity and presence of the body in pain, which may seem contradicted by the evident spectacle of the photographs of *I Miss You!* in performance, art, and other venues and publications. In this publication, Manuel Vason's photographic documents of *Don't Leave Me This Way* approximate the work's existence at the edge of visibility, as Franko B's figure is captured emerging and receding into a darkened void.

Don't Leave Me This Way, which makes the artist's body visible in increments only to erase it through surplus light (blinding the viewer(s)), produces the live body *as already representational*, but also as "there" in front of the viewer; as both resolutely material and always already an image. *Don't Leave Me This Way* burns the performer's body into our memories as both live and representational at the same time, reminding us that we are (as phenomenologists would say) both a lived body and one apprehended from the outside. A body that enacts thought and memory (and is thus a "self") and one that can be seen and positioned externally – but that also inevitably escapes being fixed, its complex significance hovering in the processes of enactment and engagement.

Amelia Jones

Notes

1. I discuss this and other works at greater length in my essay "Corporeal Malediction: Franko B's Body/Art and the Trace of Whiteness," in Dominic Johnson (ed.), *Franko B, Blinded by Love*, Milan: Galerie Pack, 2006.
2. Parts of the press release are available at: www.franko-b.com/don't_leave_me_this_way.htm. Accessed 2 May 2011 (editor's note).

Franko B and Kamal Ackarie, *Don't Leave Me This Way*, 2007. Photographed by Manuel Vason for Franko B and Kamal Ackarie, London 2006. Photomontage edited and put together by Franko B Studio in 2008 for an exhibition titled *Posizione e deposizione* by Franko B and Zhang Huan, curated by FAM for Galleria Pack, Milano, Italy. Courtesy of Franko B, Kamal Ackarie and Manuel Vason 2006.

Chapter 19

Make Me Stop Smoking

Rabih Mroué
Translation: Ziad Nawfal

Introduction

Since I started doing videos and performances, I have been obsessed with titles.

I always had a hard time picking a title for a new performance or a new video. I was looking for attractive titles; titles that sound light but intellectual, beautiful and at the same time intelligent; deep and catchy. A title that is easy to memorize, easy on the ear, and easy on the tongue.

It used to take a long time before finally settling on one. I would ask people around me for their thoughts. I used to take their comments into consideration. And I would change it, hesitate and even ask for help … I lived under pressure. On the one hand, the play, and on the other hand, the title. What name shall we give the work? What name shall we give this child? Yes, just as parents would do when trying to decide on naming their newborn.

I used to believe, as we say in Arabic, a letter is understood from its title. It took me a long time to understand a title doesn't have to be related to the work. The moment a title or name is given, it acquires its own meaning, its own dimension.

It takes a different meaning from what we had intended. The same way you can hate or love a name because of its holder. My relation with titles and names has changed.

With time I found a solution to this problem: a list of good titles. Any phrase or sentence or word that I thought could make a good title, I would write it down in a special notebook. This way, I created some lists of titles for my unknown projects. Titles of works for which I have no idea what they are yet.

I will show you one of these lists:

List # 13
Covered with Honey and Blood
I, the undersigned
Out of Dust
Switzerland is no longer Lebanon
Life is short, although the day is long
A birthmark on my left toe
Come in Sir, we are waiting for you outside
Cry me cats and dogs
The general security of Hezbollah denies any responsibility for what might happen tomorrow
You'd be so nice to leave me so soon
My wife and I love Al Pacino, but she loves him even more
Is there any chance of dying after dying
Stolen moments
Distracted bullets
Eye is complete darkness
Wings of desire or gone with the wind
The sun sets tens of times a day
Borrow your expressions
Round corners
The old man who is still thinking of his mother and of the way he had licked her ear by mistake
Something of something
Learning to survive the desire to simplify
Tate mon amour
Who's afraid of representation?
Make me stop smoking

Make me stop smoking is the title of this presentation. I chose it for an unknown reason.

Since 1986, the year I started working in theater and visual arts, I have been collecting various materials: cut outs from local newspapers, photographs, interviews, news stories, excerpts from television programs, written ideas, proposals for performances, objects, press articles, and other things; material from the past still waiting to be used in the future. From time to time, I return to this material to see if any of it can be used in the present; a piece of news, an image, an idea worth working on which might develop into an art project to present in the future. It will then speak of the present, I mean, the present of that future: material from the past, as potential for future artworks to talk about the present.

What a complicated process to talk about, the present.

How do I speak of today without going back to yesterday, or going to tomorrow? How do I speak about the present? About how we know that this "NOW" has already passed, gone and it is no more now? I wonder how long does a moment in the present keep on going as a moment in the present! I know that a moment can be just a moment or sometimes it can be an eternal hell.

Plays an old videotape on Beirut in the 1960s, duration about 30 seconds.

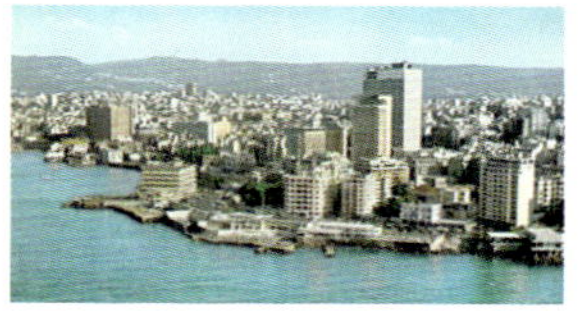

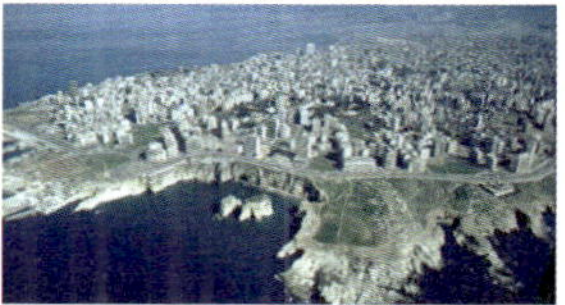

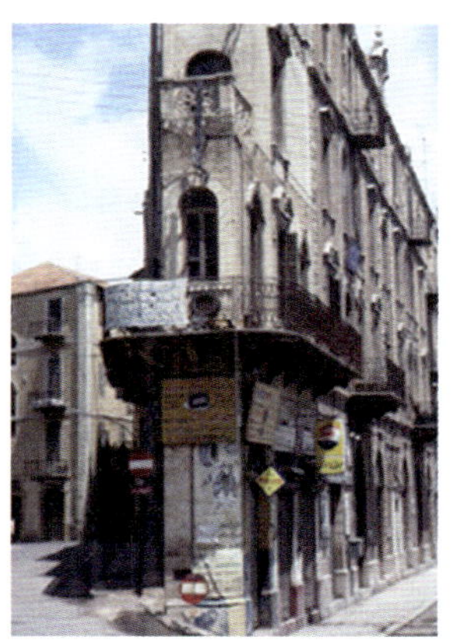

After 20 years of collecting bits and pieces, I can say that:

Today I possess what resembles an archive. I call it: my personal archive.

My personal archive consists of four different types of collected material:

1. Documentation of the projects I made and already presented … All the papers, writings, preparations, drawings, photographs, etc …
2. A press archive related to my work. Everything written about my projects, articles, interviews, and publicity.
3. Proposals that I wrote, ideas for upcoming and unfinished projects.
4. A general, non-personal archive from newspapers, televisions, radio, and other sources relating to the public sphere. Part of this material I collected myself, while other parts I got from friends. I've worked on parts of this material, and there are still parts where I've no clue what to make out of them.

Personally, I am interested in the last two types of material. The first two types do not interest me in the least. Maybe because they relate to the past. Unlike the other two, which relate to the future?

Every element of my archive is waiting to take its place in a work that I will make. The problem, however, is that I have kept many things, I don't know if I will live long enough to use them all. It's depressing. The same feeling I have each time I go to a library and look at all the books standing on the shelves; I ask myself: how many lives do I need in order to read all these books. It's really depressing.

Plays a videotape capture by a CCTV camera showing a hold-up operation in a small office for changing money.

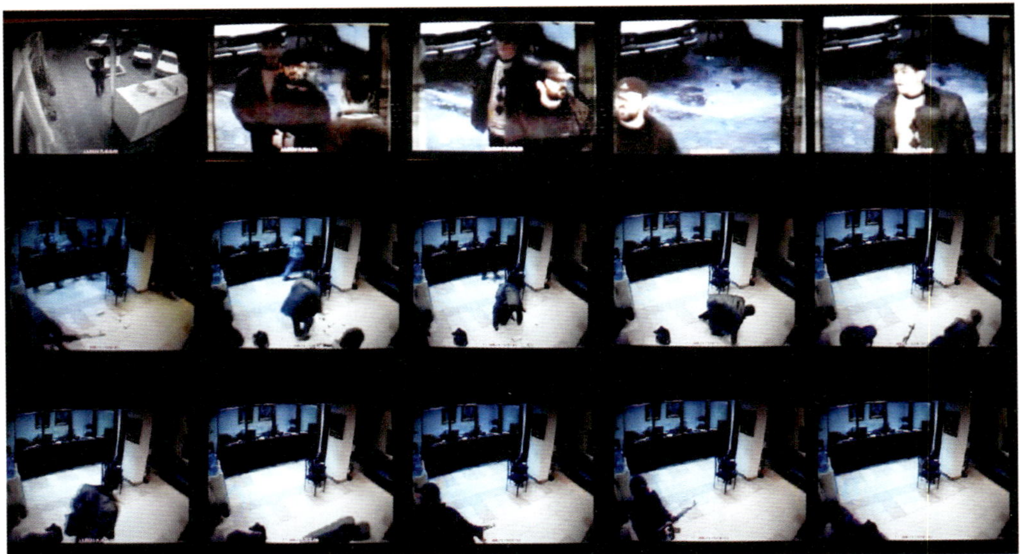

What is all this for? Why should I collect all these things, if I knew that I would not live long enough to work on them? Why would an artist collect material? Is it related to the fear the artist has of the future? I mean the fear the artist has of no longer knowing what to do in the future? Do we collect material so it keeps us secure, so that we will always have something to produce in the future? Is it fear of being devoid of ideas and proposals, a fear of being unproductive, a burden on society?

A fear of death!

To clarify, my archive doesn't have the logic of institutional archives. I mean my archive is not "archived" or organized in any way. I am not taking good care of it, not indexing it; not preserving it from any possible damage. I come across it all around my house. It has no specific place for safe-keeping. At times I stumble on it by chance.

It lives with me. A part of it remains on my mind. It follows me, I don't know how to use it. It tires me to the point I keep saying: I must tear it up, destroy it, burn it, throw it away, get rid of it. And every time I am about to do so I hesitate and tell myself: you don't know what might happen tomorrow, you might need something from it you will regret throwing it away. So, I keep it.

This is one strange relationship, material that has become part of my life. An archive. I invented and it became part of my memory. This kind of memory is unlived, but it lives with me. It's an added memory. But the difference between my memories and my archive is that my own memory forgets, erases, transforms, and throws away things without consulting me, even without my knowledge. Whereas this added memory, this archive, does not diminish.

It doesn't change without my saying so, unless some catastrophe happens.

As long as it is there I can consult it at any time I want; remember everything in it, and in detail if I so wish.

Stops the videotape.

So, the idea for this presentation is to show part of these two types of archive: the coming and unfinished projects archive and the general and impersonal materials. On the basis that if I show it to you I might be able to move them to the other types of archive. The ones related to the past. So, in this way, I will be finished with them. Hence, this presentation is an attempt to get rid of the burden of a part of my archive.

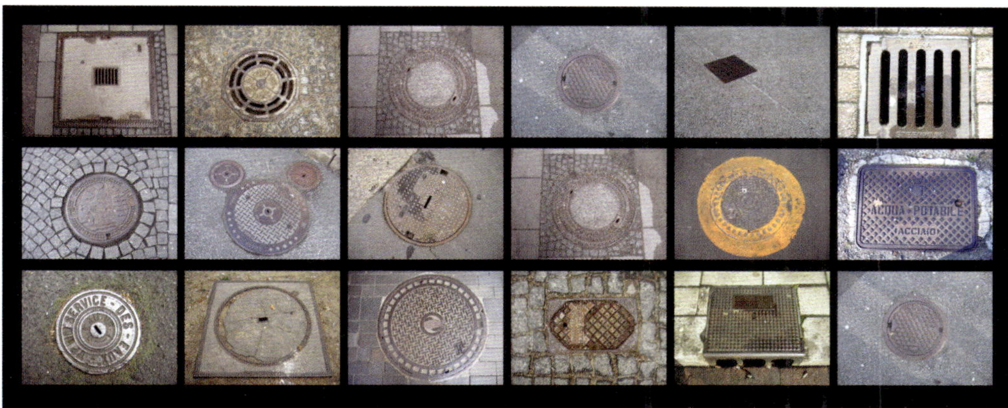

I took these photographs between 2003 and 2006. Every time I would visit a city outside Lebanon, I would photograph its sewers and the manholes. My plan was to collect pictures of all the sewers and manholes in the world. So I would make a portrait of each city from its sewers.

I stopped this project when my friend Hatem told me that it has already been done, and there is no reason to continue with it. The publisher Taschen already printed the book, which is now available in bookstores around the world.

I stopped it …

I was so frustrated that I decided to make a photo collection that no one has thought of before me. I thought and thought until I had the idea to photograph the street lamps. But I feared

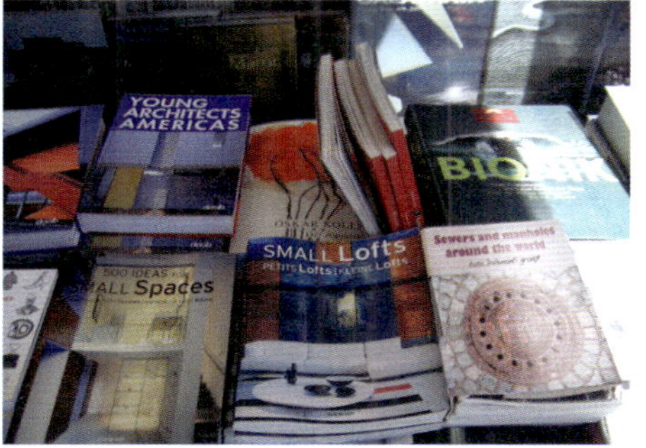

that this idea was already taken, that someone had done this before me. So I decided to photograph only one lamp post located on the way between my house and my workplace. I was sure that this collection will be an original and that no one had done it before me.

These are some photos from this collection.

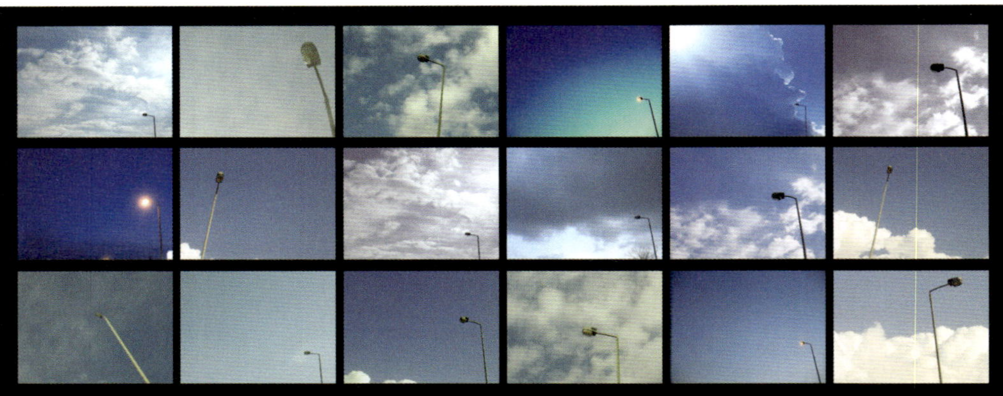

Later, I noticed that there is a relation between these two collections which is the position of my head as a photographer.

In the sewers collection, which was taken in different cities in the world especially European cities my head was dropped down, while in the streetlamp collection which was taken in Beirut only, my head was lifted up.

I always wonder; why is it that in my city I raise my face up to the sky, while in foreign cities I stab my face to the ground?

Is it something psychological, political or social?

By the way, when I tried to take photos of the sewers and manholes in Beirut, a civilian man stopped me on his own initiative, to interrogate me.

Because of his love of country, he turned into a security guard. He thought that I was studying the possibilities of planting a bomb under the street. In fact, one of the main scenarios put forth concerning the way in which our ex-prime minister Mr. Rafic Harriri was assassinated is that one thousand kilograms of TNT and other explosive materials were planted in the sewers under the street. Since then I did not dare to photograph anything related to the street. And maybe this is why I thought about streetlamps since no one would ask why I am photographing the sky. Who could I assassinate in the sky? No one would suspect me. Who is in the sky? I mean, no one would think that I am planning to assassinate anybody by putting a bomb on a streetlamp. But why not? Nobody actually thought about it yet; I mean, it could be, with our history with the car bombs.

Since 2005, Lebanon lived through the nightmare of car bombs.

Actually, one can notice that most of the walls in Beirut are filled with photos of people who were killed by car bombs …

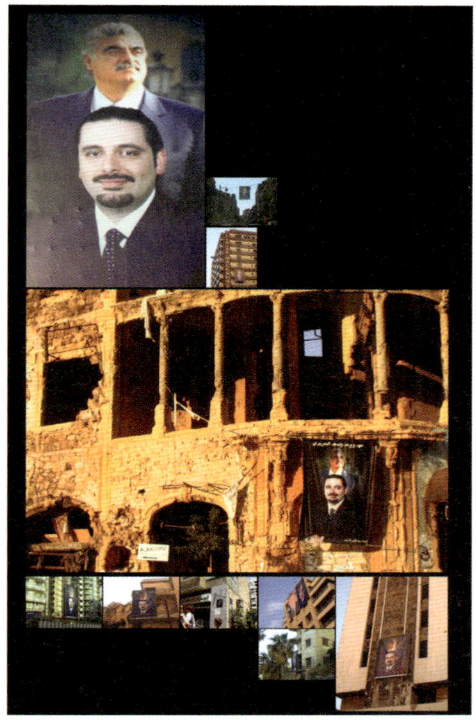

This photo appeared in the streets right after the assassination of Rafic Harriri and before the elections. It shows the ex-prime minister standing behind his son. One can see the photo in different sizes hanging everywhere in Beirut.

The assassinated father standing behind his son. It reminds me of Hamlet and the ghost of his father. But I wonder; does the son in this photo know that this is the ghost of his father standing behind him? If not then one might say that the son is not able to see ghosts in a city full of ghosts, just as Hamlet's mother can't see her husband's ghost. In that case, the son might think that what has appeared behind him in this poster is simply a photo of his father hanging in the living room.

Some day, I will do a work about this specific poster.

In fact, in 1998, I wanted to do a play based on the idea of the street poster. The idea was taken from a Lebanese novel by Rashid Al Daif.

I even wrote a proposal to get financial support from the Ministry of Culture in Lebanon. I still have this proposal, although I forgot all its details, and can't remember anything concerning the text. I forgot why I was so excited about it.

This is the letter I had sent the Ministry of Culture to receive financial support for my play *The Poster*.

He shows a photo of the letter.

The last sentence I wrote says: I hope to receive your approval and financial support, as has always been the case.

In reality it has not been the case at all; we've never received any financial support from our government, simply because our government has other priorities to pay for. And I really understand this. At that time, Beirut was considered the cultural capital of the Arab world, so the minister of culture made a call, inviting the Lebanese artists to apply for financial support. One can never know what will happen. So I applied for this fund. This is was my proposal:

Page 1:
The title: The Poster
Page 2:
Synopsis:
Who tore the poster?
The news spreads fast, and causes fear and panic in people's minds
Chaos fills the city
Everyone searches for the perpetrator
Everyone is innocent of the charge,
And everyone asks:
Who tore the poster?
They accuse each other, in grotesque and sometimes violent, irrational ways
Until they discover that they are all accomplices to this "crime"
Then, none of them remains interested in answering this question:
Who tore the poster?
Page 3:
about the play:
The play relies principally on working with the actors in structuring the theatrical performance and writing up its text under the direction and supervision of the director. The methodology applied will be based on improvisation during rehearsals; its goal is to achieve a contemporary theatrical language, where the vehicle of meaning are not the words, but the visual aspects that talk with all of the spectators' senses. … Bla blab la … nonsense …
Page 4:
Team work
Page 5:
Is the most important page in my proposal: The budget
I asked for 23.000 US Dollars.

On the last page, I put my address, just in case they decided to grant me the fund.

Four years after I submitted the proposal, I was notified by the Ministry of Culture that I had been awarded $1000 for having produced and presented my successful play: *The Poster*, the play which in fact I had neither produced nor presented.

Of course I kept the money.

Usually, when I finish a work or am about to start one, I return to my archive, look through it, rediscover it, re-read it, looking for a catalyst for my next project. This is how I came across the proposal I showed you, and this is also how I came across this proposal: *Cry me cats and dogs.*

In 2001, I had the idea to take a photo of every cat and dog I'd find killed by a car. Statistics show that each day, cars in Beirut hit between 30 and 60 cats and dogs as they cross the streets.

This is the first photo I took for that project.

He shows the first photo.

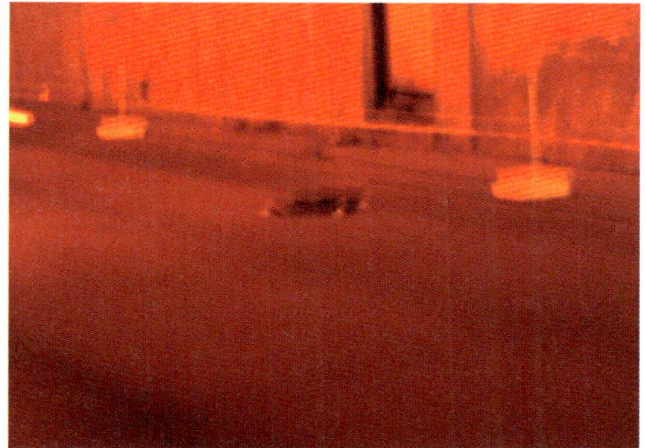

I took it from my car, but it was unclear, so I parked my car and came closer to the cat's corpse, and took this photo.

He shows the second photo.

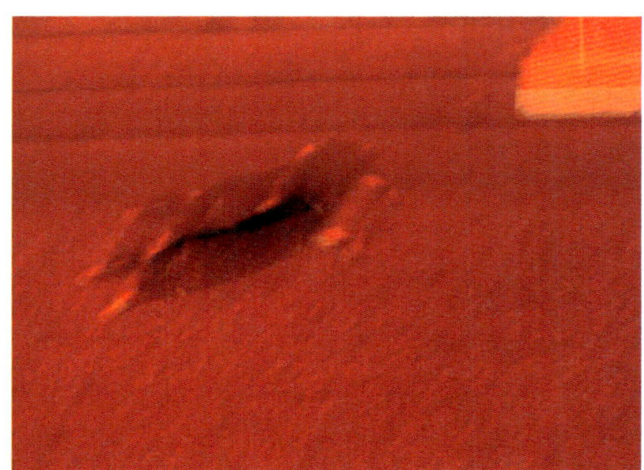

It was still unclear as there was not enough light, so I used the flash.

He shows the third photo for less than one second before he takes it off.

But suddenly I got perturbed and annoyed. So I decided to put a stop to this project. But the three photos still exist in my archive … and I am always tempted to take a look at them …

This video animation was supposed to be shown in a performance that I presented in 2003, but I never used it. I think it's time to show it.

Plays on his laptop a very slow animation showing his portrait disappearing.

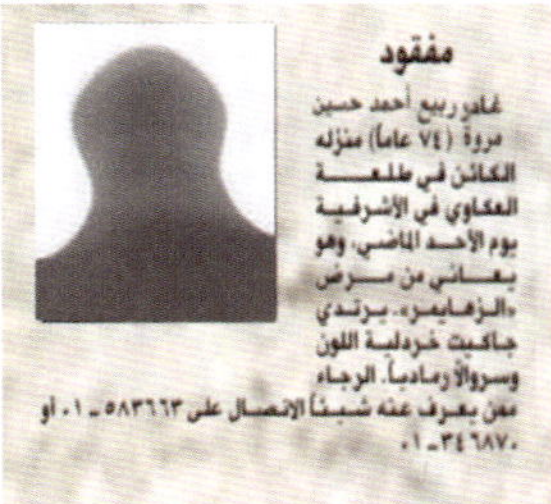

مفقود

غادر ربيع أحمد حسين مروة (٧٤ عاماً) منزله الكائن في طلعة العكاوي في الأشرفية يوم الأحد الماضي، وهو يعاني من مرض «الزهايمر»، يرتدي جاكيت خردلية اللون وسروالاً رمادياً. الرجاء ممن يعرف عنه شيئاً الاتصال على ٠١ـ٥٨٣٦٦٣ أو ٠١ـ٣٤٦٨٧٠.

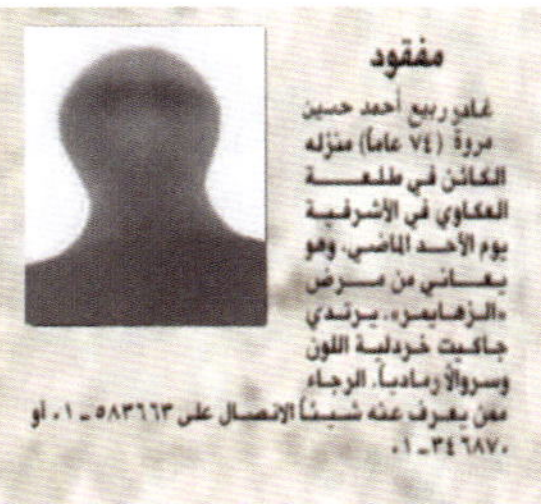

مفقود

غادر ربيع أحمد حسين مروة (٧٤ عاماً) منزله الكائن في طلعة العكاوي في الأشرفية يوم الأحد الماضي، وهو يعاني من مرض «الزهايمر»، يرتدي جاكيت خردلية اللون وسروالاً رمادياً. الرجاء ممن يعرف عنه شيئاً الاتصال على ٠١ـ٥٨٣٦٦٣ أو ٠١ـ٣٤٦٨٧٠.

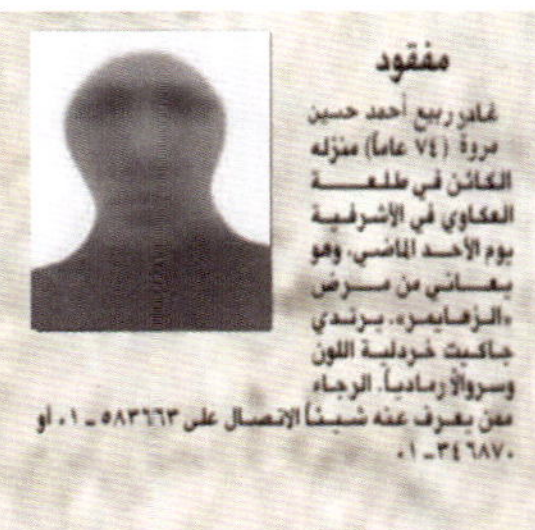

مفقود

غادر ربيع أحمد حسين مروة (٧٤ عاماً) منزله الكائن في طلعة العكاوي في الأشرفية يوم الأحد الماضي، وهو يعاني من مرض «الزهايمر»، يرتدي جاكيت خردلية اللون وسروالاً رمادياً. الرجاء ممن يعرف عنه شيئاً الاتصال على ٠١ـ٥٨٣٦٦٣ أو ٠١ـ٣٤٦٨٧٠.

Last Sunday, Rabih Mroué (74 years old) left his home in Beirut. He suffers from Alzheimer disease. He was wearing a mustard color jacket and grey trousers. If anyone has seen him, or knows of his whereabouts, please call us at: 01-583663 or 01-346870

Since 1995, I've been collecting pictures of missing persons that appear in the newspapers. I cut them out and keep them in a special notebook, with no idea as to why I do this. It seems that, without my knowing, something was attracting me toward these persons. Intriguing me. And I keep asking myself: to where could all these individuals have disappeared? Especially in a country such as Lebanon, so very small, where everyone is supposed to know everyone else. And the little that has been written about its society clearly states that it follows the tradition of the family, the tribe, the village, and the religious.

I think about it, and frankly I feel happy and comforted, in a way, that no matter how much we control this country or any country, there will always be holes a person can disappear into. Slip through cracks, get lost and vanish, possibly commit a crime, and all this without leaving any trace.

Does this mean that the disappeared are a sign of modernity, in a city that is still looking for its modernity? There is no answer. But it seems to me that, in order to achieve our individuality in my city, there is a heavy price to pay. Such as getting kidnapped, disappearing, getting murdered, or becoming a martyr. And frankly, I'm not sure that all of these are nearly enough.

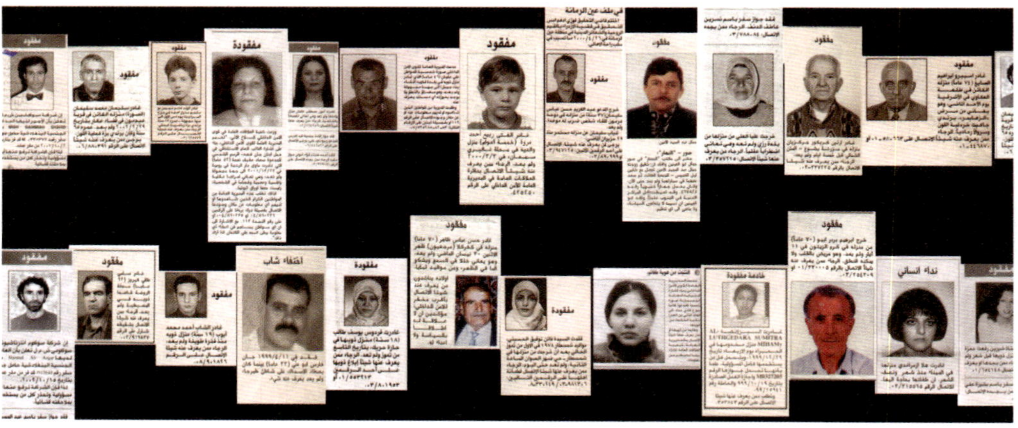

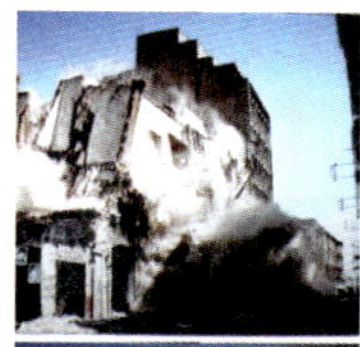
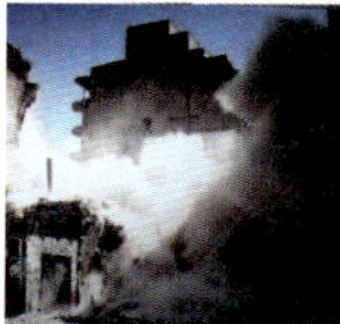
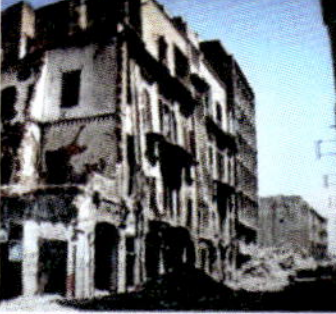
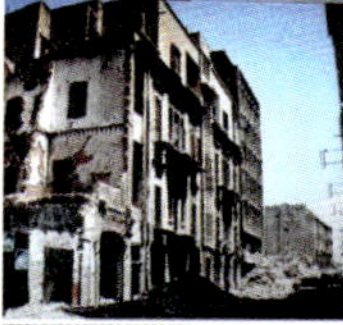
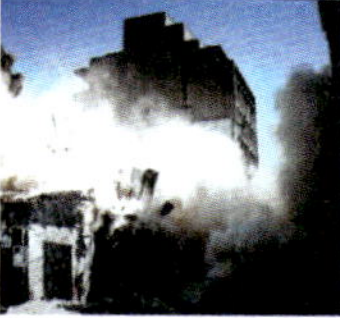
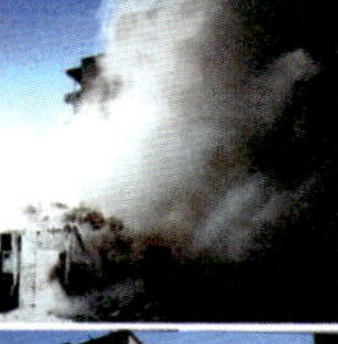
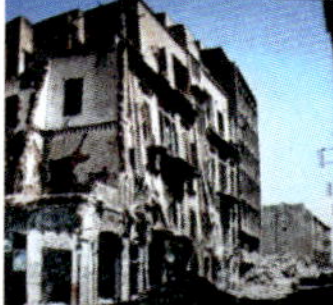
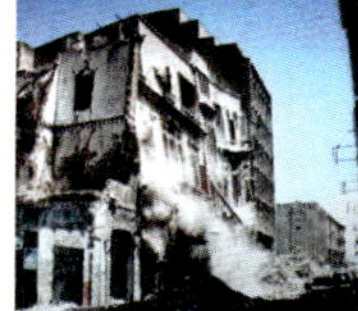

Sleiman, Shereen, Hala, Espiro, katia, Nazmole, Ali, Abdel karim, Jamal, Meya, Fouad, kasem, souad, Ammoun, Ali, Oum Hassan, kamal, Arteen, Mihami, Faten, Hassan wa and daher, Abbass, Fatema, Jean, Kamal, Ahamd, Sami, Alia …

These are missing people who disappeared after the Lebanese war. Hence, their case has nothing to do with the civil war. Knowing that there were 17,000 missing persons who disappeared during the civil war. To this moment, nobody knows whether they are alive or were killed, including those responsible for this war. Those responsible prefer that nobody mentions this subject. If they could kidnap this topic and wipe it out, they would do, just to make us forget about it. In fact, most of the Lebanese society prefers not to talk about this issue, which belongs to the period of the civil war that is already covered for the most part by collective amnesia.

To forget and to remember: this is what concerns the archive.

In his video *Still Life with 12 Minutes and Sounds*, Jalal Toufic says:

> Were one to videotape a person for years, wouldn't one be shortening the latter's "active" life by the same amount of time, since the one who was videotaped will be highly tempted to watch the tapes, especially if they are of his childhood, the period covered for the most part by infantile amnesia. The one who was extensively videotaped asked his father or uncle: "Why did you rob me of the ability to forget, thus making me sick?"

End of quote.

Amnesia by definition is: loss of memory as a result of shock, psychological disturbance, or medical disorder. Loss of Memory.

Would the role of the archive be to fill the gap created by this loss of memory?

In spite of fifteen years of living through the civil war, we are still tempted to watch again and again all the films and video rushes covering this period. But still the gap is not filled and forgetting wins over remembering. Furthermore, we agreed on a general amnesty in spite of the unknown destiny of 17,000 missing persons.

In that case, would the role of the archive be to participate in creating this gap of the loss of memory?

He plays a videotape that shows an old house falling down. The image goes backward and then forward then backward and so on so forth, sometimes the speed of the images is slow and sometimes it is very fast.

This videotape goes along with the following text:

I am not telling in order to remember. On the contrary, I am doing so to make sure that I've forgotten. Or at least, to make sure that I've forgotten some things, that they were erased from my memory. When I am certain that I've forgotten, I attempt to remember what it is that I've forgotten. And while attempting to remember, I start guessing and saying: perhaps, maybe, it's possible, it might be, probably, it can be, it looks like, it seems that, I am not sure but, etc … This way I reinvent what I had forgotten on the basis that I have in fact remembered it. After an indefinite while, I retell it. Not to remember it, no, but to make sure that I've forgotten it, or at least parts of it, and so on and so forth.

This operation might appear repetitive, but it is the contrary, because it is a refusal to go back to the beginnings, and what do you know of beginnings? This way I keep oscillating between remembering and forgetting, remembering and forgetting, remembering and forgetting, till death comes. I am betting on death to make me rediscover everything anew. Even if it happens that there will be nothing new; that will be in itself a discovery.

Once, I wrote a proposal for a performance. I still have it in my archive.

This performance is based on the concept of apology. Officially, the Lebanese war ended in 1990 and, until now, none of those responsible, who are still to this day in positions of power, have presented an apology to the Lebanese people for the crimes they have committed. With the exception of one person, who counts among those who lost the war; his name is Asaad Shaftari. His apology was a small text he published in a newspaper in 2002. That is, around twelve years after the war ended. Almost nobody took this apology seriously. Regardless, it remains registered as the first official apology given.

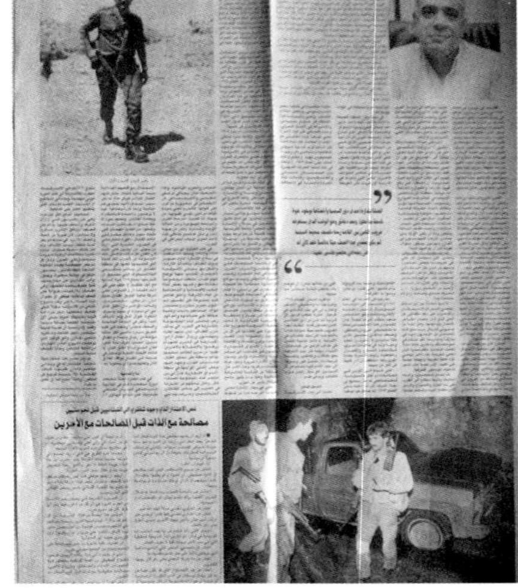
مصالحة مع الذات قبل المصالحات مع الآخرين

Like many Lebanese citizens, I have waited for apologies from many of those responsible, but in fact nothing appeared. One can tell that some of those responsible presented a sort of self-critique, or the pretense of one. Some admitted direct responsibility for the war, some recounted details of their involvement and the involvement of other parties. Some confessed, but none apologized. Why, I don't know. What does it mean to apologize? Is it necessary? What good does it do, or what would the apology of these particular people effect, since the émigré had emigrated, the kidnapped had been kidnapped, the wounded had been wounded, the mutilated had been mutilated, the destroyed had been destroyed, who had gone mad went mad, and who had died died. To clarify: there is a big difference between confession and apology. I care not for confession. And today, even apologies no longer concern us. The performance I wanted to make was based on this idea. I no longer wish to show it, but parts of it remain in my archive. I would like to show some lines of its text.

I, the undersigned, Rabih Mroué, present to all the Lebanese people, a public and sincere apology. But before I begin, I don't wish my position to be understood as a reaction, or even an action.
Since the end of the war I have been possessed by this idea and this feeling, but I hadn't until now gathered the necessary courage to make this step. Perhaps cowardice and fear stopped me from fulfilling this desire.
But now the time has come to proclaim my apologies to you brothers and sisters, friends, comrades and companions, enemies.
I apologize to all those who were my victims, whether they knew it or not, whether I knew them or not, whether I had hurt them directly or through mediators.
I apologize for I what have done during the Lebanese war, whether in the name of Lebanon or Arabness or the Cause, etc.
I apologize for my ignorance of the meaning of many words and my total ignorance of concepts I was fighting for. As I apologize for not knowing the roots and reasons for the civil war, which I had claimed to understand.
I apologize because I considered the Lebanese war a war of social-classes only.
I apologize for considering that my comrades and I were right and forever in the right.
I apologize because I fired bullets towards the sky in glee over Brazil's victory over Germany.
I apologize for promoting and chanting in private and public gatherings political and revolutionary songs that excite crowds and push them to continue with the war until victory is won.
I apologize for accepting to be a bodyguard for a Soviet diplomatic delegation and for staying with them at the "Beau Rivage" hotel for almost one week.
I apologize for accepting different kinds of weapons and arms without getting proper training or knowing how to work them.
I apologize for accepting to go to Cuba for a month to train in guerilla warfare.
I apologize because at one point I considered myself to be a policeman with the right to give orders in the name of keeping order.
I apologize for being proud of my "Lebaneseness" while at the same time aspiring to get another nationality.
I apologize that during the war I incurred no physical wounds, that I wasn't kidnapped, that no one attempted to assassinate me, and that I received no personal threat.
I apologize because I sometimes steal other people's writings and pretend they are my own.
I apologize because I enjoy playing with other people's feelings.
I apologize for working in a medium that I dislike.
I must insist that this is not a confession, and this is not an apology.
These are only words, words words words …

Respectfully yours,
Rabih Mroué

The title of this performance was supposed to be *I, the undersigned.*

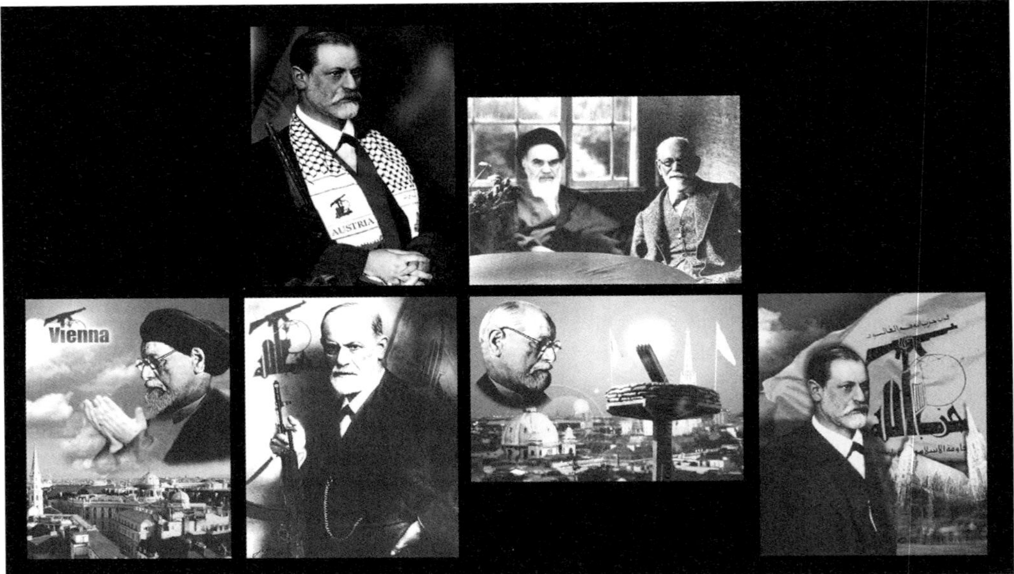

Among my unfinished works, I found six postcards that were supposed to be presented in Vienna.

My aim was an attempt to bring the Beiruti kitsch culture to Vienna by presenting Sigmund Freud, the intellectual figure, as a religious man and a saint and leader in Hezbollah. But nobody in Vienna recognized this man as Freud and when I told them they still did not react; maybe because they also don't consider it strange that Freud would be a member of Hezbollah. Why not? He can be whatever he wants. Freud is free to be in Hezbollah, Al-Qaeda, in the socialist party, or the democrats if he wanted. It's none of anybody's business. And I could not explain it further to them.

Then I proposed these postcards to an Iranian art magazine for publishing, but they refused because they were afraid their government would consider them insulting to Islam and to Khomeini. The photos might cause them trouble with censorship.

And till now, I did not present them in Beirut either, because I could not find any relationship between Freud and us, I mean why would I portray Freud as a member of Hezbollah, now?

By the way, concerning Freud, he says that the archive has a strong relation to the lapse in memory.

Initially, the archive guarantees the possibility of remembering; the possibility of repeating and duplicating. The basic reason behind this possibility of repeating and duplicating according to Freud can't be separated from the human desire for death.

Thus, the desire for destruction: the destruction of self; the destruction of the other.

Actually, for an archive to be acceptable to an authority it must suit it. In other words, before this material becomes an archive, it must be shaped, molded, and painted to become suitable. So it would become: "A truthful memory." That means this archive will be shifted into a principle of that supposed Truth. But what truth and what principle? Anyway, death stays out of any principle, because it destroys all principles.

Death threatens all archival desires.

After I presented *Looking for a Missing Employee* in Beirut, a performance based on documents from Lebanese newspapers and in which I tell a true story, with the real names of the people involved, many people started giving me actual files and documents to work on. The people felt that these were worthwhile topics, so they collected information and presented it to me, to archive and work on in the future. That is how I got my hand on a video that I will now show you.

This video is of the Mount Lebanon battles that took place between the Lebanese Druze and the Lebanese Maronites in 1983. During these battles massacres were committed by each side. No one has talked about this for a very long time. A friend of mine gave me this video so that I may talk about it. When I played the video, I was shocked. I saw corpses strewn across fields, under cars, everywhere, piled on top of each other, rotting corpses, cut into pieces, burnt, split in half, mutilated. If it were not for the teeth, we might not be able to identify them as human. I watched this tape once, and was afraid to go near it again, but the images were burnt into my mind. Moreover, I know that the tape is still at my house. I hesitated whether I should show you this video, so you may see how images can burn the eyes. I hesitated and finally decided that yes, I will not show it to you. This belongs to my censored archive … but I will show you a part of it, where a group of Druze militiamen are saluting the unknown cameraman.

By the way, the Druze won this particular battle.

He plays the videotape

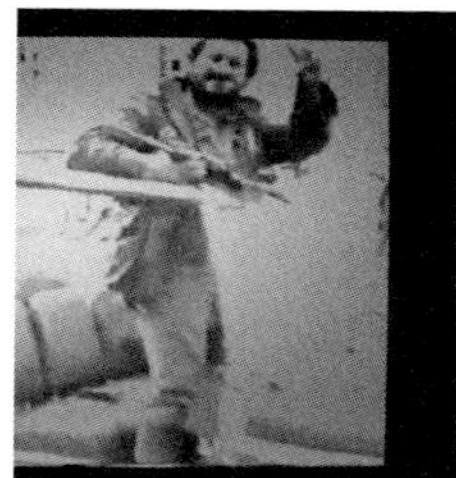
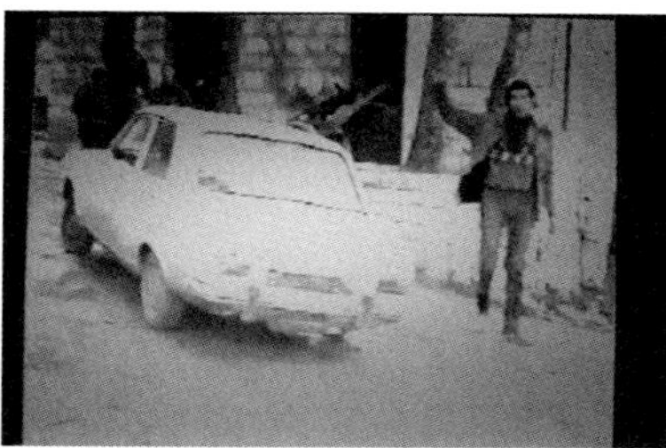
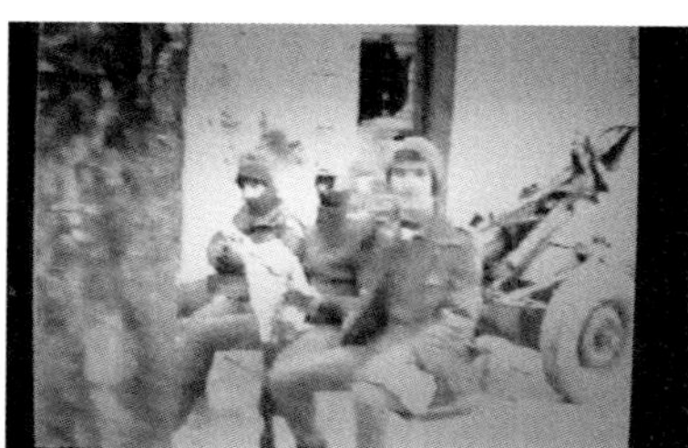
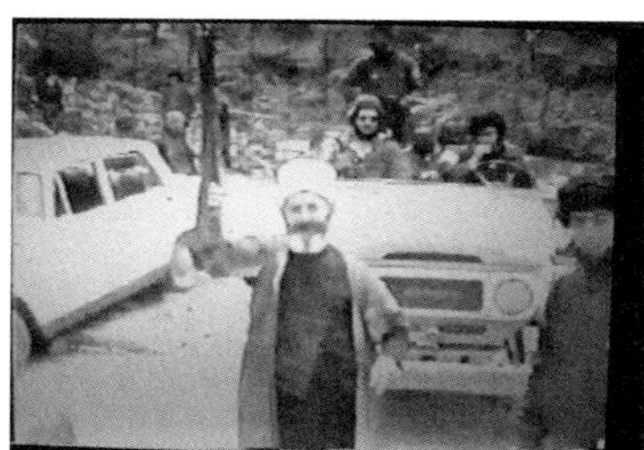
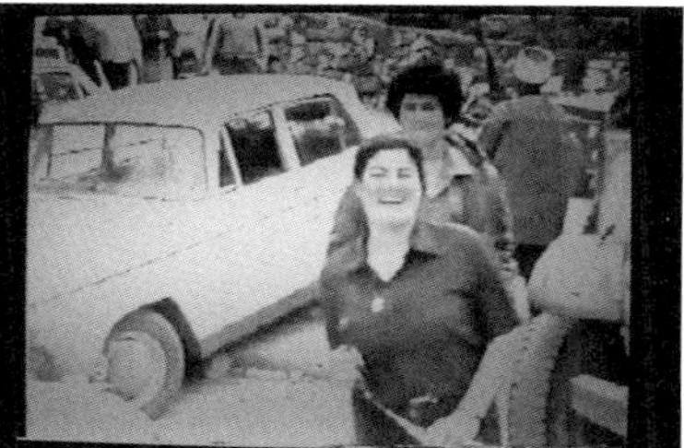
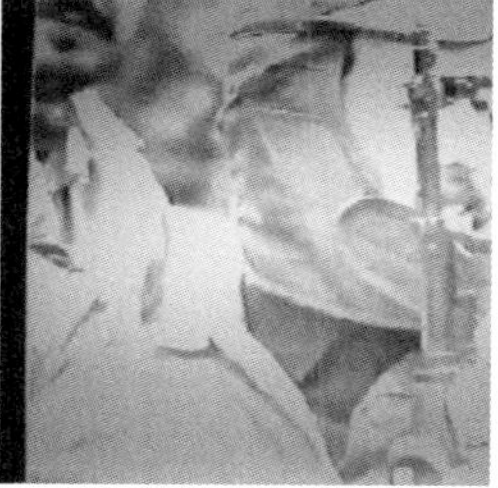

I have been collecting material for twenty years. Basically, this material is worthless. Something anyone can find. As long as you make the effort to collect it and keep it for the future, eventually this material acquires some kind of value. It could be historical, anthropological, scientific value. That is how the idea of the archive is constituted. The danger lies, I believe, in the archive becoming the property of one side that can manipulate it as it pleases. In the sense that that side will decide what is worth archiving and what is not; what should be made available to the public, and what shouldn't; what remains hidden, and what should be destroyed. The archive, in this sense, is an authority given over to historians.

I think that one of the signs of democracy appears when every citizen, with no exceptions, will have the right to see all the contents of any archive that belongs to any side, wherever it could be.

In the year 2000, Elias Khoury and I presented *Three Posters*, a performance-video. This performance was based on suicidal operations done by leftist and nationalistic groups in Lebanon.

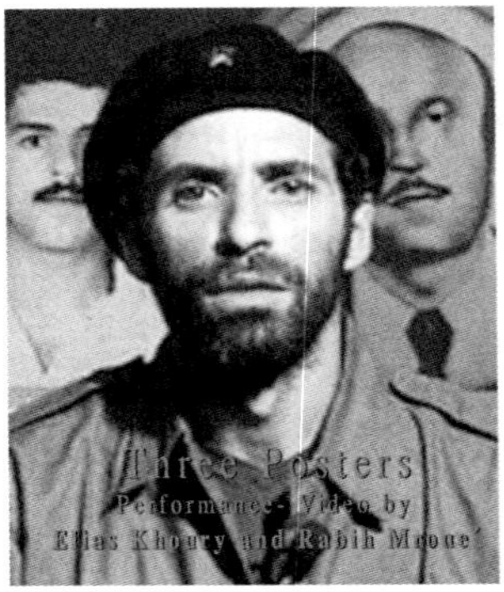

The performance was questioning the failure of the Lebanese left, and the reasons behind its marginalized role in active political life.

One of the questions posed at the time was how and why the resistance against the Israeli occupation was transformed from a secular nationalist resistance to a religious Islamic resistance, namely Hezbollah.

Actually, after the Israeli invasion of Lebanon in 1982, the National Resistance Front was born to liberate the occupied land. This resistance was declared by and consisted of fighters from the communists and secular Lebanese parties.

Between 1982 and 1987, and beside the military operations, the resistance fighters initiated some suicide operations against the Israeli army, which was still occupying the south of Lebanon.

The fighters used to record their testimonies on VHS tapes just before they went to die.

The suicide bombers used to start their recorded testimonies with the same opening phrase: I am the comrade martyr.

In fact I am always taken by the power of this phrase: I am the martyr. It intrigues me and keeps me thinking of its meanings. I mean, how can someone say I am the martyr, when he or she is not yet dead? And when we will be watching the video tape, will he or she be a martyr? How can one speak about past, present, and future in relation to this phrase: I am the martyr?

Knowing that, the purpose of these video testimonies is in fact to be archived.

Hence, how does such documentation represent or deceive reality?

In my personal archive, I can find most of these testimony tapes. I watched them all.

One of them kept haunting me: it was the testimony of Wafa' Noureddine.

Almost nobody remembers her name in Lebanon.

I will show you part of her testimony for a reason I will tell later.

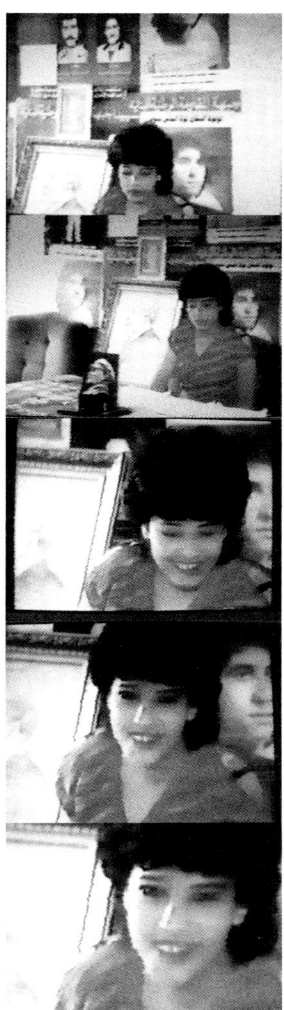

He plays the videotape
As her last words in her testimony, Wafa' says: "Finally I shake the hands of all my patriots so that the rifle remains alert until the liberation of our land. And everyone must know that we love life, and because we love life we have chosen death and martyrdom. So that the children of Lebanon, of Syria, of Palestine and all the children of the Arab nation may live, until the last grain of our land is liberated."

One day I will do a work about the most beautiful smile I ever saw:

Wafa's Smile.

Since in this world, there is not only one suffering but there are thousands.
There is not one memory.
There is not one experience.
There is not one war.
There is not one enemy.
There is not one friend.
There is not one confessional.
There is not one religion.
There is not one god.
There is neither one truth nor one origin.
Thus, there is not one archive.
But there is only one death.

He closes the file he was using, on the screen people can see the desktop of his laptop, he drags all the files related to this performance into the trash and presses empty trash.

The archive is not a diary. It seems that we collect an archive to cover our daily experiences, and to hide behind it. We create an archive of pictures, notes, stories, texts, CVs, all these in order to hide our daily life.

We hide behind the archive so no one sees us naked.

Thank you.

Chapter 20

The Personal Evolution of the Performance Object (Or, What to Do with Leftovers)

Nao Bustamante

The bulk of my performances are built, live, from fragments or flashes of images.

I had done an initial version of the work, *Given Over to Want* (before it was titled) in Nagano, Japan, in a punky rock club (Figure 1). That was March of 1999 and I was invited by Seiji Shimoda to participate in the Nippon International Performance Art Festival. I was planning to do a different work (*Sans Gravity*) as part of the festival, but was inspired by all the activity to experiment.

It was there I conceived the shadow play transforming into the ghost image, with the oranges taped on to the feet, etc. I wanted to continue to sculpt my body with tape – much like in my 1995 work *America, the Beautiful*. But, always felt that in *America* the shadow was, or should have been the main feature. So with *Given Over* I did away with the body and only worked with the shadow, the projection, the object, the other (Figure 2). Of course there is nothing new about shadow play, as it has been the basis for theatrical traditions in many cultures. If I were to compare my work to those skilled in the art of shadow play, there would be no contest. But, as with so many of my works, I approached this new method with the enthusiasm of an amateur.

Some of the elements from *America* remained, such as the taping of the body and the physique manipulation. But I added a girdle dance, illustrating the ridiculousness of squeezing one's body into a small sheath. The girdle was also a partial solution to minimize taping directly onto my skin as the bruising and marking over the years with this kind of work has become tiresome. I've often said the performance in my work happens "backstage," me with scissors pulling the carpets of tape off of my thighs. Several times while performing *America* I removed the tape in front of the audience. I found this to be helpful as I was still

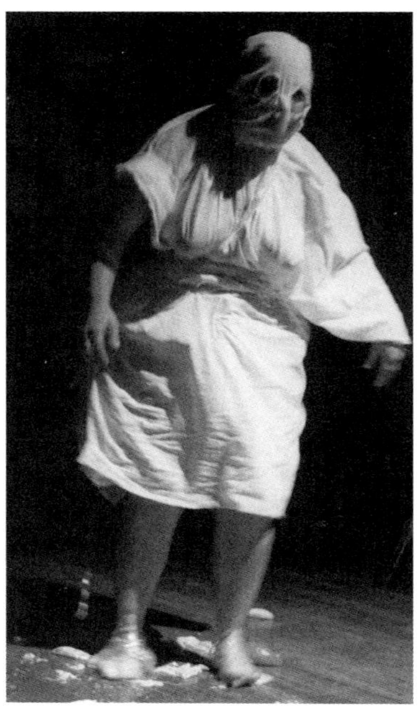

Nao Bustamante, *Given Over to Want*, 1999, performed in a rock club, Nagano, Japan.

in an altered state and the empathy exuded in the groans of the audience lessened the pain of pulling the skin, or at least made me feel tough.

So we have the shadow, the sculpting with tape, the high heels have been replaced by taping oranges to my feet. I think initially there were many oranges sitting around for us to have as a snack and I just grabbed a couple for the performance. Fresh oranges are more precarious and prettier than high-heels. One must walk delicately or the oranges will turn to mushy disks within a few steps. Something else happens that can only be experienced live. That is the citrus scent squeezed into the air from the rind, while exerting pressure. It's a fragile magic.

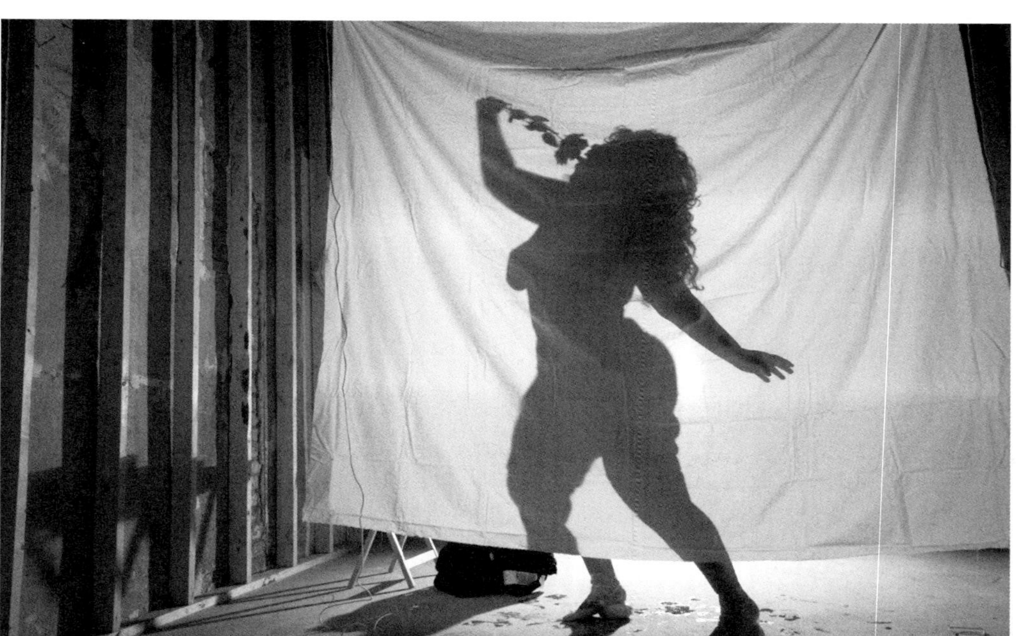

Nao Bustamante, *Given Over to Want*, 1999, shadow play.

Fast forward to November of 2006, I took the performance work *Hero* to the First International Performance Biennial, *Deformes*, at the Museum of Contemporary Art in Santiago, Chile. The work posed technical and linguistic difficulties and after the performance I was left feeling misunderstood and unfulfilled. Within a day's time I had conjured the notion to bring back "the ghost" character and add the box of wine as a provocative additional element (Figure 3). The work took on various connotations due to the atmosphere of the festival and the history of so many disappeared persons in Chile. As usual I had not had a rehearsal – but I needed only the simplest of technical set-ups.

My thought was that I would suspend the time between taping the box of wine to my head and the wine spilling on to my face, with body posturing. Once the wine began to spill I would chase it, trying in vain to drink the ancient elixir. Thus the title: *Given Over to Want*. I wanted a pretentious title to contrast with my base actions. It was here that I also brought back the rose, which appears here and there in different works. Probably most significantly in *America, the Beautiful*, where, toward the end I take a bow and a bouquet of roses is thrown to me. I act surprised, but then milk the applause until it is exhausted, uncomfortable and no longer clapping. At this point I throw a tantrum and begin biting the heads off the roses (à la Ozzie Osborne) and chewing – while pacing in a menacing style.

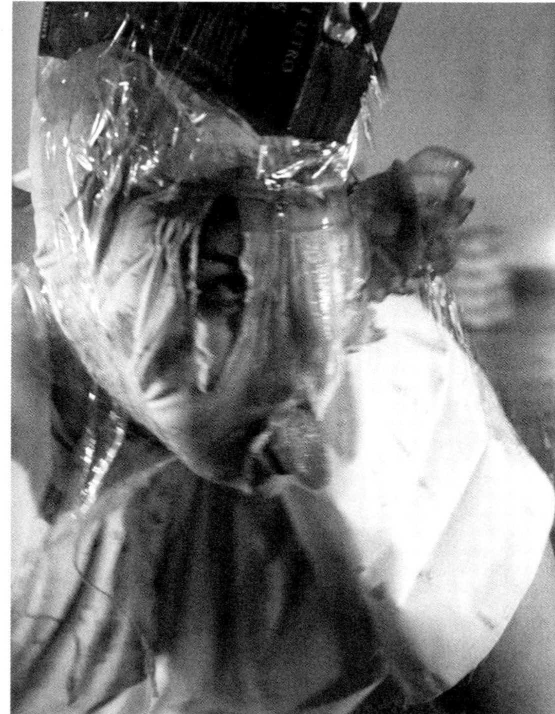

Nao Bustamante, *Given Over to Want*, 1999, wine and "the ghost".

I spray the front row with the chewed rose saliva and look like a bloody mess – often during my fit, I run into the back wall suddenly, "out of control," and spit out the red saliva. It's an old slapstick gag, where it seems you are hitting your nose, but you actually hit the wall with your foot to create the impact. But when I come away from the wall, there is a violent splat of red.

A separate untitled work was extracted and isolated from the chewing of roses and leaving marks on the (gallery) wall. I outfitted the audience with newspaper with the eyeholes cut out of the photos of faces. The audience could watch through their newspaper masks, essentially appearing to ignore me, while protecting themselves from the possibility of me spitting on them.

Back to Chile and the rose. At the Museum of Contemporary Art there were these incredible rose bushes surrounding the building with huge softball size roses. I asked a security guard if I could have one of the roses for a performance and he agreed. I taped the flower to the side of my head like I was a proper Spanish lady from a matchbox image.

I think of my "props" and gestures as a sculptor may think of materials – clay, plastics, shag carpet, etc. And since I make installations, objects, and video works, it's not such a stretch. In fact I have no hierarchies – not of materials, not of mediums, not of art as it sits in relation to the world. But I do experience the art as separate from the product and the process.

The product is a snapshot that you must take somewhere in your process of understanding or forgetting (the art).

Here is the thing I didn't count on: the leftover or the remnant having its own afterlife. After my performance Antonio Becerro, a well-known Chilean artist, approached me to go to his studio for a photo shoot. His studio was an abandoned dog pound in the middle of a city park, cum art space called "La Perrera Arte" [the dog house or pound]. We waited for his collaborator, photographer, Jorge Aceituno and attempted to re-gather or purchase new versions of my props, although it was late and all the *tiendas* [shops] were closed. His rugged assistant trotted off in the park and came back with what looked like white lilacs. Someone had stopped at a street stand and gathered a couple of tomatoes, instead of oranges. We used wine from a bottle to refill the box on my head. Cheto Castellano re-sewed the face of the sheet, which I had ripped after my performance, in desperation to breathe freely (Figure 4).

Everyone worked to keep me comfortable (Figure 5); it was a performance of collaboration, trying to renew the original spirit of the work. In the end the photo that resonated is that of a pose of refinement, which hadn't occurred in my performance. Although now when I do the performance I tend to incorporate this gesture (Figure 6). I think I left my sheet there after the shoot; it looked so great hanging on the ladder drying, painterly and ghostly.

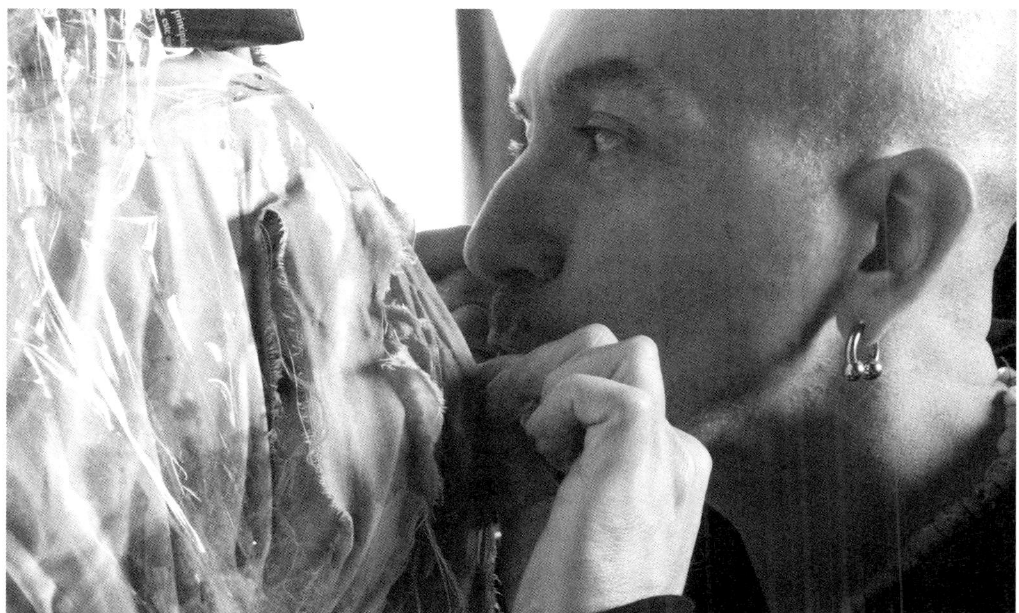

Cheto Castellano re-sewing Bustamante's sheet for photo shoot at Antonio Beccero's studio after her performance of *Given Over to Want* at the First International Performance Biennial, *Deformes*, at the Museum of Contemporary Art, Santiago, Chile. Photograph by Jorge Aceituno.

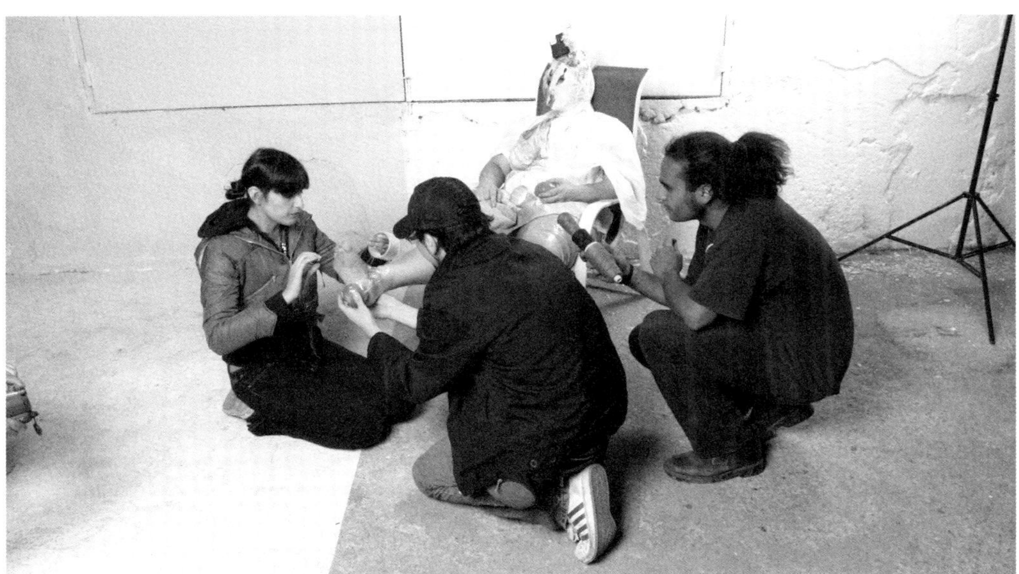

Assistants and friends make Bustamante comfortable for the photo shoot. Photograph by Jorge Aceituno.

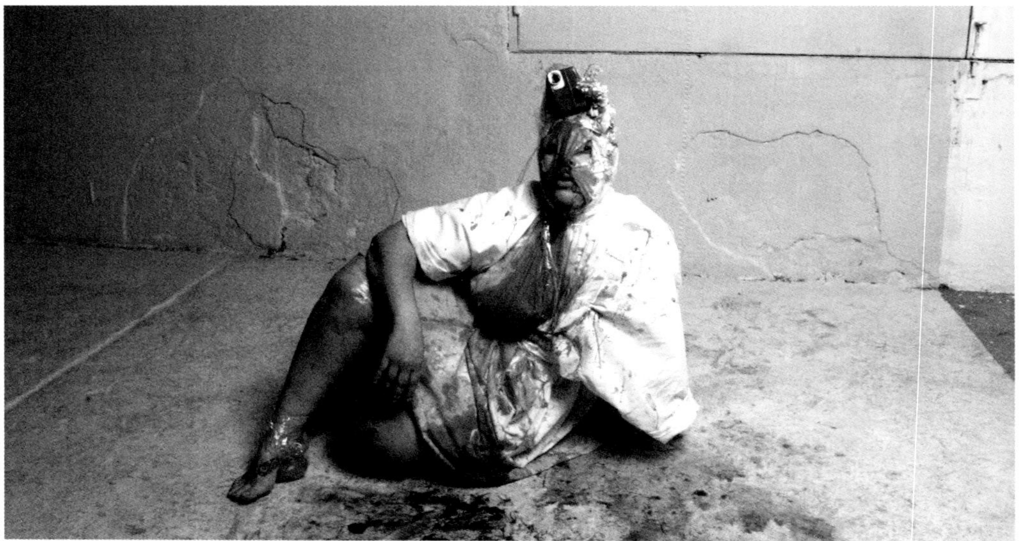

Image produced at Beccero's photo shoot, which has now become iconic in representing *Given Over to Want* (and has inflected Bustamante's performance of subsequent versions of the piece). Photograph by Jorge Aceituno.

Later, in May of 2007, I performed the work in Mexico City at Escuela Nacional de Artes Plasticas invited by the Museo Universitario del Chopo.

After the performance I kept the fake (by now) rose but ditched the "bloody" sheet in a sculpture yard dumpster; there it mingled with various "traditional" materials. I remember seeing the sheet stare back at me in disbelief that I would just leave it there, still moist, still warm. I went out drinking, but kept thinking of my bloody ghost left behind.

Now, I've begun collecting the sheets from previous performances. Two from Canada, two from New York, one from San Jose, California, three from Los Angeles … I'm building an army of bloody ghosts. Each tie-dyed with wine and sweat and grime. For now they are dried, folded, and tagged in my closet, but sometimes at night they surround my bed and caress my dreams.[1]

Note

1. Editor's note: Bustamante's blurring of the lines between the "real" and "representational" has ratcheted up since her debut as a contestant on the new prime-time television show *Work of Art: The Next Great Artist*, which premiered on Bravo channel on 9 June 2010. For her commentary on the show, see her website and twitter feed: http://naobustamante.com/wordpress/?tag=reality-show-contestant; and twitter feed http://twitter.com/naobustamante. See also the Bravo website on the show, featuring Bustamante and the other contestants, http://www.bravotv.com/work-of-art/season-1/. All sites accessed 16 July 2010.

Chapter 21

Cai Yuan and J.J. Xi, Mad For Real

Cai Yuan and J.J. Xi were both born in China, in 1956 and 1962 respectively, and have been working in Britain since the 1980s.[1] One of their first performances in collaboration was their "intervention" in Tracey Emin's *Bed* (1999). They have been working together since that time producing radical political works that enact a commentary on various contemporary political narratives and belief systems.

Cai and J.J.'s performative "interventions" shift the cultural meaning of both major works of art, Duchamp's *Fountain* (1917) and Emin's *Bed*, changing their meaning and their place in cultural history. The numerous newspaper accounts of Cai and J.J.'s *Two Artists* pieces further exemplify the way in which successful acts of intervention gain their own narrative momentum, in turn transforming the historical understanding of the "original" objects.

More specifically, both of the interventions illustrated here engage with works of art that already challenge the definitions and cultural value attached to "high art." Duchamp's readymades were epochally important: putting found objects in the context of aesthetics (the art gallery or juried exhibition)[2] during the period of high modernism, he put pressure on definitions of art as something autonomous from the social realm. Emin's Turner Prize project, which infamously offered her actual bed, replete with stains and rumpled sheets and documented with tales of her sexual exploits, once again in the context of high art, reiterates this set of questions from a postmodernist, feminist point of view. If Duchamp's presentation of a mass-produced plumbing fixture as "art" in 1917 questioned modernism's assumption that art involved skill and the hand of the "genius" artist, then an installation documenting a woman's sexual encounters in 1999, placed in the highly rarified space of the Tate Modern, claims a different shifting of boundaries between the aesthetic and lived experience. For Cai and J.J. to intervene in both works is yet again to question value judgments attached to institutions such as the Tate and the Turner Prize show.

By aggressively *performing* the works as objects to be used (as in the urinal) or played with and on (the bed), Cai and J.J. rearticulate the questions originally posed by Duchamp's readymades and posed in a different way by Emin's feminist project: what are the boundaries between everyday use value and aesthetic value? What are the boundaries between art and life? They point dramatically to the way in which Duchamp's anti-aesthetic gesture had (by the year 2000) been so thoroughly aestheticized that it had come to represent one of the most celebrated objects in the Tate's collection. The paradox of this status of *Fountain* lies in the fact that Duchamp's gesture was to erase the use-value of an industrially made object and call it art, clearly with his tongue in his cheek; remaking the lost urinal in the 1960s, he made a further ironic statement on the fetishization of the art object as an "original" expression of a genius-artist's intentions.[3] Recapturing the spirit of the readymades in the late twentieth-century, Cai and J.J. *reverse* Duchamp's gesture – resolutely insisting on the urinal's use-value to point to the artificiality of its designation as high art. In so doing they retain the most crucial critical tension of the original act of the readymades: they were *performative*. Rather than reflecting a skilled process resulting in a final fixed object, the readymade involved an *act* of choosing, which defined an object as "art."

When interviewed about the Duchamp intervention, Cai noted, "the urinal is there – it's an invitation. [...] As Duchamp said himself, it's the artist's choice. He chooses what is art.

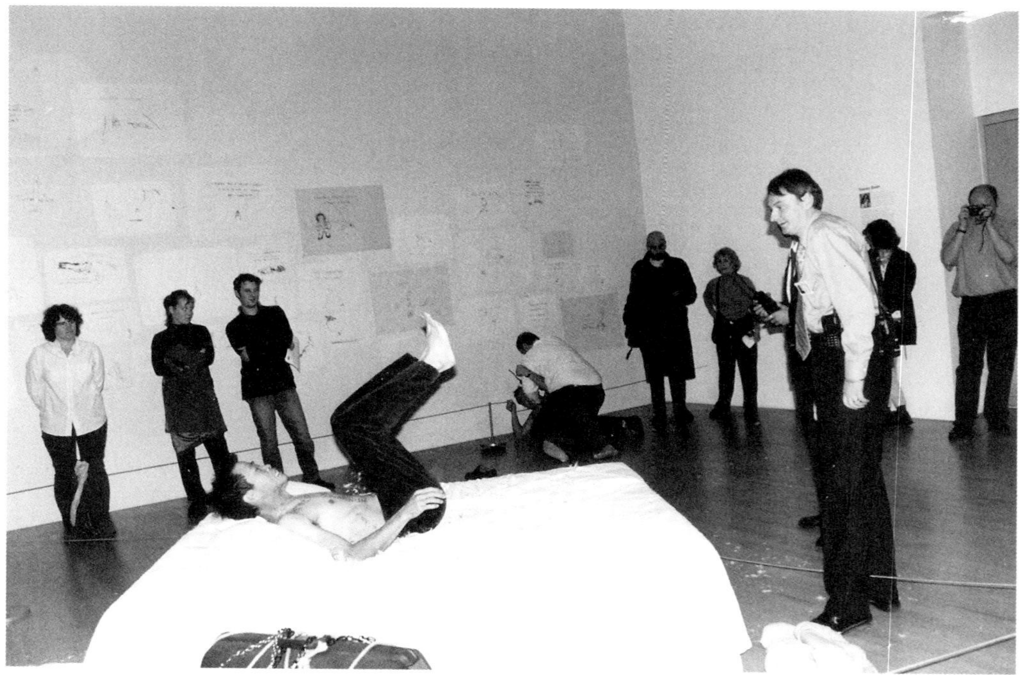

Cai Yuan and J.J. Xi, *Two Artists Jump on Tracey Emin's Bed*, 1999, Tate Gallery, London. According to their website (www.madforreal.org) this intervention took place during the Turner Prize exhibition, for which the Emin was being displayed. Cai and J.J. were arrested and then released without charge.

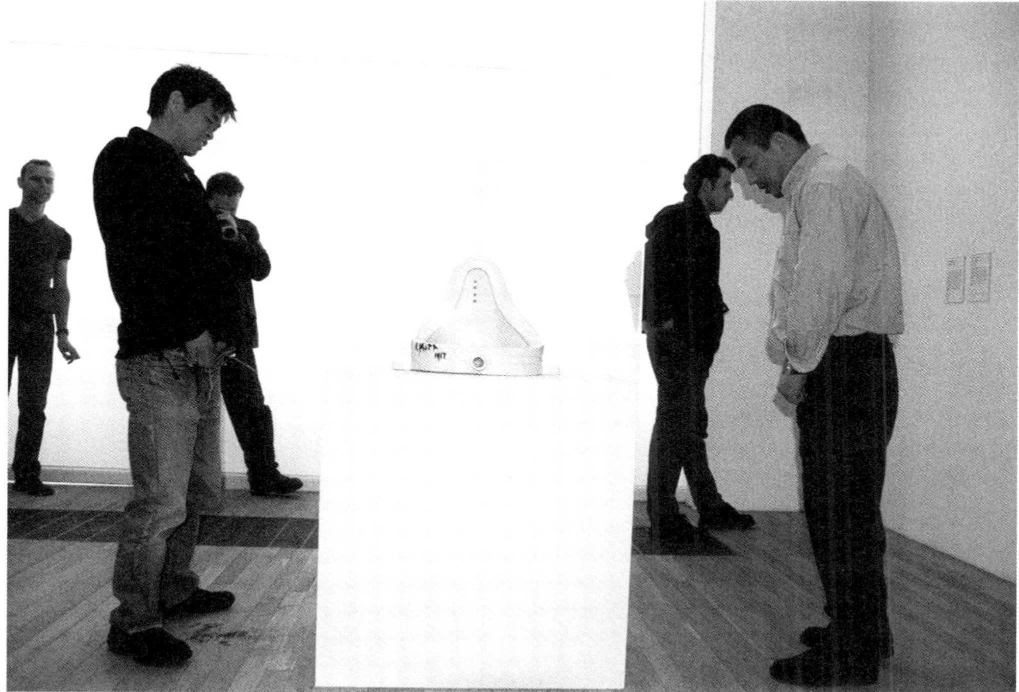

Cai Yuan and J.J. Xi, *Two Artists Piss on Duchamp's Urinal*, 2000, Tate Modern, London. Their website notes: "This intervention took place on Duchamp's iconic work *Fountain* in Tate Modern, the urinal which revolutionized the concept of modern art in the twentieth-century. The artists employed the concept of Qigong, channeling the internal energy after storing it for a few hours before releasing their Qi (spirit). They intended to broaden the context of the urinal, with the suggestive act of pissing on it to celebrate the spirit of contemporary art. Subsequently the performance was made into a film commissioned by Dazed & Confused/FilmFour." In fact, the artists could only piss on the vitrine in which the *Fountain* was fetishistically contained and protected in its vaulted status of high art.

We just added to it."[4] Far from "just adding to it," actually Cai and J.J. profoundly (if subtly) shift the terms of its place in history. This is a "re-enactment" of a still work of art that opens out the performative dimension through which it originally challenged beliefs about art in the most radical way. To return even a vestige of the radical to such a now canonized work in 2000 is no small thing.

Amelia Jones

Notes

1. For this and other information on the artists and their work, I have drawn on two sources: their website (www.madforreal.org) and the catalogue, Cai Yuan and J.J. Xi, *Mad for Real*, London: Carrots Press and MadforReal, 2005.
2. Duchamp signed the *Fountain* "R. Mutt" and submitted it, infamously, to the Society of Independent Artists exhibition in New York, which, although it claimed to be unjuried, rejected the "urinal" and removed it from the exhibition hall. The "original" *Fountain* was lost in 1917 but Duchamp made a number of replicas in the 1960s, of which the Tate's *Fountain* is one.
3. The *Fountain* was voted the most influential object in the history of art by 500 British art world professionals (see "Duchamp's urinal tops art survey," BBC News, 1 December 2004. Available at: http://news.bbc.co.uk/1/hi/entertainment/4059997.stm; accessed 27 June 2011. One of the replicas was sold in the USA at auction in 2003 for almost two million dollars; see Francis Naumann, "Marcel Duchamp: Money is No Object," *Tout Fait*, 2003, issue 5. Available at: http://www.toutfait.com/issues/volume2/issue_5/news/naumann/naumann1.htm; accessed 27 June 2011.
4. Cited in Nick Paton Walsh, "It's a New Cultural Revolution," *The Observer*, Sunday, 11 June 2000.

Chapter 22

Hayley Newman, MiniFlux

Working from a visual arts background, Hayley Newman is known for her deconstructive, analytical, and historical approach to performance and to the broader investigation of the history of live art. Her 1998 series *Connotations – Performance Images 1994–1998* is one of the most important (and was one of the earliest) interventions to date in the process through which live art works become historicized. The series involved Newman carefully staging photographic "documents" of performances that supposedly took place over the years 1994 to 1998 with elaborate textual explanations. The first part of the series includes twenty-one photo/text works (in her words) "documenting the fictional career of a performance artist … made as both a celebration and analysis of the performance canon, revisiting performances by artists such as Adrian Piper and Dennis Oppenheim."[1] Newman's relationship to re-enactment is well developed and highly critical.

The photographic components of *Connotations – Performance Images 1994–1998* thus eerily echo photographs documenting classic 1970s live artworks by artists such as Piper (specifically her *Catalysis* series, the documentary photograph of which is mimicked by the photograph documenting Newman's *Crying Glasses* in *Connotations*). The *Connotations* works might seem on first glance to be an earlier example of work motivated by the kind of yearning for authenticity motivating more recent re-enactments. The various individual works in Newman's *Connotations – Performance Images 1994–1998* series, however, have been exhibited widely in contemporary art and performance-related shows with wall text explicitly revealing the performances to have been faked. The installations are thus generally accompanied by a variation on the following text:

> The photographs in the series *Connotations – Performance Images* are constructed images intended to explore the role of documentation in performance. The photographs in the series were staged and performed by myself with most of the images being taken by the photographer Casey Orr over a week in the summer of 1998. The dates, locations,

> photographers and contexts for the performances cited in the text panels are fictional. In all instances the action had to be performed for the photograph but did not take place within the circumstances or places outlined in the supporting text.

In spite of the clarity with which Newman points to the artifice of the images and the series as a whole, the power of our desire for performance photographs to document the "real," to instantiate the having-been-there of the live body, and performance art in general to maintain the status of authenticity to which so many live artists from the 1970s and following aspired has meant that the project is often misread as, in fact, documenting "actual" performances.[2] The series exposes these desires, laying claim, as Aaron Williamson argues, "to having collapsed the traditional nexus between work and documentation by inventing documentation as a work itself."[3]

In the more recent *MiniFlux* installation documented here, Newman returns again to performance history – this time a moment in which performative actions were intimately linked to the manipulation or production of sound, environment, and rough, everyday objects: the Fluxus movement, which flowered in the 1960s in Europe and the USA. Newman's self-proclaimed desire to present a collection of "over 1000 objects used in Fluxus musical scores" was thwarted by the difficulties of managing to reproduce some of the objects called for by the scores, including a full-scale orchestra and live animals. Newman's solution was to "document" these 1000+ objects by molding them in plasticine – producing a fantastic and phantasmagorical large-scale installation of colorful toy-like (and clearly hand-made) objects to be approached as obviously compromised versions of the "originals."

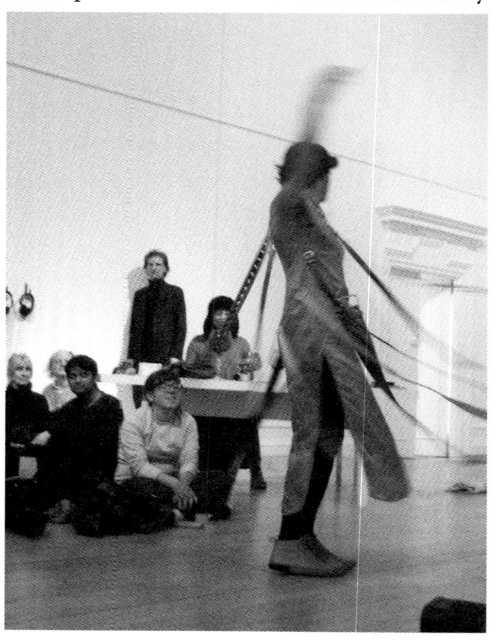

Hayley Newman, "A Concert," performance as part of *MiniFlux* event, 26 November 2005; photograph by Marie Roux, courtesy the artist and Matt's Gallery, London.

Paralleling the insights afforded by her *Connotations* series, Newman's *MiniFlux* reminds us that history can never be fully retrieved. Objects and performative acts from the past can only be recreated in the present in ways that involve new bodies and new ways of interpretation and seeing.

Amelia Jones

Hayley Newman on *MiniFlux*, 2005[4]

MiniFlux: South London Gallery, 10 November 2005–18 December 2005. Installation/ Performance; dimensions variable.[5]

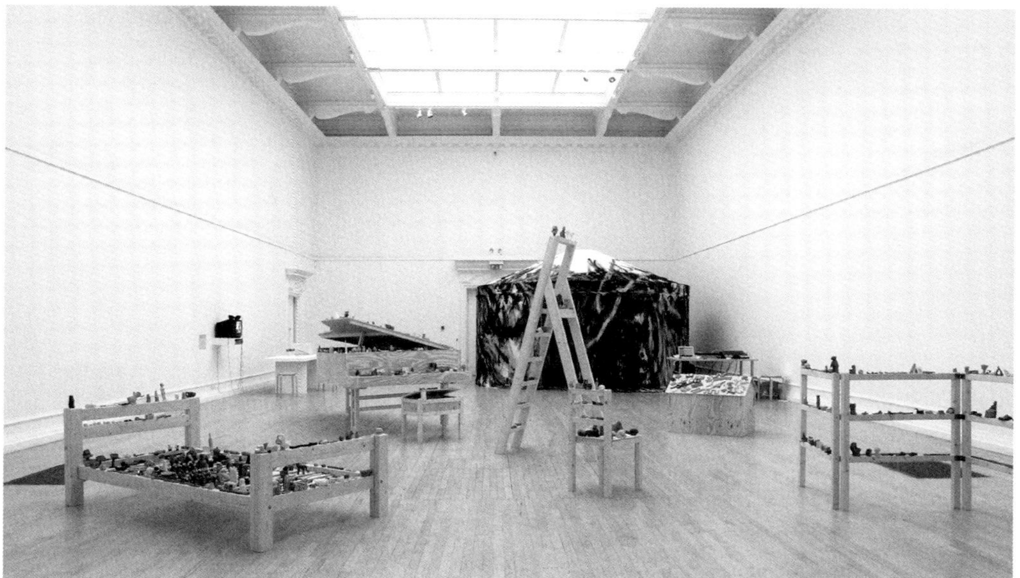

Hayley Newman, *MiniFlux*, overview of installation (in the background is a video installation by Kim Gordon and Jutta Koether, *Reverse Karaoke*, c. 2005); photograph by Marcus Leith, courtesy the artist and Matt's Gallery, London.

For *MiniFlux* I compiled a list of over 1000 objects referenced in Fluxus music scores and then reproduced them in miniature ... The work comes out of a long term interest in Fluxus; their strategies, events, and humor. Part of my motivation to make *MiniFlux* stemmed from my interest in how everyday objects were and continue to be used in performance work.

On 26 November 2005 musicians and artists were invited to devise a series of musical performances in response to the list. The evening was titled *A Concert* and took the form of a conventional concert with works by Anne Bean, The Bohman Brothers, Bruce Gilbert, and Margarita Gluzberg. The performance event *A Concert* suggests the comprehensive nature of the inventory; that is how similar objects continue to be used in contemporary performance work.

Some of the objects on the list:

- Adhesive tape
- Needle
- Quarter
- Rubber tubes
- Drum skin
- Airmail envelope
- Marching band
- Screw
- Red spray-paint
- Hoist
- Vin Rosé
- Change
- Mirrors
- Bowler hat
- Pants
- Megaphone
- Racket
- Cup of coffee
- Plasma tank
- A second item
- Double bass
- Foot switches
- Gravedigger

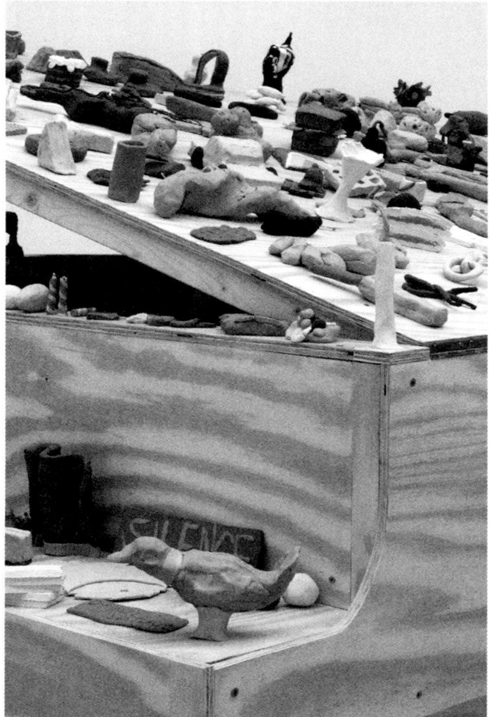

Hayley Newman, *MiniFlux*, detail showing piano and objects; photograph by Marcus Leith, courtesy the artist and Matt's Gallery, London.

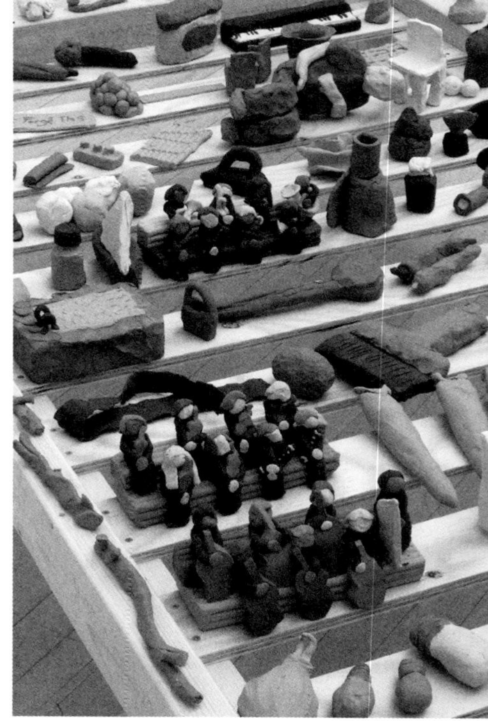

Hayley Newman, *MiniFlux*, detail showing objects; photograph by Marcus Leith, courtesy the artist and Matt's Gallery, London.

Notes

1. Newman, entry for *Connotations – Performance Images 1994–1998*, 1998, on her website. Available at: http://www.hayleynewman.com/artworks/show/15; accessed 27 June 2011. The second *Connotations* (presented at Birmingham's Ikon Gallery in 2002) involved video and "actual performances" addressing the specific cultural history of Birmingham. As Newman has noted to me in an e-mail, the second version also raised questions about the artist's role in gallery programming (running workshops and participating in events) and how this relates to the "desire to address place"; e-mail to the author, 22 July 2008.
2. On this point, see the excellent analysis of *Connotations – Performance Images 1994–1998* by Aaron Williamson, "An Introduction to Hayley Newman's *Performancemania*," *Hayley Newman Performancemania*, London: Matt's Gallery, 2001, especially p. 9, where he cites specific newspaper articles misreading the series in this way.
3. Ibid., p. 9.
4. Edited text taken from: http://www.hayleynewman.co.uk/artworks/show/3; accessed 27 June 2011.
5. *MiniFlux* took place in the context of the exhibition *Her Noise*, South London Gallery, 2005, and was commissioned by Electra Productions, with funding from The Henry Moore Foundation, Elephant Trust, and ACE. For more information on the show see the *Her Noise* catalogue, edited by Lina Džuverović and Anne Hilde Neset, Newcastle upon Tyne: forma, 2005.

Chapter 23

Daniel Joseph Martinez, Call Me Ishmael or The Fully Enlightened Earth Radiates Disaster Triumphant

Daniel Joseph Martinez has been a central figure on the Los Angeles art scene for decades and burst into international consciousness with his now infamous contribution to the 1993 Whitney Biennial, which consisted of admission tags handed out to visitors, each of which was emblazoned with a word or words from the phrase *I can't remember ever wanting to be white*. This piece demanded that the visitor become a walking interlocutor addressing the broad and deep social question of racial positioning – a question with particular urgency in the US context (and with specific valence in the context of the largely white middle class art world).[1] Whether one liked it or not, as a visitor to the show, one became part of an enunciated rejection of whiteness as the implicitly dominant social order.

Making art that constructs interactive, reciprocal situations among spaces, objects, and subjects, provoking political engagements and critical thinking, Martinez has in the past decade deployed various modes of reproducing the human body (primarily photography and robotics) to push this mandate in new directions. In his recent works he specifically makes use of the *fake* to demand particular emotional and intellectual and political responses from visitors. This latter strategy has moving and profound effects when the fake is the "live" body itself (in this case, the body of the artist). Around 2000 Martinez produced a series of photographs of a body (usually his own) being ripped apart, sliced, or otherwise mutilated; the images are entirely believable visually and one doubts them only because they are so excessively violent (in one triptych Martinez rips his own guts out of a bloody slash in his belly).[2] Expanding on this fascination with the fake or simulated, for a recent series titled *The Portrait of the Artist as a Young Man or There is a Splinter in Your Eye*, Martinez photographed himself at historic sites of political violence (at locations such as that of Bloody Sunday in Derry, Northern Ireland; and the Jewish Ghetto in Venice, Italy) wearing a crude mask based on a photograph of his own face. Photographs of photographs of himself being worn by himself, the images beg the fascinating question at the core of representation: is a photograph of a person a substitute for the person in some way? Is it a supplement or a version of the person himself? Given the specificity of Martinez's choice of locations, this series of representational substitutions also functions as an acerbic comment on the way in which particular bodies are made absent (destroyed, violated) through political violence.

As Martinez has commented in relation to his romance with the fake, "my approach is a type of simulation of simulacrum: I can make you believe that a machine has made images that I have made by hand"; he adds, "[d]oes it really matter if it [the work] is real or simulated? Isn't the result the same?"[3] Consisting of a life-sized moving robotic figure based on Martinez himself, *Call Me Ishmael* is a "simulation of a simulacrum" – in Marisa Olson's terms, a photo-realistic animatronic sculpture of Martinez himself.[4] As with the previous projects, it enacts Martinez but through the form of something else, a body that looks like him and is "live" in the sense that it moves in space (seemingly unpredictably) – and yet it is clearly *always already representational*: we do not believe it to "be" Martinez himself, any more than we mistake the mask for Martinez's actual face in *Portrait of the Artist* or other robotic works, such as the 2002 *happiness is overrated* (another life-sized "self-portrait" robot who slices his wrists repeatedly while periodically bursting into laughter).[5]

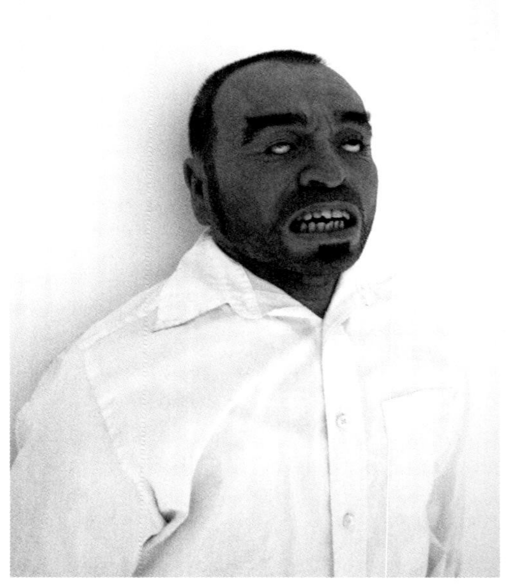
Daniel Joseph Martinez, *Call Me Ishmael*, showing close-up of face; photograph courtesy of the artist and The Project, New York.

With *Call Me Ishmael*, as with other robotic works, Martinez turns the premise of the live act on its head, throwing into question whether a body moving there in front of us can be believed to be any more "real" than a photograph (of a photograph?) of a person on the page. Martinez's robotic "self-portrait" figures are both live and not live at once, both "representational" and "real" (in the sense that they are there before us "acting"), throwing in question, of course, whether the body in motion is ever anything but representational.

Amelia Jones

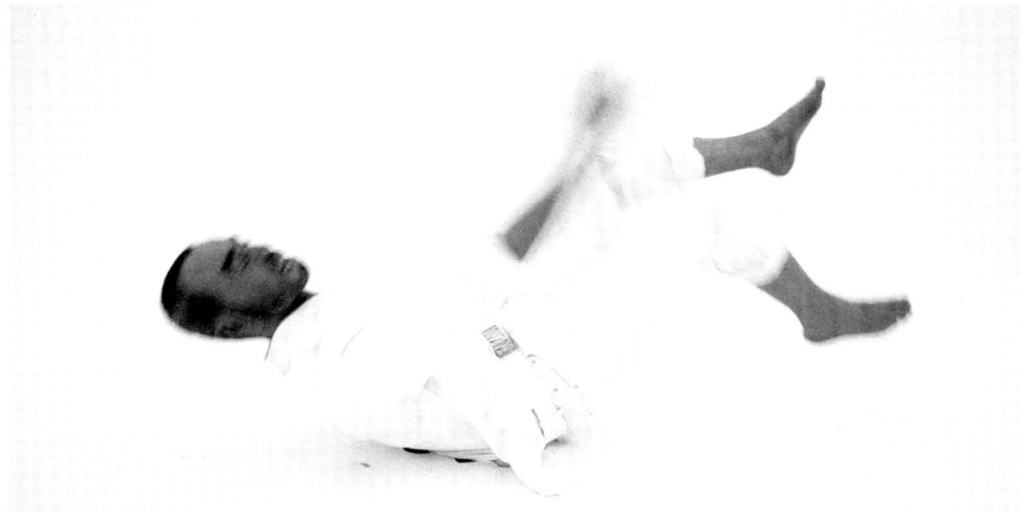

Daniel Joseph Martinez, *Call me Ishmael: The Fully Enlightened Earth Radiates Disaster Triumphant*, installation of robotic figure in motion; silicon over fiber glass skeleton, animated using computer-controlled pneumatics; United States Pavilion, 2006 Cairo Biennial, Cairo Museum of Art. Photograph courtesy of the artist and The Project, New York.

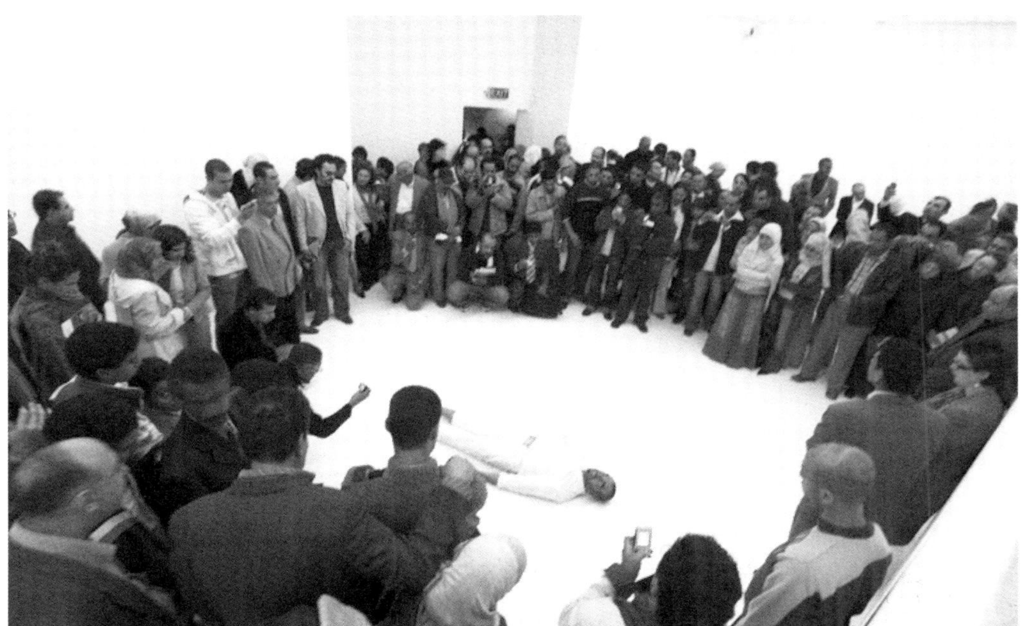

Daniel Joseph Martinez, *Call me Ishmael: The Fully Enlightened Earth Radiates Disaster Triumphant*, showing crowd; photograph courtesy of the artist and The Project, New York.

Notes

1. I examine this project at greater length in Chapter four, "Multiculturalism, Intersectionality, and 'Post-Identity,'" in my book *Seeing Differently: A History and Theory of Identification in the Visual Arts*, New York and London: Routledge, forthcoming.
2. These and other recent works are documented and discussed in the issue of *Camerawork* devoted to Martinez's work; Marisa Olson (ed.), "Daniel Joseph Martinez: Without Anesthesia, or, This Isn't a Nice Neighborhood," *Camerawork*, Fall–Winter 2002, vol. 29, no. 2. Martinez's strategy is entirely compatible with the logic of analogue photography – the photographs are based on his manipulations of bodies, not photoshopped or digitally manipulated.
3. Martinez from an interview with Cuauhtémoc Medina, "A Dialogue on the Sublime and the Fury," and cited in Sharon Bliss, "Needles and Pins," in Olson (ed.), op. cit., pp. 21, 24.
4. Marisa Olson, "I Am Real," in ibid.
5. I write about this piece at greater length in my book *Self/Image: Technology, Representation and the Contemporary Subject*, New York and London: Routledge, 2006, pp. 163–66. See also Eric Wilson's discussion of this piece and *Ishmael* in his essay on Martinez's robotic figures, which traces a history of animatronic figures, "The Sacred Technology of Daniel Joseph Martinez," in Ginger Wolf (ed.), *Interview*, 2008, manuscript version provided by Martinez. Wilson points out that the first part of the title of *Call Me Ishmael* comes from Herbert Melville's 1851 novel *Moby Dick*, a story about a huge, phantasmagorical white whale; the subtitle comes from Theodor Adorno's *The Dialectic of Enlightenment* (1947). He notes that these links bring up a vast range of connotations having to do with exile, wandering, and whiteness as a coding of "a plenitude of all meaning" as well as "a void of no meaning at all" (manuscript page 17).

Chapter 24

Multiple Journeys: A Performance Chronology[1]

Guillermo Gómez-Peña

Journalist: "What do you do when a writer or a curator wishes to deport you from performance art history?"

GGP: "You mean someone like RoseLee Goldberg? ... You write yourself back into it on your own terms. Chicanos taught me that." [...]

Prenatal: [prior to my birth]: I wish to share two facts about my ancestors: like so many Mexican families, they have been migrating to the United States since the mid-1800s and, if you review my family photo album from the late 1800s to the present, they've always had a highly developed sense of theatricality and an unselfconsciously baroque aesthetic. I'm just following suit.

1955: Born Guillermo Lino Liberio Gómez-Peña in the *Sanatorio Español* of Mexico City on 23 September at 11:10 pm. My hairy face and bizarre intensity shocked my father. He was a gallant sportsman and civil engineer who devoted his life to bringing electricity to the Mexican countryside, putting food on our table, and playing *jai alai*. My mother was a fundraiser for social causes, hostess extraordinaire, and the irrefutable nerve center of the family. Now at 86, she is still gorgeous and socially active. [...]

1961–6: I go to elementary school at the *Colegio Vanguardias*, play guitar and *futbol* [soccer], traveling constantly to the Mexican countryside with my family.

1967–72: Jesuits and Marista priests provide my *secundaria* and *preparatoria* education. I make surrealistic drawings and cheesy collages that I hope never to publish. Mexico is fairly stable and the United States a mythical place north of our imagination – a place to vacation, access modernity, and dream of the future. My sister Diana and brother Carlos migrate to Southern California.

1968: The Mexican student movement erupts like magma out of the Popocatépetl volcano. My older brother's and sister's friends are part of it. Some end up in jail; others disappear for good. Tanks surround my neighborhood. The Tlatelolco student massacre takes place five minutes away from my home.

1970: I write *El hombre de la coladera*, my first self-conscious performance, about a young activist who becomes a misanthrope and chooses to live beneath the city, inside the sewage system. The piece is presented in my Catholic high school with spoken word and slides. After the performance, a priest sends me to the school psychiatrist.

1971: The Normal de Maestros student massacre takes place a few blocks away from my home. I write and perform *Smogman*, a sci-fi piece based on one of my first alteric selves, an activist super-hero who fights against pollution in Mexico DF. The third act includes a museum of "things past" with purified water, plants, and taxidermied, extinct animals. These ideas will re-surface in my work years later.

1974: I form my first collective, a group called Anarquía SA. We produce ritual happenings, bad atonal music, and practice "ritual drugs and sex." Gurdjieff, Artaud, Nicanor Parra, and Carlos Castañeda are our textbooks. I join Swami Pranavananda's ashram in Tepoztlan, Mexico.

1974–8: I study *letras*, philology, and linguistics at UNAM (Universidad Nacional Autónoma de México, Mexico City). The campus is an open laboratory of radical politics and student activism. We read about the Latin American literary "boom" and liberation movements, and discover the French symbolists and the Beat poets. Everyday life feels like a Jean-Luc Godard movie.

I engage in a series of involuntary performance art pieces using the streets of Mexico City as a gallery without walls. I still don't have a name for what I do. My main accomplices are my cousin Eugenio and Argentine poet Mari Carmen Copani. My conceptual godfather is Felipe Ehrenberg, bless his tattooed heart, and my guru is Alejandro Jodorowsky.

1978: I receive a scholarship to study at the California Institute of Arts (CalArts) near Los Angeles. I cross the US–Mexico border in search of artistic fresh air and my lost Chicano family. I suddenly become … brown, a "wetback," a "beaner," a "greaser." I do not know the implications of these words. I begin my process of Chicano-ization with the unsolicited help of the LA police.

1978: I walk from Tijuana to CalArts in two and a half days, my head covered with gauze. I wear my father's suit and carry a briefcase containing my passport, talismans, and a diary.

1979–82: At CalArts, conceptualists Douglas Huebler and Jonathan Borofsky take me under their wing. My best friend is painter Ashley Bickerton. I explore the LA performance art scene. I am lucky. I hook up with the *High Performance* magazine crowd, meeting Linda Burnham, Steve Durland, Paul McCarthy, Chris Burden, Bob & Bob, Rachel Rosenthal, and Asco.

1979: *The Loneliness of the Immigrant. Part I.* I decide to spend 24 hours in a public elevator wrapped in batik fabric and rope, a metaphor for painful birth in a new country, a new identity "the Chicano," and a new language, intercultural performance. It's my first performance "documented" by the art world.

1979: *The Loneliness of the Immigrant Part II.* I spend 12 hours lying on the downtown LA streets as a Mexican homeless person. Despite the fact I am wrapped in a serape and surrounded by candles, most people ignore me. I discover that as a Mexican (and a "homeless" person), I am literally invisible to the Anglo-Californian population. Performance is my strategy to become visible.

I am trying to find my place and voice in a new country. One evening, I bring my audience to the edge of Interstate 5 and scream at the cars to "stop and save me from cultural shipwreck." When I am first busted by the Californian police for "looking suspicious" – meaning for being Mexican – my response is to make a performance in which I burn a photo of my mother while screaming at the top of my lungs, "*Madre, hazme regresar a la placenta!*" [Mother, bring me back to the womb!]

1979: *Spanglish Poetry Reading in a Public Bathroom.* For a whole day, I sit on a toilet and read aloud epic poetry describing my journey to the US. My audience is composed strictly of people who want to piss, shit, or wash their hands. Through these types of experiments, I become interested in the notion of performing for "involuntary audiences."

1980: *Mexiphobia: Post-Revolutionary Situations.* I begin to experiment with images of fear of the Mexican other. My friends and I start showing up at various public places dressed as "typical drug dealers," caricatured "illegal aliens," and stylized "banditos," yet we behave in ways that contradict the stereotypes. Once we show up at a restaurant dressed as "typical Latino terrorists." The place empties out within five minutes of our arrival. I wonder what would happen if I were to recreate this performance nowadays.

1980: At CalArts, choreographer Sara-Jo Berman and I form an interdisciplinary arts troupe named Poyesis Genetica (from the Spanish word "pollo," a derogatory term for migrant workers, and the Greek "genesis"). The members are newly arrived immigrant students from Latin America, Europe, the Middle East, and Canada, bound by a shared sense of cultural displacement. Our objective is "to develop syncretic languages capable of articulating our condition of cultural outsiders and aesthetic freaks."[2] Poyesis becomes a revolving door for rebel students.

We develop an artistic strategy of fusing various cultural traditions, utilizing performance as a syntactic thread. We mix indigenous rituals from various parts of the world (or rather our romanticized perception of them) with installation and video art, combining sexual and political imagery, personal pathos, and pop culture. We perform in art spaces and theaters as well as in the street, and often use live animals on stage. We also experiment with "altered states of consciousness" induced by fasting, alcohol, or lack of sleep. Though extremely important in our development as artists, these performances are more interesting to us than to our poor audiences.

1982: I graduate from CalArts and spend six months touring Europe with Sara-Jo and a few Poyesis members. It's our first tour ever. We begin performing in small theaters and artist's lofts, and end up working the streets. I lose my virginity as a performance artist. At the end of the tour, I am hypoglycemic, hungry, and weighing just 60 kilos. I write a book titled *The Misadventures of Mr Misterio and Salome*. The manuscript gets lost. Only a few performance poems survive.

The first Mexican financial crack occurs and our family's savings evaporate. My father advises me not to return to Mexico. "Stay in Southern California and wait for better times," he says. [...] I am still waiting ...

1983: Poyesis Genetica relocates to the Tijuana–San Diego border region, where we find an ideal terrain to explore intercultural relations and become more overtly political. Sara-Jo and I reconstitute the troupe with local artists. We perform on both sides of the border as political praxis, making an average of $50 per performance, enough to buy props, tacos, and an occasional drink.

One day I receive a phone call in San Diego: my beloved cousin Alfonso, who grew up with me, has been murdered in Mexico City, stabbed twenty-two times. The murderer, a bodyguard of pop celebrity Enrique Guzman, spends only one month in jail.

1983: I run the cultural section of *La Prensa San Diego*. I also work as a correspondent for *La Opinión* and *High Performance Magazine*. Journalist Marco Vinicio Gonzalez and I begin to publish the border arts magazine *La Línea Quebrada/The Broken Line*, connected to its Mexico City twin publication *La Regla Rota/The Broken Rule*.

1984–90: With visual, performance, and conceptual artists, we form BAW/TAF (Border Arts Workshop), a bi-national arts collective involving Chicano, Mexican, and Anglo artists. Our objective is to explore US–Mexico relations and border issues using performance, installation art, video, and experimental poetry. We proclaim the border region "a laboratory for social and aesthetic experimentation," and propose "the artist as a social thinker and bi-national diplomat." Similar activist groups are forming in other parts of the country, including the Guerrilla Girls, Group Material, ACT UP, and the Los Angeles Poverty Department. Performance, political activism, and community concerns are completely intertwined in the spirit of the times.

1985: BAW/TAF's strictly artistic activities help to protect our backs and legitimize our more activist work. In addition to art shows, publications, radio programs, and town meetings, we organize performance events right on the borderline, where the US meets Mexico in the Pacific, literally performing for audiences in both countries. When the border patrol gets too close, we cross to the Mexican side. During certain performances, we invite our audiences to cross "illegally" to the other side. We exchange food and art "illegally," caress and kiss "illegally" across the border fence, and confront the border patrol in character. We are protected by the presence of journalist friends and video cameras. The political implications of the site and the symbolic weight of these actions garner immediate attention from the international media. These are the origins of the border arts movement.

1985: I begin *The Velvet Hall of Fame*, a long-term collaboration with traditional velvet tourist painters from Tijuana who reinterpret my performance characters. The process is very matter of fact; the more I pay, the better the painting is, period. They don't care about reviews or openings, but they get a kick out of my madness. My "conceptual velvet art" project will last for a decade, during which I get to exhibit these paintings at the Walker Art Center, the Detroit Institute of Arts, the Corcoran Gallery, and MACBA (Barcelona). When I see these paintings hanging within walking distance of a Gauguin or a David Salle, I somehow feel historically vindicated. I love to cross the border between "high" and "low" art.

1985: Within twenty-four hours, two major earthquakes destroy entire sections of Mexico City, killing more than 100,000 people. Poet Ruben Medina and I return immediately. Most artists and intellectuals participate in the rescue efforts. My nephews, neighbors, and I form a humble brigade. We carry corpses from a police station to the morgue. The city will never be the same. A powerful civic society and a new culture emerge out of the debris. *Superbarrio*, *Rock en Español*, and the *nuevo periodismo* and radical cartoon movement are born. Felipe Ehrenberg declares the reconstruction of the barrio of Tepito his ultimate art project.

1986: I become interested in the interface between performance and photography. I work with artist/theorist Emily Hicks on a series of performances titled *Documented/Undocumented*, playing on the double meaning of the terms vis-à-vis immigration status and as an art piece. The performances are staged for the camera and documented in photojournalistic style. My interest in what I term "photo-performance" will continue until the present day.

1987: My collaborators and I stage several "performance pilgrimages" in different border cities. In Tijuana–Niagara, Emily and I spend a month working along the US/Canadian border between Ontario and New York State, using Art Park as a base of operations. We travel in a mobile temple created from pseudo-indigenous souvenirs and religious kitsch purchased in Tijuana and Niagara Falls. We carry out fifteen "performance actions" including the auctioning of border art, spiritual consultation "for tourists," begging for money in costume, photo sessions with "authentic border shamans and witches," and broadcasting bilingual poetry with a huge megaphone from one shore of the Niagara River to the other.

That same year several Tijuana performance artists and I gather at the municipal cemetery of Tijuana and attempt to cross the US–Mexico border checkpoint in costume. From 1987 to 1990 I attempt several times to cross the border in costume. I am rejected three times, and those rejected personas never find their way into my performances.

1988: Emily and I stage our "performance wedding" right on the Tijuana–San Diego borderline, with poets and musicians performing on both sides, and family and friends crossing "illegally" into each other's countries during the ceremony. The media labels the event "a masterpiece of symbolic politics." Emily is seven months pregnant.

My only son Guillermo Emiliano is born in San Diego. A few months later, my beloved father dies in Mexico City. Both events accelerate my process of Chicano-ization. I no longer can afford to think that one day I will return to Mexico (my place in the Chicano Olympus will continue to be contested by Chicano essentialists until the mid-1990s). I wear my father's clothes for one year. I inherit my family's oldest house, which soon becomes "Chicano Central" in Mexico City, a gathering place and party den for *chilango* and Chicano artists and writers.

1988: The performance monologue movement is officially born. Many performance artists including Tim Miller, Karen Finley, Eric Bogosian, Spalding Gray, and myself feel that performance has become so artificial and technically complex that we need to go back to basics and recapture the power of the spoken word. The result is a low-tech, language-based type of performance that literally fits in a suitcase. […] We all share an interest in the transformative power of the live word and a desire to explore the flaming intersection of personal identity and social issues.

1988–9: My main contribution to the performance monologue movement is *Border Brujo*, a spoken word monologue dealing with border identity. The script is written in English, Spanish, Spanglish, gringoñol, and various made up "robo-languages." My portable altar (which functions as set design) as well as my hand-made costumes are composed of "pseudo-ethnic" objects, tourist tchotchkes, and cheap religious souvenirs.

With *Border Brujo* I become a migrant performance artist, spending two years on the road, going from city to city, from country to country and back, reproducing the migratory patterns of the Mexican Diaspora. As I travel I incorporate new texts, props, and costumes into the piece. The project is documented in two videos by film-maker Isaac Artenstein. The Brujo and I end up back at the US–Mexico border in late 1989 where I bury his costume and props and stage his performance funeral. I receive both a New York "Bessie award" and the "prix de la parole" from the International Theater Festival of the Americas (Montreal). I am suddenly propelled into the center of the art world, and my personal life becomes extremely complicated.

1989: A group of artists including Linda Burnham, Tim Miller, Steve Durland, Susan Dakin, and myself jumpstart Highways Performance Space in Santa Monica. I begin ongoing collaborations with Tim Miller, Elia Arce, Keith Antar-Mason, and Rubén Martínez. The LA art scene is imbued with a utopian spirit of collaboration and poly-amorous hedonism.

Glasnost and Perestroika spread like wild fire throughout the Soviet bloc. The right perceives this phenomenon as the defeat of socialism. I want to see for myself. I travel to Russia with a bi-national human rights commission, performing my art as a form of radical diplomacy.

1990: The US experiences yet another seasonal "Latino boom," and border art becomes fashionable. The original BAW is invited to the Venice Biennale, after which we feel it's time to dismantle the group to avoid becoming a parody of ourselves, "the Grateful Dead of border art." But as so often happens, the only Anglo male in the group copyrights the name and appropriates the project, turning it into an art maquiladora.

It's time for me to search for a new place from which to speak. I begin a series of collaborations with writer and artist Coco Fusco, the first a multimedia installation titled *Norte/Sur*. Nola Mariano becomes my long-term manager, art bodyguard, and macabre accomplice.

1991: I move to New York to live with Coco and to work on the first part of my trilogy *The Re-Discovery of America by the Warrior for Gringostroika* at the Brooklyn Academy of Music's Next Wave Festival. One day, during rehearsal, I get the magical phone call announcing that I am a "MacArthur Genius." Two months later, my ex-wife sues me, taking half of my fellowship in court, and some of the original members of BAW/TAF suggest that I split the other half amongst the group. I ask myself: "Is this my true birth ritual into the American art world?"

1992: Artists such as Fred Wilson, Adrian Piper, James Luna, and Jimmy Durham begin to interrogate the way museums represent cultural otherness and start a dialogue with radical anthropologists.

I begin to experiment with the colonial format of the "living diorama." My collaborators and I create interactive "living museums" that parody various colonial practices of representation including the ethnographic tableau vivant, the Indian Trading Post, the border curio shop, the porn window display, and their contemporary equivalents. These performance/installations function both as a bizarre set design for a contemporary enactment of "cultural pathologies," and as a ceremonial space for people to reflect upon their attitudes toward other cultures.

1992–3: During the heated debates surrounding the Columbus quincentenary, Coco Fusco and I decide to remind the United States and Europe of "the other history of intercultural performance," the sinister human exhibits, and pseudo-ethnographic spectacles that were so popular in Europe from the seventeenth century until the early twentieth-century. [...]

In *The Guatinaui World Tour*, Coco and I live for three-day periods inside a gilded cage as "undiscovered Amerindians" from the (fictional) island of Guatinau (Anglicization of "what now") in the Gulf of Mexico. I am dressed as an Aztec wrestler from Las Vegas and Coco as a taina straight out of Gilligan's Island. We are hand fed by fake museum docents and taken to public bathrooms on leashes. Taxonomic plates describing our costumes and physical characteristics are placed next to the cage. We tour the US, Europe, Australia, and Argentina. Sadly, over 40 per cent of our audiences believe the exhibit is real yet do nothing about it. [...] The tour is chronicled in the film *The Couple in the Cage* (1993).

1992–3: Coco and I tour *New World (B)order*, a sci-fi piece based on the following meta-fiction: border culture and hybrid identities become official culture as Anglo-Americans become a minority culture. We begin to practice "reverse segregation" of our audiences as they enter the art space, with members of "minorities," immigrants, and bilingual audience members entering the space first. The idea is to assume a fictional center and force monolingual/monocultural Americans to feel like foreigners and "minorities" in their own country, even if only for an hour or two. Coco abandons the project in the middle of the tour and Roberto Sifuentes replaces her. To continue the tour we are forced to reconstitute the entire performance in less than a week. It somehow works. Roberto remains as my main collaborator until this day.

1993: Roberto and I become interested in Spanglish pirate radio. We stage our first pirate radio project in a performance festival in Hull (UK). With a low-tech radio transmitter, we broadcast from the top of a ten-story high building. Local radio pirates explain to us that it will take twenty minutes for the police to locate the source of our transmission and get to the site. As the police are circling the building, Roberto and I escape through the back door.

1993: The backlash era begins as multiculturalism gets a bad rap. I move back to LA and reconnect with the Highways performance scene. The LA earthquake transforms the city into a compassionate place. We see racial, social, and generational borders break down in front of our eyes as people help each other and speak with each other as never before. Sadly, this only lasts for a few months.

1993: I start a long-term collaboration with Native American artist James Luna. In *The Shame-Man Meets El Mexi-can't at the Smithsonian Hotel and Country Club*, Luna and I share a diorama space at the Museum of Natural History in Washington DC. I sit on a toilet dressed as a mariachi in a straightjacket with a sign around my neck announcing, "There used to be a Mexican inside this body." I unsuccessfully attempt to get rid of my straightjacket while James paces back and forth, changing identities. At times he is an "Indian shoe-shiner," at other moments he becomes a "diabetic Indian" shooting insulin directly into his stomach. He then transforms into a janitor of color (like most janitors in US museums) and vacuums the diorama floor. Hundreds of visitors gather in front of us. They are sad and perplexed. Next to us, the "real" Indian dioramas speak of a mute world outside of history and social crises. Next to us, they appear much less "authentic."

While rehearsing the second part of our project (to take place at the Natural History Museum Auditorium), James lights up some sage. The security guards phone the DC police and we get busted in the dressing room for "smoking pot." Furious with such a ludicrous claim, curator Aleta Ringlero calls museum administration demanding an apology on our behalf. For James and me, such a situation is just a good anecdote. As James put it, "simply one more day in the life of an Indian and a Chicano." We re-enact the bust in a series of photos.

1994: NAFTA comes into effect. The Zapatista insurrection takes the world by surprise. Organized crime makes its home in Mexico. To exorcise my own fear of losing the streets of Mexico City to the new culture of fear, I engage in a series of street performances in downtown Mexico City.

Grandma Carmen, the moral center of my family, dies in our Mexico City home. My relatives and I surround Grandma's bed as her soul tenderly leaves her body.

1994: Roberto Sifuentes and I crucify ourselves for three hours on 16-foot high crosses at Rodeo Beach, in front of San Francisco's Golden Gate Bridge. The piece is designed to protest the xenophobic immigration politics of California governor Pete Wilson. Inspired by the biblical myth of Dimas and Gestas, the two petty thieves crucified next to Jesus, Roberto and I decide to dress as "the two contemporary public enemies of California" [...] Using a flyer, we ask our audience "to free us from our martyrdom as a gesture of political commitment," but we miscalculate. Paralyzed by the melancholy of the image, it takes audience members over three hours to figure out how to get us down without a ladder. By then, my right shoulder has become dislocated and Roberto has passed out. The media picks up photographs of the Cruci-fiction Project and the piece becomes international news.

1994: Greywolf Press publishes my first book, *Warrior for Gringostroika*, a collection of writings and photographs from 1979 to 1992. It's my "border art period." With this book, my work slowly begins to be embraced by academia.

1994: Roberto and I create the interactive pirate television project *Naftaztec TV* in collaboration with Adriane Jennik and Branda Miller (from the iEar Studio at Rensselaer Polytechnic). This simulacrum of a pirate TV intervention is broadcast to hundreds of cable television stations across the country, as well as over computer networks via early broadband technology. The content is a strange blend of radical politics, autobiographical material, and a parody of traditional TV formats gone bananas. [...]

1994: Colombian ballerina-turned-radical performance artist Michelle Ceballos joins our troupe.

1994–ongoing: My colleagues and I begin to take our personas out of the museum or theater and into the streets, often crashing politically charged sites in costume. […] Though these types of interventions are central to our performance praxis, they often go unnoticed by critics and art historians who concentrate almost exclusively on work that takes place within the confines of the art world, which is why I have written extensively about these adventures in my books.

1994–6: Roberto and I tour *Temple of Confessions*, a performance/installation combining the format of the ethnographic diorama with that of the religious dioramas found in colonial Mexican churches. For three-day periods, we exhibit ourselves inside Plexiglas boxes as "end-of-the-century saints." Those visitors who wish to "confess" their intercultural fears and desires to us have three options: they can either confess into microphones placed on kneelers in front of the Plexiglas boxes (their voices are then recorded and altered in post production to ensure their anonymity), or if they are shy, they can write their confessions on a card and deposit them in an urn. If they are extremely shy, they can call an 800 number.

The "confessions" are quite emotional and intimate. They range from confessions of extreme violence and racism toward Mexicans and other people of color to expressions of incommensurable tenderness and solidarity with us, or with our perceived cause. […]

By the end of the third day, we leave the Plexiglas boxes and are replaced by human-sized wax effigies. […] The project is documented in a PBS documentary, a radio documentary for NPR, and a book (Power House, NY), with the same title. The last performance of the tour takes place at the Corcoran Gallery of Art in Washington DC.

1995: I move to San Francisco and begin the long-term project of tattooing my torso and arms. Nola Mariano and I found *La Pocha Nostra*. The objective is to create a loose interdisciplinary association of rebel artists interested in collaboration. Inspired by zapatismo, our collaborative model of concentric and overlapping circles functions both as an act of civic diplomacy and as a means to create ephemeral communities of like-minded artists. We are more of a conceptual laboratory than a company, a strategic gathering of politicized artists thinking together, exchanging ideas and aspirations.

We begin a fruitful bi-national exchange project with Mexican performance artists titled *Terreno Peligroso/Danger Zone*. It's a good time for Mexican and Chicano artists to collaborate. We create a Free Art Agreement, an ongoing exchange of ideas and artwork, and begin to collaborate across the border.

1995: I begin my long-term association with the National Public Radio program, *All Things Considered*. I write and record a monthly commentary from the position of a performance artist. I suddenly have a national voice in a society in which mainstream media covers artists either as celebrities, human-interest stories, or social monsters but rarely as intellectuals.

1995–7: Roberto and I tour *Borderama*, a proscenium piece that subverts and parodies pop cultural formats such as the talk show, the self-realization seminar, a hypnotist lounge act, a French anthropologist's lecture, and an ethnic fashion show [...]At the end of the piece, Roberto and I auction ourselves as "sexy, AIDS-free Third World performance artists."

1996: Like many Chicano artists at the time, Roberto and I visit the zapatista area. We travel through various military checkpoints posing as "eco-tourists."

1996: City Lights publishes my next book, *New World Border*, a collection of writings and photos from 1992 to 1997. In this book, perhaps my most experimental, I develop my thesis of hybridity and my critique of global culture. The whole book reads like a hypertextual performance script. It receives the American Book Award. Luis Valdez forgives my aesthetic sins. That same year, I begin a three-year collaboration with Nuyorrican maestro Miguel Algarin.

1996: I become interested in the politics of new technologies. I write extensively about "racism in the net" and develop the concept of "poetic and imaginary (or rather useless) technologies," meaning technologies with strictly aesthetic or ritual purposes. My colleagues and I begin to construct "Chicano cyborgs" with lowrider prosthetics and braces. The basic idea is: if we don't have access to this technology, we have to imagine it.

1997: The art world begins to talk about "relational aesthetics." Roberto, radical choreographer Sara Shelton Mann from the dance troupe Contraband, and I jumpstart a three-year project titled *The Mexterminator*. The idea is to use the Internet as a tool of "reverse anthropology" to research America's psyche regarding Anglo/Latino relations, then to develop an ever-evolving repertoire of performance personae based on this research. For this purpose, we develop "confessional" websites asking individuals to suggest how we should dress as Mexicans and Chicanos, and what kind of performance actions and social rituals we should engage in.

The Internet confessions are much more explicit than those gathered during live performances such as *Temple of Confessions*. [...] As performance artists, we embody this information and reinterpret it for a live audience, thus refracting fetishized constructs of identity through the spectacle of our artificially constructed identities on display. A gorgeous photo-portfolio by Mexican photographer Eugenio Castro is made out of the Mexterminator personae. [...]

1997–ongoing: Chicana writer Sandra Cisneros invites the Latino MacArthur fellows to form "the MacArturos" or "MacCabrones." Part ombudsmen and part cultural instigators, the group meets once a year in a different city with a sizeable Latino community in turmoil. These gatherings are designed as informal think tanks and a means to insert a Latino perspective into current national debates. We strategically use our name to empower local communities, generate public dialogue, and confront local authorities. [...]

1998: I team with producer Michael Milenski and theater director David Schweizer to create a Chicano-ized version of *The Indian Queen*, a seventeenth century opera by composer Henry Purcell and poet John Dryden. In collaboration with Elaine Katzenberger, I rewrite the original script in Spanglish. In our version the Indian Queen is a fallen Hollywood starlet and her throne is a lowrider car shaped as a red stiletto.

1998: Enrique Chagoya, Felicia Rice, and I publish a book art piece, *Codex Espangliensis*, first as a limited edition of fifty for collectors (Moving Parts Press), and then in paperback form (City Lights).

1998: La Pocha tours *Borderscape 2000*. Described by critics as a "high-tech Aztec Spanglish lounge operetta," the performance critiques the corporate appropration of multiculturalism, attempting to reintroduce the political discourse absent since the backlash against mulitculturalism began, when audiences grew tired of "political" art. One image lingers in my mind: a stylized gang member clubbing a chicken to the tune of "Hotel California." We cross the Political Correctness border. The performance is heavily criticized by theorists for contributing to the fetishization of extreme Latino imagery. It's clear to La Pocha that we have reached a deadend and that we need to open a new door.

1998: I become obsessed with trying to understand X-treme pop culture. What ten years ago was considered fringe "subculture" is now mere pop. The insatiable mass of the so-called "mainstream" has finally devoured all "margins," and the more dangerous, thorny, and exotic these margins, the better. In fact, *stricto sensu*, we can say that there are no margins left. "Alternative" thought, fringe "subcultures," and so-called radical behavior, as we knew them, have actually become the mainstream. Stylized racism and sexism are now daily spectacle. This poses all kinds of questions for us: if we choose to mimic or parody the strategies of the mainstream bizarre in order to develop new audiences and explore the *zeitgeist* of our times, what certainty do we have that our high definition reflection won't devour us from inside out and turn us into the very stylized freaks we are attempting to deconstruct or parody? And if we are interested in performing for non-specialized audiences, what certainty do we have that these audiences won't misinterpret our "radical" actions as merely spectacles of stylized radicalism? We risk these possible misinterpretations by embodying these personae in live performance and find that each context delivers different reactions, which keeps us developing new strategies to reach these complex audiences.

1998–9: We gradually begin to surrender our will to the audience, allowing them to shape the content of our work by manipulating us in tableaux and joining us in performing composite identities dictated by the fears and desires of museum visitors. *El Mexterminator* project becomes even more participatory, encouraging audience members to interact with us in various modes. They can touch us, smell us, hand feed us. They can spray paint our bodies, point fake weapons at us, braid our hair, change our make-up, put different wigs and headdresses on us, using the performers as life-sized paper dolls. They put dog leashes on us, engaging in consensual power games. [...]

1999: I marry gorgeous Colombian curator and writer Carolina Ponce de León. Our loft in San Francisco becomes an informal roadside museum, salon, and hostel for Mexican, Colombian, US, and European artists who pass through. A local TV station does a reportage on the house calling it "the Smithsonian of the barrio."

1999: Film-maker Gustavo Vazquez and I create *The Great Mojado Invasion*, a mock documentary that presents an ironic twenty-first century reversal of US–Mexican relations, as "dastardly mustachioed bandits" reconquer the United States and impose their own language and culture upon Anglo-Americans.

1999: There is major internal turmoil in La Pocha Nostra. Roberto Sifuentes and Sara Shelton Mann step out for personal reasons, while Juan Ybarra and Michele Ceballos join on a more permanent basis. All projects must be reconfigured overnight.

1999–2002: The new Pocha Nostra troupe tours *The Living Museum of Fetishized Identities* internationally. The next step in our performance research is to develop large-scale interactive performance/installations that function as "intelligent raves and art expos of Western apocalypse." Every "living museum" is site-specific and involves a different group of local artists [...] In these intoxicating environments, we exhibit ourselves on platforms as intricately decorated "ethno-cyborgs" and "artificial savages" for three to five hours a day. The structure is open and non-coercive, allowing the audience to walk around the dioramas designing their own journey. They can stay for as long as they wish, come in and out of the space, or return later on, fully participating in our performance games or keeping to the sidelines as voyeurs. [...]

2000: While touring Brazil I catch a mysterious parasite and experience a total "liver crash." My recovery takes eight months. The doctors forbid me to perform and rehearse. My mother and Carolina take care of me. During this time I write *Califas 2000* and *Brownout*, two of my darkest and most personal performance scripts ever. Also during my recovery, my new book comes out. *Dangerous Border Crossers: The Artist Talks Back* (Routledge) is a collection of writings and photos from 1997 to 2000.

2001: I begin touring my solo performance *Brownout*, using Spanglish, acid Chicano humor, and hybrid literary genres as subversive strategies. The script intertwines two discourses. One is a poetic/political account of the times. A parallel discourse recounts my inner hell during the recovery from my liver crash. I often broadcast live from the theater to a local radio station.

Gustavo and I re-edit *The Great Mojado 2* with newfound footage.

2001: The US experiences on its own soil its worst terrorist attack. The neo-cons in power rapidly transform the country into a closed society ruled by paranoid nationalism and fear. An unprecedented era of censorship for artists and intellectuals begins. This climate forces La Pocha to spend more than half of the year outside the country, becoming Chicano expatriates abroad. We begin to compare notes with Arab and Persian artists based in the United States and the United Kingdom regarding the demonization of the brown body.

2002: In response to the challenges of 9/11 we create Re:group, a San Francisco-based performance laboratory dedicated "to re-conquer the artistic freedoms being taken away by the Bush administration." The group lasts two years. A documentary of Re:group is commissioned by PBS and later on censored by them. Their version of Re:group is very light. With the original footage, we edit our own version.

I publish my first book entirely in Spanish titled *El Mexterminator: La antropología inversa de un performero post-mexicano* (Editorial Oceano, Mexico City).

2002–4: La Pocha begins to incorporate workshops as part of every project we tour. It's like a nomadic performance workshop. We resume the exploration of ceding our will to the audience, begun in *El Mexterminator* project, with a performance titled *Ethno-techno* or *Ex-Centris* in which we completely reverse the gaze and step out of our dioramas. We create tableaux vivants with audience members, manipulating their body positions and decorating them with costumes and props. We then invite them to create their own imagery. We call this experiment "performance karaoke." It's our response to the extreme culture of mindless audience participation and role-playing created by talk shows and reality TV.

2003: La Pocha performs *Ex-Centris* at Tate Modern, a humongous coup for us brokered by performance curator Lois Keidan. A few months later, the troupe is confronted with harsh reality as Juan Ybarra steps out due to serious health issues and Michelle Ceballo's father is kidnapped in Colombia. Roberto Sifuentes returns; Violeta Luna becomes a full-time collaborator, and Emiko R. Lewis joins in. All our upcoming presenters are perplexed by the abrupt changes. It takes half a year for La Pocha to settle into the new troupe.

2004: I become interested in the search for a radical spirituality that can emerge from living against the backdrop of war and censorship. Emiko and I begin workshopping *Mapa/Corpo* as a response to the invasion of Iraq. The performance/installation is a poetic, interactive ritual that explores neo-colonization/de-colonization through "political acupuncture" and the re-enactment of the post-9/11 "body politic." It's clearly an anti-war performance and for the first two years, we are only able to present it in Latin America, Europe, and Canada. Only after mid-2005 do US presenters dare to book it.

Michelle Ceballos' passport gets confiscated as we are trying to catch a plane for Argentina for a project titled *Tucuman-Chicano*. It will take three years for Michelle to recover it.

2004–ongoing: I begin a long-term project with Spanish curator Orlando Britto-Jinorio, a series of "photo-performance" portfolios created specifically for the camera. The initial portfolios are shot in Mexico City, San Francisco, Madrid, and the Canary Islands. It is the first time in my life that I make art-objects strictly for the gallery. My hope is that they function as a prosthetic extension of my live performances.

2005: As I approach my fiftieth birthday, my then 83-year-old mother and I collaborate in a performance ritual "to prepare me for the 2nd part of my life." She tenderly washes my body in an old-fashion bathtub, then dries me with a towel and dresses me up with my father's clothes. The site is the garden of her Mexico City home. The audience is composed of forty relatives and neighbors who were alive and around during my birthday, including my nanny and first friends ever. The next morning my family takes me to the airport and sends me to the next stop in my tour. A film of the ritual bath by filmmaker Gustavo Vazquez is in the works.

2005: I publish *Ethno-Techno: Writings in Performance, Activism and Pedagogy* (Routledge), a collection of writings from 2000 to 2005. Despite the fact that it may be my best book to date, the price of the book is so high that it does not have the distribution I expect. My literary heart is broken.

2005: We begin to conduct a yearly Pocha Nostra Summer School of radical performance art in the state of Oaxaca in Mexico. Artists come from all over the world to collaborate with indigenous Oaxacans working in experimental art forms. We offer two seven-day intensive workshops on "the human body as a site for creation, reinvention, memory and activism." The first workshop is for young artists, and the second for established artists, culminating in a public performance at MACO [Museum of Contemporary Art of Oaxaca]. The Pocha Summer School becomes an amazing artistic and anthropological experiment in how artists from three generations and many countries, from every imaginable artistic, ethnic, and subcultural background begin to negotiate common ground. Performance becomes the connective tissue and *lingua franca* for our temporary "globcal" (local/international) community of rebel artists.

2005–7: Violeta Luna, Roberto Sifuentes, Gabriela Salgado, and I workshop and tour *Mapa/Corpo 2: Interactive Rituals for the New Millennium*. Violeta's nude body lies on a surgical table covered by the flag of the United Nations. Above the body, an acupuncturist dressed in a lab coat prepares for surgery, laying out forty needles. A small flag is attached to the tip of each needle, each representing a nation of the "coalition forces." As I deliver a multilingual poem dressed in my *chaman travesti* persona, the acupuncturist peels the UN flag from Violeta's body, working from the feet up, exposing her. The acupuncturist methodically inserts the forty needles into the body/map, leaving the audience to ponder the after-image of a "colonized" female body/world. I ask the audience to "de-colonize the Mapa/Corpo" by carefully removing the flags with the assistance of the acupuncturist. [...] Parallel to this, at a second station, a curator ritually shaves and washes the body of Sifuentes as if preparing it for burial, representing the brown body of "the universal immigrant." [...] Different versions of *Mapa/Corpo 2* are performed in fifteen different countries. Sometimes Violeta is replaced by Colombian performance artist Maria Estrada. [...]

2006: I premiere a new solo performance titled *The Mexorcist: America's Most Wanted Inner Demon*. Shifting between languages and performance personae, I reflect on the post-9/11 condition, the "War on Terror," the new anti-immigration hysteria, and their impact on our notions of identity, community, nationality, and activist politics. Americans of all ages and ethnicities are finally fed up with the war and with the Bush administration.

2006: *Bitacora del Cruce* is published by *El Fondo de Cultura Economica* (Mexico City). The book contains a selection of my border diaries and performance texts from 1970 up to the present. It starts in 1970 Mexico City (in Spanish) and as I move north, the text slowly incorporates more Spanglish. The last chapters are in English and "robo-esperanto." It is the first time a book of this multilingual nature has ever been published by a major Mexican publishing house. [...]

2006: My Chihuahua son "Babalu" is born in Northern California. He will soon become a regular troublemaker on YouTube. His series are titled "The Chihuahua diaries."

2007: I complete the first part of my tattoo project: my torso and arms are all connected in a sort of total "skin mural." I work as "image consultant" and "performance adviser" for the campaign of Krissy Keiffer, a San Francisco activist lesbian dancer who runs for Congress under the Green Party ticket. My job is to produce provocative photo-portfolios for the media and suggest performative strategies for her campaign. The Green party campaign officers are weirded out by my suggestions.

2007: Due to the militarization of Oaxaca, The Museum of Contemporary Art in Tucson invites La Pocha Summer School to relocate temporarily to Arizona. They provide us with a huge warehouse for the month of August where we hold workshops for artists from eight different countries as well as indigenous Arizonians. We continue to nurture multinational communities of rebel artists that ignore the existence of borders.

2007–ongoing: James Luna and I reconnect to begin working on *La Nostalgia*, last in the series *The Shame-Man Meets El Mexican't*. The project researches the symbolic and iconographic dimensions of nostalgia both in the Native "reservation" and the Chicano "barrio," through a series of live performances and photo shoots. We launch it with two performances: first, we stage our own ritual death inside coffins in a piece titled *The Shame-Man Meets El Mexican't at a Funeral Parlor* and then we engage in a poetic dialogue while Luna cooks an Indian stew and I play roulette.

2007: Video Data Bank (Chicago) publishes *Border Clásicos*, a collection of my collaborative video artworks from 1988 to the present. The "conceptual box" contains four DVDs with twelve video art pieces and an accompanying catalogue with critical writings by Amelia Jones, Richard Schechner, Carol Becker, and others. The goal is to use this box as a teaching tool in multiple university departments.

2007–8: We jumpstart *El Corazon de la Misión*, a unique bus tour guiding the audience through history, vernacular anthropology, and social reality into the heart of the Mission District of San Francisco, a place that spends a lot of energy dreaming of a better future. The passengers of this performance tour ride the legendary "Mexican bus," and are invited to participate in a processional as if they, too, were characters on a parade float. They witness "the creative neighborhood" and the city as a bohemian theme park, using the windows of an immigrant bus as a vantage point to watch the streets while eavesdropping on my mind as a pre-recorded tour guide and Violeta Luna performs live. [...]

2007: La Pocha premieres *The New Barbarian Collection* commissioned by Arnolfini on the two hundredth anniversary of the abolition of slavery in the UK. Working with an international troupe of fifteen performance artists and a fashion designer, we appropriate the format of "an X-treme fashion show," engaging the audience with a variety of fashion-inspired stylized performance personas stemming from problematic media representations of foreigners, immigrants, and social eccentrics, as both enemies of the state and sexy pop-cultural rebels. [...] What is actually being "sold" are a new designer hybrid identity and the human being as a product. The piece ends with the disturbing auction of Abu Ghraib-like imagery and couture.

2008: La Pocha premieres *Divino Corpo* at the New Moves Festival in Glasgow, Scotland. As part of our ongoing *Mapa/Corpo* series, this new work continues to examine the brown body as a site for radical spirituality, memory, penance, activism, and corporeal reinvention. We pose as living saints and Madonnas of unpopular causes (border crossers, undocumented migrants, sex workers, bohemians, the infirm and the displaced invisible others). [...] Our goal is to invite audience members to engage in this ritualized interactivity and embrace a new form of radical faith – the faith in the art process to be a personal and political force through which the intimate human body becomes a transformative site against a backdrop of global despair and war.

2008: Gustavo Vazquez and I premiere *Homo Fronterizus*, a video project in two parts: *One-on-one* includes reinterpretations of some of my classic performance pieces, as well as "homages" to other performance artists who have influenced my work (Roi Vaara, Marina Abramović, Stelarc, Melquiades Herrera, and James Luna).

In *Duelos* we explore the unspoken tension between performance and video asking such questions as: who is the real author? The performance artist who creates the concept and offers his body/identity/map/arte-facto in sacrifice to the camera, or the video artist who filters it, frames it, and, in doing so, inevitably recreates it?

2008: *La Nostalgia Remix*: James Luna and I continue our exploration of the cultural and political implications of nostalgia both in the Native American "res" and in the Chicano barrio. We deal with nostalgia as style, resistance, false identity, and reinvention, in a series of re-enactments of our "best hits and outtakes for an imaginary bar." We also create a digital mural with photographer RJ Muna.

To Be Continued ...

Notes

1. This performance chronology is a conceptual artwork in progress. It includes information and projects that connect my life and family to my art, which I embed in a political and art historical context. The project is inspired by the archival work that Diana Taylor and the Hemispheric Institute of Performance and Politics is doing, by Amelia Jones' reflections on performance documentation and by the work that Carolina Ponce de Leon is carrying out with the visual histories of Galeria de la Raza in San Francisco. In the process of writing this Proustian text, I have asked several colleagues and collaborators to help me rebuild the bizarre edifice of my memory. I particularly wish to thank Gretchen Coombs, Lisa Wolford, Linda Burnham, and Roberto Sifuentes for helping me prepare the manuscript; Emma Tramposch for archiving the extensive photographic material; and my jaina Carolina for designing the amazing powerpoint that accompanies the live version. Many names and projects are still missing and I hope that future versions will be more thorough. [Editor's note: cuts have been made by Amelia Jones to the original version of this chronology for this publication.]
2. Poyesis Genetica flyer.

Chapter 25

Attending to Anthony McCall's Long Film for Ambient Light

Lucas Ihlein

In March 2007, The Teaching and Learning Cinema, an artist group from Sydney, Australia, coordinated by Louise Curham and myself, recreated the conditions for a contemporary experience of Anthony McCall's *Long Film for Ambient Light* (1975). *Long Film for Ambient Light* is a work of Expanded Cinema, comprising the bare minimum elements required for "film": light, time, a screen, and an audience. Here I discuss some aspects of this recreation, with particular focus on the compilation of an "experiential document" as a way of understanding how the work affected individuals who encountered it.

Expanding What Cinema Might Be

Experimental films from the 1960s and 1970s which reached beyond the convention of a single rectangular projection screen were sometimes called "Expanded Cinema." "Expanded Cinema" events often involved fragile and ephemeral situations: light bulbs that flashed in front of the screen, puffs of smoke which illuminated the cone of light from the projector, or performances involving "mini-cinemas" utilizing the sense of touch rather than sight.[1] This emphasis on the contextual elements of space, time, and the social transaction of the performance situation places Expanded Cinema alongside 1970s conceptual and performance art.[2] Like other manifestations of performance art from that era, often these events were so specific to time and place that it is impossible to experience them ever again. Some, however, possessed certain characteristics – such as prepared film material, or a set of written instructions – which might enable a future recreation.

During the last ten years, the re-enactment, or recreation, of performance art from the 1970s has increasingly been employed as a method of historical "research," as well as an art form in itself. Importantly, re-enactment has placed artists (as "action-researchers") at the center of a discipline traditionally dominated by (non-artist) scholars.[3] The Teaching and Learning Cinema engages with the history of Expanded Cinema through such re-enactments. Our "cinema" is not an architectural space, but rather a collective that pursues a program of action-research around the histories of experimental cinema.

The Teaching and Learning Cinema's interest in re-enactment began with a strong belief in the inherently *experiential* (rather than simply "conceptual") nature of Expanded Cinema events. In this, the group draws from the writings of pragmatist philosopher John Dewey, and radical educational theorist Paulo Freire – each of whom emphasized the primacy of lived experience over "propositional" learning.[4] In light of this emphasis, this chapter presents a brief account of our 2007 recreation of a 1975 work by Anthony McCall, focusing on the experiences of visitors to our new version of the work.

John Dewey, in his 1934 book *Art as Experience*, argues that art is not simply the painting or sculpture as a discrete object. The "work of art" is rather *the work that art does* in lived experience. Art, he wrote, "intensifies the sense of immediate living" – and this intensification of the present moment needs to be considered as an intrinsic part of the work of art itself, rather than one of its by-products.[5] In considering art as a sphere of human activity – a *practice* rather than an object (albeit a practice often mediated by objects) – Dewey shifts the definition of art from a noun to a verb. The work of art is not a singular, autonomous object or action, but a bundle of relations and artifacts that come together (differently at different times) in the creation of an aesthetic experience within the mind and body of the human subject.

The advantage of thinking about the work of art in these terms is that it potentially releases us from the disabling trap of mythologizing the past. One's own experience is an important node in the network of interlaced relations that make up "the work of art." Thus, instead of privileging a prior moment in history as somehow more "authentic," we are urged to value our own encounters with art in the present moment.[6] The push to validate the present experience of the audience was a key tenet of much of the work produced by Expanded Cinema artists in the early 1970s. Malcolm Le Grice, a British film-maker and theorist of Expanded Cinema, criticized the paradigm of the commercial motion picture industry for creating illusory worlds that (mis)represent the creative work as a *fait accompli*. In narrative commercial films, all aesthetic decisions appear to have been made at some moment *prior* to being projected for a passively seated audience. By contrast, Le Grice and his colleagues at the London Film-makers' Co-op were concerned with composing events that emphasized the here-and-now – what he called "real time/space" – as a shared aesthetic encounter.[7] In the context of Expanded Cinema, this meant the foregrounding of the cinematic apparatus: the passing of film through a projector, the projection of light onto a screen, and the architectural space of the theater. Together with the communal experience of the audience, assembled at a particular time and place, these apparatuses became tangible elements of the artwork itself. In this, Expanded Cinema shared many of the concerns of performance art and happenings – in which audience members were not merely passive consumers of material created prior to their arrival, but actually participated (to varying degrees) in the making of the work.

Le Grice's desire to *work together* with the audience to develop an aesthetic experience echoes the writing of radical Brazilian educational theorist and activist Paulo Freire. Writing at around the same time as Le Grice, Freire attempted, in his book *Pedagogy of the Oppressed* (1970), to overcome the active/passive dichotomy in the teacher/student relationship. Freire criticized what he regarded as the "banking concept of education," in which the student is merely the destination for deposits of knowledge that are complete and pre-formulated. For Freire, the banking concept of education is fundamentally oppressive because within its system, success means becoming a docile subject accepting propositions on face value without testing them through lived experience:

> The more students work at storing the deposits entrusted to them, the less they develop the critical consciousness which would result from their intervention in the world as transformers of that world. The more completely they accept the passive role imposed on them, the more they tend simply to adapt to the world as it is and to the fragmented view of reality deposited in them.[8]

Conversely, Freire writes, when educational curricula emerge from the interests of students in collaboration with their teacher, the pedagogical process is more empowering and liberatory. Education then becomes a tool for enriching and improving the lives of students wherever they are in the here-and-now, rather than a means for creating model citizens. In fact, in *Pedagogy of the Oppressed*, Freire renames the partners in pedagogy as "teacher-student" and "students-teachers."

I would like to propose that the recent growth in the desire to re-enact performance art and Expanded Cinema is compatible with this liberatory pedagogical movement. Rather than regarding the past with white-gloved reverence, re-enactments by younger generations of artists can be seen as a process of active intervention in history in the pursuit of vital knowledge. In contrast to the kind of knowledge that is generated through reading about artworks after the event, re-enactments seek to provide a different kind of knowledge by making it possible to *encounter the artworks ourselves*. If (as suggested by Le Grice) the spirit of Expanded Cinema was to have an experience in the present time and space, then to consider such works after the event might mean their re-assembly wherever and whenever we happen to be. The process of re-enactment goes beyond polite homage, or slavish devotion to the "authentic" work of art. Instead, re-enactments are an interaction with, and reflection on, history, transforming our experience (and therefore our understanding) of the original work.

In preparing to re-enact Anthony McCall's *Long Film for Ambient Light*, we discovered that very little had been recorded about the specific experiences of audiences who encountered the film at its debut in 1975. Essays about the piece, and interviews with McCall, mainly discussed the work in light of the artist's intentions, or placed it in a linear history of avant-garde or conceptual art practice. Connections had been made to John Cage's musical compositions, Minimalist sculpture, structuralist and experimental film, and anti-spectacular performance art. But nowhere could we find an account from someone who had actually been there.[9] Before describing McCall's work, I should note that The Teaching and Learning Cinema uses the term "re-enactment" only out of convenience. Given the nature of *Long Film For Ambient Light*, there is actually not very much to "enact" – and thus we prefer to describe our role as "re-creating the conditions for a contemporary experience" of the work.

Long Film for Ambient Light: New York, 18-19 June 1975

Long Film for Ambient Light was among the last of McCall's "minimalist" films, in which he drew attention to the structure of cinema itself. In his earlier work, *Line Describing a Cone* (1973), focus was brought to the sculptural cone of light thrown by the 16mm film projector as it illuminated particles of smoke and dust in the air.[10] *Long Film for Ambient Light* takes this process a step further. Even for a work of Expanded Cinema, the piece represents a rather radical "expansion." The work was in fact only nominally a "film." It did away with celluloid, projectors, and a passively seated audience. Believing that these were merely the technologies commonly assumed to be associated with cinema (but by no means indispensible to it), McCall stripped his work back to what he regarded as the fundamental elements in the creation of a cinematic experience – "an architectural container, a light source, a given duration."[11]

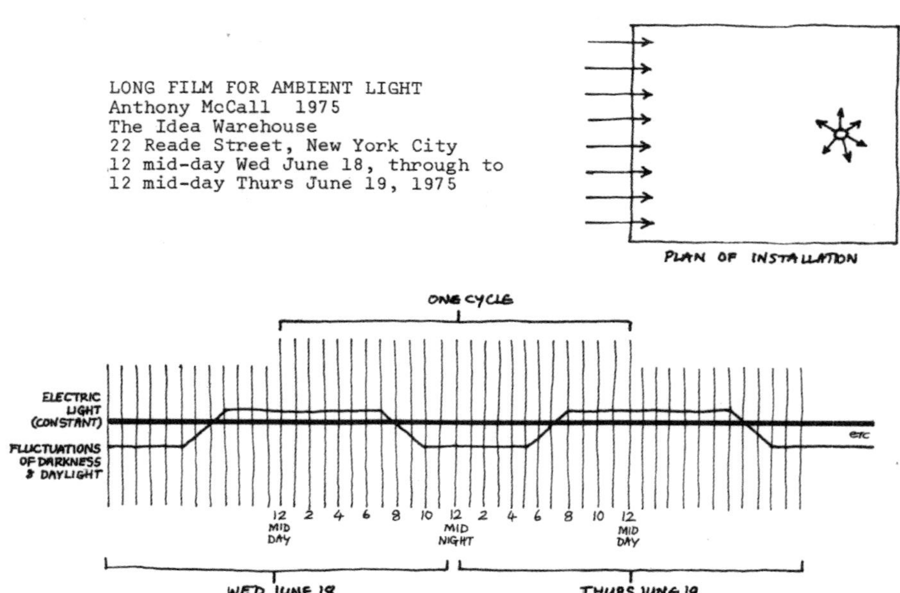

Anthony McCall, *Long Film for Ambient Light*, 1975. Invitation Card. Courtesy Sean Kelly Gallery, New York.

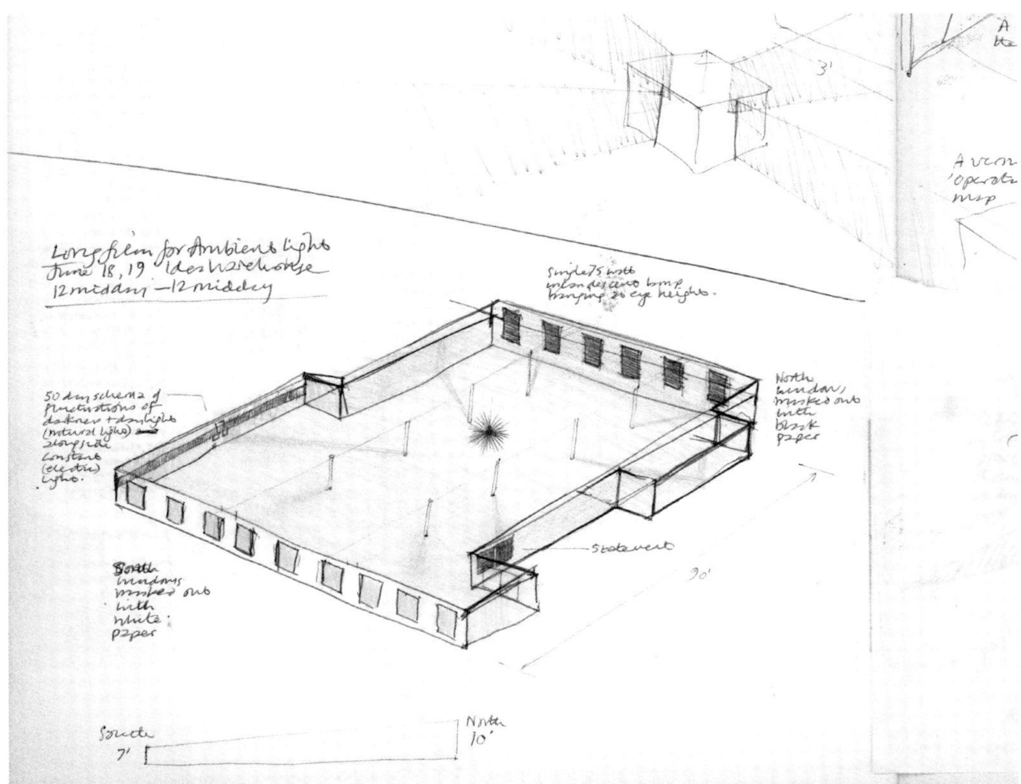

Anthony McCall, *Long Film for Ambient Light*, 1975. Installation drawing (from 1 May–26 June 1975 notebook). Courtesy Sean Kelly Gallery, New York.

Long Film for Ambient Light consisted of a specially prepared room, made available for a period of 24 hours, beginning and ending at 12 noon. Unlike standard film viewing situations, the audience could enter and leave as they wished. The windows along one side of the room were covered with translucent paper, and this was the only source of natural light. In the center of the space, at about head-height, hung a single light bulb. The bulb was continuously illuminated throughout the course of the piece.

On the walls were mounted two paper documents: a text entitled "Notes in Duration," which outlined McCall's philosophical framework for the piece; and a "Time Schema Drawing," which graphically represented the fluctuating relationship between the natural and artificial light sources in the room.[12] McCall did not consider these documents to be simply an explanation of *Long Film for Ambient Light*, but an intrinsic part of the work itself. In his "Notes in Duration" statement, McCall argued that the quality of human attention is the key to understanding our relationship with "art objects":

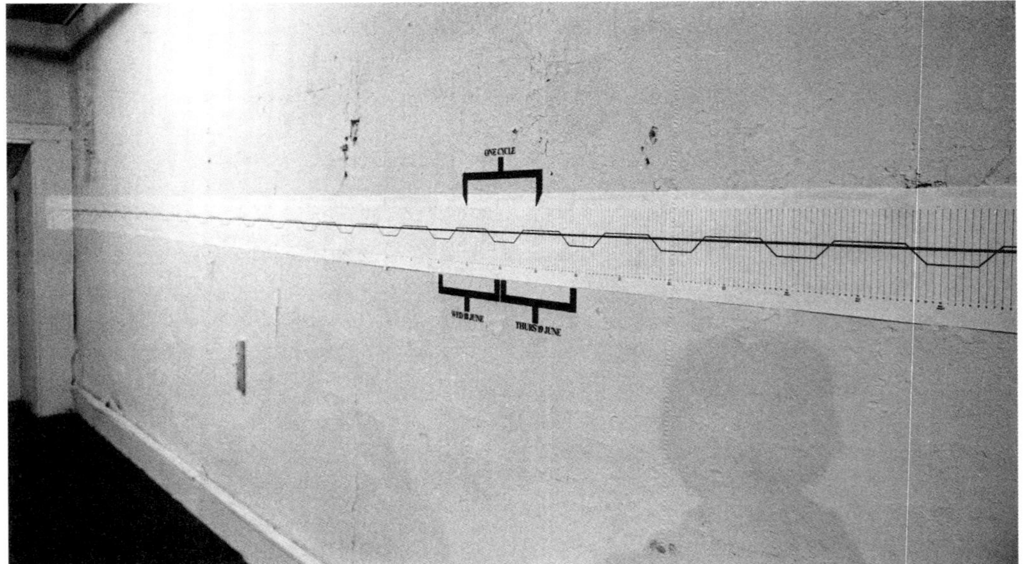

Anthony McCall, *Long Film for Ambient Light*, 1975. Time schema installation view at Idea Warehouse, New York, 1975. Courtesy Sean Kelly Gallery, New York. Photograph by Anthony McCall.

> Art that does not show change within our time-span of attending to it we tend to regard as "object." Art that does show change within our time-span of attending to it we tend to regard as "event." Art that outlives us we tend to regard as eternal. What is at issue is that we ourselves are the division that cuts across what is essentially a sliding scale of time-bases. A piece of paper on the wall is as much a duration as the projection of a film. Its only difference is in its immediate relationship to our perceptions.

Paradoxically, this radical statement at the heart of McCall's film has, to date, only been considered as a hypothetical proposition. If, as McCall states, it is true that "our attending to it" (or, as Dewey would say, *our experience of it*) is a crucial part of the work of art, then surely it follows that any analysis of *Long Film for Ambient Light* should begin precisely there – in the actual experiences of its audience.

Creating an "Experiential Document" for *Long Film for Ambient Light*

In order to document the experiential qualities of our recreation of *Long Film for Ambient Light*, The Teaching and Learning Cinema invited visitors to participate in recorded audio interviews, during or after their encounter with the work.[13] The intention with these interviews was to create an "oral history" of our 2007 version of *Long Film for Ambient Light*.

In this way, we hoped to contribute a different way of knowing McCall's work – through actual lived experience – to the prevailing theoretical and conceptual analysis.

Working with curator Lizzie Muller, we encouraged visitors to participate in "semi-structured interviews." Adapted by Muller to access the often difficult-to-describe experience of interactive digital (or "new media") artworks, semi-structured interviews elicit experiential narratives, in which audience members "tell the story" of their encounter with an artwork. This method of audience research draws out information about the particular events that make up an encounter with the artwork. The process often produces a deepening of reflection in the interviewee, and thus an intensification of the experience itself.[14]

Experiential Narratives: *Ambient Light*

As might be expected for a work that runs for a full twenty-four hours, the interview responses varied greatly, depending on the time of the day or night the recording was made, how long the interviewee spent in the room, and the conversations and social interactions which occurred in and around the work. For the sake of brevity, my account here considers only one of many themes which emerged from the interview transcripts – the audience's response to the ambient light sources from which the film takes its name. Curiously, neither McCall's published notes, nor later theoretical analyses of *Long Film for Ambient Light* hint at the strong visceral and emotional effect of the light. And yet, in the transcripts from our interviews, the quality of light is repeatedly and vividly described and evaluated. In the following summary, I draw from a selection of responses from twelve visitors. Our recreation was carried out between Friday, 16 March, and Saturday, 17 March 2007 in a very large room at Performance Space, a center for experimental art in Sydney.

The following account traces transformations in response to the light in the room over the course of the work: from afternoon, dusk, night, dawn, to the return of natural light the following morning.

Long Film for Ambient Light: Sydney, 16–17 March 2007

During the first afternoon, the room was flooded with light entering through the large translucent windows on the northern wall of the room. Because of this abundance of sunlight, the light bulb, although continuously glowing, contributed very little to the overall illumination. At this stage, one visitor, Anne, observed the bulb with a sense of curiosity – primarily as an "object," rather than as a source of light. Her eyes, having adjusted to the natural light flooding the room, were able to gaze unflinchingly at the light bulb. She saw the bulb as a "sharp point in the centre of the space," and studied its glowing incandescent filament. Imagining the flow of electrons running along the wire inside the bulb, Anne said: "I feel a bit scared of it … it's very electric, the light bulb. The 'thing-ness' of it is for me very strong."

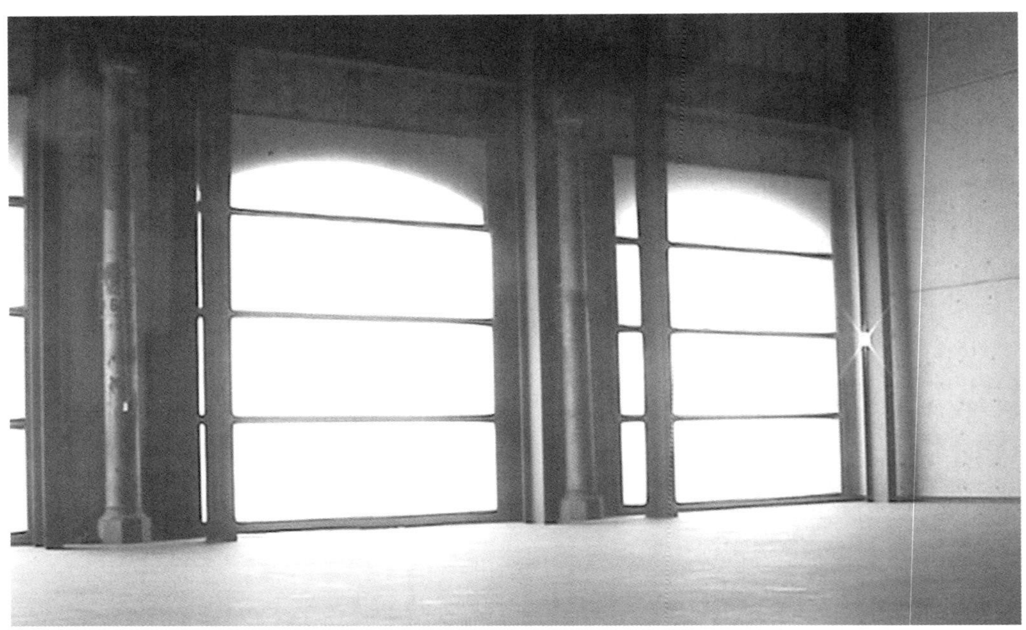

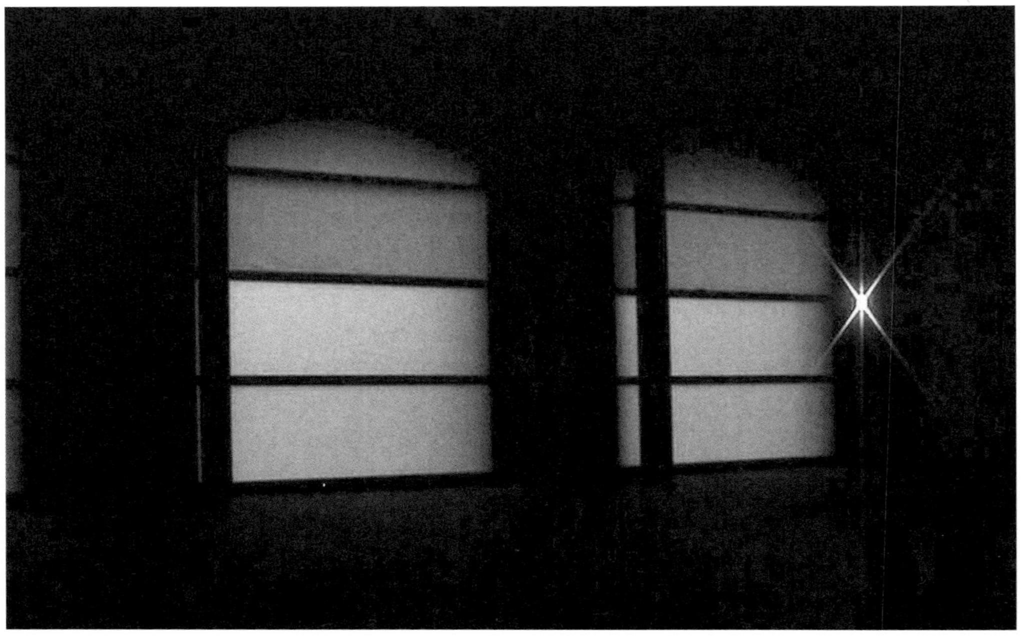

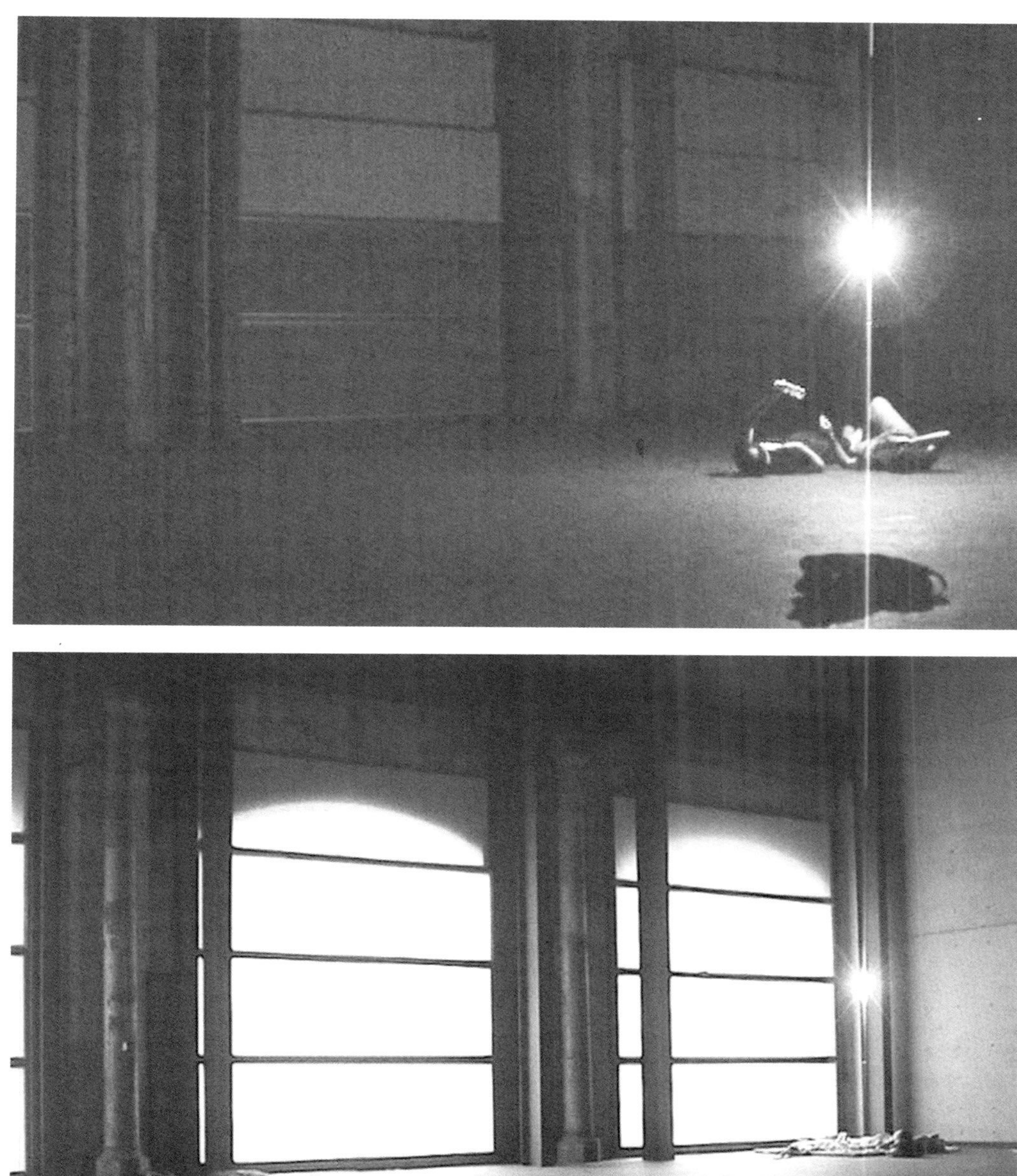

Long Film for Ambient Light, recreation, Performance Space, Sydney, 16 March: 2pm, 8pm, 11pm; 17 March, 8am; 2007. Photos by Lucas Ihlein and Louise Curham.

Another visitor, Sam, arrived just before dusk. He too admitted that he had given the light bulb a great deal of attention. "For the first fifteen minutes," he said, "I couldn't stop thinking of the light bulb as an art object hanging in the room." For Sam and Anne, the balance of light in the room, tipped strongly in favor of the natural light streaming through the translucent windows, reduced the artificial light source to an "object" in the space. But with the coming of dusk, this balance changed.

From about 6pm, the intensity of the natural light began to slowly decline. Visitors' eyes gradually adjusted to the darker space, and it became increasingly difficult to look directly at the light bulb. The transition from day to night, via this slow shift in the balance of light, was described by visitors as a "heightened" period in the narrative of *Long Film for Ambient Light*. McCall's work had managed to frame and dramatize the everyday occurrence of dusk. It was one of two extended moments (the other, of course, being dawn) in which the changing light conditions were almost perceptible in relation to the human attention span.

Sam's awareness of this fact was triggered after studying McCall's time-schema graph fixed to the wall: "I could see that I was probably there at a dramatic time just by looking at the little up and down lines, when things were changing light-wise." Lizzie, who was recording interviews with visitors, observed: "that was a magical moment with no specific beginning or ending but I remember that there was a peak, a moment of acceleration when change seemed to be happening more perceptibly."

After this "dramatic" period of change, the natural light disappeared completely, and the room was lit only by the bare light bulb. Some visitors (especially those who were planning to stay in the room overnight) reported "feeling time stretching out" ahead of them, with almost "no end in sight." One visitor, John, who arrived after 8pm, likened the room's nocturnal appearance (a seemingly empty space with a single light bulb blazing at head height) to a theater set suited to a play by Samuel Beckett or Harold Pinter. For John, the passing of time in such a situation could potentially be experienced with physical awkwardness, or jarring psychological self-consciousness. And yet, instead of this awkwardness, John reported a sense of deep relaxation in the room: "It's funny, I was thinking about stuff before I came in here," he said, "but now I feel my whole brain's just switched off. And I felt like I could go in there and switch out, and I wasn't wasting time. There was a kind of guiltless non-doing about it that I really enjoyed."

The experience of visitors Vanessa and Tim was more playful. They arrived around 10pm. Not having any awareness of what the room had been like prior to sunset, they began playing with the light cast by the single bulb, creating shadow puppets on the walls and floor. Throughout the night, I observed other visitors lying on the floor under the bulb, chatting sociably while "basking" in its glow.

However, many other visitors who spent time in the space between dusk and dawn were physically and psychologically "bothered" by the incessant glow of the artificial light. Some began to develop an antagonistic relationship with the bulb, viewing it almost as a kind of aesthetic torture device. Lizzie, who arrived at 6pm on Friday, and stayed until noon the following day, reported:

> the light bulb bothered me unbelievably. In my eyes and my head, it hurt [...] this aggravating insistence of it. I couldn't look anywhere else: it totally dominated my field of view no matter where I was. I feel like it's been printed on my retina possibly forever, that light bulb. Every time I shut my eyes, there it is on my retina.

Sleeping, for Lizzie and those of us who decided to stay overnight, involved strategically positioning our bodies in the space, facing away from the "aggravating insistence" of the light bulb, or else covering our heads with blankets or towels.

For the "survivors" of the long night, the return of daylight was generally greeted with a sense of relief. One particularly enthusiastic visitor, Chris, arrived in the dark, at 5am on Saturday, in order to witness the sunrise. Like Lizzie, Chris found himself unable to escape the light bulb's glare, describing it, at first, as a "horrible insistent little monster of a thing." However, when dawn broke, and as his eyes adjusted to the natural light coming through the translucent windows, Chris welcomed the emerging sunlight with great pleasure: "Yeah it's just real nice, and it's got a nice full spectrum of color. It's full and juicy, and it represents all the good things in life." This "evaluative" interpretation of the ambient light conditions in the room was common across the recorded interviews.

A fresh batch of visitors arrived in the early morning. One of the first to arrive, Bob, observed the prevailing mood during this period as "quiet and meditative." He explained that he had read about *Long Film for Ambient Light* in advance, and actually planned his visit at this time precisely for that reason: "It sounded like a work you should contemplate and meditate on. I thought, you know, you're half asleep in the morning, so I thought that would be good." Like Bob, many of the early morning visitors reported experiencing a calm and contemplative mood. Although the balance of light had tipped toward the natural again, curiously, nobody reported observing "the light bulb as an object" as Anne and Sam had done the previous afternoon. Bob suggested that this might be related to the meditative, rather than analytical, state of mind of the early morning visitors.

This brief account of various responses to the changing balance of light in our re-enactment of *Long Film for Ambient Light* is fragmented, anecdotal, and by no means "scientific" in its methods or results.[15] However, it does point to the clear correlation between the actual, physical conditions of the work in the here-and-now, and the audience's experience of the piece. Besides reflecting upon the ambient light conditions in the room, other major themes that emerged from visitors' interviews included:

- an increased sense of self-consciousness due to the relative lack of visual stimuli in the room;
- the observation of, and participation in, the social relations among people in the room;
- reflections upon the nature of the artwork itself – as the "original piece," and as the documented re-enactment.

It seems almost unnecessary to point out that our recreation took place at a different latitude, and during a different season, to McCall's presentation of the work at the Ideas Warehouse, New York, in June 1975. One can only imagine that, depending on these variables, as well as the peculiarities of the architectural container in which it is set up, and the cultural context of the place in which it is staged, the work itself must always engender a dramatically – or subtly – different experience. And yet, in the sense that the original concept for the piece explicitly encompasses a situated, evolving form, *Long Film for Ambient Light* remains "the same work" of Expanded Cinema, regardless of temporal and geographical shifts.[16] That is, for Anthony McCall (as for John Cage before him), the creation of an artwork is not simply the bringing forth of a static object into the world. Rather, it is the creation of a *framework for experience.* This framework is able to be expanded and elaborated upon over time, and be set up in different places, allowing us to imagine our own re-enactment as "the actual work." The difference, of course, is that our version of the work is not only *Long Film for Ambient Light*, but also its "second coming" – a separate and distinct work of art.[17]

For those who encountered it in Sydney in 2007, the work was imbued with doubleness: the here-and-now laid over New York, 1975; the thrill of accessing the original work overlaid with the pedagogical focus of the re-enactment; the direct encounter with the ambient light conditions in the room, enhanced – or perhaps mitigated – by our request that visitors contribute to our experiential document: a request that reminded them of the historical and theoretical motivation of the re-enactment. The ability to perceive an artwork such as *Long Film for Ambient Light* depends on a myriad of embodied conditions – perceptual apparatuses such as eyes, ears, and their associated cognitive processes, the body's movement in space over a period of time, social interactions, and so on. All these components need to be brought into the equation when considering, and reflecting upon, a work of art like *Long Film for Ambient Light*. While the method we utilized – semi-structured interviewing – can only capture a fragment of the whole experience of visitors to the work, we believe it represents, at the very least, the beginnings of a broader understanding of the piece. As Lisa Lefeuvre writes:

> [A]s the work has become situated within history, each presentation of *Long Film for Ambient Light* will slightly shift it, and as documentation of each realisation is distributed, expectations of future manifestations of the work are layered upon past representations of experience.[18]

The Teaching and Learning Cinema takes seriously the idea that *Long Film for Ambient Light* was not simply a conceptual gesture to be imagined only in the mind. Rather, McCall's film, along with many other works of Expanded Cinema from the 1960s and 1970s, was made to be attended – and attended to – in a specific time and place. The flux of light in a room, the gradual (or rapid) sense of time passing, the waxing and waning of one's own attention span – these are phenomena which can only be encountered in lived experience. By re-staging the work, we create an opportunity for a direct encounter in the here-and-now. Attending the re-enacted work offers an embodied alternative to shuffling through paper documents and archives. It allows us to compare our own experiences with the artist's statements and theoretical assertions. Since one of our own frustrations with the historicization of live art events from the 1970s is the absence of first-person accounts, we attempt to address this problem by making a new deposit in the archive. If *Long Film for Ambient Light* were to be "experientially documented" in a similar manner in several different times and places, a rich, expanded, and plural picture of the artwork might begin to emerge.

Notes

1. A few iconic examples of Expanded Cinema: Malcolm LeGrice's *Castle One* (1966) which involved a light bulb that switched on and off during the screening of a 16mm film, momentarily blinding the audience members, whose eyes had adjusted to the darkness of the cinema; Anthony McCall's *Line Describing a Cone* (1973), which utilized particles of smoke and dust in the atmosphere to create a sculptural cone of light; and VALIE EXPORT's *Tapp und Tast Kino* (Tap and Touch Cinema) (1968), a mini-cinema strapped to the artist's chest – audience members could 'view' the 'film' only by reaching their hands through the cinema curtain and touching the artist's body.
2. For a contemporary reflection on 1970s Expanded Cinema, see Lucas Ihlein, "Pre-Digital New-Media Art," *Realtime*, April–May 2005, no. 66. Available at: http://www.realtimearts.net/article/66/7779; accessed 27 June 2011.
3. For one recent reflection on this field, see Jessica Santone, "Marina Abramović's *Seven Easy Pieces*: Critical Documentation Strategies for Preserving Art's History," *Leonardo*, 2008, vol. 41, no. 2, pp. 147–52.
4. See John Dewey, *Art as Experience*, New York: Perigee, 2005 [1934]; and Paulo Freire, *Pedagogy of the Oppressed*, New York: Continuum Press, 2005 [1968].
5. Dewey, ibid., p. 5.
6. Dewey's theory of aesthetics drew from his much deeper desire to reform the American public education system. For Dewey, teaching and learning should be interactive, experiential processes of critical engagement, rather than a mechanical acquisition of "facts." See John Dewey, *Experience and Education*, New York: Macmillan, 1938.
7. Malcolm Le Grice, "real time/space," *Art and Artists Magazine*, December 1972, reprinted in Lucy Reynolds, *Defining FILMAKTION*, 2005. Available at: http://www.studycollection.co.uk/filmaktion/Frameset7.html; accessed 27 June 2011.
8. Freire, op. cit., p. 54.
9. One account that approaches a description of audience experience is that of Lisa Lefeuvre, "The Continuous Present," in Helen Legg (ed.), *Anthony McCall: Film Installations*, Warwick: Mead Gallery, 2004, pp. 33–41. However, even Lefeuvre's experiential descriptions are of a hypothetical, rather than an actual, visitor to the work. For further critical analysis of *Long Film for Ambient Light*, see Anthony McCall, "Line Describing a Cone and Related Films," in *October*, Winter 2003, no. 103, pp. 42–62; and Brandon W. Joseph, "Sparring with the Spectacle," in C. Eamon (ed.), *Anthony McCall: The Solid Light Films and Related Works*, Chicago, Illinois: Northwestern University Press, 2005, pp. 94–9; Jonathan Walley, "An Interview with Anthony McCall," in *The Velvet Light Trap*, 2004, no. 54, pp. 65–75; Jonathan Walley, "The Material of Film and the Idea of Cinema: Contrasting Practices in Sixties and Seventies Avant-Garde Film," *October*, Winter 2003,

no. 103, pp. 15–30; Deke Dusinberre, "On Expanding Cinema," *Studio International*, Nov–Dec 1975, vol. 190, no. 978, pp. 220–4; and George Baker, "Film Beyond Its Limits," *Grey Room*, Fall 2006, no. 25, pp. 92–125.

10. In 2005, The Teaching and Learning Cinema (in its former guise as Sydney Moving Image Coalition) coordinated an Australian tour of *Line Describing a Cone*. Although presented in artists' lofts during the 1970s, in recent years Anthony McCall's films have increasingly been displayed in art museums. We chose to reconnect the piece with its "rougher" history, showing the work in small artist-run warehouses in Sydney, Melbourne, Brisbane, and Perth. For McCall's reflections on the changing context for the presentation of his work over time, see Mark Godfrey and Anthony McCall, "Anthony McCall's *Line Describing a Cone*," in Tate Papers, Autumn 2007. Available at: http://www.tate.org.uk/research/tateresearch/tatepapers/07autumn/godfreymccall.htm; accessed 27 June 2011.
11. Baker, op. cit., p. 110.
12. The "Time Schema Drawing" graphically contrasted the daily changes in natural light entering the room, with the constant lux of the artificial light bulb. The drawing described twenty-four hours as "one cycle" – seeming to suggest that *Long Film for Ambient Light* could be presented for a longer period. In fact, Anthony McCall has subsequently confirmed that the work has a potentially infinite duration: "The piece is imagined as continuous, with no maximum duration, but the minimum duration would be a single cycle of 24 hours." McCall, e-mail correspondence with the author, 10 April 2007.
13. It is worth noting that the visitors invited to our 2007 recreation, in general, belonged to a social network of artists and art-enthusiasts, rather than representing a broad spectrum of the wider community.
14. Muller, who demonstrated the method for us, agreed to be interviewed about her experience as well. For detailed description of Muller's audience experience techniques, see Lizzie Muller, *Towards an Oral History of New Media Art*, Montreal: Daniel Langlois Foundation. Available at: http://www.fondation-langlois.org/html/e/page.php?NumPage=2096; accessed 27 June 2011; and Caitlin Jones and Lizzie Muller, *Between Real and Ideal: Documenting Media Art, Leonardo*, 2008, vol. 41, no. 4, pp. 418–19. Muller's adaptation of semi-structured interviewing draws from the qualitative research methods described by Steinar Kvale in his book *Interviews: An Introduction to Qualitative Research Interviewing*, London: Sage Publications, 1996.
15. The full transcripts of the visitor interviews are available on the Teaching and Learning Cinema website. Available at: http://teachingandlearningcinema.org; accessed 27 June 2011.
16. As Lefeuvre writes in "The Continuous Present": "*Long Film for Ambient Light* was inspired by the space of the Idea Warehouse; however it is not dependent on it, and has been exhibited elsewhere: for example in 1975 at Galerie St Petri in Lund, Sweden (a small storefront gallery) and the following year at Neue Galerie, in Aachen (a large Baroque hall within a museum)." Interestingly, since our own re-enactment in Sydney, Anthony McCall has recreated *Long Film for Ambient Light* himself, in a dramatically different context at the baroque Musée de Rochechouart, France, 2007 as part of the exhibition "Anthony McCall: Elements pour une Retrospective (1972-1979 / 2003-)."
17. In a similar vein, McCall himself has considered a (hypothetical) future digital remake of his 16mm Expanded Cinema film *Line Describing a Cone*: "It will be titled *Line Describing a Cone* 2.0, thus marking it not as a re-make at all, but as a second version. It would not replace the film version. It may be that over time, 2.0 gets looked at more than the film version. Or it may be that 2.0 drives people back to the film version." Godfrey and McCall, op. cit.
18. Lefeuvre, op. cit., p. 37.

Chapter 26

ReCut Project

Ming-Yuen S. Ma

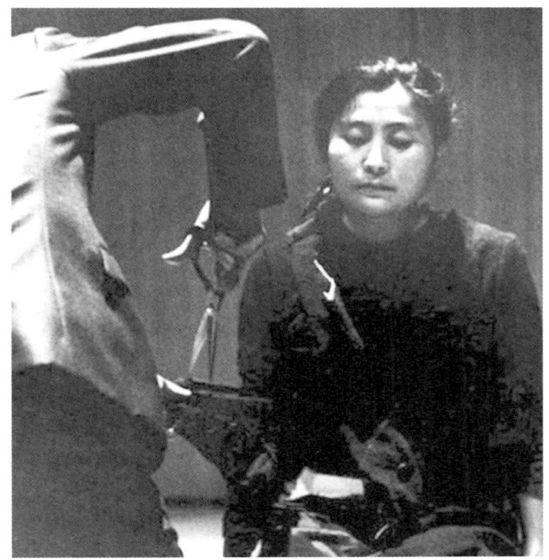

Yoko Ono performing *Cut Piece*, on 20 July 1964 at Sogetsu Art Center, Tokyo, Japan. Photo: Minoru Hirata, courtesy of Yoko Ono.

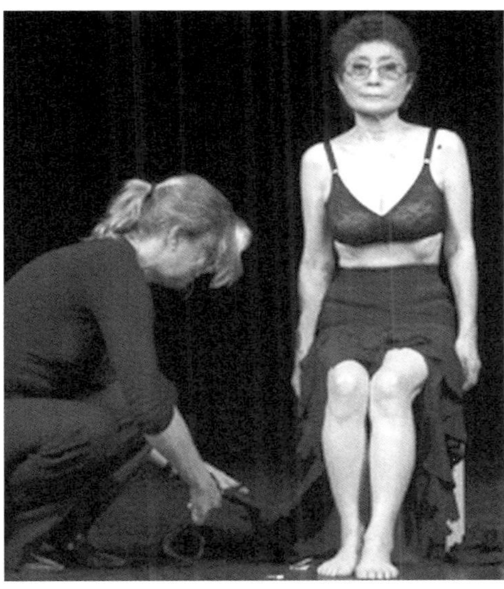

Yoko Ono performing *Cut Piece*, on 15 September 2003 at Theatre Le Ranelagh, Paris, France. Photo: Ken McKay, © Yoko Ono.

Cut Piece, from *The Strip Tease Show* by Yoko Ono, 1966

First version for single performer: performer sits on stage with a pair of scissors in front of him.
It is announced that members of the audience may come on stage – one at a time – to cut a small piece of the performer's clothing to take with them. Performer remains motionless throughout the piece.
Piece ends at the performer's option.
Second version for audience: it is announced that members of the audience may cut each other's clothing.
The audience may cut as long as they wish.

The ReCut Project (2006)[1]

Dear Members of the Audience,

The *ReCut Project* was conceived at the Getty Research Institute. When I was looking through the Fluxus material in the Jean Brown collection for this exhibition, I came across a publication for Yoko Ono's exhibition *This is Not Here* (1971). It was a two-page spread collaged with newspaper clippings about Ono. As John Lennon said in one of the articles, "Yoko Ono is the world's most famous unknown artist. Everybody knows her name, but nobody knows what she does"; the amount of reportage and commentary around her was phenomenal. This, I suppose, was a part of life as the wife of a famous rock star. I was fascinated by how these journalists – not just the art press, but also society writers, gossip columnists, music writers – responded to Ono's artwork. It seemed that the same actions, performed in different contexts, could yield very different interpretations.

I based my concept for the *ReCut Project* in this realization. I chose the *Cut Piece*, one of Ono's most well known actions, and one that was frequently mentioned in the newspaper clippings, as my starting point. I found Ono's instructions for the piece, and invited a group of participants to interpret them in a series of performances. I want to find out if the same instructions, performed by different individuals, could yield different interpretations, different meanings.

Among the artists associated with Fluxus, Ono's artwork consistently challenged the socio-political issues and gender politics of her time. I very much share her concerns. The *Cut Piece* has been canonized within the annals of feminism, performance art, conceptual art, and other cultural practices, its reference to Buddhist self-sacrifice has also been pointed out by a number of scholars.[2] Yet, it seems to me that at its center, behind the provocation of its performance, is a blankness. This blankness does not signify lack, but rather a plural void that makes it possible for the simple action in the *Cut Piece* to encompass the contradictory notions of active and passive, violence and peace, violation and self-sacrifice.

In other words, the meaning of the *Cut Piece* is embodied in the bodies and acts of the performer and the audience. This is evident in the varying accounts and interpretations in the newspaper clippings I found, and is also demonstrated by Ono's own re-staging in 2003, when, at age 70, she performed the action at the Ranelagh Theatre in Paris. Billed as her "hope for world peace," this version of the *Cut Piece* produced markedly different reactions from when she performed it in Japan and the US in 1964–5.

In the *ReCut Project*, I have invited a diverse group of individuals to present their interpretation of Ono's instructions. They represent a wide range of positions in terms of age, nationality, gender, vocation, and practice; some are immigrants, some are troubled by what the US represents in the world today; a few are recent college and high school students, while others are tenured university professors. They are Asian, Iranian, Latino, queer, feminist, or none of the above. At least one embodies the Ono/Lennon dichotomy: a Japanese woman artist rock star. They have different relationships to their bodies: living with HIV, battling cancer, being mistaken for a terrorist, being a virgin, being bi-racial. I am so very curious to see what bodies and what notions of self are revealed when their clothing is cut off, piece by piece. It is also possible that some of them will decide to keep their clothes on, or have you, the audience, dress them up as you desire.

And perhaps you, dear audience member, will decide to stage your own version of the *Cut Piece* in the spirit of Fluxus; here at the exhibition in LACE,[3] on the streets outside, at a concert hall, museum, in a classroom, on TV, on the Internet ... the meaning of your version will be determined by your actions, and the actions of those who are your audience. The possibilities are infinite.

Sincerely,

Ming-Yuen S. Ma
17 June 2006

Editor's notes

1. DVD documentation can be requested through www.mingyuensma.org.
2. See, for example, Jieun Rhee's essay "Performing The Other: Yoko Ono's *Cut Piece*," *Art History* 28, n. 1 (February 2005), 96–118.
3. This project was part of the "Draw A Line and Follow It" exhibition at LACE (Los Angeles Contemporary Exhibitions) held from 30 June to 18 August 2006. LACE is an alternative art space, founded in 1978, and currently located in Hollywood. For more information, visit www.welcometolace.org.

ReCut Project (2006)

Conceived and directed by Ming-Yuen S. Ma
With interpretations of Yoko Ono's *Cut Piece* (1964) by Justin Chin, Catherine Lord, Ming-Yuen S. Ma, Jocelyn Matsuo, Lun*na Menoh, Amitis Motevalli, Osuna, and the Toxic Titties.

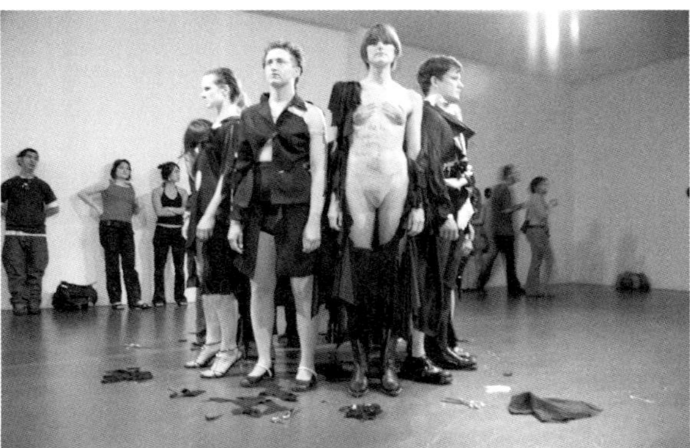

Ming-Yuen S. Ma, performance still, *ReCut#2: Untitled*, the contribution of the Toxic Titties (Heather Cassils, Clover Leary, and Julia Steinmetz), 7 July 2006. Photo: Ming-Yuen S. Ma, courtesy of the artist.

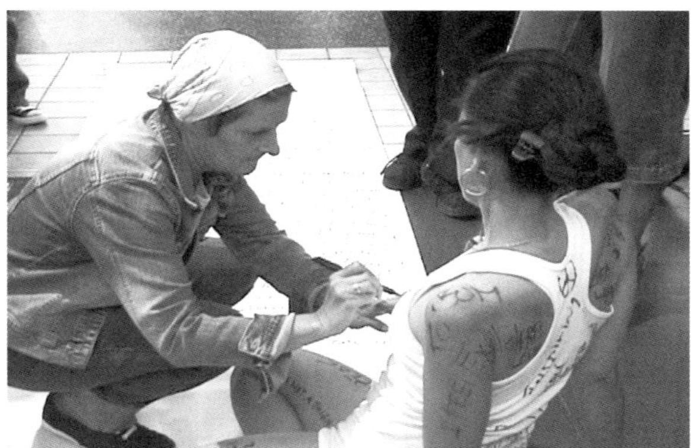

Ming-Yuen S. Ma, performance still, *ReCut#5: Right; Rite; Write Piece*, the contribution of Amitis Motevalli, who is being written on by an audience member, 4 August 2006. Photo: Ming-Yuen S. Ma, courtesy of the artist.

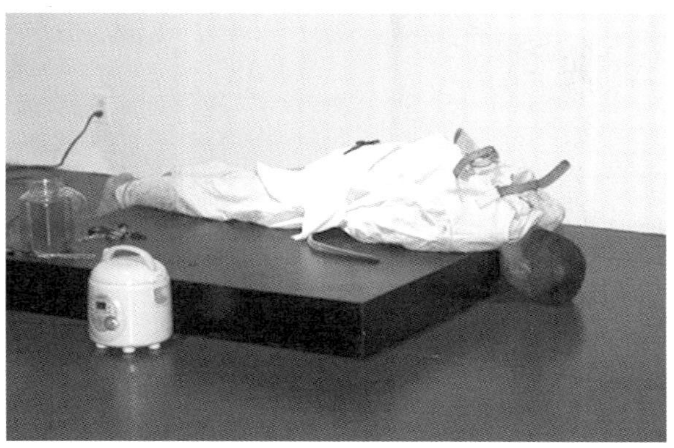

Ming-Yuen S. Ma, performance still, *ReCut#1: Cut Piece Remix*, Justin Chin's contribution (Chin is lying face down with a white straitjacket on), 30 June 2006. Photo: Ming-Yuen S. Ma, courtesy of the artist.

Chapter 27

Assuming a Migrant Woman's Identity

Tanja Ostojić

First, with *Illegal Border Crossing*, I directly familiarized myself with border-crossing strategies that migrants have been using for decades. The work consisted of two actions on the Slovenian–Austrian border, at the time when the Austrian border was the Schengen border, as well as the border to the European Union. At this tiny border, approximately eight or nine illegalized persons were captured each day in an attempt to cross the border non-registered.

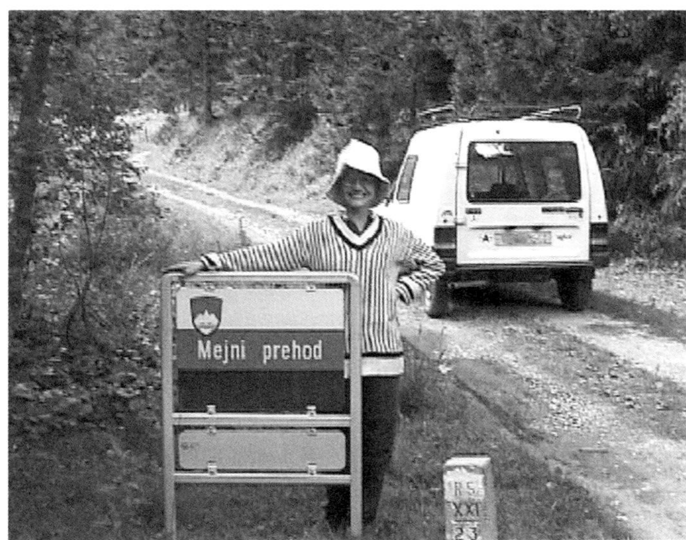

Tanja Ostojić, *Illegal Border Crossing*, 2000. Art action (duration: 3 days)/photo-installation. Location: Schengen border, Slovenian–Austrian border. Copyright: Tanja Ostojić.

For some administrative reason that is not worth describing here, my application for a Schengen/Austrian visa in June 2000 was not taken into consideration. At the time I was living and working in Ljubljana, and I wanted to join an informal international artists' workshop taking place in Austria. Thus, as I was without a visa and therefore prevented from passing the Austrian border normally, I decided to realize this border action and attend the workshop in this way. Going through the non-registered border crossing was possible only thanks to the enormous help of my friends from Austria, who picked me up in Slovenia and guided me through tiny mountain roads to Austrian territory. They helped me in both directions. The person driving me by car through small mountain roads risked a lot.

We were equipped with detailed maps of the territories, as well as with a small digital camera we used for basic documentation of the event. It was exciting and still less stressful than the legal procedure that I went through when I had gotten a proper visa a few weeks earlier, when I took part in an exhibition in Carinthia.

The presentation of the project consists of three video stills and a text that describes the action, each: 20 x 30 cm. The text is glued on the wall, while video stills are mounted on aluminium, hanging on the wall.

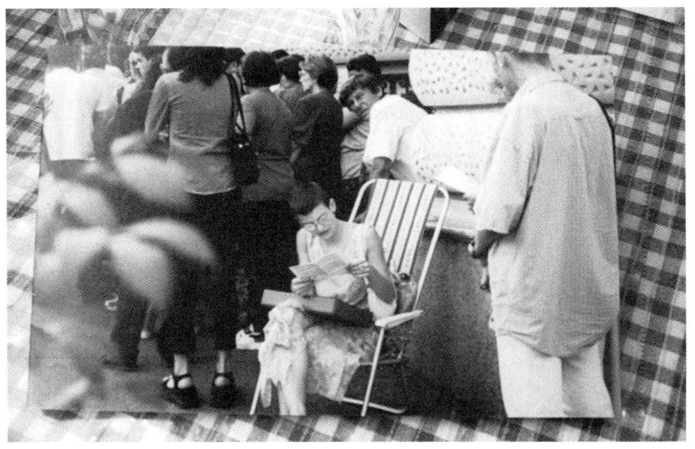

Tanja Ostojić, *Waiting for a Visa*, 2000. Situationist performance (duration: 6 hours)/photo-installation. Location: Austrian Consulate, Belgrade. Photo: Nenad Andrić. Copyright: Tanja Ostojić.

As a consequence, I went on exploring the topic in *Waiting for a Visa* (August 2000). The title refers to a queuing action in front of the Austrian consulate in Belgrade with "no result": from 6:00 am until noon, I lined up in the regular queue with hundreds of people, with about twenty pages of documents and guarantee letters, in order to apply for a visa. At noon, the embassy closed, so I shared the destiny of failure with more than a hundred others who were "too late." Every day in Belgrade one can see the same scenario, which one is prohibited to document with cameras or other devices. This goes on throughout the whole year and almost twenty-four hours a day: people queue for visas. The Austrian, German, and Croatian consulates are among the most popular, as they issue visas for different purposes: transit, tourist, student, business, etc.

The presentation of the performance consists of a series of 12 photographs and the text describing the action; 12 photographs and the text sized 20 x 30 cm each are mounted on aluminium, and hang on the wall.

In August 2000, I started the project *Looking for a Husband with EU Passport* (www.scca.org.mk/capital/projects/tanja). After publishing an ad with this title, I exchanged more than five hundred letters with numerous applicants from around the world. After a correspondence of six months with a German man, K. G., I arranged our first meeting as a public performance in a field in front of the Museum of Contemporary Art in Belgrade in 2001. One month later, we were officially married in New Belgrade. With the international marriage certificate and other required documents, I applied for a visa. After two months, I got a family unification visa, limited to a single entry for a three-month stay in Germany, so I moved to Düsseldorf, where, on the basis of my next visa, I lived officially for three and a half years.

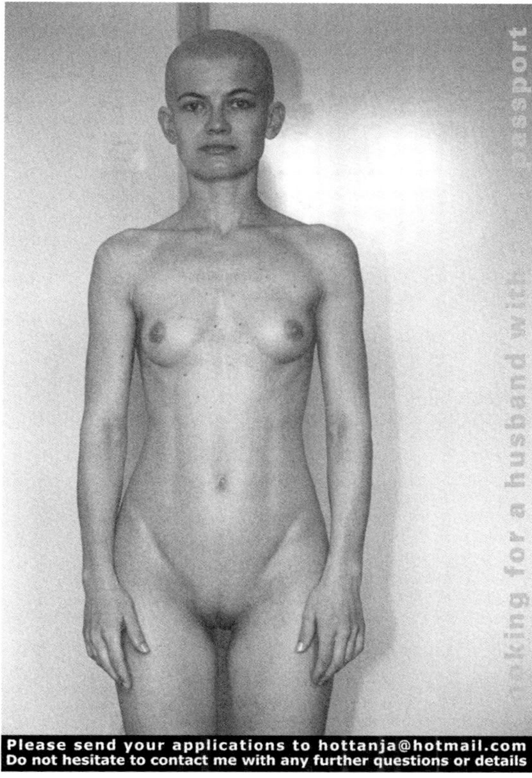

Tanja Ostojić, *The "Ad"* from: *Looking for a Husband with EU Passport*, 2000–5. Participatory web project/combined media installation. Including: *CrossingOver*, 7 min. video DV, 2001, in collaboration with Klemens Golf, with English subtitles. Photo for the "ad": Borut Krajnc.

In spring of 2005, my three-year visa expired, and instead of granting me a permanent residence permit, the authorities only granted me a two-year visa. After that, K. G. and I got divorced, and on the occasion of the opening of my *Integration Project Office* installation at Project room Gallery 35 in Berlin (1 July 2005), I organized *Divorce Party*.

In order to claim my own rights, which I had been deprived of under current EU law, I explicitly applied the strategy of tricking the law (as earlier with *Illegal Border Crossing*) to gain the right to move freely, and live and work in diverse locations.

Migrants are constantly abstracted by the media and discriminatory laws, and often treated as a single alienated group. The aspect of personal and direct speech, as opposed to abstract speech, is an important element throughout my work. I showed myself in that position, with my own story, as well as later collecting the individual stories of others whom I met, so that the audience would get a chance to understand the variety and depth of the matter, and identify with me, with them, with us.

Tanja Ostojić, The "Applications" from: *Looking for a Husband with EU Passport*, 2000–5. John H. from Texas, André S., Svenja Sch.

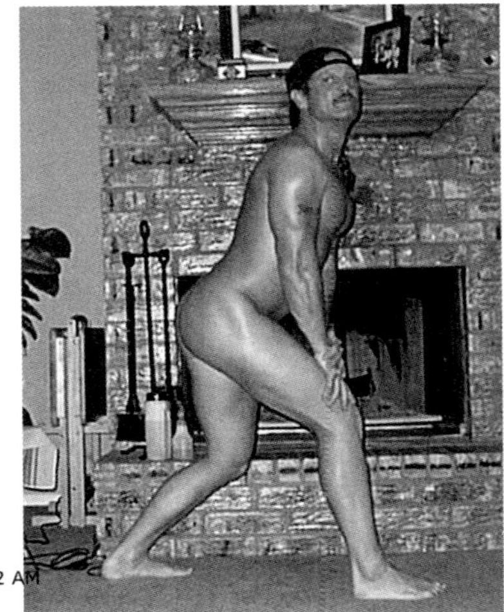

From: John H
To: t @diplomats.com
Sent: Saturday, January 05, 2002 5:32 AM
Subject: Looking for a Husband

Hello Dear Lady,
I know this is a bit late but I just now found your add and site. Are you still in the market for a husband? I don't want to go into any great details if I am wasting my time.

John, 43 years old in Texas

From: andre <andre@ . .co.uk>
To: tanja@ .net>
Sent: Monday, August 21, 2000 7:08 PM
Subject: Re: +Looking for a husband with a EU passport

dear tanja..

what? you want to marry someone...are you serious...you can't find anyone... I can't believe it..you're so beautiful and sexy !! Is it only for staying in EU...??? a marriage of covenience??? That would be a pity.

why not marry someone for real that you love....???..and who loves you....??? I think this is something very serious to consider...

Where exactly are you now anyway...where are you living?? I thought you where living with someone and in a relationship??

love and best wishes
andre XXX

Within the entire *Crossing Borders* series and the *Integration Project* (2000–5), the aim was to introduce certain aspects of reality into the arts in order to utilize the channels of the latter for broader transmission. I was continuously learning through the complex process of this project and, on that basis, making further decisions for the next step of the project. Compiling an archive proved a very helpful device for my continuing work. The *Integration Project Archive* (which consists of over eighty hours of unedited video interviews, audio materials, books, an essay, interviews, documents, photos, flyers, brochures, etc.) stands in an important relation to the ongoing research. Whenever the archive is exhibited as part of the *Integration Project Office*, it is openly accessible to whoever is interested.

From: Svenja Sch <svenja .de>
To: hottanja@hotmail.com
Subject: looking for a husband with EU passport
Date: Wed, 23 Jul 2003 04:31:27 -0700 (PDT)

hi tanja,

i'm very sorry that i found your 'real-life-internet project' called 'looking for a husband with EU passport' too late, means today.

i'm not male but an attractive female. my name is svenja and i live in south germany. i'm 23 years old and a lesbian since the age of 16. i have a shaved head too; is your head still bald?
i read that you already found a husband, that german guy. are u interested in a meeting with me nevertheless? i would be very happy if we could meet here in stuttgart.

i'm looking forward to hear from you soon.

best wishes

svenja

p.s. i addes a pic of me which was shot after my headshave

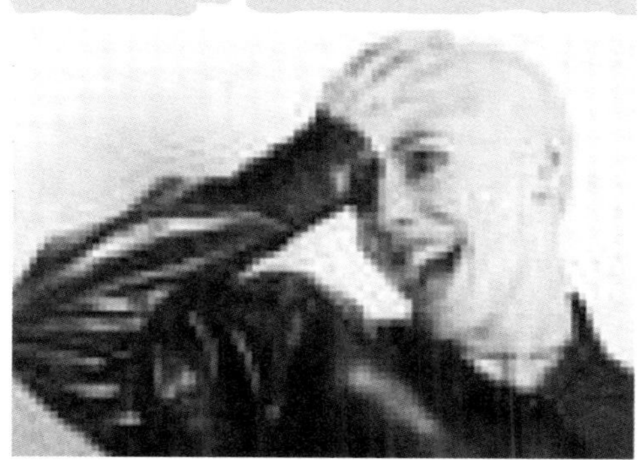

Chapter 28

Barbara Smith, Intimations of Immortality

Barbara Smith has long been a key, but underappreciated, figure on the American performance art scene; her work is particularly crucial in histories of California performance and feminist art since the late 1960s. While colleagues she worked with such as Paul McCarthy have become internationally known, Smith's practice has been promoted and written about only by McCarthy and a handful of feminist curators and writers – testimony to the lingering sexism determining how histories of various art forms get written and institutionalized.

Smith's *Intimations of Immortality* is a relational work, involving her in-depth interaction with three homeless women. Her invitation for each of the women to sit in the gallery while she took their place in a public park nearby involved an intense engagement with them (and winning of their trust), but also a kind of substitution of their bodies for hers in the gallery situation – in the sense that visitors knowledgeable about performance art might expect the artist to appear herself in the gallery space. The piece offered a potential exchange of identities due to her empathetic identification with the homeless women she met and worked with to make the piece, and the potential identification between gallery visitors and the homeless women or visitors to the park and Smith herself.

If *Intimations of Immortality* involved substituting homeless women for Smith then histories of the work must engage with different (representations of different) bodies – all of which were equally central to the work's effects across these varied public spaces – to attempt to retrieve the work and place it again in public view. Accordingly, here is included a range of documentary "evidence" of the piece, including a photograph of Smith in MacArthur Park being interviewed for the Super-8 film documenting the piece; a still from the film showing "Olive" being interviewed in the gallery; and a reproduction of a spread documenting the piece from the "spare" 1994 catalogue (effectively a broadsheet); an interpretation by an art historian (Jennie Klein) from a retrospective catalogue; and even reminiscences by Smith herself, as written in an e-mail to the author.

Amelia Jones

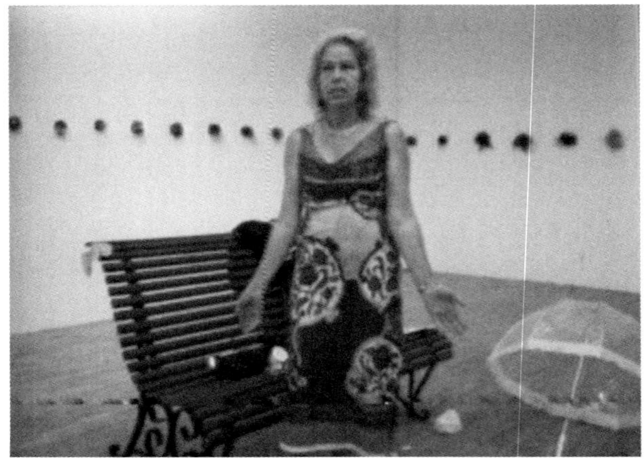

Still from the original Super-8 film footage documenting the homeless woman in Grandview Gallery I & II, Women's Building, Los Angeles; captured from Smith's DVD compilation of her performances, Barbara T. Smith Performances 1969-1999; in this section of the film, the woman is being interviewed, and notes "We're a long way from MacArthur Park!," followed by Barbara Smith's voice over noting "I was so poor, I was afraid of living on the street."

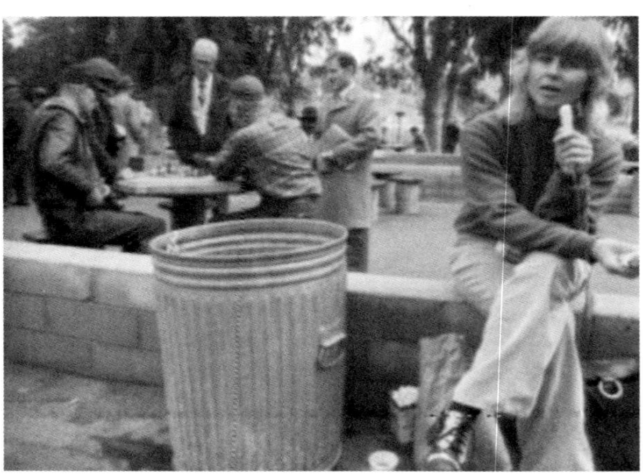

Still from the original Super-8 film footage documenting Barbara Smith in MacArthur Park; captured from Smith's DVD compilation of her performances, Barbara T. Smith Performances 1969-1999; in this section of the film, Smith notes to a male interlocutor, "My name is Barbara Smith… I'm an artist… I'm exchanging places with a number of women who ordinarily spend a lot of time in MacArthur Park."

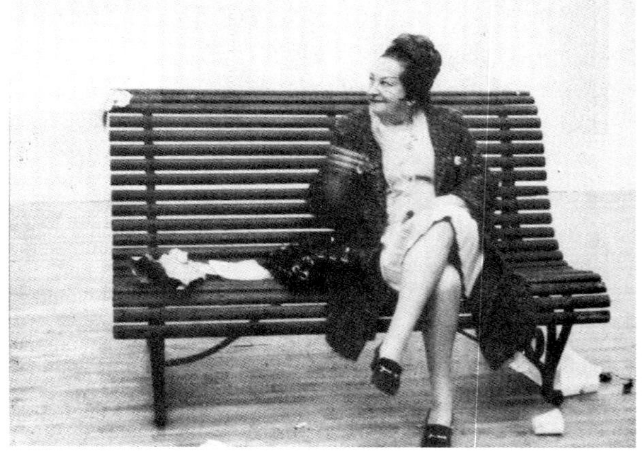

Spread from Barbara Smith's self-published pamphlet documenting her work, Barbara Turner Smith (1994), showing a still photograph from *Intimations of Immortality*, a homeless woman on the bench in Granville Gallery. Courtesy of Pomona College Museum of Art.

Excerpt from Jennie Klein's "The Body's Odyssey"[1]

For *Intimations of Immortality* [... as] was the case with *Feed Me*, Smith opened herself to collaboration with people unknown to her. [...] Homeless or simply lonely, these elderly and/or alcoholic women – Alice, Bertha, and Olive – were hardly individuals one would associate with immortality. Capitalist detritus, they spent their days, and possibly nights, sitting in the park [...]

One might view *Intimations of Immortality* as exploitative of these women, making them into art material to shock the typical gallery visitor. Grandview Gallery, however, was not a typical gallery, nor were those who visited the Woman's Building typical gallery goers. That was not Smith's intention. She did not think of the women who participated in *Intimations of Immortality* as mere curiosities. Rather, she intended the piece to honor a group of women – the elderly and the homeless – that was virtually invisible in 1974. The title of the piece came from a poem by Wordsworth ... Smith chose the title because she felt these women deserved a chance at immortality rather than simply being forgotten. At the time she conceived the piece, Smith was desperately poor, barely able to make ends meet. Although nominally an "artist" – a profession that in most cases yields very little money but at least suggests a life devoted to a higher calling – Smith saw very little difference between herself and the women whose place she took in the park. Yet at the same time, her decision to involve these women in her art transformed their marginalized existence into an historical event worthy of documentation (hence their inclusion in this exhibition). [...]

Barbara Smith, an e-mail to Amelia Jones

Subject: Intimations of Immortality
Date: 20 July 2008 00:13:07 BDT

July 19, 2008

Dear Amelia,

[...] I am trying to see what I think you need from me. Perhaps I will just write based on your e-mail of July 8 and see if that gives you what you want. You can send me any edits you want to make or things you want added. Now I wonder what tone to write in.

The time was 1974. I belonged to a feminist collaborative gallery called Grandview I and II housed in the Women's Building in LA. I and II because there were too many of us and so we rented 2 gallery spaces and exhibited often two artists at a time in each space. (If you notice in the images from this piece, there are artworks on the walls behind the women on the bench in the gallery, little round things in a row around the room. They are Nancy Buchanan's work, human hair pieces attached to Styrofoam half rounds. It was a shared exhibition.)

I was then […] extremely worried about survival. I had a studio in the "skid row" part of Pasadena, no job, and my ex-husband owed me money he was not paying. Nancy and I shared the membership in GV because it was all we could afford. I had recently realized that I would never see my daughters again. (And I didn't until 17 years later.)

I felt an intense psychic pull and identification with homelessness. My inner soul was being enticed as if by a drug, like "You WILL come down here." It felt like an anguished struggle and Macarthur Park held it all. It was a trash-strewn place where indigent people, homeless men, and impoverished, even then mostly Mexican families gathered. Grandview Street where the Women's Building was abutted into the park. The physical feeling I experienced was like gasping for breath and being scraped with thorns as I walked through although of course I barely acknowledged it.

But I felt a curiosity about the park, the people there, whether there were any women who were homeless too. (Called then "bag ladies.") In the mysterious way that an artwork invades the mind and becomes, Yes!, the actual thing I wanted to do, I decided to go into the park and find out.

I spent weeks walking around and sure enough there were a few [homeless women]. Here it was that I realized I had an enormous compassion for them. That indeed they were no less heroic, no less worthy of respect and dignity than any other human being. I wanted by my piece to honor them and for me to find out in some small way how it felt to be them, i.e., to live like they did. Soon I saw clearly I would find a park bench and ask them to sit on it in the gallery as the art.

The name of the piece floated into my mind, "Intimations of Immortality" […] recalled from my studies at Pomona College. It was perfect without reason for I had no recall of the author nor his exact meaning. For me, it meant that these women like all women are immortal […] for no reason except their innate human dignity.

Finding a park bench was near impossible until I remembered my college friend, Frank Wells, who was then president of Warner Bros. He got a bench from their prop department and delivered it to the building.

But the women! It was delicate to approach them and some would not talk to me. Some did not understand and I could see would not remember from one day to the next that we had spoken. I got Olive fairly quickly because she had the sophistication to understand an art gallery; she had been an artist's model. On a very cold rainy day I found Alice. All the park people were hanging out in a long dark shed out of the rain and at a distance I saw her hunched over in a dark grey coat. I approached and she and I began to talk. I told her my wish and she agreed with the proviso that I understand that "I am an alcoholic you know," said in her rough and raspy voice. There is a whole story about her but one of the issues was getting booze out to her while she sat. […] The last was Bertha, who I found hanging out with a group of men who gathered every day to play and sing on all manner of instruments. […]

They, all three, were great! [...]

The whole experience was an ordeal, psychically demanding and exhausting. I worried at first about how the women would be perceived because I absolutely did not want them to be objectified; instead gallery goers could talk with them and I wanted them to be appreciated. I wrote a text for the wall hoping it would set the correct tone. Given that it was at the Women's Building, I think it worked.

But it seemed there was no happy ending. Alice had a terrible sore on her leg that wouldn't heal. I got my doctor to agree to look at it, and it turns out this wasn't needed because someone else procured a doctor for her. Only at the end when I invited the guys who Bertha sang with to come over and play [...] did there seem to be humanity and hope. As stated, the men were shy and only a visit by me with Allan Kaprow and Ransom Rideout convinced them that it was OK. Then spontaneously as we cruised through the park to get to the building, they began to play the Battle Hymn of the Republic. It was very moving. Once inside they were again shy but eventually one by one they took the lead with a song or two, all ones everyone knows, and a crowd gathered. And we all, persons of all sorts began to sing and dance.

I went back with pictures for them but never saw any of them again. You ask about this exchange of me with them. It was not an exact exchange. I was honoring them and exploring something of what their lives were like. No one was acting. All of us were being who we are, just in a new circumstance. For me, the park became friendlier and more familiar. Suzanne Lacy and I even made a short comical film of me trying to catch pigeons to hang out in the room with the women. [...]

This piece was typical early performance art, i.e., Body Art, in its focus on the real experience of lived bodies in a non-theatrical, durational setting. One can think of Chris Burden in his several incarnations in gallery settings, my *Feed Me* piece [her influential 1973 performance], Marina Abramović, etc., etc.

How does this work get documented into history? I myself shot the photographs of Olive, Alice, and Bertha and printed them myself. A friend, whom I cannot remember, interviewed Alice, and me ... segments of which are in our DVD. There were no art historians, or curators breathing down our necks wanting to show and validate or analyze any of our/my work. So like all my other pieces, I simply stored the info away and moved on, having I think received the transformative healing value of actually doing it.

There it sat until 1994 when Judy Hoffberg in company with 18th Street Arts Complex [in Santa Monica] and Sue Dakin wanted to turn a space there into a gallery and then to do a two-person show of my work with Hirokazu Kosaka. Judy pushed the idea of some sort of a catalogue for which we had zero money. She and I pasted it up and it was self published on newsprint in about a run of 1000 copies. It had to be inclusive, a sort of history of my work, and spare, so it only contains photographs of key pieces with captions and defining chapter headings according to the issues on which I focused. The catalogue, called *BARBARA TURNER SMITH*, contains a picture of Bertha from the *Intimations of Immortality* piece.

Time goes by and in 2002 Diane Fuller put together a feminist history exhibition called "Parallels & Intersections: Art/Women/California 1950–2000" at the San Jose Museum of Art. And she asked me to include several of my key pieces. The only way I could imagine doing this was via a DVD. I engaged Kate Johnson of EZTV to be my collaborator and we made a DVD (called *Barbara T. Smith Performances, 1969–1999*) that included this piece. It is clear that the public history of this piece and others has resided in the memories of key (women) who are now in position to include it in shows.

Next Rebecca McGrew and Jennie Klein began a plan for a retrospective show at the Pomona College Museum of Art. (Jennie had been writing about my work and that of other less well-known women.) It was four years in the making (since my work was termed by some curators as impossible to show in a gallery setting). The show opened in 2005 and included *Intimations* … Finally in a conversation with Catherine Grenier this piece was chosen for my inclusion in the "LA–PARIS 1955–1985" show at Centre Georges Pompidou in 2007. I was very relieved to show this work rather that the ever-present images from *FEED ME*, as if that piece is the only one I ever did.

In 2007 the Pomona College Museum of Art bought the piece, which includes the four photographs, the 3 contracts the women signed to agree to be in the piece, and various of my handwritten notes, for their collection.

Slowly my work has gained visibility many times through the influence and support of my friends. I am not sure if this is usual but … I rarely repeat a piece so it is not commodified and I haven't written about it as much as one could. Etc., etc.

So this is lengthy and very narrative in structure. I hope you can cull what you want and ask any questions you still need answers for. Thanks for doing the book, I hope it is a big success!!! My best wishes,

Barbara T.

Note

1. Jennie Klein, "The Body's Odyssey," *The 21st Century Odyssey Part II: The Performances of Barbara T. Smith*, Pomona, California: Pomona College Museum of Art, 2005, pp. 13–14.

Chapter 29

Santiago Sierra and the "Contexts" of History

Santiago Sierra's performative projects take their meaning and power through their relationship to context and documentation. The importance of documentation is indicated by his spare but effective website, which consists simply of a gray home page with dates; on each date page, each of his projects is simply documented with text and images.[1] Institutional and geographical *context* is also absolutely crucial to how his works play out, how they engage with institutional constraints and frameworks, and how they end up being documented and historicized.

Sierra developed his now signature practice of hiring laborers to perform various demeaning and/or difficult tasks in Mexico and nearby countries such as Guatemala, where laborers are exploited for a pittance and are desperate for work. In that context the pieces principally engage broad structures of labor and capital rather than art world politics or economics per se. In the early 2000s Sierra's work was widely recognized on the international (particularly European) scene and he began to be commissioned to do similar pieces or to re-stage earlier Mexican works (such as the 2000 *Lifted Out Wall Leaning Over by 60 Degrees*) in Europe. The transfer of this kind of project from the difficult economic conditions of Central America to the "first-world" standards and pretenses of the European art world transformed the practice into commentary on the economically driven politics of the global art market.

Sierra himself claims that this shift in site and audience "essentially didn't change my work [because the] same fundamental labor mechanisms are in place nearly everywhere, though expectations are quite different."[2] I would argue, however, that while labor conditions may be similar in the broadest sense of all areas of the world being under the sway of late capitalism, the "expectations" particular to the context in which the performance is completed and documented are crucial to how the works function politically and historically. Attempting to shift *Lifted Out Wall* to the context of the Munich Kunsthalle in 2001, for example, Sierra was forced to give up because the constraints of the gallery demanded an entirely new approach; the gallery demanded he employ legal workers and refused to consider allowing the artist's workers to tear down a wall – these different conditions resulted in *Elevation of Six Benches*, a completely different piece responding to what Sierra called the "clean and prosperous" character of Munich.[3] Attempting to produce *Lifted Out Wall* again in 2001 in New York City at P.S.1, Sierra again gave up, given the fact that the gallery did not have the funds to hire five people for the period of time demanded and, as Sierra noted, this was shortly after the terrorist attacks of 9/11 and "I didn't want to fly to New York – not out of a fear of terrorist attacks, but out of a fear of American immigration officials."[4]

If the location and specific conditions of a work – in Sierra's case installations produced from performances, usually completed before the audience enters the gallery – are crucial to its effects, then understanding the work in history involves close attention to these contextual elements. Produced at Lisson Gallery in London, one of the most important commercial galleries in one of the centers of the global (Euro-American dominated) art world, Sierra's *Polyurethane Sprayed on the Backs of 10 Workers* takes on a particular set of political and social meanings. He paid the Iraqi workers, in his own words, "as little as possible" in an economy in which they are already used to being exploited.[5] This clear exposure of unfair labor practices (signaled mournfully in the final installation by the evacuated husks of dried foam, which highlight the absence and erasure of the bodies that support structures of capital in "first world" societies) is in tension with Sierra's own tendency to disavow art's potential to create political change. Sierra has described contemporary art as "a narrow margin through which one can convey blame."[6] He also notes the significance of his chosen materials (including, clearly, the "material" of Iraqi immigrant workers, linked in the Euro-American imaginary since 2004 to the abuses at Abu Ghraib):

> I used the foam because I wanted to bring the guns used to apply it together with the system of protection from it – a dual way of administering power: with love and hate. Polyurethane protects aggressively because it releases toxic fumes. I also wanted to re-create certain memorable images – for instance, of the 2002 oil spill off the northwest coast of Spain [where cleanup crews wore protective suits identical to those used in handling polyurethane] and of Abu Ghraib. It's an image of disaster, a painting of power trying to objectify the body.[7]

Re-building an overall "picture" of this project (without, sadly, having seen it at Lisson), I understand it in relation to this constellation of "documentary" sources: website, texts, images, and analyses, including Sierra's own. This does not secure "the meaning" of the work. As presented here, it simply provides another cluster of descriptive modes of re-presenting the work.

Amelia Jones

Santiago Sierra, *Polyurethane Sprayed on the Backs of 10 Workers*, Lisson Gallery, London, UK, July 2004

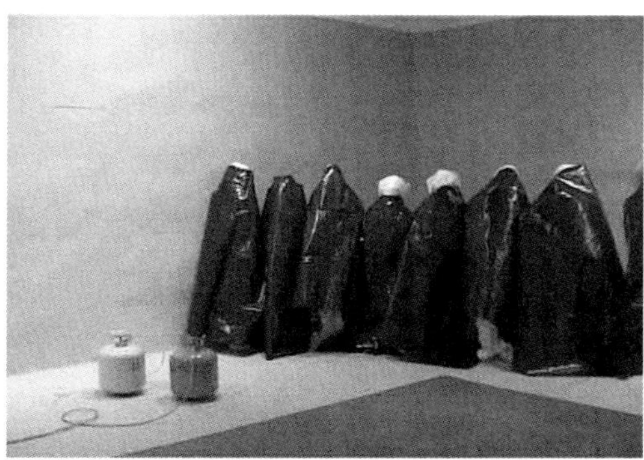

Santiago Sierra, *Polyurethane Sprayed on the Backs of 10 Workers*, still from the video documentation. Lisson Gallery, London, UK, July 2004. Courtesy the artist and Lisson Gallery.

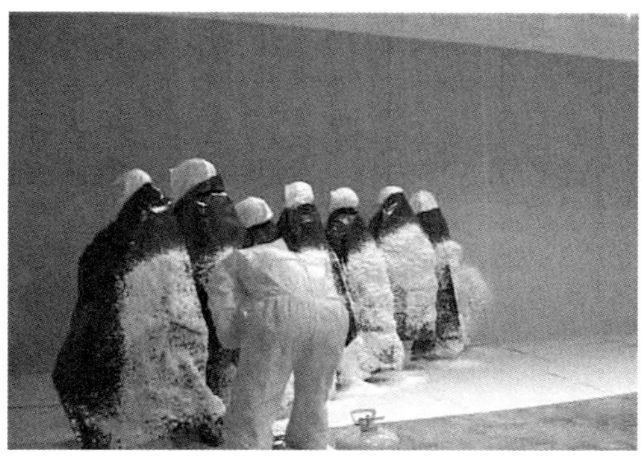

Santiago Sierra, *Polyurethane Sprayed on the Backs of 10 Workers*, workers being sprayed; still from the video documentation. Lisson Gallery, London, UK, July 2004. Courtesy the artist and Lisson Gallery.

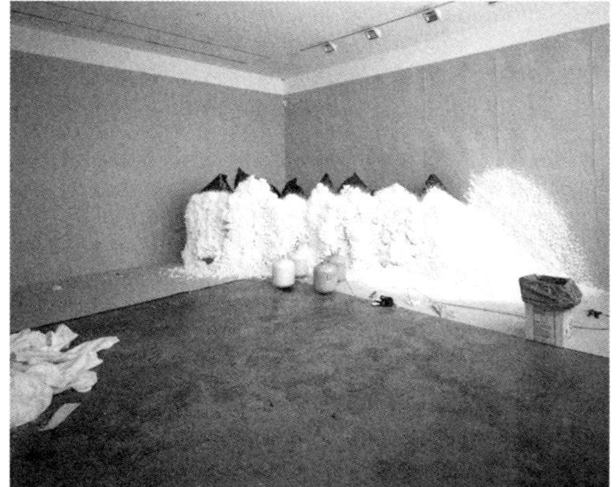

Santiago Sierra, *Polyurethane Sprayed on the Backs of 10 Workers*, 2004, hulks of sprayed workers on display at Lisson Gallery, still from the video documentation. Lisson Gallery, London, UK, July 2004. Courtesy the artist and Lisson Gallery.

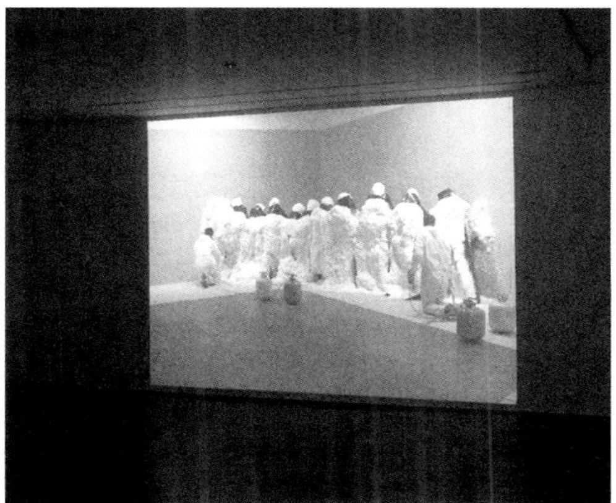

Santiago Sierra, *Polyurethane Sprayed on the Backs of 10 Workers*, video projection of documentation of spraying of workers, on display at Lisson Gallery. Lisson Gallery, London, UK, July 2004. Courtesy the artist and Lisson Gallery.

Ten immigrant Iraqi workers were hired for this action. They were protected with chemically resistant clothing and a thick sheet of plastic, then they were placed in various positions and sprayed on the back with polyurethane until large formations of this material had been obtained. Only a very small group of people involved in the making of the work was present during the action and its recording. Two technicians took care of all practical and technical aspects of the spraying of the polyurethane. The exhibition displayed the video documentation of the action, as well as the sculptural remnants and all of the elements employed in the action.

As in most cases, Santiago Sierra's work is the action as well as its documentation, although in this case visitors could not be present during the action, and the only way to experience the work was through its photographic and video documentation. The casts were only shown during the exhibition.

Notes

1. See http://www.santiago-sierra.com/.
2. Sierra comments on this shift in Klaus Biesenbach, "A Thousand Words: Santiago Sierra Talks about his Work," *Artforum*, October 2002, p. 131.
3. Ibid.
4. Ibid.
5. Sierra is cited by Martin Herbert in "Material Witness: Martin Herbert On Santiago Sierra," *Artforum*, September 2004, p. 211. One guesses the workers are *illegal* immigrants but (for obvious reasons) this is not clearly stated by the gallery or website.
6. Ibid.
7. Ibid.

Chapter 30

Reconstruction2[1]: On the Reconstructions of Pupilija, papa Pupilo and the Pupilceks

Janez Janša

Pupilija, papa Pupilo and the Pupilceks [*Pupilija Papa Pupilo pa Pupilčki*] was performed in 1969 by a group of poets, visual artists, musicians, and amateurs. It consisted of twenty scenes, including elements of everyday life, popular culture, folklore, children's games, contemporary dance, performance, and improvisation. The performance is an iconic event of Slovenian theater neo-avant-garde and one of the most influential experimental performing works. It introduced an interdisciplinary approach into Slovenian theater and constituted the grounds for the understanding of performing arts as an area, where different artistic and social practices come together. *Pupilija* included elements of happening, body art, performance, improvisation, contemporary dance, everyday life, pop culture, ritual theater, cabaret, and political protest.

The records of the 1969 performance *Pupilija, papa Pupilo and the Pupilceks* are quite extensive. The performance was recorded in Viba studio with five cameras and was also excellently edited. The Slovenian Theatre Museum has numerous documents on the performance, its media reception and public response; most of the participants are still alive and serve as an important oral source; a quite detailed scenario of the performance is preserved. In a strictly historical and analytical sense the documentation of the performance is well conserved, accessible in public archives and there is no need to reconstruct it due to the loss of historical evidence. The motives for reconstruction, therefore, lie elsewhere. The point of reconstructing *Pupilija* is not to re-experience a performance from the past, but to experience the very relationship to history: what we are watching when we see the reconstruction is our relation to history. Together with Inke Arns, we could say that re-enactments "are *questionings of the present* through reaching back to historical events that have etched themselves indelibly into the collective memory."[2]

An extract of an essay originally published as Janez Janša, "Reconstruction2: On the Reconstructions of Pupilija, papa Pupilo, and the Pupilceks" in *Dance on Time*, eds. Gurur Ertem and Noémie Solomon, Istanbul: Bimeras, 2010, pp. 44–63.

What can we conclude from the fact that, in 1969, *Pupilija, papa Pupilo and the Pupilceks* was recorded without the presence of an audience?[3] What makes a performance part of its time is not only the performance itself but its audience. In this sense, the only real reconstruction would be the reconstruction of the audience. By being shot without the audience, both recordings of *Pupilija* (the original and the reconstructed one), at a certain level, want to blur the time in which the performances were created. Many of the actors of the original *Pupilija* were skeptical about the possibility of its reconstruction, especially because they had doubts about the possibility of re-enacting the time at the end of the 1960s. The answer that the reconstruction had to give was that the performance does not deal with the time of the original performance but with the present time.

In a sense, the reconstructions have to "betray" the original in order for it to even function in the time of the reconstruction. The approach I used in the reconstruction is nevertheless essentially different from a contemporary interpretation of a classic, since a reconstruction demonstrates its procedures; it discloses and screens documentary material and constantly questions the status of the truth of a historical event, whereas in an interpretation of a classical text, the historical evidence, documents and procedures are part of the creative process and are, as a rule, excluded from the final staging. In reconstructions, one first needs to prove that the object of a reconstruction actually existed.

The fundamental directorial and dramaturgical move used in *Pupilija, papa Pupilo and the Pupilceks – the Reconstruction* is the displacement of the gaze. What we are watching constantly eludes us; there is something else that constantly wants to appear before us. When we think we are watching the original *Pupilija*, the present, a reconstructed one, shows itself to us. Underneath today's *Pupilija*, the one from 1969 always creeps up on us, but we do not know to what extent we can believe it. I call this displacement of the gaze *zooming*, a procedure of watching in which spectators focus, zoom in or out, on a certain segment, a certain part of the performance or the events in front of them, or use the same operation to distance themselves from the performance; they can even bracket it and, for a moment, apply themselves to side perceptual effects, which at first sight do not seem to be related to the performance, yet are enabled by the dramaturgical structure and thus become part of the performance for the audience. For the spectators, the performance is not only that which the creators perform in front of them, but all that happens in this space-time.

On the Interpretations of Pupilija

Each age operates with a certain interpretative language and, at a certain level, it is understandable that the predominating interpretations of *Pupilija* operated with terms such as "death of literary theatre," "anti-literariness," etc.[4] Most of the interpretations point out the ritual nature of the performance, above all, because of the last scene of slaughtering a chicken. In the actors' performance, the distance from the expressiveness typical of the 1960s was very visible – in it, we can note an essential difference between *Pupilija* and, for example, the Living Theatre. Acting in *Pupilija* is much closer to what Michael Kirby named "non-acting."

The reconstruction attempts to stress the procedures used in the original performance, especially openness and non-formality. What is especially interesting for the reconstructors is how to re-enact the following elements: everydayness and unskillfulness; non-spectacularity and extremity of execution; open improvisation, folklore and military discipline; collective mind and mindlessness; the open, non-aestheticized and non-linear language of the performance and its political engagement.

Pupilija's *politicalness* – in Jacques Rancière's terms – lay primarily in its resistance to all forms of authority and not in the direct expression of a political protest. *Pupilija* distances itself, mocks and subverts authorities, from the external (state, nation, party, church, market) to the internal (theater and aesthetics). With its suggestive, yet almost innocent speech, it also easily attracts today's spectator. This is why *Pupilijia's* politicalness has to be understood in a Rancièrean sense: the politicalness lies in admitting into the public sphere voices that can otherwise not be heard. *Pupilija* is definitely a generational performance, a performance of members of a generation who did not want to wait to get the permission to enter political life, but rather strengthened their voices themselves. At another level, *Pupilija*'s politicalness should be understood in the way that Hans-Thies Lehmann writes about political theater, namely, through the format of the performance. By this, we mean the structure of the performance and especially the stance of the creators on and off stage, in the media, at the court, etc.

The next dimension that the performance attempts to lay open is the introduction of dance. It was typical of all the socialist and communist countries that they hindered the development of contemporary dance, which therefore had to make its way to the forefront in experimental performance forms. In a conversation, Rok Vevar said that "if we look at *Pupilija, Papa Pupilo and the Pupilceks* as a dance performance, we will see what has been happening in dance in the USA since the 1960s."[5] *Pupilija* introduced various choreographic procedures without defining them as dance. These procedures were conceived through appropriated forms of movement, from spontaneous children's games, folklore parody, and military exercises to improvised scenes. We can look at the structure of the performance, the twenty more or less arbitrarily composed scenes, in the way Slavoj Žižek understood happening in pop art, at the time: "The happening is directed into the exhibited object, which is not there just like that, but in order to be there just like that. The object is arbitrary and determined (i.e., eliminated from the environment) by this arbitrariness."[6] The arbitrary combination of fragments becomes one of the key structural procedures of postmodern theater of the 1980s. In the dramaturgical and structural sense, *Pupilija* is much closer to this postmodern theater than to the experimental theater of the 1960s and we could even say that the structure of *Pupilija* is similar to the structure of *Baptism Under Triglav*, the fundamental performance of Slovenian postmodern theater.

The Reconstruction of Pupilija for the Past, Present, and Future

In his review of *Pupilija*, Blaž Lukan wrote that, in the reconstruction, we actually see three performances:

> The first one is the original that no longer exists; the second one – today's performance – has contemporary performers who are more than mere substitutes for the original ones; the third one is a reconstruction as a whole. [...] This whole seems like some kind of a superstructure, supra-performance which upgrades both (or more) of the others and establishes itself in front of the spectator as the only possible performance "based on the model," as performance as such which no longer is an imitation or something that feeds from imitation while it seeks its own mechanisms and effects.[7]

Drawing on this view, I propose that the performance and the whole strategic specter encircling it is where the past, the present, and the future intertwine.

We look at the present as projected documents. Together with the author of the projections, Samo Gosarič, and the projection matrix designer, Igor Štromajer, we thought about what MTV or a news channel would look like if it had existed in 1969. We thus composed the framework of the projection from an uninterrupted screening of clips from the original performance, the statements of original creators, and media reactions. This resulted in a parallel media layer of the performance, conceived entirely through historical sources. We translated the past into history by projecting it. We thus literally used a procedure that every historical process already employs: because there is no past, we are left with no other alternative but to project it. Each projection is actually a construction of the view (of the past). A document as the place of truth is *mediated*: it exists only as mediatized event. By being presented *in* a performance, it is additionally mediated.

In the same text, Lukan wonders: "What or who – to say this with a certain amount of drastic irony – should be slaughtered today to achieve a similar effect in public?" Since we were forbidden to perform the last scene, the scene of slaughtering a chicken, by the manager of the Old Power Plant, the venue where the reconstruction was staged, we decided that, rather than performing this historical component, we would stage the current fact of the prohibition. We asked the spectators to decide on the last scene of the performance: they could choose among three recordings (the recording of a reconstructed slaughtering of a chicken, the statements of Junoš Miklavec and Dušan Rogelj, who slaughtered the chicken in the original *Pupilija*, and an excerpt from the regulations on the protection of animals at the time of slaughter), the fourth option was slaughtering the animal live. We thus made the audience responsible for the execution of the event. But what was more interesting for us than this participatory dimension was the tension between the legal and the legitimate. The legislation allows animals to be slaughtered only in appropriate places (slaughterhouses) or at home, for domestic use. If we wanted to perform the slaughter of a chicken legally, we would have to put on the performance in a slaughterhouse or turn the theater into our home. Instead, we enabled the micro-community of spectators to oppose the legal order, which is what usually happened, since, except on one occasion, the audience always chose the live slaughter of a chicken. In view of this, let us not judge too quickly that every audience wants blood and that our times are like old Roman times. For it was because the course of the performance itself, the dramaturgy of its execution, was predominantly playful and at times easygoing that the audience wanted to play a joke on the performers. What we wanted to show with the last scene was that the performance had become here and now, that the reconstruction cut into the time in which it was created and thus staged the present.

I have already said that every historicizing is a construction of the past. We construct the past through the gaze of the present, with the gaze being constructed by a set of social, political, cultural, methodological, interpretative, and other factors. We historicize the past in the present, but we do it for the future. Every historicizing includes, on the one hand, the opening of the overlooked and concealed; it brings and strengthens the unheard voices, while, on the other hand, it closes or, better yet, uses this operation to *package* a certain chapter of the past.

On the basis of this, we thought about building a mechanism into the reconstruction of *Pupilija*, which would resist this packaging and would demand two different packagings from the outset. Let us first take a look at how two of the most important critics, Rok Vevar and Blaž Lukan, interpreted the ending of the reconstruction of *Pupilija*:

> In compliance with the changed political context the spectators democratically vote whether or not the Chicken should be slaughtered. […] When at the premiere slaughter was voted through, the conditions for the Event were re-established. "If you have voted for the slaughter, we call to a member of the audience who has voted for it, to come to the stage and perform it." The answer/responsibility of the gaze, what else! What followed was painful waiting and to be honest: democracy has upset the Chicken too. In those painful moments I, as signed below, could not help thinking: "Well, well, the Chicken is watching us …" Right after that I was overcome by a thought: "Mother Chicken! Is it at all possible to have a more genuine experience of (Slovene) democracy?"[8]

> At the most recent staging in the Old Power Station, despite the ambiguous ending – it remained unclear whether Grega Zorc in his white butcher's apron actually slaughtered the chicken or not – there was suddenly painful silence which went on and on; in it we could feel discomfort because it awakened the memory of the "slaughter" from almost four decades ago, and of which we knew something about, because of the – not quite provable – death of a living being which happened in front of the spectators' eyes; but the horror was actually the result of an exceptionally well constructed scene or epilogue, from the point of view of dramaturgy, direction and acting, which concluded the whole performance.[9]

So we have projected into the future a doubt as to which ending actually took place. Did Vevar and Lukan see the same performance even if they saw it on different nights? Was the chicken nevertheless slaughtered? And if it was, how come its slaughter was so unproblematically received, although outraged writings about the possibility of a chicken being slaughtered on stage had appeared already before the opening night?[10]

Scandalizing as Censorship

At this point, we should speak about one of the reasons for reconstructing *Pupilija*. The 1969 *Pupilija, papa Pupilo and the Pupilceks* is generally remembered in Slovenia as a scandal. When Slovenians think of this performance, the first reaction, the first memory of it, is the slaughter of a chicken, while those who have seen it may add nudity, homosexuality, intercourse with a globe, etc. *Pupilija* is not the concealed part of the history of Slovenian contemporary performing arts; there is reference material on it. We could sooner say that it is a *skipped* part of this history. But it exists as a scandal in collective memory. And, paradoxically, this scandalizing excluded *Pupilija* from the main course of history. Approaches that devoted attention to *Pupilija's* artistic qualities have been exceptionally rare.

What we were interested in, in the reconstruction, was the manner of acting. At first sight, we could say that it was a youthful, amateur approach, but, still, what has remained, what we can read from the tape, is a whole range of performing poses, from everydayness, non-acting, over-identification, and ludic acting to parodying the sublime. These approaches to acting were kept secret and were ousted from the academic canon, wherein lies one of the fundamental censorship moves of the cultural circle.

The second censorship took place at the level of production. In reconstructing *Pupilija*, the focus was also on affirming the mode of production that emerges on the basis of group affinities, the need for experimenting and a different kind of expression, the need to cooperate in non-hierarchical conditions, conditions that essentially differ from working in the theater, which is one of the most hierarchically organized art forms. The reconstruction of *Pupilija* was not created in the same group way as the original. I put together the cast so that the interdisciplinarity of the original performance would be even more pronounced, with various expert knowledges brought to the performance by the performers' backgrounds. I cast a dancer (Dejan Srhoj), actors (Grega Zorc, Ajda Toman, Alja Kapun), a film actress (Aleksandra Balmazović), a TV host (Dražen Dragojević), a writer, a radio host and a musician (Matjaž Pikalo), a singer and dancer (Irena Tomažin), and musicians (Boštjan Narat, Gregor Cvetko and Lado Jakša). On average, the original cast had fifteen members. We could afford eleven at most, due to the production conditions. This is why, when they were not musically engaged, the musicians performed in the acting and dancing scenes. At the same time, we thus additionally emphasized the interdisciplinary nature of the performance.

The Western Reception of *Pupilija* and the East Dance Academy

When *Pupilija* was on tour in Austria and Italy, doubts were raised as to the existence of the original.[11] We can find the reason for such comments in a sort of a stereotypical view that the West has about the theater and art of Eastern Europe during socialism. Behind the Iron Curtain, the West saw depression, suffering, and oppression, which is why the ideal theater artist who embodied this perception was Jerzy Grotowski. The West could not imagine that a non-authoritarian performance such as *Pupilija* could have been created under a socialist regime. And it is still hard for the West to accept that important performance experiments took place in Eastern Europe, which belong to the context of European experimental performing art practices on an equal footing.

Because *Pupilija* is not an isolated example, my colleagues Bojana Kunst, Aldo Milohnić, and Goran Sergej Pristaš and I developed an idea for a platform called East Dance Academy (EDA), which will contribute to the articulation of a different history of contemporary dance and performance art in Eastern Europe and Europe in general. The aim of EDA is to detect the Eastern European places, areas, and events where contemporary dance and interdisciplinary performance appeared. Contemporary dance was not institutionalized until the decline of the communist regimes in the 1980s, but it was constantly present and it developed in interdisciplinary experimental forms, such as, experimental music and theater, video, performance art, etc. EDA emphasizes interdisciplinarity and a strong social contextualization of artistic production. In this sense, it brings together an audience from different fields and different perspectives.

EDA is a working space in which the participants display historical examples of performances and actions in their local context and which considers contemporary dance and performance art within a broader cultural perspective. We can understand EDA as the continuation of the processes of articulating the history of contemporary art in the context of Eastern Europe, which started in the field of visual arts and resulted in the East Art Map project conceived by the Irwin group.

Pupilija would not have had such a contemporary feel to it, had it not given room to contemporary dance, contemporary choreographic procedures, and the movement practices of everydayness.

Document and Documentary Theater

Perhaps we could suggest a difference between documentary theater – a theater that deals with a real event and is based on facts – and the *theater of documents* where the focus lies on the demonstration of a document as the bearer of truth. What makes *Pupilija* part of documentary theater is the fact that the content and dramaturgy of the performance are, in large part, conceived through the use of documents. Thus, the tension between the real and the performed is constantly being produced. In this, the question of the status of truth is not crucial; what is crucial is the continual displacing of the point(s) of reference. If we, for example, used the facsimiles of newspapers from 1969, we would probably want to show that what we are watching is taking place in 1969. Newspaper documents are additionally mediated by projections. When a document becomes a projected citation, we tear it away from its concrete temporal dimension and it thus becomes not a document of the time it was created in but of the time in which we are watching it. If at the time of the first performance of *Pupilija* the artists were looking for the real on stage – the reason that they staged the death of the chicken, death as ultimate reality – it is exactly the confrontation between the real and the performed that creates the real in performance today. In that sense, we could even say that reconstructions were not possible before media and that reconstructions are a paradigmatic performative format of media culture.

Procedures

In her lecture titled "Re-Enactment of Performances and the Productive Potential of Calculated Failure," Astrid Peterle differentiates between a copied and a reflected reconstruction.[12] She wants to establish a difference between reconstructions (in English, we could use the standard term "re-enactment") that try to re-stage the original performance art piece or theater performance literally and the reconstructions that try to provide an analytic space in which to reflect the original event and the present performance. In this case, the approach we used in the reconstruction of *Pupilija* belongs to the reflected reconstructions.

Copying

Copying is one of the essential layers in the reconstruction of *Pupilija*. We approached it through various protocols, but the basis of our decision for copying was the difference between the two periods. The original *Pupilija* belonged to that spirit of the time that searched for an authentic language, immediacy, and directness not only in art but also in everyday life. The ultimate gestures in this sense were Tomaž Kralj and Manca Čermelj kissing (some of the performers say it was sexual intercourse) in the bathtub and the slaughter of the chicken. In the period of the reconstruction, a subject no longer searches for the point of authenticity, honesty, and immediacy of an undistorted identity, but deals with many identities, with how he/she is mediated, how every act is contextualized and how every gesture is an object of a network of meanings, which inhabit the gesture through complex receptive operations. In each scene of the reconstruction that is being copied, we show precisely the procedure of copying.

Copying in Real Time

In the Photoromance scene, the actors watch the recording on the screen and copy it in real time. The action is not learnt; all that is learnt is the text. The recording appears as a point of reference and a dictation of action.

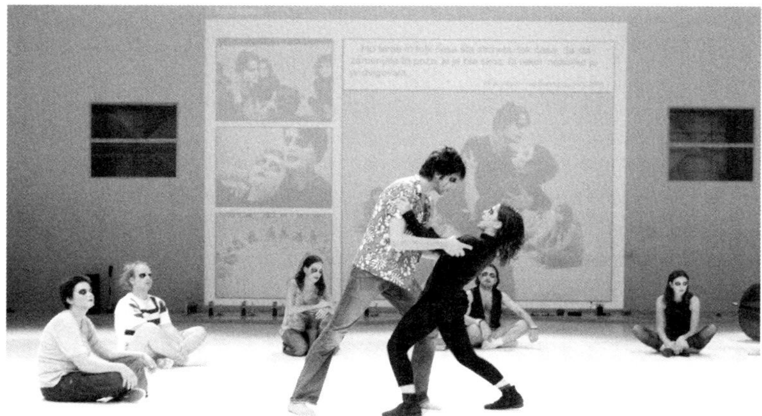

The Bathing scene is not preserved in TV Slovenia's recording. We shot it with the same aesthetics present in the preserved recording of the original. The black-and-white film stock and the white, sterile set at the Viba film studio are reminiscent of silent film aesthetics, which is why the text from the scenario was projected in the form of inter-titles. The actors on stage use mime to copy themselves in the recording. There are no props, no set, and even the musicians mime playing on imagined instruments.

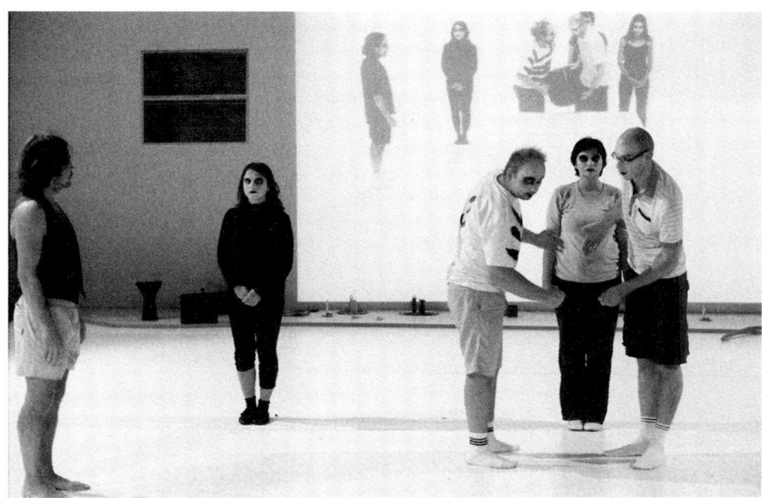

Pupilija, papa Pupilo and the Pupilceks – reconstruction. Directed by Janez Janša. Maska Production, Ljubljana, 2006. Photo by Marcandrea.

Copying as a Choreography of Space

We used copying as a mode of distributing the bodies in space and made it an obvious procedure. In the Elle scene, the actors on the right-hand part of the stage copy the action on the left-hand side of the stage.

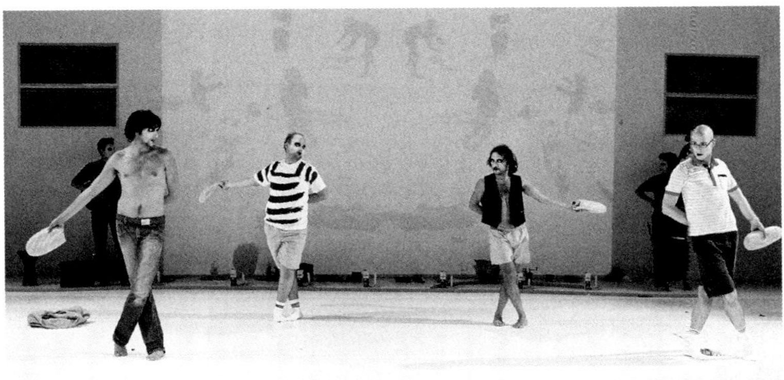

In the Snow White scene, the chorus in the back copies the performance of the couple in the front, the triangle of copying is completed by a trio of musicians who copy the performance of the chorus in the background. In addition to the scene itself, the procedure of copying is demonstrated.

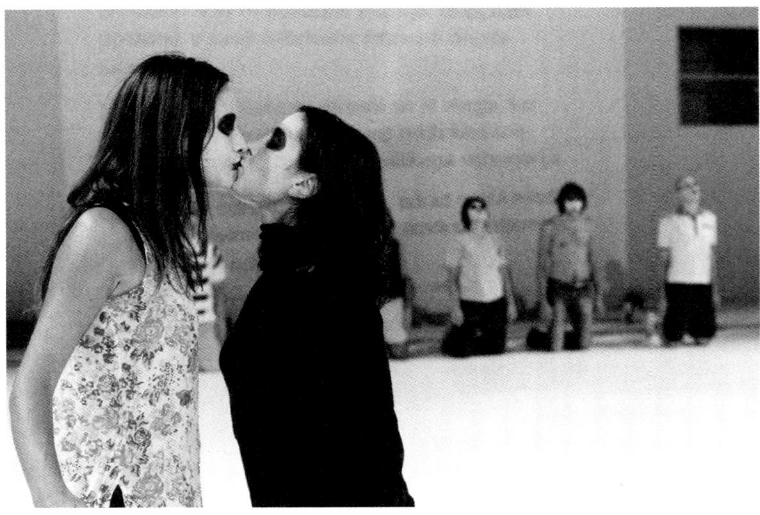

Pupilija, papa Pupilo and the Pupilceks – reconstruction. Directed by Janez Janša. Maska Production, Ljubljana, 2006. Photo by Marcandrea.

To Be in the Picture

In the Computer scene, a photo from the original performance in which the actors are in a formation is projected onto the actors in the reconstruction standing in the same formation. The actors in the reconstruction are thus a literal projection of the original actors and they thus function in a similar way as the projected documents.

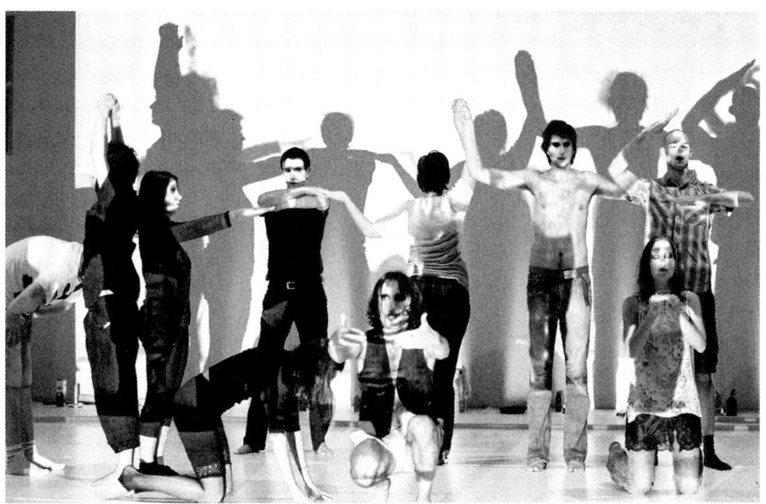

Looping

The only document related to the Gibberish scene available to us during the preparations for the performance (a year later, Slavko Hren found a recording of this scene in the archives of RTV Slovenia) was the reminiscences of performer Milan Jesih, whom we recorded during the preparations for the performance. We edited his performance into a loop in a rhythmical structure that enabled the creation of a music and dance score. Just as the original gibberish was not something to be understood, so, too, the music and dance sequence stands in the place of something that need not be understood, but is there to show that there is a constitutive place in the performance that need not be understood, that is, that the very moment of incomprehension is inscribed in the understanding of the performance.

Rotating the Cast

In the original cast, there was a great fluctuation of performers. A total of thirty different performers cooperated in the performance although the original cast was composed of fifteen members (three of whom were musicians). The main reason for the great fluctuation was the youth of the performers who were mostly between eighteen and twenty-one years of age and under great pressure from the environment and their parents. Many performers left the performance after its opening night. We included this moment in the reconstruction by rotating the tasks performed by the performers in the reconstruction. The cast of every individual performance was determined just before the beginning. All the actors knew most of the roles/tasks. At the same time, we thus maintained the freshness of repetitions, while the performers took on the responsibility for the whole performance and not only their particular part/task.

Chance

Although this procedure was not used in the original *Pupilija*, some of the decisions in the performance were a consequence of chance. We emphasized this procedure in two scenes: the cast of Snow White rests on the elimination game in the previous scene – the two performers that remain at the end of the elimination game appear in the next scene. In the Alpine Milk scene, the actor chooses his or her co-actor in the scene.

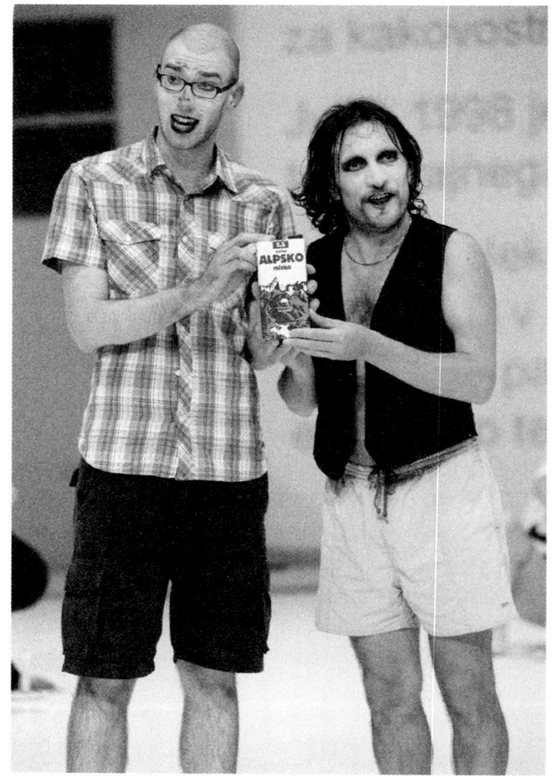

Pupilija, papa Pupilo and the Pupilceks – reconstruction. Directed by Janez Janša. Maska Production, Ljubljana, 2006. Photo by Marcandrea.

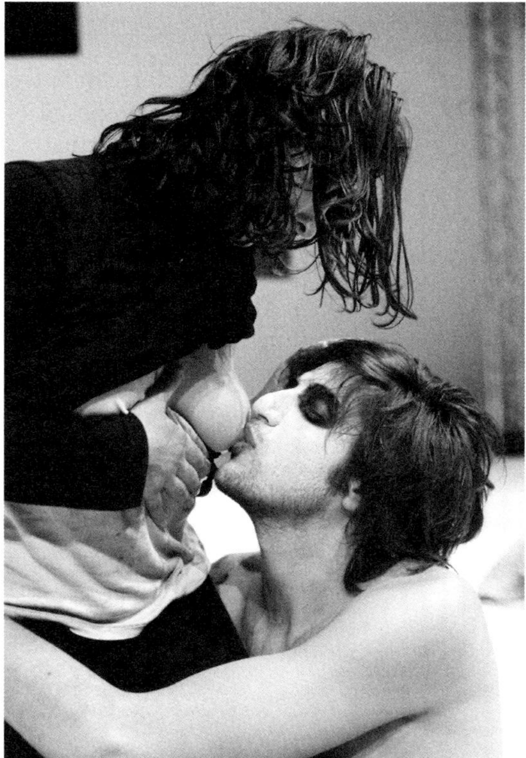

Pupilija, papa Pupilo and the Pupilceks – reconstruction. Directed by Janez Janša. Maska Production, Ljubljana, 2006. Photo by Janez Janša.

Performing the Scenario/Practicing the Task

In the Breastfeeding scene, we hear the voice of Dušan Jovanović, the director of the original performance, reading the scenario and, after his every sentence, the actors perform the described task. Thus, the director of the original performance directs the performers of the reconstruction.

De-Construction of the Conductor

For each cast, we engaged a conductor, who was either a member of the original cast of *Pupilija* (Barbara Levstik, who was the conductor in the original, Dušan Jovanović) or artists, festival directors, etc. (e.g., Jovan Ćirilov, Dragan Živadinov, Tone Partljič, etc.). We thus follow the logic of the relationship between the orchestra and the conductor: the orchestra is always composed of the same members, while the conductors change, the repertoire remaining practically the same.

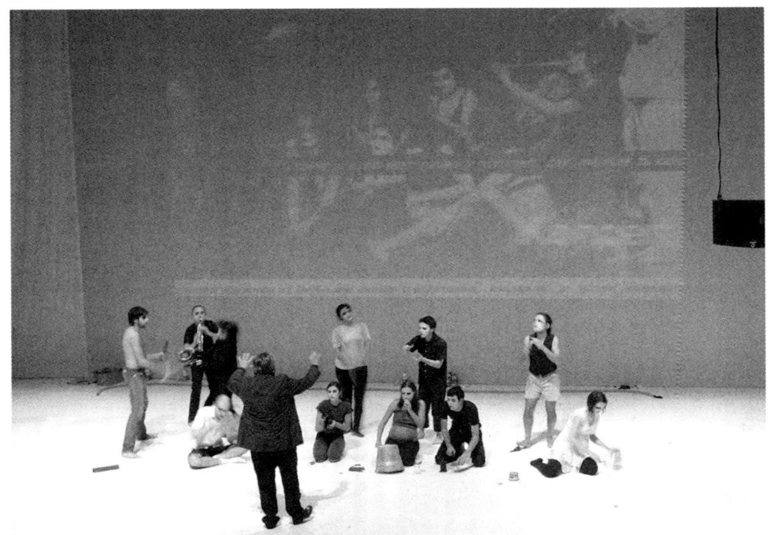

Pupilija, papa Pupilo and the Pupilceks – reconstruction. Directed by Janez Janša. Maska Production, Ljubljana, 2006. Photo by Janez Janša.

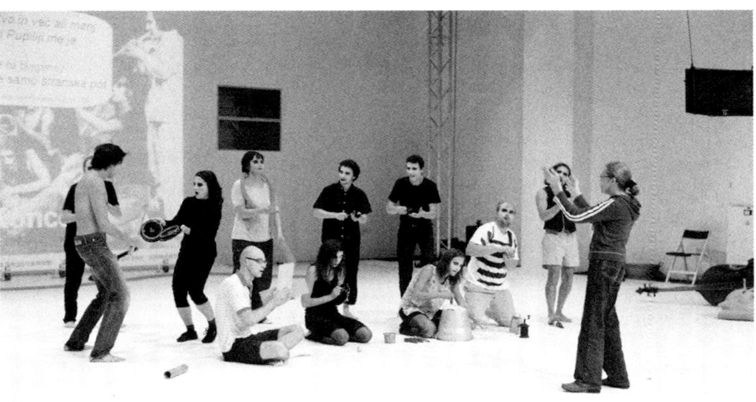

Pupilija, papa Pupilo and the Pupilceks – reconstruction. Directed by Janez Janša. Maska Production, Ljubljana, 2006. Photo by Marcandrea.

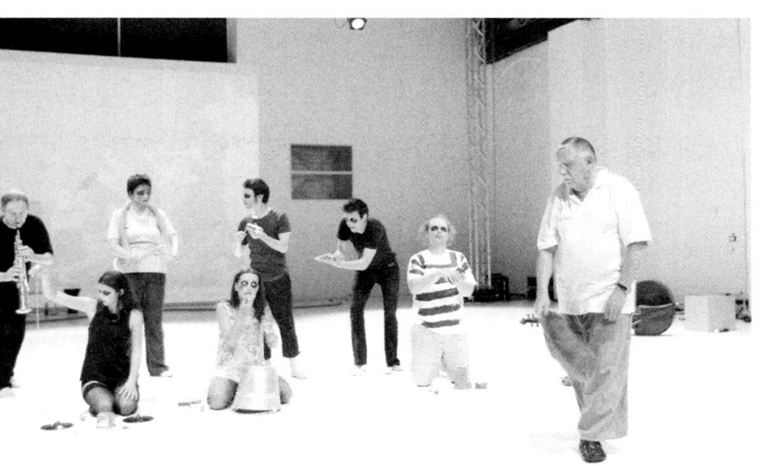

Pupilija, papa Pupilo and the Pupilceks – reconstruction. Directed by Janez Janša. Maska Production, Ljubljana, 2006. Photo by Marcandrea.

Over-identification

We played Koseski's Poem as the original Pupilceks – with an over-identification stance, which produces an ironic distance, on the one hand, and an ideological effect, on the other.

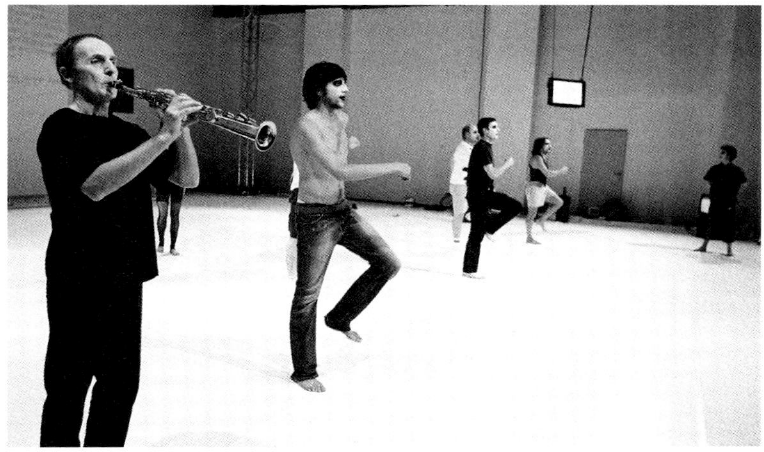

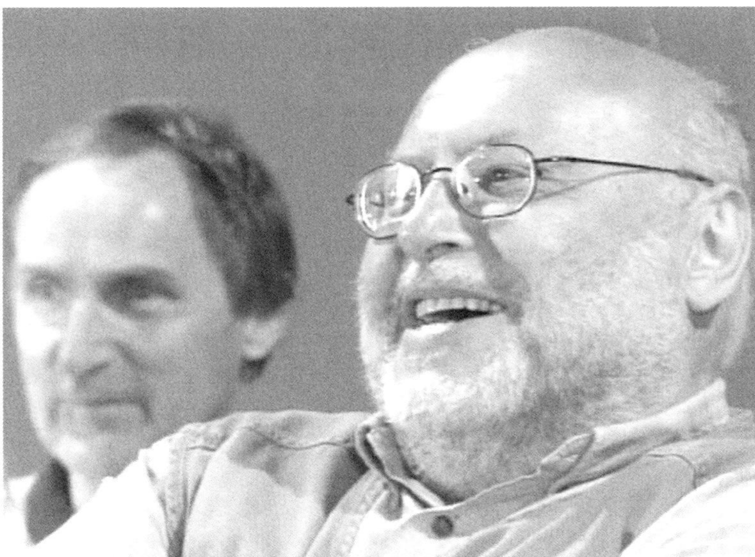

Pupilija, papa Pupilo and the Pupilceks – reconstruction. Directed by Janez Janša. Maska Production, Ljubljana, 2006. Photo by Marcandrea.

The Structure of an Open End

The length and course of the Alpine Milk scene are uncertain. The actor has to cut a log in two and if this does not succeed in the first try (which happened at some of the performances), the scene can be transformed into a negotiation between what is real and what is staged, what is improvised and what directed. It is a particular task with an improvised end.

Staging the Gaze

In two scenes, a recording of the original Pupilceks appears on the screen, shot at a joint viewing of the recording of the original performance organized at the end of the opening night at the Križanke Knight's Hall in May 2006. The Pupilceks watch themselves (in the recording from 1969), while we watch them watch themselves being reconstructed on stage. The direction of the Pupilceks' gaze on screen is what leads the movement of the actress playing beautiful Anka, who directs the movement of the round dance.

Notes

1. In 1990, Emil Hrvatin's article "Reconstruction" was published in *M'ARS*, Moderna galerija – Museum of Modern Art, Ljubljana, 1990, no. 3, 20–6 (the journal was discontinued). The author-artist Emil Hrvatin later took on the name Janez Janša as part of an evolving artwork.
2. An interesting terminological paradox arises in reconstructing the historical avant-garde or neo-avant-garde. In Europe in the 1980s, there were many reconstructions of Russian avant-garde performances: Schlemmer's ballets, Picasso's *Parade*, Kandinsky's *Yellow Sound*, etc. In English literature, the term "reconstruction" became established for these performances. Upon the emergence of reconstructions of works from the 1960s, the term "re-enactment" started to appear in specialized literature, which used to refer to the re-enactments of historical events. It should be explained why this terminological change arose, linked as it was to some other related concepts appearing at the same time (for example, appropriation art).
3. The reconstruction was also recorded without the presence of an audience. You can see spectators in the final version of the filmed material, but they were recorded during another performance. The original recording by TV Slovenia was made at the same venue (Old Power Plant), but without an audience.
4. "Whether we agree or not, and even if we throw a scrap of a pear on stage, as it happened on the opening night, the death of the white chicken was also the death of literary, solely aesthetically functional theatre in Slovenia." Veno Taufer, "Experimental Theatre at Križanke: Pupilija, papa Pupilo and the Pupilceks," *Naši razgledi*, 7 November 1969. It is interesting that nobody wonders what Rapa Šuklje was doing at the performance with a pear.
5. Rok Vevar, *Dnevnik*, 18 October 2006.
6. Slavoj Žižek, "The Theory of Happening," based on Allan Kaprow, *Tribuna*, vol. 1967–8, no. 6, p. 11.

7. Blaž Lukan: "Tri predstave v eni sami [Three Performances in One]," *Delo*, 28 September, 2006, p. 13.
8. Rok Vevar, "Original, ponovitev in razlika [The Original, the Re-Staging and the Difference]," *Večer*, 28 September 2006, p. 12.

   "Let there be no mistake; when upon the reconstruction of *Pupilija, papa Pupilo and the Pupilceks* last week, whose original at the end of the 1960s ended by a performer slaughtering a chicken, but now this cannot be done as easily nor in accordance with the law (how quickly awareness develops!), they provoked a volunteer from the audience to do it, I came very close to stepping out and doing it. To take the killing upon myself, to the outrage of those who, in private, stuff themselves with kebabs and chicken sausages and, at receptions, 'only' with salmons and basses fattened on slaughterhouse waste, and to thus reveal social propriety and hypocrisy like Hermann Nitsch and Franc Purg in their slaughtering performances. Bravo!" Matej Bogataj, "Najboljši ribiči rib ne lovijo več [The Best Fishermen No Longer Fish]," *Večer*, 30 September 2006.
9. Blaž Lukan, "Tri predstave v eni sami [Three Performances in One]," *Delo*, 28 September 2006, p. 13.
10. For example: "History must repeat itself, first as a tragedy and then as a farce. This is why I suggest to Hrvatin that, instead of the chicken, he slaughters himself. It would be even better if a giant chicken slaughtered him and Jovanovič together. The scene should look like the scene from a Woody Allen film in which he is chased by a giant pink breast. Dušan Jovanovič and Emil Hrvatin will thus choose the most powerful immortality, neither a Small (a person remembered only by their personal acquaintances) nor a Big immortality (the deceased being remembered also by the people who did not know him personally), but a Funny one. They will be so immortal that they will even end up in joke cycles. Something like the Irishman jokes. Yay!" Matjaž Pograjc, "Brezglava kura napadla brezglava režiserja [A Headless Chicken Attacked Headless Directors]," Blog - Življenje je najboljše maščevanje [Blog – Life is the Best Revenge], 19 October 2006. (Matjaž Pograjc is a well known theater director from Slovenia of Janša's generation.)
11. "Upon the reconstruction of the avant-garde event *Pupilija, papa Pupilo and the Pupilceks* in Vienna, a journalist tried to persuade Emil Hrvatin to admit that the original of the reconstruction, the 'cult performance' directed by Dušan Jovanović, is really his idea and that the reconstruction is only an ingenious bluff. Maska's performance became a real rebus of Mittelfest's Thursday evening, since the confused spectators were wondering whether the company actually pulled their leg with a theatre document which is as 'original' as the name of its author, Janez Janša." ROP, Predstava *Pupilija, papa Pupilo pa Pupilčki* pretresla občinstvo [*Pupilija, papa Pupilo and the Pupilceks Shocked the Audience*], *Primorski dnevnik*, 26 July 2008.
12. Astrid Peterle, "Re-Enactment of Performances and the Productive Potential of Calculated Failure," lecture given at Perfomance Studies international, Zagreb, 25 June 2009.

Chapter 31

Documents of Chinese Time-Based Art: Three Impressions from Three Fragments

Meiling Cheng

A sheet of rice paper. At first, it shows a face of immense whiteness, disturbed by a tiny inconsistency in its texture: white on white. Then, such whiteness becomes interrupted – repeatedly, if intermittently – by black ink, which seeps into the paper in the impression of classical Chinese characters inscribed by calligraphy. The white paper, having transfigured from a surface into a background, now bears the writing of a commemorative text, known as "*Lantingxu*" ("*Orchid Pavilion Preface*"), originally authored by the master calligrapher, Wang Xizhi on 3 March 353.[1] The paper's unmarked spatiality gradually loses ground, as Wang's text – composed of 324 words in the *xinshu* (literally "walking-writing") style – is inscribed again and again, in vertical after vertical line, onto the remaining whiteness. After having been duplicated ten times in this layering fashion, Wang's text disappears, like whispers in cacophony, into an intricate ink painting made of overlapped columns of lines, curves, tilts, and dots. After fifty times, the painting evolves into a rectangular inky mass, its individual patterns no longer discernible. After a thousand times, Qiu Zhijie, the calligrapher who has labored for seven years to reproduce Wang's *xinshu* on the same sheet of paper, concludes his durational exercise. He has fulfilled a performance plan, promised by its straightforward title, *Chongfu shuxie yiqian ci "Lantingxu"* (*Repeatedly Duplicating a Thousand Times "Lantingxu,"* 1990–7).

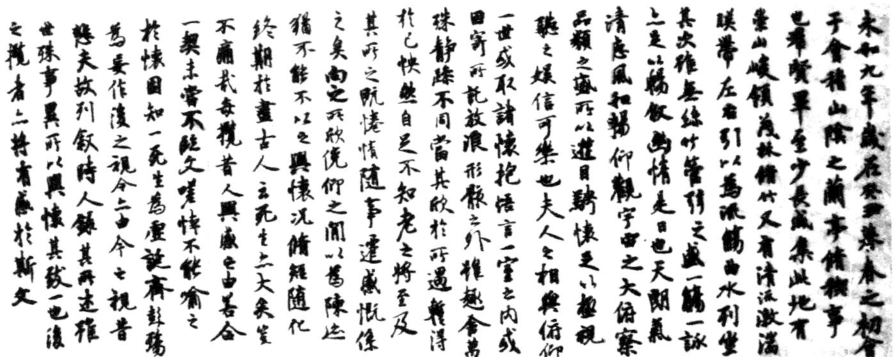

Wang Xizhu, *Lantingxu* [*Orchid Pavilion Preface*] (353) inscribed by Qiu Zhijie, 1990. Courtesy of Qiu Zhijie.

A mid-point image of *Repeatedly Duplicating A Thousand Times "Lantingxu,"* undated. Courtesy of Qiu Zhijie.

A closing image of *Repeatedly Duplicating A Thousand Times "Lantingxu,"* undated. Courtesy of Qiu Zhijie.

A black-and-white photograph. A Chinese man stares at me, the one who reads, from inside the page of a book bilingually titled *Document/Xianchang* (*Live Action Site*).[2] His gaze is steady, his expression calm, and his crew cut overgrown. The man wears a long-sleeved shirt, which is cut diagonally across by the canvas strap for a canteen. His shirt's partially shaded surface looks like an extension from the weather-torn brick wall in the background. The picture's caption identifies the image as Yang Zhichao. The artist has the snapshot taken to document the moment before he departs for his *xingwei* (behavior/performance) project, *Sihuan zhi nei* (*Within the Fourth Ring Road*, 26–30 July 1999). I turn the page and find a grayish reproduction of a Beijing map, superimposed with a diagram made of thick white arrows and dotted lines, marking Yang's itinerary within the downtown area circumscribed by the Fourth Ring Road. Five circles, accompanied by handwritten notations of dates and places, record the departing, resting, and closing spots for Yang's action. On the next page appears a list of rules for *Within the Fourth Ring Road*:

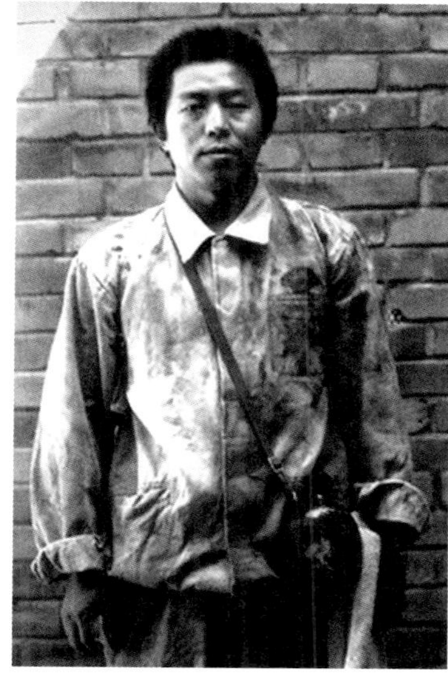

Yang Zhichao's documentary photograph for *Within the Fourth Ring Road*,1999. Photo credit: Ai Weiwei. Courtesy of Yang Zhichao.

> Xingwei Rules
> Process: To beg within Beijing's Fourth Ring Road
> Regulations: 1. The beggar has no money whatsoever.
> 2. Does not accept any help from acquaintances or friends.
> 3. Does not contact friends or family during the begging process.
> 4. Does not stop the begging activity without reason.
> Time: 26 July 1999, 12PM–30 July 1999, 12PM (lasting four days)
> Range: Beijing, East to East Fourth Ring, west to West Fourth Ring, south to South Fourth Ring, north to North Fourth Ring.
> Records: 1. Handwritten journals, 2. Photographs.
> (Note: Ai Weiwei serves as the witness for this activity. Ai is entitled to supervise the one who executes this action and to interpret the action's rules.)[3]

An Internet announcement. First posted on 28 December 2005, the notice consists of a list of facts and regulations outlining the plan for an artwork titled, *Wang Mian Liang Yu Shangdian dang an* (*Wang Mian Rice Oil Shop Document Files*). The disclosed facts include the authors' names [Wang Chuyu and Wang Hong], the date when *Wang Mian Rice Oil Shop* began operation (20 August 2005), the location of the shop (in Tongzhou, a suburb of Beijing), the family who manages the shop (Wang Hong (husband), Tian Haijen (wife), Wang Mian (son)), and the family's financial source (incomes from the Wang Mian Rice Oil Shop). Such basic information is followed by the artists-developed rules:

> The Artwork's Execution Plan and Process:
> 1. The artwork will be executed beginning 1 January 2006, until this Rice Oil Shop is forced to close by external factors beyond its control.
> 2. During this period, everyday a financial record for business and living expenses and incomes will be kept. Every month all these financial records will be presented. Every year an overall balance sheet will be sorted out to evaluate the shop's operation. All incomes and expenses will be publicized.
> 3. Once the artwork is finished, the resulting product will be the compilation of all document files for the *Wang Mian Rice Oil Shop*.
> 4. The artwork will produce documents of operation for the Rice Oil Shop, literature and documents for [Wang's] family life, and financial records for the business and life in the Rice Oil Shop.

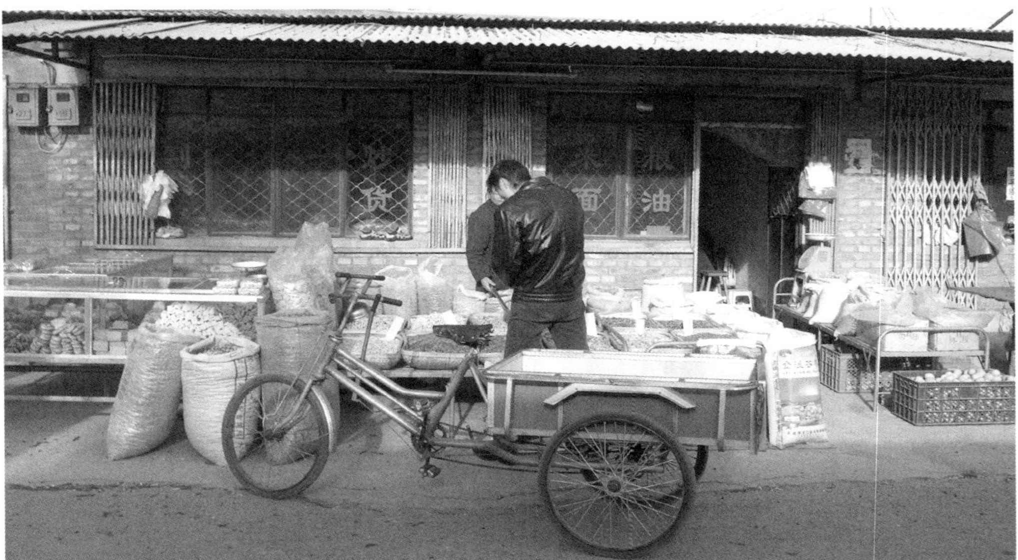

Wang Mian Rice Oil Shop Document Files, an image of the shop in June 2006. Photo credit: Wang Chuyu. Courtesy of Wang Chuyu and Wang Hong.

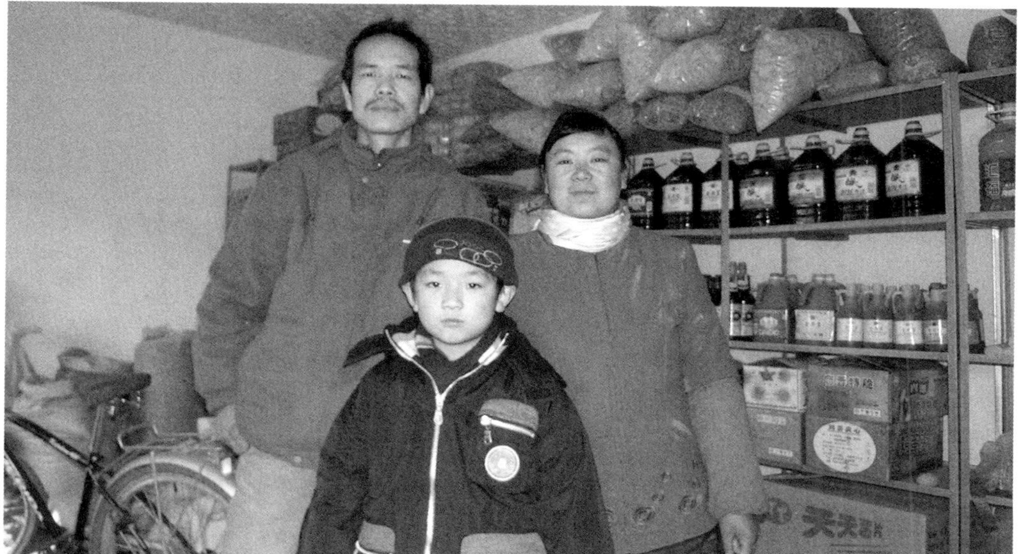

Wang Mian Rice Oil Shop Document Files, a family snapshot of the shop owners, Wang Hong, Tian Haizhen, and their son Wang Mian. Photo credit: Wang Chuyu. Courtesy of Wang Chuyu.

The Artwork's Methods of Display:

1. Monthly web-posting the financial records of *Wang Mian Rice Oil Shop* and the operators' itemized records for living expenses.
2. Monthly web-posting a photograph of the live operation site in *Wang Mian Rice Oil Shop*.
3. Producing a documentary video, *Wang Mian Rice Oil Shop*.
4. When the artwork is finished, an exhibition will be held to display all pictures, document files, literature about the operators' lives, and the documentary video.[4]

Notes

1. See *Baidu baike* (online). "Lantingxu." Available at: http://baike.baidu.com/view/43384.htm, first accessed on 14 December 2007.
2. Zhichao Yang, "Dangan 15: Yang Zhichao xingwei yishu dangan," in Wenguang Wu (ed.) *Document/Xianchang*, Guangxi, China: Guangxi shifan daxuei chubanshe 2005, pp. 6–147, at p. 6.
3. Ibid. Although *Document/Xianchang* has a bilingual title, its text is published only in Chinese. I translated this list of rules from its Chinese version. Yang Zhichao had devised these rules before he undertook the action, but he noted "four days" as the duration of his action when the list of rules was published as part of his performance documents.
4. Chuyu Wang and Hong Wang, 2005, "'Wang Mian liang yu shangden' dangan' zuopin jihua." Available at: http://www.tianya.cn/publicforum/Content/develop/1/71482.shtml, first accessed on 15 December 2007, translation mine.

Chapter 32

Both Sitting Duet

Jonathan Burrows and Matteo Fargion

Both Sitting Duet is the first of five duets made and performed by Jonathan Burrows and Matteo Fargion.

The principle behind the making of *Both Sitting Duet* was "Counterpoint assumes a love between the parts."

Both Sitting Duet is a direct translation, note for note and bar for bar, of the violin and piano piece *For John Cage* by the American composer Morton Feldman (1926–87).

The translation was made from the score of the music, and no recordings were listened to while the piece was being made. *Both Sitting Duet* borrows, therefore, the structure but not the atmosphere of the original.

The piece is performed sitting down, in silence. The choice to sit down was made in order that the two performers, one a composer and the other a choreographer, could be seen either as musicians or as dancers.

The material is mainly built up of hand and arm gestures. The principle for finding these gestures was "to accept what came easily."

The speed of the performance begins at the metronome marking of the original music, 120 beats a minute, but speeds up two thirds of the way through.

The documents assembled here are copies of both performers' scores, one written in classical musical notation and the other as a series of written numbers. These scores are placed at the feet of the performers and read throughout the performance.

In addition to the formal means of the structure, the performance is also mediated by a series of principles for performance, which include: "how the audience sits is how we should sit," "how we feel is how we behave," and "there are no mistakes."

Jonathan Burrows

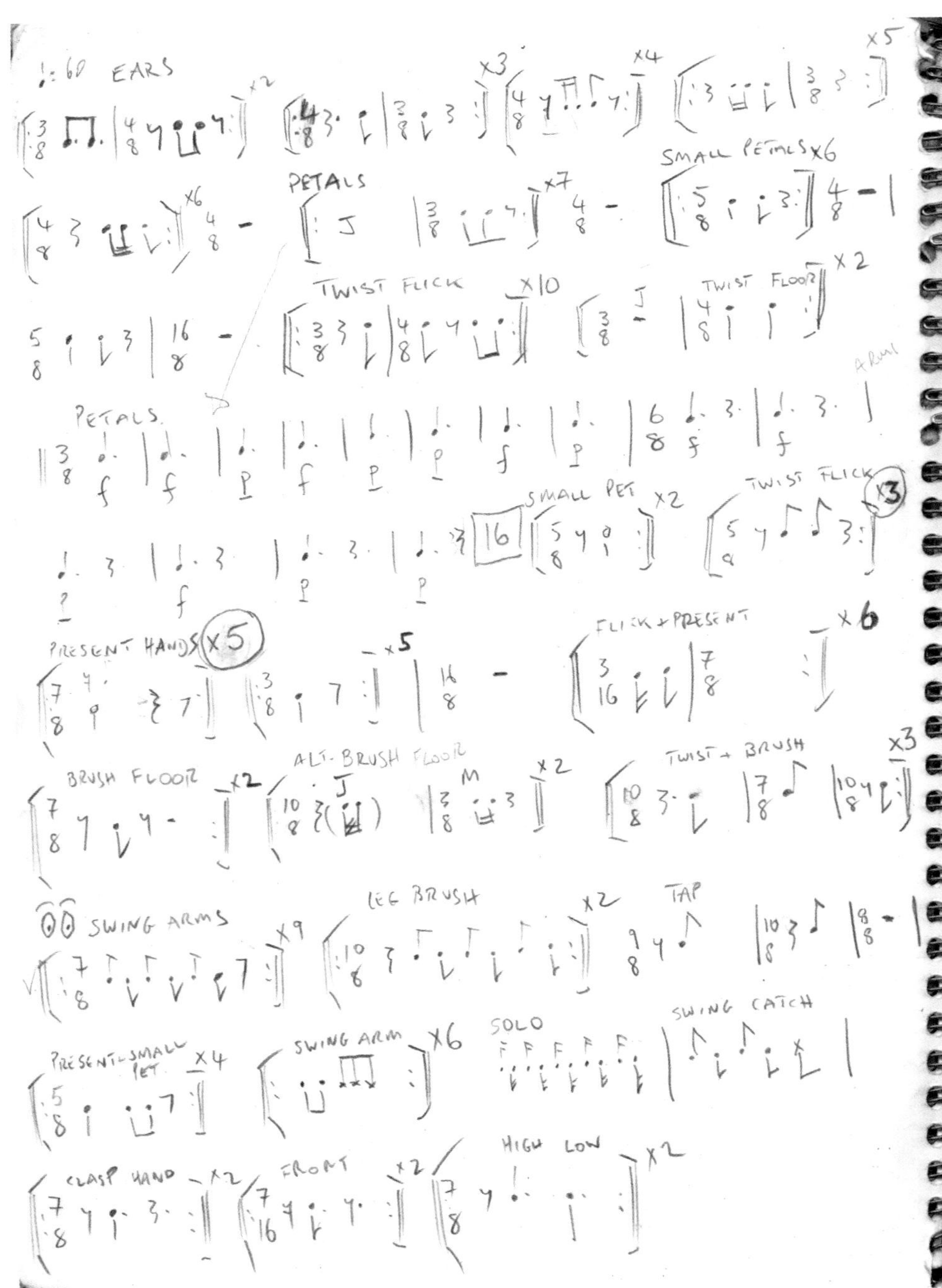

Matteo Fargion, score for *Both Sitting Duet*.

TWIST ON LAP	1 2 3 4 5 ×3 PRESENT HANDS
PRESENT ON KNEES	1 AND 2 3 4 5 6 7 ×5 BACK
EARS / PRESENT	1 AND 2 3 ×5
	WAIT 16
R HAND PETAL	1 23 / 1 2 3 4 5 6 7 ×6 M J
2 HANDS BRUSH FLOOR	1 2 AND 3 4 5 6 7 ×2
BRUSH R	1 2 AND 3 4 5 6 7 8 9 10 M BRUSH WAIT 3 } ×2
TWIST BRUSH FLOOR	1 2 3 / AND 4 5 6 7 8 9 10 AND / 1 2 3 4 5 6 7 1 / AND 2 3 4 5 6 7 8 9 10 } ×3
	MEETING PLACE
DOUBLE ARM SWINGS	1 2 3 4 5 6 7 8 9 ×7 STOP
BRUSHES ON LAP	1 2 3 4 5 6 7 8 9 10 ×2 TAPS 2 OF 9 / 3 OF 10 / WAIT 8 → PRESENT / PETAL

Jonathan Burrows, score for *Both Sitting Duet*.

Matteo Fargion, score for *Both Sitting Duet*.

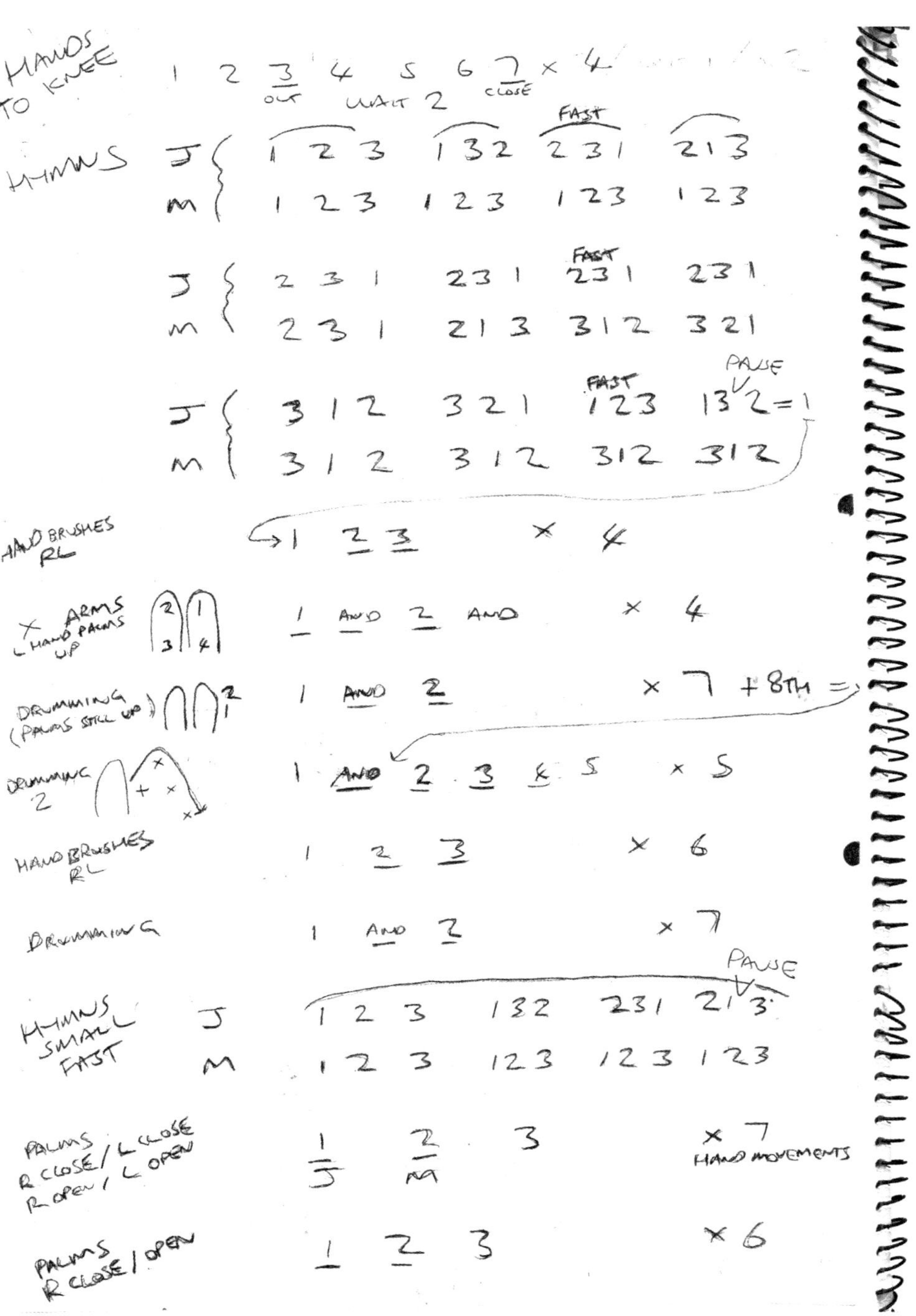

Jonathan Burrows, score for *Both Sitting Duet*.

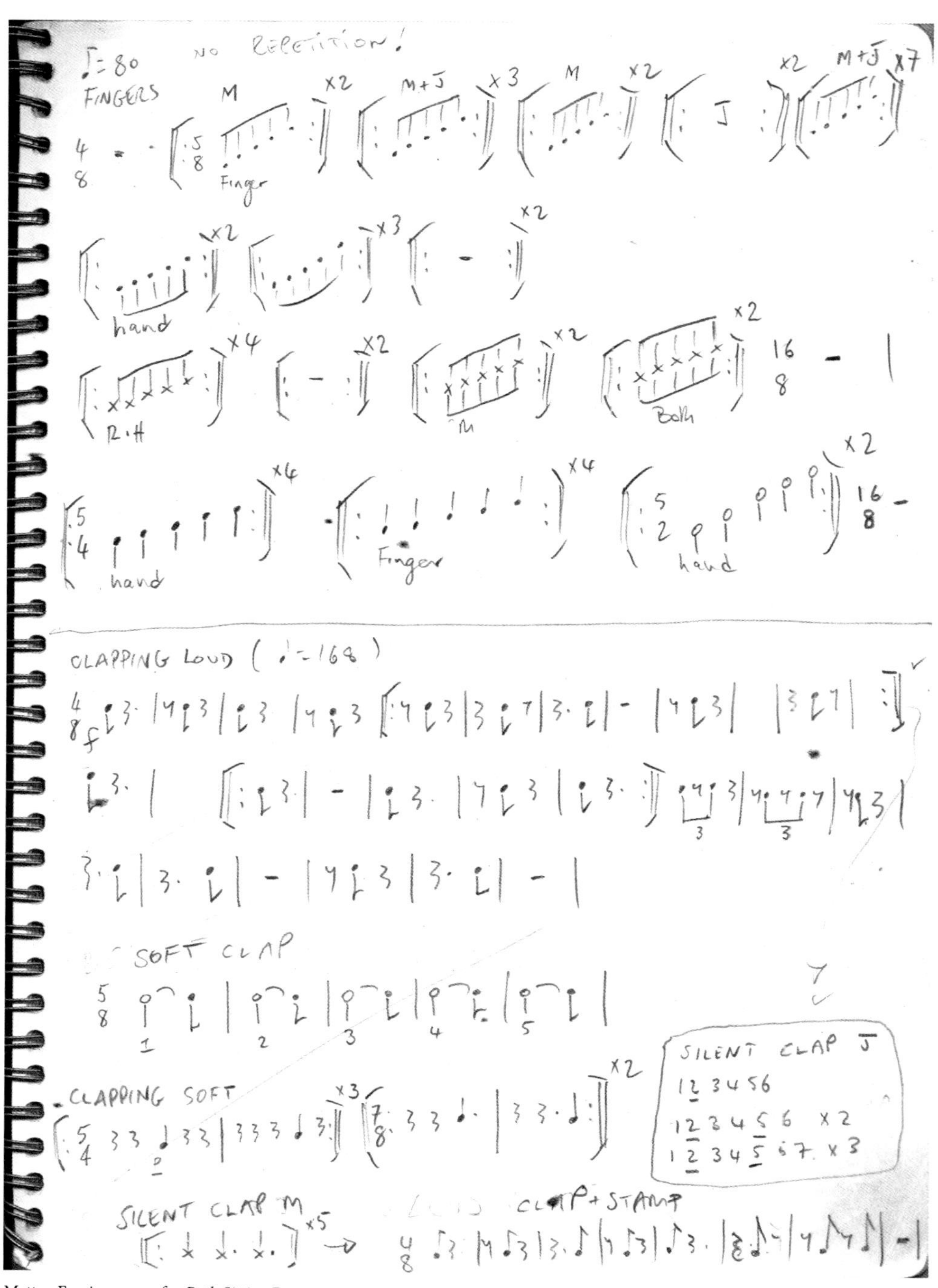

Matteo Fargion, score for *Both Sitting Duet*.

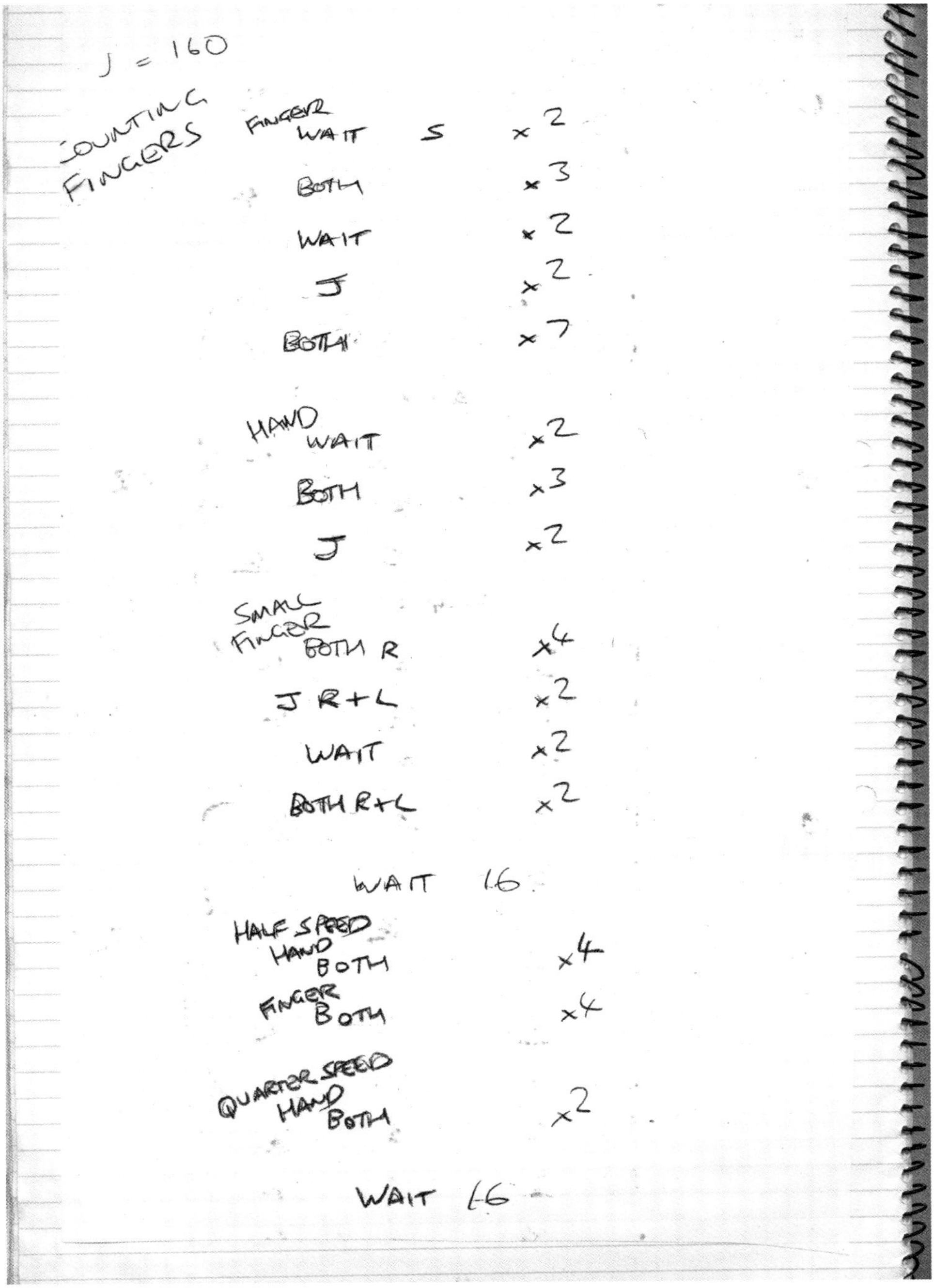

♩ = 160

COUNTING FINGERS

FINGER WAIT S ×2

BOTH ×3

WAIT ×2

J ×2

BOTH ×7

HAND WAIT ×2

BOTH ×3

J ×2

SMALL FINGER BOTH R ×4

J R+L ×2

WAIT ×2

BOTH R+L ×2

WAIT 16

HALF SPEED HAND BOTH ×4

FINGER BOTH ×4

QUARTER SPEED HAND BOTH ×2

WAIT 16

Jonathan Burrows, score for *Both Sitting Duet*.

Cheap Lecture

Jonathan Burrows and Matteo Fargion

Cheap Lecture is the fourth of five duets made and performed by Jonathan Burrows and Matteo Fargion.[1]

Cheap Lecture is a translation of *Lecture On Nothing*, written by John Cage in 1949.[2] *Lecture On Nothing* is a talk on composition, written in the manner of a piece of music. When we say translation, we mean that we have followed the structure of what John Cage wrote, which he described as a rhythmic structure, meaning by that a predetermined shape of time which would accept anything.

The rhythmic structure of *Lecture On Nothing* is built up of smaller units of 7, 6, 14, 14 and 7, and these are then repeated 7, 6, 14, 14 and 7 times so that the larger shape reflects the smaller shape.

Cheap Lecture follows this micro-macrocosmic structure, replacing Cage's words with new words and adding a layer of piano music, most of which is drawn from Schubert. The words and music are counterpointed throughout the performance by 139 projected words and phrases.

In the score that you see here, the shape of the text is a visual image of the rhythm of the words when spoken, and each line represents a beat. The gaps between printed words suggest the flow or hesitation in our speaking, and an asterisk is a counted pause.

Jonathan Burrows and Matteo Fargion

Notes

1. *Cheap Lecture* was commissioned by Cultureel Centrum Maasmechelen and Dans in Limburg, 2009.
2. John Cage, "Lecture On Nothing," from *Silence*, London: Marion Boyars Publishers, 1995 (1961), p. 109.

This talk
began
with empty
hands and they
continue to be
empty.
*

As soon as we
think we
know what might
happen
nothing
happens.

If
on the other hand
we accept
that our hands are
empty then
something
usually turns
up to
fill them.
*
*
*
*
*

If
we hold on
tight to
things we
value saying
"This would make a
very good
ending," for
instance, it
usually
doesn't make
a very good
ending at
all.

We prefer
to use our
favourite material
first and we
have no
idea how
this will end.

We must
neverthe-
less try our
best,
maximum strength,
best we can
to continue.

The expression
maximum strength
comes, by the
way, from our
yoga teacher
Shiv Sharma,

who is famed for
a number of
expressions
including our
personal favourite:
*
"Kundalini?
*
You want
*
Kundalini?
You can't even
touch your
toes!"

This talk is a
negotiation with the
space of the
page and the
written
form and the
room we are
in:
together,
under the same
roof,
together.
*
*

The space of the
room, and the
written form
create the time
within which this is
happening.
*

There are
other
times
also
overlapping around us.
The time
                of the

changing   of the
projected
words   is in
counterpoint
to the flow of our
speaking.   This

beat   of the
projected
words   is in
counterpoint to the
flow of our
speaking
marking
boundaries of
thoughts   as they
pass,   as they
pass.
*
                As they
pass.

Hidden   from
you   but
present   to
us   is the
time   of the
earpiece   which
guides us   through the
slipperiness of the
temporal
storm   of
adrenaline in our
bodies
anchoring   our
words.

The earpiece
distracts us
enough, we
hope, from
ourselves that
ourselves might become
visible.

Each   of the
times   we're
describing is
talking   to the
time   of the
music
behind us,   and

around us.
The music   is a
wall   of
rhythm against which
our thoughts   can
lean.

The pulse   of the
music   is an
emotional
map
by which   we might
navigate
the watery
meanderings of
language.
The silences -
*
*
the silences between
words   and the

*
silences
               between
sounds   are
different
*
silences,   but
both
arrive   at a
punctuation   which
guides   our
reactions   and   gives
time   for our
responses.

Even the most
simple
conjunction of
times   becomes
complex and we
love   that
complexity.

If you have difficulty
putting together
what you see and
hear,
allow it
gently, perhaps, to
flow over you, and

if you have difficulty
understanding
what we might call
poetry,
allow that to flow over you
also.

What you want to hear
will have done its work
anyway
and you can relax and
trust that
slowly, as we
continue, some
sense will
slowly
be
made.
*
Slowly.
*

Meaning is what
accumulates in
collaboration
between what
happens in the
gaps
between
words and the
gaps
*
between
thoughts.
*
*

It's not
necessary that
all of us
immediately
understand
everything that is
happening.

*
*
*
*
*
*
*

*
*
*
*
*
*

We are trying to
perform in the
present, but you are
living
also the
past of
your
recognition and the
future of
your
expectations,
which are our
constant
companions.

With us, in the
room, are our
histories and
our hopes,
not least
the hope of a nice
meal   and a
cold
beer.
With us are
all of the
people we have
spoken with
today.

With us
*
are all   of the
people   we have
spoken with
*
today.

Some of the times
deliberately
collide, and
some have
just
collided.
*

Counterpoint
                assumes a
love
between the
parts.
*

I must be exactly
myself,
and at the same time
I must give up
myself,
myself
exactly to the
person
next to me.
Counterpoint
                assumes a
love
between the
parts. In this

act of
relinquishing
self we
experience
a momentary
freedom, as
though we had
looked
briefly
away.
Sharing time can be as
awkwardly
intimate as
sharing the lift.

Sharing
time
can be as awkwardly
intimate as
sharing
the lift.
*

Our simultaneous
histories
also
awkwardly
overlap.
*
*

Events which we
perceive as
points on a
timeline,
coexist in our
memories.

This piece was
written and is
being performed in a
line,
starting at the beginning
and continuing until the
end.
As soon as we
begin to
perform
however
time
begins to
riot.

What comes first
determines
what can happen
next, and what
happens
next,
alters what has
come
before:
our perception of the speed
at which time is passing
is completely shifted by a
darkened room and an
enforced state of attention:

things
appear to
either speed up
or
alternatively to
slow
down.

Not only must
things
change but the
rate at which they
change should
also
change.

Or:
Patterns of
predictability and
unpredictability must be
both predictable and
unpredictable.
*

Composition
is what
happens   in the
gap   between
one thought
*
and the
next thought.
Meaning
arises
between things,   and is
altered by their
relationship.

Flow is an
accident   of the
attempt   to
get   from
one event   to the
next event:
things   which
only flow
give us nothing
against which to
read   the
flow.
*
*

Rhythm
is about
heightened
attention   in an
open
field.
*

Think of
pulse and we
think of a
heartbeat:
boom boom,
boom boom,
boom boom.

Or
perhaps we might
think of
walking:
boom boom,
boom boom.

When we dance to a
beat, our
bodies
organise and
coordinate
themselves around the
rise and
resolution of each
moment, in a
gentle
collaboration between
falling and
standing.
*

When we dance
together to a
beat,
we are usually not
trying to
express ourselves,
but
rather to
lose ourselves in a
field of
expression.
Most of the
world likes to
dance to a

beat. Most
of the
world likes to
dance to a
beat.
*
*

In the second part of the
evening
you may see us
dance,
perhaps, just a
little.
*
The rhythm you will
see   when we
dance,   is
different   to the
rhythm   you might
hear.

The rhythm you will
see   is
weaker   and more
delicate   than the
rhythm   we
make   when we
speak,   or walk
loudly,   or play
music   and we must
try,
best we can,
maximum strength   to
balance the two.

Things that
appear complex
             when you
see them,   may be
rendered
simple   when you
hear them, and
things that are simple
             when you
hear them, may become
complex when you
see them.
We call
these two kinds of
rhythm
visual rhythm and

aural
rhythm.
Placing these two
rhythms
together
creates the thing
called
choreography.

This talk is a
translation of the
talk
given by John Cage in
19-
50   which he
called

"Lecture on Nothing."
"Lecture on
Nothing"   is a
spoken
performance
written in the

manner of a piece of
music.
When we say
translation,
we mean that we have
borrowed   the
structure   of what
John Cage wrote, which he
described   as a
rhythmic
structure,
meaning   by
that   a
predetermined

shape   of
empty time which would
accept
anything.
The structure is
built up of
units   of
48 measures each,
subdivided in the
following
proportions:
7
6
14, 14 and

7, and the
5 larger sections of the
piece have the same shape
so the smaller parts
reflect the form
                 of the
larger parts.

1
2
3
4
5
6
7

1
2
3
4
5
6

1
2
3
4
5
6
7
8
9
10
11
12
13
14

1
2
3
4
5
6
7
8
9
10
11
12
13
14

1
2
3
4
5
6
7

This delight in
patterns does not
suit everybody, but it
suits us
because
we're not the world's best
improvisers.

Pattern is what
allows me to
recognise your
face in a
crowd and
you to recognise mine. We have

called this piece
"Cheap Lecture" in
reference to the
piece John Cage wrote when he
wanted to use
Erik Satie's Socrate for a
choreography by
Merce Cunningham, and
they could not afford to
pay the rights for the
music: so
John Cage wrote a piece
to replace it which he called
"Cheap Imitation."

Some people who will
see our
performance might
think to themselves
"Aha, it's
that kind of
thing." But we've
discovered we're only
good at
that kind of thing. It's a
preconception that an
artist can make what they
want, whereas
an artist can only make
what they are able to

make.
We, for
instance, would
love to
make a
Pina Bausch
piece.

Chapter 33

Aftermath: The Performance/Installation Nexus

Blair French

Located in an old warehouse on the Sydney waterfront, Artspace functions as a lightning rod for experimental and ephemeral practices within a local art scene that is otherwise largely committed to sustaining a commodity-based understanding of art as object across a commercial–institutional axis. For many years steadfast in advancing frameworks of site-specificity, Artspace has historically privileged self-reflexive practices; the gallery is engaged in cultural, theoretical, and art-historical critique through a curatorial program supporting, via residency, the development and realization of new installation, media, and performance art projects by artists from both Australia and abroad.

Rather than functioning as a gallery in which artists simply locate their work, Artspace acts as a site in which artists *work*. Working bodies inhabit the three large, interconnected, and crucially rough-hewn gallery spaces, thinking, talking, making, performing. Projects are invariably ephemeral, occupying the gallery for limited periods of time (around a month) – the corollary of initial utterances, propositions, or short, fierce arguments, rather than carefully crafted theses. This is a dialogic model of art, intended as dynamic, generative, and consistently performative.

Within such a curatorial program, installation itself becomes a consciously performative mode of practice, creating a post-event sensibility through installation both *as* and as *producer of* mnemonic traces. I am thinking here about the temporal limits of installation. As the current executive director of Artspace, I have come to be increasingly interested in this paradoxical reliance of installation on aspects of temporality (and thus of the performative): however strongly installation might be considered less a particular mode of practice than a code for contemporary art's preoccupation with space in its material, perceptual, and social forms, and no matter how weighted in materiality (how laden with mass) installation, at least in its various gallery-exhibition permutations, tends to be, installation is also a fundamentally ephemeral practice that takes place both in space *and* over time.

I suspect that regular visitors to Artspace have become attuned to the almost relentless programming of material appearances and disappearances in the series of installations commissioned from local and international artists, which has dominated exhibition programming. However, the conventional understanding of installation in its most institutionalized forms carries with it profound implications for the work itself, an in-built fatalism of sorts. Just as the best installation work encourages the visitor to experience (an often familiar) space in a significantly new manner, or utilizes given spatial contexts to cast its own core qualities in relief (a sort of post-minimalist mirroring of the self), its very "active" material presence within the space also generates a heightened sense of its inevitable and imminent absence. Installation work anticipates its own erasure.

Whilst certain forms of installation art have certainly become commodifiable and collectable, available for multiple public incarnations, within the gallery spaces of a non-collection base institution focussed upon the presentation of singularly new projects, the historical experience of installation art is conditioned in part by an accumulation of erasures, of fading memory traces, of photographic documentation, and of sedimentary layerings of now absent presences over the architectural linings of those spaces. Here installation art evokes an experience of haunting, perhaps even of mourning. Of course, each visitor will remember certain installations more clearly than others – some installations will leave more profound absences than others, more significantly determining subsequent encounters with the spaces of their "once having been," staining subsequent encounters with other works installed in the space. Foregrounding their own transitory nature, certain works enact strange compressions of time, on one hand anticipating their own disappearance or future condition as documentation even at their moment of presence in a gallery, on the other existing in space as little more than traces of past action. These are often elusive works that utilize contradiction and indeterminacy as means of both evading clear categories of meaning and embracing the fragility associated with their impermanence. They are necessarily always incomplete and ongoing in some manner. There is no particular moment, no point of final resolution in the work on which to hang acts of apprehension and comprehension. There is just a continuing generation of associations, readings, and speculations provoked by the work in mnemonic form; an ongoing, quiet amplification of its reach across time. How like performance.

Elements of the preceding two paragraphs are drawn from an essay I wrote in response to an Artspace installation project, two years before I joined the organization.[1] To a large extent, the thinking behind this essay gave rise to the first major performance/installation program of my Artspace tenure.[2] With this program – *Aftermath* – I sought to provide a critical and public focus to the complex relationship of performance to installation art, sharing a genealogy, as they do, in early conceptual and post-object art. The project centered on the installation "aftermath" of performance, or conversely, performance as a strategy for creation of material environments – the bleeding back and forth of active modes of performance and its post-life remainders.

Running over eight weeks and bringing together six major performance installation works, two further discrete performances, a screening program, and symposium events, *Aftermath* posed a range of questions regarding the relationship of performance to installation.[3] The exhibition series was aimed at addressing a number of crucial questions about the importance of performance to the development and understanding of installation art. To what degree, for example, do the coordinates of site-specificity and temporal ephemerality, so important to installation art of the 1990s for example, find their basis in performance? After all, both are practices of ultimate disappearance, depending on documentation or re-enactment to stake a claim on history.

A range of Artspace projects over the years, such as two in 2003 – David Burrows and D. J. Simpson's *Sample Scatter Synthesis (Amplified)* and *Islands in the Stream* by Hany Armanious, Koji Ryui, Mary Teague, and Natsuho Takita – have approached installation as a material trace of performance action. Such projects have raised the important question of whether such an approach functions to reposition the gallery viewer from participant in the work, as installation often claims to do, into bystander always appearing a moment too late on the scene, always missing the main event. Another tendency is toward models of installation as performative environment – in which activity continues throughout the run of the "exhibition" – work to reintegrate the gallery visitor into a shared time experience of performance and installation. An example of this approach is the 2005 *The Universe as Mirror* project at Artspace by Australian artist Domenico de Clario in which for a fortnight the artist undertook an improvised performance between moonrise and sunset each day, seated blindfolded at a piano within a space full of his belongings delivered and deposited by removalists. And then, of course, further models of a spatial conflation of performance-installation treat the gallery more as a space to realize and/or present social engagement and collaborative action. This could be seen, for example, in the 2005 *Gift* project at Artspace by visiting Dutch artists Jonas Ohlsson and Jennifer Tee, which drew on the sociological imperative described in Marcel Mauss' celebrated 1925 book of the same title and involved forms of collaboration with local community including activities such as a mask-making workshop that resulted in masks being "gifted" to the exhibition whilst a limited edition artist book was made from this workshop and gifted back to the participants.

These Artspace projects,[4] and the performance–installation relationships they are based in raise the following questions: in its relationship to performance, to what degree does installation and by implication the gallery itself come to function as culturally loaded stage-set? (Or laboratory?) When performance prefigures installation, does it necessarily place action in an impossible position of always becoming (but never arriving)? Or in such cases does installation inevitably come to serve as a document or memorial of the event?

Insomuch as *Aftermath* was intended to engage with a loose epistemological inquiry into the relatively recent trends in contemporary or post-conceptual art, it was also hoped that, in its own "aftermath," it might begin to draw out from within the projects a perhaps covert commentary on the inevitable, oft-times relentless propensity of Artspace to inscribe all practices as, above all, "installation." I never publicly articulated this latter somewhat latent curatorial drive to either artists or audiences, but rather it constituted something of an internal dialogue with the hegemony of installation within the particular history of Artspace. And so perhaps further questions should have been asked: does performance offer a strategy for either deconstructing or further radicalizing the spatial rhetoric of installation? Or does it inevitably serve to further sustain installation as a form of host, feeding and embellishing installation with more material and representational possibilities (as may well be argued of its attendant recording media, particularly photography and video)? Can performance resist co-option into the dominant gallery and museum convention of "installation"? Is there a purpose to even attempting such resistance?

Interestingly from this perspective, whilst the spatial frame of installation tended in the final instance to define each individual work within *Aftermath*, whatever its point of origin and form of activity, related discussions throughout the program and in the concluding symposium focussed almost exclusively on performance as a subject. Installation remained a form of opaque default setting for the program – a given platform – while performance somehow implicitly pleaded its own need for the certification of language, a public testimony or witness to presence (in a manner installation just as implicitly abhors).

From the outset the curatorial framework of *Aftermath* was never intended as prescriptive. Half of the six major artist projects were already in the early stage of development before dialogue began regarding the overall structure of the program, whilst each project pitched itself, whether consciously or not, at a very point within the performance–installation nexus (or it might be said, launched itself from a different ground-point within performance and/or installation). Importantly, the framework created a further performative space in the relationship between projects. As the overall program rolled out – one new work a week – new relationships formed across spaces between the "aftermath" of preceding performance works and new activity. This constantly evolving structure was crucial to the conception of performance taking place within installation, rather than simply providing an opening party piece or the "sexy supplement" lightly mocked by Melanie Gilligan in a recent *Artforum* essay,[5] although in the final analysis three of the works did in fact conflate performance with the occasion of an installation launch.

This was most notably the case with the first two projects in the series: *Maximum Commune (Ugly Business … on the basis of disbelief.)* by New York-based Australian artist Guy Benfield, and Sydney artist Anne Graham's *In Between Space*. Benfield drew on a range of self-consciously "retro" aesthetic and cultural models, building a pavilion in the center of the gallery reminiscent of the utopian dwelling structures of 1960s and 1970s communities such as Drop City,[6] populating it and the surrounding gallery space with various props including furniture, a mannequin, and a huge lump of clay on a potter's wheel, and then undertaking a range of actions on opening night ranging from clambering over the structure while pouring and spraying fluorescent paint to parodically working, wet, spinning clay while dressed in cardigan, slippers, and blacked out glasses. Benfield's series of actions, "droppings"[7]or situational episodes reanimated apparently obsolete tropes such as ritual,

Aftermath: Performance Installation
Artspace Visual Arts Centre, Sydney. Curator: Blair French. 05 July–8 August 2007. Photograph: Silversalt.

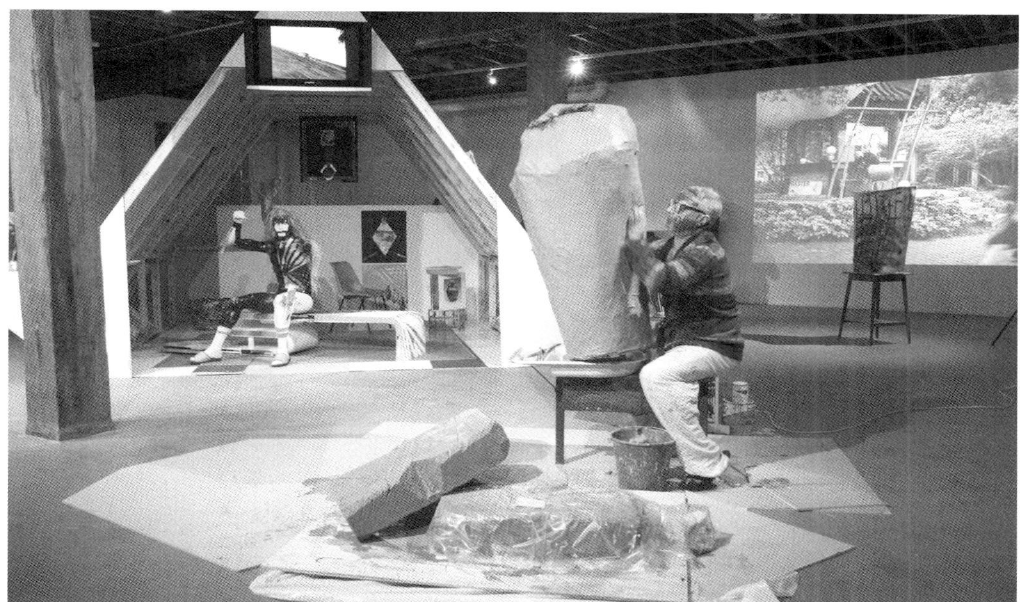

Guy Benfield, *Maximum Commune (Ugly Business ... on the basis of disbelief.)* Performance, 05 July 2007; Installation, 06 July–21 July 2007. Courtesy the artist and Artspace Visual Arts Centre, Sydney. Photograph: Silversalt.

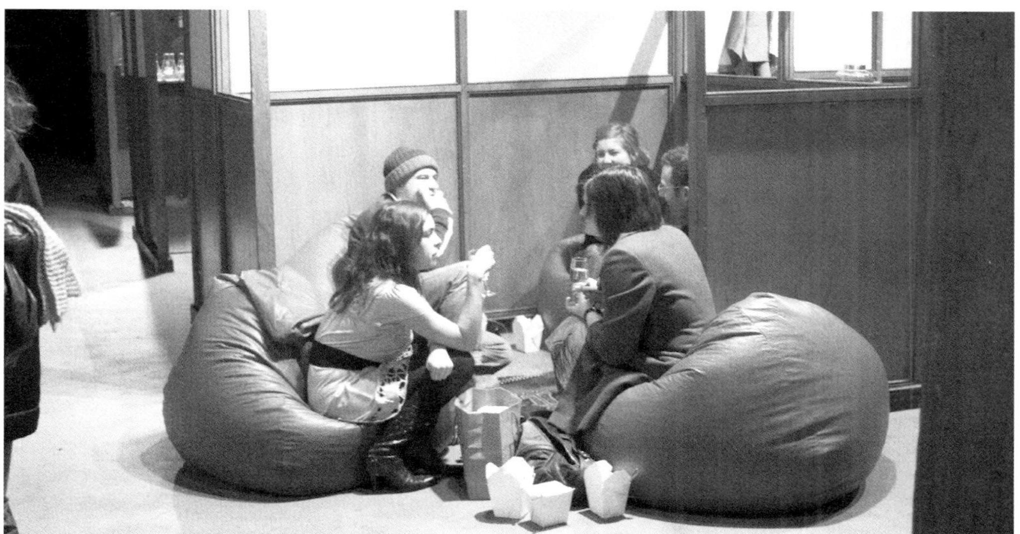

Anne Graham, *In Between Space.* Performance, 12 July 2007; Installation, 13 July–28 July 2007. Courtesy the artist and Artspace Visual Arts Centre, Sydney.

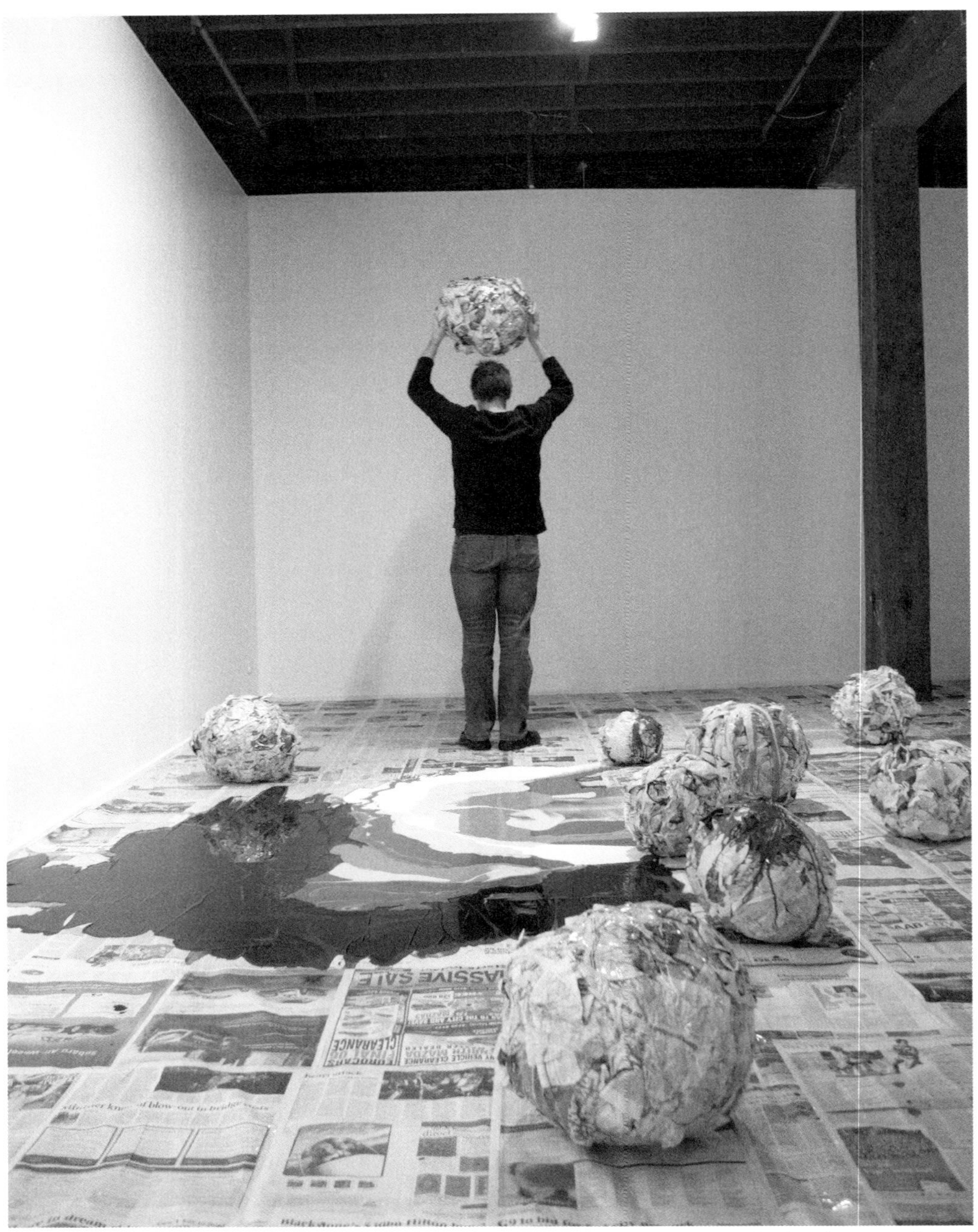

Franz Ehmann, *Forever Young*. Performance, 19 July 2007; Installation, 20 July–11 August 2007. Photograph: Silversalt. Courtesy the artist and Artspace Visual Arts Centre, Sydney.

Japanese and European models of live action painting, 1960s west coast American ceramic funk, and plain old 1970s suburban Sydney bourgeois bohemian craftwork.

Like Benfield, Graham constructed an architectural space within the space, providing physical parameters and structural context for live action. In her case, however, this took the form of old timber room partitions whose utilitarian finishing imparted more than a whiff of institutional compartmentalization (schools, hospitals, and the like). Each of eight spaces corresponded to a particular function – so a bedroom, bathroom, kitchen, studio, library, living room, office, gallery – and were occupied on opening night via a range of intimate participatory activities. Food was cooked and consumed, hands washed, hair cut, "work" undertaken in the study, the remnants of all such activities simply left as "aftermath." Of all the projects in *Aftermath*, Graham's work clearly operated most in synchronicity with the now well-recognized tropes of relational aesthetics.[8] As performance it is gentle, barely present and yet as such somehow self-conscious, the literal domestic leftovers of activity straining to signify anything other than the simple everyday experience of sharing a few hours social time with a group of family or friends.

Benfield's work by contrast was far more structurally self-referential. A built environment literally served as a platform for a particular mode of gesture, which in turn reanimated that environment through its reassertion in video form. This is a typical Benfield strategy, and an important one in the context of thinking through the inscription in the present of performance as document. Benfield's performance included a large wall projection featuring documentation of an earlier Benfield performance in China (involving hair and paint) along with further work featured on an LCD screen fixed to the apex of the pavilion structure. These were then newly reactivated performance documents relocated within a new performance that in turn immediately displaced them: Benfield placing footage of the opening night performance back into the space (in projection and screen forms). There was more than an endless circularity here. Rather, the dynamic, hand-held performative quality of much of the footage ensured that its reinstallation amongst the stage setting of its creation imbued the overall work with both a spatial presentness and temporal liquidity, as if to make the point that documentation is always a mark of something current.

This approach of using video documentation to create a feedback loop between past and present within an installation scenario was partially shared by Brisbane-based artist Franz Ehmann's *Forever Young*, although here the work was more stripped back, wry, and propositional. Ehmann also prepared a gallery space in a particular manner, carpeting it with newspaper that in one area was "decorated" with a spill of bright paint. A large rubbish skip was placed near the gallery entrance, painted in bright stripes like some post-minimal-pop sculpture. Projections into the skip and onto an end wall showed Ehmann undertaking discrete actions or live sculptural works in his Artspace studio situated in another part of the building, above the gallery – fixing and unfixing his body to the wall for example, or balancing a small table. Paper balls, a paper suit, and a space where visitors could crawl under the newspaper skin of the gallery all created the potential for spatial rupture of the environment on the part of visitors (although this rarely occurred), whilst Ehmann consistently refreshed

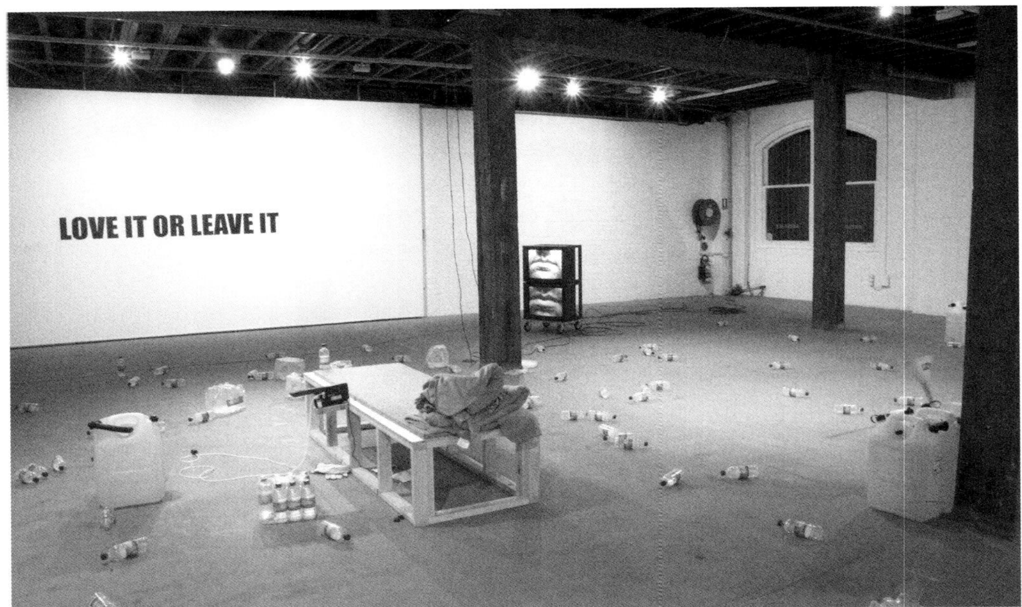

Tony Schwensen, *Rise*. 100 hour performance, from 8pm 24 July 2007; Installation 31 July–04 August 2007. Photograph: Silversalt. Courtesy the artist and Artspace Visual Arts Centre, Sydney.

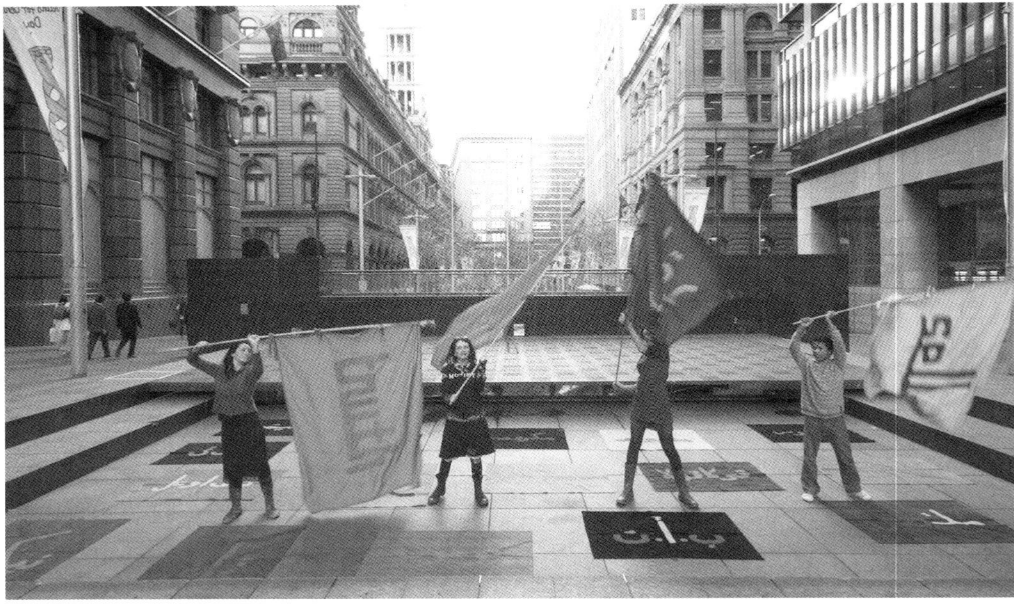

Arahmaiani, *Make-Up or Break-Up*. Installation, 02 August–18 August 2007. Photograph: Silversalt. Courtesy of the artist and Artspace Visual Arts Centre, Sydney.

the video elements of the installation every couple of days by replacing it with new footage of him working, inferring perhaps that the installation might best be treated as a psychic frame for exploratory actions – phenomenological experiments, performances – taking place elsewhere (literally upstairs – out of sight but on-camera). Visited just once, the video component of the installation read simply as *documentation* of some past performance. However, encounters with a different video element on each of multiple visits shifted this reading, more firmly placing the video performance components of the work in the same present moment – or experience of temporal flux – as the visitor. The video component here not only continually refreshed but re-performed the installation space.

Two other works directly worked at the question of the "liveness" of documentation, although in very different ways. Visiting from Jakarta, Arahmaiani worked with a loose group of local students and activists to stage banners with slogans such as "faith" and the names of multinational corporations written in Jawi (Malay-Arabic) script at various public sites around Sydney, ranging from Bondi Beach to the Aboriginal housing area known as "The Block" in Redfern. The stagings, however, were more simply photographic constructions than acts of public intervention – whether in mock protest or advertising mode – as if models for the work might be sourced in a history of performance documentation rather than that of performance itself (in turn nudging the work closer to the status of post-conceptual photographic art). Indeed, the "performance" aspect of the work resided primarily in an amalgam of engaging structures of community organization and photo-shoot direction. Banners and photographic documentation then made up the installation – *Make-Up or Break-Up*. As performance, this was the most tangential work in the program, but also that in which performance was most clearly inscribed in the representational content of the work.[9]

Like Benfield, Australian artist Tony Schwensen (then local, now based in Boston) reinserted video documentation of his performance into the subsequent installation element of his work *Rise*. Of all the projects, this distinction between live and mediated body was most problematized by Schwensen. The artist inhabited the space for one hundred hours, dressed in blue coveralls, framed by the Beckettian slogan "Hopes None Resolutions None" writ large on one wall, while on another was "Love It Or Leave It" – the aggressively jingoistic catch-cry of Anglo-Australian rioters on Sydney's Cronulla Beach in late 2005.[10] This latter statement also echoed at regular intervals throughout the space via a recording of the artist's voice (accompanied by close up video images of his mouth). Schwensen had originally planned to process one hundred liters of salt water through a hand desalination pump, whilst also processing a more internal liquidity – as ever-increasing numbers of empty water bottles were strewn across the space, so rose the levels in his urine containers. However the pump malfunctioned on the first night, leaving the artist with little to do but to simply exist in space, pace the gallery, banter with the occasional interlocutor, and attempt to ignore the large numbers of late-night visitors banging on the gallery windows (this gallery opens out onto a busy street, with an iconic fast-food cart across the road). The initial one hundred hour period was followed by a further week in which another monitor was placed

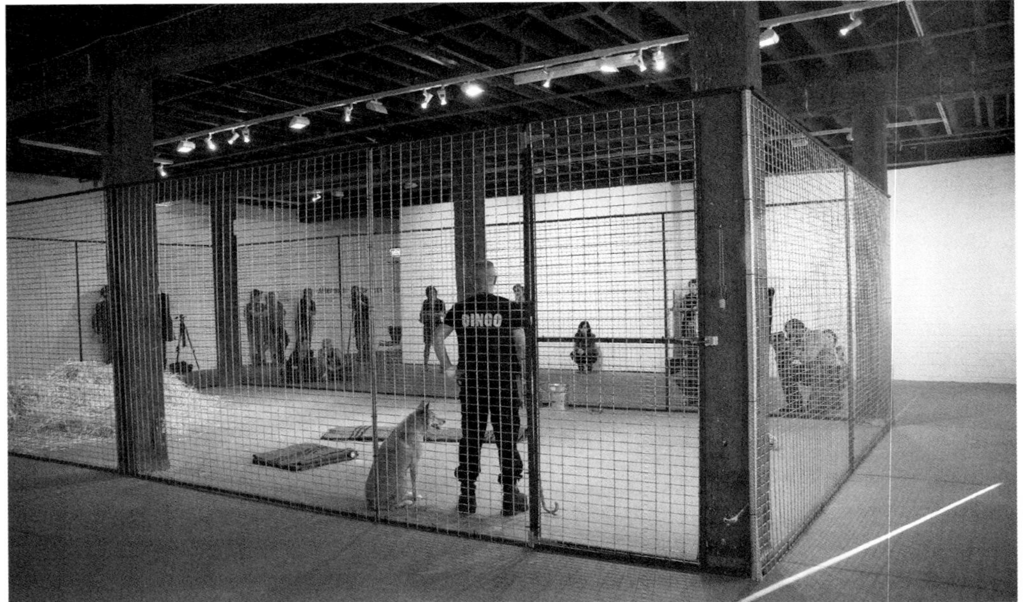

André Stitt, *Dingo: A Treatment towards a New Communionism.* Performance, 4–7pm 09 August–11 August 2007; Installation 14 August–18 August 2007. Photograph: Silversalt. Courtesy the artist and Artspace Visual Arts Centre, Sydney.

in the space, screening in real time those seemingly interminable one hundred hours again, in real time. Shot with a fixed camera that could not track his wanderings about the gallery, the footage did not always feature Schwensen; nevertheless the forlorn weight of the "failed" performance (that was, in turn, the crux of its success) was magnified in this dogged, one-to-one revisitation of a state of absence in presence.

Whereas Schwensen compounded his performance practice with an insistent drive not only to document everything in digital video form but to treat that material as a 1:1 real time record of the work, the final participant in the program, Cardiff-based André Stitt, treated the digital video record of his nine hour work *Dingo: A Treatment towards a New Communionism* as raw material for the production of what might almost be considered a discrete moving image work. Stitt's performance treated Joseph Beuys' *I Like America and America Likes Me* (or "Coyote") performance of 1974 as a loose score. Stitt certainly did not recreate or re-stage Beuys' work in the precise manner of other recent "re-enactment" works such as those comprising Marina Abramović's *Seven Easy Pieces* series of 2005. Rather, Beuys' work offered a template for undertaking a new work dealing with the cultural confrontations both explicit and implicit in acts of arrival in sites, lands, and contexts inhabited by others, along with the resultant undertows of collective cultural trauma.

For three three-hour sessions over three days Stitt thus shared a caged-off area of Artspace with a dingo, taking a cue for various actions from photographic documentation of Beuys' performance (published in this instance on a large poster for a travelling exhibition of Beuys' work organized by the Arts Council of Wales), but also introducing elements consistent in his own practice (bandaged wrists, small effigies) and others specific to the place (news photographs of the 2005 Macquarie Fields "riots" in outer suburban Sydney).[11] Press and public interest in the work was high, but in the case of the latter mainly from passers-by clustered outside the gallery windows, willingly distanced from the space of performance both by the gallery architecture and the caging within. The work was ultimately most affecting for its intimacy and literal quietness, as artist and dog took to long periods of resting in piles of straw, or laid out on the concrete floor, punctuated by brief phases of activity, play, and in Stitt's case the marking of paper, photographs, and objects with red mud.

As was so with all the artists, even Schwensen, Stitt created an architectural or material frame for his performance work in such a way to suggest, in response to questions posed at the outset, that installation rather than performance was (and is) necessarily figured by the institution itself, in the case of Artspace as an implicit institutional principle. In the majority of the projects, performance then undertook a certain transformation of space, with perhaps the most memorable works being those in which the finally absent body of the artist remained inscribed within installation form, often in documentation mode (or with Stitt, via remnants of clothing), in such a way as simultaneously to mark past time (in an act of mourning) but also to insist upon the presentness of the work. In this way then, the works in *Aftermath* pointed collectively to the fact that installation and performance depend upon the other, and documentation becomes a form of re-membering in the most literal way.

Notes

1. See "After-Image," published in David Burrows and D. J. Simpson, *Sample Scatter Synthesis (Amplified)*, exh. cat., Artspace Visual Arts Centre, Sydney, 2003, pp. 4–8.
2. Performance art had formed a core element of Artspace programming for some years previously, including major works by Australian artists such as Mike Parr as well as short programs of work by younger local artists and a range of works by international visitors.
3. The full *Aftermath* program also included single performance works by Yiorgos Zafiriou (*Malignant Mother*, 16 August 2007) and senVoodoo (Fiona McGregor and Aña Wojak) (*Font*, 17 August 2007). Further documentation of and commissioned texts on individual projects have been published in *Column #1*, 2008, a periodical published by Artspace Visual Arts Centre.
4. All these aforementioned projects were presented within the Artspace program developed by former Executive Director, Nicholas Tsoutas. The *Gift* project was curated by Sally Breen.
5. Melanie Gilligan, "The Beggar's Pantomime," *Artforum*, 2007, vol. 45, no. 10, p. 430.
6. Drop City was a community formed in the mid-1960s in Colorado by art students and film-makers Gene Bernofsky, JoAnn Bernofsky, Richard Kallweit, and Clark Richert. Inspired by the architectural ideas of Buckminster Fuller and Steve Baer the community constructed domes and zonohedra to house themselves, using geometric panels made from found metal and other materials.

7. The term "droppings" or Drop Art dates back to the early 1960s and the young artists noted above who were to soon establish Drop City. Related to Allan Kaprow's "happenings" and the performance work of John Cage amongst others, "droppings" were works of art literally formed in the act of "dropping" materials.
8. This is Nicolas Bourriaud's model, in which art is figured as primarily a mode or context of social exchange, its "value" or "quality" being bound up in that experience of engagement. See Nicolas Bourriaud, *Relational Aesthetics*, translated by Simon Pleasance and Fronza Woods with the participation of Mathieu Copeland, Paris: les presses du réel, 2002 [1998].
9. That the re-staging of photographs and banners in the gallery space could also be considered a performative, transitory act was challenged in a class discussion by one group of art students who criticized what they considered the museological ossification of the work's original live impulse in its gallery presentation.
10. The Cronulla "riots" were a series of racially based violent group confrontations following the gathering of approximately 5000 people on Sydney's Cronulla Beach on Sunday 11 December 2005 responding to what they believed to be earlier instances of violent and intimidatory behaviour on the beach by youths of Middle Eastern background.
11. The Macquarie Field "riots" were a series of disturbances over four nights in the suburb of Macquarie Fields in south-west Sydney sparked by the deaths of two local youths killed when the stolen car in which they were passengers crashed into a tree following a police chase. Rioters confronted police with rocks, bottles, and bricks as well as setting cars alight. Macquarie Fields is a disadvantaged area, with a high percentage of housing commission homes (cheap, often poorly maintained housing stock provided by the state) and suffering high levels of unemployment.

Timeline of Ideas: Live Art in (Art) History, A Primarily European-US-based Trajectory of Debates and Exhibitions Relating to Performance Documentation and Re-Enactments

Amelia Jones

1950s: *The "Live" Erupts into the Visual Arts* **1950–1:** Hans Namuth photographs films Jackson Pollock Painting and edits footage into *Jackson Pollock*; the film and photographs are disseminated internationally. **1951:** Abstract Expressionist Robert Motherwell edits and publishes *The Dada Painters and Poets*, introducing the performative works of European Dadaists such as Marcel Duchamp to an English-reading public. **1952**: Harold Rosenberg publishes "American Action Painters" in *Artnews*, in which he famously described American abstract painting in terms of action (with the canvas "an arena in which to act"). **1952:** John Cage, Merce Cunningham, David Tudor, Charles Olson, and Robert Rauschenberg perform the time-based multimedia work *Theater Piece No. 1* at Black Mountain College in North Carolina, considered by many to be inspirational for the development of Happenings and Fluxus in the late 1950s and following. **1954:** Yoshihara Jiro founds the performative arts movement Gutai in post-war Japan. **Mid-1950s onward:** Georges Mathieu produces his performative paintings in Europe and Japan. **1956:** R. G. Collingwood's *The Idea of History* proposes the idea that all history is performative. **1957:** In the journal *Dance Observer* experimental musician John Cage writes of his work with choreographer Merce Cunningham: "We are not, in these dances and music, saying something [...] We are rather doing something. The meaning of what we do is determined by each one who sees and hears it." **1957–8 onward:** American artists Allan Kaprow, George Segal, and later Claus Oldenburg and Jim Dine develop the first Happenings in the New York/New Jersey area. **1958:** Inspired by John Dewey's 1930s book *Art as Experience* and by classes in New York City with John Cage, Kaprow publishes "The Legacy of Jackson Pollock," in which he shifts attention from Pollock's paintings to the "diaristic gesture," the bodily *act* of painting. **1959:** Erving Goffman publishes his hugely influential book on the performance of the self, *The Presentation of Self in Everyday Life*. **1960s:** *Consolidation of* *the Performative within the Visual Arts.* **1960:** Yves Klein produces his *Leap into the Void* photographs and begins his public *Anthropometries* performances in which he uses naked female bodies as human paintbrushes. **1961:** The first official Fluxus event at AG Gallery in New York City; organized by Lithuanian born artist George Maciunas, who went on to develop Fluxus festivals across Europe, presenting works by artists such as Nam June Paik and George Brecht. **1961:** Niki de Saint-Phalle performs the first "shoot" painting in Paris. **1961:** Andy Warhol supposedly completes his first "piss" (or "oxidation") painting during this year. **1962:** J. L. Austin publishes *How to Do Things with Words*, in which he elaborates speech act theory, which (via the work of Jacques Derrida and Judith Butler) will become central to theorizing meaning and identity as performative. **1964:** Carolee Schneemann's first performance of *Meat Joy* in Paris and New York. **1964–5:** Yoko Ono performs *Cut Piece* in Tokyo and New York. **1966:** Michael Kirby publishes the book *Happenings*. **1966–70:** A series of articles and debates by artists making minimal abstract sculpture or environmental works (Robert Morris, Donald Judd, and Robert Smithson) and critics such as Michael Fried and Lucy Lippard debate the pros and cons of the opening of the artwork to temporality and spectatorial desire, or what Lippard calls the "dematerialization of art." **1967:** The UK's first modern historical re-enactment group, *The Sealed Knot*, is founded. **1968:** *The Southern Skirmish Association* is formed to re-stage incidents from the American Civil War. **1969:** New York-based artist Lee Lozano produces *The Dialogue Piece* in which she aims to produce a live work without remaining documentation, noting: "The purpose of this piece is to have dialogues, not to make a piece. No recordings or notes are made during dialogues, which exist solely for their own sake as joyous social occasions." **1969:** VALIE EXPORT produces a photograph of a supposed performance of *Genital Panic*, a performance that only occurred *as* the photographic pose. **1970s:** *From Performativity to Body and Performance Art.* **1970–5:** A series of articles in US and European publications by Willoughby Sharp, Cindy Nemser, Lea Vergine, François Pluchart, Ira Licht, and others defines the emergence of body-oriented (or "Body Art") works by artists from Vito Acconci to Gina Pane. Meanwhile vital performance centers take shape in Europe and on the East and West coasts of the US and Canada. **1976:** Martha Wilson co-founds performance space Franklin Furnace in New York City; by the early twenty-first century, Franklin Furnace is raising funds to establish one of the most extensive and sophisticated online version of their massive archive of images, texts, and video and film footage documenting the live art events they have mounted over the decades. **1976:** Adrian Piper produces *This is Not the Documentation of a Performance*, in which she reworks a newspaper story about protesters in New York City by replacing one of their placards with the text "This is Not a Performance." **1976:** Guy Sherwin executes *Man with Mirror* for the first time; he re-enacts the piece numerous times over the decades. (See 2009 for another redo.) **1979:** PS122 (Performance Space 122) founded in New York City. **1980s:** *The Institutionalization of Performance Art as Spoken Word Theatre.* **1980s:** "Performance art" begins to be defined and solidified as a sub-genre of contemporary art in US discourse, pulled away from theater studies while at the same time the trend was for artists such as

Laurie Anderson and Tim Miller to develop further the narrative aspects of theater and autobiography in contrast to the simple body-oriented practices dominating the 1970s practices. A series of publications in English by authors such as Mel Gordon, Mary Emma Harris, and RoseLee Goldberg begin to document the history of experimental performative techniques in the visual arts and to define performance art as a particular genre with a Euro-American history. **1980:** The first performance studies department is co-founded by Richard Schechner, Brooks McNamara, and Michael Kirby (joined by anthropologist Barbara Kirshenblatt-Gimblett in 1981) at the Tisch School of the Arts at New York University out of their graduate Department of Drama, indicating a new awareness of performance as a separate, interdisciplinary genre of creative production with a history and theory of its own. **1982–4:** Mike Bidlo produces his first one-man show, the installation *Jack the Dripper at Peg's Place*, which functions as an homage to Pollock painting as documented in the Hans Namuth film; and produces *Add One Blue Poles for Germany*, a redo of the images of Pollock painting by Namuth from 1950. **1986:** Mel Gordon's Mastfor 2 Company reconstructs various events from Russian/Soviet Constructivist movement c. 1920 at Franklin Furnace, New York. **1989:** DADAnewyorkDADA Company, headed by John Wilson, reconstructs a number of performances by Dadaists such as Marcel Duchamp, Tristan Tzara, and Hugo Ball at Franklin Furnace, New York. **1989:** Founding of Los Angeles performance space Highways by Linda Frye Burnham and Tim Miller. Miller, along with Karen Finley, John Fleck, and Holly Hughes – all of whose works typified the turn to autobiography in US performance art – is involved in the Culture Wars, the national debates and lawsuits regarding state funding of controversial artworks in the early 1990s. **1990s:** *Expansion and Development of Performance Art in Relation to Art's Histories.* **1991:** The founding of the National Association of Re-Enactment Societies, UK. **1992–4:** Coco Fusco and Guillermo Gómez-Peña perform *Two Undiscovered Amerindians Discover* in various cities around the world, a piece documented through still images and the film by Fusco and Paula Heredia *Couple in a Cage: A Guatinaui Odyssey*, 1993, as well as by Fusco's 1996 article "The Bodies that were Not Ours." **1993:** The exhibition *In the Spirit of Fluxus* takes place at the Walker Art Gallery in Minneapolis; along with the scholarly catalogue accompanying the show, *In the Spirit of Fluxus* exemplifies a new approach to displaying the ephemera relating to one of the key performance movements of the 1960s. **1993:** Babette Mangolte, originally a stills photographer who documented performances in New York in the 1970s, produces a series of films for Robert Morris's retrospective at the Guggenheim Museum in New York in which the artist's classic body artworks are re-enacted by hired performers. **1994:** The Live Art Archive is founded at the Nottingham Trent University; the archive is transferred to the University of Bristol Theatre Collection in 2006. **1994:** Curated by Robyn Brentano and Olivia Georgia for the Cleveland Center for Contemporary Art, the exhibition *Outside the Frame/Performance and the Object: A Survey History of Performance Art in the USA Since 1950* includes a range of documentary materials as well as a live art program, indicating a new consciousness in the gallery world of the objects and images involved in the memorializing of performance in history.

1994: German-Swedish artist Felix Gmelin inaugurates *Art Vandals*, a series of works rethinking works by artists from Pablo Picasso to Robert Rauschenberg to Robert Gober; the "redos" include researched texts that provide a context of historic debates about the original works' meaning and importance. **1994:** In a gallery in Amsterdam Barbara Visser re-enacts Yoko Ono and John Lennon's 1967 *Bed In*, documenting the re-enactment in the videotape entitled *Hilton/Bed Piece.* **1995:** Performance Studies international, the professional organization for performance studies, is founded by Peggy Phelan and her students at New York University's Performance Studies Department. **1995:** Dan Graham re-stages *Performer/Audience/Mirror* as *Video/Architecture/Performance.* **1995:** The show and accompanying panel *Action, Performance and the Photograph* at Craig Krull Gallery in Los Angeles explore the relationship between live art and its photographic remains. **1995:** Keith Boadwee redoes Jackson Pollock's drip paintings by squirting paint out of his anus in a series of works displayed at Ace Gallery, Los Angeles. **1997:** Amelia Jones publishes "'Presence' in *absentia*: Experiencing Performance as Documentation" in *Art Journal*, debunking from an art historical point of view claims of live art as "authentic." **1997:** In their video project *Fresh Acconci*, Los Angeles based artists Paul McCarthy (active in producing live art in the early 1970s) and his protégé Mike Kelley redo several classic Vito Acconci body artworks as soft porn, replacing Acconci with naked aspiring young Hollywood actors. **1997:** The exhibition *You Are Here: Re-Siting Installations*, Royal College of Art, London, explores the "redoing" of famous installation works. **1998:** Paul Schimmel organizes *Out of Actions: Between Performance and the Object, 1949–1979*, an exhibition focusing on the objects and images associated with historic live art at the Museum of Contemporary Art, Los Angeles. **1998:** Jane Pollard and Iain Forsyth begin their project of staging re-enactments of classic rock gigs using tribute bands, beginning with the performance *Rock n' Roll Suicide* sponsored by the Institute of Contemporary Art, London, with Steve Harvey as Ziggy Stardust in the famous final concert by David Bowie in 1973. **1999:** In London Lois Keidan and Catherine Ugwu establish the Live Art Development Agency to support and develop live art practices in the UK. **1999:** *Skirmish: The Living History Magazine* is founded in the UK, covering performative and cinematic re-enactments of historical events. **2000s:** *Fascination with Performance Histories and the Historicizing of Live Art.* **2000s:** Demonstrating a new fascination with the passing of time and histories of visual and live arts, a massive spate of exhibitions addressing various aspects of live art in history are held around Europe and North America; most of these are accompanied by catalogues with documentation and essays exploring the problem of documenting or remembering the live act in history. **2000:** Pierre Huyghe's *Third Memory* is a two channel installation that reworks the bank robbery filmed in Lumet's *Dog Day Afternoon* (1975) including reminiscences by the robbery's protagonist whose recollections have been sifted through the lens of having seen the film. The major feature film *Pollock*, directed by and starring Ed Harris (channeling the artist) is released, "re-enacting" Pollock painting in scenes showing Harris explicitly imitating Pollock from the 1950 Hans Namuth film. University of the West of England lecturer Rod Dickinson stages a re-enactment of a series of events leading up to the massacre of cult members by Jim Jones at Jonestown in 1978. **2001:** Jeremy Deller conceives and produces his re-enactment of the famous 1984 miner's strike against the Thatcher administration as the *Battle of Orgreave*; this re-enactment is filmed under the direction of Mike Figgis and the film is aired on British television in 2002. **2001:** *A Little Bit of History Repeated* is curated by Jens Hoffmann at Kunst-Werke Berlin, a two day survey of noted performance art pieces as translated by younger contemporary artists, including Laura Lima's redo of Yoko Ono's *Cut Piece*. **2001:** Andrea Fraser produces *Art Must Hang*, a performance in which she re-enacts a drunken lecture by Martin Kippenberger from 1995; Fraser's re-enactment takes place at Galerie Christian Nagel, Cologne. **2002 and 2003:** Whitechapel stages re-enactments in *A Short History of Performance*, including Carolee Schneemann's 1964 *Meat Joy*. **2002:** Rod Dickinson recreates Stanley Milgram's infamous 1961 social psychology experiment on obedience and authority for the Glasgow Centre for Contemporary Art. **2002:** *Draw a Line and Follow It*, held at Los Angeles Contemporary Exhibitions, includes works following scores held in the Jean Brown Collection of Fluxus-related materials; the show includes Ming-Yuen S. Ma's reworking of Ono's *Cut Piece* in *ReCut*. **2002:** Lebanese artist Walid Raad, founding member of the Atlas Group, prints a series of photographs he supposedly shot as a teenager during Israel's 1982 occupation of Beirut; he titles the series *We Decided to Let Them Say, "We are Convinced," twice*. **2002:** Robert Longo produces *Seeing the Elephant*, a series of photographs documenting American Civil War re-enactments. **2002:** Irish artist Gerard Byrne produces a three-channel video entitled *New Sexual Lifestyles*, in which amateur actors re-stage a roundtable published in *Playboy* magazine in 1973. **2002:** Felix Gmelin produces *Farbtest die Rote Fahne II* (*Color Test: The Red Flag II*), a videotaped performance remaking a 1968 film by Gerd Conrad of a student action in which Gmelin's own father had participated, carrying a flag through the streets of Berlin. **2002–3:** PS1 Museum in New York City exhibits *Video Acts: Single Channel Works from the Collections of Pamela and Richard Kramlich*, performance-based videotapes. **2003:** New York-based artist Sharon Hayes re-stages the monologues from the famous audiotapes disseminated by Patti Hearst and fellow members of the SLA in her work *Symbionese Liberation Army (SLA) Screeds #13, 16, 20 & 29*; her re-enactment is disseminated in the form of VHS tapes given away free to gallery visitors. **2003:** Brandon LaBelle orchestrates *Learning from Seedbed* at the Standard Gallery in Chicago by re-staging the ramp Vito Acconci had built at Sonnabend Gallery for his *Seedbed* in 1972, inviting visitors to enter its interior as a social space; in addition to the ramp LaBelle staged a performative action across the city with participants adopting the position Acconci seems to have occupied in the original work as visible in photographic documents from the period. **2003:** Franklin Furnace, New York, launches its online database *The Unwritten History Project*, documenting their three-decade long history of performances. **2003:** Omer Fast's *Spielberg's List* is a two channel installation showing footage of the replica of the prison and gas ovens at Auschwitz that were built a short distance from the actual prison for the 1993 blockbuster Steven Spielberg film *Schindler's List*. **2004:** Yoko Ono redoes her own *Cut Piece* at Ranelagh Gallery, Paris. **2004:** *Re-Enact* performance event at Mediamatic, Amsterdam. **2004:** Velveeta Krisp is joined by Leena Minifie, Rachel Racecar, Karen Moe, Tyler Wheatcroft, Ali Lohan, Julie Sargosa, and Julianna Barabas to present a collection of performative interpretations of Carolee Schneemann's 1975 *Interior Scroll.* **2004:** *Experience, Memory, Re-Enactment*, an exhibition and series of lectures and screenings exploring experience and memory in relation to the visual arts, is organized by Anke Bangman and Florian Wuest at Piet Zwart Institute, Rotterdam. **2004:** *Art, Lies and Videotape* opens at Tate Liverpool, an exhibition curated by Adrian George exploring the range of performance documentations, including "fakes." **2005:** Marina Abramović stages *7 Easy Pieces*, six re-enactments of major performance works from the 1960s and 1970s (including her own *Lips of Thomas*) and presents a new work, *Entering the Other Side*; Babette Mangolte makes a film out of the live footage of the events. **2005:** *Once More … With Feeling*, an international selection of art responding to the phenomenon of re-enactments, is curated by Robert Blackson and takes place at Reg Vardy Gallery, University of Sunderland, UK. **2005:** Nicola Hood works with Martha Wilson and Britta Wheeler to mount *History of Disappearance*, a show addressing the archives of performance space Franklin Furnace, at the Baltic Centre for Contemporary Art in Newcastle, UK. **2005:** Artur Żmijewski produces *Repetition*, for the Polish Pavilion at the 2005 Venice Biennale, a live historical re-staging for an audience of Philip Zimbardo's 1971 Stanford Prison Experiment. **2006:** Mark Tribe's Port Huron Project produces its first re-enactment of a famous protest speech from the 1960s and 1970s; *Until the Last Gun is Silent* consists of actress Gina Brown redoing Coretta Scott King's 1968 speech at a peace march in Central Park, New York City just after Martin Luther King was assassinated. **2006:** Franklin Furnace exhibits *Trace*, displaying a range of documentary materials from the archives of the Trace Installation Artspace in Cardiff. **2006:** *A Historic Occasion: Artists Making History*, an exhibition of work by artists deploying re-enactment strategies, takes place at "Mass MoCA," Massachusetts Museum of Contemporary Art in North Adams. **2006:** Johannes Zits re-enacts Yves Klein's early 1960s *Anthropometries* at Grunt Gallery in Vancouver. **2006:** The 1966 Los Angeles *Peace Tower* is reconstructed for the Whitney Biennial in the museum's courtyard. **2006:** Barbara Clausen edits the collection *The (Re)Presentation of Performance Art*, Nürnberg, Verlag Moderner Kunst. **2006:** The show *Playback_Simulated Realities* is held by Edith Russ Haus for Media Art, Oldenburg, Germany. **2007:** *Live Art on Camera*, organized by Alice Maude-Roxby, exhibits a range of photographic documents of performance at the Hansard Gallery, University of Southampton, UK. **2007:** André Lepecki and colleagues re-stage Allan Kaprow's 1959 *18 Happenings in 6 Parts* as part of the Performa series organized in New York City by RoseLee Goldberg. **2007:** The National Review of Live Art in Glasgow includes a panel titled "Live Art Documentation: Responsibility of the Artist?" Organized by Malik Gaines and Alexandro Segade, "Talks about Acts," a panel addressing the link between text and performance, is held at LA><Art gallery in Los Angeles, with presentations by Eleanor Antin, Ron Athey, Andrew Fraser, José Muñoz, and others. **2007:** Harun Farocki's *Deep Play* debuts at Documenta 12, Kassel, Germany; the piece consists of a twelve-screen video installation

replaying the 2006 World Cup final between France and Italy using footage from a range of computerized expert and surveillance systems. **2007:** Austrian artist VALIE EXPORT re-stages her 1973 performance for film *Remote … Remote …* as *Remote … Remote … Passagen* at the Venice Biennale, installing the film projection in front of a large pool of black ink. **2007:** *After the Act: The (Re)Presentation of Performance* and *Wieder und Wider: Performance Appropriated*, curated by Barbara Clausen at the Museum Moderner Kunst Stiftung Ludwig in Vienna, present various modes of artistic redos of public and artistic events, including the re-enactment of an entire 1990 Dia Center for the Arts conference on the "Politics of Images" by New York-based group Continuous Project. **2007:** Art and Re-Enactment conference takes place at The Australian National University in Canberra, Australia. **2008:** *Not Quite How I Remember It*, organized by Helena Reckitt at the Powerplant, Toronto, displays artists' works that engage with time-based events, highlighting forms of re-enactment and reconstruction. **2008:** André Stitt and a group of performers enact *Trace* at the National Review of Live Art, Glasgow, in which, in a set mimicking the appearance of Trace Gallery in Cardiff, they explore objects and documents reminiscent of performances completed at Trace in the past. **2008:** *Live Art Unpacked, Geneva*, developed by La Ribot and Centre d'Art Contemporain Genève in collaboration with Live Art Development Agency, London, presents a range of events addressing performance in history as part of La Ribot's *Rite of Spring.* **2008:** Lilibeth Cuenca re-enacts a number of earlier performance works at the Renwick Gallery in New York City, including Piero Manzoni's *Living Sculpture* (1961), Janine Antoni's *Loving Care* (1992–6), Ana Mendieta's *Blood Signs and Body Tracks* (1974), Orlan's *The Artist's Kiss* (1977), Marina Abramović's *Art Must Be Beautiful, Artist Must be Beautiful* (1975), Yves Klein's *Anthropometries of the Blue Period* (1960), and Shigeko Kubota's *Vagina Painting* (1965). **2008:** The exhibition *Re-Enactments* is organized by John Zeppetelli at DHC-Art Foundation in Montreal, Canada, featuring the work of six artists who appropriate and rework existing cultural texts. **2008:** As part of the Allan Kaprow retrospective at Museum of Contemporary Art, Los Angeles, artists are commissioned to re-enact a number of his performance works across the city. **2008:** New Zealand artist Alex Monteith produces a dual-channel video piece *Reenactment of the Return of the Maori Battalion C. Co. Nga Tama Toa*, documenting in real time a parade of 2000 family members and descendents of the original WWII Maori battalion returning from Gisborne Train Station to Te Poho-o-Rawere Marae. **2008:** The event *A Little Bit of History Repeated* is organized by Jens Hoffmann at the Kunst-Werke Berlin Institute for Contemporary Art, including three performance evenings with work by artists including Tania Bruguera and Tino Sehgal. **2008–9:** *Re.Act.Feminism: Performancekunst der 1960er und 70er jahre heute*, an event including an exhibition, video archive, live performances, and a conference aiming to recapture 1960s and 1970s feminist performance art takes place at the Akademie der Künste, Berlin. **2009:** The Tate Modern commissions Robert Morris to redo his *Bodyspacemotionthings*, a large-scale environment of minimal objects to be engaged with by visitors, originally commissioned by the Tate in 1971 but cancelled after four days due to dangers posed to visitors. **2009:** Iain Forsyth and Jane Pollard present *Radio Mania: An*

Abandoned Work at BFI Southbank Gallery, London, in which they re-enact a film from the 1920s, *The Man from M.A.R.S.* **2009:** *NOTES on a Return*, curated by Sophia Hao, takes place at Laing Art Gallery Newcastle, featuring "recalls" of live artworks that took place at the Laing in the late 1980s; younger artists are asked to respond to the earlier works rather than to re-enact them directly. **2009:** Art Gallery of York University, Ontario, mounts a reconstruction, based on elaborate archaeological and archival research, of *The 1984 Miss General Idea Pavillion*, a conceptual art piece by Canadian artist collective General Idea. **2009:** Lucas Ihlein and colleagues Nick Keys and Astrid Lorange re-stage Allan Kaprow's *Push and Pull: A Furniture Comedy for Hans Hoffman* at Performance Space in Sydney, and mount an information and blog center to document the experience: http://www.pushandpull.com.au/about/. **2009:** Organized by Jennifer Doyle, *Resonate/Obliterate I.E.*, a group of performances at University of California, Riverside's Sweaney Art Gallery includes a signature piece by Ron Athey (*Self-Oblitaration Solo #1: Ecstatic*) and a simultaneous "archiving" of his piece by Julie Tolentino titled *The Sky Remains the Same: Tolentino Archives Athey's Self-Obliteration #1: Ecstatic.* **2010:** Plymouth Arts Center, UK, works with the Marina Abramović Institute for Preservation of Performance Art and the Performance Re-Enactment Society on a project titled *The Pigs of Today are the Hams of Tomorrow*. In the PRS portion of the event participants are invited to "focus in on a particular moment or image from a memorable performance," and bring an object to recreate it at the event, in order for "a series of new works to be produced" through "original performance photographs." The event is followed by the publication of a book, *Marina Abramović and the Future of Performance Art*, edited by Paula Orrell. **2010:** The exhibition *Gestures – Performance and Sound Art* opens at the Museum of Contemporary Art, Roskilde, Denmark, redoing and exhibiting documentation of past sound/performance pieces by artists such as Allan Kaprow, Yoko Ono, and John Cage. **2010:** Spearheaded by Boris Nieslony from Black Market International (a European durational performance group), The Performance Anti Re-Enactment Organisation is formed on Facebook, promoting the "notion that performance art is not an object nor an ahistorical reproduction." **2010:** The Academy of Fine Arts, Vienna, hosts a conference titled *This Sentence is Now Being Performed: Research and Teaching in Performance Art*, addressing the question of live art in history. **2010–11:** *Push and Pull* takes place at Museum Moderner Kunst, Vienna (2010) and the Tate Modern, London (2011); the two shows include works by artists invited to engage with Allan Kaprow's 1963 performative installation *Push and Pull: A Furniture Comedy for Hans Hofmann* by investigating its elements through performance and/or installation. The collaborative performance and installation series is curated by Barbara Clausen, Walter Heun, Achim Hochdörfer, Kathy Noble, Sandra Noeth, and Catherine Wood. **2011–12:** A major publication, edited by Nick Kaye, Gabriella Giannachi, and Michael Shanks, and titled *Archaeologies of Presence: Acting, Performing, Being* addresses the concept of "presence" in relation to live art, including issues of memory, documentation, and simulation.

III

Dialogues

Introduction

Adrian Heathfield

Through a series of exchanges between artists and between artists and theorists, this zone seeks to emphasize a vital dynamic in both the creation and historicization of performance and live art: dialogic discourse. As several contributors to this volume have already noted, the artist as an individual voice and identity still occupies a privileged place within the economies of production and reception of contemporary art practices.[1] Following Roland Barthes' deconstruction of the powers of authorship in "The Death of the Author" (1967), the reductive rooting of an artwork's meanings and affects within a single authorial figure – one who acts both as the primary source for and repository of interpretations of the work – has become a suspect critical gesture.[2] Contemporary art and cultural criticism would more readily assess the significance of an artwork in a complex network of interdependent productions of meaning, arising from, between, and through diverse agents and factors, including the artist, the reader or spectator, and the many material and discursive contexts of the forging and understanding of a work. The very notion of the singular artist as an originating, exceptional, elevated, and isolated figure has been criticized as a projection of modernist ideologies, and contextualized as culturally and historically specific.[3] Nonetheless, the individual author–artist persists as the dominant figure in the systems of production of western contemporary art and in the critical and financial modes of art evaluation by the art institutions, press, and market. Recognition and reward route to a single name, even if that nomination is a stand-in for a complex set of collaborative relations. Live art and performance practices have sat somewhat uneasily in relation to identitarian economies, as public physical enactment in both its preparation and realization is often dependent on complex social creative relations. Whilst there are some striking examples of performances made in solitary conditions and "unwitnessed" by spectators, more often than not performance arises from situations involving collaboration, whether visible or invisible, explicit or implicit, stratified or non-hierarchical.[4] Historically, across its somewhat distinct visual art and theatrical genealogies, performance has also been the chosen form of loose and tight collectives, the necessary modality of mutual and relational artistic expression.

A mode of discourse that emerges not simply from the individual but from the space of relation between agents would seem, then, highly appropriate for a discussion of performance and live art and its passages into historical record. The cultural status of the dialogic in relation to art production and discourse has been made more complex by the resurgence, in late twentieth- and early twenty-first centuries' global visual art scenes, of practices that are socially engaged and whose content arises from processes of extensive relational production.[5] Here art is refigured as a dialogic process, and the transient, intersubjective, and affective dynamics of these works necessitates complicated and highly politicized negotiations around its containment by and lasting presence within art institutions, evidentiary and archival registers. No account of the powers of the dialogic within the contemporary could be complete without consideration of the general information explosion arising from new technologies, and its accompanying cacophony of continuous interpersonal babble. What qualities of the dialogic might distinguish it from the incessant noise of the general economy of prodigious information exchange? Conversation (and its common textual manifestation in the form of the interview) is now an established form of art discourse production, rather than an intriguing minor biographical supplement. The ambiguous status of the interview form in terms of its enmeshment within identitarian and market forces is made evident, for instance, in the phenomenon of the high profile curator Hans Ulrich Obrist's prolific "collection" of interviews with key "names" in the contemporary art world. Cumulative collection and nomination here are in tension with Obrist's commitment to the practice of exchange, its epistemological and pedagogic dimensions, his interest in a kind of "endless conversation."[6] But what might be the potentials of dialogic exchange in this context? What does dialogue disclose that is inaccessible or illegible in other forms of discourse or historicization? And how might dialogue be particularly enlightening as a critical force in relation to the practices of performance and live art?

While the interview can easily become a means of reinforcing notions of individual "genius," dialogic discourse can open up more critical relations. One potential of such exchanges may well be, if the dialogues' participants choose to utilize its inherent capacities, the further dismantling of the cultural and critical powers of both the figures of the artist and the art theorist-historian. Contributors to this volume have previously discussed the discursive mechanisms of mythologization that have sprung up around particular performance acts and artists, and the disclosures of artists in such exchanges may work in a counterfactual mode. Equally, particular figures within the fields of art criticism and history have acquired elevated status through their formalized interpretive powers, so much so that the authority of the figure overrides the truth-claim of what is said. The epistemological imperatives of both art and theory are obscured by these operations. In contrast, the openings occasioned by dialogue – to the informal, the unplanned, and the interpersonal – can be deployed to estrange the participants from their habitual perceptions of the relation between their selves and their work, to unpick cultural and critical projections and upturn sanctioned knowledges.

These exchanges can thus provide an opportunity for the power relations that define the cultural positions of artist and art theorist to be tested and loosened. This is the loosening not only of positions occupied by participants, but of the language and vocabulary deployed by speakers to mount a discourse on a subject. As a form of discourse that is within and partly about the present context of encounter, dialogue is an intensely social and provisional affair that is not readily subject to closure. Here language is gripped by differentiation: as the philosopher Maurice Blanchot stated, conversation "turn[s] language away from itself, maintaining it outside of all unity, outside even the unity of that which is. To converse is to divert language from itself by letting it differ and defer, answering with an always already to a never yet."[7] In particular, for the practicing artist to speak theoretically or for the art theoretician to discuss the practicalities of making or reception may involve each in a leaving of established formalities, languages, and logics, a departure that produces new ways of knowing and of speaking about the work. What might it mean for the practice of art criticism to attend less to interpretation, speculation, placement, and narration, and more to the kinds of knowing that emerge through doing? What place might the artist's voice occupy in this changed context? What claim does the author–artist have over the work, what understandings are particular to their voice? If the powers of the author are diminished and transformed, what discernible remains are there of the author in the work, what traces of style or signature? These questions are the implicit grounds of the exchanges between performance artists and theorists assembled here, though they range over many other subjects.

In the interviews assembled here between Amelia Jones, myself and established figures in the recent history of performance art – Carolee Schneemann, Tehching Hsieh, Marina Abramović and Janine Antoni – dialogue that crosses positions between artists and art theorists becomes an opportunity for the evaluation and extension of existing historical narrations. The object here is not simply the elaboration of informative details or the creation of new material for consumption by art history. The dialogue enables a space for the artists to examine and contest their critical and historical reception, to make interventions in the discourse upon their work, in ways other than those the work itself makes. This interrogation of the enfolding of the artist's work into art historical narration makes apparent those dynamics of artistic production and reception that trouble the logics of the work's smooth assimilation. One recurring dynamic here is the gap between an artist's intention and effect, and the tendency to read art through intentional fallacies. In Schneemann's interview for instance, we hear how elements that are retrospectively read as intentional content may just have been the product of circumstances or of chance. The title of this interview, *Interior Squirrel*, a perverse mutation of one of Schneemann's most celebrated, cited, and analyzed works, thus suggests that misunderstanding and misinterpretation are constitutional elements of art discourse and history. For Abramović, caught in the complex questions of the redoing of the work of others, intention emerges as an unobtainable goal of the unavoidable labor of the interpretation of the work of others. Here it seems that intention is an unknowable entity for an artist who is never "fully conscious," an unstable object in the folding into each other of works in different times, and the interplay between one artist and another. In Hsieh's account of the making of his one year performance works, his promises to carry out specific acts over long durations are tested out in the enactment of the work, and in its modes of documentary verification, which emerge as part of the process. The whole body of his work appears as a kind of test site of the relation between intention and effect, will and enactment, event and document, with most art spectators only having retrospective access to the work through its evidentiary traces. In Antoni's interview, we hear how a minor comment in an earlier interview meets other cultural forces at work in the times and becomes the foundation for a dominant reading of a celebrated work; moreover we hear how art discourse is itself a mobile feast, respondent to particular changing cultural and historical conditions.

Other interviews are concerned with the exclusionary dynamics of art history and art discourse, the restoration to record of significant acts of invention from subjectivities and voices whose labor and creations have been under-acknowledged. In Tilda Swinton and Joanna Scanlan's exchanges with Amelia Jones, the back-story of a particularly renowned exhibition, *The Maybe* (1995), is told for the first time. As its co-creators narrate its genesis and the storm of interest around its realization, we hear how complex collaborative relations meet existing structures of legibility, evaluation, and authorial designation, and in particular how Swinton's contribution is elided through her previous identification as actress rather than artist. Modern art's "anti-theatrical prejudice" is strikingly operative here, and Swinton's commitment to a durational performance within the installation is used by the institutions of art exhibition and reception to de-authorize and de-value her labor, making her exhausting central action in the work a kind of ineligible and illegible gesture, consigning her to the status of a staged, passive, and silent object.[8] The issue of the feminine subject's relation to art economies based on the values of the static material object is one that is also strongly taken up in Antoni's interview, as she narrates the logics of her presencing of her absence in the matter of the sculptural or installation object. At stake here is the tracing of feminine subjectivities, sensibilities, and affects in a visible material register. If one of the mechanisms of art institutions and art history is its policing of what can be made visible and legible through the establishment of proprieties of identity, Dominic Johnson's interview with Ron Athey makes apparent the resilience of artistic practices that have remained at the margins of what is seen, read, and discussed. Athey's conversation is a means to acknowledge and examine a network of figures and acts, or as Johnson terms it, the "mostly unwritten sub-history of experimental practitioners." Athey's sustained and powerful engagement with bodily limits is seen then as a nexus through which those cultural locales, identities, bodies, and acts that have slipped under or over cultural and critical registers can be marked and evaluated. This recognition requires examination of the "phobic refusals" upon which existing histories have been written, and a continuing investment in the counter-values of work that takes place at the margins of "official culture."

This questioning of the sanctioned space of art is equally present in Shezad Dawood's discussion of his live and filmic works that hybridize "high" and "low" forms and cross-fertilize culturally distinct popular and avant-garde sources. Fabrication and theatricality emerge as aesthetic tactics in a practice that moves fluidly between performance and film, to explore culture clashes, globalism, and the politics of difference and disadvantage in local urban contexts. "High" art and "low" culture recur as contested notions in Iain Forsyth and Jane Pollard's interview about their re-staging of key events in popular music and counter-cultural history. In these sonic redos, Forsyth and Pollard pose questions on the nature of the relation between the culturally elevated and the devalued, the "original" and the copy, the past and the present. Their exchange with the art theorist Andrew Renton, and their assemblage around this conversation of other witness voices, places these events into a polyphonic discussion on their cultural and art historical resonances. The function of music within cultural and personal recollection, its highly emotive content, and its association with the operations of nostalgia are brought into play within a broader discussion on the politics of the redo. If music is a vector of transport from the present to the past and back again, it raises fascinating questions around who is speaking (and singing) in these performances, what it might mean to possess or find ownership in the presence or voice of another, and the relative powers of sonic and visual mimesis.

Interestingly, Forsyth and Pollard's work in this area moves away from visual rhetorics of veracity, and into questions of the ethereal spirit of figures and works as they are transported across time. This conversation is also taken up by Abramović who speaks of her redoing of canonical works of performance art by other artists as a form of dialogue in the present with those living and dead artists. Abramović's thoughts here, in correspondence with Jones, transect the complex issues of any mimetic relation to the past: how important is the notion of faithfulness to an original work that you are redoing; what would it mean to stay close to the "spirit" of a work; where does authorship and ownership rest in the space of the redo; what space of re-invention is both taken from and sanctioned by the parameters (relational, legal, institutional, historical) that sit around the new event?

In Forsyth and Pollard's and Abramović's interviews, as well as the performance-lectures of Hugo Glendinning, Tim Etchells, and myself, and Lin Hixson and Matthew Goulish, the tendency of the visual record, whether filmic or photographic, to consume the event, to become its memory, is repeatedly noted. In each, a certain desire is differently expressed: to wrestle memory from the grip of the image. One might think of this desire as one that seeks to restore to memory the capacities of the fuller sensorium neglected through the privileged sense of sight. Equally one might say that this desire aspires to return memory to movement, unlocking it from the fixed coordinates and distillations of the plane of imaging. These themes recur in detail in the three dialogic works published here, of Mathilde Monnier and Jean-Luc Nancy, Hixson and Goulish, and Glendinning, Etchells, and myself. Across these works the written dialogues were particularly composed in the context of performance and the spoken word, and so might be read more as fragments of a scripted event of relation. Each of these pieces to some extent concerns itself with choreographic works of performance, and consequently with considerations of the relation between body and image, movement and writing, the unknown quotient of the event and its memory or recall.

In Monnier and Nancy's text, movement arises as a question of the relation between flight (or escape) and a ground, and as a quality of enactment where the undecidable play inherent to the "language" of dance – between the unmediated and the mediated – results in the suspension and endless deferral of meaning. Turning over the documents and memorial residues of their collaborative relations in the work of the now disbanded Chicago-based performance company Goat Island, Hixson and Goulish's composed performance-lecture is an evocative enactment of such deferrals in writing. The piece returns to particular images, most strikingly of Goulish suspended in the air – in the flight of movement – not simply to distinguish memory from the document but to elaborate a conversation on the tireless creation of the past in the present, and on the interdependency of forgetting and remembering in the constitution of histories. The performance-lecture thus acts as a way to narrate, remember, and mark the ending of the company's work (valuing, as the work did, the fragmentary nature of knowledge and experience), but also its continuation and rebirth in other forms and other collaborative constellations.

Most significantly in this piece, it is dialogic relay, and the interruption of another person (reminding them of what they have forgotten and of the aporias in historical record), which keeps the restless movement of narration and recall alive. Movement is similarly evoked in the exchange between Glendinning, Etchells, and myself as a primary quality of a performer's presence. The dialogue works through the highly contested subject of the presence of the performer, anatomizing its constituent parts – the voice, the face, and embodied gesture – as they meet modes of mediation (linguistic, sonic, photographic) to consider how the fluidity and instability of presence troubles critical discourses and documentary practices that seek its capture. Glendinning narrates his practice as a performance photographer through the notion of the witness, but significantly this witnessing is marked by his absence from the scene that he depicts, and the images produced are marked as moments whose "happening" is below or beyond human perception. For Glendinning, "the camera lets us know these invisible moments," the documentary function is surpassed by the photograph's powers of invention: "these pictures are *only* photographs, they make new memory, new knowledge."

Notes

1. Eleonora Fabião, Hannah Higgins, this volume.
2. Roland Barthes, "The Death of the Author," *Image, Music, Text*, ed. and trans. Stephen Heath, New York: Hill and Wang, 1977 [1967], pp. 142–8.
3. See for instance Rosalind E. Krauss, *The Originality of the Avant-Garde and Other Modernist Myths*, Cambridge: MIT Press, 1986.
4. Interesting examples of this approach can be found in the work of Bas Jan Ader, Ana Mendieta, Allan Kaprow, Yoko Ono, and Tehching Hsieh amongst others.
5. Key texts in this area include Nicolas Bourriaud, *Relational Aesthetics*, Dijon, France: Les Presses du réel, 2002 [1998]; Claire Bishop, *Participation*, London: Whitechapel and MIT Press, 2006; Claire Bishop, "Antagonism and Relational Aesthetics," *October*, Autumn 2004, no. 110; Grant H. Kester, *Conversation Pieces: Community and Communication in Modern Art*, Berkeley: University of California Press, 2004; Shannon Jackson, *Social Works: Performing Art, Supporting Publics*, London and New York: Routledge, 2011.
6. Hans Ulrich Obrist, *Interviews*, vol. 1, New York and Milan, Charta Art Books and Fondazione, 2003 and Hans Ulrich Obrist, *Interviews*, vol. 2, New York and Milan, Charta Art Books, 2010.
7. Maurice Blanchot, *The Writing of the Disaster*, trans. Ann Smock, Lincoln and London: University of Nebraska Press, 1995 [1986], pp. 34–5.
8. See Jonas A. Barish, *The Antitheatrical Prejudice*, Berkeley, Los Angeles and London: University of California Press, 1981.

Chapter 34

Interior Squirrel and the Vicissitudes of History[1]

Carolee Schneemann and Amelia Jones

Amelia Jones: I'm Amelia Jones and it is my great pleasure to introduce (well, she needs no introduction really!), Carolee Schneemann, who has very generously agreed to talk a little bit about the live in relation to issues of history and her particular body of work.

There is a resurgence of interest in performance histories on the part of younger generations of scholars and artists who are using various kinds of technologies or engaging the body over time in new ways. They have a particular relationship to the question of history and live, being at the beginning of their careers. For you, however, the question of history is pressing – you have to deal, among other things, with how your work has been and continues to be written into history and via what kinds of evidence. So, what I'd like to do here is to draw out some issues that relate specifically to your practice. One of the brilliant things about your work is the way in which it crosses over different media and modes of creative expression, all of which collect around the body.

So I wanted to start by asking you to sketch briefly first for the audience how you came to do live art works. You trained primarily as a painter in the late 1950s - so what happened that by the early 1960s you were doing incredible group performance pieces such as *Meat Joy* [1964] and individual pieces such as *Eye Body* [1963].

Carolee Schneemann: My – I can't use the p word – I'm so sorry I just can't say it. I don't have a "practice" and I don't have a career. [audience laughter] What else is it that I don't I have …?

AJ: Well you do have a body.

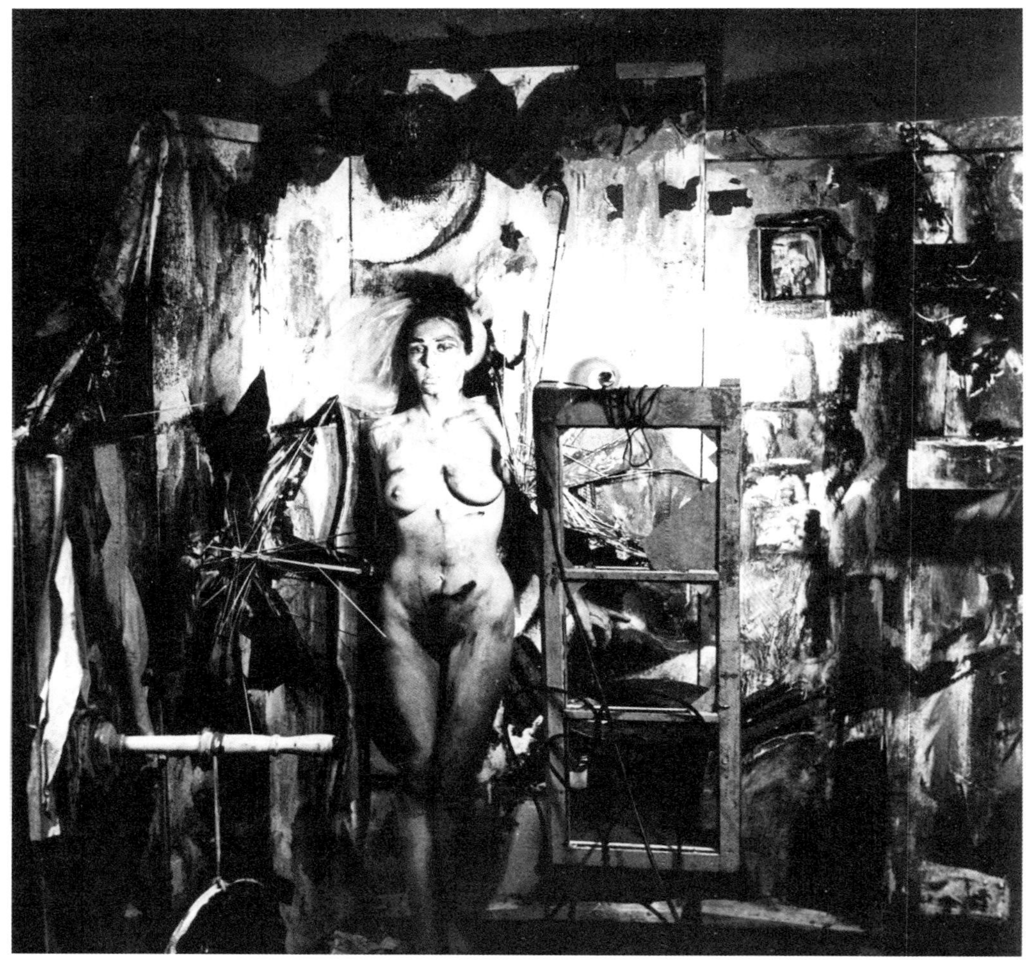

Carolee Schneemann, *Eye Body – 36 Transformative Actions*, 1963. Action for camera. Showing her studio installations and sculptures and Schneemann's inclusion of her body as a collage element. Photo: Erro. © Carolee Schneemann.

CS: Yes. That's right we can go with that. The increased dimensionality, the kinetic optical requirements of abstract expressionism were what were driving me into a terrible conflict with my painting: it was getting increasingly dimensional. I began working with technology early in the 1960s because I wanted to motorize some of the elements in my constructions [as in *Eye Body*] …

"Performance" was certainly something I never wanted to do in itself. [I was driven] to actually activate space with my body.[2] There was some conjoining motive with the energy of the painting, the urgency of the materials and the physicality with which I was engaging the materials; my body comes in as a kind of large question mark. I think aspects of technology were driving me also.

All of this early work was considered impossible and wrong; everything that I've done seemed to [emerge] at a moment when it wasn't quite right; [this might because it is always] too soon, [ahead of its time]. I was in college [at the time when I started these mechanized sculpture works] and it was an aesthetic grief for me to feel that I had to move off the canvas.

And once again, the pure inspiration, as many of you know, because I've written about it,[3] was from my cat Kitch, when a tree hit our shack – where we lived outside the University of Illinois – it literally smashed into the little kitchen and it destroyed the walls. There was a tree in my kitchen sink and it was a complete disaster. Except that my cat studied this fracture, the outside now inside and went right out into the landscape. And I thought that's what I have to do! I'm a landscape painter [but] I'm trying to get in when I have to get out. That week I made my first landscape activation in space with people having instructions – friends and students – picking cards: to walk, to crawl, to climb, to get wet, to get dry …

[CS and AJ discuss images from that period of Schneemann's work]

CS: This [activation of the body] was [around] 1960. At that point I had read about [Allan] Kaprow.[4] I was already heavily influenced by the abstract expressionists and the energy that was required kinetically, optically; you had to have a muscular perception to see their works.

AJ: And then how did you at that point pick up with the Fluxus group?

CS: Oh everybody was wandering around! But actually I was excommunicated by the chief of Fluxus, George Maciunas. He sent out a little broadsheet saying "Schneemann is nothing to do with us, she's operatic, messy, personalised." But we're all good friends, still. They've never been in my work, but I would sometimes be in theirs. It's like family.

AJ: So when you started with this more spatially oriented time-based practice did you think about documentation? Was that something that was even in the foreground?

CS: No, we weren't organized. It was enough to have a vision. I went into Judson [Memorial Church][5] and was the first visual artist to choreograph for the Judson group. What we call performance, activations, live actions were so demanding; it was such an unknown territory that we'd never had time to remember that we needed a document. Fortunately Peter Moore, the quintessential New York photographer of the early work, was usually everywhere with his six cameras hanging all over him and somehow always invisible,

Carolee Schneemann, *Interior Scroll*, 1975. Performance photograph. Photo: Anthony McCall. © Carolee Schneemann.

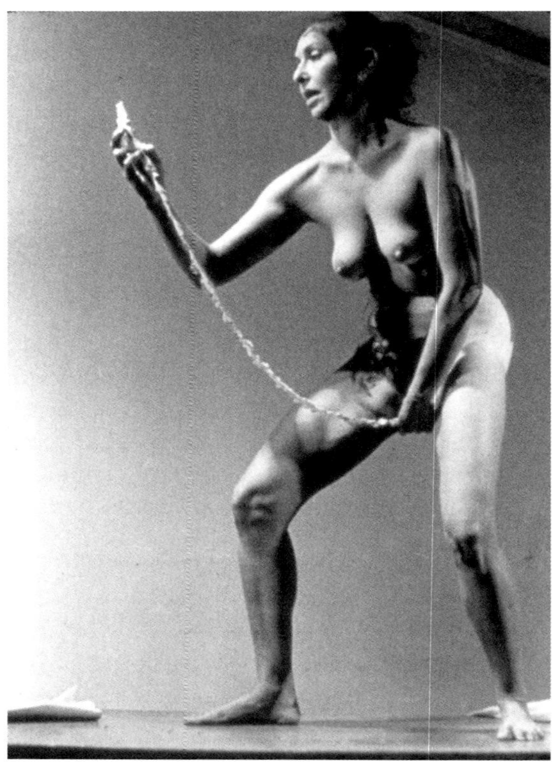

but he was there really for each kind of unique moment. This begins another layer of what my work is about - how photographs become an instrumentality of the [moment being documented]. The photograph became a memento of live actions even for the artist - who couldn't see what she was making at the time.

AJ: Peter Moore's photographs are a great example of how such pictures become iconic and reduce the event to a single moment. How does that feel as someone who was a participant or even a generator of the live moment, which in the instance would have been complex, open-ended, impossible to pin down. You and I have been in dialogue about *Interior Scroll* [first performed in 1975], which has become an iconic piece, partly because of the power of the primary images – used as documentation – photographed by Anthony McCall. So how does this dynamic play out for you?

I'm wondering if you have moments when the live richness of the event escapes you in the face of the photograph?

CS: Oh, yes. Yes. Say that again that's an important one.

AJ: The live richness of your experience of the event – I mean I know this happens with me just in terms of snapshots, my memories of my childhood are largely clustered around photographs and so I wonder what are the things in between that I can't access any more, can't remember?

CS: With *Interior Scroll* I also wanted to say that it was [originally] filmed by a seemingly feminist friend who was documenting a lot of women artists' work. That was a time when I really was organized and my friend said, "I'm a wonderful videographer, I'd be thrilled to document this work." She did and it was an excellent video but then she withheld [the footage] and she said, "it's mine. You can't have it." She did that also with Eve Hesse, Judith Bernstein, Hannah Wilke, Lil Picard. Some of Hannah's last events [she died in 1993] are withheld by this videographer. We did a class action suit and there was a choice – either you can sue her for the tape, or you can get a settlement, and I didn't have a job [so I went for the settlement].

So that's an interesting part of the problem of documentation. All of the images of *Interior Scroll* that exist were shot – with one exception – by my partner at the time, Anthony McCall. We loved each other, so we don't tear up negatives. These images become the work and a substantiation of it.

[But while] I'm doing the work, I'm in some trance state. Part of me doesn't know what I'm doing – there's another aspect of self that enters the urgency of the image making. I never know if "she's going to turn up." Before an action, I'm very sick, petrified and then there she is! She's inhabiting this whole thing and it's crystal clear. Then I'd want to see what happened.

AJ: So when you see the image does it feel like you're looking at this other performed self?

CS: Yes. And I'm hugely critical. Actually I can't bear to watch the documents; what I have to do [when I have access to it] is edit the documentation. That's an odd position, because to be me generating the image and to be central to the image and then to have to assume aesthetic authority over the image [as it exists historically] – particularly the images that exist in time as video – is a fierce demand.

AJ: So, you've implied that the moving image is somehow more revealing than the more frozen moment of the still photograph?

CS: No. Let me think about it. The frozen moment is deeply – it's like an archaeological discovery. It's layered and it's charged. It's also very changeable, and history is so changeable.

I'm just amazed that we're all here in this room for this conference on performance – how did this happen? When we were all alone in our lofts [in the 1960s], dripping materials on ourselves and having six people gathered around in aesthetic bewilderment and pleasure [we never could have guessed].

AJ: Well, how do you feel about this resurgence of interest in performance or body art – exemplified in Marina Abramović's recent [2005] re-enactments at the Guggenheim and in the fact that she's having a retrospective at the Museum of Modern Art [in 2010]. Is this acknowledgement by the art world a good thing?

CS: Sure.

AJ: Doesn't it institutionalize a mode of creation that was initially meant to escape institutions and commodification? Is it unequivocally good that live events are being written into history and becoming part of the most established institutions?

CS: I don't know. I live off in the woods. So no judgement; talking about the shifts of history, this is also so unexpected and unpredictable. We're in the middle of these tremendous [social] shifts and re-organizations, and we're also in the middle of a huge fascist techno militaristic cultural moment - what do we really mean in the center of all that? Not much is now focussed on expressivity and personal materials [because artists are more interested in] examining the more menacing issues.

AJ: Do you think the sense of political desperation of many creative people particularly in the US since the rise of the Bush administration and the events of 9/11 [2001] is part of the resurgence of interest in live art? And particularly in retrieving its history – is this sparked by a desire to go back and retrieve a moment of political activism in the face of kind of defusing of political agency?

CS: We really don't have what I recognized [in the 1960s] as an effective activism – everyone seems kind of asleep while the dynamics around us are so potentially enormously destructive.

AJ: Do you think it's possible that for a young student today seeing an image of a piece from the early 1960s suddenly a portal might be opened as it were into this wide embodied history of activism? Could that new knowledge make a difference politically?

CS: Well it certainly did for me. I have to remind myself how obsessed I was with process. Joan Mitchell's work was another link to physicalization of the body since with her work, I recognized the stroke as an event. All of the theoretical elements that come around my work, I keep tracing them back to elements of painting and [realize] that I'm a kind of classicist. My inspiration comes from [Gaston] Bachelard and D'Arcy Thompson's *On Growth and Form* (1917) – the biology and pre-history [of forms] and that's what's really nourishing my unconscious.

[Looking at images of Schneemann's *Venus Vectors*, 1986–8]

AJ: The quality of these images isn't great, I'm sorry; they were all dragged off of Carolee's website at the last minute in desperation, just to make sure we had some images [to project digitally]. That's a whole other conversation we could have, the googleability of images does open up another way of doing a history of visual art but how does it change our relationship to the work?

Carolee, you had wanted slide projectors and this produced great bafflement among the conference organizers – which is an interesting comment on technology and its effect in conveying histories.

I want now to get back to that issue of actual ownership of the image. You've talked in the past about how you don't hold copyright to much of the documentation of your early work (as you described above) – literally you cannot access it or reproduce those images. Who profits from the documents? Of course I'm wondering if this woman you call the "supposed feminist" who filmed some of your early works is marketing this footage?

CS: She said it's like wine: the longer she keeps it, it will either turn to vinegar or become more valuable. It's become more valuable.

AJ: It's also decaying! We had better be careful. But in terms of how you get written into history, does that feel like big pieces of your career are missing if somebody else is controlling this copyright?

CS: Yes, yes. You have a budget and you need certain photographs and you go to someone we won't mention for images of your own performance and they demand huge fees!

AJ: Well I'm against copyright, that's my position, partly because … well that's another discussion, but I do take that view precisely because of these issues of control; I think that the overall picture is that it causes more trouble than it protects artists who rarely make any money from the publication of their images anyway.

CS: Exactly, I hope everybody knows every time they buy a book of mine that I don't get paid.

AJ: Copyright has created a false marketplace.

CS: There's actual copyright [with my work], but the virtual copyright allows appropriation day and night.

AJ: Yeah, but it does touch on the subject of how stories get written – copyright fees affect what scholars and critics can write about. With university presses and journals, scholars actually have to pay these fees out of our own pockets, so if there is a photographer, like

Peter Moore, whose photographs get priced out of the market … the images will get taken out of circulation [or, rather, will be reproduced only in commercial venues such as art magazines, which have a budget for such things]. Because effectively no scholar can afford high reproduction fees, there are all sorts of false economies in terms of which histories get written.

CS: A footnote to what you're saying is that Peter Moore gave me these incredibly beautiful documents, these photographs that are unique, but his estate is refusing to let me use them. They're gifts; I have them, but I can't print them.

AJ: So I do think this is an issue in terms of what gets written about and how it gets written about, and what becomes iconic.

CS: It's true. [History is] edited by factors we can't control.

AJ: Can we talk about the relationship between your films and your performance work in terms of the live? [Your 1964–66 film] *Fuses* of course conveys a temporal, textured narrative – or semi narrative – of bodies making love, carefully edited into a final product, which is very different from a live event that gets documented maybe through film or still images.

CS: You're giving me a chance to tell everybody that *Fuses* shot in 16mm has been restored, and converted.

The reason it's been restored is because in 1966, the original collage on film was so thick that it could only be pushed through the developer by hand. So anyone who's seen *Fuses* has already seen it at least one generation removed from the original; but with new technology they've restored it to the original. It's more brilliant, it's more sexy, plus there's ten missing minutes that I hadn't been able to afford originally to print at all, so it's all there!

I want to respond to this question of "enacting yourself" which has nothing to do with process. When I'm working there is no "self" – it's not about me – it's about the materiality, about the body I activate. It's about being able to merge with the need to question certain image possibilities. [My work] always comes out of uncertainty. I can't bear to pose. I don't like to look at this "self." I don't like to look at photographs. It's a body as an instrumentality through which certain energies might become manifest. But again, [these ideas are] not predictive when I use the body; it's not a kind of conceptually predetermined process. [My process is] conceptually tough because I'm involved in phrasing and the musicality of time, the duration of gesture. So in all the work there is an implicit aspect of structure within it and it has to be rigorous. How to describe [my multi-layered process] I really don't know – but I know when it's available to me, and I certainly know when it's not happening.

AJ: So actually with film you can wield a lot more control because you're going in to edit and fuse theory into the images – so does that then appeal to you more than doing live performance? You haven't produced these kind of more unpredictable live events so much in recent years.

CS: No I haven't done anything performative as such for fifteen years because – here's my little mantra – the inclusion of my body as part of my work has obscured the major body of my work. I never thought that would happen. You know with *Eye Body* [1963] and *Vulva's Morphia* [1995] I always thought the material would overcome this so-called self.

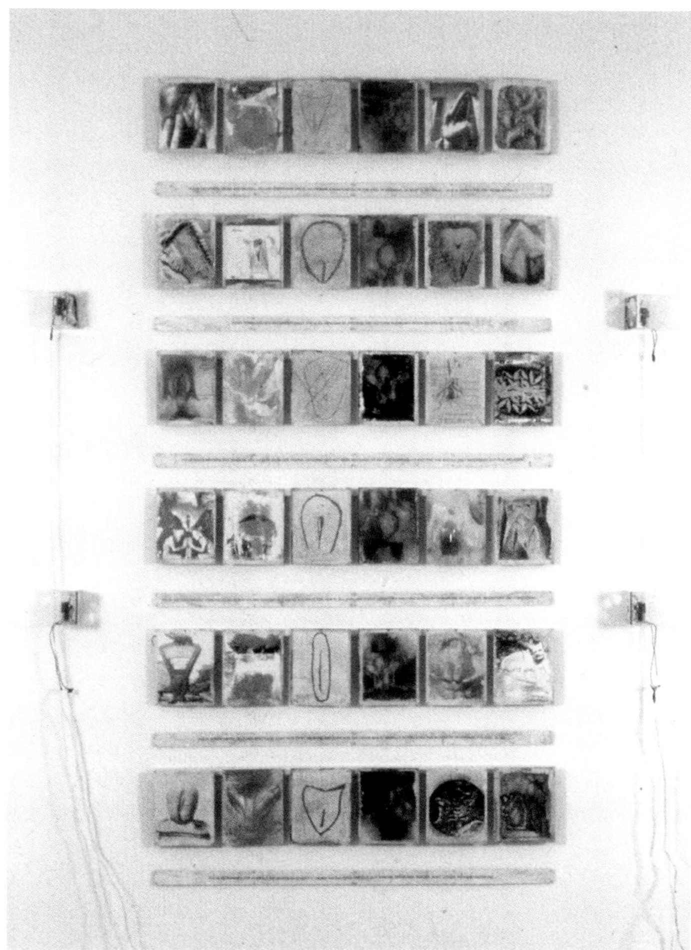

Carolee Schneemann, *Vulva's Morphia*, 1995. Photogrid wall installation with 4 fans. Total 8 x 5 feet; each image 11 x 8.5 inches; text strips 2 x 58 inches. © Carolee Schneemann.

AJ: So what *is* the "body" of your work then?

CS: I don't know. Well actually I do think it's the projections, the big installations, that I never get a chance to show. I feel these are where the work is most developed – works like *Mortal Coils* [1994–5], *Cycladic Imprints* [1991–3], *Vesper's Pool* [2000], the recent multi-channel political rumination, *Devour* [2003–4].

AJ: Does your body, which gets conflated with your work by the viewer or the art world, give viewers access (or the illusion of access) into your self in some perverse way? Does this relation function differently in film versus the performance documents where your body is central?

CS: I don't know. I'm behind a veil when all this is happening and I have to stay behind the veil so that the next possibility can develop apart from this mythological self. It's odd.

AJ: There are different receptive audiences for your work, too, which is interesting – there's obviously the avant-garde film community, then there's the performance community and then there's the art world. Obviously these overlap to a degree. And all of them in different ways want to construct you as an author of some sort.

CS: But that's fabulous! [This idea of my multiple audiences] implies that at least the complexity of the work is coming into view.

AJ: If they're viewing across all these different media. But one of the problems, as you know, is that the reception, theorization and historicization of your work is often fragmented according to these separate audiences: there's the avant-garde film scholarship which addresses only *Fuses* (not even some of the other films like *Plumb Line* [1971]); and then there's the art world that writes mostly about *Interior Scroll* through the iconic documents and so on. I think that this is getting better – I do think younger scholars are starting to see more of a range across not just your practice, but all of the artists in the 1960s and 1970s who were reaching across media, but has that been frustrating for you in the past to have these different kinds of practice isolated out and do you feel that each one, each approach, constructs your work differently?

CS: I have no control over any of that, but there's wonderful scholarship and it's getting stronger and more coherent; and then there are also absolutely terrible reviews and stupid things and I get the book and I write in it "oh no stupid jerk" and put it away.

AJ: How do audiences, based on the way in which you work with all these different permutations, engage with the remains of your live process in history, including photographic documents but also the installations, films, and objects?

CS: I never work with a specific sense of audience. I work sometimes with a cultural idea that, well, I think they need this – this kind of imagery, this eroticizing, this politicizing, this contact with the dead. But it's not certain, my audience. I don't have an economic structure that supports the work, never have. I have a gallery that subtly markets the work; the work is rarely collected. You will not see it in any museum in the United States of America with the exception of the Hirshhorn [Museum and Sculpture Garden, Washington, DC], which just bought the original 1963 sequence of *Eye Body* photographs. MoMA [the Museum of Modern Art, New York] has a tiny thing and the San Francisco Museum of Modern Art initiated a purchase fifteen years ago [of *Infinity Kisses*, 1981–7].

AJ: Well that actually leads to this rather pompous question I have before opening this up to the audience, which is how you want to be viewed in history. I know you can't determine this yourself, as you say, but understandably you have a lot of frustrations about certain tendencies to conflate your work with your body or to look at your images without looking at the full body of work.

CS: I think it would be splendid if the eroticization of technology was recognized. The other would be to have recognized my being kissed by my cat – [in terms of me being] an emissary of the shameless erotic structured by unexpected mercurial zen forms.

AJ: Thank you for amazing and thoughtful answers. Well let's open it up to the audience as I'm sure people have thoughts or questions.

Audience Questions

Q1: I remember my first encounter with *Meat Joy* was a black and white photograph I think in RoseLee Goldberg's book[6] and later as I studied more about the piece I saw a video of the piece and it was blue paint that was being used, and I remember the shock of realizing it was blue paint not blood. I had always imagined [based on photographs published of the piece] that there was blood, that the stuff smeared on the body was blood because there were actual animal parts as well; [this discrepancy produces] sort of a gap for performance art scholars clinging to the evidence of black and white images. [We read something from the photograph], only to realize that [our assumption may be at odds with] what took place. [There is a] slippage between the document and the real performance.

CS: It's a nice mistake.

AJ: Well, that's the kind of thing that Carolee would catch me on in our dialogues over my interpretations, as I would write some political rumination on blood and she would say "that's not blood." You know obviously we project our own expectations and fantasies as we interpret works from the past, or for that matter in the present!

CS: I think there are a lot of reasons to suspect that it might be blood. Shall I tell you my favorite mistake story? It's an interview by phone with a Danish art historian and so there's distance and a little language [problem]. We were talking about *Interior Scroll*, and discussing how the dream produced it and such, and then she's sounding very upset and she says, "but the pain," and I say, "no, it's not painful. I do endurance work, but I don't do painful work;" and she says, "but no, it must hurt, it must really hurt." I said, "no, no, no, it doesn't hurt." She said, "but the edges, the edges." I said, "oh, I use cream so it doesn't hurt," and then she says, "but the claws the claws," and I said "what?" and she said, "the claws." "The claws?" "Of *Interior Squirrel*."

[widespread laughter]

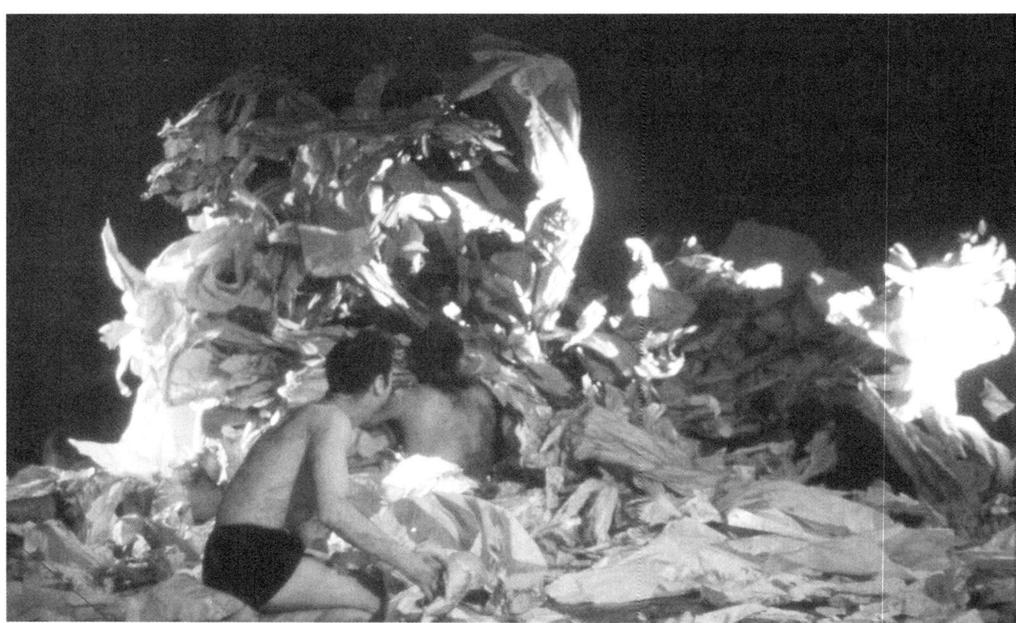

Carolee Schneemann, *Meat Joy*, 1964/2002. A Short History of Performance: Part One. Whitechapel Art Gallery – London, England, 16 April 2002. Photo: Manuel Vason. © Carolee Scheemann.

Q2: [Lois Keidan of Live Art Development Agency, London] Carolee, about five or six years ago [2002] the Whitechapel Gallery in London did a short history of performance and they invited you to do a re-enactment of *Meat Joy* in a completely different time and different place. How was that for you?

CS: Oh chaos, re-enacting *Meat Joy*. I thought it would be interesting. The problem was that I had a motley crew of volunteers.[7] They couldn't really be trained to have the intense trusting sensuous relationship to each other [required by the piece]. We did the best we could, so it was very crucial to have the lighting sequences, the elements that were set really had to be precise so that whatever happened between us could evolve, that there was [also] structure around our improvisatory interactions. But what happened was that the audience was so huge we were pushed towards a wall [in the] back area [of the gallery] where the lights were never on us properly, and the sound wasn't coordinated. It was pretty good, it was OK. Were you there? What did you think?

Q3: [Lois Keidan] I was there. I thought it was a really fascinating event, mostly because of the audience, really, because the first time you did it [in 1964][8] it would have been in a loft with a kind of unexpected audience not knowing what was happening and this [Whitechapel performance in 2002 in contrast] was like the hottest ticket in town! People were killing each other to get in, and there was this real sense of expectation; people knew what they were going to see, so it was the idea of seeing it for real, so there was this very kind of strange dynamic with the audience. It was a fascinating experience and it was fantastic to see it, but it was sort of trying to work out what we were seeing.

Q4: [Kathy O'Dell, from University of Maryland, Baltimore County] I just wanted to follow up on the question behind me about black and white photography versus color representation and your *Meat Joy* in New York is so beautifully represented in this John Hansard [Gallery, Southampton] show that's up right now [called] *Live Art On Camera*.[9] They're black and white and color photographs, some I've never seen before, by at least four or five different photographers who were there, so Harvey Zucker, Al Giese, Robert McElroy, Peter Moore, of course, and Tony Ray Jones. And there's something about this show – nothing has reoriented me to the history of the use of the body in live art more than this exhibition.

What's interesting about it is that it's a show that features the photographers – not in the way that it privileges the photography over the performance, but it's very democratic in [showing] the importance of all these players [making the live art event]. All these different photographs show so many different layers of that particular performance [*Meat Joy*], which emphasizes the importance of all the different positions that live art opens up – the photographer's position, the critic's, the viewer's, the performer's and it all gets messed up like *Meat Joy*! Which is great!

So I'm wondering how you felt at that time about so many different photographers [being there to document] – because every artist did that very differently. For Gina Pane the audience couldn't even see the work because she had a photographer in front of them, because it was more important [to her] to get the work photographed in a particular way. You seem [to have been] much more open about who was photographing; [looking back via the documents left behind, this leaves us with] so many different positions from which we're an audience.

I would also like to hear about your interactions with the photographers and how you made that decision to be much more open and democratic about who was doing the photographing.

CS: Oh I had no money. I had no way of controlling anything. It was enough trying to get the piece together and one thing that those of you who are doing performance know is that it prepares you, it seeks to prepare you for any possible disaster. You're touring in a car, or a bus, a truck, you parked in the wrong place, you come back and your tyres are all slashed. You set up your projection system and the structure collapses, the main person you need to work with never shows up, the other one gets a raging fever, your boyfriend runs away, your equipment is not there despite months of preparations. What was the question? Oh so yes, then you have to arrange for a photographer? I've never had a producer or manager, I've had to do every detail so if I see somebody with a camera, yes, what I try to do is get their name and say you can do whatever you want but you have to share prints with me at cost, and you can sell – you can do whatever you want but I need access to the documents.

The photographers deserve [an exhibition like *Live Art On Camera*]; they're the heroes.

AJ: Do you ever think of live art as a collaboration – does having the photographers there turn it into a collaborative process? I attended some performances yesterday [in Chelsea, New York City] and I was actually really shocked by the way in which these performers were in a very packed gallery and were obscured by extremely aggressive photographers who were literally a foot away – the audience seemed almost irrelevant. So, I was struck by that as obviously a massive shift from the 1960s and 1970s where by happenstance people would happen to have cameras and take photographs. Now there's just this hyper realization of the market with the document.

CS: Yes. We've got to get it into the magazine.

AJ: So you have these photographers – and the event becomes about the photographers – it's not about the audience at all. With the works I saw last night there was no sense that the performers were engaging the audience. They were engaging the cameras. And of course there has recently been published a spate of very glossy books of performance photographs that substantiates this trend.

CS: Read the book!

Q5: It seems like in the last two or three years there's been sort of a resurgence of attention paid to the 1960s, I mean with Marina Abramović's reconstruction of all those [performance] pieces,[10] Anna Halprin's doing a re-staging of *Parades* and *Changes*, the Whitney [Museum of American Art, New York] show on the 1960s and psychedelic art – it seems like an obsessively reflective moment on the 1960s right now and I'm just wondering … [Like many] I have this nostalgia for something I never experienced you know … but its also interesting how it seems to be a trend right now and it's getting a lot of attention [in New York]. It seems like it's almost a strategy for artists to get attention by rehashing the past, and I don't know why we're obsessed with it at the moment.

CS: I'm sure you have some idea of your own. What do you think? Why?

Q5: There was an experimental fervor that was happening in the 1960s at Judson, where artists were able to just unleash their sense of experimentation; there was a sense of risk. And I don't think artists of our generation, we don't have that space, we don't have 50 dollar rents, we have 1200 [or] 1500 dollar rents; we're being pushed to the margins, so maybe there's this attempt to recapture that [moment]?

AJ: Well somebody in this country has to figure it out pretty soon – figure out how to stop being so acquiescent. As an American, even though I don't live here now [but rather in the UK], I include myself in this warning. The government is becoming more and more coercive and invasive and nobody knows how to resist that any more. I mean part of the interest in the 1960s, and actually the resurgence of interest in feminism as well, I'm sure comes from this desperate desire to rekindle what is perceived as that moment's methods of resistance – but of course the conditions are completely different. The problem is that we live in this late capitalist moment where we've all internalized our own oppression so no one on the left is sure what to do.

Q6: [To Schneemann] I'd like you to go back a little bit to the recreation of *Meat Joy* just to what you were saying about what it means now [that it's been recreated]. [This] also relates to where you see yourself in the trajectory of history.

CS: Well I think that *Meat Joy* and *Fuses* and some of the other works still represent an aspect of shameless pleasure, shameless eroticism – the viscerality of the body, the body conjoined with energies that are [now] commodified, commercialized, taken away from our cultural moment. I suppose that's why we're still looking at it. And [our desire to look back at this work] of course is a measure of how suppressive some cultures remain and how synthetic sexuality [and its representations] have become, [the extent] to which the sacred erotic has been psychically and completely banished from the cultural consciousness.

AJ: This is a nice point to end on – returning to embodiment, eroticism and the "present" (to be written into history in the book I am co-editing!). Thank you.

Notes

1. This conversation took place at the Performance Studies international #13 conference "Happening/Performance/Event," New York University, New York, 10 November 2007.
2. All clarifications in brackets and endnotes have been added by the editor, Amelia Jones.
3. See her *More Than Meat Joy: Complete Performance Works and Selected Writings*, New Paltz: McPherson & Co., 1997 [1979].
4. One of the founders of the Happenings movement in the late 1950s and an important theorist of live art in his practice and writing.
5. Located in New York City, the Judson Memorial Church was the location for many experimental dance and Fluxus events.
6. See Goldberg's *Performance Art: From Futurism to the Present*, 1st edn, 1988; 2nd rev. edn, London: Thames & Hudson, 2001.
7. Schneemann herself also participated, but in a role different from her original role in the 1964 version.
8. *Meat Joy* was actually first produced as part of the Festival of Free Expression at the American Center in Paris, then at Judson Memorial Church in New York City.
9. *Live Art on Camera* was curated by Alice Maude-Roxby and up from 18 September to 10 November 2007.
10. In *Seven Easy Pieces* (2005); see Abramović in this volume.

Chapter 35

I Just Go in Life

Tehching Hsieh and Adrian Heathfield

Extracts from an Interview

Adrian Heathfield: One of the most radical dynamics of your performance pieces is the way that they make art and life simultaneous, so that the two activities cannot be separated. This collision is made absolute by your use of long durations. When you started making work, why did you decide the performances would take a year? And did you know that you would be making a long series of *One Year Performances*?

Tehching Hsieh: The reason I used such a long duration in my first piece was to do with my life experience. At that time, I had been an illegal immigrant in the States for four years. I earned money to survive and tried to do my art but without smooth advance. One day, after work, I was walking back and forth doing my thinking in the studio. Suddenly, I thought "why don't I make the process of thinking about art in my studio an artwork, and present it using a long duration?" I had spent a lot of time in this situation of isolation, as if I was doing time. Giving the thinking process an art form, my idea would be embodied. Also I knew that to present life, I needed to use a long duration. One year is a basic unit for human beings to calculate their life, and it is also the time the earth takes to circle the sun completely. [...] The whole series of my *One Year Performances* was not constructed at one time. I was not certain I would have a series at the beginning of that first piece; it was only during it that I came to know how I should do my next work.

AH: It interests me how much your work assimilates and plays back the language and processes of the law: the phrasing of the declarations that begin the *One Year*

An extract from an interview originally published as "I Just Go in Life: An Exchange with Tehching Hsieh," in *Out of Now: The Lifeworks of Tehching Hsieh*, London and Cambridge, MA: Live Art Development Agency and MIT Press, 2009, pp. 318–39.

Performance works and lays down their rules, the processes of signing seals, the repeated use of a witness …

TH: As an illegal immigrant it was natural for me to be concerned with the law. As an artist, I tended to use accurate language to present my concept. The language of the law was appropriate to support my ideas. But I was the one who built rules, executed them, and broke them as well.

You could see my work in some part as being about representing the illegal immigrant, the refugee, or the homeless person. But I don't think of art from this view, I think of it as being about the struggle in life, and I'm inside it. You could say a work is about this or about that. It is not about something only. It continues to be open. It is possible for you to see it in many ways.

AH: Sure, it's important not to collapse the work into single readings. But there are some very strong themes. People's tendency is to do this collapsing all the more because your work is so ungraspable …

TH: Hard to understand?

AH: and to touch.

TH: Yes, you see something in it, but still something is missing.

AH: Do you see documentation as a trace and as a source for a re-imagination of the artwork?

TH: For me, the document is secondary. It has been handled subjectively, and so it can be seen as another art piece. But the document can hardly restore art. I think art and the document should not be treated identically. Instead of approaching art through the document, we need to go back to art itself; to feel art, we need to use our own experiences and imagination. But what is closest to the origin of art, this will always be a question.

AH: When I read and hold these documents, or see the film of the second "Time Clock Piece," it makes me want to touch the performance. The documents draw me in physically, but at the same time you are resolutely not there.

TH: Art exists by itself and has its own life. When time has passed, only art documents stay as a trace for the work to remain. To get the message of my art, an audience's presence is not vital. As long as audiences know my concept and the real action I did, they can use their own experiences and imagination to feel these artworks. Most of my art documents were published twenty years after I made my performances. Before that, people knew of my work through articles or by passing words around. If art has the quality of truth, people will get the message that art conveys. Like Kafka's novels, even though they are fictional, they have a truth in essence; or like Van Gogh's work, if we know his dedication and enthusiasm for life, even if we just see his prints instead of original works, we can feel his spirit as well. On the contrary, being present physically may not be helpful. While I was doing "Cage Piece," one day an old lady came to my studio, looked around then came close to my cage. She held the bars of the cage and asked me "where is the work?" I gave no response of course.

AH: In the first *One Year Performance* the audience could come to see you, but only on specific days?

TH: That's right. Every three weeks it opened to the public: nineteen times a year. During the nineteen public days, what the audience saw was no different from the other three hundred and forty-six private days. No talking, no reading, no writing, neither listening to the radio nor watching TV. Whether people saw me or not, I was in the same situation: not communicating with others at all. The viewers didn't need to come every day because every single day was almost the same. This emphasized my isolation effectively. For those nineteen days alone, I brought my isolation to the public while still preserving the quality of it.

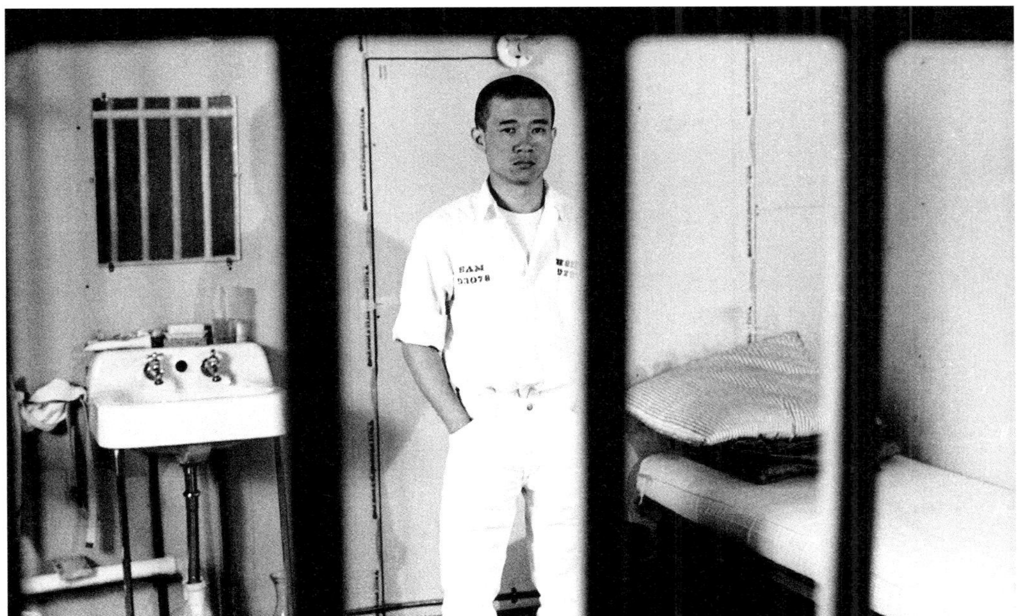

Tehching Hsieh, One Year Performance 1978–1979, New York, Life Image. Photograph by Cheng Wei Kuong, © Tehching Hsieh.

AH: On those days when you had an audience did you feel that the meaning of the work was changed by the presence of the people watching you?

TH: Yes, I did, although I didn't look at them directly. I didn't want to communicate with them through the eyes. It was my first *One Year Performance*, there were just a few people coming to my studio for the whole year. But I want to say that the most important thing is that I do art for myself. For me the audience is secondary. However, without them, my performances couldn't exist.

AH: How do you think of the thinking that you did in this piece?

TH: Thinking was the focus of this piece and was also my way of survival. While doing this piece, thinking was my major job. It doesn't matter what I was thinking about, but I had to continue thinking, otherwise I would lose control not only of myself but also of the ability to handle the whole situation. It was difficult to pass time. I scratched three hundred and sixty-five marks on the wall, one for each day. I had to calculate time; although I may have broken the rule of no writing, it helped me to know how many days I had passed, how many days I had to go. In such a condition, I had no work to do, so I had more work to do. I tried to bring art and life together in time, and to be in this as a process. I was so concentrated on thinking about art. Everything I thought about art was about this: how to survive? I thought mostly about my past, sometimes about the outside world, or when Cheng would deliver my meal. Whatever I was thinking, what's important to me is that people can see that in this special period of time, one year, the artist's thinking process becomes a piece of art.

AH: All of these pieces work on a rule system; the performance attempts to stay within the regulations. But because this is human life the rules get broken or are insufficient. Are there many times in the different pieces where the rule is broken?

TH: Yes, I allowed myself an exit. I don't think that if I punched the time clock 100% it would make the work perfect. But of course, the rules could not be broken too often; otherwise the work would collapse. A little bit of damage is good for the system.

AH: What interests me about the *Outdoor Piece* is that you have put yourself in the situation where the social conditions that prevail in this circumstance operate very powerfully upon you. You live for a while in the world of homeless people: a precarious life, with violence and penalties. You give yourself over to powers that you cannot control, and by doing this you make a profound commentary on these powers. I would say that you allow these powers to show their nature; this is very different from an artist setting out to say things about political powers.

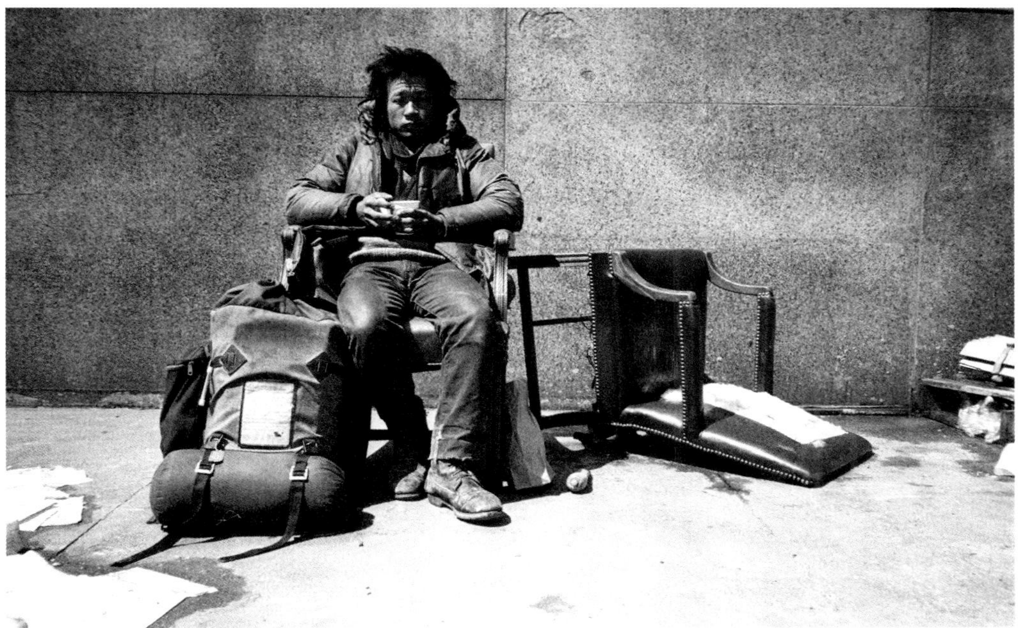

Tehching Hsieh, *One Year Performance 1981–1982*, New York, Life Image. Courtesy of The Gilbert and Lila Silverman Collection, Detroit.

TH: I think this has to do with my attitude to life. Maybe I am pessimistic. I don't think that art can change the world. But at least art can help us to unveil life. I do have political awareness, but I am not a political artist. It is my reality that compels me to confront political issues. I know that my work would fit in a political frame in such a way that people can have their own interpretation of it. But I am inclined to observe the universal circumstances of human beings instead of pointing to issues. My understanding is, the more I give a critical commentary on political powers, the less powerful my art will become. Political powers are close to the truth of reality; on the contrary, the power of art is leaning towards the exploration of essences.

AH: Talking in this way we are trying to reconstruct pieces from over twenty years ago. Each of us is a transformed person across that time and we are dealing with quite distant and unstable memories.

TH: Time makes some memories unstable; meanwhile it embeds the profound memories in one's body, and makes them even more solid. I didn't write anything down; however I still remember those pieces vividly. When I was doing the *Time Clock Piece*, my dreams were always interrupted. Nonetheless, they tried to free me. I dreamt that I didn't want to be an artist anymore. Many times my dreams were about my illegality and the immigration authorities trying to catch me, or sending me back to Taiwan, and I would try to cross the Mexican border to come back again … For me, when dealing with memories the biggest matter is not about their accuracy. Rather, it is about how to manage and rearrange these fragments of memories, transfer them into language and a process of discourse. This is what we are doing right now.

AH: You have spoken before about the notion of the performance works "wasting time" and the idea that there is another kind of value in wasting something.

TH: This is a discussion we have had regarding my future retrospective. The curator needs a waste of space in order to show the waste of time in my works. It's ironic. In many ways in life I am working so hard, but I still feel that this is wasting time. In my art, I make it reverse. So you can see why in my work I stayed in a long duration. I had to let time waste in order to prove how hard I was working.

AH: You think of this process as having another kind of value?

TH: It doesn't really matter how I spend time: time is still passing. Wasting time is my basic attitude to life; it is a gesture of dealing with the absurdity between life and time.

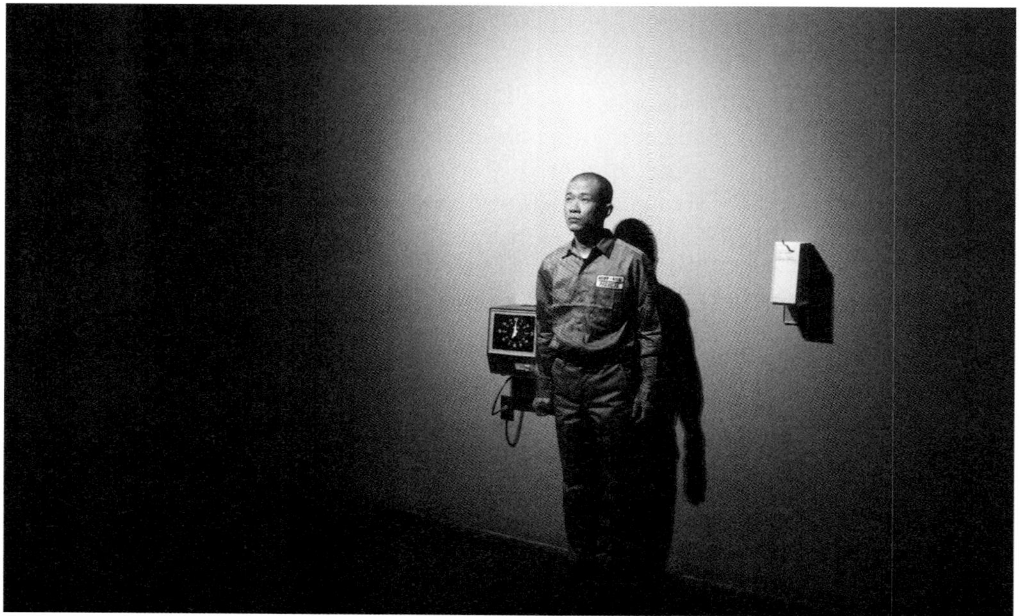

Tehching Hsieh, *One Year Performance 1980–1981*, New York, Taking the Picture. Photograph by Michael Shen, © Tehching Hsieh.

AH: Perhaps one of the reasons that the art world finds it difficult to take up this work and value it is because it is so absolute in its dissolution of art into life. The art world needs this distinction for it to function.

TH: I only did six pieces of art. To me these pieces are more about time. My art certainly has a life quality. But I don't really blur art and life. The gap between each *One Year Performance* is life time. But the pieces themselves are art time, not lived time. This is important. Each piece is very clearly a piece of art, but this art has a life quality: that is its rhythm. The time of the performances is art time, and my life has to follow art.

AH: If there is life time in between the time of the pieces (the art time), is there any life time inside the art time? Because while you are making this art you are also living, and while in all of the pieces this living is very constrained, it is still life.

TH: Sure. Each piece has a different way in which it uses time. If you look at it in any one moment, say the moment of punching the clock, you cannot say whether it is life time or art time. But generally to me, this is art time with the quality of life. But it is very tricky. How to see the quality of life in art? It depends on which piece you are looking at. In my "Time Clock Piece," in one hour I could not do much, my mind and my body have to be totally concentrated on time. Even if I were talking to someone I would be thinking, "I have to go and punch the time clock"; I could not miss that. I couldn't use my energy too much.

AH: Would you say that the "Time Clock Piece" consumed your life in a way that the other pieces didn't?

TH: All the pieces consumed my life, but each consumed me in a different way. "Cage Piece" confined me physically, which caused an extreme mental struggle. In "Outdoor Piece" I needed to pay a lot of attention to public spaces, because of the violence out there – artificial and natural; in "Rope Piece" Linda [Montano] and I had to face each other without any intermission. Or in "No Art" and the "Thirteen-Year Plan" there was no external energy from an audience; I had to use my own generator. All of these consumed my life intensively or slowly, and some still continue to affect me.

AH: We have talked about the earlier pieces and not so much about the last three. In the earlier pieces you controlled the presence of an audience; there were very strict mechanisms in place to shape your relation with them. In doing this you negotiate the question of what is private and what is public. In making an art frame around your life you make the private public, but you also carefully control how public it is. The first three pieces are very much about isolation in different ways, even though you give yourself over to art and to the public, there is still something very private about this giving over, but when you got to the relational piece with Linda Montano, you could not control the work as much as you felt you needed to.

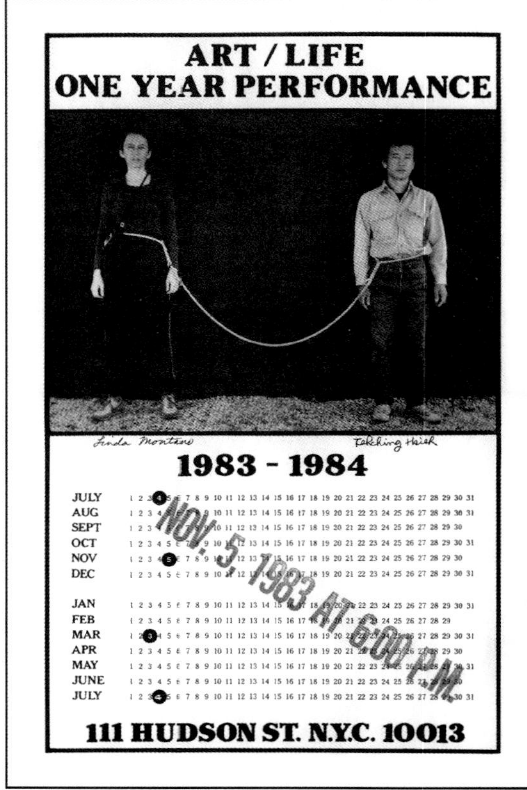

Tehching Hsieh, Linda Montano, *Art/Life One Year Performance 1983–1984*, New York, Poster, 11 x 17 in. (27.9 x 43.2cm.) © Tehching Hsieh, Linda Montano.

TH: In the previous three works I know that no matter how isolated I was, there always existed "the other." The "Rope Piece" intended to deal with this issue of "the other." The point here is not about what kind of person you've selected: good or bad, wrong or right. They are part of the piece, like in life, marriage, etc. This piece needed both of us to have a normal daily life like everyone else: dealing with people, doing jobs, etc. This is what makes this piece more real. Meanwhile Linda and I were exposed to each other. That brought complexity. The bottom line was that we should not cut the rope; whatever happened would be a part of this work. I could not desire privacy or control in this piece. I could only struggle for the value of my view.

AH: In breaking with the isolation of the previous work you locked yourself into a year of cohabitation with an artist that you barely knew. Was this lack of knowledge of each other essential to the piece and to its paradox of distance within intimacy?

TH: In this piece the intimacy and the distance between the collaborators is artificial: Intimacy is restricted to the intimacy of a one-year contract; distance is limited to the distance of an eight-foot rope. To do this piece with two people unfamiliar with each other, with no previous emotion involved, gave a kind of clearness to the work. But even if the two people were familiar with each other, this kind of intensive artistic collaboration still would not have been experienced before.

AH: It was not so much the relation with Linda that was problematic then, after all that was at the heart of the concept, but the relation with others that this relation necessarily entailed. By admitting another into the space of the work you inadvertently let in society.

TH: Some people had a strong subjective inclination toward this piece; some wanted to be a part of it. It was like letting many people into your home. For example, a photographer wanted to document the whole piece for the whole year. I didn't want anyone else to be "tied" with us. We documented this piece ourselves using a camera on a tripod. […] Compared with the solitude of the earlier pieces, this work was more out of control. It allowed for that. What matters is that you stay within the rules, it doesn't matter how good or how terrible it gets.

AH: In the "Rope Piece" you made tapes every day of the dialogues between yourself and Linda. Those tapes are now sealed and no one, not even a keen researcher, will ever hear what transpired between you. In each of the first three pieces you kept something private, by withholding your time, but in the piece with Linda there is no chance of private time but you somehow retrieve a space of privacy through the withholding of the tapes.

TH: Privacy also contains darkness, which we sometimes do not want to confront. In this piece we were forced to see our own and each other's darkness; this was a double quandary. We used tapes to document our conversations across the whole year and sealed them. These tapes are the witness of the "Rope Piece"; they are like the aircraft's black box. We keep them sealed to keep our privacy. Like Pandora's box they cannot be opened. They make a question; they give you imagination.

AH: In the first four pieces you are incredibly rigorous in your dedication to the rules. So later in the work, in the fifth "No Art Piece", it seems that you are making a rule system that tries to accommodate the decay inherent within rules themselves. One cannot stay inside the rules you set up in the fifth piece, they hold a certain impossibility, and so your duty to the rule is quite different. At this point, something that is latent within the work emerges quite strongly: the press toward invisibility over a long duration.

TH: Right. This "No Art Piece" would have happened sooner or later, although it happened too quickly to be accepted by the art world. At that moment, it was a new dilemma I had to face, also a necessary stage I had to pass. Since the concept of my work is passing time, not about how to pass time, I had to give this piece an equalized position, place it within the series of *One Year Performances*. There is no accurate rule formulated in this piece; the rule cannot give this piece powerful support, it is just used for distinguishing life and art.

AH: But the "Thirteen Year Plan" really says "I don't want to play the art game anymore"? Of course this conversation is a "making public" and if you answer the questions I am dying to ask you, about what you made in this thirteen-year period (of the "Thirteen-Year Plan" piece), you break the spirit of the rule. Can you break the spirit of the rule and discuss what you made in this time?

TH: The rule is over now. In the public report on 1 January 2000 I made a statement, "I kept myself alive"; this is the best I can say because I hadn't finished the artwork I was doing. If you are asking me what work I was making, I can tell you: I tried to disappear. I only did half a year and I didn't finish this plan, but at least it can show the direction in which I practiced art. When an artist does works but doesn't show them in public for thirteen years, he cuts himself off from communication. This is a sort of exile. In such a situation, how could he do art which would still maintain its meaning in that moment? I had this idea of disappearance: a double exile. This would give me communication in reverse whether at that moment or in the future.

AH: This is very important and I don't want to get this wrong. I think this is one of the most extraordinary things that you did, but you don't think of it as an artwork?

TH: It is a concept that's all.

AH: OK, but it is a very important concept. You made this incredible gesture, you said: "For thirteen years I will make art but I won't show it." So in terms of the art world and in terms of public presence as a figure you become invisible. And then in the midst of that anonymity, five years into this project you say "I am not invisible enough. I will make myself more invisible. I will disappear from human contact." And this wasn't just for one year, but for the rest of the thirteen years?

TH: Yes. I started it in 1991 and I tried to disappear until the end of the thirteen years. I had a huge internal struggle while I was doing it. I knew, as an art piece, "Disappearance" could be powerful. I could have done it in order to prove myself. But at the same time, I was thinking if I stayed in this double exile status for such a long time just for art's sake, it was not my ideal response to life and art. That's why I gave it up.

AH: In the first *One Year Performance* you were an illegal immigrant, and after this, when you became legal, you seemed to press yourself further and further into invisibility, into the conditions of an outsider.

TH: As an illegal immigrant, realistically, I was an "outsider;" as an artist, mentally, I was approaching an "outsider." This double identity of "outsider" propelled me to create works in a particular way. When I became legal, I used an invisible way to present my work, but in fact, I was showing my "outsider" mentality.

For me to make art in the present time is good. But to stay in the present you have to change direction, you have to keep turning different ways. It doesn't matter if you are a young or an old artist, you have to try to explain what art is in a different way in order to make art go ahead. I still went ahead, went my own way, although there was no response from the art world. I just tried to develop my philosophy of where I should go. In this I have freedom.

AH: Will you make art again?

TH: I haven't finished my art, but I will not do art any more. After I went through such a persistent exile, it was hard to go back to my previous state of doing art; not doing art is an exit. People may ask me if the things I'm doing right now, like making this book [about my work] or participating in exhibitions, are making art. For me by doing these things I'm dealing with my reality, not doing art, but I will do things with the same attitude I had to art. The only thing I'm sure about is that I'm still in the process of passing time, as I always am. Life becomes open and uncertain once again.

Chapter 36

The Maybe: Modes of Performance and the "Live"

Tilda Swinton and Joanna Scanlan

Introduction by Amelia Jones

The Maybe (1995) was a hotly debated and highly influential installation/performance work conceived and executed by the now world famous actress Tilda Swinton, and exhibited at the Serpentine Gallery in London (and later once again in Rome in 1996) to crowds of up to 25,000. The most striking, and controversial, aspect of the piece was the placement of Swinton herself in a vitrine, apparently sleeping (and with the wall caption "Matilda Swinton (1960–)"). The version of *The Maybe* that took place at the Serpentine included installation elements in adjacent galleries, a variety of objects chosen from London collections by internationally renowned artist Cornelia Parker in collaboration with Swinton. (Each of these marked a famous person's passage through time, her or his former state of embodiment, motion, weight, being-in-the-world: Lord Nelson's cutlery; Queen Victoria's stocking; Charles Babbage's brain; Wallis Simpson's ice skates, etc.)

The Serpentine urged Swinton to collaborate with a known artist and Parker was thus brought into the project – partly due to the fact (noted below) that the funding for the project was to come from a national Arts Council grant that specifically required collaborations. Swinton and Joanna Scanlan, former Arts Council staff and producer of *The Maybe*, also hypothesize that the Serpentine felt the need for an additional ("real"?) artist on the project as Swinton was known as an actress.

Published widely (for example, on the cover of the 2004 book *Difference and Excess in Contemporary Art*[1]), the iconic image of Swinton in the glass case has come to represent a signature moment in the exploration of the links between the "live" (performance art) and the "death" of the gallery space (its tendency to freeze in time and space that which is displayed there). Swinton's project is in dialogue with the earlier histories of artists enacting the everyday in the gallery space (such as Chris Burden, with his *White Light White Heat* piece from 1975, in which he lived and slept at Ronald Feldman Gallery for the three week run of the show) and has informed subsequent explorations along these lines (such as Marina Abramović's *House with the Ocean View*, Sean Kelly Gallery, New York, 2002) but comes from and arrives at a different place.

Swinton's work is informed by her particular relationship to performance, as someone active in working with artists to produce experimental films. A unique figure in art and film worlds, she crosses over art making, acting in feature films, modeling (she has worked with renowned designer Chalayan, who produced a work for the 2003 Venice Biennale featuring Swinton), and collaborating with experimental directors and artists (in addition to Derek Jarman, she has worked with Lynn Hershman, Sally Potter, Isaac Julian, Doug Aitken, and others). She comes to performance as someone who acts within the auspices of others' projects, but is a crucial collaborator in determining the meaning of the final product.

The Maybe is both mundane and elegiac. Swinton's "death" (her making of herself into an object) was, like the life-in-death of sleeping beauty, only partial as visitors could see her breathing, her eyelids move and (in fact) she was often awake and feigning sleep. It was the engagements of visitors (who talked about and to Swinton all day long) that revitalized her still breathing body into something much more than a corpse, something equivocal (both the *artist* and the *object*).

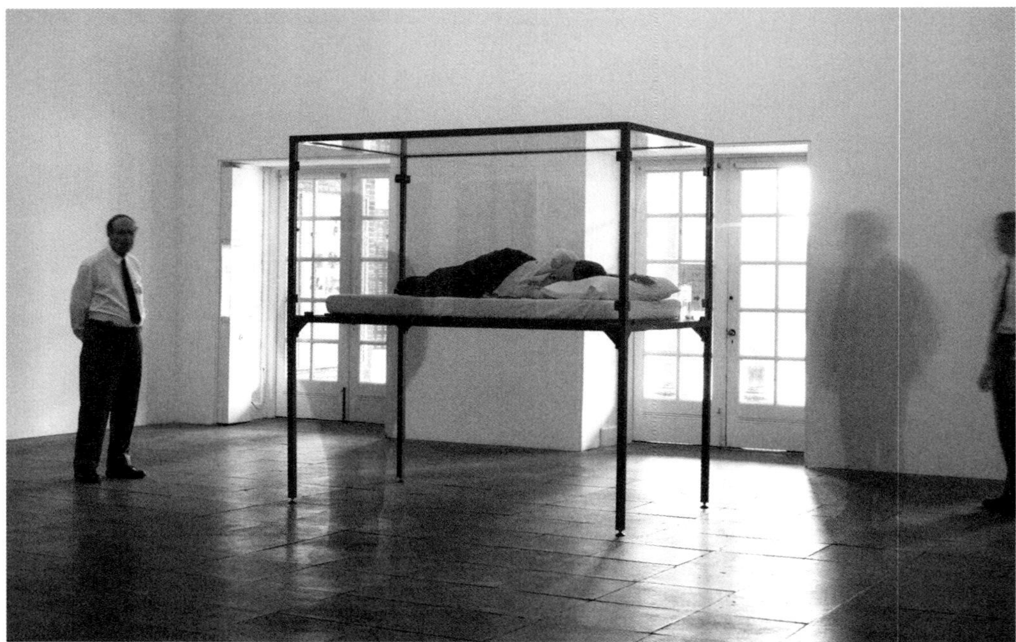

Tilda Swinton and Cornelia Parker, *The Maybe*, 1995. Photograph by Hugo Glendinning. © Hugo Glendinning.

Interestingly, too, and partly as a consequence of her willfully presenting herself in a vitrine as an "object" or fetish (like an artwork), *The Maybe* provides a case study for how the shift of the "author" to a position of objectification – and the participation of "authors" outside the conventional parameters of the artworld[2] – can affect the way the work is historicized. As the following dialogues make clear, *The Maybe* also throws in relief important issues in relation to how the art world constructs and defines authorship (which also of course relates to how art's histories get written). In part because Swinton was asleep, and literally unavailable to the visiting press, the piece was from 1995 onward increasingly discussed and labeled, particularly in the art press (in mainstream venues such as *Artforum* and in art history books such as the above-mentioned book, *Difference and Excess in Contemporary Art*) as a *Cornelia Parker piece*. This attribution has progressively taken hold in spite of the fact that, in its genesis, conceptualization, and the initial fundraising (through Arts Council), *The Maybe* was clearly Swinton's project.

Innumerable examples could be cited of the elision of Swinton as author (as "subject" of *The Maybe*). For example, an interview with Parker appears in the *Difference and Excess* book in which *The Maybe* is initially defined as a "collaboration" by the interviewer Lisa Tickner, but then more or less examined as Parker's work. Although Parker clearly admires Swinton and in no way erases her creative "presence" overall, her language clearly subordinates Swinton to her (Parker's) aesthetic project:

> Tilda had an idea to do a performance where she slept as a Snow White character – a fictional character – but through our collaboration it changed to her sleeping as herself [...]. I created an installation around her in the form of a reliquary [...]. In *The Maybe* the history of the object [I chose from museums] had been conferred by someone else [the original owner], and my role was to isolate these objects and put them together like sculptural material [...]. I liked playing around with these little histories. I wanted to breathe new life into these objects by their juxtaposition and their relation to Tilda, living and breathing only a few inches away. I was interested in an orchestration of objects, in the sense that each object is itself, its own sound, but that all the objects together create something larger than the sum of the parts [...].Tilda stood in for everyone; she was still alive, like us, where all the other objects belonged to dead people.[3]

By the end of this quote, Swinton is simply another object in Parker's installation. This elision of Swinton's authorship is common in the general press as well. As *The Guardian* recently put it in two different gossip columns: "Tilda Swinton [...] whose career highlights include sleeping in a coffin [...] *in an installation by the artist Cornelia Parker*"; and "Cornelia Parker [...] famous for *her installation of the artist Tilda Swinton* in a glass case."[4] The following dialogues between myself, Swinton, and the producer of *The Maybe*, Joanna Scanlan, tease out some of the complexities of the work in terms of how live art gets written about and marketed, and enunciate from Swinton's and Scanlan's point of view a longer and more personal genesis for the piece that completely changes how it might be positioned in (art) history.

Sparked by their mutual friendship with Lynn Hershman Leeson, Amelia Jones visited with Tilda Swinton at her home in Scotland 30 September–1 October 2006 where their initial dialogue about *The Maybe* took place. This dialogue continued over e-mail.

Swinton Answers A. Jones's Questions Sent via E-mail 22 August 2007, in an E-mail of 29 April 2008

Amelia Jones: What different "subjects" (authors/identities) come through in each project? In film versus performance art? Via celebrity journalism (as a kind of narrating of the meaning of films and the identities of directors and actors) versus the art press?

Tilda Swinton: I find that I am conscious of operating my own personal circus parade of work through a variety of identities. Indeed, the more work I do, the clearer these different identities become. When I am asked to play the Angel Gabriel in Francis Lawrence's *Constantine*, for example, I know that this is a direct link to the kind of androgynous, fantastic, iconography explored in *Orlando* – ditto the White Witch in the *Narnia* films.[5] Then again, the strand of "self," the particular calibration of naturalism asked for in the performance of Karen Crowder in *Michael Clayton* is a direct relation of the work we explored in *The Deep End*.[6] These simultaneously spinning worlds – Maybury/Hershman are stable mates in sensibility and spirit of performance – are stimulating to run alongside each other.[7] Another world away, the work with fine artists like Doug Aitken, Hussein Chalayan, Joan Jonas, Isaac Julian:[8] video and film installation art that occupies an entirely different territory to the commercially distributed cinema and is exhibited in galleries and museums as part of a fine art context. This is the arena within which *The Maybe* operates.

AJ: Could you elaborate on working with Derek Jarman: where did the agency lie in this work? Who determined the dialogue, gestures, nuances of performance? Whose authorship is at stake? In terms of the topic of this book I am co-editing I'm interested in how the films become in a sense "documents" of a complex creative process in each case. Can you elaborate on this process in relation to each director/project?

TS: Jarman was a painter first and foremost and when he came to make films it was as much in search of the collaborative process as anything. He would put together the group of people – throw the party, if you like – and see which way it rolled. In this respect, each of his collaborators were in no doubt as to how much we were held responsible for our own contribution: not to say that one was abandoned, exactly, but there was a fair bit of sinking and swimming. Derek was a believer in what happened happening, was not so fixated on product that he didn't value the process above all.

In the case of the 35mm films – which needed big cameras, expensive lighting, filmstock, ergo budgets and funding – there were scripts with designated scenes, dialogue and prescribed locations and mises-en-scène. So there was a pre document if you like. The films I worked on in this way with him were *Caravaggio* [1986], *Edward II* [1991], *Wittgenstein* [1993].

On the Super8 films – released from the need to raise money for industrial working practices – we had no scripts, no dialogue, no characters prescribed, no story, no nothing. We had a dressing up box attitude, flexible handheld cameras, no pressure to make any sound, were intent only on recording a certain kind of image that became, somehow, kind of kinetically determined. One could feel it when a "performance" filmed thus held a power likely to hold on the screen. All gestures were entirely improvised on these films, with a modicum of direction from Derek in the first place to get the energetic ball rolling. But the sequences generally played themselves out of their own momentum: a fine example of this being the sequence at the end of *The Last of England* [1988] when the Bride is spinning around the fire. I remember Derek asking me what I wanted to do in that awful wedding dress and I said "cut myself out of it" – so we got his huge shears and started shooting – and then somehow I started spinning. In this respect, the performance in these films is pure "live art" recorded.

The question of authorship in filmmaking is constantly vexed by the fact that it takes so many individuals to make a film. However, I firmly believe that the authorship of an individual film is that of the director. The authorship non-directing filmmakers can lay claim to may be revealed over time and a history of many projects, where an individual voice, sensibility, spirit and agenda may be glimpsed more easily.

Another E-mail from Tilda Swinton to Amelia Jones, 29 April 2008

dear amelia, [....]

In 1994, things happened in my life which set in my mind a chain of reactions that eventually – among other responses – gave birth to *The Maybe* project. [....]

First and most significantly, Derek Jarman died. He had been ill – with HIV infection and AIDS related diseases – for a very long time, we had all been aware for a couple of years at least that he wouldn't be around for very much longer, that his filmmaking, at least, was slowly coming to an end. Quite apart from the natural and usual impact of losing an extremely close and beloved friend, his dying over these preceding years had begun in me a set of questions, ranging from the practical to the metaphysical, to the critical.

I had found with Jarman a real artistic home in which, as a performer, I felt I could develop in a free and individual way, outside of the proscriptions of theater or the dramatic "acting" practices in the narrative, fictional, cinema at the time. His passing left me open to a sense of void, a real loneliness and a lack of context within which I could easily see myself continuing as an artist. [....]

Naturally, having lost my "mentor," my teacher in filmmaking, my "author," the question of my own call to authorship raised its head. [....]

At this same moment, it also occurred to me that I was becoming impatient with a preoccupation in the art world with all things un-figurative and specifically non-human. The emblematic gesture embraced by the art world of the time was without doubt the 'Shark in a Box': *The Physical Impossibility of Death in the Mind of Someone Living* [1991] by Damien Hirst, exhibited with much attention at the Saatchi Gallery, a piece of work which I admired unreservedly, not least in the context of its title, but the overwhelming celebration of which I found disconcerting. It felt as if the critical authority was only too happy to laud a figure in a frame just as long as it was not human. I began to ask myself if it were not also the fact that such an "object" would also have to be *not living*, to boot.

Lastly, I was at a point in my life when I began to think about having a child. (The year after we presented *The Maybe* in Rome, in fact, I had twins.) I started to contemplate the encasement of the child in utero, the vulnerability/security/passivity/activity of this stage of life, this limbo state, this promise, this maybe.[...]

With the end of Jarman's freeform cinema with its myriad opportunities for experiment in performance, I asked myself about what made me a performer in the first place (see my former responses sent earlier). With the impetus of profound soul-searching, I asked myself to distill the essence of performance that keeps me interested in it at all: specifically, I needed to identify clearly what it was about live performance that most intrigues and sustains me, and then to discover the same basic formula for cinematic performance. I see this question as a genuinely humanistic and existential one about energy and exchange: an essentially spiritual exchange between performer and spectator. I approached the matter scientifically, scrupulously sifting through my responses. It occurred to me that it is this humanistic exchange that is the lowest common denominator that keeps me fascinated in performance as a ritual and cathartic endeavour, the sense of shared witness to basic mortal experience between viewer and practitioner: this is where "truth" comes in and becomes the deal breaker, and where the dance with fiction and with interpretation becomes intricate and dense.

I asked myself to propose a gesture, a hybrid between that essence which I value most in live performance – namely, that kinetic experience of human beings all (wholly – as in, every part of them) present together in the same space at the same time and in the thrall of time and the unexpected – with that essence which I value most in cinematic performance – namely, the possibility of the scrutiny by the viewer of the "unwatched" who cannot "watch" back. I began to conjure the sense that at the heart of both these scenarios is a rich seeding ground for real compassion and understanding between people: the idea that in witnessing another human who voluntarily puts themselves up for scrutiny/to lead the energy of the space, we see ourselves mirrored back at us, in all our privacy, in all our skinlessness.

(Here I began to realise why, maybe, I am so uncomfortable with the idea of the classical repertory as an "actor" – the reality of holding the gesture of a situation in a drama that many/ most people in the audience know just as well as you, outcome, previous interpretations and all, wastes for me the jewel of the spontaneous at the centre of the live performance magic formula. I mean, we never can doubt what Hamlet will end up doing, and while we all know that Iggy Pop is very likely to throw himself into the audience at one of his gigs, but at least you can never be *quite* sure *when* …)

Building on this idea of compassion within the exchange, I thought of a simple experience from childhood, very likely shared by most: the moment of being on the verge of sleep and largely ignored and hearing someone whisper "Is she asleep?" and the thrill of someone answering "Yes" … the sensation of a blanket being laid incredibly softly onto one, surely more softly than ever in "life" … the feeling of being between worlds/states … an alien, visible, but not truly encountered as when awake …

I thought about a kind of loving attention – pretty much unconditional – that is accorded only to those sleeping, ailing, dying or dead … that is rarely given freely to those standing hale hearty, upright and eyes open before one …

I thought about the experience of being witnessed sleeping … so run of the mill in the life of children and lovers, so rare for everyone else …

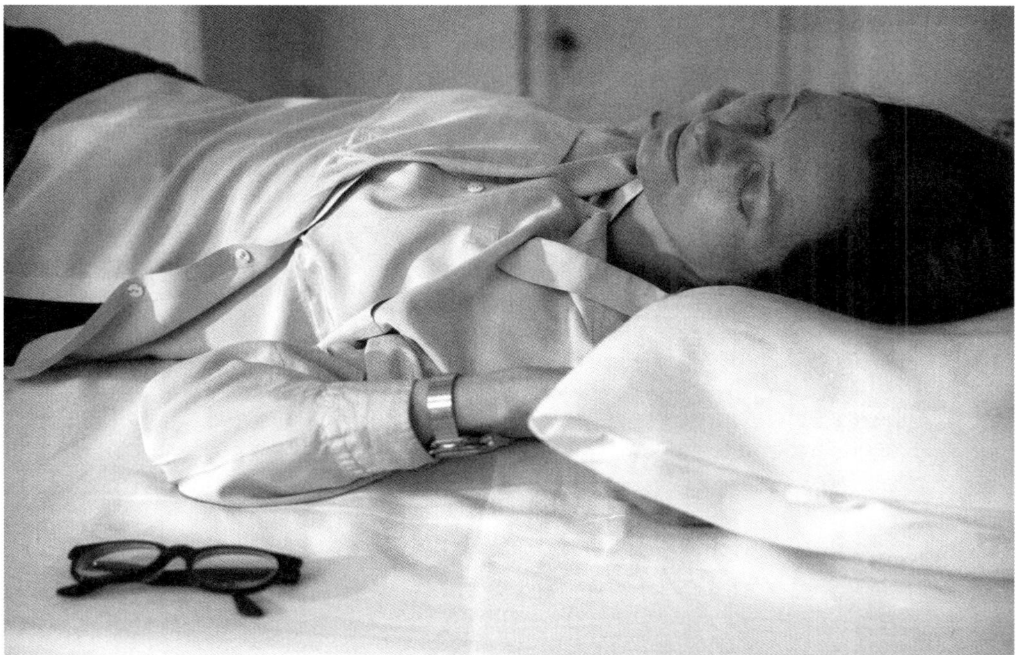

Tilda Swinton and Cornelia Parker, *The Maybe*, 1995. Photograph by Hugo Glendinning. © Hugo Glendinning.

I thought of the thousands of homeless people that those passing through our world's cities "witness" every day as if invisible ... as if sealed away ... as if behind glass ...

I thought about the recurring image of the sleeping woman in the fairy tales of our culture ... woken into love and life out of nightmare and cruel oppression ...

I thought about how tired I was ... how much I longed to sleep ... how much time I had spent over the past two years at the side of my friends, prone and living – although maybe only just – and how energetically engaging it had been, how exhausting, how inspiring to life ...

And I thought of Lenin in his tomb, and all those relics of saints and holy men and women, displayed as talismans to inspire the populace ... I thought how much more inspiring it might be to contemplate a *living* body in a case, a *living* one of my contemporaries, a *living human* in a case in a London gallery ...

Voilà.

When I began to talk to Jo [Joanna Scanlan] about my idea for this piece of live art, her enthusiasm meant a lot, not least because she was, at the time, in a strong position to give an opinion about whether it would be likely to raise funding.

The rest of that development story you know, told, not only brilliantly clearly and evocatively, but also, I think, more appropriately, from Jo's angle [see below]. My own objectivity on the whole development process is a harder thing to rely on, so caught up was I in a naiveté about assumptions being made: for example, it never *occurred* to me that anyone could ever doubt my original authorship of the piece, as the generator of the project over two years and the physical "body" in and of the work ...

What I can add is that when Connie [Cornelia Parker] and Jo came to Los Angeles, expressly in order for me to persuade Connie to help me achieve the installation for the other three rooms of the Serpentine around the room in which I would be lying, I remember with real fondness our conversations about relics, about fame (a friend of hers had asked her to bring him back a pair of my knickers, I remember ...) and about the *evidence* of life. We spoke about what generally ends up in glass cases in exhibition spaces, about my love of the "wunderkammer" [cabinet of curiosities] and the randomness of human attention.

I remember telling Connie about people very close to my heart in terms of this dialogue about fame: Arthur Askey, old music hall entertainer, for example, the first famous person I ever heard of: his granddaughter was at nursery school with me and my nanny was all of a twitter when she found out (she was a fan) and had to explain to me why she was delighted even though she had never met the man. So when Connie went back to London, agreed to work on the piece and started sending me lists of available things she had researched from a variety of collections around London, Arthur Askey's suit was a no-brainer for me, it felt like a lucky charm ...

Ditto a piece pertaining to Virginia Woolf, ditto Joe Orton, ditto Charles Babbage, ditto Freud: all supremely personal choices which I made from the lists she submitted, according to my own personal resonances. When an LP of Mahler, allegedly recovered from Hitler's bunker, was at the eleventh hour questioned by the gallery on the grounds of sensitivity, my

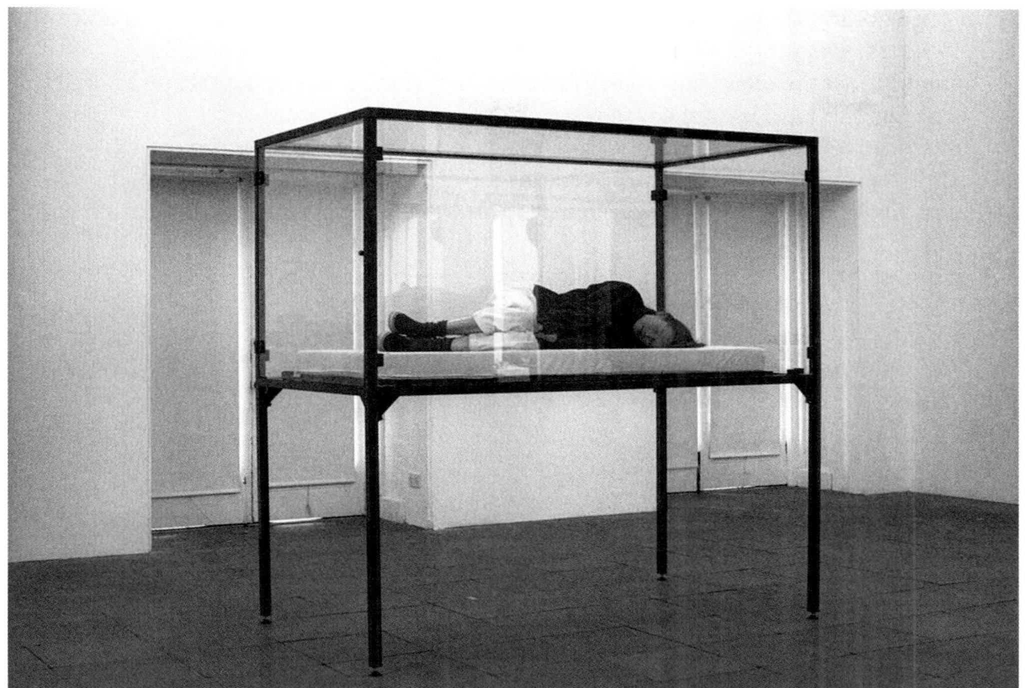

Tilda Swinton and Cornelia Parker, *The Maybe*, 1995. Photograph by Hugo Glendinning. © Hugo Glendinning.

insistence that it be replaced with a camera that once belonged to Lee Miller, in order to keep the WWII reference in place, was carefully adhered to.

This was an installation achieved by Cornelia according to the resonances each element presented to the central hub of the show: me, not as artist, only, but as the living sensibility at the germ of the environment, the subject *and* the object at the same time, the essential text source, whose spider's web of references was positioned around her, like a material dreamscape, a tangible unconscious map, while she slept.

This felt like the collaboration to which I was used: I was blissfully unaware of any risk of any hijack. I was aware that the Serpentine needed me to work with an artist "legitimate" within the art world, I was aware that our grant was a Combined Arts Grant and that it was expressly geared towards collaboration. What I never felt aware of was the danger that my first public gesture of authorship, albeit shared in collaboration with an established sculptor with fine art credentials, might be undermined, let alone ignored or never imagined.

We made a limited edition to be sold in the gallery shop of 100 small sealed Perspex boxes in which Cornelia and I placed "relics" of ourselves: tellingly, Cornelia's contributions were exclusively small bits of her work, fragments from the development process of her previous pieces. My contributions were exclusively, uniquely, personal: old passport, childhood photographs, baby shoes, curls of my hair etc … there feels like a significance in a difference in approach, here. I noticed it at the time, but never understood then how distinctly differing were our individual angles on the work we were both involved in, and how unbalanced was our alliance. It seems clear now that there was something Cornelia and the Serpentine never truly grasped about the nature of the investment in the live aspect of the work – and, I also believe, its enormous impact which resulted directly from this aspect – its coordination with *reality*, out with the realm of art, quotation, intellect … essentially, I have to name it, its *spiritual* value.

Fortunately, an audience of over 25,000 people were more open. They came, stayed very often for hours, choosing carefully their optimum distance from the case, some of them visibly moved, some of them angered, some amused. [….]

The painful irony – and it *is* painful still, however fascinating I find it – is that escaping the concept of "being put in a box" by someone else – as the majority of the art press labelled my contribution to *The Maybe* eventually – was the *very reason* I had developed the piece in the first place.

E-mail from Joanna Scanlan to Amelia Jones 26 April 2008

[In the Spring of 1995] Connie [Cornelia Parker] and Tilda spent the weekend talking about ideas and by the return Connie had agreed to come on board. She would be responsible for the installation that provided a context for Tilda in The Box. The two elements were clearly separate but in relation. The diamond and the ring. The woman and the dress. The living and the dead.

It is so interesting to me that the visual art world annexed this work for one of its own, making the assumption that Connie put Tilda in the box. I wonder whether there wasn't some notion to colonise and suppress Tilda by surrounding her with the falsely analogous to claim and possess her, and in the process "deaden" her. Tilda is Victoria's stocking. Tilda is Lee Miller's camera, no more no less.

Certainly one problem exists in the retelling of the event; when people came to the work itself Tilda was undoubtedly the main attraction. People stood for hours in her presence. The vitrines were interesting, fascinating, but never compelling. There was no sense at the time of a competition between the two elements because it was pyramidic: the viewer experienced the installation as the wide base and climbed to its pinnacle, the living, breathing, sleeping woman. But after the live work was over, only the dead remained in which the energy, physicality and life of the living woman was reduced to the same state as the objects in the vitrines – photographs, reportage, etc. – and could be claimed by the sculptor as her own. There is a way in which the objects in the vitrines were reduced to dross by the death of their owners. And the end of the performance reduced *The Maybe* to a nothing. [….]

At that point historically in the development of art and culture in the UK, partly through the new Lottery funding and partly through the deep alliances built with the corporate and business communities and the press, the commodification of art was becoming complete. Performance has never sat easily in that sphere, being of the moment in its totality, and looking back I now see that the vitrine notion so prevalent at that time (Damian Hurst's cow, sheep, shark) was a very clear parallel with the death of life and the death of the chaos it brings, and the ultimate buy-ability, tidiness, of the remains.

The Serpentine was a hugely ambitious organisation during the early 1990s and I wonder whether the only viable means of containing the live for them was within the consumable container of art, the vitrine. The art became an animal from the wild brought into captivity, and put behind bars for the safety of the public when they came to gawp. [....] There was a mismatch between our ironisation of the culled and the art world's containment and consumerisation of the Live. In short, I don't think we were speaking the same language.

As we installed the piece in that first week of September and Connie's objects arrived, the piece, as a whole, began to come clear. It spoke, amongst the notions that I have already mentioned, about notoriety and fame. The questions raised as to the value of a life, one against another, of the time in which the liver lives, the somebody-ness or the nobody-ness and the ways in which individuals influence the future, all spilled over and on to Tilda, making us ask ourselves who is she? And does she matter? And if she does, what matters about her and why? I always answered that myself by recognising the presence in her, her elemental essence as her value, contrasting that with the absence of the other individuals cited in the work, through their possessions. They became Ozymandias and her life his countermand. Of course, her "sleeping" put her into a demi-world, a half life, representing a woman yet *to be*, maybe. She had yet to decide to live and to make her life, and in the suspension of sleep remained nascent. The privilege afforded to us, the spectator, of watching that state was the ultimate power of the work.

On 3 September we opened with a press call. All of us were expecting a few desultory press folk sent by their art desks. Nothing could have prepared us for what happened. About a hundred news photographers and TV camera crews arrived, with lights, ladders and notebooks. There was about half an hour of tussling and pushing before they were all expelled and the show was opened to the public. Julia Peyton Jones and I were astounded. The appeal of Tilda lying in a glass case had taken us all by surprise. That was the story. We made it on to the BBC news that night and from then on the show was a huge cause célèbre.

At that point, as I remember, there was no assumption that Cornelia Parker put Tilda Swinton in a box. Gradually over the week the public descended, and by the end of the seven days 25,000 people had come to visit the show. The most we had hoped for was about 5,000. The weather was beautiful; it was silly season in the press who were looking for good news stories, and the imagination of London had been caught. I was in the gallery at all times. I watched power shift over that week as the art world descended. I watched Julia entertaining her peers from other galleries and I began to feel distinctly excluded. I remember watching her have a conversation with Nicholas Serota (still yet to open "his" Tate Modern) which made me feel very uncomfortable. At the same time Connie was in the gallery frequently and she became the spokesperson for the work, as more and more press enquiries were made and Tilda was, of course, unavailable. Connie's point of view was limited by her own contribution to the work, which had commenced rather late in the process as a whole. This too made me uncomfortable. In addition Tilda was now feeling the strain of the performance itself, which was hugely demanding on her body and mental health. As she emerged from the box each evening at six o'clock, the Serpentine staff having gone home, job done, John Byrne (Tilda's sweetheart), Dean Proctor and myself would sit in the kitchen feeding her baked beans on toast and encouraging her to drink liquids so that her kidneys would revive overnight, as of course by the next morning she would be unable to drink again so that she would not have to go to the loo during the day in the glass case.

Tensions began to emerge between the performance group and the Serpentine and Connie. It felt that the huge success of *The Maybe* was becoming a battle ground for ownership. Art or performance, object or subject, time/space or commodity, the visceral or the vestige? [....]

Over the next few months the toll of the project was felt by us all. Tilda became very ill with shingles as a consequence of the dehydration she experienced during the performance and in addition she had to psychologically recover from the extreme nature of her experience. The project was also being reported in the press, by now, as Cornelia Parker having put Tilda Swinton in a glass case. This essentially emanated from the art press [writers], who simply annexed the work for one of their own. Tilda and I employed a solicitor to ensure that this could not take place again, and apologies appeared in a couple of papers, I think *The Telegraph* and *The Times*. This was followed by a very uncomfortable meeting at the Serpentine Gallery headed by Julia Peyton-Jones at which wording was agreed between us and Cornelia Parker that accurately apportioned the contributions of the project.

Notes

1. Gill Perry (ed.), *Difference and Excess in Contemporary Art: The Visibility of Women's Practice*, Oxford: Blackwell, 2004.
2. Other examples might include the projects of American David Blaine; trained as a magician, his website describes him as "magician and endurance artist" (http://davidblaine.com/). Media coverage of his stunts, such as the 2003 suspension of himself in a Plexiglas case above the River Thames in London for forty-four days without food, is extensive and international, but he is not by and large covered by the art press. This comparison is not by any means meant to conflate Blaine with Swinton (who has extensive experience working as an artist and with other artists), but simply to make a point about the art world's ability (or willingness) to incorporate authors that cannot be marketed through conventional channels – a fact confirmed by the difficulties I have faced trying to publish a book on *The Maybe* through various art presses, who clearly do not view Swinton as "an artist." This is especially odd considering how much more marketable Swinton is in terms of international celebrity than the vast majority of visual and/or performance artists!

3. Lisa Tickner, interview with Cornelia Parker, "A Strange Alchemy: Cornelia Parker," in Gill Perry, op. cit., pp. 65–7.
4. These are two "People" columns, *The Guardian*, respectively on Swinton (26 January 2007, p. 10); and on Parker (13 December 2007, p. 10); my emphases. These off-hand attributions mirror the increasing tendency, once the installation had opened and Swinton was immobilized, to describe the work as a "Cornelia Parker." It was only before the show opened, when Swinton was being interviewed by the mass media (*not* so much the art press) that it was described as a Swinton project; see, for example, Rowena Young's column, "Glass Act," in the gossip section "*Vogue* notices," *Vogue* Magazine (September 1995), from the Serpentine Gallery press file, no pages visible. I am deeply grateful to the Serpentine Gallery, and archivist Clare Colvin, for making these files available to me.
5. *Constantine* was released in 2005; Swinton plays an androgynous but powerful angel; Sally Potter directed *Orlando* (1992) from Virginia Woolf's 1928 novel by that name, and Swinton plays the range of male, female, and androgynous characters. The Narnia films, *The Chronicles of Narnia: The Lion, the Witch and the Wardrobe* (2005) and *The Chronicles of Narnia: Prince Caspian* (2008), were directed by Andrew Adamson. Swinton plays the villainous White Witch in both films.
6. *Michael Clayton* (2007) was directed by Tony Gilroy; Swinton won Best Supporting Actress Oscar for this role, indicating her recognition as a major actress in Hollywood. *The Deep End* (2001) was directed by Scott McGehee and Swinton starred in the highly acclaimed film, which premiered at the Sundance Festival. Sundance straddles the Hollywood and "independent" worlds of feature film production.
7. Maybury and Hershman have both made independent "artist's" films; Maybury has moved more into feature film-making since the release of his 1998 bio-pic on Francis Bacon (*Love is the Devil*), while Hershman has continued to work across film, art, performance, and new media. Hershman's most recent film, *Strange Culture* (2007), is a documentary taking up the case of artist Steve Kurtz, who was unfairly arrested by the FBI in 2004 and accused of bioterrorism; Swinton plays Kurtz's wife in a parallel narrative recreating the couple's creative relationship.
8. Of particular interest is Swinton's participation in Julian's 2008 film in homage to Jarman entitled *Derek*. Swinton appears in the film (as herself?) speaking her "Letter to an Angel," a text she wrote in 2002 in remembrance of Jarman. The film is an unabashed homage, creating a tension between Jarman's own admissions of being difficult (an impossible lover, etc.) and Swinton's performance of melancholy in her reminiscences. The complexity of Swinton's personae and performances of self are more fully revealed in personal correspondence; Swinton thus wrote in an e-mail to me on 26 May 2008 in response to my appreciation of her role in *Derek*, "the truth about the albeit beloved derek was he was unfazed as only a true narcissist can be …"

Chapter 37

Photography as a Performative Act

Shezad Dawood and Amelia Jones

This dialogue first took place "live" at Shezad's then-studio in London on 15 January 2007. Unfortunately Amelia's tape recorder was substandard and the original dialogue was inaudible – hence a reliable transcript of the "authentic" event could not be recreated. The "live" discussion was then recreated over e-mail with Amelia reconstructing passages through her spotty memory, and running them by Shezad for elaboration.

Amelia Jones: Can you describe the development of your interests in photography and film in relation to your interest in live art? How did you come to the kind of complex interweaving of all of these media in your work?

Shezad Dawood: I actually began working in photographic studios when I was about 14, initially being a very junior assistant – cleaning cameras and lenses, helping set up studio lighting. In a way, this was a crucial beginning to an ongoing interest in both a notion of artifice and also the performative in that for me, working in a studio, behind the scenes everything was in motion, it was far from the notionally static end-result of the photographic process.

This idea of process was something that was becoming foregrounded in art schools in the 1980s and 1990s, even if we weren't sure what it meant. Actually, the fact that it was less well defined than it is now was an advantage in that it allowed a more open approach to practice in art schools, without such a focus on the outcome. This open approach encouraged a more playful, and often less rigid agenda – an approach I still use to good effect these days, and which on balance allows for a far more complex series of references and layers within the work.

As far as growing up with different and evolving technologies, I'm not sure how much of a factor that was, as I came late to computers. To be honest most of my work is very low tech – all the way through college I was staging very lo-fi performances relating to the films I had grown up with and photographing these. For me the faux-artifice of Hammer films, the texture of 1970s Kung Fu films and the stilted acting in a lot of Jean-Luc Godard's movies really carry on the legacy of avant-gardism begun with Bertolt Brecht and Samuel Beckett. For me this legacy bears a light of truth on proceedings, the idea of alienating people, making them aware of artifice, of the text as foregrounding the action, takes away the suspension of disbelief. Performing is a form of proselytizing, and the moment we slip into the pleasure of cathartic, or immersive "watching," we have abandoned some of our intelligence.

AJ: You have used the words "representational regime" and spoken about your intervention in the real estate market and the complex interweaving of value systems in the 2005 *Make it Big* and *Paradise Row* projects – with *Make It Big* involving your re-staging in Karachi (with yourself as the protagonist) Michelangelo Antonioni's 1966 film *Blow Up*, and *Paradise Row* being the project in which you purchased real estate in London, lived and worked there, and had the *Make It Big* project displayed to the public through

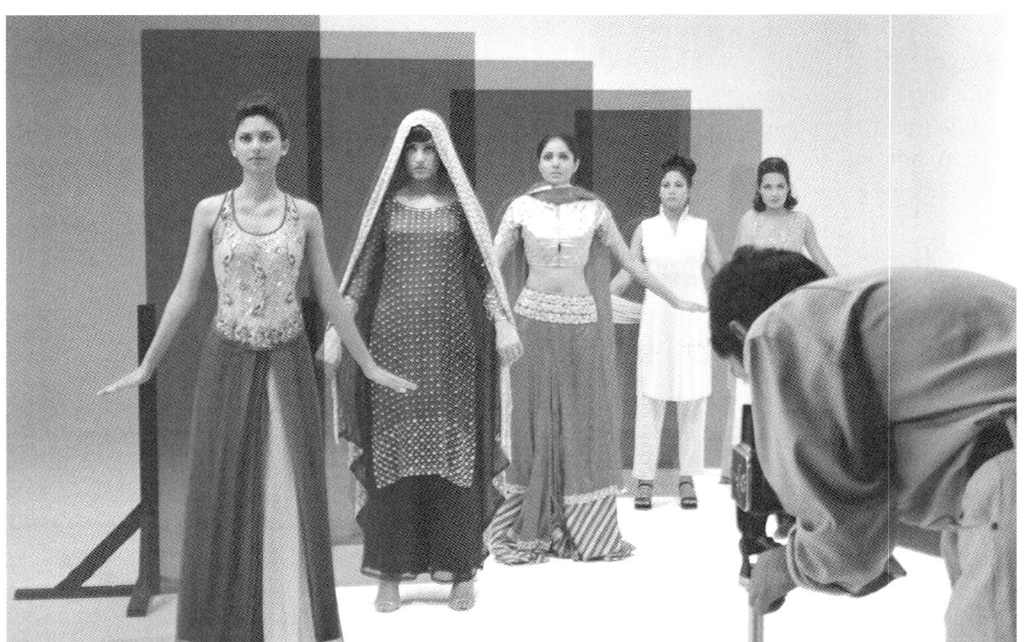

Shezad Dawood, *Make it Big (Blow-Up)*, 2002/3, Film still (set of 5 prints), C-print diasec mounted, 44 × 58 cm. Courtesy of the Artist and Paradise Row, London.

an estate agent.[1] Can you expand on what you mean by "representational regime" and relate it to your interest in interweaving live performance with photographic imagery?

SD: By "representational regime" I mean a complex structure where meaning and value are interwoven and exchanged through the mediums of the image, the distribution of capital and the currency of ideas (or prevailing notions). This regime represents human culture (with all its concomitant archetypes, prejudices, and injustices) at this point in planetary evolution.

What I tried to do – in a very small way – with the *Make It Big/Paradise Row* project was to go some way toward articulating these relationships, that is, between the distribution of wealth in the real estate market in London and the circulation of capital in the art world. I wanted to explore how artists become a factor in creating and opening up new areas for investment by developers but are ultimately priced out of the very areas they have opened up in this way. I wanted to look at how this process of capital following and displacing creativity can be mapped on to the way in which exotic archetypes are made and framed on a sliding scale of racial acceptability and assimilation, ever at the expense of some new group. In a simple way, I wanted to point out how the East/West divide in property in London can be mapped out in relation to Edward Said's notion of the "West and the Rest." (The East of London has been a shifting ghetto, more associated with poverty whether this was white English at the time of the French Huguenots, Hogarth, or the Jewish or latterly Bengali diasporas – I'm very keen to make these associations, and this is what I mean by a sliding scale of racial acceptability, that race is ultimately bound up with notions of class and privilege.) I take Said's argument further than a merely postcolonial standpoint, applying it to the slightly childish need to always prefigure a center, from which all hierarchical relations are maintained. My visual art projects employ performance, photography, film, and other aspects of the market (such as the real estate system) in order to explore and expose this dynamic.

AJ: Is there something particular about the way in which your generation of artists (born, say, in the 1970s) works in relation to the connection between the live and the representational?

SD: Artists born after the 1960s have a certain amount of distance from a previous generation of artists and from the debates about authenticity that surrounded work such as the fetishized low quality video documentation of early Dan Graham performance pieces. I think for us there is less of a preoccupation with the honesty or truth of a particular performance. Or perhaps more of an awareness of the untruth of a particular performance, and so this becomes the focus of understanding. For example the re-introduction of historical or cultural texts, as a basis for performance, becomes in my mind a very politicized use of "play" in its disruptive sense, my "re-stagings" of a conversation between Hegel and Crazy Horse, or between Krishna and Camus (fictionalizing the encounters as well as the dialogue) to undermine notions of duality, that underscore a particular western philosophical trajectory are at once much more theatrical than the previous generation, and much more about the text. Similarly Spartacus Chetwynd's "re-stagings" of scenes from "Star Wars" and the "Incredible Hulk" to re-assess notions of gender and racial archetype, are less concerned with a "high" aesthetic, but more with a sense of rupture, through their use of home-made props and costumes.

AJ: While artists in the 1970s performed themselves partly as a way to counter modernism's imperatives (producing a non-commodifiable kind of artistic moment) this is clearly no longer what motivates artists to perform live or to incorporate live elements in their works. Can you discuss/explore this in relation to your practice? What does the "live" mean in your practice?

SD: For me the live in my practice is what opens it up to several things: to failure, to chaos and, when performing (as I often do) with other artists, writers etc., to a multiple set of texts and modes of authorship. Which for me is very important: to find ways to enlarge upon my own limitations as a practitioner.

I think as well, my fascination with film and with theater as texts, particularly the often unexplored relation between the two, creates a strange tension that I like to explore through, on the one hand, staged performances and, on the other, highly performative

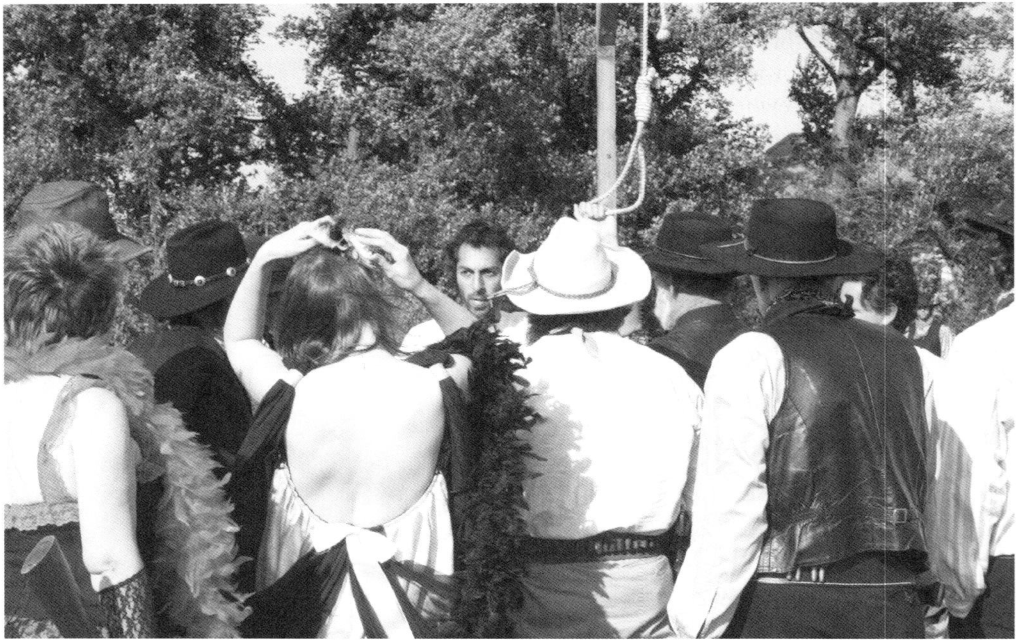

Shezad Dawood, *Feature* (Production Still), 2008, from Super 16mm and HD, 55 mins. Courtesy of the Artist and Paradise Row, London.

filmed works. Although putting it this way is to oversimplify the recipe, as strategies of improvisation, sabotage, and acting (i.e., what the "actors'" in the performances I stage, some of whom are themselves artists, bring of themselves and their practice to a character I have assigned them) play a part across both my live performances and film works. In fact, I don't even make a separation between the two (the live and the cinematic), viewing my practice as a continuous text.

I view the live performance and whatever documentation comes out of it (film, photographs), as well as the mode of display through which the various aspects are shown (such as the house I had renovated in *Paradise Row*) as interdependent. They need each other in order to take on their meaning and value and to sustain their mystery and interest. I kind of view it like the Eleusinian mystery plays from Ancient Greece (1600 BC to approx. 400 AD) which "performed" the myth of Demeter and her daughter Persephone, who was kidnapped by Hades God of the underworld, thus bringing on the cyclical pattern of Spring, Summer, Autumn, Winter – you had the live experience of a complex allegory, while at the same time the text exists as a way of analyzing the functioning of that allegory. In the same way, in *Paradise Row* all the different elements of the project (including the original performance and re-staging of *Blow Up*, the posters I commissioned from Bollywood billboard painters advertising the Urdu versions of *Blow Up*, and the documents scattered throughout the house) reflect on one another. The house itself was totally white, and therefore echoed both the studio and the gallery, as well as activating a sense of agency (through the very market forces of encountering it through a real estate agent). And then set within this live encounter was the mystery of the document, or texts of a performance that had taken place elsewhere. My intention was thus to set up a circuit of meaning and value, in which various elements, normally separate and distinct – notably the value of the property, the question of the authenticity of the documents, the presence/absence of their author (I performed in the David Hemmings role within the recreation of *Blow Up* in *Make It Big*) – were set in counterpoint.

AJ: What models of photographic and/or cinematic practice have inspired/interested you?

SD: Definitely more cinematic than photographic. While I know a lot of photographic practices, and have often taught them as theory, they don't have the same fascination for me as cinema. And with cinema it is endless, I have a great love of American B movies by directors such as Sam Fuller and Herschell Gordon Lewis, movies that performed as over-the-top and psychological critiques of their societies well before the more popular but watered-down high budget films such as *Deliverance* (still a good film). To Godard's and Chris Marker's works with image and text, which explore the displacements between time and memory. To Robert Altman and Marco Ferreri's highly performative, improvised Westerns (such as *Buffalo Bill and the Indians* and *Ne Touchez pas a la Femme Blanche*, respectively). And finally the high integrity and commitment of film-makers such as Amar Kanwar and Trinh T. Minh-Ha. But this is just scratching the surface.

AJ: What modes of live art practice have inspired/interested you?

SD: Two examples really stick out, the first is Hayley Newman's *Crying Glasses* 1998, the documentation of which made such a profound impression on me when I first encountered it that it is still with me today. I'm still not exactly clear on how staged this was, and whether it was just staged for the camera, or extended at all beyond it, and it is this play on constructedness that fascinates me within the work. The work itself, or what it proposes, is quite simple: a special pair of sunglasses that emit tears, to test the reactions of a jaded public on the London underground network.

The other example would be the work of the Living Theatre, particularly in their heyday in the 1970s. Again I love the received mythos – the idea of invading the everyday experience of your audience, following them home, forcing an awareness of the performed nature of our every little action. And again the documentation of their performances at the Venice Biennale in the 1970s (*Six Public Actions to Turn Violence into Concord*, 1975) are remarkable, and also remarkably filmic, albeit consisting merely of still images – they make me want to see the rest of the film that doesn't exist, for me the ultimate achievement of good documentation. The whole piece looking like some crazy, performative political rally with a cast of thousands, and the Living Theatre regulars, right in the middle of it, writhing about, haranguing audiences via microphones – it just looks like sheer madness, and there's something really liberating about that. Call me an enthusiast, but I just love that scale of activating people and place – the results can't help but be spectacular, looking like the set of some crazy psychedelic protest film, of which only fragments remain. Particularly if one is considering the shift outlined previously between generations of artists, the Living Theatre in a way provide the missing link. Although perhaps more concerned with authenticity and immediacy than a lot of their contemporaries, the results end up so burlesque and public that one can't help think of Fellini's *Roma* (1972).

AJ: What is your relationship to history? Do you think about how your work relates to the past and how or whether it will be viewed in the future?

SD: I like to think it will be viewed in the future, and mythologized in some way – at least that is my hope and intention. It might sound a bit romantic, but it is that historicizing function of performance, and the documentation thereof, which has always attracted me, and something I definitely play with in relation to previous performance texts I am referencing. At the same time I wouldn't want to limit the spheres within which my work might be written, equally happy between the fields of art, film, and performance discourse. And to be honest it is the slippage between them that interests me, rather than one specific field of endeavor. Performance didn't use to have this separate function, which although I am in favor of live art getting a greater degree of recognition, I also saw it as a subversive strength of the performative.

AJ: Is the body more than representation? Is it always representational? How does the body (yours; that of the actor; that of the viewer) function in your work?

SD: As a cipher. A cipher for meaning, which in itself is an empty signifier. Hence my choice to try to work with people I know, or other artists, so that their personalities/ practices bring something to bear on these soulless machines of documentation such as the camera! Ha ha! In a way that's a bit dramatic, but it is important when setting up a piece of work that one considers the function of documenting it; a lens is pretty neutral, so what is it you are recording, and how and why? What level of mediation are you intending, as this will be important to know from the outset (e.g. the editing of performance footage into a secondary text, such as a film, with its own duration and narrative).

Hence also my interest at other times to work with actors/ models, to play with and highlight their function as ciphers, that is, that an actor or model is in a way a "professional cipher," as their function is to take on a meaning prescribed for them as a form of method and exchange. And then set this against someone whose function

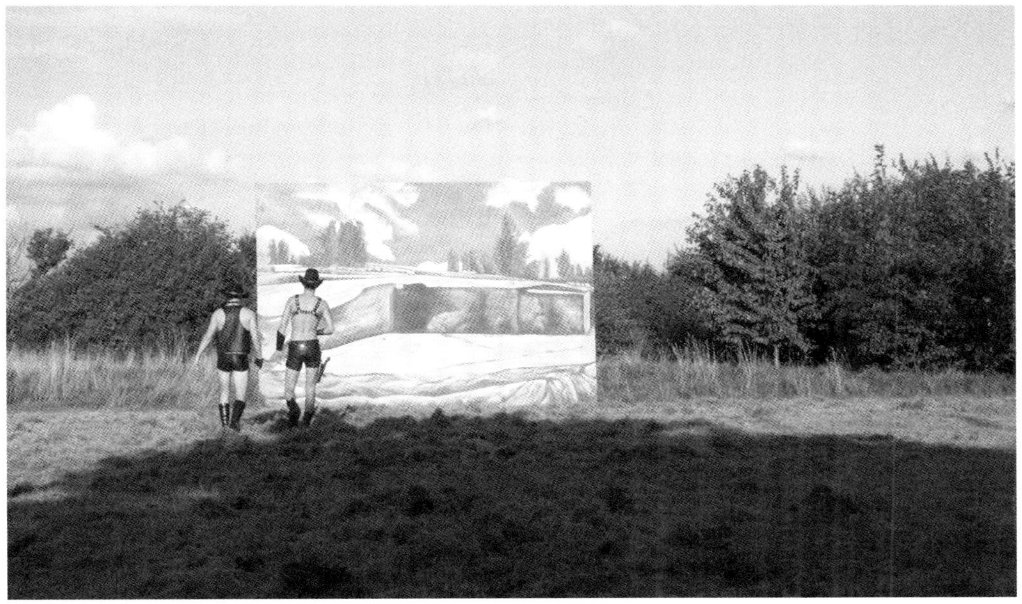

Shezad Dawood, *Feature* (Production Still), 2008, from Super 16mm and HD, 55 mins. Courtesy of the Artist and Paradise Row, London.

is very much their self-image/projection, that is, an artist, who when playing a role is always going to be in tension with the role they are already playing in the art world, and you have an interesting mapping of how these different bodies can function. Which is obviously an oversimplification, as there is a whole range of possibilities depending on the individual personalities involved, but you get the idea.

AJ: How do you view your relationship to your audience members? Are you concerned about what is said/written about your work and how it might be exhibited later? Do you try to influence what is said?

SD: No I think that is a losing battle. And whereas I think making art is something of a losing battle, it has a bit more nobility if you don't try to affect the outcome.

AJ: How do you see your work relating to conventional models of understanding artistic authorship, particularly in the art world today where artists (whether living or not) are still often referred back to as guarantors of the works' meaning and value?

SD: The paradox for me is that the use of my body, far from positioning me as somehow a predictable or knowable source for the works' meaning, denotes a kind of absence, or the impossibility of reading me as fixed. This floating signifier/author is something I try to highlight through the necessarily collaborative aspects of most of my projects. And the fact that perhaps I have never felt fixed, in terms of my allegiances, nationhood, personality etc. is linked to this strategy. I find that quest for security/fixity in art history and art criticism a bit conservative, and a bit disappointing.

Without giving too much away, this strategy is also prefigured in the intuitive jumps I make between projects, and the constantly self-critical shifts I make in the intentions and thoughts behind them. Hopefully this is a way to keep the practice fresh, and asking necessary questions of the world and of the practice itself.

AJ: Can we talk briefly about your relationship to identity politics, extending earlier discussions we've had in Manchester and London? What is your sense of where you fit in relation to identity politics and to the performative works pivoting around identity in the 1970s and 1980s? In interviews and our discussions you have resisted personal connections yet admitted that a lot of how the British and European art markets position your work has to do with the perception of you as a "hot," "young," British South-Asian etc. Can you expand on this?

You have also described to me your interest in "finding a way to make the subject remain elusive," and linked this to your distrust of identity politics; but then you also described your interest in the *Make it Big* project in reversing the masculine/feminine, Occident/Orient relation. How does this all fit together?

SD: Ha ha, yeah it's a difficult game to play. I just hate the fact that lots of well-meaning people would like me to be defined solely within some kind of South Asian conurbation. As if that nice cohesion exists even in South Asia. It is simplistic and ignorant, but it seems a lot of people feel it is a necessary stage to pass through on the way to enlightenment. Hence my desire to keep the subject elusive. It's unfortunate to have to play this game of double-bluff, in order to make people aware of the reductive nature of their gaze, but then it does keep me on my toes and my practice continually changing.

And I think it makes for a more complex reading of the work, say in *Make It Big*, alluding to the performance, of which the documentation is the representation of the fabrication central to the performance. In this case the hoax remaking of an Antonioni film in Pakistan was actually a myth played out on those who performed within it, thereby doubling the prurient gaze of the viewer, above and beyond the masculine/ feminine relationship within the piece. And making my position even more untenable within an ethics of art making, in that the piece overtly foregrounds the exploitation and exoticizing that so often underlies the making and viewing of art, historically in its traffic between peripheries and centers.

AJ: We've talked also about whether or not your work creates friction in the art system. How does your relationship to the "institution" (whether it be the art market or the real estate market) differ from that of artists in 1970s, 1980s, 1990s? If those artists took an oppositional stance to the market (at least in the 1970s), do artists of your generation take more of a networked approach relating to the logic of the Internet?

SD: More of a self-destructive rhizomatic axis!

Ha ha, sorry couldn't resist that as a rejoinder to our previous conversation. Friction I hope so; contradiction inevitably.

I think I create a certain sense of distrust, playing with notions of capital and real estate, in relation to a critical, somewhat politicized practice. Almost as if these elements should be mutually exclusive. I kind of see this paradox as a parallel to organic fruit and vegetables in supermarkets that come from countries hundreds of miles away and therefore have a far worse environmental footprint when you consider the impact on both the transport of the goods, and their eventual quality. It's a no-brainer: If you don't address honestly and critically the representational regime within which you exist, you are building ivory towers.

I guess for me I can't help but see the interconnectedness of dialogues around identity, history, real estate, and global capital. And their functions as modes of social control – and by extension their philosophical underpinnings (in notions such as the absolutism of linear time or the inherent worthiness of vertical integration) as presenting no possibility for dissent. I try to enact this within my work, even if it means going against the grain of notional dissent, and its often worthy approaches to identity management, and the policing of gender or other kinds of otherness. By these worthy approaches I mean any number of propositions that seek to promote art or artists from a particular breed, but can't fail to get trapped in positive discrimination: that is, promoting video art from Uzbekistan, or by five hermaphrodites from Scandinavia. If the work is good it should be shown, and not relativized, otherwise I see little difference from a colonial gathering of trinkets, and we all know there's blood underlying those stories. For me I don't mind having a go, trying to make intuitive leaps and connections between places, maybe this makes my practice a bit unwieldy, and confusing to some – for example the fact that I might be re-staging *Blow Up* in Pakistan one year, and then working with western re-enactors in Cambridgeshire in another,[2] are equal and horizontal acts of translation to me, and fall within my scope as an artist.

Notes

1. See Amelia Jones, "Seeing Differently: The Subject of Viewing in Antonioni's *Blow Up*" (1966) versus Shezad Dawood's *Make It Big* (2005)," *Journal of Visual Culture*, August 2008, vol. 7, no. 2, pp. 181–203.
2. *Feature* was presented in the following exhibitions in the UK, 2008: Feature – Archaeology: Leeds Met Gallery, Leeds, 20 June–13 July 2008; Feature – Image: Castlefield Gallery, Manchester, 7 August–21 September 2008; Feature – Architecture: Eastside Projects, Birmingham, 6 December 2008–31 January 2009.

Chapter 38

Do it Again, Do it Again (Turn Around, Go Back)

Iain Forsyth and Jane Pollard, with Andrew Renton

Andrew Renton: I'd like to start by talking about the idea of witnessing: one of the things that you are trying to solicit is the different stages of witnessing. I think that in terms of your reference points, collective ownership is important. It's like the performances belong to each one of us. Our favorite pop songs belong to all of us; they deliver a whole series of different experiences in different ways to different people but somehow there is a shared ownership. It's not just to do with distribution but also to do with the effect they have on us.

And so your performances, in a sense, cut across that and they set up this second act of witnessing. A kind of re-witnessing, of something that's already mythologized, un-witnessed except by the lucky few. So, "un-witnessable." In fact, if you had witnessed it, you wouldn't have known you were witnessing it because you wouldn't have known its significance. Even when Bowie says, "this is the last show we'll ever do" you wouldn't have got it at that moment. Most of us got that one only a few days later when it was printed up in *NME* (*New Musical Express*), and then you realized the significance of it.

So, this idea of witnessing and really re-entering these immovable building blocks of the culture that we value – that, for me, is what these performances do. They cut cross something we all own and that produces another interesting problem, which is, where does your work reside? Whose work is it? Who owns this chain of referral?

The reason why you make these performances might be to get a grip on the previous work. A somehow, dare I say, Kantian ownership of the previous work. So it is slippery. If your work is about getting a grip on this nostalgic moment, and nostalgia is the word I want to really talk about, then it is very hard to pinpoint exactly what your work is.

I can say in formal terms, "Ah, there's a reconstruction of an event." There's an attempt to create something, with as much veracity as possible, but all the time we know that it is a reconstruction, all the time we know and we cannot totally immerse ourselves in it unless we are somehow connecting back. And then maybe a miniscule percentage of each of those audiences can say, "Ah, I was there … and I'm here." Even that double witnessing interestingly enough does not authenticate. It parodies something else. "I was there then, and I am here now," produces what you might call a cognitive dissonance. It's not quite what it was but it's exactly the same.

What you're doing in each of these performances is related to music. I've been trying to figure this out in relation to visual art; why I see your work as very much within the visual realm. This thing called nostalgia really brings things up for us in terms of how we understand works of art, because it never lets us read an object formally, neutrally, objectively. This consideration will always be colored, affected by our relationship to it: nostalgia. Now, nostalgia is a misnomer, but it's the only word I can come up with. I think of nostalgia not in terms of something deep in the past, but I think of it in the all-but-present. I think of nostalgia as a microsecond lagging behind the present and as something that music alone can articulate effectively. Because I get a sense that when one listens to a song for the first time, not for the second, but the first, one is already nostalgic for it. That is to say you place things upon music and they get embedded into the songs: they are about you and the moment you experience them. By the time Kylie has gone, "La la la, la la la la la," you're in, and you remember that moment. The experience is formative and totally embedded in your or anyone's version of that song. These performances articulate the embedding of ourselves into these objects of contemplation – either a piece of music or a work of art – and you can never separate yourself, or be objective, once you are bound up.

Instant nostalgia: that's what I would call it. When you hear a song you are instantly implicating various versions and intensities of this. So you get push-pulls going on. There are a few examples of this; here is the classic one: you go on holiday and as you're checking into a hotel you're standing in the lobby and there's a woman in front of you looking at the computer, looking up your name. You look around. What you do at that moment is tune yourself in. You're spending five hundred quid and you want to know that this week is going to be great. So you take it all in. There is a sofa. There is a palm tree. There is muzak going on in the background. A table over there, and so on … Then she says, "Oh yes, here is your room," and then gives you the key. A week later you've come back to check out, and as they make up your bill you look around again and everything is in exactly that same place as it was a week ago. But it looks completely different.

So we've got this complication – the sofa, the palm tree, the table – if you got out a ruler and measured them everything would be exactly the same, and yet they look different. They look different because of your familiarity with your surroundings. Philosophers and scientists have never figured it out. The only philosopher who came close was Bergson because he said that matter is affected by memory. I think our relationship to the work of art is constantly moving backwards and forwards: this is the bit I am intrigued by. Our experience of the object is never unencumbered.

I remember the conversation we had several years ago about *File under Sacred Music*, your re-enactment of The Cramps performing at Napa State Mental Institute. And I've just realized that the thing I envy here in your studio is something that I took out of my life several years ago, and now I mourn it: my copy of David Bowie's *The Rise and Fall of Ziggy Stardust*, with the original scratches. Of course I now have a digital version of it, but it's not my version of the original vinyl. Playing it was never an unencumbered act of listening, but a psychologically charged act of listening, because the crackles and the physicality of the object interfered with my listening: that's what made it mine. Technology is obsessed with clearing away all of that materiality. In contemporary culture we haven't begun to think of the consequences of all of our offloading of materiality.

Jane Pollard: I remember you talking to us about the "hotel experience," and it's something that we've come back to repeatedly. It's an exercise in thinking how the mind reinterprets a situation or an experience. The "lobby" too is a wonderful metaphorical space. Every time you pass through this incredibly anonymous space, it changes. It changes because you change. It's the same as that act of listening. In the process of listening, the mind changes. As you listen to a song, especially "popular" songs, as they tend to be structured with repetition, you understand their structure almost immediately. We know they will have an introduction, verse, chorus, verse, etc. We pretty much know how the song is going to flow – so much so that by the time the chorus comes back in for the second or third time we are able to preempt it and sing along or hum the melody. And in this sense of brain programming there's also a change.

Iain Forsyth: the most perfect example of this for me is "Jesus' Blood Never Failed Me Yet" by Gavin Bryars. Because of its remarkable length, and because the actual recording of the tramp singing doesn't change, the music just swells and effects you, so much so that you feel like the singing has changed, but it hasn't. There's something else going on. Your mind hears it differently. The intonation changes, the speed warps, but in actuality it stays the same. For me, this is such an incredibly powerful passage of music because of this physiological thing that occurs to you as you listen to it. It's similar to the track "Slow" by My Bloody Valentine, which must be the only piece of recorded music that does, I swear, actually slow down time.

AR: So how do you see these ideas relating to your own performance work?

JP: Well, our very first live project was *The World Won't Listen* in 1996, when we placed a Smiths tribute band in a gallery in East London. There was something of this thinking in our naïve undeveloped brains when we saw the band at The Venue in New Cross, near where we went to college at Goldsmiths. We only went to see them because we thought it was a bit odd.

IF: At that time there weren't really tribute bands in the same way there are now. There were a handful of more theater-based acts that toured, but they were very mainstream, just bands like the Doors, Abba, the Beatles and the Stones. The Smiths just didn't fit in there at all.

AR: The Smiths were the antithesis of that. In theory they were not going to be fetishized, but of course the irony is that they ended up being exactly that. I remember going past Morrissey's house when he lived in Camden and there were always people who looked like Morrissey sitting outside. It used to torture him: he really hated it. I remember going there with Linder Sterling and she

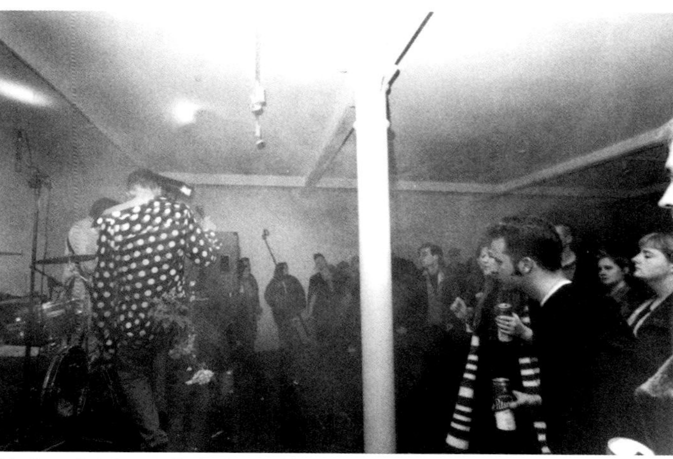

Iain Forsyth & Jane Pollard, *The World Won't Listen*, production still (Underwood Street, London, 1996). Photographer credit: Arnold Bogerth. Image courtesy of the artists and Kate MacGarry, London.

The World Won't Listen

Critic David Barrett recalls attending Forsyth Pollard's first live art event staged on 22 November at 30 Underwood Street, London N1. It was also first experiment with the diametric status of the "tr band." The event, described by Barrett as a "mock took as its starting point the music and legacy of Smiths, one of the most revered English bands o 1980s, and included a live performance by The Stil

There was clearly something unusual going o wasn't uncommon for groups of East-End art t to arrive for an exhibition opening at Underw Street, a low-rent exhibition space beneath a ric set of workshops and artist studios. But it was ra find an equally sized group of die-hard Smiths here. Which is not to say the art crowd weren't Smiths fans – many of them would be – it's just they weren't all dressed as Morrissey. The Smiths were. All of them.

The crowd arrived at seven. I make my downstairs. You can buy a can of beer. You can We all stand about. The space makes no pretens to being a music venue; it is demonstrably an ar run gallery space. White walls, concrete floor, wh painted iron columns, tracklighting with mini s – the usual elements. No high-wattage lamps, black backdrop, no theatricality, no dressing ro off behind the wings. There is a stage, but it is low doesn't create any real barrier. Nobody quite kn what to make of it all. For the bemused art cro their familiar environment has become unheimli literally "unhomely" – with the introduction of t überfans, who, in turn, are gathered in prote knots, and are perhaps as at home here as anyw (or not; they are a proudly self-conscious and il ease set).

It is cold outside, a November night, uncomfortably sticky in the basement. Not happens for a long time, just a crowd and a sh sense of dislocation. Usually art events are opposite of gigs: a trial of patience while th happening, rather than while you wait.

The band arrives at nine. They just walk thro the crowd from the back, get up on stage, Instantly, this is a full on Smiths concert. Half crowd are dancing, devotedly lost in the music. M of us know every word to every song, but some torn between the rapturous pleasure of the music, and the dispassionate, cerebral apprecia of a knowing, layered artwork. This isn't a gig, ar isn't a gig crowd. It is an artwork: the band mem are props, the crowd extras. A night of awkw delicious uncertainty.

was standing there as all these little Mozzers were sat on the ground next to the door asking, "Is Morrissey in? Is Morrissey in?"

You can say imitation is a form of flattery. With the tribute bands of course they only really work on the basis of them being bands on that superstar level. Did you resent the Smiths tribute band because it "de-cooled" them? It's fine to have an Abba tribute band, But somehow the Smiths held something sacred?

: On a purely personal level it represented something that I could completely understand, but at the same time I have never been one of those really obsessed Smiths fans. When I was at school you could either be into The Smiths or The Cure – you had to go one way or the other. A sort of Beatles or the Stones thing, and I went with The Cure. That cut me off from the Morrissey obsession. I didn't feel defiled in some way by seeing a guy on stage pretending to be Morrissey. Had it been a Cure tribute band I probably wouldn't have wanted to go, it would have messed with a deeper meaning for me.

: That "push-pull" was right in the middle of the experience. I also didn't feel possessiveness over The Smiths. My best friends' older sister had been obsessed with them and Billy Bragg, so I always saw them as quite romantic. And on the other side, it was a tribute band, which was totally uncool. We did and still do go to a lot of gigs together, but we would never have thought of going to see a tribute band; it was right on our doorstep, so we went. I remember feeling that I was witnessing it and attempting to understand it at the same time. I also remember we stood at the bar, to the side of the venue, not getting involved with the crowd, we just stood there trying to figure it out. Really watching: the band, the audience and this kind of past–present oscillation, which is still difficult to articulate.

R: I guess most other tribute bands then would have been closer to what you would perceive a tribute band

Eventually, the band members conclude their set. They leave the stage, walk through the crowd once more. Morrissey passes right by me. This is what sticks in my mind most vividly. I want to reach out to touch him, just to say that I have. But self-consciousness prevents the contact; in galleries, you don't touch. I immediately regret my inaction, wish I had reached out a hand. Curse my hesitancy, my diffidence. From that moment, my overriding memory is not of the musical performance, nor of the displaced fans, but of not touching someone who wasn't Morrissey, and rueing it. There remains of the evening a lingering sense of regret, which I know is absurd, but this feeling has outlasted the gallery and the century – and what could be more authentically Smiths than that?

David Barrett

to be: nostalgic bands from a past era. Our culture is wound up in a tightening coil: it revisits itself much more quickly. And then we have something else that we've not witnessed before: rock stars over sixty-five. You don't need a David Bowie tribute band because he is his own tribute band. David Bowie is the pastiche of David Bowie. I saw him a few years ago and it was an excruciating experience. He's on stage and says, "This one's from my new album," and everyone over forty in the audience groans. Then he says, "This one's from the

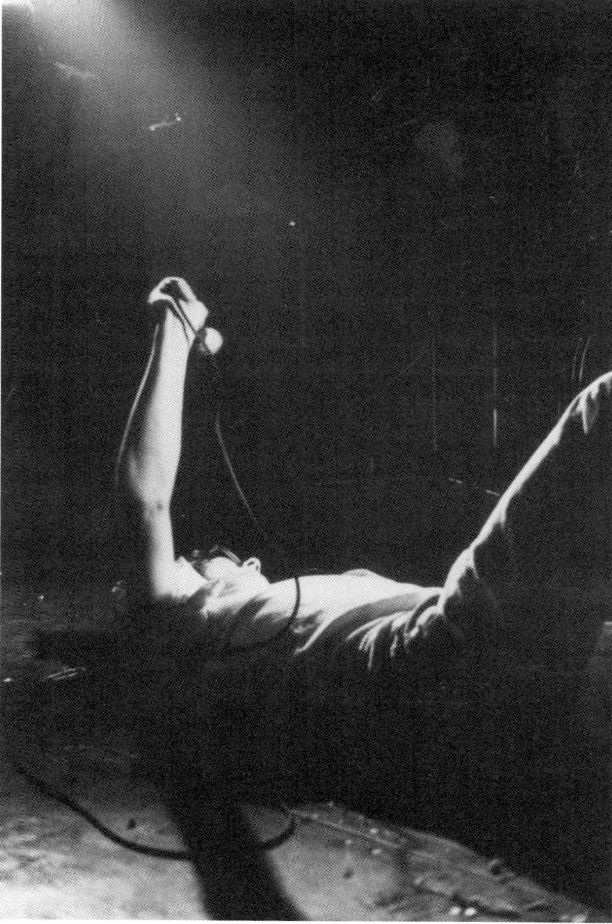

Iain Forsyth & Jane Pollard, *The Smiths is dead*, production still (ICA, London, 1997). Image courtesy of the artists and Kate MacGarry, London.

The Smiths is dead

Vivienne Gaskin is a contemporary artist's agent, consultant, and curator. In 1997 she commissioned Forsyth and Pollard's third live art project, the first o a series of projects she would go on to present with th artists at the ICA, London. Building on The World Won't Listen *and taking place on 1 August exactly ten years after The Smiths had split-up, Forsyth and Pollard engineered this to be the last ever performan by The Still Ills.*

My memories of *The Smiths is dead* are quite vivid. There was a lot riding on this project as Iain, Jane, and myself were in many ways enacting ideas above our station. They were fairly fresh from Goldsmiths and I had a largely self-appointed title of "bar event manager" at the ICA, London.

I had read in *Frieze* about the duo presenting a similar project in an event space in East London. Th review was brief but succinct, the project involved presenting a found Smiths tribute band not as a pastiche but as a cultural cipher connecting past wit present. I was both intrigued and a Smiths fan. On o first meeting Iain and Jane explained in detail what they sought to achieve in that event and that in man ways the experiment had failed. What soon emerged was that the aim of the project was a re-enactment, a replication of a moment which resides somewhere between historical fact and a communal cultural memory. This project appealed to me on two very clear levels: a love of pop and its relevance to those who loved pop.

The process of developing the project was unexpectedly intense. It involved two meetings a week stretching to daily meetings in the run up where Iain and Jane armed with a clipboard of questions and action points raked through the minutia of what was needed to create this event. The night was to be staged on the somewhat tenuous anniversary of 10 years since the split of The Smiths. Its intention was to present the only known Smith tribute act – The Still Ills – as convincingly authentic as the originals. This nigh was for the fans, yet presented in the sacred halls of the art world, tribute became simulacrum and the art world voyeurs dutifully filled the safe hav of the back rows.

In the process of creating this project, unwitting the core "rules" of what has become the cultural genre of "re-enactment" were sketched out. It was agreed that no trace of "the original" was to be present – no film clips, photos, press clips, etc. The desire was that for the time and space of the event early seventies," and they all cheer. The whole audience knew every word to every song up until 1978.

: We quite quickly turned our back on tribute bands as subject matter. In themselves they didn't interest us, it was simply that act of a person enacting or re-enacting something. There is a detachment between the role and the person, and a collapse of those two things. Often this period of our work is talked about as being about fans or fandom. For us, it was not that. We were looking at this experience and this psychological maneuver when reaching something familiar. The subject matter leads you to think that this is an act of being a fan. But that was only ever tangential to what really got us fired up: to try to make work as powerful as the gigs we were going to. We wanted more freedom, which working with music would allow, but we wanted to have the potency, the effect, the directness of that experience. Taking that physiological playground was where we could begin to find a way of working that worked.

: I think in terms of the wider context it's also important to understand that when we left college it really did feel like an extremely dull time to be an artist. Especially coming out of Goldsmiths in the mid-1990s, there was a huge weight of history, with everyone hoping to catch a bit of stardust in Damien Hirst's vapor trail.

R: So the solution that you tentatively reached is centered on a very unstable object. You were producing work that was all about the instability of representations. If art is about the history of representations or about making visible the things in the world which may not have been visible otherwise, your representation is extremely problematic, because it signals something else. You can't really put your finger on what it is that you have constructed, and because you're not fetishizing, you're not celebrating the "holy relic," your relation to those moments or objects is ambiguous. It produces an unstable ambiguous thing, the spectators don't know what to think, where to put themselves, how much to

this was "The original," "The memory" and "The reality."

And so on a break even budget of £1,600, with vats of cheap sunflowers from the local florist (Gladioli were out of season alas), a one-night-only cocktail "The Oscillate Wildly" on sale at the bar and adapted versions of the album sleeves as backdrops, the doors opened for the event *The Smiths is dead* on 1 August 1997.

Anticipating a modest turn out, the fortunes of the night were quickly upturned as the sight of swathes of Morrissey look-a-likes began a parade down The Mall toward the ICA, surely a performance in itself? It was clear that the event was selling out. As the first tunes were played, the sight of dejected impersonators sat in silence in the bar prompted within me a moment of rebellion as I passed them through security and into the theater space. Throwing the critical and thoughtful to one side they swelled the front rows as a five deep wave of quiffs jostled to rip at the shirt of The Still Ills lead singer (a builder from Birmingham by day I recall?)

By the last few numbers a certain magic had taken hold of the audience. Those at the rear were no longer pondering on the cultural attributes of the event but joining the general fray. Meanwhile those at the front had taken hold of the stage, lurching for the touch of the band and hugging the security guards. The re-enactment's ability to engender a suspension of disbelief in the audience has been exhaustively debated. In the case of *The Smiths is dead* I would question if this had not already taken place in the minds of the mass of the audience long before the doors opened. This night however held a certain magic for me. Art felt relevant, instant and had impact. Art felt okay for the likes of me and them; we weren't simply the right audience – as the audience we were the main conduits of the event.

In comparison with the following three much larger scale re-enactments I worked with Iain and Jane on at the ICA over the next eight years, this was in many ways rather rough around the edges, yet it came to form the pro-forma for a generation of artists from Rod Dickenson to Jeremy Deller to explore the possibilities and limitations of this genre and gave the sad lads of Salford a great night out in the process.

Vivienne Gaskin

be inside it and how much to be outside of it. That is what is deeply disturbing about these performances. The viewer is implicated in the work of art in an ethical relationship. The ambiguity of this work is an intriguing counterpoint to what happened in the immediately previous generation. What I like about these works is that they resist their own materiality. The performances are not separate from you. They resist our ability to frame them.

Have you seen the film *Rock Star*? It's a really terrible film…

JP: No I haven't seen it but I remember the trailer.

AR: You have to see it. It's an hour and a half of your life you'll never get back, but the Mark Wahlberg character is the lead singer of a tribute band and the singer in the real band dies or disappears. So the singer of the tribute band ends up being singer of the real band. The whole message is that the authentic experience was when he was in the tribute band. As terrible as the film is, it is interesting because the really authentic moment is the moment of fetishizing that which is already a copy of an original.

IF: The story came from Judas Priest. They replaced their singer with a singer from a tribute band. The original singer Rob Halford left the band and he was then replaced by Tim 'Ripper' Owens who was in a Judas Priest tribute band at the time called British Steel. They seem to have come full circle because I think Rob Halford is now back singing with the band.

AR: Beautiful, beautiful!

JP: I heard a rumor that Kiss were going to do a reality TV series in which they would audition and find replacements for every single member, then the new band would continue to exist as Kiss.

IF: I heard Gene Simmons on the radio describing it as a franchise. He said he could see no reason why there

A Rock 'N' Roll Suicide

Artist Dan Howard-Birt reflects on the cult landscape at the time of A Rock 'N' Roll Suic Forsyth and Pollard's largest live event to be preser at the ICA. The project was developed over eight months, and this was the first time the artists specifically re-enacted a complete performance. original event had taken place at Hammersmith Od in London exactly twenty-five years earlier, w David Bowie performed as Ziggy Stardust for the time, before killing his creation with the words "th the last show we'll ever do."

There once were great cult bands whose mus differences at some point acrimoniously fractu their delicate center leaving them for years i wilderness of solo projects and diminishing crit and financial returns. In the twenty-first century isn't really a problem. Six and sometimes seven fig advances seem to be enough to encourage musici to put aside previous grievances and mount the st once more, united, in order to re-hash career defin moments with all the enthusiasm of a Sun morning spent washing the car.

But the 1990s were a different time. The trib industry was taking off. Pink Floyd-alikes would t the world, tributes to past legends were manif Good, solid gig venues around the country wo start to replace new band nights with Oasisn't, Cured and Who's Who, and of course *Stars in Th Eyes* was fast becoming a Saturday evening televis staple.

These live events back then were p pantomime, part greatest hits tape. I went o or twice, reluctantly, though hoping to h favorite songs once more in that awkwa sweaty, adolescent crucible of the gig. I always disappointed. What these events in fact seemed offer was the spectacle of some normal guy (j like you and I) hamming the cherished words "lo love will tear us apart …"

A Rock 'N' Roll Suicide happened right at center of this particular time of camp nostalgia a indulged ordinariness, and from this distance co be seen as its very quintessence. Only it wasn't.

What set this event apart wasn't the fact tha happened at London's ICA, the home of measu knowingness, nor, as Nick Coleman in *Independent* reported, "because it was Art." W distinguished this night was the desire to recre not a band, or an album, or period, but an even single evening in 1973. And the fact that this, uncelebrated, evening was itself a complex ficti

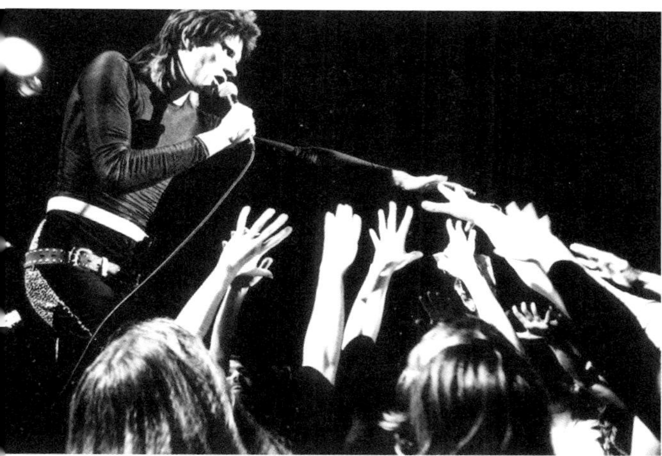

ı Forsyth & Jane Pollard, *A Rock'N'Roll Suicide*, production still (ICA, London, 1998). otographer credit: David Cowlard. Image courtesy of the artists and Kate MacGarry, ıdon.

couldn't be twelve authorized versions of Kiss touring at the same time. The fantastic thing is that you still don't have to do away with tribute bands: you could have twelve official Kiss bands touring as well as all of these Kiss tribute bands.

R: Which is phenomenal. I mean, what helps us here with that experience is that because Gene Simmons says, "This is the authentic," he's recognizing that the authenticity of the thing resides in a place where you may not think it does. Kiss can do that because they work through a rule of disguise.

': Which is exactly what drew us to Ziggy Stardust for *A Rock 'N' Roll Suicide.*

': Because there was a characterization – Ziggy rather than David – it felt like at least on some level it was possible for somebody else to play the character. In fact during the several months of research we did for the project I remember finding an interview from the 1970s in which Bowie talks excitedly about how he conceived Ziggy as a character who could have been played by other people.

meant that the fastidiousness evident in every detail, served to add precarious storeys to this already elusive edifice.

The small theater was a sell-out, and as Ziggy entered the stage dressed in a metallic blue and red cape accompanied by his Spiders From Mars, and launched into "Hang Onto Yourself," a fragile crystallization occurred; the exotic look, the nonchalantly affected movements, the surge of the first chords.

Twenty-five years ago to the day, Bowie had used the Hammersmith concert to loose himself from his strange creation Ziggy Stardust. Ziggy was more than a mask and an elaborate wardrobe, to be put on and taken off at will and yet he is less than a man, and this strange and potent specter was incarnate once more before us on the stage of the ICA in July 1998. Ziggy Stardust and the Spiders From Mars is a peculiar proposition, and inevitably there were a few minutes of incredulous disconnection evident within the massed audience. My own self-consciousness was overcome as helpless grins began to break the poised faces around me and the crowd began the small appreciative and inclusive movements that bond such a group of strangers.

As the set list moved through "Moonage Daydream," "Space Oddity," the stark "My Death," and "Cracked Actor," and Ziggy's attire was again and again changed from crouch length white kimono, to one-armed-and-one-legged knitted leotard, to see-through gauze top and sequinned trousers, the crowd became more animated and involved. A tangible sense of being present within a particular place while this baroque spectacle, rich and excessive with every new turn, unfolded grew and the evening palpably assumed the status of an historic moment.

The performance ended, as all Bowie fans present knew it would, with the mortal utterance "this is the last show we'll ever do" and the dying strains of "Rock 'n' Roll Suicide." And then it was over; the audience shuffled out from the theater, onto the street; then into bars or tube stations; and then homes, and Ziggy disappeared again into pop mythology, only now his myth carries a strange and unaccountable afterglow witnessed by a mere few hundred.

Dan Howard-Birt

JP: The distance allowed our performer to take possession of that character. He became an authentic act amidst the inauthentic act of pretending to be Bowie by following literally his every move and note.

IF: The character, and the entire original show became a script or a text: essentially something we could analyze and he could learn to perform in the same way.

AR: There's always going to be authenticity, simultaneously to the inauthentic, or the reproduced, or the depicted, or copy, or clone. There's always going to be a layer of authenticity.

JP: It's funny: that work was the first time we got a huge amount of feedback. We got lots of letters after the event, people saying they hadn't really "got it" until a few days afterwards. This goes back to what we were talking about with new experiences. Often it seemed to take something like reading a review or talking to someone else about it, that act of digesting what happened allows you to understand it. I think it has always been our expectation that you should be able to experience our work in the present moment. The analysis comes later, either a few days later or in a split moment, but the first experience is emotional not analytical. When you look at a picture or a photograph, a sculpture or an installation, your very first response should not be a psychological mess, pulling your head in different directions. That might happen a moment later, of course, as you're starting to walk away from the gallery and thinking about what to say to your friends.

AR: It's usually only when you start to walk away that it makes sense, because when you are standing in front of it you don't know what to think. That's what the work of art is about today. Art is no longer didactic and moralizing. The point of art today is that you don't know what to think, and the ethical encounter with the work of art is that moment when you are trying to figure out where you stand in relation to it but you can't compute it. The only way you really can compute it is with the re-encounter.

I just noticed on your shelf the book about Ian Curtis that his wife wrote. Then I thought about the film *Control*, which also in a way solved some of these problems. It could have gone all sorts of different ways. They actually performed the songs rather than miming to original recordings: it was courageous to do that. They didn't sound like any of the recordings we have, but it felt like what it felt like then. You start to see a really interesting scenario where a reconstruction can be more authentic than the original.

JP: Here we get to The Cramps. We really grappled with the change between the sort of work we had been making such as *A Rock 'N' Roll Suicide*, and the transition into *File under Sacred Music*.

: I think when we made *A Rock 'N' Roll Suicide* we were essentially putting together a tribute band. Because we didn't work with an existing band, which tend to come from groups of friends playing together, we had the luxury of picking from all over the place. We auditioned endless potential Ziggys and handpicked the band. We had some beautiful moments. Finding a piano player had been really problematic – on that tour Bowie worked with Mike Garson, who was this fabulous off-kilter avant-garde influence on the shows. Someone else just replaying the same notes would have done nothing to capture the spirit of the performance, of what Garson actually brought to the stage. We were lucky to be able to get Tom Cawley, a pianist who had just won Young Jazz Musician of the Year. He'd never played in a rock band and couldn't believe that he was allowed to have a pint and a cigarette during rehearsals! That said, he would rarely turn up to the rehearsals, but he had this incredibly intuitive approach to performing with the band and he just got it. He was an extraordinary influence on the rest of the band, who were all coming from a "rock" background. Tom, in a way, was our Mike Garson.

: Of course we were aiming for a visual similarity as well as a sonic one. Casting the band, and Ziggy in

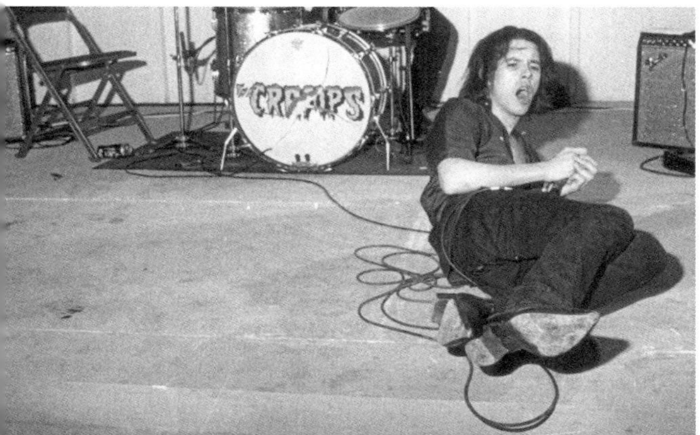

a Forsyth & Jane Pollard, *File under Sacred Music*, production still (video with sound, nins, 2003). Photographer credit: Claire Norman. Image courtesy of the artists and Kate cGarry, London.

File under Sacred Music

Writer and artist Tom McCarthy was one of a small group of writers invited to attend the closed-set where Forsyth and Pollard were filming their first "video re-enactment." Constructed inside the ICA theater in London the set mirrored the Napa State Mental Institute where The Cramps had performed for the patients in 1978. Exactly 25 years later a band of garage-punk luminaries put together by the artists performed for the camera in front of an audience made up of users and survivors of the UK psychiatric care system.

Before the gig began Jane strolled onto the stage to thank people for coming and to explain that the event was a re-enactment but they should feel free to express themselves as the mood took them – which, of course, is what the Napa crowd had been doing. Then she stepped down and the band came on. As soon as they started playing the audience, effectively, split into two sections: the mental health patients and carers occupied the main floor, bobbing and dancing, while the ICA staff, film crew, and art journalists kept further back. There wasn't a concrete border between the two groups, but what border there was pretty much coincided with the sweep-range of the video camera, whose operator acted on instructions relayed to him through a set of headphones by the director of photography, who was counting the shots off against a carefully time-coded transcription of the original. "Zoom in on drums – two, three, four – and jerk back, across to stage left – one, two, three – go out of focus and then – four, five – up and in on Lux Interior's face." Lux Interior, meanwhile, re-enacted Lux Interior, worked his way through the play list, panting and yelping: "I see you on my TV set! I hear you on my radio!" I can confidently write, just like some awe-struck if verbally ungifted rock critic, that the words seemed to flow not from him but rather through his mouth from somewhere else.

Lux Interior, it must be said, was very good. The whole band were. This isn't just some vacuous compliment: it made a huge difference to the event. I'd seen the Napa video, and knew that this was meant to happen at this moment. "We heard you people were all crazy, but I'm not so sure about that!" said Lux Interior, also bang on cue.

The re-enacted Cramps kicked off again, with the same set. This time round, waves of recognition rippled through the audience; we were already part of a fraternity. "We heard you people were all crazy, but I'm not so sure about that!" said Lux Interior again, again-again. The Cramps played even better than the first time, and the crowd went wild.

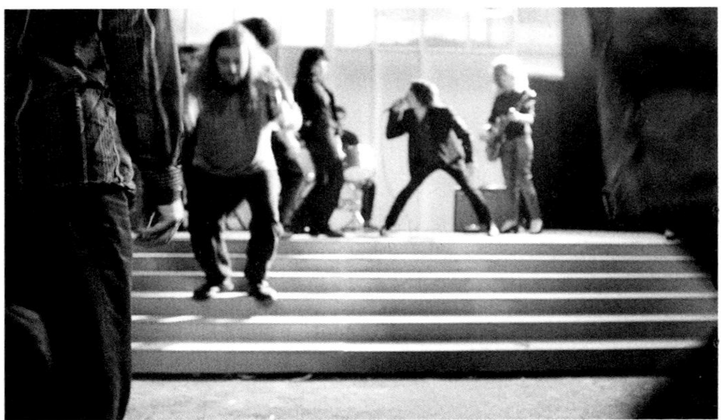

Iain Forsyth & Jane Pollard, *File under Sacred Music*, production still (video with sound, 22mins, 2003). Photographer credit: Claire Norman. Image courtesy of the artists and Kate MacGarry, London.

particular, we wanted someone who looked very authentic, who had the same characteristics. Steve Harvey, who eventually played the part, was very similar physically – his height was right, and his weight was identical to Bowie's when he was 26. While looking and sounding right remained important, the big shift for us into *File under Sacred Music* was that we now understood that we also needed people who felt right. Our performers needed to have the right attitude to not only recreate the look and sound of the original text, but also the spirit.

AR: When we look at things the act of looking is also the act of unseeing. We choose to overlook and to not worry about certain things so that we can engage on some level.

JP: In this context, I think the word spirit is to do with context. You intend to do something in a certain way and in doing so you imbue a spirit into it. It became incredibly important to us to find people to work with who understood this. The performers we worked with for *File under Sacred Music* were already established and respected musicians. They were able to follow our script but at the same time be utterly spontaneous and react to whatever happened on the day in a genuine way.

I'd talked to Iain and Jane before about the sta
of the copy both in art and in experience, and
relation to the notion of authenticity. We'd agreed t
copies never reproduce originals completely. "T
shortfall is where the real emerges," they had sa
"where understanding can begin," demonstrating
perfect comprehension of the secret all real arti
come to know: good art always, at some level, fails.
Iain and Jane's position is simple: they
activating an event-field, and activating with i
whole set of aesthetic, discursive, ethical, ideologi
and you-name-it fields as well. They make no atten
to "work through" or "resolve" these fields, and ev
less of an attempt at "therapy" or "cure." "We're
interested in foisting on people our own, perso
understanding of the questions our work raises," th
say; "our work replays them as unresolved." Arti
can do this, and should do this, even – especially
when the results are uncomfortable or shocking. I
and Jane are good artists – very good artists, b
sincere and bold. Their work exposes and blo
away the limits of the liberal culture whose Proz
like language they had had to learn to speak in or
to get funding and permission to carry out the w
in the first place. The Cramps re-enactment was
an outreach exercise. Like much good, dynamic
it was concocted from a mixture of generosity a
exploitation, of dark cynicism and extraordin
innocence. Iain and Jane were barely thirty.

Tom McCar

Our audience too: they came from two organizations who work with users and survivors of the psychiatric care system, Core Arts and Mad Pride.

AR: The work of art is obviously no longer something you can direct or stage-manage or art direct, even. You can put in a few parameters but something else happens: the "What if?" scenario.

IF: A friend of ours used to work at the Hacienda back in its heyday. He was also on the set they built for the film *24 Hour Party People*. He told us that they'd managed to construct the set almost perfectly and fill it with familiar faces: the original DJs and clubbers whom he recognized. He said it was completely the same, and completely different. Everything was there, but nothing was there.

AR: There is a limit to how much someone can sustain their role within in this context – it's an example of how pastiche enters into this – the people who took roles in that film could only ever be ironic. Any other way would have meant the authentic reconstruction didn't work.

JP: It also had the perfect operational disguise of Steve Coogan as Tony Wilson. It would have been impossible for another person to step into taking the personality of Tony without irony.

IF: It's impossible. Think about the guy who played Tony in *Control*. It was impossible for him to do that. Like watching Bowie playing Warhol in *Basquiat*. That was like watching Bowie playing someone impersonating Warhol. It doesn't really work.

AR: And of course it's a classic Wilson-ism to have Coogan amplifying himself in that way. That's why it worked. You get this peculiar discrepancy because the film constantly reminds you it's reconstructing something. The real characters keep popping up. Do you remember that weird moment when Howard Devoto pops up in the toilet? He's not playing Howard Devoto, but you can't help going "oh, there's Howard Devoto."

IF: Isn't that the scene where Tony's wife is in a cubicle with someone who is playing Howard Devoto, then Devoto appears as the janitor and says "this never happened." He's essentially in the film to correct the film.

AR: Classic Brecht. If you interrupt the drama to tell the truth that this is a performance you are getting a more authentic performance; the alienation effect, but you're not seduced by the performance.

JP: You are seduced, but you are not tricked. I think you're seduced by the emotion of it. I remember stepping into the audience of *A Rock 'N' Roll Suicide* at the end of the first half. At the end of the last song Bowie plays "My Death" by Jacques Brel, and there was this moment in the original show when he holds back on the last word of the song before the audience fill the space by shouting the word "me" back at him. At the ICA there was a pregnant pause because people wanted to get the timing right. There was a knowledge and familiarity with this participation, and a strange sense of community; everyone knew what was going to happen, utterly acknowledging that this was simply an act of repetition, but they were trying to complete something, and get it "right."

IF: For some people they were also literally creating their own re-enactments. I spoke to one guy afterwards who said he was there in 1973, and he showed me a silk scarf with B-O-W-I-E printed on it. He said, "I was there, this is the scarf I waved at David twenty-five years ago."

AR: They don't know this, but it wasn't how they remembered.

JP: I remember the discussion we had about lighting.

IF: That was revealing, because it threw up the question of reality versus memory. D. A. Pennebaker filmed the original performance and of course that became really important source material for us. But we also managed to locate several bootlegs: mostly stuff people in the audience had shot on Super 8. We also traced a lot of people who had been at the show and interviewed them. When it came to the lighting, the Pennebaker film has a strong red wash over the whole image. The people we spoke to who were there also described the lighting as being almost entirely red, but when we watched the stuff shot by the audience it just wasn't there. There were red stage lights, sure, but there were very distinct other colors too. This sense of everything being bathed in red light just wasn't there. We did a great deal of research and eventually found out that the stock that Pennebaker had shot on had caused the reds to be exaggerated. This film was released on video in the 1980s and is obviously now available on DVD. Even for the people who were there in 1973, they saw the live show once, but they've probably seen the video a hundred times: it has completely warped their memories.

JP: That left us with a difficult decision to make. If we'd completely gone for the authentic – what actually happened – nobody would have been convinced! You're going into a project like that pursuing the authentic, but all the time you're aware that it's the sum of the details that will create this remarkable experience; the combination of them will be the trigger that sets off someone's emotional and psychological connection. You don't know which will hit, so you try to take care of them all and create an environment in which as many people as possible will experience something emotive. In the end we actually went for using more red lights than had been there in 1973, because we knew that without them, people wouldn't connect.

R: They made a kosher prawn in Israel. Prawns are not kosher but some manufacturers decided to make a fake looking prawn, and it comes with a kosher stamp. Why do they exist? They exist for Jews who want to fantasize about the authentic experience of something forbidden. The irony is that the Rabbi went to the factory to check it was kosher. So the Rabbi says it's okay to have this inauthentic fantasy of prawns, and still nobody knows what a real prawn tastes like.

: Beginning to understand this space for interpretation even within an "accurate" re-enactment ultimately led to the thinking that fed into *Silent Sound*, the project we did in Liverpool with Jason from Spiritualized. *File under Sacred Music* helped us understand that an original text was still a fluid thing.

We also began to realize that a lot of the words we were using really tied into the ideas of Spiritualism – we were talking about using the event as a medium to channel the previous event, the performers as somehow resurrecting the spirit of the original performance. We weren't remotely interested in speaking to the dead, but somehow that language and rhetoric seemed useful.

: I think we were also coming to realize that re-enactment in itself no longer had the potency it once had. Its position within culture had shifted, people had become much more aware; remember, it had been ten years since we began making these projects. So *Silent Sound* came out of us looking for a new way of using these frameworks from the past to make something happen in the present, right here, right now.

: We've never really understood Performance Art. When it is expressive, in the sense of bicycle tyres and blood letting, it has a way of being read as art meaning, where an audience can begin analysis simultaneous to experiencing it. This just doesn't appeal to us.

: There is a knowingness in the role of the audience. We're always looking to experiment with other frameworks

Silent Sound

Ceri Hand is director of Ceri Hand Gallery, Liverpool's first commercial art gallery. In 2005 she was Director of Exhibitions at FACT and met with Forsyth and Pollard several times during their frequent visits to Liverpool developing Silent Sound *for A Foundation. The piece was presented initially as a live performance for an invited audience in the Small Concert Hall at St. George's Hall, a public performance space that had sat unused for over 20 years.*

I met a friend of a friend outside in the queue for the performance, who was resplendent in a grimy rock star coat. We were to become goofy mutual admirers of each other's camp dress sense and thrill each other by pseudo-misbehaving out and about town. Sadly I no longer catch flashes of his stumbling wicked heels, as he has since committed suicide.

My memory of him is framed by that night, however, which was charged with exhilaration, desire, and a tantalizing otherworldliness, sensations Forsyth and Pollard are experts at revealing.

On entering the domed concert hall we were parted from friends and deliberately positioned next to a stranger, facing the rest of the audience and configured in a circle around a stage, which immediately heightened our senses. Eyes darted around the luscious room, soaking up the staging and nervous whispers anticipated our fate.

It is fair to say I had fallen headlong into the piece before Dr Ciarán O'Keeffe even took to the stage. The audience performance, the echoes of time, the arrival and formation of the flock of musicians – all the details resonated for me.

The swell of the spine-tingling music carried me through belief, sadness, and joy and I was captivated by the haunting prescience of the artists, entombed in their beautiful silver pods, illuminated on the stage like lovers in separate call boxes a million miles apart.

As they transmitted, the room's yellow glow intensified and my elbows throbbed and tickled. The backs of my knees were injected with a weird pulsating sensation that bizarrely felt somewhat like I was about to have an epileptic fit. I felt all pressure points within my body rustling, vying for attention and I wanted to reach out. My neighbor and I restrained from communicating, but sensed each other acutely. It felt like being on a tipping point, trying to stop your insides leaking out. Only occasionally did I wonder if anybody else was feeling "it," mostly too dedicated to the sights, sounds, and vibrations stinging me like nettles.

that could set out different languages and challenge that.

IF: Through talking about these terms borrowed from Spiritualism, we began doing some research into Victorian public performance. The sort of thing that people did at the weekend before there were gigs to go to. What excited us was the way that an event like a public séance also has an audience and a performer as well as a series of co-conspirators who were essential for the whole thing to work. The event itself would be a hybrid: part belief structure, part science, part spectacle, part interactive performance, part pure entertainment.

JP: We wanted to work with this idea of using science and psychology to affect an audience. We were setting out a proposition and putting in place an environment in which we stood a chance of creating a remarkable experience. Everything was borrowed, but not necessarily from the same place this time.

AR: So what were the reference points?

IF: I suppose the most overt one was the Davenport Brothers. William and Ira Davenport were two brothers from upstate New York who became famous soon after the birth of modern Spiritualism. It started with two sisters, Kate and Maggie Fox, who produced rapping sounds using their toe joints. Their parents and older sister attributed these unexplained sounds to communications from the dead, and Kate and Maggie played along and went on to become famous, delivering public séances all over the world. The Davenports were also from New York and toured the world performing. They would be tied inside a box that contained musical instruments. Once the box was closed the instruments would sound. Then the box would be opened and the brothers would still be tied in their original positions.

What was really interesting to us about their performances was that they themselves never claimed any supernatural powers. Their act would be introduced

At the end I remember feeling irritated oth didn't stay seated in order to come back do together, as was suggested by ringmaster Ciarán, a bamboozled that friends weren't as intoxicated by all as I was.

I think the artists told me I was in a seat wh "something" was likely to occur. I know I asked th if they were talking about love.

For me it was all about hope and the impossibi of being. I am a believer.

Ceri Ha

by an esteemed gentleman, usually a minister called Dr. Ferguson. Before they performed their box trick Ferguson would deliver a lecture on the afterlife. The suggestions laid out in this lecture would lead the public to reach the conclusion that it was spirits playing the musical instruments.

JP: It was the conspiratorial nature of the relationship between William and Ira that we were really drawn to. This had also been there with Kate and Maggie Fox, and I guess working so closely in collaboration, as we do, something just connected.

IF: We had been asked by A Foundation to make a new project for the opening of their new space at Greenland Street in Liverpool. During our research into the Davenports we discovered that they had been to Liverpool in 1865. They had been scheduled to perform two public séances in a small concert hall inside St George's Hall. Part of their routine was to invite members of the audience to tie them into their cabinet. In Liverpool the knots were tied too tightly and they were unable to perform. This lead to what the newspapers described as a "riot": their cabinet was smashed to pieces and the Brothers fled to Hull. We went to visit the hall in Liverpool, which was undergoing renovation and had been closed to the public for over twenty years. There were of course the usual stories about the building being haunted, and we were also told that the small concert hall had been a favorite of Charles Dickens, who had given several public readings there. It was immediately obvious to us that we wanted to work in that space.

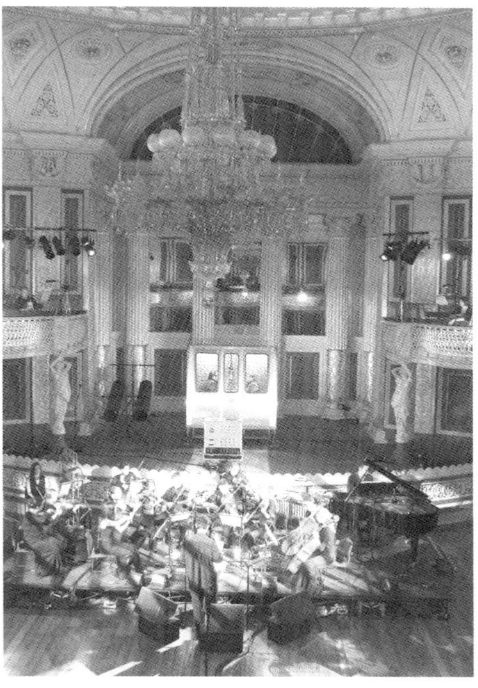

Iain Forsyth & Jane Pollard, *Silent Sound*, production still (St. George's Hall, Liverpool, 2006). Photographer credit: Anne Worthington. Image courtesy of the artists and Kate MacGarry, London.

JP: The project was also drawing on other sources. The history of Spiritualism overlaps in so many places with the development of technology. Thomas Edison, for example, was obsessed with trying to talk to the dead, and many of his experiments were trying to create an apparatus for exactly that purpose. We were fascinated by this and really wanted to explore the idea of science as public spectacle.

IF: It was such a big thing. All these great minds, inventors and scientists, drawn to Spiritualism: Marconi, Alexander Graham Bell, Logie Baird, Sir Oliver Lodge, who was heavily involved in the development of radio, Alfred Russel Wallace, who co-developed the theory of natural selection with Darwin, Sir William Crokes, the chemist who developed atomic theory and produced the first cathode rays. It's just mind-blowing; these guys are all obsessed with trying to talk to the dead, something that these days is consigned to daytime cable TV shows and theaters in seaside towns, but these were the same brains that gave us radio, the phonograph, the microphone, the telephone, television. So as well as channeling, we became seduced by this idea of transmission.

JP: We began investigating subliminal messaging. There's so much material, from academic studies to complete junk science and conspiracy theories lurking in the darker corners of the Internet. We spent several months gathering and going through this material and working with two audio specialists: a sound engineer who works with experimental bands such as Wire and Throbbing Gristle, and a former Ministry of Defence employee who was an engineer in their non-lethal weapons department. They helped us filter all this material and together we worked on developing our Silent Sound Machine, a device that tries to embed a subliminal message within music. Music apparently acts as an effective carrier for the subliminal signal.

For the live performance at St George's Hall we were on the stage that the Davenports had performed on, inside a cabinet we had built based on their original dimensions. A microphone inside this cabinet fed a message that we were repeating into our Silent Sound Machine, where it was converted into a subliminal signal that was then embedded into the music, which had been specially composed by Jason Spaceman for the project.

IF: We had other things going on too: infrasonic pipes, which create a deep bass sound that is almost entirely below the range of human hearing, so you don't hear it, but you feel it. We also charged the room with negative ions and added elements specifically designed and manipulated to amplify the experience. We worked with a parapsychologist, Dr Ciarán O'Keeffe, and essentially he helped us to reverse-engineer the atmospheric conditions that are regularly present at sites where hauntings or other paranormal activity is reported. That was for the performance. For the installation in the gallery we made a recording of the performance using a sound-field microphone and then played it back using Ambisonics, which is a three-dimensional speaker system that allows you to map the physical space a sound is recorded in then play it back in a different space with the sounds plotted to their original locations. So in the gallery we actually recreated the physical sound of St George's Hall. We worked with the acoustics department at Arup, who use the technology to model the sound of buildings before they're built. The recording plays endlessly inside this specially constructed listening chamber.

You know, Marconi had this idea that sounds never really die, they just carry on, the signal getting weaker and weaker. Just before he died he had been working on a listening device that he hoped would be so sensitive that one day he'd be able to hear Jesus delivering the Sermon on the Mount.

Chapter 39

Touching Remains

Janine Antoni and Adrian Heathfield

Adrian Heathfield: *Perform, Repeat, Record* shares a set of concerns with your body of work, in that it deals with questions of how you make present something that is absent, how the traces of actions or events are left in material things. Because this is a book, we have mostly been concerned with textual remains, but your work frequently focuses on the residues of actions in the sculpted object. What prompted this focus in your work?

Janine Antoni: my initial interest came from the belief that meaning comes from how a thing is made. I realized that I could draw the viewer's attention to this aspect through the performative object. This comes from discomfort about my lack of understanding of any object: how it works, who made it, and what it is made of. I guess one way for me to feel more at home in the world was to think about trying to follow an object back to its birth and then somehow, to do that for the viewer. My problem is "how can I tell the history of the object on its surface?"

AH: Is your work affected by how it is read and historicized?

JA: Yes, I continue to be fascinated by what is communicated by my objects. I enjoy the dialogue and I have noticed that viewers who have a pre-existing relationship with my work come to my objects and say, "what has she done now?" Early on I had to call a work *Gnaw* (1992) or *Lick and Lather* (1993) to give an indication of what I had done. I noticed that people enjoy telling the story of how I made my work. It made me think about my relationship to 1970s performance and oral traditions. Story telling is another form of documentation. While I weave the blanket in *Slumber* (1994) I talk to viewers so those people are the ones that experience the fairy tale and they become the storytellers. Hopefully that story then gets passed on. *Slumber* is a performance, an object, and a relic. Some of the performance is unseen and some of it is witnessed. So within the space of the show, art can exist in different ways and that's the reality of most objects. They have this kind of life. It is fascinating for me to watch my work have a life. Sometimes it has a life that I didn't intend and this makes me look at what I'm making differently. I made *Gnaw* with a set of intentions. I showed it at Sandra Gering, a small gallery at the time and through mere coincidence I met someone who wrote about it for a New York magazine. We did a long interview and there was a moment when the idea of bulimia came up. I talked about my action as a metaphor for a culture that's consuming then spitting out. The article came out around the time when the show opened; it triggered a deluge of popular press wanting me to talk about bulimia. It was interesting to me that I made a piece about eating and the world comes back to me and says it has a disorder. I tried to engage this interest while redirecting conversation to my original intentions, but I was naïve. It didn't work. Then I showed at the Whitney Biennial (1993), which became known as the politically correct Biennial; at that time feminism and identity politics were the concerns so it was read from that perspective. At a later date, I was asked to be on panels about minimalism alongside other artists of the time who were hiding social and political content in minimalist form. The next part of its history was that it was put up for auction and MOMA bought it. If it is in MOMA, it should last forever! So then the dialogue began to be about its ephemeral nature. I was asked to do radio interviews and panels about conservation. I guess in the end I could link each one of those readings to something in my original interest in making the work but it is fascinating to watch this unfolding. At the time I really struggled with how these readings seemed to hijack my other intentions. In time though, the breadth of the work was acknowledged.

AH: Well, forces that you have little control over produce these readings: fashionable discourses in journalism or the academy, currents within the art market, or dynamics in society and politics more broadly. But each has a tendency to dominate the work with a particular set of metaphors. It must have been strange to see your work move through so many discourses or moments of reinterpretation so swiftly.

JA: As much as it is painful, it is the success of the piece: that's why it is known! Because it could hook into all these different readings, but at the same time I've had to fight my way out of each one of these boxes. With *To Draw a Line* (2003) I tried something different. I walked across a tightrope at the opening. I was offering my source of inspiration for the sculpture. This time I was very consciously giving the story to certain people to re-tell. For me it was a kind of christening. So the audience became my documentation. In this showing the emphasis remained on the performance. Now that the object exists on its own I hope it will be considered as a sculpture in its own right, beyond the performance.

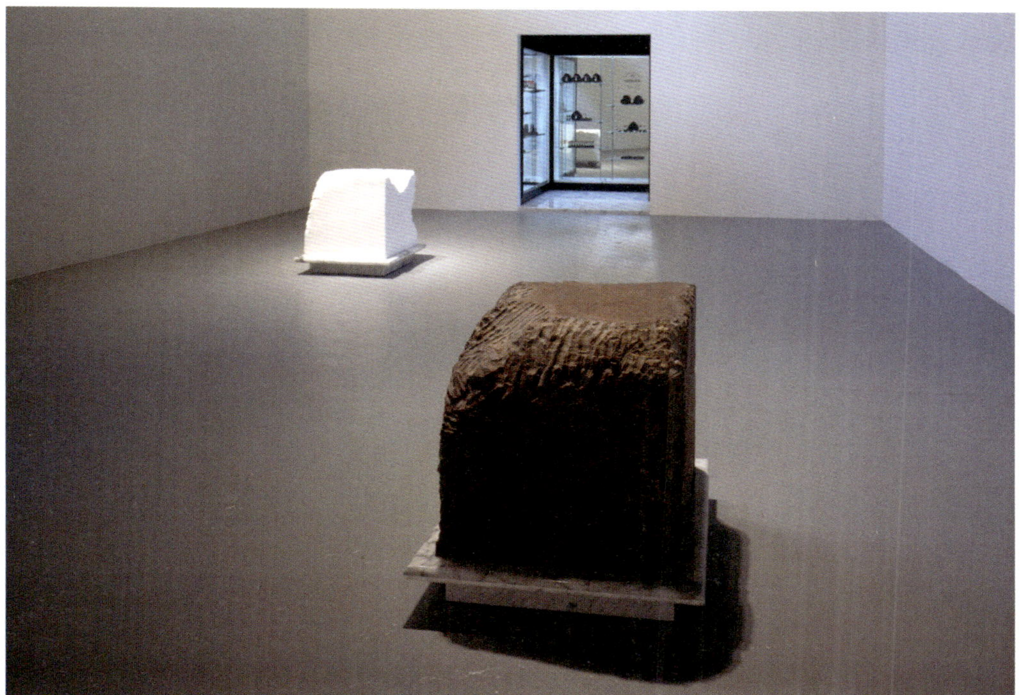

Janine Antoni, *Gnaw*, 1992, Installation shot (LA Moca). 600 lbs. of chocolate gnawed by the artist (24 × 24 × 24 inches), 600 lbs. of lard, gnawed by the artist (24 × 24 × 24 inches), 45 heart-shaped packages for chocolate made from chewed chocolate removed from the chocolate cube and 400 lipsticks made with pigment, beeswax and chewed lard removed from the lard cube. Courtesy of the artist and Luhring Augustine, New York.

AH: I wondered what it is about your work that lays it open to so many different interpretations but also to a certain desire to fix it, perhaps it is something that happens when you make objects that are not finalized or resolved. You open the object to human processes; then there seems to be an access for the spectator's imagination. Perhaps this is also something to do with touch, because the works are touching the spectator they are touched in return; the spectator's point of entry is very physical and deeply felt. So, intellectually and imaginatively, you have to work on what it is that this thing before you is doing to you.

JA: I have always been interested in an object that leaves you wondering. But lately I have become interested in leaving an intentional gap in the work for the viewer to fill in. It is funny how we use words like "touched" or "moved." I am interested in how the physical and emotional are conflated in these words. I want to make full use of this conflation in my work. There are certain responses to my work that I don't know how to take, like with my work *Lick and Lather* (1993). Three different viewers in three

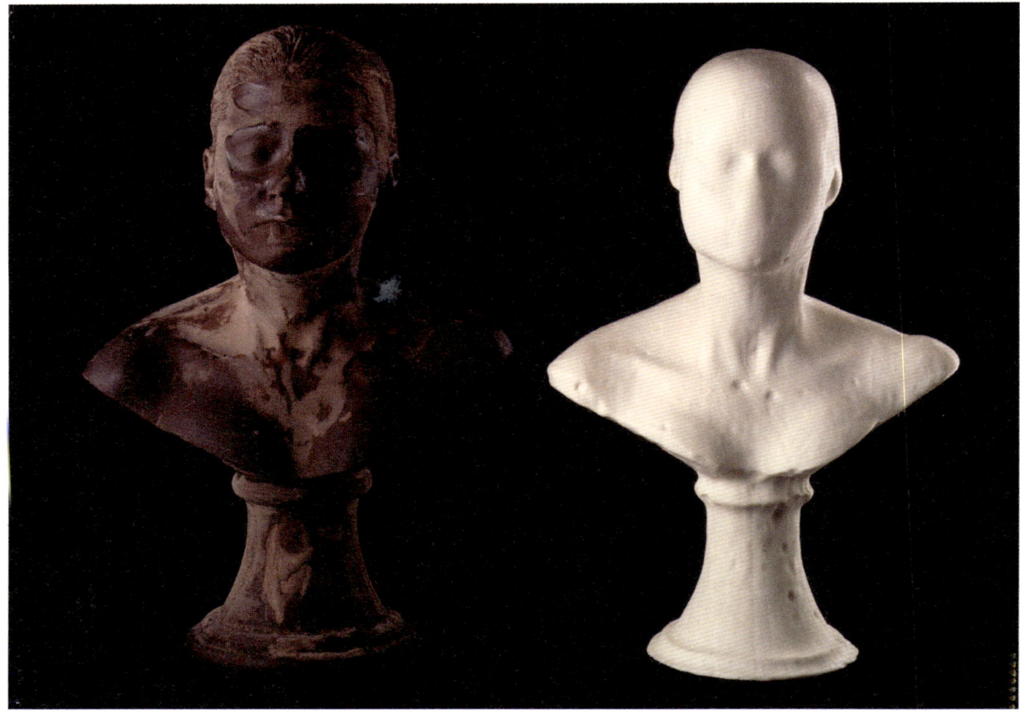

Janine Antoni, *Lick and Lather*, 1993. Two self-portrait busts: one chocolate and one soap. Edition of 7 + 1 full set of 14 busts, seven of each material. 24 × 16 × 13 inches (60.96 × 40.64 × 33.02 cm). Photographed by John Bessler. Courtesy of the artist and Luhring Augustine, New York.

different countries have bitten into my chocolate busts. The first time I thought, ok it is just a crazy person, and then after it has happened repeatedly I have to think, "how have I provoked this response?" I was trying to make a piece that's all about desire and then somebody succumbs to *his or her* desire. How can I be mad when someone responds in such a conceptually correct way!

AH: It is a somewhat narcissistic piece, even if the self-attention goes beyond the visual: your actions are oriented toward a sculpted record of yourself.

JA: Yes, you are right. It is about me having a relationship with myself. But these viewers want to intrude on the relationship. Their response has an implied violence that I wonder about. Performance brings out a lot of strange things in people. It challenges people. From the perspective of the artist, I see it as the most vulnerable position I can put myself in, but it is amazing to me how people read that as aggression. I've seen it in my work, but I've also seen it watching Marina Abramović perform and seeing certain people in her audience; they can't take it. It passes through certain boundaries and gets a person all worked up. It is asking something of the audience.

AH: The vulnerability is reciprocal. Maybe some don't have the capacity to deal with the vulnerability that they find in themselves when they enter that space of relation?

JA: I feel that this is one of the prerequisites of being a good viewer. You have to lay your prejudices to rest and be open to the artwork. This is the only way an artwork can truly move you. Otherwise, viewing art is just an intellectual exercise. I guess for some this kind of intimacy is reserved for the deepest relationships of their lives. So to find themselves exposed is startling. Then there is the desire of the viewer for you to act out on their behalf. So no matter how far I push myself it is not enough for them. When I made *Gnaw*, not only did people want it to be about an eating disorder, they felt it wasn't messy enough. When I fell from the tightrope in *To Draw a Line*, some critics felt that there should have been more risk involved, which misses the point.

AH: I read that review.

JA: I had worked so hard to fall with skill, not to hurt myself, not to deliver the drama people were waiting for. Instead the fall was quiet, controlled, and graceful. For the room it was a cathartic moment. You just never know what you are tapping into. People used to refer to my work as obsessive compulsive. It took me by surprise; I was interested in the discipline it took to bring myself to an edge, being very aware of that edge and not going over it. I am fascinated by what happens emotionally when the body goes to that extreme. Things are revealed.

AH: Maybe you have found a lighter touch with ritual, with repetition, and durational processes? The mark of the ritual is very strongly felt in *Gnaw* in the heaviness of that act and the evident difficulty that you engaged with. Thinking about the work, *To Ply*, that you have just made in Laos for The Quiet in the Land, there is a deep ritual structure to that work, but it has a less punishing feel.

JA: I began that piece by tapping into a needlepoint tradition used to create heirlooms that I received from grandmothers on both sides of my family. In the Hmong tradition, the women have a very developed form of appliqué and embroidery that is also passed down through matrilineal gifts. I used this commonality to both acknowledge our differences and to allow us to bypass the language barrier and communicate visually through the stitch. The work is called *To Ply* because for two strands to intertwine and lock together they must be spun in the same direction but twisted together in opposite directions. This is how they become strong. This is the model I tried to follow with this project.

AH: Coming back to objects that are marked by actions or processes, the spectator may feel disappointed, as the object appears incomplete. Perhaps one thing people find difficult in your work is its movement between performance and the object, your insistence on the artwork being a movement between these things.

JA: I find this movement incredibly dynamic. There is no place to rest. Everything points to something else. It's funny. I feel like I am creating space for the viewer but some viewers want to be told. Disappointment is a really interesting thing with an artwork, and it has meaning. When I do *Loving Care* (1993) and people are pushed out of the room, the fact that they are frustrated that they cannot see me is in fact the meaning in the work. I am extremely conscious of my physical experience – how it influences my understanding of the world – and I try to move that out into the viewer's realm. I like the works that start you spinning and then push you out the door. Those are the ones you can't stop thinking about.

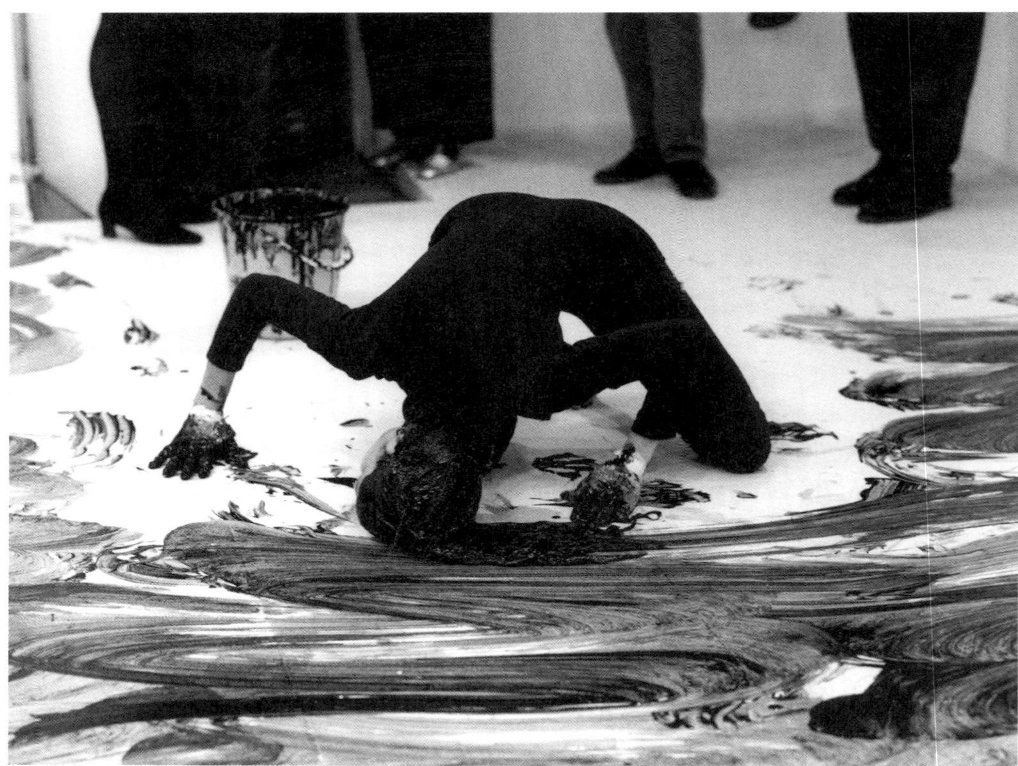

Janine Antoni, *Loving Care*, 1993, Performance with Loving Care hair dye Natural Black dimensions variable. Photographed by Prudence Cumming Associates at Anthony d'Offay Gallery, London, 1993. Courtesy of the artist and Luhring Augustine, New York.

AH: The refusal is a form of communication, and because there is an obstacle in some way, we are drawn in further.

JA: So how can this longing be fruitful? How long can we float in the not knowing? This space is pregnant with potential; it calls the viewer into that absence.

AH: *Slumber* (1993) seems very different from your other works. You are present in the work in duration. The other night you spoke of your ambivalence about being in this work, you narrated your being in it as a discovery of things. I was fascinated when you said that, in a sense, the piece is infinite. But isn't the meaning of the work very much to do with your presence and your ownership of those invisible but somehow materialized dreams. Whilst it has a durational life as a work, doesn't that stop with the singularity of your life? Or is it more of a conceptual piece that could be passed on to another body to enact?

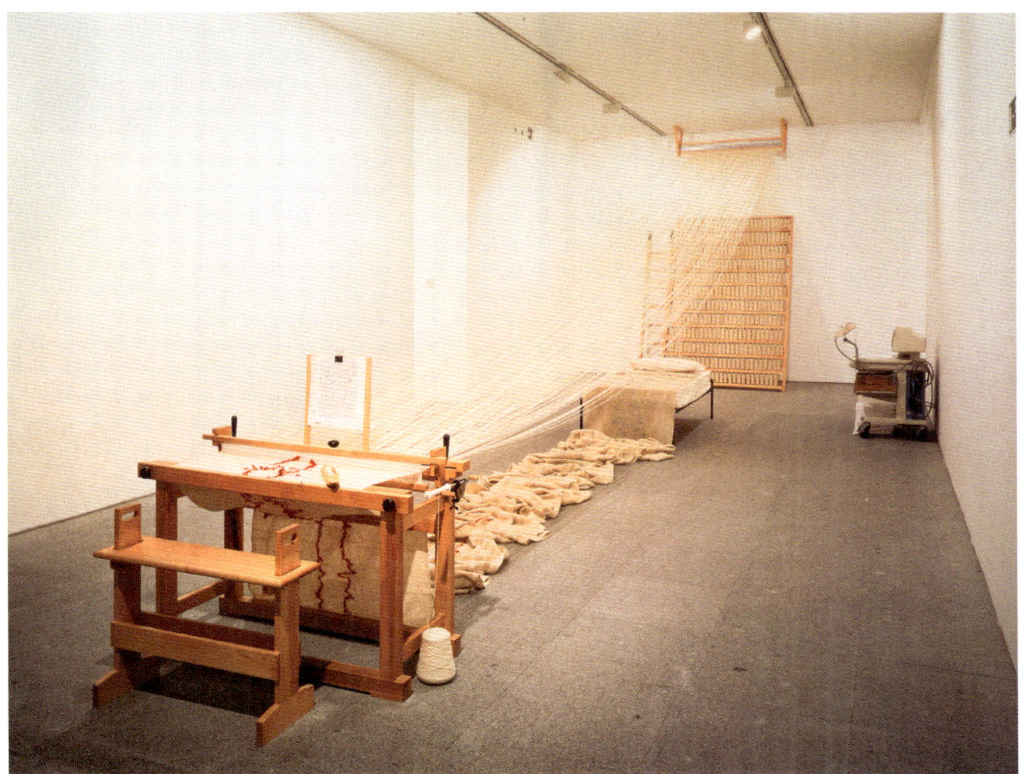

Janine Antoni, *Slumber*, 1993. Performance with loom, yarn, bed, nightgown, PSG machine and artist's REM reading, variable dimensions. Courtesy of the artist and Luhring Augustine, New York.

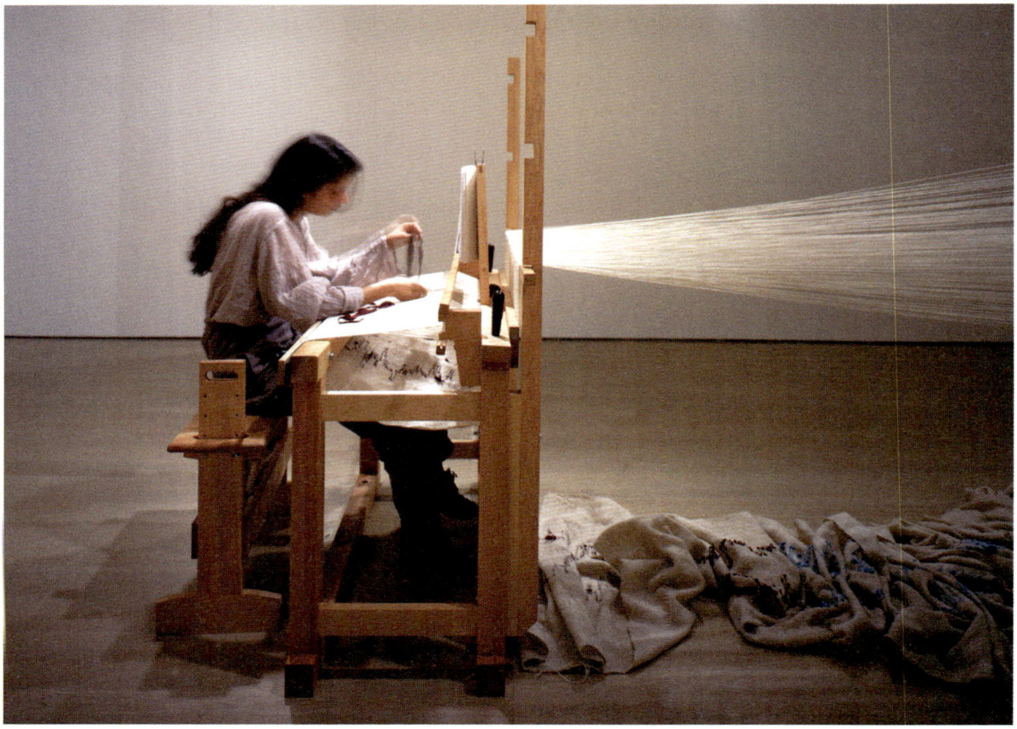

Janine Antoni, *Slumber*, 1993. Performance with loom, yarn, bed, nightgown, PSG machine and artist's REM reading, variable dimensions. Courtesy of the artist and Luhring Augustine, New York.

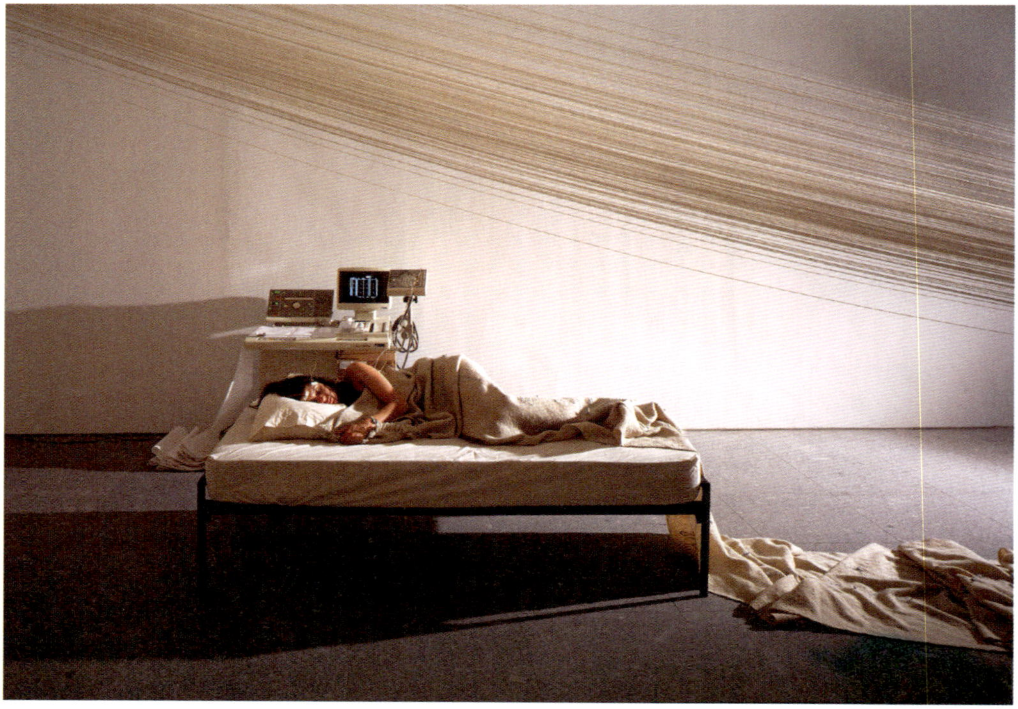

JA: No, it wouldn't make sense for someone else's dreams to attach to mine although I might make a piece that has that structure someday. It is funny that you bring this up because I have just made the decision to stop weaving and sleeping in the piece. *Slumber* is a very porous work. There is the performance that you do not see which is me sleeping at night in the museum. There is the performance that some people have seen which is me weaving during the day when the exhibition is open. Then there are the objects that bear the marks of my time spent with them. I feel that I have lived the fairy tale long enough for it to continue to tell its story without my presence. I think that my decision to keep the warp threads connected to the spools allows the object to remain open. The blanket is never quite complete even though it is over 200 feet long.

AH: But at the same time you also left yourself open to the kind of engagement with spectators that artists rarely get. Durational performance in itself is fairly rare, but durational performance where the content of that work is the exchange with the audience is pretty taxing.

JA: Every time I did the performance I would get somebody who would come every day, and I received notes under my pillow and presents and letters. I just couldn't help thinking about Penelope and her suitors: was I pulling on something deeper than I could understand in that piece? Doing something while waiting is really interesting to me; it makes me think about labor in a totally different way and the creative process for that matter. Maybe one gives oneself a good excuse to do something and then one waits for something to happen.

But I want to tell you about one of my favorite objects in the world. My grandmother made it: it is a half-finished doily. It was carefully folded and fixed to a spool with a crochet needle stuck through the middle. She died before completing it. I found it next to her bed and I've been carrying it around with me ever since. It is an open object. Sometimes it is calling me to finish it or I just meditate on its unfinished nature and how life just stops and things are left open. Then years later I realized that *Slumber* is a remake of that object. I am afraid when I let go of the object. When I put it into the world it closes and when I sell it, it closes. And so I made an object that, although it has been sold, still needs me. I did the piece here in London and I slept with it for a month and a half. I came back home for the first night sleeping in my own bed and I was awakened by a phone call. I woke up startled from a dream where someone from the gallery had cut the blanket away from the loom. Do you know the story of the three fates? One spins, one weaves, and one cuts and that's the story of life.

AH: I am intrigued by this figure that keeps recurring across your work: the thread that connects people, or connects people to things, or the thread that binds histories together. I am wondering about the idea of lineage, which seems increasingly strong in your work. Is this because of a deeper sense of memory, history or loss?

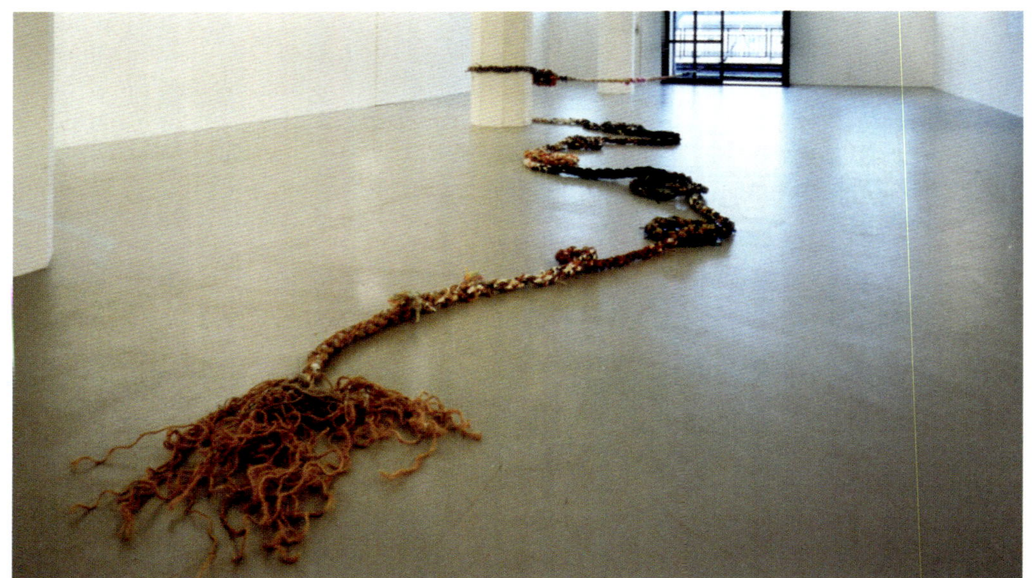

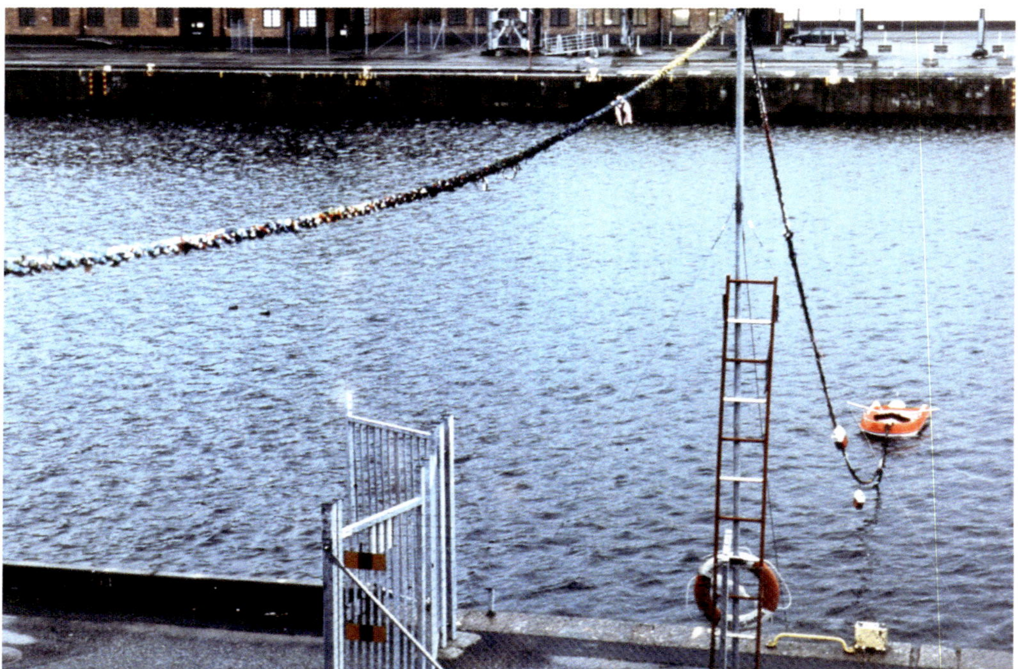

Janine Antoni, *Moor*, 2001, Installation, mixed media (and details). As of 8/18/09 Moor is 326.9 feet (99.63 meters), Moor will continue to grow. Source: Magasin 3. Courtesy of the artist and Luhring Augustine, New York.

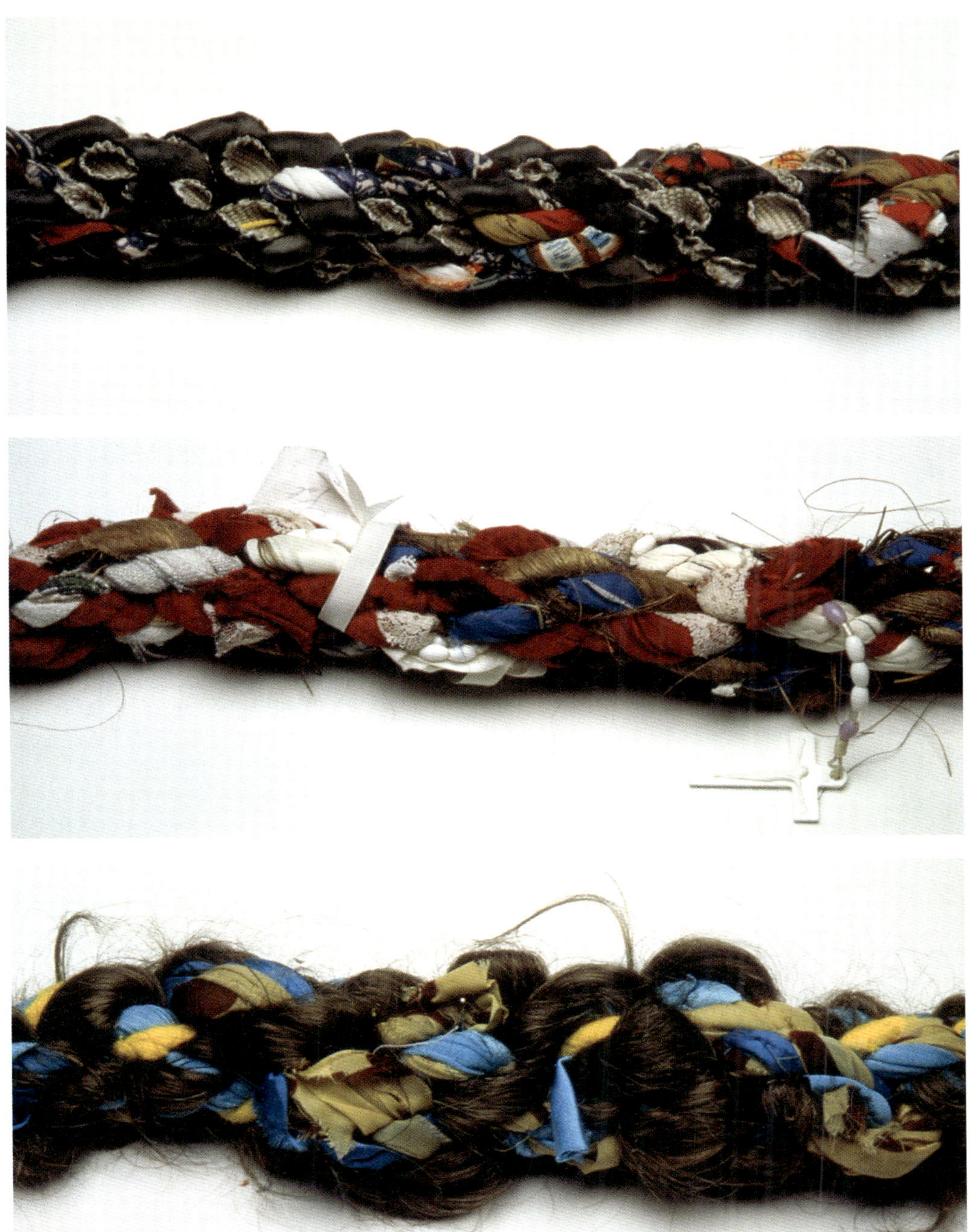

JA: Or having a baby? I don't know.

AH: Maternal lineage is a recurring theme isn't it, but more broadly female lineage.

JA: I address my matriarchal lineage both biologically and art historically. It always makes me feel very old fashioned. I just can't throw it all out in order to make space for myself, I have to take it and rework it. If you want to talk about female lineage, it is easy to say this generation is different now, but it is not my experience. I cannot pretend that I'm doing something new because my lineage is such a part of me: I am made by the things my mothers taught me, what I've observed or what I've unconsciously absorbed through osmosis. Frankly, having a kid has made me rethink all of this, because it is really complicated in terms of gendered roles. I had to rethink my beliefs on equality. We have to make sure that being equal doesn't erase difference.

AH: Complicated because you relive your own childhood through your child and you also relive your relationship to your parents?

JA: And that's all you know: your parents and the way they treated you. So you have to work hard not to fall back on that at times and use it at other times. Regarding the thread, did you know that *Moor* (2001) is ongoing too but this time I'm trying not to trap myself in the fairy tale. I've sold the work with the understanding that I can change the piece according to my creative process. The problem with *Slumber* for me is that my creative process is moving along and then I have to keep going back to my old ideas. That takes discipline and is really painful, especially because the viewer is getting enchanted with it for the first time. So with *Moor* I tried to create an object that could grow along with my thinking. So every time I show it I add to the rope with materials given to me by new friends that have entered my life. When I install it I respond to the place, so it takes on a different form each time. This way I can have a piece that keeps growing but has the ability to change.

AH: So it is an object-centered, site-specific, and process work. That's quite an achievement.

JA: That's me wanting to have it all. Making *Moor* it occurred to me, what if you make a piece more like the way a plant grows, so that it is responding to its environment – and its response to its environment makes its form.

AH: What would its relationship be to the art market? It's an unresolved object, and worse still it gets bigger and bigger. Presumably there's a moment of ownership at the beginning?

JA: A collector who is proud of collecting difficult work purchased *Moor*. In one way it is great for them, because they have a piece that grows, if they can afford to keep storing it. The idea is that anyone who wants to show it has to provide a situation for me to be able to add to it. The first time it was shown it was tied to this little tugboat at the center of the harbor and some of it was under water and I was thrilled about that. I didn't care if that section rotted. But then they went to conservators who said it would continue to degrade. So they treated it, but it was exciting for me that even the showing of it would be changing it. This directly comes out of my experience of *Slumber:* at the time of its making I couldn't afford the polysomnograph, so I borrowed it, and then the piece was sold. I had to write to the collector and explain to him that the piece could not live without the polysomnograph – that it was actually part of the piece – and he was kind enough to purchase it for me. Each time I weave he has to supply me with more yarn or pay for me to get more yarn, so we go back to this plant idea. It is a funny idea that we have with art, that it is about this thing being sealed: you have this object and it should last forever and it should not require anything of you besides maybe climate control. So what if you ask the collector or the institution to take care of the object, what if you pass some responsibility on to them? What happens to their relationship to the object?

AH: Well, the market wants art to be timeless, and if it isn't closed in time it can't be timeless, because it is timely …

JA: So I have asked this question with *Lick and Lather*. They tell me that the chocolate has a hundred year shelf life, which is the food industry's way of gauging its archival possibilities. I always say to collectors "It's going to outlive you. What do you care after that point?" Then this whole question of them immortalizing themselves through the object comes into play. When I was asked to do all those conservation lectures, I couldn't think about anything more boring to talk about, I just decided I would talk about the fear of death as a way to make it more interesting for myself. When I sold *Lick and Lather* I made a contract saying that the person buying it understands that the transformation of the material is conceptually part of the meaning of the work. And of course many people said, "Thank you very much but I guess we won't get it." All the time I'm getting letters from collectors saying, "My soap is cracking," and I say, "Well, if you have any old soap around, that's what it does. That's the piece." Then all of a sudden the piece starts to be about something else in the collectors' relationship to it, which is great.

AH: But then, as you mentioned with the rope in *Moor,* there is no end to the ingenuity of the institutions and technologies of preservation.

JA: Well, they have a field day with me.

AH: You're a challenge and that's what they love.

JA: When I am reinstalling my work I have to resist the urge to improve it. Of course, I am not supposed to alter it. The institutions don't want me to touch it, but they bought it because it has been so touched by me. So this relation is about me touching at a certain moment, and not again at another moment. All of this is so curious to me.

AH: In terms of the question of your touch and your relation to objects, the caress seems to be a recurring figure. I notice that the caress is always with the extremities of your body, the parts that are associated either with sex or with death: the fused nails in *Interlace* (1998), painting with ones hair in *Loving Care* or the caress of the eyelashes in *Butterfly Kisses* (1996–9) …

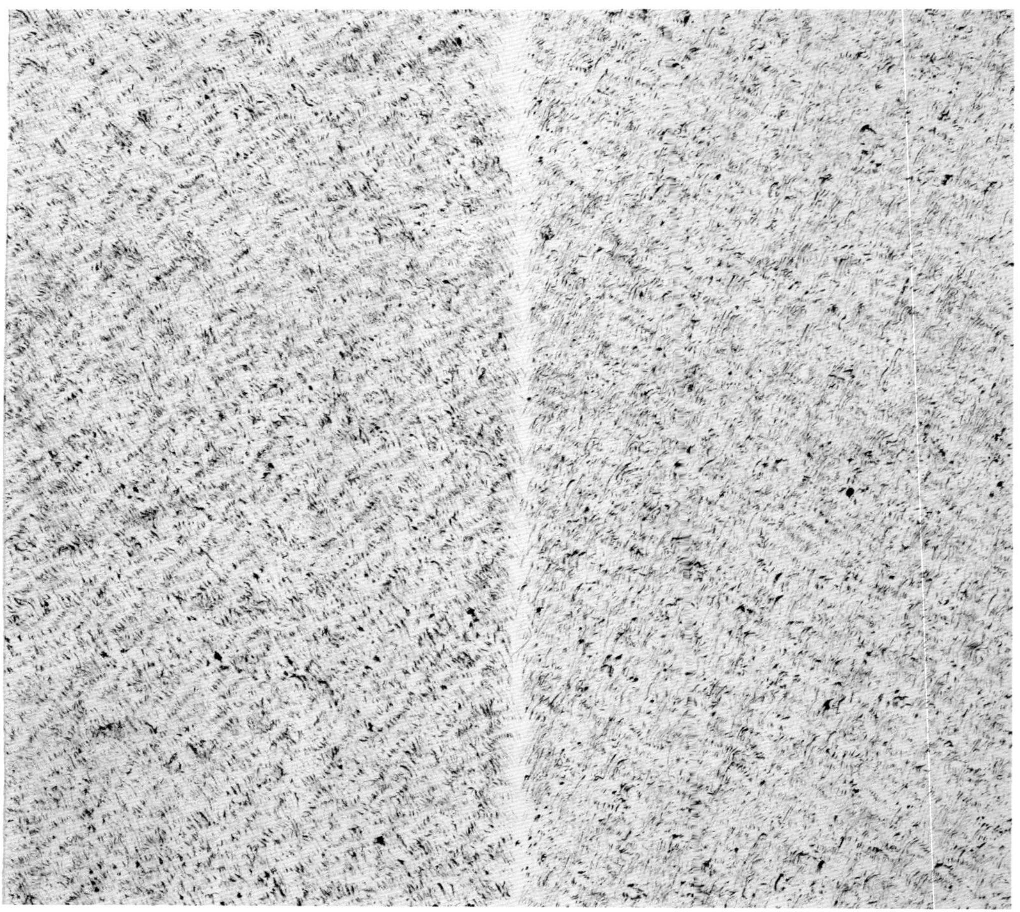

Janine Antoni, *Butterfly Kisses*, 1996–99, Cover Girl Thick Lash Mascara, 32¼ × 32¼ inches (81.92 × 81.92 cm). Collection of The Museum of Modern Art, New York. Courtesy of the artist and Luhring Augustine, New York.

JA: That's where I meet the world: at those extremities. Do you know *Coddle* (1999)?

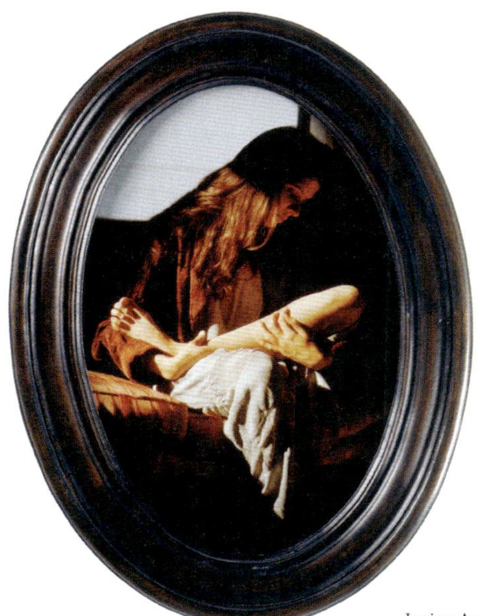

Janine Antoni, *Coddle*, 1998, Cibachrome print, hand carved frame, 21½ × 16 inches (54.6 × 40.6 cm).

AH: I have seen an image of it, but only on the Web.

JA: Ok, so there's this problem:

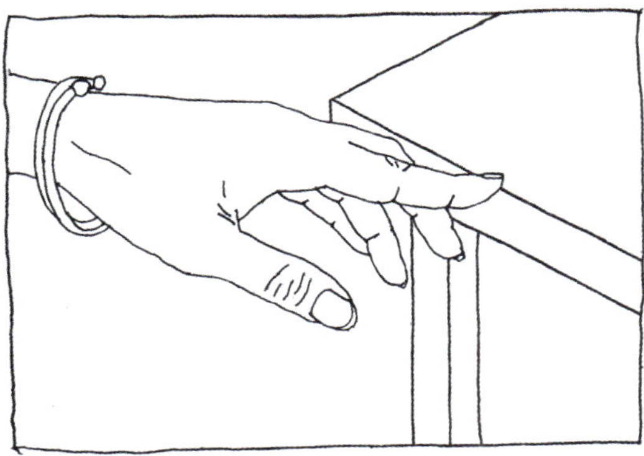

Janine enacted gestures to illustrate her idea. These gestures were then re-drawn by Paul Ramirez Jonas.

and this problem:

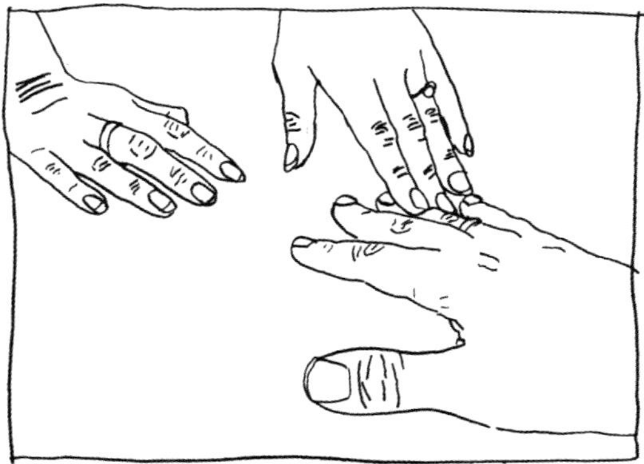

And then there's this problem:

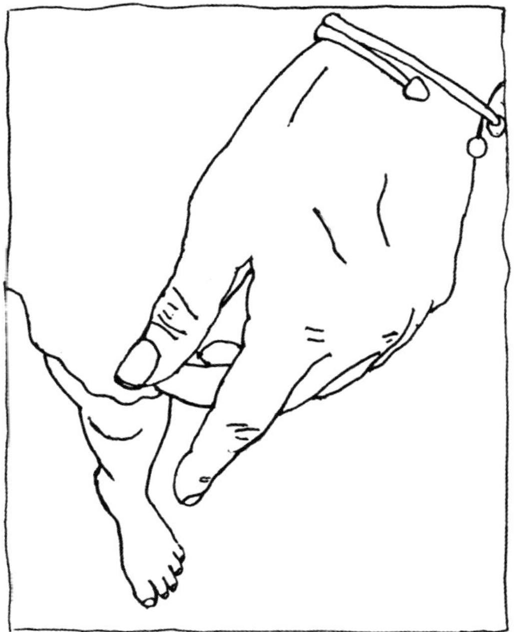

Now let me see if I can articulate those gestures. First there is the perception of things that are not my body. There is my effort in understanding how my body meets the world. You are also a problem. Being separated by our skin is a bit of a tragedy. Don't you think? I even look down and feel separate from my foot. Your feet are the part of you that are the farthest from you. This is why it is a great comfort to be in fetal position, to bring the body back to this place that I perceive as my center.

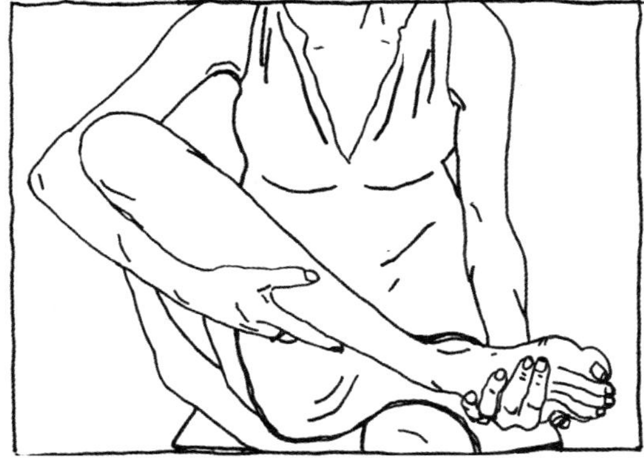

So this is how I can see myself in the world. I've never tried to explain this to anyone before. In *Coddle* my leg is not mine and I am contemplating it. It has become my baby. When you give birth to a baby, you have the opportunity to experience something from the inside existing on the outside. One would think that this lets you see yourself but of course it is more complex than that.

AH: Yes. This gap between you and the thing that is you, produced by your seeing of yourself …

JA: Yes, this is the conundrum of *Lick and Lather*. Licking oneself or washing oneself with an image of oneself. And then there is touching. Sometimes I feel that if I am intimate enough with the object it will come alive.

AH: … trying to resurrect things that are dead in a sense?

JA: … are dead for me. But I am also saying that I am here now, for those moments of touching, I exist, I am in relation.

AH: The last piece you have made – *To Ply* – seems very different, in that it touches a bigger community. It is very much about distance in relation and how one can travel across that distance – this is another kind of touching of otherness that is not immediate …

JA: When I work outside myself I get a bit overwhelmed by my desire to empathize and to connect. Laos is foreign to me in everyway and I find it problematic to use it as a material so I decide to try and keep my identity and help preserve the identity of the women that I worked with. The piece was a kind of conversation. I like to say that we were pen pals through the stitch. I was as interested in our ability to communicate as I was in our miscommunication. I want the piece to show our connections while maintaining our differences.

AH: But *To Ply* is very closely connected to your previous methodology in the sense that you are giving yourself over to things that you cannot control or contain. There is a deep methodology of self-extension through this relation to the unconscious or to unconscious performance: you give despite yourself. Yet here the giving is much more located in a social realm, and connected to complex cross-cultural histories.

JA: The two Hmong women who I worked with, Mo Ly and Xia Song, were my primary audience, so I was making something to communicate to them and then they were responding. I purposefully chose to talk about my life story through the tracing of DNA, knowing that this is the farthest point from the Hmong's belief systems. It is impossible for me to know what those Hmong women took from my project. But I am sure they understood and appreciated my desire to connect with them.

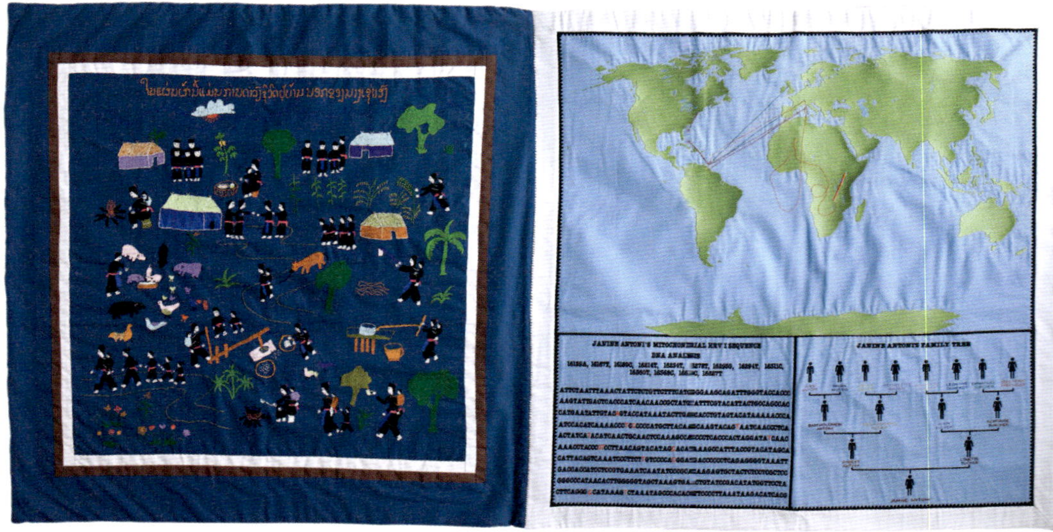

Xia Song and Janine Antoni, *To Ply* (Xia Song's Life Story Cloth with Janine Antoni's mapping of her DNA and family tree), 2006, fabric and embroidery thread, 35 × 70 inches. Photo Credit Edward Addeo. Courtesy of the artist and Luhring Augustine, New York.

Chapter 40

Perverse Martyrologies

Ron Athey and Dominic Johnson

Ron Athey has been a key figure in the development of performance art since the early 1990s. His influence has been felt especially strongly in Europe, where he continues to tour new performances and, more recently, also curate events. However, institutional acknowledgment of his practice in the United States has been obstructed, arguably because of his stigmatization in the Culture Wars. The enduring political fallout of the scandal, and its conservative observance by curators, has seemingly prevented some cultural institutions from showcasing his work, despite its increased critical attention, and the debts owed to his influence by a generation of younger practitioners. While histories have indeed acknowledged Athey's major contribution to the development of performance and visual art, rarely has his work been afforded the focused critical weight that it demands. Commentaries such as those by Jane Blocker, Marvin Carlson, C. Carr, and Carole S. Vance discuss his work in terms of the National Endowment for the Arts controversies;[1] writers such as Amelia Jones, in her influential book *Body Art/Performing the Subject*, discuss his work through critical propositions that engage more extensively with other artists;[2] historical surveys, most notably RoseLee Goldberg's, include his work but only in fleeting (and perhaps misleading) terms.[3] A thorough study of Athey's practice on its own terms is clearly overdue.

In *Performance: Live Art since the 60s*, Goldberg gestures to a further problem in the reception of Athey and other artists. In her grand overview, Athey's "extraordinary and breath-stopping actions" signal a curious historical development, in that "[the] body art that has re-emerged in the '90s is of a far more virulent and highly publicized strain than before," that is, its emergence in the late 1960s.[4] Appropriating the language of contagion, Goldberg attributes this "virulent" return to the contemporary horror of AIDS, and the widespread anger aroused by punitive retaliations and legislated homophobia. Lea Vergine

---

An extract from an interview originally published as Dominic Johnson, "Perverse Martyrologies: An Interview with Ron Athey," *Contemporary Theatre Review*, Autumn 2008, vol. 18, no. 4, pp. 503–13.

stages a formally similar historical reading of performance trends in the 1990s, arguing that the decade is notable for a critical mass in artistic practices that explore "the phenomenon of shifting identities, technological contaminations, and [...] hybridizations," specifically centered on the body. In naming Athey, Matthew Barney, Franko B, and Marcel.Lí Antúnez-Roca as archetypes of this re-emergence, Vergine foregrounds such bodies as "martyred and exultant flesh" reconfigured as the "mangled appendage of a post-human condition." Like Goldberg, therefore, Vergine summarizes the 1990s as a decade in which "the body made its return – at nearly thirty years of distance from the scandal (which it once had been) of Body Art – as the seat and arbiter of multiple identities."[5] While Vergine is a persuasive and sensitive reader of Athey's practice, describing his aesthetic as "the birth of sinister delight and an air of fable in the midst of the [...] demented and abject," her periodizing account seems to fix him, problematically, as a curio from an obscure and apparently distant time.[6] I suspect that this effect has been naturalized to some extent, in the familiar but outmoded assumption that "Body Art" is a meaningful yet historically remote category of work.

In the conversation below, Athey discusses his performance practices as a staging of crisis, sexuality, and the death drive in the time of AIDS. In works such as his celebrated *Torture Trilogy* (1992–5), Athey has challenged the purported sanctity of the body, and specifically those meanings and values that claim sovereign command of it through religious, moral, and other disciplinary logics. Athey has written, "In my performance material, I am guilty of enhancing my history, situation and surroundings into a perfectly depicted apocalypse, or at least a more visual atrocity."[7] As such, in these earlier works, Athey explored the relation between body and text in terms of his experience of intravenous drug abuse and HIV infection, often rehearsing the traumatic emergence of verbal testimony within the registers of physical crisis. Recalling also his idiosyncratic childhood, his inherited "calling," he continues, "it's taken very little work for me to parallel my experiences with the jeweled doomsday prophecies from the Book of Revelations."[8] Recent works such as *Incorruptible Flesh (Perpetual Wound)* (2007) and his current series of *Self-Obliteration* solos (2008) continue these explorations, as an "ecstatic" theater of wordless spectacle.

Works such as *Incorruptible Flesh* and *Judas Cradle* (2005) are demonstrative of Athey's extensive and rigorous research practice; his literary erudition and the subtle diversity of his sources, however, are often overlooked in critical accounts of his work. *Judas Cradle* evidences in-depth knowledge of the development of operatic traditions and the history of European torture, since the fifteenth and sixteenth centuries, respectively; *Incorruptible Flesh (Perpetual Wound)* appropriates Sophocles' classical tragedy *Philoctetes* (409 BC), referencing Ron Vawter's final performance in collaboration with John Jesurun, *Philoketetes-Variations* (1994), James Bidgood's *Pink Narcissus* (1971), and Wagner's epic *Parsifal* (1882), among other texts. Similarly, the visual vocabulary of *Solar Anus* (1998) draws on an essay of the same name by Georges Bataille, and a series of photographic auto-portraits by Pierre Molinier. In the twenty-minute solo performance, these appropriations are given life under the sign of a grisly Hollywood myth: in her later vaudeville turns, a scaffold of needles and wire was stitched into the scalp of an aging Marlene Dietrich, to hold the sagging flesh of her face in an immobile smile. The deft collision between a grim anecdote and the forefathers of Surrealism is representative of Athey's encyclopedic (and esoteric) repertoire of influences. Below, Athey discusses his influences, including Bataille, Molinier, Jean Genet, Reza Abdoh, and David Wojnarowicz.

Spending time talking with Athey is a rich primer on the fringes and beyond of the historical radars of art and performance. As he explains, he has been actively invested in developing scenes in an around punk and club performance since the early 1980s. As such, to explore his references is to learn a far-reaching and mostly unwritten sub-history of experimental practitioners, each an outsider to the cultural purview of performance scholarship. To broach the relations between Athey and varied and often uncategorizable exiles in the hinterlands of cultural practice – such as Breyer P-Orridge, Kembra Pfahler, or Johanna Went – is to ask, implicitly, why so little scholarship exists about their achievements. Such questioning also tests the strict yet unstated limits that the academy has drawn around its archive of possible referents. A relatively small coterie of accepted historical precedents have been more or less canonized in the official histories of performance after 1960. Research into a broad spectrum of performance-makers, though, perhaps reveals more familiar examples to be insufficient touchstones for thinking the full diversity of experimental performance practice since the 1960s.

Moreover, it is insufficient to argue that Athey's critical and institutional marginalization has taken place on account of his prioritizing of sexuality, bodily functions, disease, and death. To offer such an apologia for critical oversights would simply offer consolation for the phobic refusals that characterized the reception of Athey, Robert Mapplethorpe, or Andres Serrano in the early 1990s. As such, Athey affirms, in his persistence, Jennifer Doyle's assertion that "queer criticism" should seek to "call into question the disciplinary narratives that have formed around queer art that has been absorbed into the canonical record [...] or that stubbornly remains 'underground,'" a redefinition that Doyle herself articulates with direct reference to Athey's critical placement.[9] Moreover, the faithful reproduction of the canon takes place at the expense of those artists who consistently evade official culture, in its delimited estimations of the appropriate – and culturally urgent – horizons of cultural reception.

Dominic Johnson: What is your process leading up to the staging of a performance? How do you carry out research and through what processes and techniques does the piece come about?

Ron Athey: My pieces are usually not based on any "issues" defined clearly in advance. I think, initially, they come out of posing a tough, philosophical question that I work through in the process of making. When making *Deliverance* (1995) right at the point that anti-retroviral therapy was becoming standard treatment, I asked: when faced with terminal illness, how does the belief and definition of healing change; and then I made a fantastical leap. This of course referred me back to my upbringing, and to experiences of pursuing miracles, such as faith healing. I'm not always consciously motivated by the horrors of the body, but the mortal tightrope feeds this tension, whether clearly at the beginning of my career, or looking back at the outrageous exhibitionism of *Solar Anus*. In that piece, for example, I thought: how to queer Georges Bataille? The image of Pierre Molinier auto-penetrating his anus with a dildo attached to his high-heel really affects me, as an articulate expression of defiance. Once that's established as a source, a part of me wants to reinvent the costume before really establishing the structure of the piece. But I seem to be on a cycle of creating (for me) "minimal" solos and grander theatrical pieces. When I find a logic, or avenues of new inspiration, these start coming to life. I also work on images through writing down dreams, and especially cognitive dreaming. This isn't an easy part of myself to reckon with, as it goes back to the insanity of my childhood experiences, but really adds flair to problem solving. I have altered other aspects of performance with hypnosis, which at this point happens almost automatically as part of my process.

DJ: *The Monster in the Night of the Labyrinth* seemed to make such brilliant sense, in that Bataille's writings have so clearly influenced your work.[10] What is it that draws you to Bataille's writings?

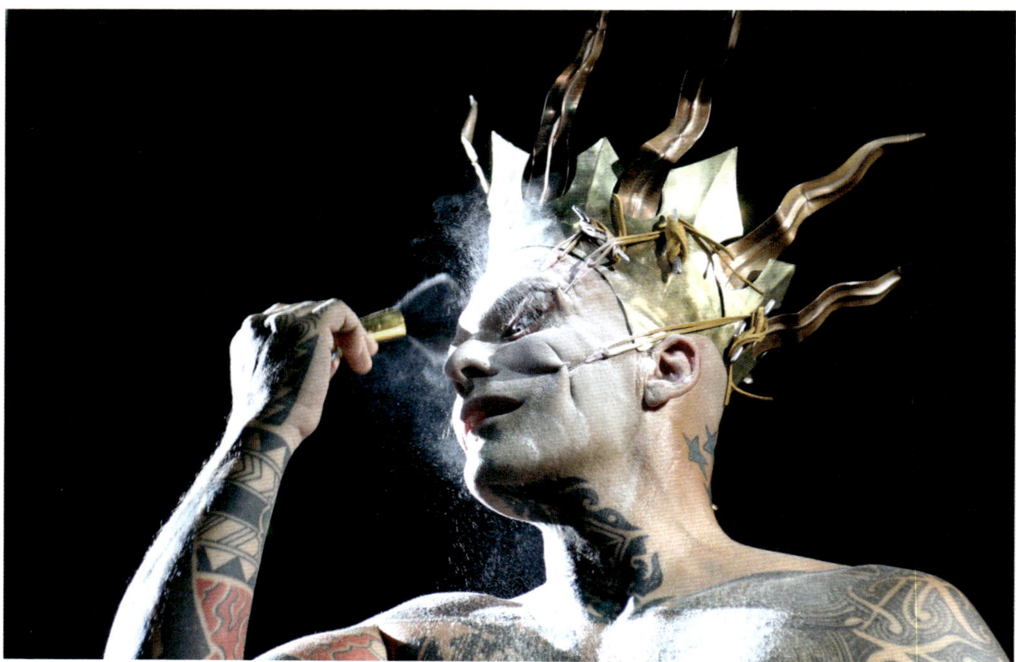

Ron Athey, *Solar Anus*, Hayward Gallery, London, 2007. Photo: Regis Hertrich.

RA: Reading Bataille – especially *Visions of Excess*, *Literature and Evil*, and *The Trial of Gilles de Rais* – definitely helped me make sense of my own work. While I am unwilling and unable to pull my punches, I also experience a paranoia about what I'm unleashing on audiences. Some of Bataille's major premises as the "excremental philosopher," and his accusations (such as his critique of conservative Surrealists in their name-dropping of de Sade), resonated deeply in me. He elevated filth to sacred status – Incestuous Mother, Perverted Priests – while completely destroying familial, cultural, and societal myths. He even claimed Jean Genet was overrated! Well, that one hurt my feelings for a minute. His essay "Solar Anus" triggered and fit my view of the magic tricks inherent in the anus. But visually it was the self-portraits of Pierre Molinier from the 1970s that fed the visuals to me. Rather than fetishizing a young girl's anus (like Bataille), Molinier was obsessed with his own 70-something-year-old asshole. With the required stockings and heels, he successfully transformed himself into a cheesecake pinup figure, the look drilled in through cut'n'pasted repeat images and mandala formations.

DJ: You've described the rectum as the "homosexual weapon," and Amelia Jones has written that your asshole "has its own place" in the history of visual art.[11] What, to you, are the cultural, political and artistic implications of the asshole? How have you explored these in different works, and to what effects?

RA: There is a homophobic repulsion at the idea of the rectum as a receptacle for sex; or further, a more general body-phobia (that many gay men also share) of the turned-out asshole as fist-hole: punch-fucking, double fisting, dark red hankies, and the elbow-to-armpit fist. There's also the pathology of shit-eaters, a direct link to cannibalism. But more importantly, in our time, this particular hole garners more phobias for its symbolic potency as a receptacle for disease. Leo Bersani's essay, "Is the Rectum a Grave?" is useful here, but closer to home is Coil's "Anal Staircase."[12] Bataille's revelation is that the anus is both the day and the night. In keeping with this idea, a brief *assholeography* of my work would read:

> *Deliverance* (1995): in the "Psychic Surgery" sequence, several meters of pink stretch banners are pulled out of my ass and draped around the central two-level set piece; an enema is then administered, and the water expelled into clear cylinders pre-filled with glitter. Later in the performance, in a section called "Rod 'n' Bob: a Post AIDS Boy-Boy Show" with Brian Murphy, after genital "castration" (using surgical staples) we ride a double dildo while I read a text in as calmly modulated a voice as possible. The double-dildo connection is severed with large shears by a figure called The Icon, an act we call the second castration.
>
> *Trojan Whore* (1995): in this short solo, devised as a tribute to Leigh Bowery, I appear encased inside a stuffed lady body. The casing is cut open, and I emerge, in drag. I'm bent over, and an endless strand of pearls is pulled out of my rectum.

Solar Anus: the pearl trick opens this work, followed by auto-penetration with dildo attachments on my high heels: a slow motion, penetrative can-can, modeled on Molinier.

Judas Cradle: in the middle of an operatic duo-drama, I climb a ladder and mount the Judas cradle – a large wooden pyramid used as a "gentler" form of torture in the Spanish Inquisition. This is penetration with a steep learning curve.

I am currently working on the second action in my *Self-Obliteration* series, *Sustained Rapture*, that will somehow capture full-throttle punch-fucking.

DJ: To some audiences, some of the sexual acts you perform may be unfamiliar, even monstrous. What is the attraction, on your part, of bringing these events to the theater?

RA: I do think about the experience-levels of audience, but mainly I acknowledge that it's so varied. If the audience provides the possibility of an entire spectrum of experiences, why does the standard focus attend to the lowest common denominator and privilege the inexperienced heterosexual? I think an image can unify the sexually jaded and naïve, and in the transformation become something else altogether. That "something else" can become beautiful, like a dripping strand of pearls, but it can also be a stand-in for violation, or, in another mood, an act of defiance. What is my attraction, or drive, in exposing these actions? Honestly, it's not a strategy of shock, but of generosity. The image or action must be shown. Pulling one's punches may be the tradition, but I still quiver when live, real-time experience happens.

DJ: I remember you saying that Annie Sprinkle suggested that you might incorporate safe sex messages into your performances. Her conception of sex as healing, as spiritual path, or as a form of public absolution at first seems diametrically opposed to your project, but in fact your work has often staged rituals of sexualized cleansing, or purging through eroticism (I'm thinking of the blood-washing scene in *4 Scenes in a Harsh Life*, and the douching segment with Patty Powers in *Joyce* [2003]). How do you respond to a holistic sexual politics?

RA: To provide a context for my response: safe sex messages seemed obligatory by the days of ACT UP in the late 1980s and early 1990s, so I can see that, in a narrative performance about sex, there could be space for that kind of information. But I couldn't imagine including a public service announcement for the betterment of the audiences for my work. Yes, sexualized cleansing acts have been staged in some of my performances, but the effect of these acts is not instructional, and they're often set in another time period: biblical, or the 1960s. I'm not sure how successful I've ever been in addressing current politics unless there's a deeply personal link. AIDS may be the exception, because it involves a complex galaxy of issues revolving around life and sex and death. But I do also reference other specific events, like the Abu Ghraib sequences in the projected video of *Judas Cradle*, or the re-imagining of queer unions in the three-way wedding scene in *4 Scenes in a Harsh Life*. In these, I was able to tease out something that's more like role-playing, which resonates differently to sincerity.

DJ: I'd like to dwell on some of the thoughts you've just raised. Richard Dellamora writes that "AIDS has not destroyed the memory of gay existence, but it has made such destruction imaginable."[13] Thinking perhaps about your early work, or about personal events in the 1980s, how has living through the height of AIDS informed your practice, or indeed your outlook?

RA: If I look through my personal photographs from that era, and see a table full of people, a small percentage of them are still alive. AIDS destroyed my world, so, how to go forward? And how to reckon with my own sickness? I still feel at odds with planning for the future. I was diagnosed HIV-positive in 1986 – a death sentence until the three-therapy cocktail. But by that time I had already lived ten years of that sentence, and had been through the deaths of too many friends. (Having been an IV drug-user, and being gay, I had a particularly high number of sick friends.) And idols I never met also died: the death of David Wojnarowicz devastated me. I wrote down a line, "The Best are Already Dead," and felt this for some time. This heaviness triggered what I call the "dissociative sparkle," which for me was manifested firstly in the grandiosity of the *Torture Trilogy*. In those three works, all the players (sick men, caregivers) recede into the paintings of Christian martyrology: my appropriation of esoterica and definitions of healing simultaneously heightened and became grim. The first part, *Martyrs & Saints* opens with Pigpen strapped into the frame of a pyramid, having blood drawn, which refers to a dying friend's morphine hallucinations; at the end of *Deliverance* (and of the trilogy) the bodies of the three men are restrained in body bags and buried under hundreds of pounds of dirt, with wailing butch women atop the mound.

From there, it's a case of "Still Here" in the "post-AIDS" era of the cocktail: the living corpse of the *Incorruptible Flesh* manifestations,[14] wrestling the death drive in the *Self-Obliterations*. For me, whether or not these images are front- or back-loaded with the specter of AIDS, it's still relevant, and representative of life: of learning to love the monster, pseudo-health aesthetics, and the giver of death, anal sex.

DJ: You mention Wojnarowicz, and I can see the links between your work and his, and why his example would be so vital to you. I wonder, though, about the importance of other artists whose lives were also cut short, yet whose influence on the official histories of performance have not been fully registered, at the level of, say, the market or the academy. I'm thinking specifically of artists who were close to you, like Lawrence Steger, Reza Abdoh, or Rozz Williams. Beyond these, also, I'm wondering about practicing artists whom I'd want to relate you to, like Kembra Pfahler, Breyer P-Orridge, Goddess Bunny, or Johanna Went. Can you say something about these figures, and what it means for them to have not, perhaps, been assimilated into cultural histories? What is it that is resistant in their work?

RA: Well, this is about access to information, exclusion from proper mediums for whatever reasons, and the validity of underground sources, such as the importance of "zines" before the Internet. *NoMag* in LA profiled bands, and published smart political satires, did features on custom tattooing (a profoundly new concept in 1980), and also covered artists like Johanna Went, Z'EV, and The Kipper Kids. RE/Search Publications was available as a tabloid, and documented "industrial culture," such as Throbbing Gristle, SPK, Monte Cazazza, and Survival Research Laboratories. I believe this not only led the curious such as myself into looking at a culture broader than the music scene, but also changed the way that my generation looked, firstly by examining body modification in tribal cultures, and eventually the Modern Primitives scene. More intimately, it seemed like people older than me kept their own archive. I spent weeks with a Yippie who owned a punk record store called Toxic Shock, while he played me everything he had that could have led to the emergence of the industrial bands: John Cage, weird Captain Beefheart offshoots, particularly interesting bits of New Music. Or Don Bolles, the Germs drummer, who collected *Alarma!* – a very graphic tabloid of accident and murder photographs from Mexico.

I remember talking to Genesis P-Orridge [now Breyer P-Orridge] at Vaginal Davis' Club Sucker – a Sunday Afternoon Punk Rock Teadance – on a particularly lively week, and he seemed to be loving the scene, but asked, "why punk"? Certainly that's a valid question, why alternative Queercore went that way. Rozz Williams was my first boyfriend, and basically lived as a deathrock woman during that time (1979–82). His band Christian Death was largely responsible for the goth aesthetic, though it had not yet been named. And the next in my "I'm with the band" moment was Edward Stapleton, of the *très* intellectual synth-punk-queer band Nervous Gender; they were 15 years ahead of the techno dance scene, using synthesizers and drum machines, and lyrics such as "Jesus was a cock-sucking Jew from Galilee, Jesus was just like me, a Homosexual Nymphomaniac." Anyway, those people were creating, not appropriating nostalgia.

There is currently an ACT UP era show at UCLA's Fowler Museum [*Make Art/Stop AIDS*, 2008], that includes the stars such as Wojnarowicz, Félix González-Torres, and Gran Fury, but also many more underground activist artists who contributed to zines like *Infected Faggot Perspectives* and *Diseased Pariah News*. This period of the late 1980s and early 1990s was one of the last issue-driven movements, and the energy, with all its rage and despair, is still palpable. Why, though, is "timeless" art considered more valid than the ephemeral? I care more if it has at least cut to the quick at some point, as opposed to it being a piece of smartypants art in a vitrine for semi-eternity. Do I need to read another queer Warhol essay?

Of course the Internet and the nature of Google searches supports and dilutes the distribution of obscure information. It's not exhaustive, but I'd imagine some of my profound isolation at a younger age would have been relieved if I had known that certain artists or events existed or had taken place. It was a slow journey through books for me. Scenes can be described superficially, and again are ephemeral, and therefore are deemed not to be of great importance, but in my life this is where creativity has been stoked and supported. That is, there are great influences on creators of work that are outside of academia. Performance created for audiences of other students rarely has the same edge as performance made for a general (even if specific) audience: it's not so easy for the latter to be masturbatory.

DJ: Continuing with the thought of relations between you and other makers of performance, I know that you worked with Reza Abdoh as a performer in his film, *The Blind Owl* (1992). I think there are some interesting comparisons to be made between your work and his. Would this be a meaningful comparison for you?

RA: I remember seeing a piece of Reza's in the early 1990s in the ballroom of an old hotel in the MacArthur Park region of LA. It was a live *telenovela* in Spanish, and he had brought up a pack of trannies from Tijuana to perform in it. I met him when he was preparing *Bogeyman* (1991), parts of which were obviously heavily researched (and cast) at Club Fuck, including our theme song, which was by Ministry. I had never seen an insane non-narrative production with a huge budget before, and I was hugely inspired by the way he was able to structure chaos. And the three-story set was extremely grandiose. It was with his usual cast plus the Goddess Bunny and the mad queen behind Club Fuck, my little sister Cliff Diller. I think I felt inspired to go large. His relationship to Burroughs' cut-ups was really effective, simultaneous and overlapping outbursts configuring something new. But as physical as it was, it was still theater. Later I saw a few Richard Foreman pieces, *Benita Canova* (1998) and *Bad Boy Nietzsche* (2000), and could see his apparent influence on Reza's work.

DJ: Tell me more about Club Fuck. More generally, too, how was club performance important to your development as an artist?

RA: The dynamics of a bona fide scene are intense, as in life changing. I don't tend to think of myself as a "scenester," but I was present and active in a series of cultural moments: ghetto gay disco (as opposed to the gay ghetto), 1977–80; the inland empire suburban and then Hollywood punk scenes, 1979–83; death rock, 1980–2; industrial culture, including bands like TG, SPK, Cabaret Voltaire, 1980–4. After 1983, the LA scene returned to big fashion-scene clubs and gigs seemed kind of sad. 12-Step recovery needed to be my residence for quite some time (1986–2007); this internal work doesn't fit here except that most of the foundational Club Fuck people were also in recovery.

DJ: How important was Club Fuck for your development as an artist?

RA: Club Fuck was in a small but high-ceilinged cha-cha bar called Tobasco's, with a corner for four go-go dancers off of the dance-floor. The regulars throughout the entire three years it was at that location (and valid) were myself, Cross [Athey's former co-performer] , Michelle Hell [Michelle Carr] (before Velvet Hammer Burlesque but same harsh look), and Christian White. Rotating were Jenny Shimizu, Bud Hole, and Jake [trans-man porn star Buck Angel]. Performances were sometimes short sets by bands like Vaginal Davis' art band PME, Rozz Williams and Eva O's Shadow Project, Drance, and Babyland. There would also be a piercing or SM demonstration, by Elayne and Alex Binnie, Durk Dehner of Tom of Finland fame, and myself. This is what led me back into making performance work again, after a nine-year hiatus. *Martyrs & Saints* was created there, as a series of individual ten-minutes pieces. In and around our group, the "first family" of Fuck, the early 1990s were really the heavy time of AIDS deaths, so the project was powered by frustration, grief, anger, despair. Sexually charged, exhibitionist behavior rattled through this group like an affirmation of life, and I'm not being wordy with the sentiments. I could suddenly dream and feel and fuck nasty again.

Three fags started Fuck: Miguel Berestain, who had worked selling fashions for years on Melrose; Cliff Diller, an amazing nutty Oklahoma queen and makeup artist; and James Stone, who had been doorman at many of the fashionette clubs in the 1980s. They pow-wowed with us (the regular dancers and performers, plus PME) and the first Sunday night happened with a bang. The music was the launch of Chicago techno dance – My Life with the Thrill Kill Kult, Ministry, as well as Nine Inch Nails and the like. We worked hard to keep it from being overexposed (including a "No" to Madonna's request to have the upstairs alcove as her private viewing perch, and different door prices for non-queer or no-kinks, as another club had opened – Sinamatic – which was larger and less focused on the theme and was good for the spillover fools). Anyway, three years of sustained intensity was an awesome second wind for me.

At this point I had no real agenda to enter the art venue circuit. Encouragement came from Lydia Lunch, Dennis Cooper, Bob Flanagan, and Sheree Rose. I did an excerpt at Highways [Performance Space and Gallery, Los Angeles] in 1991 and performed a full length *Martyrs & Saints* at LACE [Los Angeles Contemporary Exhibitions] with a cast of fifteen. That week, word spread to New York and Chicago, and this was the beginning of my relationships with Julie Tolentino and Lawrence Steger, probably the only two people who ever had their hands in my work – literally and on a mentor level – until my opera collaboration [*Judas Cradle*] with Juliana Snapper in 2004–5. Steger was a brilliant performer, writer, and curator, and programmed me into Chicago art venues. Tolentino was a member of David Rousseve's dance company REALITY, and she booked me into New York clubs. She was also behind pivotal early-1990s gigs like the ICA [Institute of Contemporary Arts] in London, PS122 in New York, the Walker Art

Center in Minneapolis, Festival Atlantico in Lisbon, and the Sigma Festival in Bordeaux. I was so into doing club shows that, when we performed *Martyrs & Saints* at the ICA for three or four consecutive nights, one night we also did a midnight performance at Fist! This was the trip when I also met Leigh and Nicola Bowery on a few occasions.

At some point I became concerned that the tableaux format of *Martyrs* and *4 Scenes* was the result of creating vignettes for clubs, and that I was unsure whether the scenes might fit together or flow in a different way if, instead, it was conceived as an entire 60-minute performance from the start. So during the construction of *Deliverance*, I mostly stopped performing in clubs, and started doing showcases in more intimate and focused spaces. I do think I would make a performance for a club if I was into the idea, as it's a completely different kind of reward to be able to grip a drunk distracted audience who didn't necessarily come to see you. But it's also a pain in the ass – low-tech, usually with impossible prep conditions.

DJ: Can you tell me about the *Self-Obliteration* series, their concerns and how you see these developing?

RA: I see this topic as a purgatory of sorts – zeroing in on it rattles me. So I'm not predicting a solution or resolution to your question. The series is not literally about suicide, and also not a metaphor for destroying the ego, but creates an aggravated, suspended state. Again, like much of my work, it's backed up by heavy life experiences: I attempted suicide a number of times between the ages of 15 and 25, and that will always stigmatize me. A brand of shame is applied to didactic self-destructions, but I've experienced a fuller range of revelation within that dark place. It can be a final act of strength, rather than a vortex of unmedicated depression. Somehow these thoughts started brewing after I explored what it means to be an Ecstatic, as a through-line in my research. I've always had a tendency to trance out, to have audio hallucinations, or visions. How lucky for me to be born into a radical Pentecostal family of five schizophrenic Scorpio women. In other pieces I've explored the vocal and movement aspects of these experiences, but the Ecstatic identification reaches from birth to my current performance practice, coming from within myself. So if I let my psycho-neurological system run wild within a framework – in *Self-Obliteration #1* that being a wig, 5 needles, and 2 sheets of plate glass – could this happen with minimal action? This glass scene came from *Incorruptible Flesh (Perpetual Wound).* Identifying myself, the decomposing post-AIDS survivor, with the eternally gaping and unhealing wound of Philoctetes, the glass was used as a barrier to press my nasty gash against the fresh wound I inflicted on your body, as a young Neoptolemus figure run through a *Pink Narcissus* filter. This is followed by an action on the floor where I shuffle the two sheets of bloody glass over my supine body: a sick frenzy, then holding a pose, and back to a display as a living corpse.

In *Self-Obliteration #1*, without the interplay of the blood from two bodies, I found pleasure in an emotional distance from the traumatized body, and a fusion of stigmata

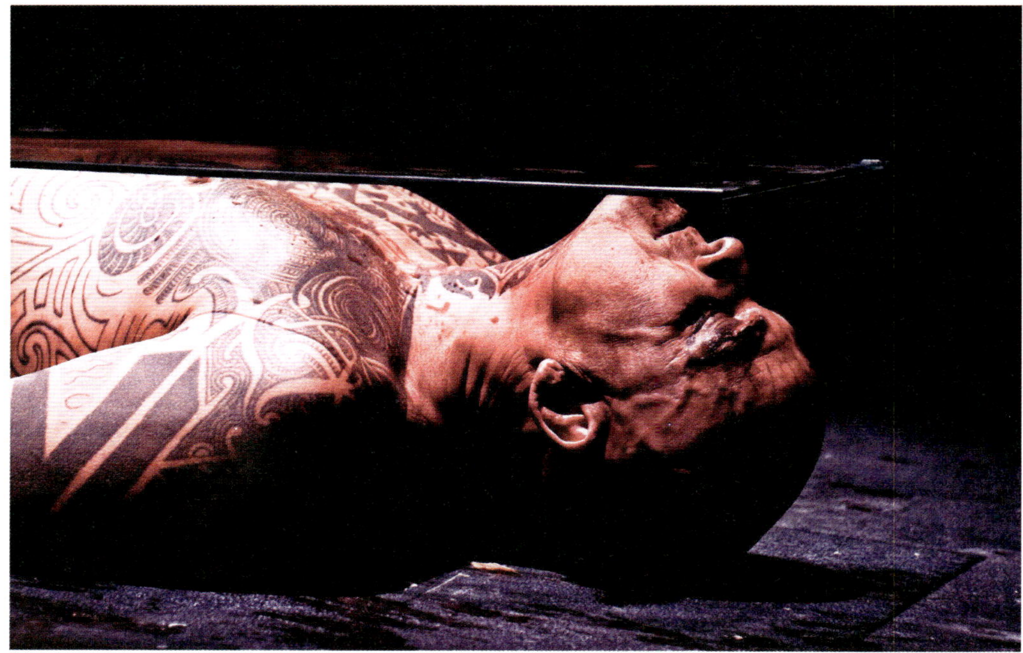

Ron Athey and Dominic Johnson, *Incorruptible Flesh (Perpetual Wound)*, Chelsea Theatre, London, 2007. Photo: Regis Hertrich.

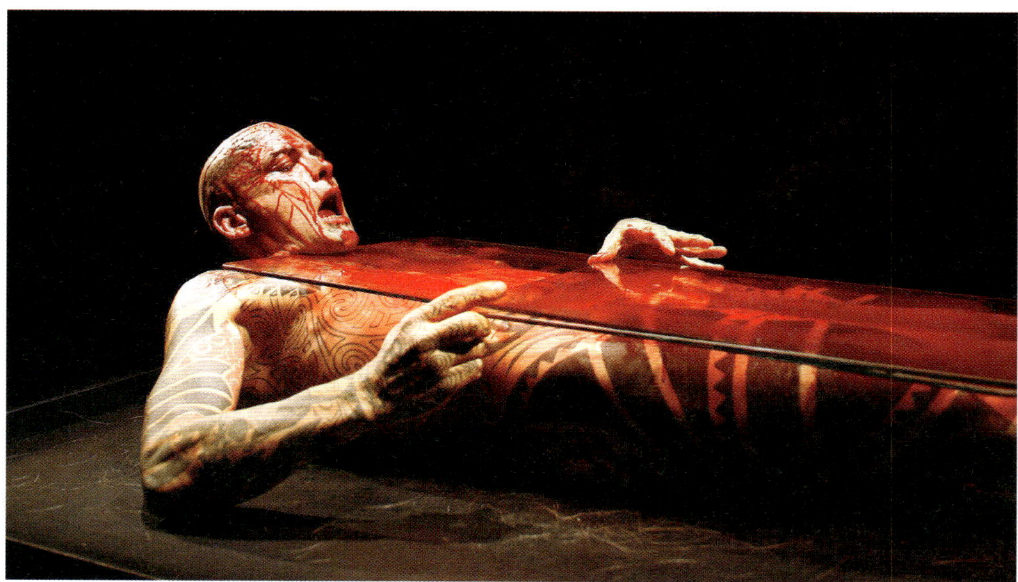

Ron Athey, *Ecstatic*, Donaufestival, Austria, 2008. Photo: Florian Wieser.

and glamour. Pinning the opening look (a shiny long blonde wig) to my scalp are thick needles, hidden under the wig cap. So the un-pinning act of removing the wig causes profuse bleeding from unexplained head wounds before my face has been revealed. Masquerading as a blonde and sliding two bloody glass sheets over my body like guillotine blades, this feels like a stand-in. I create an excuse to convulse this living "dead" body. I give out an improvised vocal that is either a death rattle, or perhaps just fucking weary.

Self-Obliteration #2: Sustained Rapture came about when images and a litany of words came to me in a dream, and I concluded that my deepest desire was to rupture to obliteration in an ecstatic state, specifically though hard sex. Is this a revelation? It did startle me that the destructiveness of my sexual fantasies has not changed since puberty. I don't believe dreams are always prophetic, but appreciate that these images can come from a well-lubricated source. In the mornings as a child, my grandmother discerned my dreams with a lap full of interpretation books. She encouraged cognitive dreaming, so many of my dreams were on repeat-play until the desired outcome was achieved or changed. I dreamed that I was facing off a man, and I was talking. I remembered the sound pattern but not the words. I was delivering a relentless litany. So I wrote to the man this was directed at, and then the dream repeated itself, but this time the words hung in the air with form, like that of ectoplasm. The content, what I heard myself saying with urgency and brutal flourishes, was more like a manifesto, calling for me to abandon conventions, emotional safeguarding, and complacency, in order to build a deeper love. This came to sex with no boundaries, a willingness to literally have no limits in the interaction of animalistic sex. This idea of intense pleasure ramped up to full-throttle, would it be able to stop before the death drive at the brink?

Notes

1. Jane Blocker, *What the Body Cost: Desire, History and Performance*, Minneapolis and London: University of Minnesota, 2004, pp. 111–5; Marvin Carlson, *Performance: A Critical Introduction*, London and New York: Routledge, 1996, pp. 158–9; C. Carr, "Washed in the Blood: Congress Has a New Scapegoat," *Village Voice*, 5 July 1994, p. 16; Carole S. Vance, "The War on Culture," in Ted Gott (ed.), *Don't Leave Me This Way: Art in the Age of AIDS*, London and Melbourne: Thames and Hudson, 1994, pp. 91–111, at pp. 107–8.
2. Amelia Jones, *Body Art/Performing the Subject*, Minneapolis and London: University of Minnesota Press, 1999, p. 125.
3. RoseLee Goldberg, *Performance Art: From Futurism to the Present*, revised and expanded edition, London: Thames and Hudson, 2001 (1979), pp. 212–3.
4. RoseLee Goldberg, *Performance: Live Art since the '60s*, London: Thames and Hudson, 2004, p. 99.
5. Lea Vergine, "Diffused Body and Mystical Body," in *Body Art and Performance: The Body as Language*, Milan: Skira, 2000, pp. 269–91, at p. 280.
6. Ibid., p. 289.

7. Ron Athey, "*Deliverance*: Introduction, Foreword, Description and Selected Text," in Joshua Oppenheimer and Helena Reckitt (eds), *Acting on AIDS: Sex, Drugs & Politics*, London and New York: Serpent's Tail, 1997, pp. 430–9, at p. 430.
8. Ibid., p. 431.
9. Jennifer Doyle, "Queer Wallpaper," in Amelia Jones (ed.), *A Companion to Contemporary Art since 1945*, Malden and Oxford: Blackwell Publishing, 2006, pp. 343–55, at p. 347.
10. Co-curated by Athey and Lee Adams, *The Monster in the Night of the Labyrinth* was an evening of Bataille-inspired performances at the Hayward Gallery, London, 3 July 2006.
11. For an extensive critical study of this piece, see Amelia Jones "Holy Body: Erotic Ethics in Ron Athey and Juliana Snapper's *Judas Cradle*," *TDR*, 2006, vol. 50, pp. 159–69.
12. Leo Bersani, "Is the Rectum a Grave," in Douglas Crimp (ed.), *AIDS: Cultural Analysis/Cultural Activism*, Cambridge and London: MIT Press, 1988, pp. 197–222. "Anal Staircase" is included in Coil's iconic album *Horse Rotorvator*, London: Force & Form/Some Bizarre Records, 1986.
13. Richard Dellamora, *Apocalyptic Overtures: Sexual Politics and the Sense of an Ending*, New Brunswick: Rutgers University Press, 1994, p. 28.
14. *Incorruptible Flesh* forms a further trilogy of works. The first part, *Incorruptible Flesh*, was a collaboration between Athey and the Chicago-based performance artist Lawrence Steger, performed at CCA (Glasgow) and Galerija Kapelica (Ljubljana), in 1997. Steger died of AIDS-related pneumonia in 1998. The second part, *Incorruptible Flesh (Dissociative Sparkle)* was a solo durational performance, presented at the National Review of Live Art (Glasgow) and Artists Space (New York), in 2006. The final part, *Incorruptible Flesh (Perpetual Wound)*, was a collaboration between Athey and Johnson, staged at Chelsea Theatre (London) and Fierce Festival (Birmingham), in 2007.

Chapter 41

The Live Artist as Archaeologist

Marina Abramović and Amelia Jones

After a long preliminary chat about Abramović's mother, an art historian who worked for the Yugoslav state and who had just died a few days before, we set down to our discussion about live art, pivoting around *Seven Easy Pieces*, the seven performance works Abramović staged at the Solomon R. Guggenheim Museum in New York City in November of 2005. In addition to six re-enactments of classic works from the 1960s and 1970s, Abramović produced a new work for the Guggenheim, *Entering the Other Side*, which involved the artist standing in a gigantic blue dress that functioned as an architectural structure, lifting the artist far above the crowd into the central rotunda of the museum (working within the terms of Frank Lloyd Wright's famous spiraled dome structure). The schedule of the re-enactments and this final work, all performed entirely by Abramović, was as follows:[1]

9 November, 5 pm to 12 am
Bruce Nauman, *Body Pressure* (1974). Nauman constructed a false wall nearly identical in size to an existing wall behind it. A pink poster with black typeface invited visitors to perform their own action by pressing against the wall.

10 November, 5 pm to 12 am
Vito Acconci, *Seedbed* (1972). Acconci occupied the space under a false floor, masturbating and speaking through a microphone to visitors walking above in an attempt to establish an "intimate" connection with them.

11 November, 5 pm to 12 am
VALIE EXPORT, *Action Pants: Genital Panic* (1969). Wearing pants with the crotch removed, EXPORT walked through an art cinema, offering the spectators visual contact with a real

female body. Walking up and down the aisles, she challenged the audience to look at reality instead of passively enjoying images of women on the screen.

12 November, 5 pm to 12 am
Gina Pane, *The Conditioning, First Action of Self-Portrait(s)* (1973). Pane lay on a metal bed above lit candles for approximately thirty minutes. Her suffering was apparent to the audience, who witnessed her wringing her hands in pain.

13 November, 5 pm to 12 am
Joseph Beuys, *How to Explain Pictures to a Dead Hare* (1965). With his head covered in honey and gold leaf, Beuys cradled a dead hare, showing it pictures on the wall and whispering to it. He wore an iron sole on his right foot and a felt sole on his left.

14 November, 5 pm to 12 am
Marina Abramović, *Lips of Thomas* (1975, Galerie Krinzinger, Innsbruck). Abramović ate a kilogram of honey and drank a liter of red wine out of a glass. She broke the glass with her hand, incised a star in her stomach with a razor blade, and then whipped herself until she "no longer felt pain." She lay down on an ice cross while a space heater suspended above caused her to bleed more profusely.

15 November, 5 pm to 12 am
Marina Abramović, *Entering the Other Side* (2005). Abramović premieres a new performance created specifically for this project.

The Dialogue

Amelia Jones: My first thought is to ask you to think about your earlier work and what you think about the recent resurgence of interest in performance; you are of course at the forefront of this resurgence because you've re-staged these works at the Guggenheim in *Seven Easy Pieces*. With this renewed interest in live art there's a rethinking of the historical performances from the 1960s and 1970s – such as the projects you did with Ulay in this period; obviously you've been making work all the way through up to the present. Why just in the past decade do we suddenly find the art world and art historians in particular taking account of that history?

Marina Abramović: It's so many things, actually related. From my point of view, in the 1970s performance kind of came out of conceptual art very much but also there was a parallel resurgence of theater and dance and these also contributed to this body art movement. But performance didn't stop in the 1970s. There was big collapse of the art market in the 1980s, there was a big push of all these guys to make some object related work, and it's very interesting because when you see the early 1980s paintings they are all like painted performances. Also the renewed interest in body art really related very much to AIDS from my point of view and the fear of dying you know. The body became a focus very much.

But then also the performances in the 1980s didn't come into the gallery right away, but really into the nightclub scene and I think that was very important for me – artists like Leigh Bowery and Charles Atlas and all these guys who did performances in nightclubs – actually, you know, the feel was away from the kind of structure of the normal gallery scene or museum scene, it was much freer in club culture, so that in London, New York, and Berlin you had all these kinds of centers developing in the 1980s after the earlier heyday of performance in the 1970s. These performances appeared so much stronger, but not as a performance art per se but actually as direct influences in dance and also in the theater, for people like Anne Teresa De Keersmaeker of the Rosas dance group, Pina Bausch and Jan Fabre, all of whom took elements and were directly influenced by performance in their attitude. And then also in the 1980s you started seeing the elements of performance in MTV culture very much. Even in advertising they started to look at performance images you know and started actually recycling them, and taking them completely out of context and making something new out of it.

All of these elements together encouraged a very young generation of artists starting to make video and performance related works. But [most of the time these newer works] are not executed for a live public; they are actually video works very much and look more like home movies. [Many of these more recent works by younger artists documented] extremely short actions, often looped so that all of them you know could be seen in twenty seconds, or one or two minutes maximum. Life was getting faster so the public wanted to have a fast view of the work so the artist really adapted to a fast way of viewing actions by making these short films. And I was always arguing that we never went to the real experience because it now seemed kind of fake, because the films were made this well so that actually it looks like the action was done forever, it goes on and on and on in the same image. But in a way by doing this kind of work artists deprive themselves of that real experience which gives the performance meaning, making us reconsider time. You really have to have time to develop the piece in a live situation.

Now performance is very much work with interrupted action; it is about not just the artist's experience but that of the public. You know, very few people know about the earlier examples of this engaged kind of live performance work, such as the work I made at the Great Wall of China in 1988 [with Ulay, *The Lovers: Great Wall Walk*[2]]. I made all these works where actually the *public* were performing. I did this work because I believe that we have to leave behind the eighteenth-century view of the museum-going public as simply voyeurs. The art has to be interrupted; there can't just be isolated works with the viewer positioned simply as an observer looking in. There are lots of artists who started making process-based works that involved the public in the 1970s and 1980s like the Chinese Wall piece.

So the resurgence of interest in performance is due to a lot of different things; looking back to that history, we can't really see or isolate what exactly happened at the time either. I believe that action performance went back into performance again in the 1960s and 1970s, through the theater, dance, and music, those three elements kind of put it back together.

AJ: Very interesting. I can tell you're related to an art historian![3]

In terms of history, obviously your work is continuous and yet also there's a sense in which people from the outside looking at your career, without knowing works such as the *Balkan Baroque* piece (which won the Golden Lion Award at the Venice Biennale in 1997 but isn't very well known in the United States) might just see highlighted your individual works in the early 1970s (such as *Rhythm 0*) and your work with Ulay from the mid-1970s and then these redos at the Guggenheim. So how do you see that as serving people's conception of your career? How do *you* view your relationship to the past?

MA: You know in a very strange way, I'm going backwards and forwards at the same time, because when I was in Yugoslavia I really didn't want to be influenced by anything which was Yugoslav there. I was absolutely not interested in the culture; nobody understood what I was doing, there was such a hostility about my work that I wanted to go far away. All other cultures were more interesting to me than Balkan culture.

So in 1980 my first actually really big trip I made was to the Sahara desert; then I went to the Gobi desert and then the great Australian desert, where I spent one entire year. The Aborigines for me were the most interesting because of their ceremonies, which are a way of living. Also, they don't have any possessions; they are just nomadic tribes who are constantly moving. And the other very important element from them was that everything was happening in the dreamtime history of the culture, but at the same time they perceive life as being about the here and now. There's no past and no future. Everything is happening *always now* when they're talking about it. So it's all about that idea of here and now, which I think is very important in relation to performance too.

And then the second culture Ulay and I explored was Tibet. Along with the culture of the Aborigines, Tibetan culture was the most interesting of all. The Aboriginals were born [with a relationship to the past but linked to the present] and Tibetans have the technique of how to get to a similar point. We learned a lot about performance at a time when performance was dying out. It was in 1979 when everything was finishing; there was only the idea of going back to painting and drawing, of going back to your studio and producing things or just radically do something else entirely.

Ulay and I didn't know what we wanted to do radically; we only knew that we needed to go to nature, but the question was which nature? The most minimal there is and that was the desert, and then from there we saw what we came up with. So from that experience and this long kind of durational work then Ulay and I had the end of our relationship with the *Great Wall of China* piece and so I couldn't make any performances at that time.

After that I went through my own performances and then I went back into my own culture with the *Balkan Baroque* piece. I was invited by the government of Montenegro to present my work in the Yugoslavian pavilion at Venice and I proposed *Balkan Baroque*. The Minister of Culture refused it and attacked me. But then the Minister of Culture had to resign and that was such a satisfaction. I was unbelievably hurt about this whole Balkan thing because of this but I had to deal with Balkan culture. I went to interview my mother, my father, and a man who was a rat catcher for the last thirty-five years of his life and from these three stories I made *Balkan Baroque*. I didn't want to do anything with Balkan culture again, but lots of strange circumstances took me back to it. Every time [I have made work about the Balkans it's because] somebody would come with the idea and I would go back to my culture. I never did it on my own. This is very strange because I always try to refuse. So Neville Wakefield from Destricted Productions asked me to work with past performances to make a piece relating to the erotic in art. The result is the 2005 video piece *Balkan Erotic Epic*.[4]

And now, the older I get and the more distance I have from my own culture, the better I can see. I could never make such a work when I was younger. I could not have this distance. *Balkan Erotic Epic* is my favorite piece addressing my own culture. It's about the old stories – such as the seventeenth-century tale in which, if there is too much rain and the fields are flooded, the women run around showing their genitals to make the gods afraid and to stop the rain. In the middle of the film I have this woman [Olivera Katarina, who was a famous Yugoslavian actress and singer], sing the song "Slavic Soul." Every time this song comes I cry, because for me, she's singing in Russian [and it reminds me of my childhood].

AJ: Were the performances in *Balkan Erotic Epic* done for a live audience or just for video?

MA: No, I filmed it for video.

AJ: You are speaking of a looping and retracing of themes and ideas within your own work with this return to the "Balkan" in these works – some of which were performed for audiences, others just for the camera. So your own career is really about retracing and redoing.

MA: I see my work as circular, as a spiral.

AJ: In terms of a spiral, a looping back to the past, can we talk about *Seven Easy Pieces*? Because you have this obviously embodied relationship to your past work, it must feel very different to redo your own work (the *Lips of Thomas*) than to redo other people's performances. How did you feel in the midst of redoing, say, Acconci's *Seedbed* in contrast to performing your own past work?

MA: Yes. First of all, *Lips of Thomas* – I had a total feeling, because it was my piece, and I changed it; I added things, I took bits out. I had this freedom to do whatever I wanted, because it was my piece, and it was to me the strongest experience I could possibly imagine to go as far as I could. All of the elements of the original performance were the same except the shoes and the stick I used when I walked the Chinese wall – I got something much shorter; the hat is the one my mother was wearing in 1943 [when she fought against the Germans in WWII] and is original. Then the last thing is the song – I reused the track of Katarina singing in *Balkan Erotic*. In the 1950s, Katarina was one of the most charismatic women. She was one of our first divas. But now she's old and living completely abandoned.

So the re-enactment of *Lips of Thomas* has elements coming from different things. First of all, this piece, it was something like two hours in the original but I expanded it to seven hours; it was like, how I can do something that was so completely crazy, how far I can go with the re-enactment?

AJ: So you broke the original actions up into different parts, extending them, and added elements from other pieces such as *Balkan Erotic Epic*. The new piece becomes a map of your career in that way.

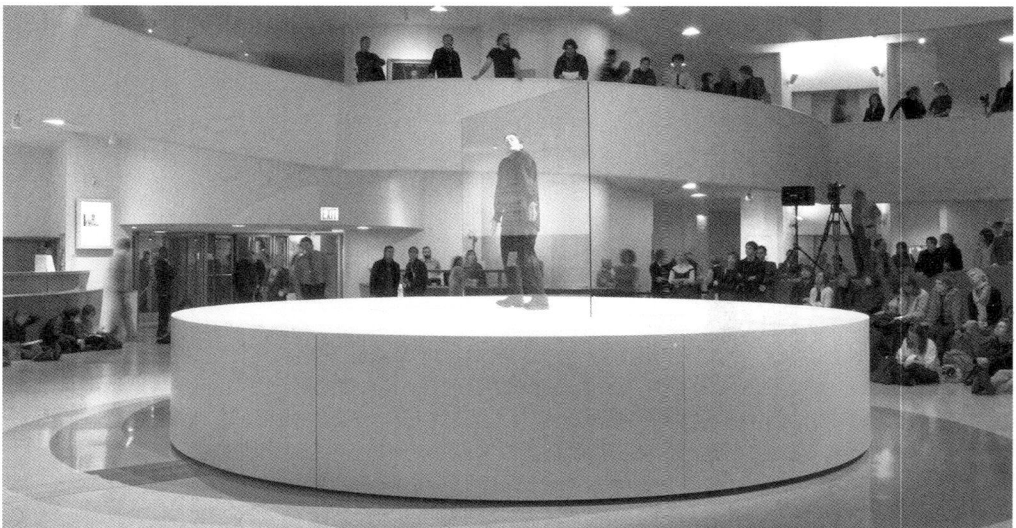

Marina Abramović performing Bruce Nauman, *Body Pressure*. Solomon R. Guggenheim Museum New York, 2005. Photo: Kathryn Carr. Original work: Bruce Nauman, *Body Pressure*. Originally performed at: Yellow Body, Galerie Konrad Fischer, Dusseldorf 4 February / 6 March 1974.

MA: Yes, different elements, step by step. With other pieces, re-enacting other artists' works, it was very different: these were not my pieces. I was feeling like an *archaeologist* really – I had to figure out how I was going to do each piece. Let me talk about each piece chronologically.

I started with Bruce Nauman for a really specific reason – because *Body Pressure* is actually the piece for which there are written instructions. I was interested [in the fact] that Bruce Nauman never performed this piece – it was only instructions stuck on sheets of paper that you could take home; the public would take these sheets home and put them on their book shelves or forget them or throw them away. So I was thinking that's a good idea – I can take the instructions and I can adapt it for the Guggenheim.

AJ: So in that sense that piece is the least of an appropriation among the other artists' works in *Seven Easy Pieces*, because you are simply performing what Nauman instructed within the original project.

MA: Exactly, except that I had to make lots of decisions, like how to translate what Nauman instructs [into an actual performance]? For example, instead of a wall as Nauman describes, I put up glass, so people can see me from any angle and then I repeat the pressing action. Then in the Acconci piece [*Seedbed*], I had no guide other than Acconci's published photographs and text describing it. A funny thing, when I talked to Acconci, he said he never recorded his voice during the original piece and he was

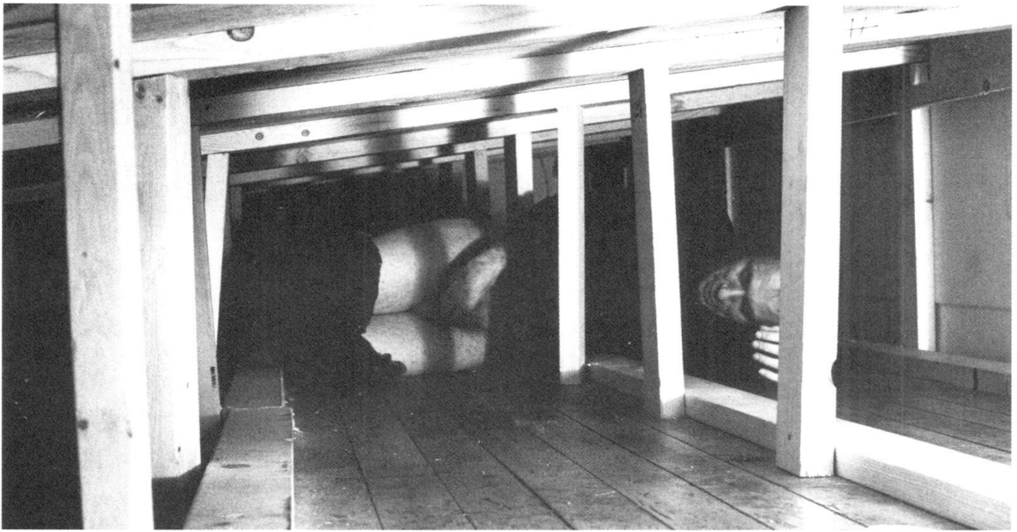

Vito Acconci, *Seedbed*, Sonnabend Gallery, New York, January 1972, view under the ramp. Performance / Installation: wood ramp 2 ½′ x 22′ x 30′; 9 days, 8 hours a day, during a 3-week exhibition.

very sorry about that. Also, he said in the published text about the piece that he is not supposed to have been visible, but there is a well-known image of him under the ramp, masturbating.

AJ: Which is the iconic image of the piece. So you had to deal with all these inconsistencies in the historical rendering of the piece.

MA: [Yes.] But basically, you're never supposed to see him. So I followed this idea and you never see me as I re-enact the piece. Also, originally *Seedbed* was about what you could do, what you could produce, and Acconci produced semen. But what did I, as a woman, have to produce?

With all of the re-enactments, I arranged it so that every time the public was coming, there would be seven of my friends, mingling in the crowd with tiny microphones, going around so they could pick up conversations among the public. It is amazing to see what the public talk about during the performances.

AJ: Especially during that piece, while you're having orgasms! Tell me about redoing VALIE EXPORT's *Genital Panic.*

MA: So the VALIE EXPORT thing again; I was the most critical and most careful about this piece because in reality she stated that she originally performed the piece in this theater at the erotic film festival in Vienna, but at the same time she made the poster as well. *Genital Panic* is a great contradiction [in terms of the issue of "live" versus documented performance] because she also made the photograph in her studio and there are lots of different images of that poster.[5] And she wouldn't give me any clear answers when I asked her about it.

AJ: Well I was going to ask you about that, because obviously she's still alive, so you could ask her about all the contradictory stories, but she clearly doesn't want to give definitive answers. Having the "original" artist around to talk to doesn't necessarily give one any more definitive access to what happened with the piece first time round, does it?

MA: No, and then she was very proud because that image is the kind of image that can work at different times, in different contexts, with different meanings and the piece has been very influential just in the form of this image.

AJ: And what was it like to engage with a non-living artist's work – such as that of Gina Pane [who died in 1992] – particularly this kind of work that's closer to your own practice in that it is more visceral?

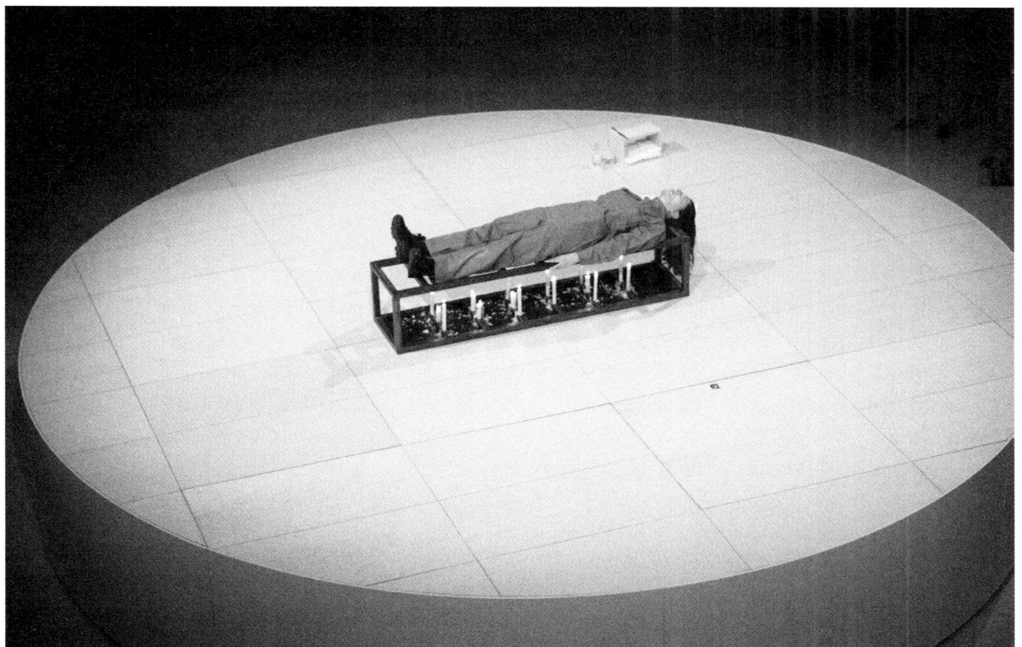

Marina Abramović performing Gina Pane, *The Conditioning, First Action of Self-Portrait(s)*. Solomon R. Guggenheim Museum New York, 2005. Photo: Kathryn Carr, video stills: Babette Mangolte. Original work: Gina Pane, *The Conditioning, First Action of Self-Portrait(s)*, 1973.

MA: The Pane was the most difficult for me because first of all I was asking to perform the entire piece, but her girlfriend, who represents the Gina Pane foundation, only gave me permission to re-enact one part of the piece. And that's the part I used – but it was also hard because two things I hate about performance are candles and eggs, I don't know why! But they always make kitschy shit. Just not me, candles and eggs.

The piece was quite hard also in physical terms – I had to deal with seven hours of pain, and every time a candle went out I had to get down and fix it. Over hours, you have to make certain adjustments because, all of that time, what else do you have to do?

The Joseph Beuys [b. 1921–d. 1986] re-enactment was also hard, because Vera Beuys, his wife, didn't want to give permission, although I finally got it from her. But the only image I knew was this single image [of *How to Explain Pictures to a Dead Hare*]. There were all these videos made of the piece, which I saw, but he didn't authorize them because there were too many problems with them. So I was again an archaeologist.

I was the most constrained in this piece, because firstly the resistance by Vera Beuys and then it was hard dealing with Beuys as a figure in the work, because in Acconci I masturbated but you didn't see me, in the Bruce Nauman re-enactment I could be anything, but in *How to Explain Pictures* [because people had in their minds the iconic images of Beuys performing the piece], I was clearly a female in male clothes. There was also the question of how to deal with all these elements, ritualistic things, to repeat and repeat like an obsessive.

AJ: So you were consciously mimicking the actual movements from the Beuys film?

MA: Yes, the actual movements, and then repeating them to make a loop of actions. But there were a few things I did on my own. Beuys had taken the hare's ears in his mouth as if to try to animate it; I understood that I actually could take the hare by his ears and hold the whole thing, but he hadn't done this. You know … I think my actions were subconscious: I had seen a movie of my grandfather, who had this young man holding a peacock in his teeth and the peacock is just hanging like this … so this element was something that came out because of my own experience.

AJ: Marina, could you talk a little bit more about the embodied relation? I'm interested in what you just described – finding yourself unconsciously repeating actions or visual elements you've seen from other parts of your life or other films or works while re-enacting someone else's piece. I would think this contrasts strongly to the experience of re-enacting your own piece, where you have a bodily memory (whether consciously or not) of doing the piece before.

MA: Yes. For me it is really going back to the journey I did know. But either way, the re-enactment does generate enormous fear. It's hard to tell from watching me perform these pieces, but finally when the date came for *Seven Easy Pieces*, for a whole month ahead I was physically sick, because I was so afraid that I would be unable to perform somebody else's piece. I thought that this was not originally my idea, that I had no idea how it would go, especially for such a long time [seven hours for each re-enactment].

Endurance is hard for me – and in the past only once was I part of an endurance piece, which I actually stopped after the halfway point. It was supposed to be twenty-four hours long, but I stopped after twelve hours. I just stood up and didn't want to do it. It was not my thing.

This was in 1975, and it was so strange because it was something that I never had thought about. It has to do with energy – perhaps this is the thing about energy, because if it's your own piece you create such a kind of energy, it's so powerful. But if it's not your own, you're not as motivated. In this endurance piece [in Prinzendorf, Austria, in 1975], Herman Nitsch poured the blood over me and it was going on and on and at one point I felt panicky. I would never do this kind of thing with my own performance. Never. But I never cancelled a performance in my life. Because it's like the passion of life for me, performing is a life and death thing.

AJ: So you're not going to volunteer for one of Vanessa Beecroft's pieces? [laughing] I actually know some performance artists, a queer feminist group called the Toxic Titties, who did an intervention by volunteering for one of her performance installations.[6] I think they found it really difficult partly for that reason – being forced to take action (or to remain in a state of inaction as the case may be) within someone else's project and, in the case of Beecroft's work, acceding to being objects rather than having agency.

MA: You know what is happening since *Seven Easy Pieces* took place, how many people are writing to me asking me for permission to redo my works? The one thing I have given permission for, this is so fantastic now, is to re-enact my work on the Internet site Second Life. Eva and Franco Mattes came to me after they saw the seven pieces at the Guggenheim to ask for permission to re-stage some of the works on Second Life [they are re-enacting *Imponderabilia* (1977) and *Rest Energy* (1980), both originally performed with Ulay, on the website]. I gave them permission because to me Second Life is a completely different medium; it's something else, and so it is not competing with the live act.

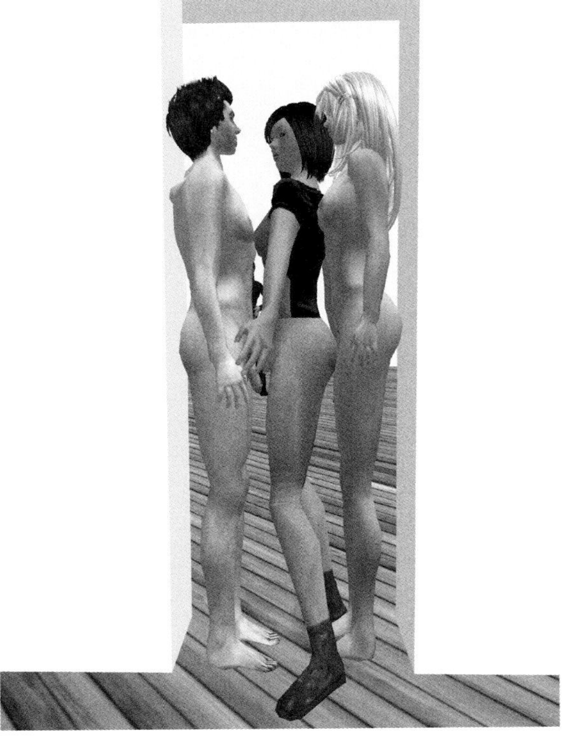

Eva and Franco Mattes aka 0100101110101101.ORG, Re-enactment of Marina Abramović and Ulay's *Imponderabilia*, 2007. Performance, Second Life and Performa07, New York. Courtesy Postmasters Gallery, New York.

I don't give permission for every request – I have to be sure that the person is capable of doing the piece. But Second Life is OK, because Second Life is the Internet, just great, a different medium – and it's called Second Life because it is a Second Life! It is not competing with live art.

AJ: Vis-à-vis *Seven Easy Pieces*, do you think performing in a mainstream museum like the Guggenheim compromises what performance was set out to do in the 1970s, often working in alternative or renegade spaces?

MA: That's all fine for the 1970s, but these pieces are part of history and this history has to be honored, as has any history, in a museum. Why not performance? Still today nobody cares at all about pure performance. Even now if you look at photography or video it really has a strong part in collections, but where is performance? Performance is always related in some way to entertainment. I get so many invitations saying oh we're having an opening of this or this can you come and do a piece? The idea is to have a drink and see the performance, which I hate. Performance is not entertainment, but that's how it's placed – it's always in between something, and for me it's such an important form of art because it's so informal, it's so direct, it's so here and now. I wanted to have a museum context finally for that.

And I'm not planning to repeat these performances ever. My idea was – because now every day I get three invitations saying can you do these pieces here, here, and here – I'm not touring! For me the point was to provide examples of work by a few artists of that generation to show how we should really address these pieces. You understand in re-enacting other artists' works you have to ask permission, you have to do your own interpretations, but there has to be a kind of seriousness about it, because there are so many artists out there making slapstick art, or making very funny Acconci, or funny this funny that. But this is wrong – art must be beautiful and any re-enactment should address the big issues that the original piece was about at that time.

AJ: But if the point of performance is that it's ephemeral, then isn't putting it in a museum in a sense at the very least creating a tension with that aspect of the live act? You are making it something more historical by doing so, taking away or mitigating the ephemeral aspect of it – turning it into an object that can be commodified and displayed.

MA: Yes and no, because this event was seven days, so it was itself ephemeral and then ceased to exist. It was not like a three-month show that you can go and see over and over again. With *Seven Easy Pieces*, you would come and see it – it was still ephemeral, still time-based art. If you weren't there between five and midnight you wouldn't see it, and if you couldn't be there every night of the seven days you would not see it all. Still …

AJ: But of course *Seven Easy Pieces* will be known historically through documentation; it's not "lost" in that sense, and can itself be commodified (per the book and film that now represent it).

Can you talk then about the problem of documentation? Your access to the "original" works you re-enacted in *Seven Easy Pieces* was through photographic, textual, and filmic documentation – does that mean you had access to the works themselves? And how does this then play out in relation to your re-enactments and *their* documentation?

MA: For me this is where you think about the body. In the 1970s most of the artists doing live art paid no attention to the documentation or gave no instructions to the film artists of how it should be done. Like with Beuys. People would record his pieces and then they would show them to him and then he would say this one I like, this one I don't like, but he didn't give instructions of how it should be filmed beforehand.

With *Seven Easy Pieces* I spent a lot of time working with the filmmaker, Babette Mangolte, to produce good documentation. I had a static movie camera that filmed each piece in its entirety over the seven hours and then I had three other cameras moving around. I also had numerous still photographs taken, which we used for the book.[7] And I gave instructions to the photographer on how to take each photograph.

With my lawyer I made a statement that I would only make photographs of my own work and never of anyone else's, so that I wouldn't benefit financially if the original ideas were not mine.

AJ: So you have photos of yourself re-enacting the Beuys performance but you are not selling them.

MA: Absolutely not. And everyone contributing to the book [*Seven Easy Pieces*] and the film will have an equal percentage of the proceeds.

AJ: So you're paying, for example, the Beuys foundation some of the profits.

MA: Yes, the estate.

AJ: There are many different intentionalities or creative agencies at play with this project. There's the artist who originally performed the piece – in the case of Nauman, for example, he's got a much more removed agency in relation to it, because from the beginning there was a set of instructions, whereas with Acconci you're dealing with his image, his description of the piece (which actually occurred, unlike with the Nauman, as far as we know), and discussions with him in the present.

But in terms of intentionality, what happens when you redo the piece – say, Beuys's *How to Explain Pictures* – and it is now seen in a sense as your piece? (If you google "Beuys dead hare" half the images that come up are of you re-enacting the piece!)

It's collaborative in a way, but it's also in a sense an Abramović. You've appropriated authorship of these pieces.

MA: That is so complicated. I'm still trying to figure it out because I think that actually the work, such as *How to Explain* or Acconci's *Seedbed*, is not my idea. The only new element I bring to the piece is time, the element of time, which is my interpretation. It's as if I am a musician performing a score – OK if you play the Bach as it is written, you are interpreting Bach, but what if you make techno-Bach? Different interpretations, different pianists, interpret the piece in different ways.

AJ: So if a famous pianist such as Vladimir Horowitz plays a Bach sonata is it a "Bach" piece or a "Horowitz"?

Isn't the main difference between music and performance art or other kinds of visual art linked to the role of the body? In a "Marina Abramović" performance, it is *your* body in particular that "is" or enacts the work. So what the audience member thinks of as the work is linked to that body (that person, that subject). Whereas with music, which is much more abstract and disembodied at least when you hear it via a CD or on the radio, one has more access to an abstract author ("Bach" as the organizing creative force) than to the body of the performer.

Does this particularity of live art – the role of the body *in* and *as* the work – relate to your plan for *Seven Easy Pieces* and your relationship to the documentation process (your desire to *redo* rather than just allow performances to be known historically through photographs, text, and other forms of documentation)?

MA: Yes – redoing is still performance and performance is somehow *living*. For me the performance only has sense when you perform; otherwise it's dead. It's the same with music that is never played. But there are no rules in performance – not any of the artists who do performance dead or still living ever actually made the rules of how the piece should be done. Musicians have rules – there are the notes and various marks indicating how the score should be played. Performance doesn't have rules, so I was actually seeing if I could give a set of rules. I am interested to find out what are the rights of the performance. Not only which performance, but who performs?

You know something happened incredible here with this performance, too: an enormous number of young people came, who had only known the works from these bad photographs – to come to see something to then reflect on it and have discussion. Here it was like in the 1970s when everybody is sitting watching an event, people would not know each other, but because they had to spend so long time together they would say "Oh, I'm going to lunch; let's have lunch together," you know, go to lunch, come back, go to dinner, come back, so they start to have a relationship. Looking at this piece becomes an experience that is something really so organic, so alive. Everyone becomes so connected, it becomes some kind of energy body.

AJ: So you create a public sphere around the work. But can you say a little more about the ethics of your taking on the authorship of each piece?

MA: Yeah, at the same time it's always a question of ethics. I will never say that such a re-enactment is my piece, because it's not my piece. I will never sell it as my piece, because it's not my piece. Because you know, for me it's almost religiously important, that every time [the piece has to be identified in relation to its original performer]. The piece, the title, have to be always [identified in] the same [way]: performance, and then you'll see the name, date and when it was really done and then the date when I redid it. So I'm like a tool, you know and then I have my interpretation and that is not the [original] piece.

AJ: But even if you admit here that it's not your piece, it comes to be talked about and written about as an "Abramović."

MA: It becomes my piece. I saw a huge difference, and the public did too, when I performed my pieces [rather than redoing other people's performances], because I never could give myself so much in the latter. In *Thomas Lips*, I lose my responsibility [of thinking about the other artist]; I could do whatever I want.

AJ: But that's really interesting, you felt restrained in working with other artists' pieces.

MA: Yeah, and I was always trying to stay in [dialogue with the original maker], even if I don't have some ideas about doing it, because I could never impose [my view of] the pieces. I had the photos and visual material and the time, so I know you can go on improvising in so many directions, because seven hours is a long time, but I really restricted myself, not to [improvise beyond what I knew of each piece].

AJ: So do you feel in a sense, do you feel yourself literally, not just in a verbal and historical dialogue, but actually embodied dialogue with these performers? Perhaps not with Nauman, because we have no direct evidence of him performing *Body Pressure*, but with what we imagine Acconci to have been doing?

MA: Yes, because this [*Seedbed*] was the piece that was really interesting for me at that time, which I wasn't originally able to see – obviously I was in Belgrade – and as everyone else I had seen the documentation – and I wanted to know how it would feel to do it. The Beuys piece was mainly set in stone [but the Acconci was more open]. And I had hoped to do a Chris Burden work, *Trans-Fixed* from 1974.

AJ: But Burden wouldn't give permission for you to re-enact it.

MA: He wouldn't give permission, which I have to respect. [I was worried about Burden because he had done a similar piece to my *House with the Ocean View*[8] called *White Light White Heat* at Ronald] Feldman Gallery in New York City in 1975, where he lived and slept in the gallery for three weeks without eating. I was really questioning how he had done it; because after twelve days in *Ocean View* I went [into a difficult psychological space] – I experienced so many of the problems physically. I found myself wondering – did he drink just one glass of water per day? Celery juice or something? So I was questioning all this with a journalist who was interviewing me. But it came out, as the journalist turned what I said around [in the newspaper story], that I didn't believe that Burden had actually made this piece, that I was accusing him of cheating. Somebody told me that actually this was the reason [he wouldn't give me permission to re-enact his work].

AJ: It's a shame that Burden wouldn't just be in dialogue with you instead of assuming a certain interpretation of what you meant.[9]

MA: I think it's not just me personally [he was reacting to]; I think there have been so many bad experiences in his past that he feels like everyone is just living off his ideas. [It's a shame] because I was just questioning physically how it would be possible to last twenty-one days – it's so dangerous – you are digesting your muscles you know without food. I was really having terrible problems after I finished *Ocean View*.

AJ: You just had water didn't you?

MA: Yeah, and only, they make me vegetable soup after twelve days and I drank it but it just went straight through. For days I was like this; I couldn't believe it, just nothing was digestible. So then I was questioning his interpretation.

Anyway, so I could not redo *Trans-Fixed*, which is a shame because I was very interested in the female psychic relation. And I wanted to do it with a Tito car instead of a Volkswagen.

AJ: Marina, can I follow up on the crucial issue of what happens with intentionality in re-enactments? I've raised this question in relation to embodiment – how you relate to another artist's work versus how you relate to your own *Lips of Thomas* in redoing it. When you look back at *Lips of Thomas*, for example, do you feel like you know what you "intended" to do at the time of the original performance? Do you feel like you can totally recapture that original moment? Or do you feel it's to some extent impossible to retrieve what you "meant" to be doing at the time?

MA: I really didn't know exactly what I was doing originally with the piece, because at that time there were so many things, the ideas were just coming, I didn't have a fully conscious relationship with the things that I was doing. Sometimes I would do things and I would say, oh, how does this relate to the rest of the work? And I always feel if you have this urge to do a thing, it does not matter what the context, you have to do it.

AJ: And then looking back, you kind of become a historian or (in your words) "archaeologist" of your work as well as of others' works you re-enact. This kind of looping back is so rich because you're adding to the works each time.

MA: Yes, when you redo your own work you can really see the bigger picture; the first time you can't see what's going on – you are just doing it. I think this re-enacted performance was much better than the original. I really did the best I could, I think, at that time, but I didn't have the consciousness I have now.

AJ: In *Lips of Thomas* you're also holding together and manipulating literal attributes from your own past.

MA: So it becomes kind of complete in retrospect – but at that time [of the original performance] it was not.

AJ: Whereas when you're redoing, say, Acconci's work you're doing something totally different. You're a historian but in a different sense.

MA: Exactly. With Acconci and other pieces you are more like an archaeologist who takes elements of some of other culture or another civilization and puts together your own interpretation, but I don't have the big picture [in redoing Acconci's work] like I have in relation to my own piece.

AJ: So, redoing another artist's performance you begin with these tiny, tiny fragments from the original – photographs, text, perhaps some film or video footage, but only fragments. When you redo the work you're not retrieving the intentionality you're just redoing the act, based on extremely fragmentary evidence.

MA: With instructions, you're just retracing. Really you are an archaeologist.

AJ: I was just in dialogue with Adrian Heathfield, my co-editor, about what he would ask you if he were here, and you know he pulled out this issue of spirit and energy which you've raised here a couple of times. Since he's not here I'll re-enact his question! What is recoverable about a performance across time, and what of the "spirit" of the work can and cannot be replicated? You seem to feel this question of spirit or energy is part of what is so important about the *live* act. I think that's what he's getting at with the term spirit.

MA: It is just the fact that it's live that makes such a big difference you know. The energy flows. Actually, I could not do when I was young the forty-nine hours of performance like I can do now. Not because I am physically stronger because I am not. But I am emotionally stronger. I have more willpower than before. Because you have to have motivation to do it – otherwise it doesn't work. It's maybe really what [Heathfield is calling] the spiritual dimension which I can [access] now. As you are getting older that becomes stronger. And with willpower you can do anything you want with your body. It doesn't matter that you are strong or weak you just have to.

AJ: And that's what you feel is being conveyed in the live situation, is something to do with that energy? That's what you mean by willpower even in the context of a re-enacted work?

MA: Actually [with re-enactments] it's not about preserving the thing; it's about finding a new one, a new energy.

AJ: It seems to me that a lot of what you're talking about with the live has to do with *time*, the structure and experience of time and how memory loops back to retrieve lost moments in the past. I'm thinking of this looping back over your career as you have done, and also with *Seven Easy Pieces*, how carefully you obviously thought through the components and the overall structure – each of the re-enactments took seven hours; overall they took place over seven days. Also the endurance element, the experience of making yourself available to the public for that amount of time, must take an incredible amount of energy on your part. The re-enactments have a rhythm and a time of their own, but also recall past live events.

So I'm interested in knowing what that felt like for you from the inside of the pieces over the stretch of time it took to enact them.

I'm also interested in the way in which your works, both the "original" pieces and the re-enactments, lend themselves to an emotional engagement, which can be very moving but also sentimental.

MA: In the works from *Seven Easy Pieces*, yes that's true.

It's very difficult, I have to tell you. Because [in each performance I'm like a totally separate person]: even my oldest friends don't recognize me when I perform – it's like I step into something else. It's like you step into this higher self which you cannot maintain.

You know one thing that really starts to be important to me is to not to be ashamed of my contradictions – which I was ashamed of for a long, long time [when I was younger]. After the Chinese Wall piece when I had so much pain, I [decided I didn't] want to put anyone through anything [so personal again]

When people see performers, they always try to make a hero out of you, always try to glorify you or make you this icon, which actually you can't live up to. [But in my work,] I'm just showing everything that is imperfect. It's not easy for me, because I'm embarrassed. I'm not living up to [their expectations] you know. Yes in performance, but not in real life.

[Perhaps because of this dynamic] my pieces all the time cause extreme emotional reactions. In the gallery where I did *House with the Ocean View* there were six or seven huge boxes in which people left handkerchiefs, bracelets, watches. The most wonderful was the little serviette from the rest room [on which was] written "this is great – let's have lunch," [signed] Susan Sontag. So, then I went to have lunch with her. But, it was all these [little engagements with people, like having lunch with Sontag] you know, which change my life.

But I took a very big risk doing *House with the Ocean View*, which I only realized doing the piece. I understood that the public looking at this, they are down and I am up, so [I became an] icon, you know. This [dynamic] amplified that feeling of sentimentality and worship, which was actually not my aim in doing the piece at all. I

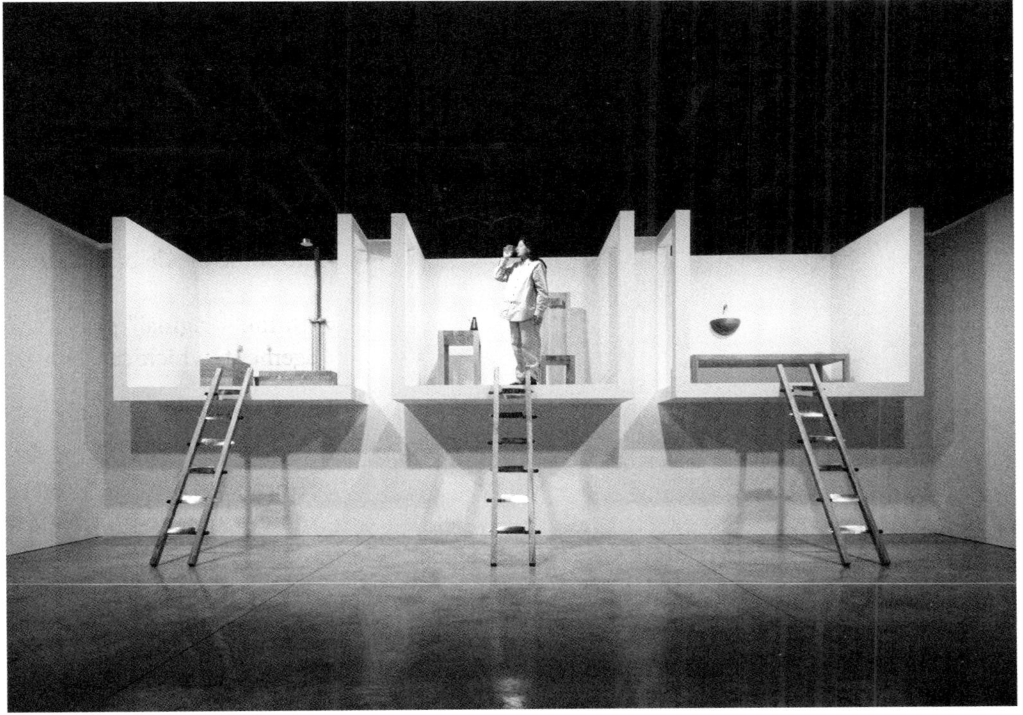

Marina Abramović, *The House with Ocean View*. Performance, Sean Kelly Gallery, New York, 2002. Photo: Attilio Maranzano. Courtesy Abramović Archive and Sean Kelly Gallery, New York.

didn't want to have this hierarchy; I'm not interested in this at all. I wanted to be totally normal and down to earth, [but] then you know something else happened.

AJ: So, expanding on this point, how you feel about the hagiographic accounts of your work? Is this approach, building you into an icon or over-identifying with you emotionally, what you want? Is that how you want your work to be seen? Or how much do you feel that you can shape how much your work is seen in history?

MA: You know that's very difficult. Before I die I have to leave as many instructions as possible to describe how the work should be performed, shown, and seen. But how it can be seen depends on the state of the spirit of society at the time.

Even now in my own testament I made very clear instructions about my funeral. It's very important to me because I went to funerals of some of my friends and I found the music wrong, and it totally went against the spirit of the person who died and so my testament is now sealed. It will [involve] three coffins, two fake and one [with my] real body. They will be in the three different places where I lived the most: one in Yugoslavia, one in Holland, and one in America. Nobody will know which has the real body. [I also insist that no one wear] any color of black or grey or any kind of beige; they must wear green, red, yellow, citron, you know, something very strong. They have to be extremely happy for the whole event, and in the background I want to have Frank Sinatra singing the really kitschy song "I did it my way." And then to make sure it's going to be exactly as I want it there'll be a rehearsal before.

In the same spirit I will leave instructions for every bit of my work. But after that I can't control [what happens with] it. You can only control it as far as you're concerned.

AJ: Can you talk about how you have trained people from different companies to redo some of your pieces?

MA: Yes. I made the biggest book of my own students redoing works. I have forty-two former students who have studied with me, from twenty-two different countries and I've now formed some of them into an independent performance group. In [the 2007] Venice Biennale there is a big performance and dance festival component and I have organized performances by fifteen of them. I've worked in the role of curator.

[I've worked up this group as a stable of performers.] So, if you wanted to look for some young performance artists, you come to me and I give you all the performers you want and then you choose.

AJ: So it's almost like you've formed a modeling agency.

MA: Yes. Exactly. I want to have "rent the performance artist," like when you want models for shooting.

There are so many artists now who are not making performances, but their ideas are performative projects. So they need people, but they are mostly looking to dancers or actors who are not performance artists. They are different; they have a different language of the body. So instead of that, we are going to rent [them] a performer [and in addition give young artists jobs]! All of my people are doing their own work, trained in long durational pieces.

AJ: Tell me about your upcoming retrospective at the Museum of Modern Art [MoMA] in New York. [Organized by Klaus Biesenbach and Jenny Schlenzka, the show, entitled "Marina Abramović: The Artist is Present," took place in April and May of 2010, two and a half years after this dialogue took place].

MA: Part of the retrospective will involve people I've auditioned to re-enact some of my performances over the three months of the show. [There will also] be installations and other stuff. And I am going to do certain things live myself.[10]

AJ: How do you deal with the fact that MoMA is the establishment?

MA: MoMA has [the potential to draw up to] 50,000–70,000 visitors a day! And I want to make my work respected.

AJ: So you don't have any issues with having your work institutionalized in the bastion of modernism?

MA: No, no, no, because it's perfect for what you have to do. You have to put something non-institutionalized in there, exactly, because they've never done such a thing. So I'm trying to do that. [I want to work within the institution because] I'd really like to change it, in order that they accept [the kind of work I do], because if they ask me, they don't expect me to make paintings!

AJ: Well just make sure that you retain some control, and that working with such an institution doesn't change the way you work entirely – I worry that you can't avoid compromising the rawness of the work. Isn't this precisely the "energy" that you talk about as essential to the live artwork?

MA: No: I told them the idea, and that the biggest part of the work is going to be one [new live] performance. I'm going to give myself two months [to do this endurance piece].

My big dream is that I can have my ex-students and all the other artists to perform in the museum at the same time a long durational work. With Artists Space I am currently curating a project called *When Time Becomes Form*; every two months one of my artists performs a durational performance for one week eight hours a day.

AJ: Right, right – so you're working with ways to recreate the temporality? So in terms of documenting or recreating the temporality of such performances, is there a method that you prefer? For *Seven Easy Pieces* do you prefer the book, the still photographs and text, or the filmed documentation? Or are these all just different and equally important ways of accessing or re-enacting the past?

MA: Documentation will never replace live performance. But you know I think that Babette [Mangolte, who filmed *Seven Easy Pieces*] maybe did it best. The best absolutely ever DVD documentation. Because she pulled 90 minutes from 49 hours of performing. The way she got all the boredom [but within only 90 minutes of footage] … cut cut cut. I think the feeling [from the DVD version] is the best. Anyway, the person who does it has to be incredibly [connected.] Because she was active in the 1970s, she saw some of these pieces live; she was the right person.

AJ: She also filmed those Robert Morris redos for his show at the Guggenheim in 1994. What's the marketing plan for the [*Seven Easy Pieces*] film?

MA: So now Babette is showing the film in festivals, and it's so expensive for us because Guggenheim never paid a fee for my performance, never paid anything for the film, nothing, zero. Nor the book.

[MA and AJ look at Mangolte's film of *Seven Easy Pieces*]

MA: [With the Nauman piece] I had to make the decision with glass, because it had to be visible by 360 degree for everybody you know. I did it for seven hours. You see, I don't have patience in real time to do what I do for seven hours in a performance. I don't!

AJ: Was there one of the pieces that was more crowded than others?

MA: *Thomas Lips* was crowded, but [the redo of Acconci's *Seedbed*] was extremely crowded. The public was really involved with this piece. Some people really got into it sexually! And for me it was a disaster because I had the eight orgasms, which I never had in my life! Mechanically I mean. And then I was so tired. And she [Mangolte] put more focus on the public, and I think it's the best in a way, for the film, the atmosphere.

You see we changed this, because people had to wait [to get up the ramp], we could not put so many on at a time, sometimes they had to go. And some people didn't want to move because they had to leave to get other people in.

[Looking at footage of Abramović's version of EXPORT's *Genital Panic*]

MA: The machine gun was so painful[ly heavy]. I never tried holding a machine gun in my life.

AJ: Is it harder to do the pieces where you're performing physical actions? Or the pieces when you're still?

MA: Still is much harder. People don't understand that. All these pieces, jumping, running slapping, you know it's so much easier actually than this kind of business.

AJ: Well, the passage of time must be so much more excruciatingly slow when you're still. Marina, I'm interested in whether any of the artists showed up to their redos?

MA: That's really interesting, VALIE EXPORT was invited. Last minute we sent a ticket. Last minute she had something else to do, she didn't come. Acconci was invited, but he had to do something in Japan. Bruce Nauman never goes anywhere. The woman from the Beuys estate never comes to America on principle. And Gina Pane's partner … I don't know, she didn't come.

[Watching the redo of Pane's *The Conditioning*]

These little movements [over seven hours] the heat of the candles. As I said, I can do it but I can't look at it!

AJ: So watching the documentation, maybe you get a sense of what the audience experiences on some level?

MA: Yes.

AJ: Was the seven hours just based on your concept of having the seven days of a week, loosely based on Biblical (Christian) time?

MA: No, no, no. It was the idea of seven hours, because most museums are open seven hours a day! But you don't see the end of the pieces. [They began] in the middle of the hours of opening, but you never see the endings – every time at midnight the gong rang, and audience had to leave so they never saw the end so the work seemed to continue endlessly.

Notes

1. Taken from the Guggenheim website: http://www.guggenheim.org/exhibitions/Abramović/, accessed 4 May 2006.
2. *The Lovers: The Great Wall Walk* (1988) is the performance Abramović staged with her lover Ulay to mark the end of their relationship. The two performers walked from opposite directions along the *Great Wall of China* until they met 90 days later, at which point they said goodbye.
3. Abramović's mother was an art historian, she worked as Director of the Museum of Revolution and Art in Belgrade, as well as being a major in the Yugoslavian army.
4. The film was included in *Destricted: Art and Provocation*, a group of seven short films with pornographic content directed by art world luminaries such as Abramović and Matthew Barney and screened at Sundance and the Tate Gallery in 2005.
5. See the chapter by Mechthild Widrich in this volume, in which new research casts doubt on whether EXPORT actually performed the piece in a theater.
6. Julia Steinmetz, Clover Leary, and Heather Cassils founded Toxic Titties in Los Angeles in the 1990s. See their article about this intervention in *Signs*: Julia Steinmetz, Heather Cassils, and Clover Leary "Behind Enemy Lines: Toxic Titties Infiltrate Vanessa Beecroft," *Signs: Journal of Women in Culture and Society*, Spring 2006, vol. 31, no. 3, pp. 753–83.
7. See Marina Abramović, *Seven Easy Pieces*, photographs by Attilio Maranzano, film stills by Babette Mangolte, Milan: Edizioni Charta, 2007.
8. Performed by Abramović at Sean Kelly Gallery in New York in 2002.
9. Since performing this interview with Abramović, Amelia Jones interviewed Burden, and asked him about this exchange. Burden stated the following:

    > Chris Burden: "I'll tell you a story about Marina Abramović—she did a performance series at the Guggenheim and she called me and wanted to 'do my Volkswagen performance,' she wanted my permission. And I said no, and she couldn't believe it and she just said, 'how can you say no?' I said, 'you asked me, so I said no.' She wanted to do on a Skoda, a Czechoslovakian car, or something and I said, 'Marina, the truth is you don't need to ask me and you don't need my permission you can do whatever you want, but now that you are asking me I'm saying no because its absolutely meaningless for you to do that performance or it has no meaning.' It becomes a parody and I think stupid."

    Interview with Chris Burden by telephone, January 20, 2010, for the Los Angeles Goes Live event, transcript available at the Los Angeles Contemporary Exhibitions Archives, p. 8.
10. For an extended analysis and description of the MoMA show, see Amelia Jones, "'The Artist is Present': Artistic Re-enactments and the Impossibility of Presence," *TDR: The Drama Review*, Spring 2011, vol. 55, no. 1, pp. 16–45.

Chapter 42

Every House Has a Door

Lin Hixson and Matthew Goulish

1: Ireland
2: Childhood
3: Berlin
4: Escaping the question
5: A micro-dissertation on clouds, in three parts
6: Last
7: *Gaslight*
– Orphic interlude –
8: Why does the dancer stop dancing?
9: Epilogue
    Out of gas
    Every house has a door

> Life in this house-island is
> riddled with light a sense of
> something last to say first
> – Susan Howe

Lin Hixson: May I show you a photograph?

Matthew Goulish: Yes.

(Photograph 1 – *Air* – on)

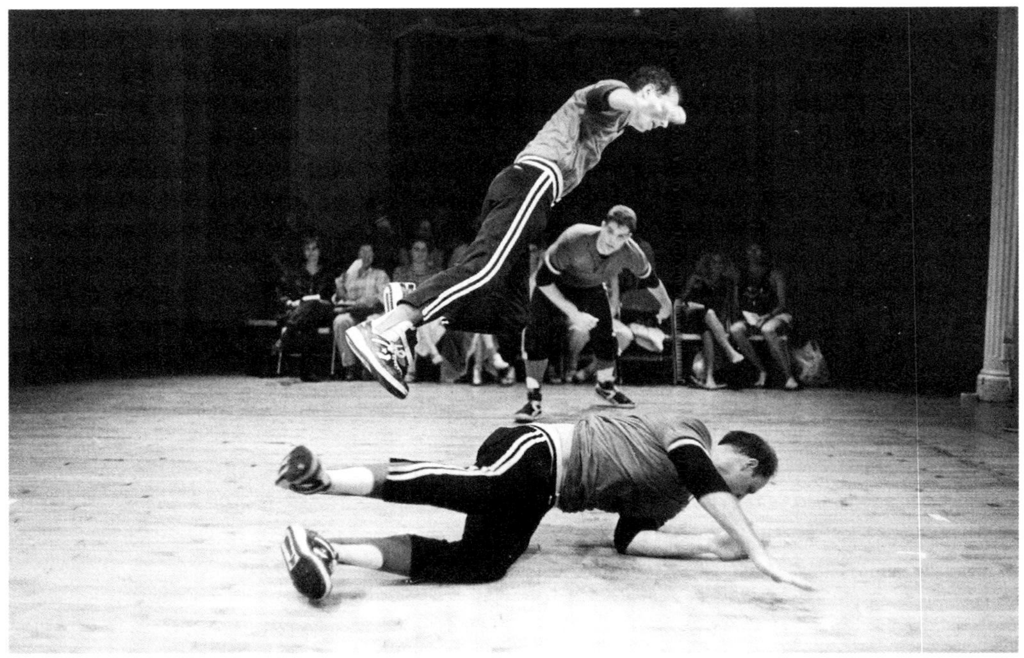

Air – Soldier, Child, Tortured Man by Dona Ann McAdams, in performance at PS122, NY, 1988. Pictured top to bottom: Matthew Goulish, Greg McCain, Timothy McCain.

MG: Part one: Ireland. I remember it.

LH: The photograph, or the moment?

MG: I remember the photograph, and I have the moment in my memory. What year was that?

LH: 1988. Performance Space 122, New York, before they covered over the wood floor and painted it black. Then it was like performing in a room. Now it's like performing in a theater.

MG: They see a wood floor and they want to paint it black.

LH: About the photograph.

MG: There is one thing. You used to tell me that when I jumped I would hang in the air for a split-second before falling. You had read that the dancer could do that, what was his name? *Prelude to the Afternoon of the Faun.*

LH: Nijinsky.

MG: I was immensely flattered by the comparison. It left me, in its implications, terrified. Only a director of real stature would notice such things, and connect them, and speak them aloud. You drew wings for the dancers who you said could float. Nijinsky, and others whose names I forget. You had the wings in frames. I could say you made the frame of the performance in which I was allowed to leap like that, to float for a split-second.

LH: The soul can farther fly
Than any feather specified
in Ornithology —

MG: When Dona Ann McAdams e-mailed this photograph recently, she gave it the title: *Air*. Of twenty years of work, I thought, here is one split-second that defined us. What is that line from *It's a Wonderful Life*, the one that repeats two or three times, about wings?

LH: Teacher says, "Every time a bell rings, an angel gets his wings."

MG: Not to talk about angels necessarily, but about bells. For those of you just joining us, this is a photograph of a moment from Goat Island's first performance, *Soldier, Child, Tortured Man*. Lin has put it up on the screen, and it has made Matthew talk about bells, specifically, how we rang a bell in a later performance titled *It's Shifting, Hank* – an actual school bell. I drove much of an afternoon to the store where I could purchase it. I remember the first time I heard it ring in the frame of the performance, I thought, "If I believed in souls, I would say my soul is in that bell." School starts now. School stops now. Greg, in the background of this photograph, with his face to the camera, he put on foamboard angel wings at the end of that piece.

LH: He was nude, like a cherub.

MG: He works now as an orderly in Northwestern Memorial Hospital in Chicago, in the psychiatric ward. Tim, the one in the foreground, Greg's brother, he got married and has a son named Beckett.

LH: You were saying, about the bell?

MG: In Irish literature, according to the convention of a *feth fiada*, the sound of a bell signals a moment of interface between this world and some other.

LH: We could be talking about *How Dear to Me the Hour When Daylight Dies.*

MG: Because we went on a pilgrimage, to start that piece, to Westport, Ireland. While on the trip Greg and Tim found out that their father had died. Old Story by Robert Creeley, from the diary of Francis Kilvert.

LH: One bell wouldn't ring loud enough.
So they beat the bell to hell, Max,
with an axe, show it who's boss,
boss. Me, I dreamt I dwelt in
some place one could relax
but I was wrong, wrong, *wrong.*
You got a song, man, sing it.
You got a bell, man, ring it.

MG: Thank you. Robert Creeley.

(Photograph 1 – *Air* – off)

LH: You were thinking of memory …

MG: I think memory is thinking. I think memory is thinking memory. Part two: Childhood.

LH: I used to think my childhood was like a beast with a lion's body and the head of a man, and the mouth of a frog and the skin of a snake, and the lips of a hippopotamus and the nose of an Encyclopedia Britannica, and whose fingers were fiddler crabs, and whose ears were plugged with wax so they would not hear the cauldron of boiling armadillos in its belly. And its veins were aphids and its nipples were wolverines, and its heart was the paw of a chimpanzee, and its penis was a caterpillar, and its knuckles were catbirds. And its left butt cheek was a bioflavinoid, and its right butt cheek was a mountain goat. And its mouth was Vanessa Redgrave, and its arms were plankton and its teeth a red bone. But now I no longer think so bleakly of my childhood.

MG: What do you think of when you think of your childhood now?

LH: Now I think my childhood is like a blue and white dress with an empire waist whose mother has climbed out of the second floor window and onto the limb of a tree, and whose party guests have all left in embarrassment. Now I want my childhood to know that she is blameless.

(Photograph 2 – *Hand* – on)

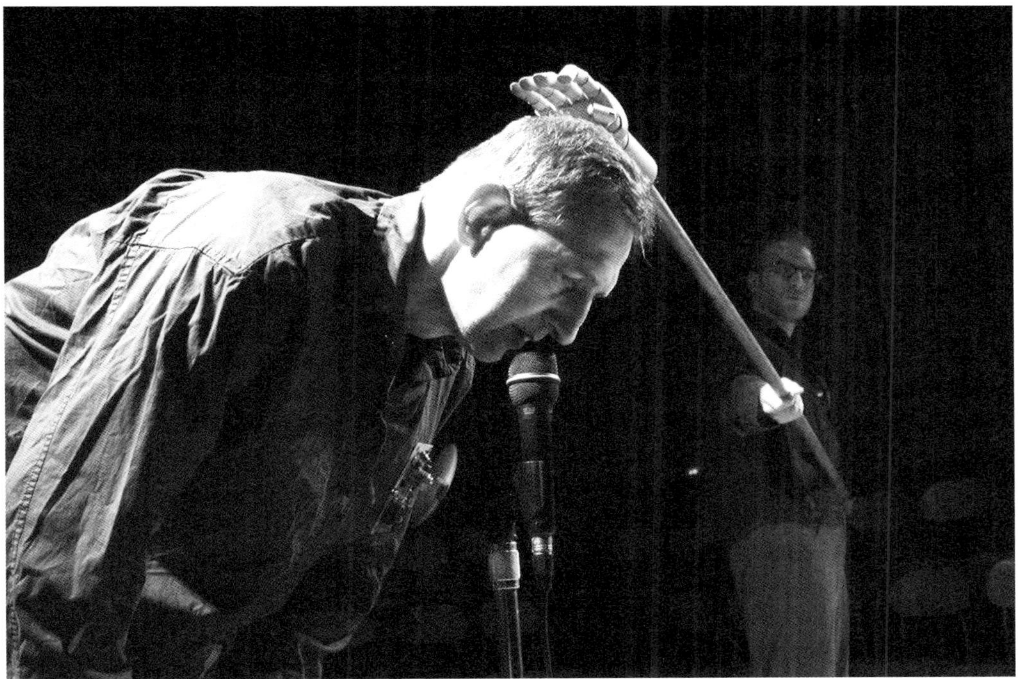

Hand – It's an Earthquake in My Heart by Rebecca Groves, in performance at Mousonturm, Frankfurt, Germany, 2001. Pictured left to right: Bryan Saner, Mark Jeffery.

MG: Part three: Berlin.

LH: When I think of the last time we saw Berlin, I think of Bryan Saner folded in half over a microphone on a low stand. I think of Mark Jeffery holding the puppet hand on a stick over his head.

MG: As seen in this photograph by Rebecca Groves, taken at a performance of *It's an Earthquake in My Heart* in 2001.

LH: I think of the following lines from Bryan's speech into the low microphone, extracted from the writing of the butoh dancer Tatsumi Hijikata.

MG: It rained often, when I was a boy. I sat on the verandah and watched the rain fall into the cabbage patch. How important the verandah is to me, I would think. The rain falls without beginning or end. As it falls, time and space become mixed and entwined, until no distinction remains between the two. And then I too deteriorate from the center, like rotting cabbage.

LH: My heart was always racing like a dog's; "thump, thump, thump," it would pound. I was possessed by the thought that if I didn't break the world apart, if I left it alone, somehow disaster would strike. I paced around and around and around. Hail would fall, and it would make no difference to me.

MG: Though I don't let anyone see, tears pour down my face when I recall my youth.

LH: The rain, the cabbage patch, the school, the movements of the next door neighbor's dog. They are like so many broken boats, drifting inside me in bits and pieces. From time to time, the boats gather, speak, and consume the darkness.

When I think of the last time I saw Berlin, I think of Bryan later after his bicycle accident, with both of his arms in casts. I think of Mark's father falling off the roof of a barn, and coming to see *When will the September roses bloom? Last night was only a comedy* at the Sandfield Center in Nottingham in a wheelchair in 2004, and then again *The Lastmaker* in 2007.

MG: The river flows on unceasingly, but the water is never the same water as before. Bubbles that bob on the surface of the still places disappear one moment, to reappear again the next, but they seldom endure for long. And so it is with the people of this world and with the houses they live in.

LH: I think of the last four sentences I wrote for *Lecture in a Stair Shape Diminishing*.

MG: How do they go?

LH: Tonight I begin to forget. My memory detaches from its locale, from the neighborhood it knows so well – the cracked sidewalks in July, the Christmas tree left up too long, the children's voices on an American fall afternoon. Perhaps if I'm lucky it will be replaced by a slow, moving cloud throwing rice. Or by a sycamore walking in the rain.

MG: I would like to return, if we could, to this question of a slow, moving cloud throwing rice, at some point in the near future.

LH: When I think of the last time I saw Berlin, I think of rain, people marching, hundreds of candles carried in the night. I think of Carl Thorne-Thomsen, who would have been sixty today. Carl was a senior in high school when I was a freshman. He was my brother's best friend. He was a quarterback on the varsity football team and the president of the student council. He held a gavel in his hand which he struck on his desk to bring the student council meetings to order. On 30 September 1967, four years after he graduated from high school, Carl Thorne-Thomsen got out of bed in Lake Forest, Illinois and into a car that drove him to the train which took him to O'Hare where he caught a plane to North Carolina and in a company of men flew to Thailand for a short stopover before flying to a piece of overgrown land in Viet Nam where a bullet broke open his stomach. Merry Christmas.

MG exits; Guest Reader enters.

For his funeral, Carl's parents hung a black sash over the front door. My brother came home from college and went to Carl's house. When leaving, he decided to enlist in the army. My father raised his voice and said, "No," and my brother received a deferment from compulsory military service. Today my brother has too much protein growing on parts of his brain. This effects his recall. But he remembers Carl Thorne-Thomsen. He repeats over and over the stories of Carl: missed football passes, nightswimming, sloe gin on the pier, toilet paper hung on trees after the prom. He asks me if I remember his tin soldiers. I do. My grandmother brought him the set from England. My brother took them and littered the ping pong table with elaborate formations. Lines of red uniformed men marched back and forth. Sometimes they faced one another with pointed bayonets. Sometimes they fell to the ground. "I was the one who should have gone," he says, "I rehearsed all those years with my soldiers. I was the one to go."

Guest: I wonder if you could put me in touch with Lin Hixson. She wrote two paragraphs in *Lecture in a Stair Shape Diminishing* (on your website) about a friend of mine who died in Vietnam in 1967, Carl Thorne-Thomsen. He and I went to France together in the summer of '64. A year or two later I visited him at Harvard. If Lin Hixson (I assume that's who LH is) knew him well I'd like to be in touch with her.

Yours sincerely,
Russell McGuirk (in London, England)

LH: Dear Russell,
Thank you for your email. I apologize for taking so long to reply. Carl was a friend of my brother Chip, who was his same age and in his same class at Lake Forest High School. Carl was a senior in high school when I was a freshman. I did not know him well. But I always admired and looked up to him. He was the first person I knew who was killed in Viet Nam and I found out this news at the same time I found out that my father was dying of cancer so the two of them are connected powerfully in my mind. Unfortunately my brother has a degenerative neurological disease and I have not been able to talk to him about his knowledge of Carl.

I hope this is helpful. Thanks again for contacting me. Lin

Guest: Dear Lin,

I found out about Carl's death in quite dramatic, almost unbelievable circumstances. In 1969 I was at Graduate School at Harvard, and in November of that year, with my fiancée and my brother, I went to Washington DC to join an anti-war march. There were hundreds of thousands of demonstrators, and some 50,000 of them were carrying placards to the Washington Monument, each bearing the name of an American killed in Vietnam. It was getting dark. It had rained, and there were fallen leaves everywhere. I noticed that one of the placards had been dropped face-down in a puddle. I went to get it, picked it up, and the name on the front was Carl Thorne-Thomsen. You will believe me, I'm sure, when I say this had the most powerful effect on me. Had the lady whom I subsequently married and my brother not been standing right there, I would have probably ceased to believe that it actually happened. That was over thirty-eight years ago. I've stopped trying to make sense of it. It simply happened.

Yours sincerely,
Russell McGuirk

LH: Dear Russell,
The gun was always with the water pistols.

Sincerely,
Lin Hixson

(Photograph 2 – *Hand* – off)

Guest Reader exits; MG enters.

MG: At one time, as far back as I can remember, I used to ask other people questions – the first person was quite certainly my mother – until I finally drove my parents to the verge of madness with my questions. Then suddenly I only asked myself questions, but only when I was sure of being ready with an answer. Everyone is a virtuoso on his own instrument, but together they add up to an intolerable cacophony. The word *cacophony* was incidentally a favorite of maternal grandfather's. And the phrase he hated more than any other was *thought process*.

LH: Part four: Escaping the question.

MG: Plant a question in a garden; define it without preventing it from flowering. Take it literally; take it allegorically; take it as a preface; take it as a mystery to decode. Ask the question five different ways before attempting an answer. Compose responses that do not annihilate the question's delicate ecology; avoid the answer that kills it, and seek the response that disarms and multiples it. One method is this: let somebody else answer, and from a place of unknowing; namely, the past. A question does not express a lack, but a creative force: propose, disarm, multiply. This is a form of escape. From what are we escaping? I will leave that as a question.

LH: Speaking of questions, certain questions have been posed to us that we need to address. Why is Goat Island ending? What will come next? Do you have a suggestion?

MG: Yes. I suggest that we return to those questions at some point in the near future. For now perhaps we could revisit the question of the slow, moving cloud throwing rice. The reference is to the conclusion of Bryan's bent-over monologue from *It's an Earthquake in My Heart*, the same monologue that began with the Hijikata extracts that we recited. The conclusion goes like this.

LH: A noise came from the sky.
It was like the rush of a mighty wind.
It filled the house where we were sitting, and tongues of fire appeared to us.
A distribution of tongues as of fire, resting on each of us.
We began to speak.
Each one of us heard the words spoken in our own language.
We came from many nations.
But each one of us understood.
I'll begin again.
The wind flung the door open.
It knocked over my water cup.
I went outside.
I looked at the sky.
This event appeared to confuse the birds.
But I was not afraid.
I saw a cloud in the shape of a country church.
The country church from my hometown.
Two smaller clouds in the shape of my parents.
A car-shaped cloud with a Just Married sign hanging on it.
The clouds showed me my parents wedding day.
It was very nice for nature to imitate reality this way.
My father wore blue, and my mother wore white.
They got in the car cloud and drove away.
Other clouds threw rice, as was the custom in those days, long before I was born.
Then it started to rain.
I held out my hand.

I caught a raindrop in my hand.
These things are miracles.
And not only miracles.
They are improbable miracles.
I never stopped loving the world.

MG: There can occur the kind of catastrophe that, rather than producing chaos from order, produces order out of chaos. Disorder is simply the order we are not looking for, and this is that, the myth of Pentecost, the lightning bolt that strikes a pile of firewood and causes a plum tree to spring up. My thoughts take the form of a genealogical tracing of this cloud through the form of three clouds, or three repetitions of one cloud, or three occurrences of cloud essence, the essence of which changes with each occurence. The first I imagined when I read the following passage by Marcel Proust.

LH: People of taste tell us nowadays that Renoir is a great eighteenth-century painter. But in so saying they forget the element of Time, and that it took a great deal of time, even at the height of the nineteenth century, for Renoir to be hailed as a great artist. To succeed thus in gaining recognition, the original painter or the original writer proceeds on the lines of the oculist. The course of treatment they give us by their painting or by their prose is not always pleasant. When it is at an end the practitioner says to us: "Now look!" And, lo and behold, the world around us (which was not created once and for all, but is created afresh as often as an original artist is born) appears to us entirely different from the old world, but perfectly clear. Women pass in the street, different from those we formerly saw, because they are Renoirs, those Renoirs we persistently refused to see as women. The carriages, too, are Renoirs, and the water, and the sky;

MG: … and the sky;

LH: … we feel tempted to go for a walk in the forest which is identical with the one which when we first saw it looked like anything in the world except a forest, like for instance a tapestry of innumerable hues but lacking precisely the hues peculiar to forests. Such is the new and perishable universe which has just been created. It will last until the next geological catastrophe is precipitated by a new painter or writer of original talent.

MG: The passage restates, in artistic terms, what Bergson stated in philosophical terms in *on the retrograde motion of truth* from his volume *The Creative Mind*. As Proust certainly understood, the world, the universe, the drama of the creative work, unfolds inside the body of the artist, and reading is a process of unfolding in the body of the reader. So we perceive the world according to the unfoldings inside us, of our understandings of the world as perceived by others. In Renoir's time, a cloud may have looked like a

Renoir – in Vermeer's time, a Vermeer. Imagine the past according to what we know of it. The landscape is never neutral, never pre-existing and objective, but only ever created and recreated by we who perceive it – landscape, cloudscape, or features of a human face. From there, of course, it is only a short leap to imagine a cloud that takes the form of a photograph from a family album. Cloud #2, of course, you will recognize from the final moments of our final performance *The Lastmaker*. When Bryan, Karen, and Litó (or Charissa) have all climbed up on the elevated planks, and I have finished my last speech and left the stage, and the music is playing, and Mark walks the length of the boards holding the artificial cloud aloft. This cloud was copied and enlarged from a template for a nametag for a children's party game. Cut out from white foamboard, it resembles a nostalgic stagecraft of the sort we used for Greg's angel wings in *It's Shifting, Hank* – a miniature theater, a stageplay within a performance, a puppet shadowbox of childhood, the past, the future, heaven, the imaginary, the land called Honalee.

(Photograph 3: *Splits* on)

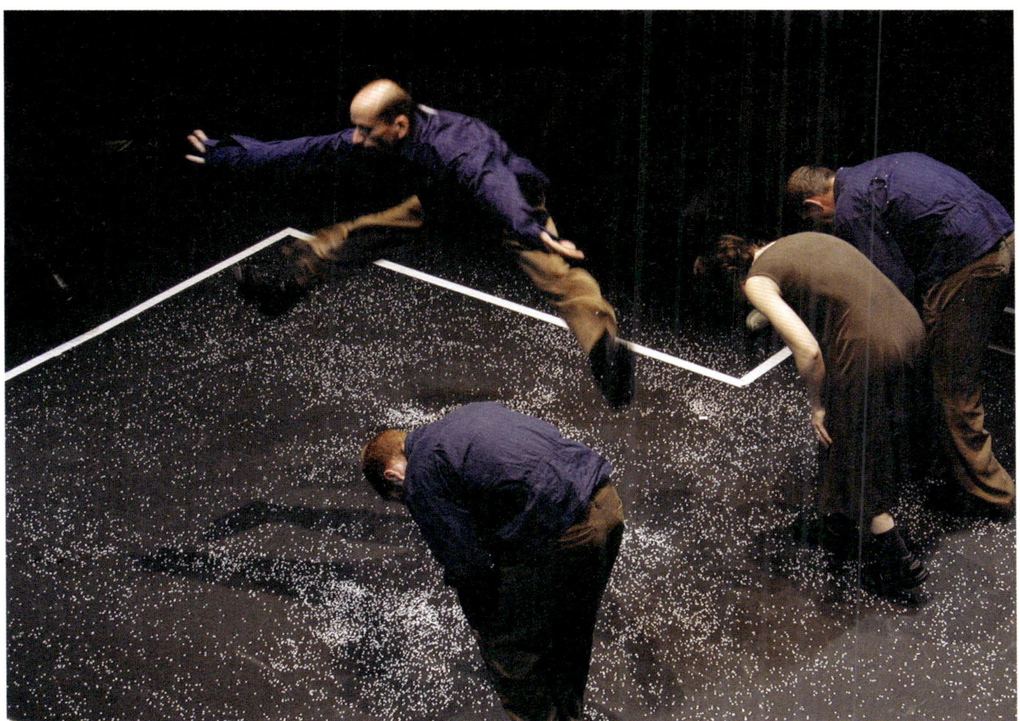

Splits – It's an Earthquake in My Heart by Rebecca Groves, in performance at Mousonturm, Frankfurt, Germany, 2001. Pictured left to right: Mark Jeffery, Matthew Goulish (in air), Karen Christopher, Bryan Saner.

LH: There you are in the air again.

MG: What's this photograph doing here? It's a mistake, I think.

LH: Imitating Dominique.

MG: No. Not yet. Can we take away the photo please? We haven't gotten to that part yet. We're still in the dissertation on clouds.

(Photograph 3: *Splits* off)

MG: Thank you. This is part five, by the way. A micro-dissertation on clouds, three appearances of clouds, or three clouds, or three repetitions of one cloud, a small cloud, part three.

LH: Do you mean part three of part five?

MG: Yes, exactly.

LH: You are obsessed with structure. Has anyone ever told you that?

MG: Obsessed?

LH: Part one, part two, part three of part five. Do you really think people follow that?

MG: Obsessed is from the Middle English, to haunt, or to be haunted by. Maybe there is a mathematics, a pattern for every desire. When one memory moves in, it appears to move the previous memory aside. Is that really the case, or does the older memory nest within the newer one? Maybe these parts fold into one another, so when we say *childhood*, then we say *Berlin*, we mean for *Berlin* to include *childhood*. Does that make sense to you?

LH: We could say it is a landscape, or like a landscape.

MG: What is?

LH: Structure.

MG: This structure, yes, the one we are inside now, and peering out of, like a hole in the wall, from where we are, or were. Which is where, exactly? I mean, where was I?

LH: Part five, clouds, part three.

MG: I'll be brief. At some point it became apparent that all the clouds of Goat Island – because don't forget *It's an Earthquake in My Heart* began as a proposal to study cloud formations, inspired by the music of Friedrich Cerha, a proposal that was rejected, which of course did not prevent the study from going forward – that all the clouds of Goat Island had descended from, or were repetitions of, or were in fact the same cloud that appears in the following poem.

LH: *Remembering Marie A.* by Bertolt Brecht.

MG: It was a day in that blue month September
Silent beneath a plum tree's slender shade
I held her there, my love so pale and silent
As if she were a dream that must not fade.
Above us in the shining summer heaven
There was a cloud my eyes dwelt long upon
It was quite white and very high above us
Then I looked up, and found that it had gone.

And since that day so many moons, in silence
Have swung across the sky and gone below
The plum trees surely have been chopped for firewood
And if you ask, how does that love seem now?
I must admit: I really can't remember
And yet I know what you are trying to say.
But what her face was like I know no longer
I only know: I kissed it on that day.

As for the kiss: I'd long ago forgot it
But for that cloud that floated in the sky
I know that still, and shall forever know it
It was quite white and moved in very high.
It may be that the plum trees still are blooming
That woman's seventh child may now be there
And yet that cloud had only bloomed for minutes
When I looked up, it vanished on the air.

LH: Whereas feet walked across my mind when I said the words Goat Island, lastness, and twenty years –

And whereas a bird flew recklessly toward my window when I wrote these words –
I now ask cautiously why we walked where we walked and at times flew.

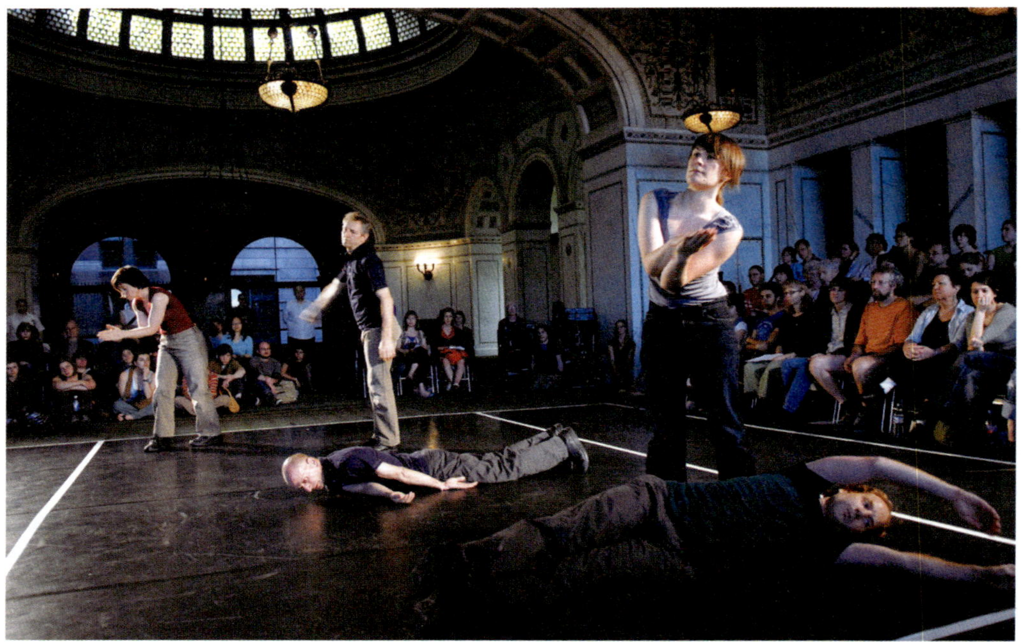

Lastmaker at Cultural Center – The Lastmaker by Nathan Mandell, work-in-progress The Cultural Center, Chicago, 4 June 2006. Pictured left to right: Karen Christopher, Matthew Goulish (on floor), Bryan Saner, Litó Walkey, Mark Jeffery (on floor).

(Photograph 4: *Lastmaker at Cultural Center* on)

MG: Part six: last.

LH: For me, it started in 1984 two years before the founding of Goat Island with feet stomping on a stage in Los Angeles in Tadashi Suzuki's production of Trojan Women when I saw history rise from the ground.

Suzuki might say, "When you strike your feet on the floor and you arouse the energy below, use it to activate a human life."

So that when, in 1987, Tim McCain, Greg McCain, Matthew Goulish, and I decided we had $100 a month to pay for a floor to make work on, we chose a gym in a church in Chicago that illegally housed Salvadoran refugees.

We never saw the floors we moved on as neutral even when they were painted black. It was a small gesture to consider carefully who we paid our money to but now twenty years later I see that small gestures grow like pages in a book to make a life.

I had the sensation for many years as we worked in the gym that things were falling in pieces to the ground. They were – in Iraq, in the former Yugoslavia, in Rwanda, in

Afghanistan, again in Iraq, in Darfur, in New York, in our bodies and in the bodies of others.

During that time, Karen and Mark struggled across the floor with wooden blocks on their feet. Matthew planted a seed on his head. Bryan stood silent with an audience. Litó stood on one foot for the length of two James Taylor songs. And all five tried to escape one of our performances through a hole in it.

Be not conformed by the limits of this world.

There was an aim upwards in these acts toward levity. Perhaps we thought we could convert into steam, fog or an exhalation and take those in the room with us. When vapors ascend into that region of the atmosphere of the same levity, they float.

But we never got that far off the ground. Instead we learned to zigzag across it and participate in its mobility and circulation.

I liked that our performances were answers to questions we never thought to ask. I like to think it was because of the conversations that we murmured with our feet.

MG: *So you're stopping because your work is finished.* A journalist said that to me. That's not at all what I said, I said. I could not make her understand, or communicate some understanding of the unknown, its importance. We stop precisely because our work is not finished. In order to continue our work, we must pursue the unknown. We capture an ending before an ending captures us – there is some truth to that. What began as a dream becomes responsibility, said William B. Yeats. Then it becomes a machine, it seems, a machinery. The work starts to work the artist, to push the unknown to the margins. Those margins call us now. Leave "the work" behind, aside, ended. It's the name more than anything. No matter how far afield you try to stray, as long as you do so under the umbrella of the name, you cannot escape. One cannot begin without ending. So we say we are ending before we end, to absorb the end into the work, in the form of *the last*. You watch the performance now, as if it has already ended. In the twilight margin, some unknown appears, a captured force.

(Photograph 5: *Lastmaker in Zagreb* on)

LH: How do you say good-bye? What if making a last performance becomes one of our directives for making a new one? *Last* is an adjective in the sense of being, coming, or placed after all others; final. *Last* is a verb in the sense of continuing in time; surviving; remaining in good condition. *Lasting* is the adjective that comes from this verb. *Last* is a block or form shaped like a human foot and used in the making of shoes. And *last (chiefly British)* is a unit of volume or weight varying for different commodities and in different districts, equal to about 80 bushels, 640 gallons, or two tons. A directive: construct a last performance in the form of a human foot that weighs two tons and remains in good condition.

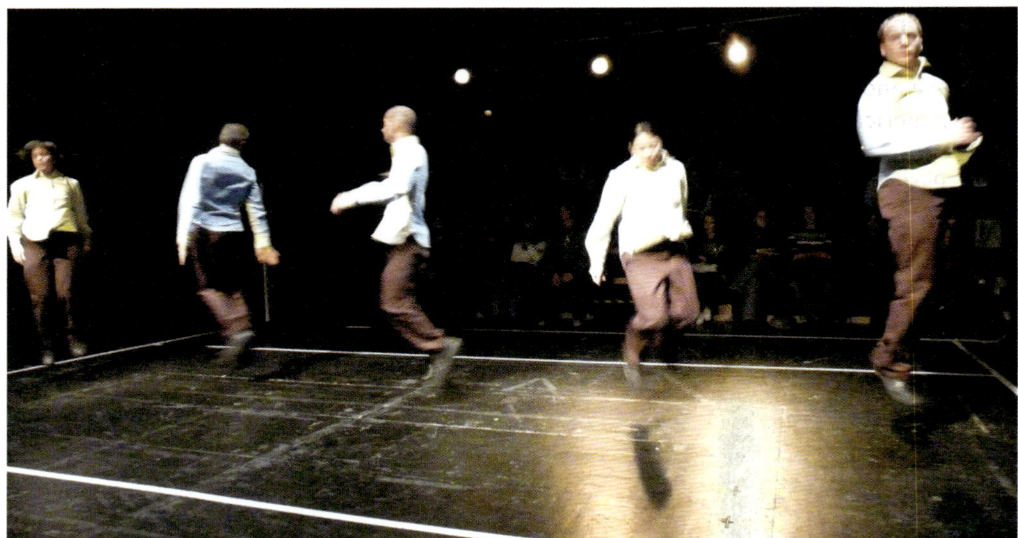

Lastmaker in Zagreb – The Lastmaker by Ivana Vucic and T. J. Kacunic, Teatar &TD, Zagreb, Croatia, 2007. Pictured left to right: Karen Christopher, Bryan Saner, Matthew Goulish, Charissa Tolentino, Mark Jeffery,

Thankfully you exceed me. You who tumble on the ground. Balance a long stick on your finger and ride the fence like a horse. You in your waking dreams provide eyes into the future. We stood in rooms that contained every moment. I think that laughter is set off when we are not afraid, says the writer Hélène Cixous. When we see that the immense is not overwhelming; as the imaginary possibility of taking a mountain in ones arms. Do not let it trouble you if you cannot walk on your head. The secret is one more step when you arrive.

MG: The one thing always still there at the end is the end. By *end* we might mean *reason*, or we might mean that which *obdurates*, hardens over the duration. *Durus*, hard; *durare*, to last. These are the insistent roots of the words that echo as we water them. Because I think lastness is less a subject and more a direction.

LH: In what sense?

MG: As director, you set us off in some direction. Lastness constitutes a point of the compass. A lastmaker makes a form, and around that form a cobbler makes a shoe. One removes the original shoe to allow others to fabricate other shoes that conform to the form of the last. The removal allows the continuation; the continuation necessitates the removal. This is what I wanted to say, not to say last, but to say next to last: the last, the void made solid.

(Photograph 6: *Mike Walker* on)

LH: We once made a performance that held the weight of Mike Walker, the fattest man in America, not in pounds but in words, spoken, by Karen, exactly.

MG: Part seven: gaslight.

LH: Exactitude – a feather on the scale, to balance the soul, weighed on the way to the afterlife.

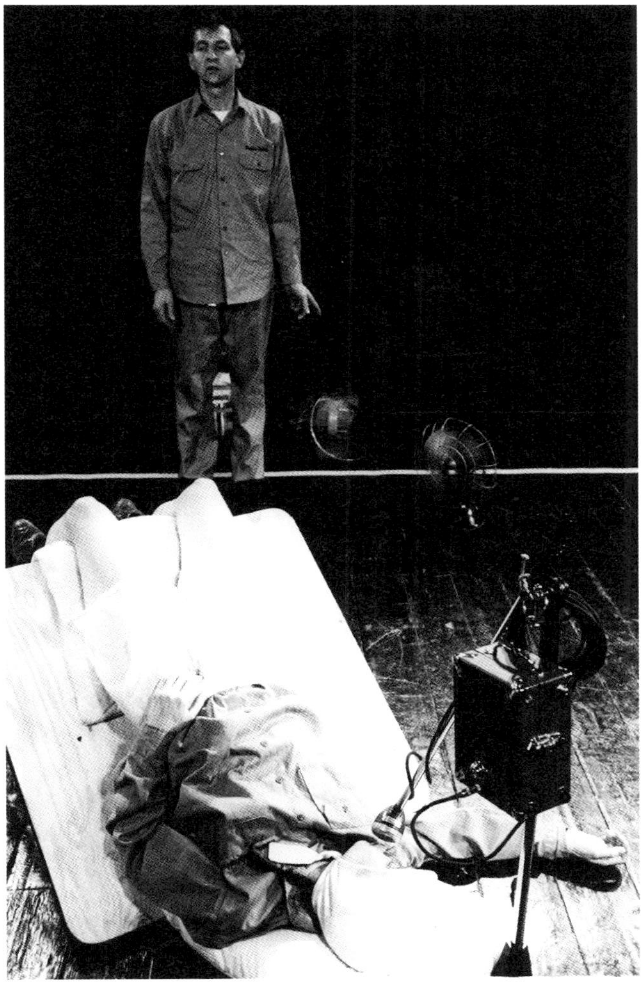

Mike Walker – How Dear to Me the Hour When Daylight Dies by Alan Crumlish, in performance at Centre for Contemporary Arts, Glasgow, 1996. Pictured top to bottom: Bryan Saner, Karen Christopher.

MG: Gas relates to *Geist* from the German, spirit or mind. The seventeenth century chemist van Helmont coined the connotation of "an occult principle present in all bodies." Can we link gas to chaos – to emptiness, disorder, preorder?

LH: And so I amend the directive: construct a last performance that weighs nothing.

MG: There are many things to be afraid of, like ghosts, and death, and climbing too high.

LH: When Goat Island performs, I shake.

But fright is formed by what we see not by what they say.

Things overlap in space and are hidden.

I write to break out into perfect primeval Consent. I wish I could tenderly lift from the dark side of history, voices that are anonymous, slighted – inarticulate.

(Photograph 7: *Splits* on)

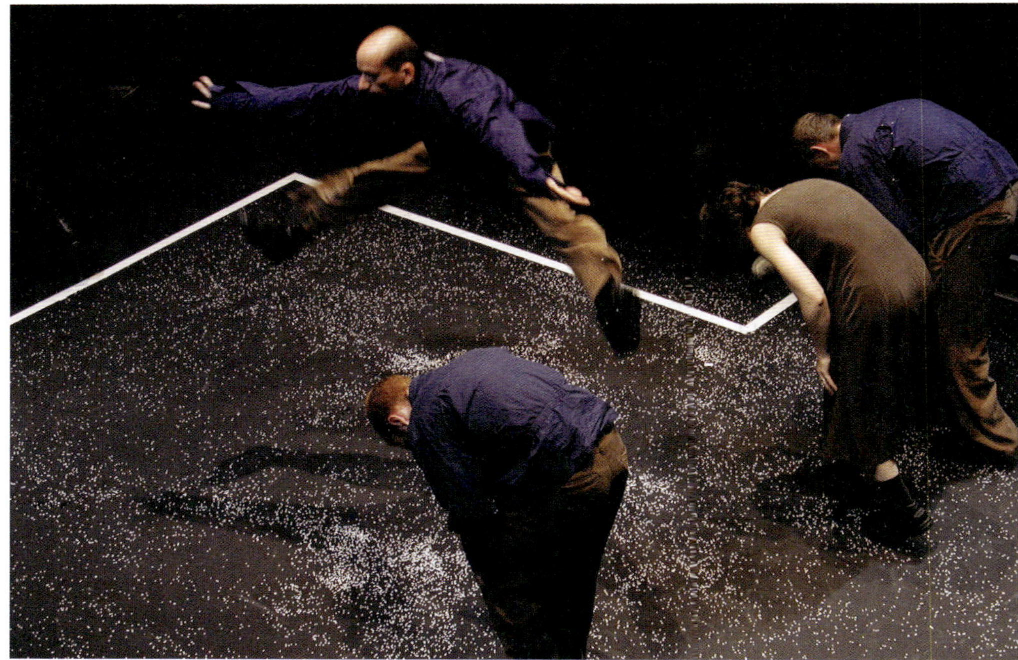

Splits – It's an Earthquake in My Heart by Rebecca Groves, in performance at Mousonturm Frankfurt, Germany, 2001. Pictured left to right: Mark Jeffery, Matthew Goulish (in air), Karen Christopher, Bryan Saner.

LH: There you are in the air again.

MG: That was when I did the dance that imitated Dominique Mercy from Pina Bausch's company. Maybe one may liken gas and geist to *spire*: inspire, respiration – the breath, the spirit. I was so small once I rode in my mother's grocery cart. At the butcher's counter, the ground beef at the front near the glass would always be molded into the shape of a pig's head looking at me. It seems strange now – a head of beef would have made more sense, but I remember a pig. If we arrived early enough in the morning we'd see the form intact rather than later with a scoop or two taken out. The wide entrance to this grocery store had plastic strips hanging. One had to walk through them, and over a grate that blasted air upward. It would always catch my breath. It frightened me, but I appreciated it. I thought of a spaceship airlock. Then once *Star Trek* came on the scene with its transporter room, the futuristic airlock became a thing of the past. That's all very good, I thought, molecules disaggregated, beamed through space, reconstituted. It makes for a nice special effect. But I am not comfortable with the destruction of the threshold. Of course the airlock made a triumphant return in *2001: A Space Odyssey*, but even that felt epilogic. Nostalgia crept into our re-enactments, because certainly one can play at an airlock in a tree house easily enough, and then the backyard becomes the surface of Venus, but how does one play at disaggregating and reconstituting molecules? Just stand still for ten seconds and say, "This is me beaming up"? What a waste of time, Jim. It could be anything. Can we bring back the airlock please? When I grocery shop now, I remember as I pause at the door, where sometimes in temperature-controlled produce areas one still encounters the blast of air, these moments of inspiration folded in upon themselves, and if I believed in the soul I would ask Dominique to have mercy on mine, because the store is named *Dominick's*, and there is nothing more to me than imitation.

(Photograph 7 *Splits* off)

LH: Here we are waiting on a platform, train station smells and sounds. A shining bright sunny morning. Bryan, Karen, Mark, Litó, John, Charissa, Margaret. Jake and Xenia, CJ and Boris. Judd and Lucy. You and me. Coffee, newspaper, a sandwich in a bag. We performed last night, and will perform again soon. The trunks have gone ahead in the van. The train is late, but not exceedingly. Again there is war. Again it is our country's doing. Again we tell ourselves our work resists the injustice, and again this is true perhaps in some small way: the poverty of image, the force of the ordinary, the collective, the extension of the faculties of attention. To open a space and not to fill it completely. Look at this, a tiny box of After the Last Supper Mints, with Leonardo's painting reproduced in miniature. A woman gave them to me after the show. A senior citizen, wise in that way, and able to smile at serious things. Pass them around. How strange the things that stay with us. Small events, small pictures, a mannerism, words spoken in a moment. We make certain decisions about significance, other decisions are made for us, made by no one, by circumstance. These are those moments, not of knowledge but of experience.

MG: Each element appears in full as it appears, not as a repetition. A tree is a tree. A cloud is a cloud. A hand is a hand. A face is just that, and nothing more. So it seems as it appears, in sequence, that everything is everything, until the end, and after the end.

LH: Then suddenly we see that all along something else has been forming. The landscape falls together into the form of a face. It has snuck up on us. We recognize it.

MG: It has been behind us, a breath, a breeze, a shade. We discover like Orpheus the danger of looking back, but only after it is too late. What we have loved has died away, and now our looking back has killed it a second time. Whatever we expected to see has vanished, and we see instead only landscape, and in the landscape, we recognize what has gone.

LH: The recognition, what is it? It is not in us. It is not part of us. It is us. It is the substance of us.

MG: To enchant is to make into a song, to invest with a quality of songness that which previously was not a song. Or something. When Orpheus sang in the underworld, it says in Ovid, *with his words, the music made the pale phantoms weep.*

LH: Why bring up Orpheus?

MG: Because we're looking back. Also because I had to pick up the poet Susan Howe at the University of Chicago last month and drive her up Lake Shore Drive to the School of the Art Institute, and during that drive she received a call on her cell phone, a poetry professor from the University reviewing notes for a lecture, asking Susan to clarify a point about an Emily Dickinson poem, and all at once Susan recited this poem from memory in the car into her cell phone.

LH: With Pinions of Disdain
The soul can farther fly
Than any feather specified
in Ornithology —
It wafts this sordid Flesh
Beyond its dull — control
And during its electric gale —
The body is a soul —
instructing by the same —
How little work it be —
To put off filaments like this
for immortality

MH: Ornithology, said Susan Howe, that's the key to the poem, because in the manuscript, Emily Dickinson has written the word *flying up the margin*, and that's what the poem is about, said Susan, it's about the word ornithology flying up the margin. And when you go into class, said Susan, take the Oxford English Dictionary, it's in the office and still open to the page. Look up the word ornithology, and look at all the other O words that occur coincidentally near it, for example, said Susan, Orpheus.

LH: Cast the nets in rivers north of the future.

MG: There are still songs to be sung on the other side of humanity.

LH: I believe we are coming to an end.

MG: I agree. Let me rephrase the question. Why does the dancer stop dancing? A.k.a. part eight.

LH: Part eight: Why does the dancer stop dancing?

MG: She does not understand dance. She realizes this because she makes a discovery. She discovers that she has not asked two basic questions – questions so basic that even her teachers have neglected them.

Why does a dancer start dancing?
Why does a dancer stop dancing?

She resolves not to dance again until she has answered these questions. She buys a tiny notebook with a photograph of a treefrog on the cover. She attends as many dance performances as possible, and she begins to compile a list of answers. She watches only the beginnings and ends. For now, she ignores the middles. In the midst of this project, she has a second realization. She realizes that she will never understand dance. She will only understand her questions and the incomplete list of answers in her treefrog notebook. At that moment she knows the difference between the dancer and the dance. At that moment she knows her way forward.

LH: The dancer starts dancing –

MG: – because the music starts.

LH: The dancer stops dancing –

MG: – because the music stops.

LH: The dancer starts dancing –

MG: – because the lights come up.

LH: The dancer stops dancing –

MG: – because the lights go down.

LH: The dancer starts dancing –

MG: – because she enters the room.

LH: The dancer stops dancing –

MG: – because she leaves the room. OR The dancer stops dancing –

LH: – because she hits the wall.

MG: OR The dancer stops dancing –

LH: – because she forgets the steps.

MG: OR The dancer stops dancing –

LH: – because she is too tired to continue.

(Pause)

MG: This needs music. It's just not right. Maybe it's fine, but I'm just not ready to let it go. Anyway, something sad but not dramatic. Not mournful. Gentle, but at the same time, merciless. For that we need brass, I think. Can we do that? We'll start again.

LH: The dancer starts dancing –

MG: – because the music starts.

LH: The dancer stops dancing –

MG: – because the music stops.

LH: The dancer starts dancing –

MG: – because the lights come up.

LH: The dancer stops dancing –

MG: – because the lights go down.

[Music: Pezel *Brass Suite* movement II. *Sarabande.*]

LH: The dancer starts dancing –

MG: – because she enters the room.

LH: The dancer stops dancing –

MG: – because she leaves the room. OR The dancer stops dancing –

LH: – because she hits the wall.

MG: OR The dancer stops dancing –

LH: – because she forgets the steps.

MG: OR The dancer stops dancing –

LH: – because she is too tired to continue. The dancer starts dancing –

MG: – because she contracts an illness.

LH: The dancer stops dancing –

MG: – when the dance has cured her. The dancer starts dancing –

LH: – because somebody forces her to.

MG: The dancer stops dancing –

LH: – because somebody forces her to. The dancer starts dancing –

MG: – because she is still alive.

LH: The dancer stops dancing –

MG: – because she has died. The dancer starts dancing –

LH: – because she has died.

MG: The dancer does not stop dancing.

LH: The dancer starts dancing because the audience wants her to, and she agrees.

[Music ends.]

MG: The dancer stops dancing because she does not want to overstay her welcome.

LH: Shall we proceed to the epilogue?

MG: After you.

LH: Part nine: Epilogue, part one: Out of Gas.

MG: Late in his career, the comedian Buster Keaton starred in a number of television commercials that he devised himself. In one, for Texaco, I believe it was, the gasoline company, Keaton comes along pushing his car up a hill, for the gas station sits atop a hill as I recall, since I am recreating the commercial from memory, there being no definitive source for the scuttlebutt on Buster Keaton's late commercial phase. "Out of gas," anyway, is the setup, and Buster, positioning the large automobile in proximity of the pump, lodges a wedge behind a wheel. He then lifts the nozzle from its cradle, and as he turns to begin pumping gas he inadvertently kicks away the wedge. The car rolls back down the hill. Buster gives chase, and the gasoline tube impossibly follows, emerging from the pump like a fireman's hose, and continuing to emerge endlessly. Some time passes. Buster's pursuit slows to a dogged walk, the gas hose trailing serpentlike on the road behind him. At last the car comes to rest. At last Buster approaches. As he lifts the nozzle to insert it into the tank – bam – he runs out of hose. He looks at the car, looks at the hose, strains with all his might, but it won't budge. It's half a mile long, but six inches too short. Eventually things end happily, of course. But I hold this commercial responsible for my recurring dream slash nightmare. I am on stage, before an expectant audience, and it goes something like this.

(MG stands and moves his chair to a predetermined spot several feet to the left side of the table. Spotlight up on chair, anchoring it in place. MG returns to the table, picks up his microphone, and begins walking toward the chair with intention of sitting in it and speaking into the microphone. Just shy of the chair, the microphone cable yanks him up short. He tries and fails to negotiate the predicament.)

MG: (awkwardly bending to microphone) Part nine: Epilogue, part two: Every house has a door.

(LH repeats the procedure to the right side of the table, only her cord is long enough. She sits in the newly positioned chair, and says the following.)

LH: In order to constitute the space of a home, of a house to inhabit, we must have an opening. We need a door and windows. We have to give up a passage to the outside world. There is no interior without a door or windows. Let me say it this way. The rain, the cabbage patch, the school, the school bell, Carl Thorne-Thompson, cloud, Orpheus, ornithology. A name face-down among the crowd, resurrected, from the thousand faces of the dead, recognized. We were in school together. And like so many broken boats, drifting inside me. Hospitality requires that we open our home; that we give not only to the foreigner but also to the absolute, unknown, anonymous other; that we *give place* to them, and take place in the place we offer them; that we not ask them to give back in return –

(Photograph 8 *Anthropomorphic Landscape* on)

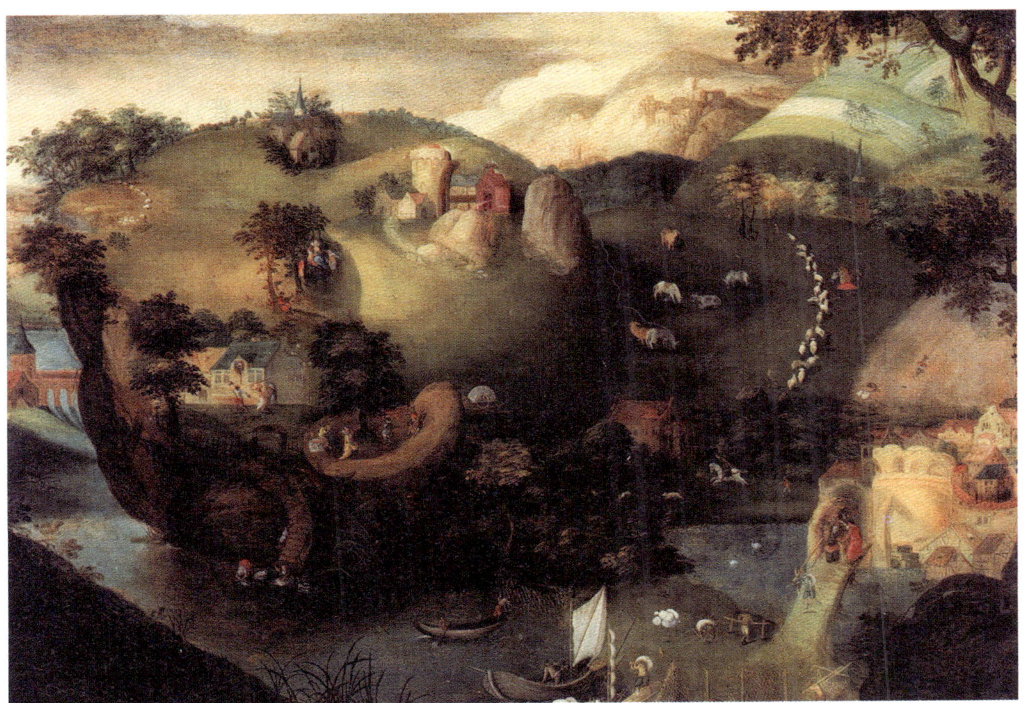

Anonymous, *Anthropomorphic Landscape*, 16th century. Musées Royaux des Beaux-Arts, Brussels.

LH: – that we not ask of them even their names, as they gather, speak, and consume the darkness.

(12 count. The lights fade. Photograph 8 *Anthropomorphic Landscape* off.)

Every House has a Door

This dialogue was a commission of Tanzquartier Vienna, for the series of events accompanying *The Frequently Asked*, organized and curated by Adrian Heathfield and Tim Etchells. It was performed in Vienna on 23 November 2007, and in revised form at the *In Transit Festival* in Berlin on 21 June 2008. Simon Will appeared as the Guest Reader in the Berlin performance.

Sources

Epigraph
Susan Howe, *Souls of the Labadie Tract, 118 Westerly Terrace*, New York: New Directions, 2007, p. 92.

The soul can farther fly…
The Poems of Emily Dickinson, Cambridge, MA: Belknap Press of Harvard University Press, 1955, p. 992.

Teacher says, "Every time a bell rings, an angel gets his wings."
Frank Capra, Frances Goodrich, Albert Hackett, Jo Swerling, *It's A Wonderful Life* screenplay, Frank Capra, dir. 1946.

In Irish literature, according to the convention of a *feth fiada* …
Paul Muldoon, *The End of the Poem, All Souls Night by W. B. Yeats*, New York: Farrar, Straus and Giroux, 2006, p. 13.

Robert Creeley, *On Earth, Old Story*, Berkeley, Los Angeles, London: University of California Press, 2006, p. 49.

SHE: You were thinking of memory …
HE: I think memory is thinking. I think memory is thinking memory.
Robert Creeley, *The Collected Prose, Listen*, New York, London: Marion Boyars, 1984, p. 249.

I used to think my childhood was like a beast with a lion's body …
Daniel Borzutzky, *The Ecstasy of Capitulation, Poem for my Mutual Fund*, Buffalo, New York: BlazeVOX [books], 2007, p. 60 [extracted and altered].

It rained often, when I was a boy.

Hijikata Tatsumi, *Kazedaruma*, speech on the eve of the Tokyo Butoh Festival, 9 February 1985, trans. Nippon Services Corp., in *Butoh: Dance of the Dark Soul*, edited by Mark Holborn and Ethan Hoffman, New York: Aperture, 1987, pp. 124–7.

The river flows on unceasingly … and with the houses they live in.
Kamo no Chomei, *Record of the Ten-Foot-Square Hut*, in *Four Huts*, trans. Burton Watson, Boston and London: Shambhala, 1994, p. 60.

Lecture in a Stair Shape Diminishing – 366 sentences for Vienna, It's an Earthquake in My Heart – A Reading Companion, Goat Island, Chicago, 2001.

Excerpts of correspondence, courtesy of Russell McGuirk.

The gun was always with the water pistols.
Jacob Brackman, *The King of Marvin Gardens* screenplay, Bob Rafelson, dir. 1972.

At one time, as far back as I can remember …
Thomas Bernhard, *Concrete*, trans. D. McLintock, Chicago: The University of Chicago Press, 1984, p. 112.

Plant a question in a garden.
Stephen Bottoms and Matthew Goulish (ed.), *Small Acts of Repair – Performance, Ecology, and Goat Island*, London and New York: Routledge, 2007, p. 133.

These things are miracles.
And not only miracles.
They are improbable miracles.
I never stopped loving the world.
Michel Serres, *The Parasite*, trans. L. Shehr, Baltimore and London: The Johns Hopkins University Press, 1982, p. 46, and chapter "Pentecost."

Disorder is simply the order we are not looking for …
Henri Bergson, *The Creative Mind*, trans. M. L. Andison, New York: Citadel Press, 1992, p. 98.

The passage restates, in artistic terms, what Bergson stated in philosophical terms …
Henri Bergson, "Introduction: Retrograde Movement of the True Growth of Truth," in *The Creative Mind*, trans. M. L. Andison, New York: Citadel Press, 1992, pp. 11–29.
People of taste tell us nowadays that Renoir is a great eighteenth-century painter. But in so saying they forget the element of Time …
Marcel Proust, *The Guermantes Way – In Search of Lost Time vol. III*, trans. C. K. Scott Moncrieff and Terence Kilmartin, D. J. Enright revision, New York: Random House, 1993, pp. 445–6.

It was a day in that blue month September …
Bertolt Brecht, *Remembering Marie A.* trans. J. Willett, in *Poetry and Prose (German Library #75)*, London: Continuum International Publishing Group, 2003, pp. 11–13.

Be not conformed by the limits of this world.
Simone Weil, *Gravity and Grace*, quoted in Introduction by Gustave Thibon, London and New York: Routledge, 1987, p. XXXV. Original Latin quote attributed to Dr. John Colet, Dean of Saint Paul's in the Reigns of Kings Henry VII and Henry VIII.

I think that laughter is set off when we are not afraid …
Hélène Cixous and Mireille Calle-Gruber, *Rootprints*, trans. E. Prenowitz, London and New York: Routledge, 1997, pp. 21–2.

Gas relates to *Geist* from the German, spirit or mind …
Stanley Cavell, *Contesting Tears: The Hollywood Melodrama of the Unknown Woman*, Chicago: University of Chicago Press, 1996, p. 73.

There are many things to be afraid of, like ghosts, and death, and climbing too high.
Low, *Dark*, from *The Curtain Hits the Cast*, Vernon Yard Recordings, VYD 18, New York, 1996.

But fright is formed by what we see not by what they say.
Susan Howe, *There are Not Leaves Enough to Crown to Cover to Crown to Cover*, in *Postmodern American Poetry*, Paul Hoover, ed., New York and London: W. W. Norton & Company, Inc., 1994, pp. 647, 649.

… *with his words, the music made the pale phantoms weep.*
Talia dicentem nervosque ad verba moventem exsangues flebant animae …
Ovid, *Metamorphosis*, Book X, lines 40–1, trans. Rolfe Humphries, Bloomington and London: Indiana University Press, 1955.

With Pinions of Disdain …
The Poems of Emily Dickinson, Cambridge, MA: Belknap Press of Harvard University Press, 1955, p. 992.

Cast the nets in rivers north of the future.
There are still songs to be sung on the other side of humanity.
Paul Celan, *Collected Poems and Prose of Paul Celan*, trans. J. Felstiner, New York and London: W. W. Norton, 2001, pp. 226–7, and 240–1 [extracted and altered].

Part eight: Why does the dancer stop dancing?
This section revises the concluding passage from Matthew Goulish "Two Basic Questions from Unwinding Kindergarten," Performance Research, 1999, vol. 7, no. 4, pp. 92–107.

In order to constitute the space of a home …
Jacques Derrida, *Foreigner Question* in *Of Hospitality*, Anne Dufourmantelle and Jacques Derrida, trans. R. Bowlby, Stanford, California: Stanford University Press 2000, pp. 25, 61 [extracted and altered].

Chapter 43

Alliterations

Mathilde Monnier and Jean-Luc Nancy
Introduction and Translation: Noémie Solomon

This dialogue between the choreographer and dancer Mathilde Monnier and the philosopher Jean-Luc Nancy is excerpted from a manifold collaborative process. Monnier, a prolific artist and influential figure at the head of the Centre National Chorégraphique of Montpellier since 1994, and Nancy, located at the forefront of a French philosophical tradition, collaborated on *Allitérations*, a creative and critical project made over a number of years and consisting of a publication and a performance. The passages translated below are a short selection of an e-mail correspondence that opens the book *Allitérations*, which also gathers a series of public exchanges, notes, and texts all issued from their common work.[1] Monnier and Nancy's encounters at the limits of dance and philosophy, language and movement began to take shape when Monnier heard a text by Nancy, then titled "Séparation de la danse" and written specifically for the Festival International de Nouvelle Danse in Montréal.[2] Monnier invited Nancy to take part in a performance project in which dance and language would be intertwined simultaneously on stage, taking Nancy's writing as prompt for movement. While Nancy conceives this text as an articulation of the shared and "im-mediate" experience of thought, birth, and dance, Monnier sees it as the description of a dance solo by and for the philosopher himself. Appearing at the end of the publication in its sixth version, the movement of Nancy's initial text can be seen as enacting the trajectory at work in *Allitérations*: as the work undergoes a series of encounters, rehearsals, and representations, it reiterates and reassembles, at each occurrence, its many words, gestures, and meanings. *Allitérations*, then, affectively connects the written form and the live event, the lecture and the performance to interrogate and reinvent the ways in which dance and philosophy can cohabit on the page and on the stage.

An extract from and translation of Mathilde Monnier and Jean-Luc Nancy, *Allitérations. Conversations sur la danse*. Paris: Galilée, 2005.

The performance premiered in Paris in 2001 and toured to several cities across Europe between 2002 and 2004. In the piece, four performers (Monnier and Dimitri Chamblas, dancers; eRikm, musician; and Nancy, talker)[3] sit next to each other across the front edge of the stage, behind four peculiar tables made of malleable latex. Each performer works from a specific field, with distinct tools and artistic modalities, yet does so in relation to the other performers, experimenting with modes of transmission and connection between the different performing bodies, media, and art forms. Gestures, words, and sounds impinge upon each other, interrupting and recomposing the ways in which meaning is produced across the performance. The pulsing music echoes Nancy's fragmented reading; the words are suspended as he leans onto the precarious surface that swiftly gives way under his body. Monnier's unfinished and lingering gestures as she hangs at the edge of a table resonate with and distort the densely imagistic text. These restless enunciations seem to perform nothing but the many gaps, frictions, and redundancies across movement and sound; the visual and the tactile; the written and the spoken word. *Allitérations* therefore emerges as a transversal event that simultaneously cuts across and undoes the distinctions between the different artistic forms and functions at work, thus exposing the porosity of aesthetic and sensorial borders.

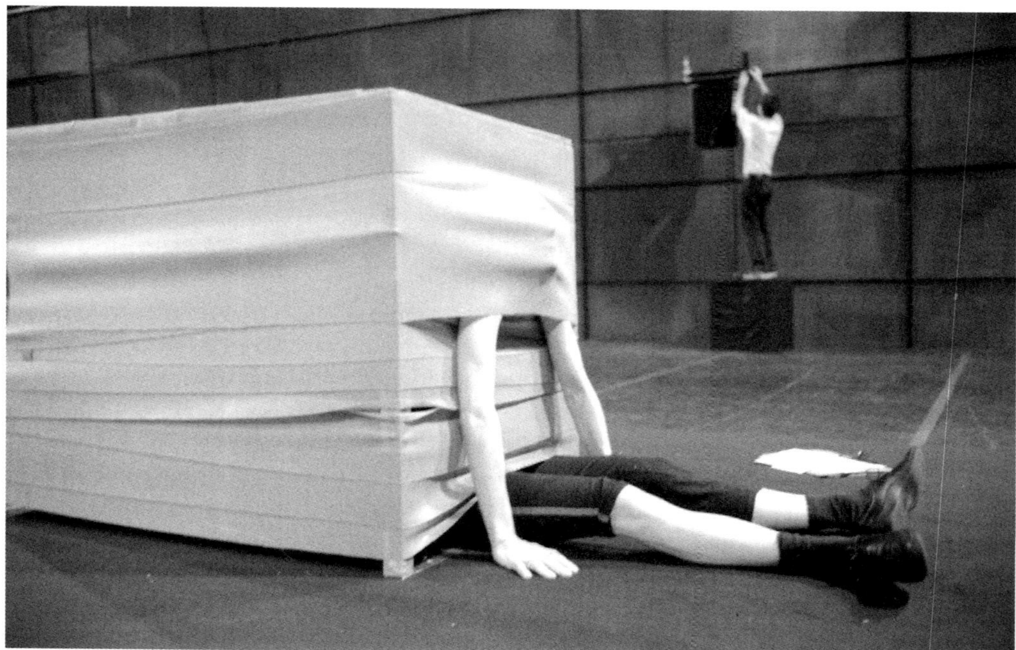

Mathilde Monnier in *Allitérations*, by Mathilde Monnier and Jean-Luc Nancy, 2002 / 2003. Photograph by Marc Coudrais, courtesy of the Centre chorégraphique national de Montpellier.

This singular articulation of relations between dance and philosophy is not an isolated phenomenon. Over the last fifteen years the European dance scene has generated new perspectives by creating affective alliances not only with other art forms such as theater, performance, live art, installation, and music, but also with different discursive fields such as literature, anthropology, and philosophy, among others. In this respect, *Allitérations* might be said to epitomize a certain tendency of what has, often mistakenly, been called "conceptual dance." If some have described contemporary dance's movement toward philosophy as a means to gain legitimacy, others have emphasized these innovative tactics as ways to refigure dance's many gestures and functions, to experiment with the sensorial and political potential enacted by the dancing body within contemporary culture. Crossing different concerns, methods, and practices, this fruitful dialogue between dancers and philosophers has increasingly generated a series of thoughts, affects, and movements, from which contemporary dance has emerged as a particularly dense site for the intensification and reinvention of forms and meanings.[4] In *Allitérations*, Monnier and Nancy step into each other's field, showing a deep curiosity for their respective practices and discourses. Throughout the excerpts below, the authors discuss a series of notions vital to contemporary performance discourse such as the body, language, mediation, repetition, and movement: in so doing they co-figure a body and the ways in which it composes *sense* at the intersections of dance and philosophy. The dialogue marks an expansion of the choreographic endeavor and registers the philosophical attempt to grapple with moving, thinking bodies at the thresholds of perception and signification. By activating potentiality in the work of the dancing body, *Allitérations* exposes not only that which a body can do – and what can be done to a body – but seeks to reinvent what philosophy might do for dance, and dance for philosophy.

Dance, in what sense?

Mathilde Monnier:
Jean-Luc, thinking again of a discussion we had, I remembered this sentence you said at the end of our conversation: "The body is the place by which sense escapes."[5] Now, thinking of this again, it seems obvious; I am thinking that dance, as well, touches upon something of that idea, of that sentence, being an art that works to hold back the escape of movement in the body and, at the same time (in the same time, simultaneously), to give sense, give sense to that which seems to escape. I feel that my work as a choreographer and a dancer is first to hold, to hold back (to write as well) the meaning in this escape, or that a movement makes sense in an escape. Besides, I feel this notion of escape quite strongly because I always have this sensation of loss in the appearance. A movement is born and loses itself; I lose the movement in making it, in producing it. Hence the necessity to redo, to start again, to re-find [*retrouver*], knowing that the goal is not to find something the same, but to re-find it in order to find it again. In the repetition process, there is always a pleasure and a disappointment. One would like to re-find the first sensation, yet one does not re-find it; one

has to mourn and reinvent it, that is to find other ways, invent new ways to access memory without letting oneself be overwhelmed by the "already seen, already known, already felt."

What does it mean: to make sense for a movement, in a movement? It is not to answer a metaphor, an image, or even a translation, it is not about giving an explanation or an equivalence to the gestures and to the movements, but to consider them as carrying meaning, as being a form of language in itself. Dance does not appear to me as the translation of a meaning, but, on the contrary, it extracts a new meaning, other, different, it opens up an effect of meaning. (I relate this to a text by Walter Benjamin on language. He writes: "All language communicates itself *in* itself; it is in the purest sense the 'medium' of the communication."[6] Gesture and movement as media, I also understand that which makes sense in dance similarly; the movement in dance, but also the posture, the energy, the rhythm, the sequence, the presence are all producers of sense and create a language that expresses itself for itself.)

I sometimes feel like an organizer or an archaeologist of movement who tries to find, to excavate gesture in order to identify it, to open an inquiry (on its origin, its history, its transformation, its mutation, etc.).

Jean-Luc Nancy:
What you say requires us to interrogate three different planes, or three registers, at least. The first would be the one of the general proposition: "to make sense outside of sense." The second would be the one of art in general, since the motive of a "sense outside of sense" seems to me to correspond to that which every art form searches for or finds – without even searching! The third would be the one proper to dance, which has its specific mode in making art, that is sense outside of sense. Of course, we won't be making a plan or a system of these three registers: I distinguish them in order to clarify things, but we will find them again without always setting them apart.

However I would like to follow on the first. "To make sense outside of sense," what does this respond to? At first glance, it is pretty clear: meaning engages in completion, in culmination and completeness.

A sentence has meaning when it is complete and has transmitted a signification. "The Earth is round," here is manifest meaning. The desire of getting outside of meaning is a desire to escape this accomplishment, this closure of meaning: "[T]he Earth is round," and I circle with that. Meaning is arrested, and us with it. Meaning is rapidly – how to put it – not exactly death, rather petrification, paralysis. Nevertheless, we know that this proposition – "the Earth is round" – is not uniformly true: it is not so for all of the Earth's experience.

Husserl even wrote a text about the fact that, from lived experience, the Earth is not round, but flat, and does not turn.[7] Moreover, one only needs to linger on the sentence to start seeing or feeling its meaning tremble. "The Earth": which earth? The celestial body or the land upon which I lie and I weigh, on which I can walk?[8] And "round": circular and flat or spherical? (Here, a problem arises in common French, since we don't use "spherical" in everyday language, yet it is in this language that we make sense between us, not with some meaning in advance referred to an horizon of objects, such as the geometry in which the "sphere" is inscribed.)

I did not intend to, but it is so: here I am already close to dance. Since this trembling of meaning immediately opens up several questions: what is this earth on which I walk and rest? Is this the celestial body known by astronomy and cosmology? What am I doing when walking? Am I heading toward a horizon that will stop me and bring me back to my starting point? Am I turning on the sphere, and with it since it also turns in space? Or is what I am doing something else, something foreign to this movement, something that relates to the earth otherwise?

I state some naiveties that can either pass for false naiveties, for a set of simplistic questions that would aim for a basic pedagogy, propaedeutic to a dance theory. But it is not so: I would rather say that this is not naïve enough. That is to say not native enough. I mean this is about the experience of being born, of falling to the ground or being thrown on it, or being set down on it – and in any case coming out of somewhere, from an elsewhere entirely "inside" and which would have been neither earth nor sky, nothing of the separation of the places, elements and tensions. Then the experience of getting up and walking. Of losing the adhesion to the ground and the fixed place.

Immediately arises a matter (I am not saying a question) of meaning, in the sense of ways of feeling the earth and one's body on it; rested, laid down or flattened, crawling, standing on one's feet, resting on the ground with just a little skin and a little time, tangentially freeing itself, jumping, bouncing, yet not flying, not entering this other regime of relation to the earth.

In sum, everything would happen between burying and taking off: neither one nor the other, but a tension between both. A way to be strictly in the world, without disappearing either under the ground or in the sky. One could explore this at length at a given distance from religion: neither becoming dust nor spirit. But in diverting another Christian concept, becoming a "glorious body," that is a body whose corporeity enlightens itself, irradiates itself, here and now – far from the functional, organic body, but also far from a body supposedly without organs and finally pure spirit, light or fire. And when you say that your work as a choreographer is to "hold, hold back meaning in this escape," I understand this as a holding and a holding back in relation to these two poles of the sky and the underground world. Those two poles are the poles of signification – a salvation and a loss, so to speak. Dance would withhold from going in one or the other. And it would hold, would play by itself the tension of this withholding. Dance would be in the world in the strictest manner: neither below nor above, neither beneath nor beyond, but just in the world – which does not mean directly at the ground level nor rising above the ground, but rather raising the ground and making it dance with or as the dancing body.

Medium

JLN:
If I come back by this road verging on the question proper to dance, I would tend to say that the proper of this art is to produce its meaning in withdrawal from every *medium* and thereby to erase as much as possible the effect of signification that a medium produces. The

latter, indeed as its name indicates, operates a mediation, a reference toward another order. Painting (as pigment or paste), the pencil, the instrument (even the voice), the stone, the photographic or cinematographic capture of luminous events, etc., all first seem to propose a *means* to an end that would be the opening out of some signification (expression, presentation, as you like). But when this means is the body proper to the artist (let us overlook here the difference between the choreographer and the dancer, which is not always at work), we are at once disposed to suspect at least another configuration. The means and the end get closer, even overlap each other. That is also why dance is an art whose spectator does not solely – nor even especially – look at: its gaze becomes interior gesture, quiet tension of its own muscles, inchoative movement. Hence, no doubt, the fact that the sight of a dancer, or of an acrobat, has been a frequent example in the research on empathy. Thence, perhaps – and I say this as an interrogation toward you – the fact that the dancer is an artist particularly "self-referentiated" [*autoréférencié*] if I can say so. I mean neither narcissistic, nor autistic, nor egocentric, but in an immediate relation to oneself: im-mediate, without mediation by a medium and yet neither simply immanent in the strict sense of the term (like water in water …), but taking oneself as one's own medium. Which, by the way, brings me swiftly back, without seeing it coming, close to the exercise of thought … At the same time, it raises a question or a decisive theme: how a being in relation to itself is just as much entirely turned toward the outside, since it does not cultivate a given "self," it interrogates a "self," an ipseity which is precisely never given …

MM:
The question of the medium – to be oneself the medium – is a question and an answer (the one you give) that is fraught with responsibilities for each dancer who has to be her/his own medium, hence the difficulty and, at the same time, the force of this (apparent) confusion. The fact that the dancer has at least the possibility to detach her/himself from the medium, to have some distance from that which is produced, from what is at stake, this encourages the necessity to work with other people and to engage in exchanges on that which is seen, perceived, felt by each. There still remains the difficulty of re-reading oneself, of facing one's medium (which explains the keen interest and frequent use of video and computer work in most dance pieces), also the fear of loss, the perpetual incompleteness that we face. At the same time, I would also mention the inherent opportunity in this immediate relation to oneself, which is the very force of our practice.

I believe that each dancer invents her/his own way of thinking this detachment that she/he must have in order to evaluate and understand that which our body produces. This is probably one of the reasons why I work more and more with the support of words (as crutches and for the pleasure of words). I look for words that are linked to movements and that allow for re-finding, memorizing movements; these words are linked to ideas, more than images. The shared language [*parole*] with other dancers seems to me to be one of the means for a constant distancing and rapprochement in relation to that which is produced. By naming, by verbalizing the performed movements, one opens up an alternative for locating movement, re-finding it, understanding and enriching it. This is a possibility of questioning again the relation to one's medium, richer than the one proposed by a filmed image. This allows for a displacement of the im-mediate you mention, which is very precarious, but at the same time absolutely necessary. But it is also important to invent one's own tools to be able to exceed this immediacy, to make the work less timeless and more reproducible.

The use of video (which again is frequent) is only a partial solution to the reading, the re-reading, since it is already the passage toward another medium, which is not entirely faithful. It is a restitution that often eliminates intensity and which denatures presence, whereas verbalizing restores a sensation of subjective truth.

I return again to the medium. That which makes a medium in dance is of course the dance, but since it is inseparable from the body and thus from oneself, that which appears behind the dance is "I." That is what I look for, this accord of the subject and the dance. One has to find this adequacy between oneself and the movement. But it is not often an adequacy, it is rather a gap, and we work in this gap. In this ever changing gap between an exposition of "I" and that which I dance. One constantly negotiates more or less consciously these gaps between oneself and the dance, that which one puts away from oneself, that which one privileges, that which one preserves of oneself in each movement. Of course dance is inseparable from the dancing body, but there is a huge margin that should always be taken into account between that "I" which dances and the dance, that is what we also call interpretation (a word that I barely use since each of us first interprets her/himself). In my work as a choreographer, I leave this margin fluid and tensile, particularly in relation to that which I can propose as movement or an idea of movement, a margin where I try to make apparent the subject who dances at the same time as the dance, and not the dance first of all. Obviously, this leads to infidelity and transformation of that which I propose. I am not looking for the restoration of my movements, I can even say that this does not interest me; I try to find how movement transforms itself when it impinges upon the singularity of each dancer.

JLN:
But "immediacy" is not a convenient word. Strictly speaking, there is no immediate (except "water in water" or A=A, the flattest identity principle). Otherwise, one could not dance. To dance at once engages the gap. If A=A in dance, it is because the "=," the equality with oneself of the dancing body gives itself in an inequality that is stretched to the extreme. What I feel in front of you, dancers, is how much my body, even active, moving, remains compressed on itself, in itself, and thus abstract. But, for all that, the gap within oneself of the dancing body – that gap which makes its thought, which makes it a thinking body – is not a "mediation": there is no mediator, no third subject or third driving force [*puissance motrice*] in the distancing.

This being said, since you mention the language between you, dancers, in the work process, I can tell you that I am struck, during the rehearsals, by your ways of saying: you designate or you name always obliquely, by means of images, comparisons, or indications that instantly renounce naming, like when you say "no, it's not that!" – a "that" that you point toward "the very same thing," toward "the meaning" to produce or to touch. I roughly remembered some sentences of you saying to the dancers: "There, it should be stronger ... longer ... less broken ..."; "at this place, I didn't know where you are at"; or "with that light, it doesn't work, I am losing my bearings." You point at identities of places, or times, or gestures, at very small or general units, but you never give their significations – or you only brush against them. One day I compared this with the experience I had with theatrical work: there is a lot of proximity, but there still remains an irreducible gap since it is not a matter of interpreting a text, thus not a matter of a given meaning nor of a deciphering. All of your work as a choreographer seems to me to be made, at once and in totality, of an incessant movement between thoughts, ideas, significations (for instance, "community," since it is around that idea that the first encounter between you and one of my texts took place), and steps, gestures, spaces, spacings, tensions – without it being possible to say it would be a "translation" or an "interpretation," and even without one register preceding the other. What I am saying here is valid for all art forms, including poetry, but with dance the stake of "non-significance," so to speak, is more sensitive, more imperious as well: right away, the body is there, it takes place there, meaning that one is, if I can say so, simultaneously in the order of a *medium*, of a mediation, and of those of an ... "immediation," to avoid saying "immediacy."

Translator's Notes

1. *Allitérations. Conversations sur la danse*, Paris: Galilée, 2005. The book also includes parts of exchanges between Monnier, Nancy, and the film-maker Claire Denis that took place during the making of the two documentary films *Vers Nancy* (2003) and *Vers Mathilde* (2004). *Dehors la danse*, Lyon: Rroz, 2001, was published earlier, as a workbook accompanying the making of the performance.
2. Chantal Pontbriand's invitation followed the introduction of Nancy's thought to the contemporary dance scene via a choreographic adaptation of his seminal work, *Corpus*, Paris: Métailié, 1992, in a work of the same title by Catherine Diverrès in 1999.
3. The dancers and choreographers Seydou Bori, Laurent Pichaud, Boris Charmatz, and Lisa Nelson occasionally took part in further versions of the performance.
4. For a broader discussion on dance and philosophy, see Jenn Joy and André Lepecki (eds), *Planes of Composition: Dance, Theory and the Global*, Seagull Books, 2010.
5. This question of the production of *sense* and its relation to the work of the dancing body is vital to the discussion. In French, one should note that "*sens*" refers both to the English "sense" and "meaning," while encompassing the signification of "direction" and "way," thus implying a slight motion or directionality.
6. Walter Benjamin, *Selected Writings: Volume 1, 1913–1926*, translated by Marcus Bullock and Michael W. Jennings, Cambridge: Harvard University Press, 1996, p. 64.
7. Edmund Husserl, "Foundational Investigations of the Phenomenological Origin of the Spatiality of Nature" [1934], translated by Fred Kersten, in Peter McCormick and Frederick A. Elliston (eds), *Shorter Works*, Notre-Dame, Indiana: University of Notre Dame Press, 1981, pp. 213–21.
8. In French, the word "*terre*" refers to the planet, but also to the ground, the land, and the soil.

Chapter 44

Intangibles

Hugo Glendinning, Adrian Heathfield, and Tim Etchells

Adrian Heathfield: five years ago now, Hugo and I made a performance-lecture in the form of a dialogue. We had been working together on a book called *Live*,[1] which blended performance theory with his photographic documents of performance. The dialogue piece was a meditation on the relation between the event of performance and the photographic record, flesh and image, the moving and the still.

Hugo Glendinning: We called that piece *LAX*; it was a title we both liked although we never discussed it, a tribute to its aptness perhaps. While we were making the book, looking at the live event from a distance we talked to each other about the work, about making things and leaving things behind. *LAX* was a kind of re-staging of these conversations; we recorded ourselves trying to find the thoughts and strands of dialogue that had so animated our lives at that time and of course we found something quite different.

AH: I had been making dialogue works for a while, as it seemed to me that everything I had written as a solo critical theorist was a kind of response, an imaginary conversation, with authors whose thought I was trying to apprehend. I had sensed that writing is not a solitary act but a gathering of figures, an arrangement of voices. And so I had started to write as if I was speaking out loud. I began to see the space of the page as a kind of séance; I was asking questions to some entities beyond. Often my "authorship" was a channelling of others' voices, more or less ethereal, more or less present. It seemed an organic step, to move into a form of writing that was co-authored and into a space of saying where the embodied differences of voices could be felt.

HG: The *LAX* conversations took place in my studio. Over coffee we chatted, watched videos, and looked at photos – threw things together. That material was re-edited so we didn't sound stupid and later we sat at a table together reading those things to other people. Really it was re-edited so that I wouldn't sound stupid. One of the questions that I asked myself when working on *LAX* and again now is "Should I be allowed to do this, should I be here?" Does everyone question the right to be in a place, or is it the question of the photographer? In an attempt to secure my rights I mailed Adrian my mission statement.

I am here to warn you about mind readers.
I am here to add physical turbulence and incoherence to thought acts.
I am a parasite and a photographer.

AH: I said I was happy. I knew we had a beginning. But something was still troubling me from the last dialogue. For all its dynamism, there was something limited about the way we related. I would say one thing.

HG: And then I would say another.

AH: And so on. We were weaving perspectives and realities, but we only had two vocal threads. It seemed to me that the dialogue was the most productive when the binary broke down, when some one or some thing came between us, when we confused ourselves, when I wasn't sure who was speaking anymore, what we were speaking of. For the critical mind, this might seem like the weakest method: the dissolution of coherent argument, the collapse of distance from the object of thought. But I enjoyed these slides into the opaque and the intimate unknown. For me these were the most rewarding passages: times spent entwined with the ideas of an other, heart in hand, ear in mouth, eyes at the horizons of thought, words slipping over lips and dissolving into air.

HG: So we asked Tim Etchells, with whom we have both had quite distinct creative dialogues for some time, to join the conversation. Tim was willing, but his body couldn't come; his life lived as it is on the road, between Sheffield and numerous places across Europe. It seemed that I would coincide with the real Tim in real time often enough in the month preceding this talk to ask him some questions and record the answers, Vienna, London, Essen.

AH: In this unlikely context of collaboration we decided to play a game of exchange, a round of call and response. I played Hugo some recordings of voices that had got lodged in my ears.

HG: And after making the videos I asked Tim to write something for us to read, so that we could do his voice or he could make our voices do his words.

AH: I asked Hugo a list of impossible questions, which he should attempt to answer however he could. Hugo gave me some images from his archive of over twenty-eight years of photography and film, bombarding me each week with new material.

We set out to trace between us the resilient coordinates of the thing that each of us quite differently calls presence. I was conscious of the lineage of thought around presence, both in terms of theater and performance practice and theory, and in continental philosophy: the frequent correspondences and divergences between these fields. Conscious too, that despite the excoriating critique of the 1960s and 1970s notions of theatrical presence with their emphasis on some essential, some whole, or some mystical aspect of humanness, the systematic analysis of presence as an impossible condition for a human subject founded, sundered, and bounded by language is haunted by phenomena and affects it can neither name nor say. These are affects whose vital force remains the lure and lifeline of performance. I imagined that I would be speaking, then, in the wake of notions of presence as an inherent integrity of enfleshed Being, but also in the wake of presence as linguistic seduction and mediated caress. Knowing only that presence persists as a question.

HG: And I was conscious that much of what I did was to mediate presence, to copy and replicate, to transpose and send. Tim was a lifeline to the actual, to things that happen only once, the unrepeatable, with no fast-forward, no rewind, no duplicate. First I asked him about the unphotographable: voice.

Tim Etchells: *(extracts from interview played on video)* If I think about Jim's voice, in my monologue *Sight is the Sense that Dying People Tend to Lose First*, the thing with him is that when you hear him speak, you really feel his body. And it's a deep voice; it's one of those resonant sort of voices. But you feel him; you feel his body in it. You almost feel the voice taking its time to work its way out of his body and into the world. There seems to be thought in the voice, but also the voice seems to come from a place. I think that's what makes you listen to it: its physicality, or its presence in the world that is quite tangible.

With Forced Entertainment what we're often attracted to is this sense of the point at which the performers' voices have to strain, or have to struggle to cope with something. I think even from the very early work there was this attraction to the moments when the performers are tired, exhausted, coming straight out of physical activity, and coming to the front and having to speak. There is something about that battle – between the desire to speak and the limits of the body as an operating machinery – that is very beautiful, and I suppose you feel the person in this extraordinary way when you sense that tension. I think in many of the works we put the performers in a place where they will have to work incredibly hard physically, and immediately after that they will have to speak. It seems very productive in performance terms.

The thing that we're often attracted to with Forced Entertainment is a quite untrained way of using your voice. It's about friction, in a way, and well-trained actors can bellow quite loud, but you don't feel any body in it at all. You feel lungs, or diaphragm, but not the throat particularly. It's actually the throat, the friction of the air and voice in the throat, that's really the interesting thing. So often performers, actors, singers, or dancers are trained to use their bodies or their voices in particular ways in order to be a good machinery for presence. Very often those trainings and excessive competences are counterproductive. You long to see the untrained, the untutored, the unframed. I suppose there is something about the professionalization of presence that makes us feel very uneasy. You see it in politicians, and in the smiles of American politicians especially. But there's something very disturbing about those things, when people are, as it were, too proficient. Clearly the routine that politicians do passes somewhere, otherwise the bastards wouldn't get elected would they? Somebody must buy it! I suspect it's not so much that it is believed, but that it doesn't set off triggers. Not so much a presence, as an absence of error. That's what they say about American beauty, isn't it: that it's not about beauty as a positive, it's about not having any blemishes. Maybe politics is like that, politicians should not check any of the negative boxes, they don't have to be anything positively. Maybe that's what it is.

AH: Hugo,

For some time now I've had an interest in those parts of songs where the singer begins to speak, where song tracks back into its more mundane constituent element. In part, my taste for these talky songs is something similar to Tim's interest, and his insistence throughout his work on the coming undone of the performing subject, on the failure of intent and aspiration, the moment when a regime of ideas or of representation collapses. For it is often here, in the break, that some unconscious, unseen, or unheard aspect of the event is made evident. I am thinking perhaps of late Elvis Presley live, synthetically plodding his way through the spoken passages of "Are You Lonesome Tonight?" where one feels the lurch between the soaring sweet voice transcending the limits of loneliness, and the clunky lyricism and naff theatricality of the recitation, his song becoming tortuous teenage love poetry, then soaring and searing, carrying us off once again. The sentiments are both inhabited and discarded; the listener can be both inside and outside. One senses that Elvis knew something about the gap between the story and the song, the held and the flown, between the thought of something and the thing itself.

I have also been fascinated by preambles to songs, not least because they are hard to find these days in recorded forms, in which so much of the raw jangle and ambient noise of the event is treated or excised. Perhaps my passion is prompted by the barely planned and somewhat unguarded nature of the preamble, the fact that it is not the performance proper, the considered object, but it is nonetheless a performance. Or perhaps it is something to do with the fecundity of beginnings, the force of the prelude, the phenomena of imminence.

Here is one of my favorite preambles, Nina Simone, beginning again, near the end of a concert, near the end of the singing and of a life.

He plays Nina Simone, "Who Knows Where the Time Goes" and after a while begins to speak over the song which fades into the background.

Hugo, do you remember Roland Barthes' "grain of the voice," that joyous phenomena of self-loss he found when intertwined in the song of another? Here is Barthes again on the grain, tumbling through words to make them sing:

> Something is there, manifest and stubborn (one hears only *that*), beyond (or before) the meaning of the words: [...] something which is directly the cantor's body, brought to your ears in one and the same movement from deep down in the cavities, the muscles, the membranes, the cartilages, [...] as though a single skin lined the inner flesh of the performer and the music he sings. The voice is not personal: it expresses nothing of the cantor, of his soul; it is not original, [...] and at the same time it is individual: it has us hear a body which has no civil identity, no "personality," but which is nevertheless a separate body.[2]

I am not as sure though, as Barthes was, and as Tim seems to be when he remembers his hearing of Jim's voice, that what emerges in these vocal performances is the direct bringing of the *materiality* of one body to another body, at once anonymous and singular. When Barthes comes to describe what it is about the voice that moves him, he makes the voice into another body, gives it a surface, a skin. Because he is touched by the song he remakes the song in writing, as something he could touch. Skin on skin. He re-incorporates the flown trace of the body, the sonorous breath, and invokes the possibility of transubstantiation.

I must confess that for all the beauty of Simone's song, I keep returning to her preamble, to its immanent content, to the space between the talking and the song. Perhaps that is why I could do something as violent as talk over it now. What I hear in Simone's softly spoken voice is not just the collapse of formal boundaries: chatting becoming poetry, becoming cultural commentary, becoming philosophy; talk becoming song. But in the passage of matter into other consistencies, from the solid to the air: the dissolution of the regimes of the senses, language becoming feeling, hearing becoming touch, touch touching the intangible. When Simone speaks at the edge of audibility, one of the things we hear is her tiredness and what her tiredness speaks of is the inability to be in the present time, the sense of already being out of time with others' time, the incapacity to meet the time of others. In this state of temporal exile Simone is taking time, and in so doing gives back time. For as she reiterates, time is not something that a subject can own or be one with. It is the immaterial in the material, the thing we cannot touch that is alive.

HG: Dear Adrian,

I have learned a lot listening back to Tim's answers to my questions, not wishing to sound trite or state the obvious, we have fallen on a very important marker of presence and that is absence. Tim is absent from this conversation, present only in voice, mediated and edited by us, a very second hand fuzzy presence if you like. Meanwhile it seems that the absence of control and technique in revealing presence is one of his recurring ideas. Yet the antithesis of Tim's thesis of inventive failure in the performance world – the world of uninhibited flawless aspiration – is also expressed as an absence. He quotes "American beauty" as being the absence of blemish and says that the slick presentation of politicians is best described as the absence of mistakes. It seems much easier to define things in terms of what they are *not* than what they *are*.

A story about singing:
In the mid-1990s Elvis Costello collaborated on an album with Anne Sophie von Otter, a soprano famous for her superb operatic technique. The process was recorded for the Southbank Show. After an immaculate rendition of one of his songs Costello is close to despair, he sends Anne Sophie away with a bag of CDs for further listening, hoping that she will understand that there has to be an expression of something more than just perfect pitch, some slippage perhaps or frailty and failure in her singing. He asks her to practice singing a Nina Simone song. The comparison when the Von Otter version and Simone's are played back to back is pitiful. Von Otter might as well be trying to knit the Simone song, or type it out on a computer keyboard for our listening pleasure – her version bears so little weight it is ash. It has no soul. I'm tempted to say that any soul comparison with Nina Simone is just unfair, that the average 21 grams cannot be enough, but my atheism prevents me. How interesting that the Americans' only other use for the gram is to weigh Class A drugs.

AH: Hugo

He plays the film of Tehching Hsieh, One Year Performance 1980–1981.

Here is a face I've been seeing a lot of lately, it is the face of the performance artist Tehching Hsieh. In the early 1980s Hsieh spent a whole year clocking on to a worker's time clock on the hour every hour. He captured his body and his face after every clocking-on with a single frame of a film. A year of a life spent in continuous sleep deprivation, social withdrawal, and severe spatial restraint winds down into a six-minute film. As you see, he started by shaving his head and he let his hair grow long throughout the duration.

I've talked a lot about Hsieh elsewhere so I won't belabor the point, but I think he might have something to say, in his muteness, about life forces that escape technological rendition. Something too, to say about the violence of surveillance: what it means to be brought to attention, to be present to a gaze, to be called to account for oneself. Hsieh's performance of the pose in relation to the economies of photography and film problematizes the idea of an authentic delivery of his presence through the acknowledgment of his interpellation by a scopic regime. It questions the very integrity of that presence through the disfiguring exposure of its multiple durations. In this conversation between performance, photography, and film the spectator is returned to an awareness of the phenomena of duration. A plural experience, as Henri Bergson once argued, resolutely inaccessible to language and thought, since it is composed of sensations, emotions, and prehensions; of qualities not quantities in a constant and indivisible state of flux.[3] Immediate experience is a flowing form of radical heterogeneity, no sensation ever being the same as a previous sensation: duration then as the continuous movement of differentiation. Hsieh's body is flickering in and out of being before our eyes: a body dis-posed and de-figured in time. This body is not fully present, nor is it self-coincident: it is not owned by its subject. It exists in a radical state of oscillation: it is trembling with durations.

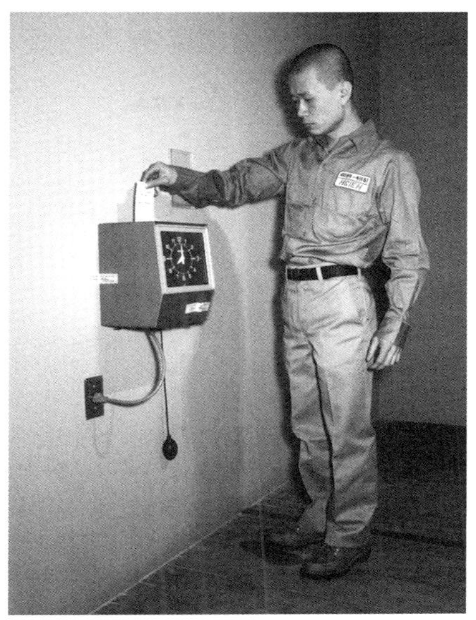

Tehching Hsieh, *One Year Performance 1980–1981*, New York, Waiting to Punch the Time Clock. Photograph by Michael Shen, © Tehching Hsieh.

Perhaps what is at stake in any communion with a presence, at once mediated and live, is this paradox of the tangible. That touching is transaction, a giving and a taking, vibrant and infinite in its deferrals. Of course the events of which we are speaking so far are predicated on physical distance, this is not the tumble of flesh of the carnival, or the rave or the riot. But could one ever find in such fleshly intimacies, or others less public, the resolution that would present a body to another, without a trace of withdrawal? Here is Jacques Derrida's thought, entwined in the chiasm of phenomenology, the sensate and the sensible, and as he goes caressing and weighing Jean-Luc Nancy's book *Corpus:*[4]

> Touching, in any case, thus remains limitrophe; it touches what it does not touch; it does not touch; it abstains from touching on what it touches, and within the

> abstinence retaining it [...] at the heart of its desire and need, in an inhibition truly constituting its appetite, it eats without eating what is its nourishment, touching, without touching what it comes to cultivate, elevate, educate.[5]

HG: Tim wrote:

Dear Adrian
Dear Hugo

I'm starting these notes about presence with an apology for my absence.

I hope you're both doing well.

I have been thinking about my fascination in performance with the ghost and the ephemeral, the human that is not human, the ethereal, the voice that emerges from no

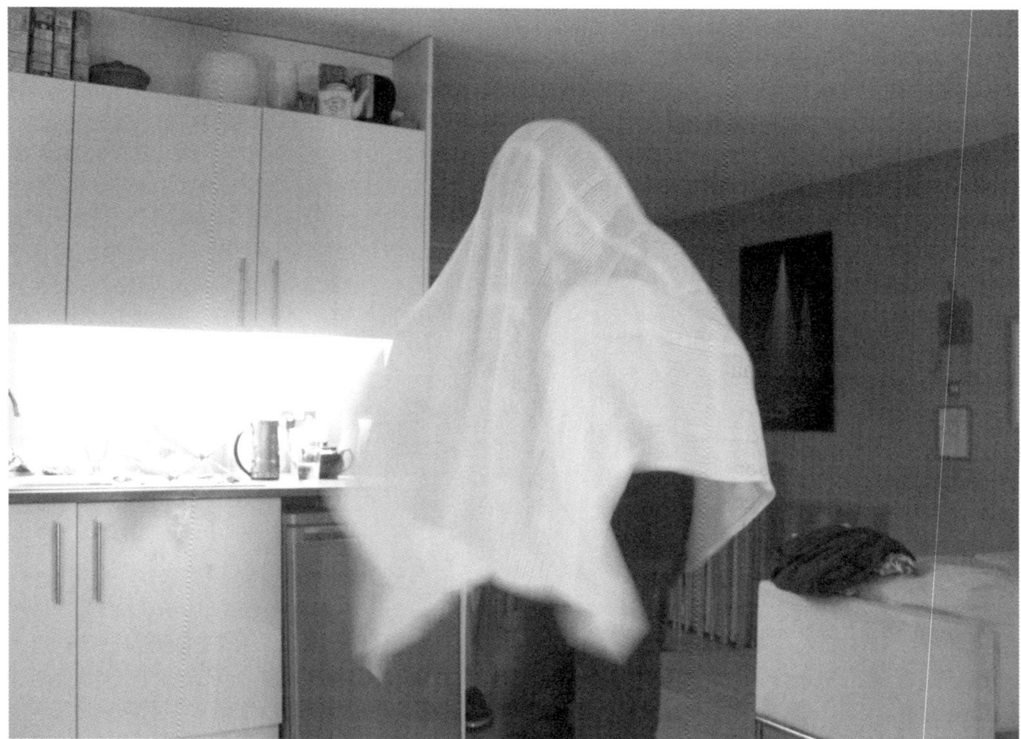

Adrian as Ghost. Photograph by Tim Etchells © Tim Etchells.

solid object. The present/not present: the human that is part air, or the air that retains a trace of the human.

You'll recall this ghost, enacted by Adrian, to the delight and terror of Louis. (HG: Louis is my son.) A repeat performance of entering from the bedroom to the dining room table and progressing closer and closer, a moving ripple in the air, a getting closer and closer and closer. In this case the ghost is just a sheet, the pathetic and most well known ruse to hide the corporeal form beneath, a crude pantomime of the intangible, a hapless impersonation, unpersonation. It was a great performance though, and all the better for its use of voice since the voice that came from this – Adrian's ghost – was on the whole never loud enough to command the room, but quiet enough to silence it. It was an unbodied voice, that seemed to come from further away than the mass before us, it was insufficiently bodied perhaps, weaker, coming from some depths, from some distance, from some vortex of air. It conjured a body, but not quite the one in front of us, bringing new form to the present absence before us.

Louis was delighted of course. Requisitely terrified and compelled each and every time until the final revelation in each case – at which point the blanket was pulled off to show not just air, not nothing or no body but Adrian beneath – a body, decidedly not an absence, and demanding with each of these final revelations a repeat of the mystery, another appearance, another unpresentation, another warp in the fabric of air.

I'm thinking of you both.

Tim

HG: So Adrian, I'm trying to think about your question "What is a face?" or "What is in a face?"

But parasites and hairdressers keep interfering.

Earlier this week I took a picture of a tiny African hairdressers called "Yinka Coiffure" in Rue René Boulanger, I did it to show the artist Yinka Shonibare whose photoworks I help make. Incidentally, I have come to see my work with Yinka as a parasitic rather than collaborative act. Not in a horrible way but just in an honest way. A Trojan Horse way but without the war. I am also reading Iain Sinclair's *Hackney, That Rose-Red Empire*.[6] I have always been a bit jealous of Sinclair's photographic collaborators (his word)

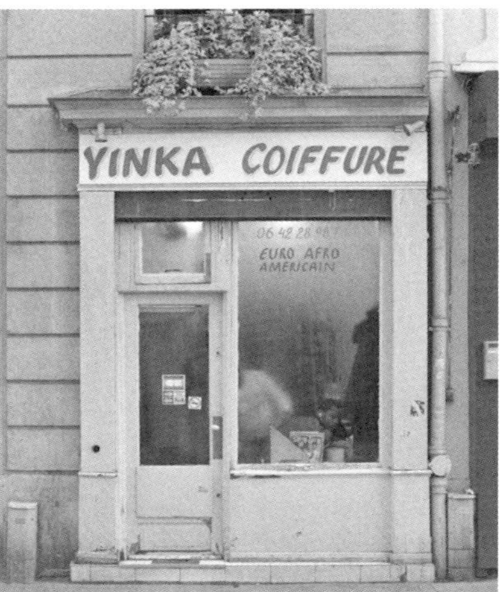

Yinka Coiffure Paris. Photograph by Hugo Glendinning, © Hugo Glendinning.

and was delighted in *London Orbital*[7] that he clearly found Marc Atkins' laziness more than just an irritation. In this new book he has a new collaborator in Stephen Gill and they set themselves a project to document the new hairdressers of Hackney, largely immigrant shops also selling mobile phones and transferring cash across continents. The project proved fraught. Sinclair writes:

> Barbers in doorways. Cameras alert them, offend them. Cameras gather evidence. They disturb the climate of managed paranoia. They stop time, that great river in which nothing is any more significant than anything else. Single images are pinned to the wall in Stoke Newington police station. Single images arranged and rearranged, create a narrative, solicit a conclusion: guilty.[8]

You may notice that in my picture for Yinka there is a man at the door. Hand on the handle, he is exiting fast, to confront me. I tell him the truth in bad French that I have a friend in London called Yinka who I think will be amused by the shop name. He backs off, too ridiculous a story in too unforgivable French to challenge further. This is one of many occasions in which I have found myself an unwanted presence as a photographer.

What do hairdressers really know? They know about glass, about the mirror and the double mirror, about the dangers and beauty of transparency. The hairdressers' shop is particular, one of the few shops to be unencumbered by the need to show product in the window. The act *is* the product, and it needs to be seen.

Looking at a detail of the man behind the steamed up glass, there are any amount of spurious versions of events to be constructed, any amount of ways to answer the question "What is in *his* face": all speculation, all noise and incoherence. Even as I crop, as I see the increase in jpeg artefacts, then sharpen which increases pixel noise in an image already streaked with steam and smeared by the window and reflections in that window, I must know that in the emerging physical complexity is also a clue to the absolute and final impossibility of knowing what that man is really thinking. The flickering and folding of another consciousness is literally interrupted by the photograph, by the photographer, transported here from Paris to London for now, soon to be at best half-remembered, until the half-remembered is half-forgotten and the Gaussian blur, Smart Blur, average blur, box blur, motion blur, the "blur more" of time returns him to the river, and then the sea.

Tim has been working with the dancer Fumiyo Ikeda on the solo performance *In Pieces*. I asked him about movement.

TE: *(extracts from interview played on video)* In the movement that Fumiyo is working with for the piece, what interests me a great deal is the fluidity. To speak really crudely, one moment it seems to be the gesture of pulling something toward you, and all these narrative flashes go off in my head around this idea of pulling somebody or something toward you. And then in a microsecond she can flip that, and it becomes the act of pushing something away. Or it is the act of internalizing something into the body, that's not about hand pulling but about her whole body folding around something.

It is this quality of the body in movement – that it is infinitely mutable and able to reference, in so many directions, so eclectically and with such fluidity – that I find really fascinating. As somebody who has been completely bound up with working with language, that's the thing about working with dance that I find really gripping: it's the floatingness. Even language at its most scattershot, and eclectic, and stream of consciousness and free, doesn't really do for me what watching Fumiyo does for five minutes in the flickering state that she can have in movement.

HG: For the past few months I have been trying to photograph a strange British business outpost that I see a couple of times every week as I travel into or out of the channel tunnel. A beer and wine shed for cross channel sales and alcohol tax avoiders a couple of miles inland from Calais in a liminal landscape now famously populated by refugees trying to find a lorry ride to London. Another photograph that has proved elusive has been a good portrait of the human fetus in the Museum of Natural History in Paris, a museum of a museum, the skeleton is still but rendered almost invisible by reflections on its glass case.

Finally, one morning in early March after a lot of practice shooting through windows, whip panning against the direction of the train with a rubber hood to avoid glare from the window and constant buffeting of camera on glass, I cracked the problem of taking pictures of the wine shed.

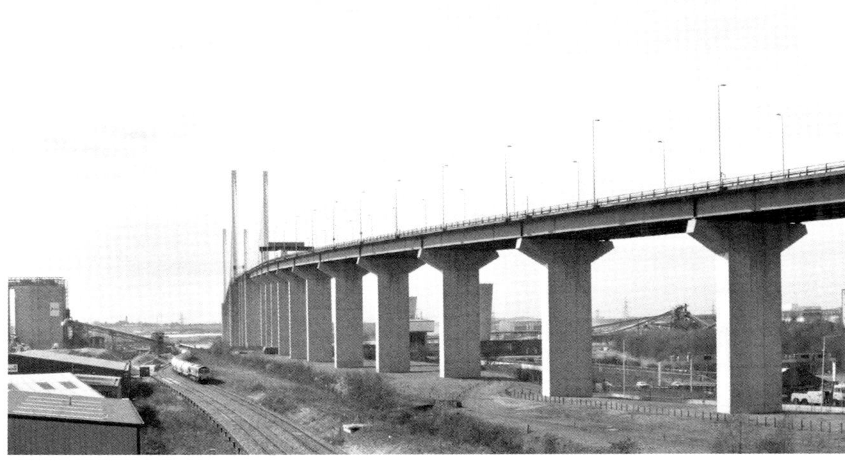

From *Trainscapes*. Photograph by Hugo Glendinning, © Hugo Glendinning.

I like it but what really interests me now is not that shot but many of the other practice images. They feel like a certain kind of considered modern landscape, like John Davies or Paul Graham, photography which affects a discourse on evidence, narrative, and the edge of things. The critical work on this kind of photography, as far as I know, always assumes that the witness, the photographer is somehow a part of the narrative, that she is in the scene. If you know how they are made and understand what it feels like to make the images, you will understand that the photographer is absolutely not in this landscape and has almost no understanding of the complex relationship of objects and forms within the frame, it all changes so quickly.

I was not really there at all. I do not remember seeing these places. I cannot compare the image with a memory of the actual place because I did not see it. On my next journey I tried to reproduce the train and the bridge photo. I managed to make another similar image but it is not nearly as interesting, missing as it does the "O. Winston Link moment," the low framing, the longer sweep of bridge. This suggests to me that the images are all about time rather than place. They are about a time made possible by technology, the camera can stop the train, both the train that I am on and the train in the picture, it can see in fragments of time that the human eye can only imagine, can only guess exist. The camera lets us know these invisible moments, these pictures are *only* photographs, they make new memory, new knowledge.

In the natural history museum I struggled again to get a picture of the foetus that would make it feel done. A friend held my big black coat behind my head, to block reflections on the glass case, an old fashioned look for a photographer, the black cloth disappearing act of the plate camera, it felt wrong but my son Louis tugged at my knee wanting to go to the zoo, my alibi. The image is nearly there. It is another image of something, someone who was never there, no memory, a scrap, just a suggestion of something that might have been.

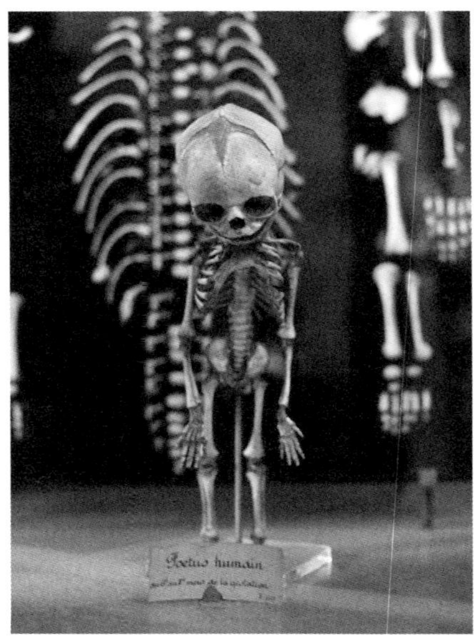

Foetus Skeleton, Museum of Natural History Paris. Photograph by Hugo Glendinning. © Hugo Glendinning

AH: Hugo,

I am glad you finally got a decent shot of that wine shed. From duty-free liquor to hairdressers with something to hide, so much of what we have been trying to speak of as a presence is the illicit, below or beyond the reach of customs or the law. It would seem that the illicit has a special relationship to the liquid, to things that flow and cannot be contained. Did I mention that while Hsieh was making his five year-long performances at the edge of public visibility, he was an illegal immigrant? When he finally got his citizenship in an amnesty, he only made art under the self-made law that it would never be shown publicly. This too was a durational work. It lasted thirteen years. Perhaps this is a little like your take on photography as the presencing of the invisible, the presentation in representation of the unpresentable. Nothing is always potential.

Earlier when you said I had been your lodger for almost two years, I was quite shocked about the length, of my parasitism. Where does the time go? I must have spent it dreaming, or like Nina Simone I cannot count the time. There's something though in all this flux, in the houses we barely inhabit, like our bodies, all the time coming and going. Perhaps we should no longer count the time, or speak of the present time, since there is no present that does not contain within it many other times. To witness something, like another life, is partly to miss it, to not be there. That's why it returns to haunt you. Perhaps we should no longer speak of presence and absence, since there is neither one nor the other, but the tireless movement between: the continuous flux of bodies with other bodies. No more talk then of a unitary or self-coincident body. No integrities, but instead intensities of exchange and flow.

When you spoke of Louis tugging at your leg, I felt him pulling me too, though it wasn't to the zoo. I was half-remembering the other side of that time in Tim's ghost story, when my daughter Anna switched roles and played the ghost, with much more conviction than I could muster. Louis was clinging on to me for protection; I think you were out doing a shoot. Louis' body could barely contain the energies it carried, as he trembled against me, ecstatic vibration, palpitating heart emanating his joy in the face of death's imminence. Of course in the game we played we managed to hold things together for some time, as in our conversation here, before things came to a close, or fell apart.

"Across the morning sky all the birds were leaving. How did they know it was time to go?"[9]

Dear Hugo

Thank you for this image, which you have titled *Something*.

A tiny fragment of a ghost voice is lodging in my ear. It is the voice of John Cage, his body speaking in another time: 1969. It is an excerpt from *Silence*. It has something unsaid in it, about *spiritedness*, about the relationship between joy and duration. The unsaid is made present in his sudden gathering of breath, in his pacing, and in the passage of intensities between us now.

He plays the tape of Cage's voice:

> We open our eyes and ears, seeing life each day excellent as it is. This realisation no longer needs art, though without art it would have been difficult – yoga, zazen, etc. – to come by. Having this realisation we gather energies – ours and the ones of nature – in order to make this intolerable world endurable.[10]

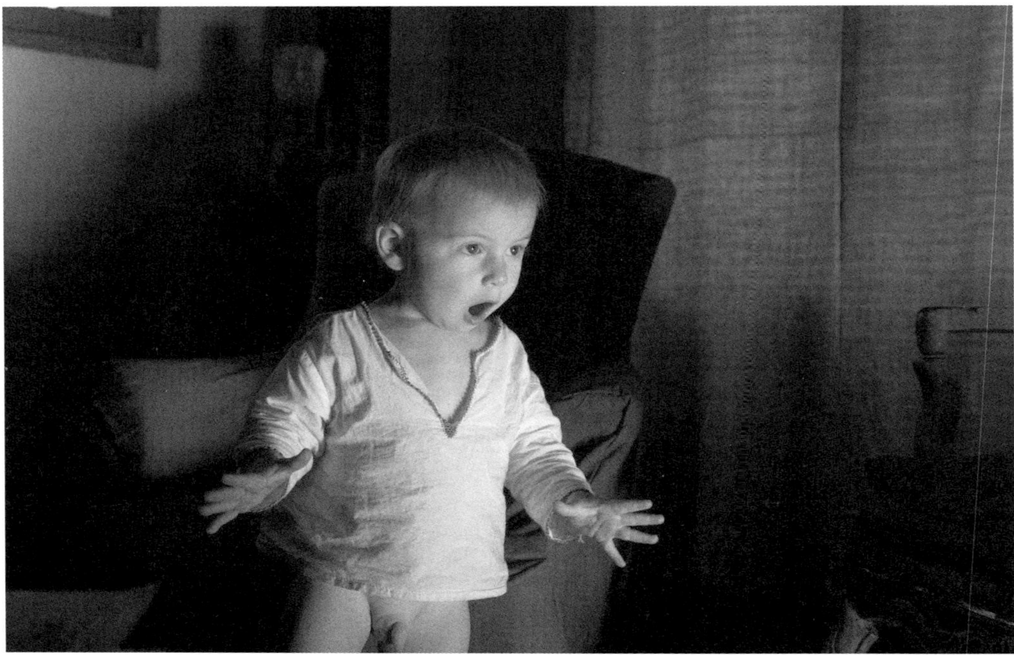

Something. Photograph by Hugo Glendinning, © Hugo Glendinning.

Notes

1. Adrian Heathfield (ed.), *Live: Art and Performance*, London: Tate Publishing, 2004.
2. Roland Barthes, "The Grain of the Voice," in *Image, Music, Text*, trans. by Stephen Heath, London: Fontana Press, 1977, pp. 179–89 (181–2).
3. Henri Bergson, *Time and Free Will: An Essay on the Immediate Data of Consciousness*, Mineola, NY: Dover Publications, 2001.
4. Jean-Luc Nancy, *Corpus*, trans. by Richard A Rand, New York: Fordham University Press, 2008.
5. Jacques Derrida, *On Touching, Jean-Luc Nancy*, trans. by Christine Irizarry, Stanford: Stanford University Press, 2005, p. 67.
6. Iain Sinclair, *Hackney, That Rose-Red Empire: A Confidential Report*, London: Hamish Hamilton, 2009.
7. Iain Sinclair, *London Orbital*, London: Penguin, 2003.
8. Iain Sinclair, *Hackney, That Rose-Red Empire: A Confidential Report*, p. 86.
9. Sandy Denny, "Who Knows Where the Time Goes," in Fairport Convention, *Unhalfbricking*, Warlock Music, 1969.
10. John Cage, *Silence (1969)*, excerpt, UbuWeb: Sound. Available at: http://ubu.artmob.ca/sound/dial_a_poem_poets/disconnected/Disconnected_07_cage.mp3, accessed 13 January 2010.

Acknowledgments

Amelia Jones

This project has taken a very long time and many from my life in Manchester (2003–2010) and Montreal (2010–2011) have supported me throughout but I will keep this brief. My colleagues and the students at the University of Manchester and, now, at McGill University have contributed much to the refining of this project, as have the discerning and inquisitive audiences around Europe, North America, Australia, and New Zealand, who have heard and commented on aspects of it.

May Yao and Melanie Marshall at Intellect have made *Perform, Repeat, Record* happen. If not for their vision and support, who knows what the history of *PRR* itself would have been? Branislava Kuburovic is a lifesaver, as are my research assistants at McGill who helped with the final threads of this book: Elizabeth Maynard, Jimmy Craig, Lauren Diez d'Aux, and Will Lockett have retrieved the last relevant sources; special thanks to Lauren for major permissions research. McGill and the Canadian government, in the form of a Social Sciences and Humanities Research Council grant have provided solid financial and logistical support and I am very grateful for that.

More than anything I want to thank the contributors to this book for their brilliance, and for their patience in dealing with the complex and seemingly endless editorial process. I have learned from every one of them.

And finally, to Paul, my heart, and Evan and Vita, my solace, without whom I would have only a "past" to repeat and no "future" to imagine performing. I thank you three from the bottom of my heart.

Adrian Heathfield

Immeasurable thanks are due to Branislava Kuburovic, who worked as the research assistant for this project from its inception to its close with forbearance, care and conviction. Thanks to the British Academy for supporting this work and Jelena Stanovnik and all at Intellect for realising it. Lois Keidan of the Live Art Development Agency has been one of the most vital and significant cultural agents in the international scenes of performance for many years and hearty thanks are owed to Lois, CJ Mitchell and to the agency for their support and facilitation of this book. The greatest thanks are due to all of the contributors for their generous gifts and especially to Noémie Solomon who, for me, makes everything possible.

Permissions

The editors and publisher gratefully acknowledge the permission granted to reproduce the copyright material in this book:

Chapter 1 was originally published as Philip Auslander, "The Performativity of Performance Documentation," *Performing Arts Journal* (*PAJ* 84), 2006, vol. 28, no. 3, pp. 1–10.

Chapter 7 is a revised version of Rebecca Schneider, "Performance Remains," *Performing Research,* 2001, vol. 6, no. 2, pp. 100–08. For the latest "re-do" of this essay, see Rebecca Schneider, *Performing Remains: Art and War in Times of Theatrical Reenactment,* New York: Routledge, 2011, pp. 87–110. This essay is altered somewhat from the original publication, modifications that bear the marks of the essay's promiscuous afterlife, including references to texts that post-date 2001.

Chapter 10 was originally published as Sven Lütticken, "Progressive Striptease: Performance Ideology Past and Present," in *Secret Publicity: Essays on Contemporary Art,* Rotterdam: NAi Publishers, 2006, pp. 161–80.

Chapter 12 was originally published as Boris Groys, "Art in the Age of Biopolitics: From Artwork to Art Documentation," trans. Steven Lindberg, *Documenta 11* Catalogue, Ostfildern-Ruit: Hatje Cantz, 2002, pp. 108–14.

Chapter 14 was originally published as Tim Etchells, "A Text on 20 years with 66 footnotes," in *Not Even A Game Anymore: The Theatre of Forced Entertainment*, eds. Florian Malzacher and Judith Helmer, Berlin: Alexander Verlag, 2004.

Chapter 30 is an extract of an essay originally published as Janez Janša, "Reconstruction2: On the Reconstructions of Pupilija, papa Pupilo, and the Pupilceks" in *Dance on Time*, eds. Gurur Ertem and Noémie Solomon, Istanbul: Bimeras, 2010, pp. 44–63.

Chapter 35 is an extract from an interview originally published as "I Just Go in Life: An Exchange with Tehching Hsieh," in *Out of Now: The Lifeworks of Tehching Hsieh*, London and Cambridge, MA: Live Art Development Agency and MIT Press, 2009, pp. 318–39.

In Chapter 38 Bertolt Brecht's *Remembering Marie A.* is used with the permission of Methuen Drama, An Imprint of Bloomsbury Publishing PLC. Reproduced by permission of A & C Black Publishers Ltd. / Bloomsbury Publishing PLC.

Chapter 40 is an extract from an interview originally published as Dominic Johnson, "Perverse Martyrologies: An Interview with Ron Athey," *Contemporary Theatre Review*, Autumn 2008, vol. 18, no. 4, pp. 503–13.

Chapter 42 is an extract from and translation of Mathilde Monnier and Jean-Luc Nancy, *Allitérations. Conversations sur la danse*. Paris: Galilée, 2005.

Author Biographies

Marina Abramović was born in 1946 in Belgrade. From 1975 until 1988, Abramović and the German artist Ulay performed together and after they separated in 1988, Abramović returned to solo performances. Abramović has presented her work in solo exhibitions at major institutions in the U.S. and Europe and a retrospective of her career, *Marina Abramović Presents*, was held at the Museum of Modern Art in New York in 2010. Abramović has taught and lectured extensively in Europe and America and has received awards internationally for her work. Her M.A.I (Marina Abramović Institute) for teaching and performance research is opening in 2012.

Kamal Ackarie is a lighting designer and technical director. Kamal toured extensively with Michael Laub's Remote Control Company and collaborated with Andrew Chetty at the NOW festival (1997–2000); the Futuresonic festival (1998–2001); with Blast Theory, Saburo Teshigawara, Dumb Type, Franko B and London's Duckie. Currently Kamal is working with Forma Arts and Media as Technical Director working closely with an array of artists.

Janine Antoni employs a variety of mediums including performance, sculpture, photography, installation, and video. She is known for her unusual choice of materials such as chocolate and soap. Her artwork takes on a physicality that speaks directly to the viewers' body, unleashing a deeply felt emotional response. Antoni has had major exhibitions of her work at the Whitney Museum of American Art, the Solomon R. Guggenheim Museum, S.I.T.E. Santa Fe, and the Irish Museum of Modern Art, Dublin. She is the recipient of several prestigious awards including a John D. and Catherine T. MacArthur Fellowship in 1998 and the Larry Aldrich Foundation Award in 1999.

Ron Athey worked in Los Angeles for the first two decades of his career and is now based in London. His major touring works include *The Torture Trilogy* (1993–95) and *Incorruptible Flesh* (1997–2008), and solos such as *Solar Anus* (1999) and his current *Self-Obliteration* series. He is working on a publication called *Pleading in the Blood: The Art of Ron Athey*, to be published by MIT Press and Live Art Development Agency in 2012.

Philip Auslander is a Professor in the School of Literature, Communication, and Culture of the Georgia Institute of Technology, Atlanta, Georgia, USA. He teaches in the areas of performance studies and music. He is the author of *Liveness: Performance in a Mediatized Culture* (1999) and *Performing Glam Rock: Gender and Theatricality in Popular Music* (2006). He is also a freelance art writer.

Vardan Azatyan, PhD, is an Art Historian. He teaches Modern and Contemporary Art History and Theory at the Academy of Fine Arts and with the Critical and Curatorial Studies Program in Yerevan, Armenia. He is the co-curator of the Armenian Pavilion in the Venice Biennial in 2011.

Franko B was born in Milan and has lived in London since 1979. He has exhibited and performed widely, including at Tate Modern, ICA, South London Gallery and Beaconsfield, and has presented work internationally in Moscow, Zagreb, Mexico City, Milan, Amsterdam, Antwerp, Copenhagen, Madrid and Vienna, Tate Liverpool, the Palais des Beaux-Arts, Brussels and the Crawford Municipal Gallery in Cork. Franko B lectures widely. Since January 2009, he has been appointed Professor of Sculpture at the Academia Di Belle Arti, Macerata, Italy. He has been the subject of four monographs, most recently *I Still Love* (2010).

David Barrett is an artist and art critic, who has written for numerous publications since 1994 and is currently Associate Editor of *Art Monthly*.

Christopher Bedford is Chief Curator at the Wexner Center. Recent and forthcoming curatorial projects include *Hard Targets* (2010), *Mark Bradford* (2010), *Pipilotti Rist: The Tender Room* (2011), *Human Behavior: Nathalie Djurberg with Music by Hans Berg* (2011), a survey of Paul Sietsema's work (2012), and a major historical painting exhibition co-organized with Katy Siegel for 2013. His writing has appeared in a variety of anthologies, journals, exhibition catalogues, and magazines including *Artforum*, *Frieze*, *October*, *Word & Image*, and *Parkett*.

Jane Blocker is Professor of Art History at the University of Minnesota. She is author of *Seeing Witness: Visuality and the Ethics of Testimony* (2009), *What the Body Cost: Desire, History, and Performance* (2004) and *Where is Ana Mendieta? Identity, Performativity, and Exile* (1999).

Jonathan Burrows is a choreographer and writer, currently working as Artist in Residence at Kaaitheater Brussels. His work includes *The Stop Quartet* (1996), *Weak Dance Strong Questions* (2001) with Jan Ritsema, and six duets to date with the composer Matteo Fargion. He is a Guest Professor at Hamburg University, Berlin Free University and Royal Holloway,

University of London. His book *A Choreographer's Handbook* was published by Routledge in 2010.

Nao Bustamante's work encompasses performance art, video installation, visual art, filmmaking, and writing. Bustamante has presented in Galleries, Museums, Universities and underground sites worldwide, including ICA in London, MoMA in New York, Sundance 2008, 2010, and the Kiasma Museum of Helsinki. In 2001 she received the prestigious *Anonymous Was a Woman* fellowship and in 2007 she was named a New York Foundation for the Arts Fellow, as well as a Lambent Fellow. Currently, Bustamante holds the position of Associate Professor of New Media and Live Art at Rensselaer Polytechnic Institute.

Meiling Cheng is a poet-philosopher interested in playing with the written word as a visual-sonic medium. She is the author of *In Other Los Angeleses: Multicentric Performance Art* (2002) and *Beijing Xingwei: Contemporary Chinese Time-Based Art* (forthcoming). Cheng teaches in the School of Theatre, University of Southern California. With Claudia Bucher and Rolf Hoefer, she cofounded the Museum of Ommmmm.

Shezad Dawood trained at Central St Martin's and the Royal College of Art before undertaking a PhD at Leeds Metropolitan University. Dawood works across many different forms of media, including live performance, film, and installation and is particularly concerned with acts of cultural translation and re-staging. Dawood's work has been exhibited internationally, including *Altermodern*, Tate Britain, and *Making Worlds*. the 53rd Venice Biennale (both 2009). He is Senior Lecturer and Research Fellow in Experimental Media at the University of Westminster.

Tim Etchells is best known for his work as artistic director and writer of the performance ensemble Forced Entertainment, one of the UK's most respected and groundbreaking experimental theater companies. He has also created diverse projects of his own in a variety of media including SMS, video and installation. Etchells has written widely about performance and contemporary culture, and has published the books *Endland Stories* (1999), *Certain Fragments* (1999), *The Dream Dictionary* (2001) and *The Broken World* (2008).

Eleonora Fabião is a performer and performance theorist. Associate Professor at the Federal University of Rio de Janeiro, School of Communication, she holds a PhD in Performance Studies from NYU. She was a fellow of the Hemispheric Institute of Performance and Politics during 2010 and is currently collaborating with the "Performing Archive" of the Berlin-based Project *Re.Act.Feminism vol.2* as a researcher on Latin American Performance Art. Fabião has been publishing, teaching and performing in the Americas and Europe.

Matteo Fargion is a composer, performer and teacher. He has worked in dance and theater for over 20 years, collaborating with leading choreographers and directors all over the world. With Jonathan Burrows, he has made a series of six duets conceived, choreographed, composed, administrated and performed together. *Both Sitting Duet* (2002), *The Quiet Dance* (2005), *Speaking Dance* (2006), *Cheap Lecture* (2009) and *The Cow Piece* (2009) are still touring, and the two men have now given over 200 performances worldwide.

Iain Forsyth & Jane Pollard began working collaboratively at Goldsmiths in the early nineties. Best known for their recreations of cultural and art historical events and documents, they have pioneered the use of re-enactment within visual art. Theirs is an enquiry into the mechanics of liveness, repetition, mediation and reception.

Blair French is a curator and the Executive Director of Artspace Visual Arts Centre, Sydney. He is author of *Out of Time: Essays Between Photography and Art* (2006) and *Twelve Australian Photo Artists* (2009), co-authored with Daniel Palmer. His edited publications include the 1999 book *Photo Files: An Australian Photography Reader* and a range of artist monographs.

A contemporary artist's agent, consultant and curator, **Vivienne Gaskin** was formerly Head of Artistic Programme at CCA, Glasgow and Director of Performing Arts at the ICA, London.

Hugo Glendinning has been working as a photographer for the last thirty years. His output stretches across the cultural industries from fine art collaborations in video and photography, through production and performance documentation to portrait work. He has published and exhibited work internationally, notably his continuing project of documentation and the investigation of performance photography with Forced Entertainment.

Guillermo Gómez-Peña's work includes performance art, video, audio, installations, poetry, journalism, and cultural theory, and explores cross-cultural issues, immigration, the politics of language, extreme culture and new technologies in the era of globalization. His performance and installation work has been presented at over seven hundred venues globally. He has been a recipient of numerous fellowships and prizes. Chronicles, essays and scripts of his large-scale projects can be found in five of his books: *Dangerous Border Crossers* (2000), *Codex Spangliensis* (2000), *Mexican Beasts and Living Santos* (1997), *The New World Border* (1996) and *Warrior for Gringostroika* (1994).

Boris Groys is an art critic, media theorist, and philosopher. He is currently a Global Distinguished Professor of Russian and Slavic Studies at New York University and Senior Research Fellow at Karlsruhe University. He is the author of many books, including *The Total Art of Stalinism* (1992), *Ilya Kabakov: The Man Who Flew into Space from His Apartment* (2006), *Art Power* (2008), *The Communist Postscript* (2010) and *Going Public* (2010).

Currently director of Ceri Hand Gallery, **Ceri Hand** is formerly Director of Exhibitions at FACT in Liverpool.

Angela Harutyunyan is an art historian and curator. She currently teaches Contemporary Art and Theory at the American University in Beirut. She has published internationally on issues related to post-Soviet art and culture, and specifically, contemporary art in Armenia. She has co-edited several international anthologies, including *Public Spheres After Socialism* (2008, with Malcolm Miles and Katheryn Horschelmann) and *The Book of St. Ejneb: Manual for Treason* (with Aras Ozgun) for the 10th Sharjah Art Biennial in 2011.

Hannah Higgins is Professor at the University of Illinois at Chicago and daughter of Fluxus artists Alison Knowles and Dick Higgins. She is the author of *Fluxus Experience* (2002) and *The Grid Book* (2009) and is completing an edited anthology with Douglas Kahn, *Mainframe Experimentalism* (2011), about the mainframe phase of experimental computer art from 1960–1970.

Lin Hixson and **Matthew Goulish** live in Chicago, where they oversee the performance company Every house has a door, which they began after Goat Island ended. They teach at The School of the Art Institute of Chicago, Lin in the Performance Department and Matthew in the Writing Program. In 2007, they received honorary doctorates from Dartington College of Arts, and in 2009 they shared a United States Artists Ziporyn fellowship.

Adrian Heathfield is a writer and curator. He is Professor of Performance and Visual Culture at the University of Roehampton, London. He is the co-author of *Out of Now: The Lifeworks of Tehching Hsieh* (2009) and the editor of *Live: Art and Performance* (2004), *Small Acts: Performance, the Millennium and the Marking of Time* (2003), and the box publication *Shattered Anatomies: Traces of the Body in Performance* (1997).

Artist **Dan Howard-Birt** is a Royal College of Art graduate, and curator at Lido Projects in St. Leonards-on-Sea.

Tehching Hsieh is a renowned Taiwanese-American performance artist. Beginning in the late seventies, Hsieh made five One Year Performances and one thirteen-year plan with which he retreated from the art world. Since the Millennium, released from the restriction of not showing his works, Hsieh has exhibited his work in North and South America, Asia and Europe. His monograph *Out of Now: The Lifeworks of Tehching Hsieh* was published in 2009.

Lucas Ihlein is an artist who works with social relations and communication. His work manifests as blogs, performances, pedagogical projects, film and video, lithographic prints and drawings. He works collaboratively with artist groups Big Fag Press, Teaching and

Learning Cinema, and SquatSpace. Ihlein's PhD thesis, completed at Deakin University in 2009, was entitled *Framing Everyday Experience: Blogging as Art*. He lives and works in Sydney.

Janez Janša is artist, writer, performer and director of interdisciplinary performances *We Are All Marlene Dietrich For – Performance for soldiers in peace-keeping missions* (2005, with Erna Omarsdottir), *Pupilija, Papa Pupilo And The Pupilceks – Reconstruction* (2006) and *The More Of Us There Are, The Faster We Will Reach Our Goal* (2010). His visual works include *Refugee Camp For The First World Citizens* (2004, with Peter Šenk), *Name Readymade* (2008, with Janez Janša and Janez Janša) and *Life [In Progress]* (2008). He is author of *Jan Fabre – La Discipline du chaos, le chaos de la discipline* (1994). He was editor in chief of *Maska* performing arts journal from 1999 to 2006.

Dominic Johnson is a Lecturer in the Department of Drama, School of English and Drama, Queen Mary, University of London. He is the author of *Glorious Catastrophe: Jack Smith, Performance and Visual Culture* (2012), and the editor of *Franko B: Blinded by Love* (2006), and *Manuel Vason: Encounters* (2007). His performances have been shown internationally.

Amelia Jones is Professor and Grierson Chair in Visual Culture at McGill University in Montréal. Her recent publications include major essays on Marina Abramović (in *TDR*), on feminist art and curating, and on performance art histories, as well as the edited volume *Feminism and Visual Culture Reader* (2003; new edition 2010). Her most recent single-authored book, *Self Image: Technology, Representation, and the Contemporary Subject* (2006), will be followed in 2012 by *Seeing Differently: A History and Theory of Identification in the Visual Arts* (Routledge).

Jennie Klein is a professor of art history at University of Ohio. She is a contributing editor for *Art Papers* and *Performance Art Journal* (PAJ), and has published numerous articles and books on feminist art. Klein curated the major retrospective of Barbara T. Smith's works at Pomona College in 2005.

Eszter Lázár is a PhD candidate at the Cultural Studies Program in the University of Pécs. She has worked as a curator at the Hungarian University of Fine Arts and as an assistant lecturer in the Theory of Fine Arts Department.

Lynn Hershman Leeson is a San Francisco based artist and film maker who for the past forty years has been internationally acclaimed for her pioneering use of new technologies and her investigations of issues that are now recognized as key to the working of our society: identity in a time of consumerism, privacy in an era of surveillance, interfacing of humans and machines. Her feature films include *Conceiving Ada*, 1998, *Teknolust* (2002), *Strange Culture* (2007), and *!Women Art Revolution* (2010).

André Lepecki is a writer and an independent curator living in New York. He is Associate Professor at the Department of Performance Studies, New York University. He is the author of *Exhausting Dance: Performance and the Politics of Movement* (2006) and co-editor of *Of the Presence of the Body*; *Planes of Composition: dance, theory and the global* (2009, co-editor Jenn Joy); and *The Senses in Performance* (2007, co-editor Sally Banes). He was the curator of the festival IN TRANSIT (2008 and 2009) at Haus der Kulturen der Welt, Berlin. His directorial and co-curatorial work in the authorized re-doing of Allan Kaprow's *18 Happenings in 6 Parts* received the 2008 Best Performance Award by the International Art Critics Association (US section).

Tevž Logar is a curator and artistic director of Škuc Gallery in Ljubljana, Slovenia. He has curated various group and solo exhibitions in galleries and art institutions in Slovenia and abroad and periodically publishes texts on contemporary visual art.

Sven Lütticken teaches art history at Vrije Universiteit in Amsterdam. He is the author of the books *Secret Publicity: Essays on Contemporary Art* (2006) and *Idols of the Market: Modern art and the Fundamentalist Spectacle* (2009). In 2005 he curated the exhibition *Life, Once More: Forms of reenactment in contemporary art* at Witte de With, Rotterdam.

Ming-Yuen S. Ma is an Associate Professor in Media Studies at Pitzer College, a member of the Claremont Colleges. He is the co-editor of the upcoming book *Resolution 3: Global Video Praxis*, and is currently working on a book exploring the relationships between experimental media and sound cultures. Experimental videos and installations by Ma have shown internationally at a wide range of venues.

Vesna Madzoski is an Amsterdam-based freelance researcher and curator. She is working on her PhD project at the European Graduate School. The project focuses on the transformations in the field of contemporary art after World War II in relation to the crisis in anthropology and the representation of the Other.

The work of Los Angeles artist **Daniel Joseph Martinez** has been exhibited in the United States and internationally since 1978. In 2006 Martinez represented the U.S. at the *Cairo Biennial.* He participated both in the groundbreaking 1993 *Whitney Biennial* and in the 2008 *Whitney Biennial,* and in numerous other international art events. Martinez is Professor of Theory, Practice, and Mediation of Contemporary Art at the University of California, Irvine, where he teaches in the Graduate Studies Program and the New Genres Department. A monograph on his work, entitled *A Life of Disobedience*, was published in 2009 by Hatje Cantz.

Mónica Mayer is a visual artists and cultural activist. With Maris Bustamante, in 1983, she founded *Polvo de Gallina Negra*, the first feminist art group in Mexico. With Victor Lerma, in 1989, she founded *Pinto mi Raya,* which is an applied conceptual art project whose purpose is to lubricate the art system. Its main axle is an archive.

Tom McCarthy is a writer and artist. His novel '*C*' was shortlisted for the 2010 Man Booker Prize.

The French choreographer **Mathilde Monnier** has been head of the Centre Chorégraphique de Montpellier since 1994, where she created a series of influential works presented internationally, such as *Nuit* (1995); *Lieux de là* (1999); *Déroutes* (2002); *Publique* (2004); and *Pavlova 3'23"* (2009). Monnier has initiated collaborations with a range of artists and intellectuals, including the songwriter Katerine; the writer Christine Angot; the filmmaker Claire Denis; and the philosopher Jean-Luc Nancy.

Rabih Mroué is an actor, director, playwright and visual artist from Beirut. He is a contributing editor for *TDR* and *KALAMAN.* He is also a co-founder of the Beirut Art Center. His complex and diverse practice spans different disciplines and formats between theater, performance, and visual arts. Mroué's works include: *Grandfather, father and son* (2010), *I, the undersigned* (2010), *The inhabitants of images* (2009), *Make me stop smoking* (2006), *Who's afraid of representation?* (2004), *On Three Posters* (2004), *Looking for a missing employee* (2003) and *Face A / Face B* (2003).

Jean-Luc Nancy is an internationally renowned philosopher, Professor Emeritus at the Université de Strasbourg. Nancy has written over forty works translated in several languages, including the seminal *Le titre de la lettre* (1973) with Philippe Lacoue-Labarthe; *La communauté désoeuvrée* (1982); *Corpus* (1992); Être *singulier pluriel* (1996); *L'Intrus* (2000); and *Vérité de la démocratie* (2008).

Hayley Newman is a Reader at Chelsea College of Art and Design in London. Her work includes *MKVH* (*Milton Keynes Vertical Horizontal*, 2006), an event in which volunteers were driven around the Milton Keynes road grid until their coach ran out of diesel. She is currently working with Gina Birch and Kaffe Matthews in their eco-feminist band, *The Gluts.*

Orlan was born in Saint-Etienne, France. She lives and works between Paris, Los Angeles and New York. She is a multi-disciplinary artist, constantly renewing herself by the use of various mediums – photography, video, sculpture and installation – but also via performance and surgery-performance. She was the first to investigate Bio-Art, in cultivating her cells. ORLAN questions the status of the body in our societies in relation to religious, cultural and political pressures, but also dominating ideologies that are imprinted in us.

Tanja Ostojić is an independent performance, and interdisciplinary artist based in Berlin and Belgrade. Ostojić includes herself as a character in performances and uses diverse media in her artistic researches, thereby examining limits of art medias, social configurations and relations of power. She works predominantly from the migrant woman's perspective while political positioning, humour and integration of the recipient define the approach in her work. She recently published the book *Integration Impossible? The Politics of Migration in the Artwork of Tanja Ostojić* (2009).

Andrew Renton works as an independent curator and writer. He has published a number of catalogues and books on contemporary art and organised more than two-dozen exhibitions in museums throughout the world. He is currently MFA Programme Director at Goldsmiths.

Joanna Scanlan is a BAFTA nominated writer and performer. She was senior lecturer in Drama at De Montfort University 1987–1992 and Live Art Officer at the Arts Council England 1992–1995 before embarking on a professional career as a creative artist.

Carolee Schneemann is a multidisciplinary artist whose work since the early 1960s has transformed the definition of art, especially discourse on the body, sexuality and gender. Seattle's Henry Art Gallery has hosted a career-spanning exhibit of her work in 2011, and MoMA in NYC has recently featured her installation *Up To And Including Her Limits* in the exhibition *On Line: Drawing Through the Twentieth Century*. In 1997 a major survey of her work was held at the NMCA in New York. Publications include *Correspondence Course: An Epistolary History of Carolee Schneemann and Her Circle* (2010); *Imaging Her Erotics* (2003, 2004); *More Than Meat Joy: Complete Performance Work and Selected Writing* (1979, 1997).

Rebecca Schneider is the author of *Performing Remains: Art and War in Times of Theatrical Reenactment* (2011) and *The Explicit Body in Performance* (1997) as well as numerous other publications. Consortium Editor of *TDR: A Journal of Performance Studies,* she chairs the Department of Theatre Arts and Performance Studies at Brown University.

Santiago Sierra's work often addresses structures of power that operate in our everyday existence and intervenes into these structures exposing situations of exploitation and marginalisation, famously hiring underprivileged individuals who, in exchange for money, are willing to undertake pointless or unpleasant tasks. Based in Mexico City, Sierra has participated in numerous major exhibitions like the Venice Biennial in 2003 (Spanish Pavilion) and has had solo exhibitions around the world, such as *House in the Mud*, Hanover 2005, and *300 tons*, Kunsthaus Bregenz, 2003.

Los Angeles-based artist **Barbara T. Smith** earned her BA at Pomona College (1953) and MFA (1971) at UC Irvine. As a founder of performance art, Smith began her body-oriented work in 1965. By 1968 she was creating powerful transformational performances continuing to the present. Iconic works include, *Feed Me* (1973); *Ritual Meal* (1969) and *Celebration of the Holy Squash* (1971); *Birthdaze* (1981) and *The 21st Century Odyssey* (1991–93).

Joanna Sokolowska, is a curator at the Muzeum Sztuki in Łódź, Poland. Her work has been focused on the intersections between art economy, politics and history. Her recent curatorial projects include amongst others *Workers Leaving the Workplace* at the Muzeum Sztuki in Lodz (2010) and *Accretions* at Galerija Škuc in Ljubljana (2010) (co-curated with Angela Harutyunyan and Tevž Logar).

Noémie Solomon is a dancer, choreographer and researcher. She is a PhD candidate in the Department of Performance Studies at New York University. She recently co-edited *Dance on Time!* with Gurur Ertem (2010) and her writing and translation work have been published in various journals including *TDR*, *Women and Performance* and *Dance Research Journal*.

Tilda Swinton is an Academy Award winning performer. She is also a writer and producer working in film.

Chuyu Wang (王楚禹) is a Beijing-based independent xingwei (behavior/performance) artist known for his sardonic, sober, and politically poignant bodyworks. Also a writer of fiction and art criticism and a prolific curator, Wang has collaborated with Shu Yang to organize the international Dadao Live Art Festival in Beijing and has founded Plaza Performance Art Workshop in Songzhuang.

Hong Wang (王洪) began making art in Xian, Shanxi Province, in 2003. He resettled in Beijing in 2005 in order to pursue a more serious art career in a culturally stimulating environment. He is primarily interested in painting and xingwei yishu (behavior/performance art).

Mechtild Widrich is senior research associate at the History of the Art and Architecture Department at ETH Zurich. She received her PhD from the Department of Architecture at the Massachusetts Institute of Technology in 2009 and has lectured and published widely on issues of authenticity and reperformance, and the contemporary monument. She is currently finishing a book entitled *Performative Monuments*, and preparing an anthology on ugliness in aesthetic discourse.

Faith Wilding is a multidisciplinary artist, writer, and educator, and was Professor of Performance, School of the Art Institute of Chicago. She co-founded the feminist art movement in Southern California in the early 1970s, where she produced *Waiting* and *Crocheted Environment*, signal works in the 1972 *Womanhouse* project. Wilding's work has been included in solo and group shows internationally. In 1998 Wilding co-founded subRosa, an internationally recognised reproducible cyberfeminist cell of cultural researchers. Wilding's publications include *By Our Own Hands* (1977) and *Domain Errors! Cyberfeminist Practices* (2003).

Jian Jun ("J.J.") Xi was born in China and has lived and worked in the UK since the 1980s. Working in performance, installation and sculpture, his major recent work includes *Aircraft Carrier Project*, Tokyo Gallery, Beijing (2008–9) and the Andy Warhol series (2010). Other best-known works include *Two Artists Jump on Tracey Emin's Bed* (1999), *Soya Sauce and Ketchup Fight* (1999) and *Pissing on Duchamp's Urinal* (2000).

Cai Yuan was born in China and has lived and worked in the UK since the 1980s. Working in various media, his work examines the way in which identity is bound up with ideologies, histories and cultural contexts. Best-known works include *Two Artists Jump on Tracey Emin's Bed* (1999), *Soya Sauce and Ketchup Fight* (1999) and *Pissing on Duchamp's Urinal* (2000).

Yang Zhichao (扬志超) is a Beijing-based independent artist known for his extreme xingwei yishu (behavior/performance art). He explored his body's endurance of pain and its capacity as an embedded archive with numerous bodyworks ranging from branding his ID number on his back, planting grass on his arm, to implanting substance-filled silicone capsules in his abdomen.

Qiu Zhijie (邱志杰) is a cross-media total artist known for his calligraphy, painting, installation, performance, video, and conceptual photography. He is Associate Professor of Mixed Medial Art in China Academy of Art, Hangzhou, and Co-Director of Visual Culture Center, CAA, Hangzhou. Based in Beijing and Hangzhou, China, Qiu has published several books on contemporary art criticism.

Index

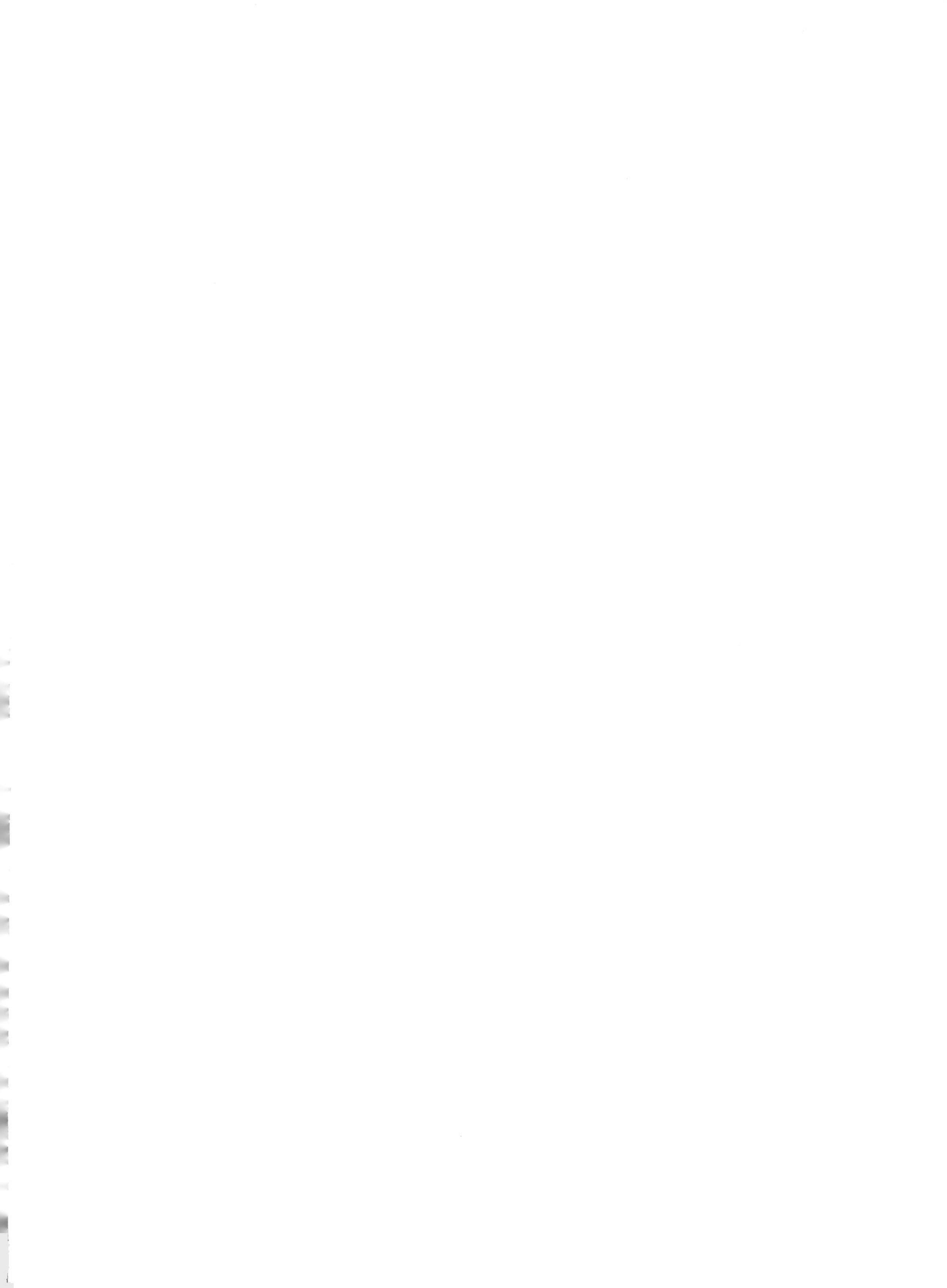